Men of Silk

Men of Silk

The Hasidic Conquest of
Polish Jewish Society

GLENN DYNNER

OXFORD
UNIVERSITY PRESS

2006

OXFORD

UNIVERSITY PRESS

Oxford University Press, Inc., publishes works that further
Oxford University's objective of excellence
in research, scholarship, and education.

Oxford   New York
Auckland   Cape Town   Dar es Salaam   Hong Kong   Karachi
Kuala Lumpur   Madrid   Melbourne   Mexico City   Nairobi
New Delhi   Shanghai   Taipei   Toronto

With offices in
Argentina   Austria   Brazil   Chile   Czech Republic   France   Greece
Guatemala   Hungary   Italy   Japan   Poland   Portugal   Singapore
South Korea   Switzerland   Thailand   Turkey   Ukraine   Vietnam

Published by Oxford University Press, Inc.
198 Madison Avenue, New York, New York 10016

www.oup.com

Oxford is a registered trademark of Oxford University Press

Library of Congress Cataloging-in-Publication Data

Dynner, Glenn, 1969–
Men of silk : the Hasidic conquest of Polish Jewish Society / Glenn Dynner.
    p.   cm.
Includes bibliographical references and index.
ISBN-13 978-0-19-517522-6
ISBN 0-19-517522-0
1. Hasidism—Poland—History.   I. Title.
BM198.D94 2006
296.8'332'09438—dc22   2005015098

9 8 7 6 5 4 3 2 1

Printed in the United States of America
on acid-free paper

For Heather

Acknowledgments

I would like to take this opportunity to express gratitude toward the numerous people and institutions that helped make this book possible. In terms of my methodological training, I have benefited enormously from the challenging and stimulating guidance of my principle doctoral dissertation advisor, Antony Polonsky, and my master's thesis advisor, Gershon Hundert. Both have instilled in me the desire to read Jewish history within its historical context, which I have at least tried to fulfill here. At the same time, scholars like Arthur Green and Rachel Elior have provided a window into the inner life of eastern European Jewry through their seminars and tutorials on Hasidic texts. While in Israel, and in other locations as well, I engaged in extremely beneficial conversations with David Assaf, Israel Bartal, Moshe Rosman, and Shaul Stampfer, among others. And Hanna Węgrzynek and Marcin Wodziński proved exceptionally helpful and gracious in assisting my research in the Polish archives. Several of those scholars, including Assaf, Rosman, Stampfer, and Wodziński, were kind enough to read earlier drafts of this book and provide extremely detailed critiques. It almost goes without saying that despite their intellectual generosity I assume full responsibility for the ideas expressed here.

Several institutions provided vital logistical support. I would like to thank the Koret Foundation for assisting in the publication of this book through their Jewish Studies Publication Prize. The Interuniversity Fellowship in Jewish Studies through Hebrew University and the Brandeis University–Hebrew University Joint Fellowship supported my research in Israel; the U.S. Fulbright Award program and Kościuszko Foundation Travel Grant enabled my research and studies in Poland; and the Tauber Institute of Modern Jewish Studies at Brandeis University contributed to my dissertation preparation. I would also like to thank the staffs at the National Library and Gershom Scholem Library in Jerusalem, the Jewish Historical Institute in Warsaw, Archiwum Główne Akt Dawnych in Warsaw, and the Center for Jewish Studies at the Jagiellonian University in Cracow for their kind assistance, diligence, and hospitality. The editors of the journals *Polin*, *Gal-Ed*, and *Jewish Social Studies* were gracious enough to publish earlier versions of portions of this book. Some chapters have been published in part in *Polin* 17 (Littman Library, 2004), *Gal-Ed* 20 (Institute for the History of Polish Jewry, 2005); and *Jewish Social Studies* 12.1 (Indiana University Press, 2006). I would also like to express my gratitude toward my colleagues at Sarah Lawrence College, who have provided a welcoming and intellectually rigorous atmosphere. Finally, I cannot envisage the completion of this work without the love and support of my father, my mother, and my wife, Heather, and now our daughter, Ela. I am so fortunate to have someone like Heather, who is my partner on many levels—emotional, spiritual, and intellectual. Her gentle yet uncompromising critiques and steadfast encouragement deserve my fullest gratitude.

Contents

Note on Place Names

Spellings and pronunciations of place names, particularly of towns and cities that were subject to eastern and east central Europe's frequent border changes, are loaded with political connotations. I have tried to remain neutral by spelling town and city names with historical context in mind. I adhere to the following guidelines.

1. As the period under review comprises both the prepartition era ("Poland," or the "Polish-Lithuanian Commonwealth," was partitioned by its neighbors in three stages: 1772, 1793, and 1795) and the postpartition era (which entailed new spellings and pronunciations by conquerors or native nationalists), I adhere to the Polish spellings of towns and cities in most cases. This is an admittedly problematic expedient for the sake of consistency and simplicity.

2. Towns with accepted or frequently invoked English names, such as Warsaw, Cracow, Vilna, Bratslav, and Kotsk, are presented in that form so that the English reader may more easily recognize them. Often their Polish equivalent is offered in parentheses.

3. Exceptions to Polish spellings also occur in the cases of L'viv and Gdańsk. L'viv was "Lwów" when it was part of the old Polish Commonwealth and interwar Poland. It became widely known as "Lemberg" during most of the period under consideration. Today it is known by its Ukrainian name, "L'viv." When discussing events prior to 1945, historians refer to "Danzig" rather than the more recent Polish "Gdańsk."

4. Yiddish town names are by and large eschewed in favor of the foregoing spellings and pronunciations. One reason is

merely practical: these names are not standardized in their transliterated rendering; nor do they appear on maps, even those preceding the tragic destruction of European Jewry. Another reason is more idealistic: it is hoped that the reader will come to realize that "Mezheritch" and "Międzyrzecz" were one town, not two. Employing a single place name constitutes another step in the direction of contextualizing east European Jewish history.

Men of Silk

All of the general Israelite population scorns them and their mystical creed to such a degree that the name "Hasidim" has become an ironic label. In several locales they are called "Men of Silk" (*Kitajcy*), because they do not make use of woolen cloth, but rather only silk, out of the fear that there might be found some linen thread mixed in with the wool. Thus they only wear silk clothing.

—Abraham Stern, "Information about the Hasidic Sect"

Introduction

In the course of their wanderings, the two brothers, Rabbi Zusya
and Rabbi Elimelekh, often came to the city of Ludmir. There they
always slept in the house of a poor, devout man. Years later, when
their reputations had spread all over the country, they came to Ludmir again, not on foot as before, but in a carriage. The wealthiest
man in that little town, who had never wanted to have anything to
do with them, came to meet them the moment he heard they had
arrived, and begged them to lodge in his house. But they said,
"Nothing has changed in us to make you respect us more than before. What is new is just the horses and the carriage. Take them for
your guests, but let us stop with our old host, as usual."
                                    —Martin Buber, *Tales of the Hasidim*

This tale, entitled "The Horses," appears in a collection by Martin
Buber, one of the pioneering theorists of "Hasidism," a movement
founded by followers of the famed eighteenth-century Podolian
(Ukrainian) mystic R. Israel ben Eliezer, known as the Ba'al Shem
Tov (the "Besht," c. 1700–1760).[1]
   The heroes of the tale, R. Zusya and R. Elimelekh, were disciples of the Besht's preeminent successor, R. Dov Ber, the "Great
Maggid" of Międzyrzecz, as well as Hasidic leaders in their own
right. In translating and publishing such Hasidic tales in early
twentieth-century Germany, Buber was attempting to recast Hasidism as an untapped repository of the authentic Ashkenazic Jewish
folk legacy, a final bulwark against a torrent of vapid secularism issuing from the West. No longer was Hasidism to be dismissed as
backward and superstitious, nor its leaders reviled as charlatans. Buber was convinced that, correctly conceived, early Hasidic leaders

were folk heroes who had uplifted the downtrodden and revitalized Jewish culture. His stylized renditions offered a refined primitive emotionalism that he hoped would animate a Jewish national renaissance. When sifting through collections of Hasidic tales, he accordingly privileged episodes that portrayed their protagonists in revolt against a stodgy rabbinic and mercantile elite, an anti-bourgeois construction that resonated with Weimar Jewish intellectuals.[2] Buber's selections seemed to promote, according to Joseph Dan, "universal ethical values of charity and compassion, social justice and generosity, the equality of all before God." They presented "not only Judaism as it was, but Judaism as it should be . . . a paradigm of human values which should serve as a basis for the Judaism of the future."[3] His *Tales of the Hasidim* achieved such wide currency that their portrayal was for many years accepted as historical, authoritative, and reflective of Hasidism's true spirit.[4]

One might sympathize with Buber's mission to forge a modern Jewish culture out of what appeared to be authentic Jewish folkways, much in the same way that the Grimm brothers had employed fairy tales in the service of early German nationalism. Undoubtedly, his collections of Hasidic tales inspired a renewed appreciation for Judaism in acculturated readers, particularly those exasperated by the rationalistic *bildung*-driven Judaism of their parents' generation. Yet the historian quickly encounters problems with Buber's neo-Romantic reconstruction. Let us take another look at our socially charged tale, "The Horses." The brothers' initial rejection by the Ludmir notables implies humble social origins, while their horses, carriage, and celebrity point to a dramatic reversal of fortune. Yet the tale's narrative interest turns not on the brothers' peripeteia but on their ironic rebuff of the wealthiest man in town and continued solidarity with their humble host, all of which is meant to signal that piety and humility are more important than wealth and social station. R. Zusya and R. Elimelekh never forgot where they came from.

But historical sources tell a rather different tale. The brothers, to all appearances vagabonds in Buber's tale, were in reality scions of the aristocratic Weissblum family. Their father, Eleazar Lipman, was a wealthy landowner and a descendant of generations of rabbinical luminaries.[5] Far from despising their exalted social station, R. Zusya and R. Elimelekh recruited followers and forged marriage alliances within the mercantile and rabbinic elite. Genealogical records indicate that R. Zusya was careful to pursue socially auspicious matches for his children. And in a letter that has come down to us, R. Zusya solicits one of his wealthy followers on behalf of a Hasid who had fallen so deeply in debt to a nobleman that his wife and child were in danger of being taken into captivity.[6] The letter not only demonstrates R. Zusya's genuine pastoral care, but also reveals that he counted the rich among his partisans. A similar pattern emerges with respect to R. Elimelekh, whose homiletic innovations bear the unmistakable mark of an elite Jewish education.[7] Despite his oft-stated preference for "self-made" disciples over highborn ones in his teachings, R. Elimelekh not only concluded propitious matches for his children but groomed his son R. Eliezer to be his successor. Through the perspective of these sources, the two folk heroes morph into astute populists who could cater to the common folk while cultivating ties with fellow elites.

Early twentieth century scholars are not to be entirely faulted for misconstruing Hasidism as folksy and subversive, for Hasidic leaders did much to encourage that image through gestures like the one described in "The Horses." In tale after tale, R. Zusya fashions his persona after the Slavic archetype "fool for God" (pious pauper), while R. Elimelekh seems to thrill in cutting elites down to size and favoring common workers. R. Elimelekh's preeminent disciple, R. Jacob Isaac "the Seer" of Lublin, is said to have proclaimed: "the rank and file of people either have turned completely to God, or can, at any rate, do so. They present no obstacle. It is the superior people who constitute a hindrance. . . ."[8] Such sentiments indeed suggest a folk revival. But in light of the elitist backgrounds of these and most other Hasidic leaders, which will be more thoroughly established in later chapters, they must be understood as populist rather than popular.

Although populism is often viewed cynically as an effort by elites to garner grassroots support and sociopolitical power by merely affecting identification with the common folk, we shall try to consider Hasidic populism in a less pejorative light. After all, the assumption of folksy personas by scions of the rabbinic elite may have served a spiritual purpose, in addition to a political one. The pioneering Hasidic theorist R. Jacob Joseph of Połonne was probably sincere in counseling his disciples that a spiritual leader is sometimes compelled to disguise himself as a commoner in order to ensure a wider reception of his message.[9] Nevertheless, it remains incumbent upon the historian to try to see through disguises.

Hasidism as Ideology

In mid-eighteenth-century Podolia, in present-day Ukraine, a number of Jewish mystics under the inspiration of the Besht broke with the Kabbalistic custom of praying and studying in exclusive circles and began espousing a popularized version of Kabbalah in increasingly permeable circles. As their movement gathered force over the next fifty years, they would attain such prominence that their authority would come to supersede even that of the rabbis and powerful kahal lay elites. Despite the challenge they posed to the traditional hierarchy, however, their eschewal of overt messianism and antinomianism, as well as their continued fidelity to Jewish law, prevented the more extreme backlashes that had recently quashed eastern Europe's more untethered mystical upheavals.[10] In the long run, their spiritual revival and social revolution would prove conservative enough to avert a permanent schism. Initially, however, their ascendancy excited jealousy and resentment among many religious traditionalists.

The Besht, as a *ba'al shem,* or "master of the Name(s) of God," could communicate with supernal personages and induce theurgical effects. He was a type of Jewish mystical practitioner comparable to an itinerant witch doctor or shaman, in that he mediated between this world and the other, performed exorcisms, sold amulets, and offered herbal remedies for physical or spiritual maladies (illness, difficulty in childbirth, etc.).[11] While it is natural to assume that such popular religious types inhabited lower or middling social ranks, Immanuel Etkes has shown that ba'alei shem could enjoy positive relations with rabbis and communal elders and even hold rabbinical posts themselves.[12] Nevertheless, complaints against "false" ba'alei shem who swindled unwary Jews began to proliferate by the second half of the eighteenth century, and ba'alei shem began to encounter increased skepticism.[13] But the Besht distinguished himself by assuming a more public role, serving entire communities instead of individual clients. Immanuel Etkes attributes this to the Besht's sense of mission, derived from his exposure to the region's various social, political and economic ills during his itinerant services, as well as from his perceived "powers of a prophetic nature: remote vision, prognostication, ability to hear decrees from on high, and so forth."[14] The Besht took it upon himself to rectify souls of the dead and convey prayers to their destinations through public ascents of the soul; while in the earthly realm he attempted to stave off catastrophes like blood libels and intervene in appointments of ritual slaughterers and arrendas (leases) in order to prevent ritual or moral infractions.[15]

The Besht also innovated in the theological sphere. He formulated radically simplified mystical teachings to facilitate devekut (communion with God), developed an ecstatic prayer-centered regimen, and repudiated the strenuous asceticism of the old-style mystics by arguing that one can serve God more effectively with a joyful countenance.[16] While these innovations rendered the divine pathways more accessible to the average Jew and implicitly challenged the hegemony of Talmudic study, it is doubtful that the Besht deliberately set out to create a mass movement.[17] Nor did he intend to subvert the social hierarchy, for he and his small circle of colleague-disciples were self-styled "men of form," while all other Jews, conceived as "men of matter," could only attain spiritual fulfillment by cleaving to them.[18] Occasionally, a member of the circle might criticize normative Jewish leadership.[19] But most sought to avoid public controversy and refrained from social criticism.[20] In fact, Hasidism's chief organizer, R. Dov Ber, the "Great Maggid" of Międzyrzecz, attempted to rein in his more combative disciples.[21] Perhaps he had learned from the demise of Sabbateanism and, most recently, Frankism—popular mystical movements that had directly challenged the rabbinic elite and had been suppressed.[22]

But the Great Maggid could not fail to appreciate that now that the Kabbalistic genie was out of the bottle, with secrets of the godhead having circulated in cheap pamphlets for over a century, it was pointless to continue to attempt to confine Kabbalistic study, prayer, and practice to a small segment of the Jewish elite.[23] Kabbalistic notions had entered the shared public sphere, and they could be marshaled to justify palpable sociopolitical power. Thus, instead of conceiving Hasidism as a reaction to "Talmudic aridity" (a formulation akin to Christian anti-Jewish polemics), scholars now regard it as a result of a groundswell of Kabbalistic enthusiasm.[24] However, Hasidic leaders were careful to neutralize the more antinomian and eschatological possibilities inherent in Kabbalah, leaving only traces of danger to delight many a young person. By the first decades of the nineteenth century, Hasidism approached such dimensions that, in terms of sheer influence, it had emerged as the most important cultural development in modern East European Jewish history before the rise of the new Jewish politics (Zionism, Socialism, and Autonomism) at the century's close.

Most Hasidic leaders began to receive the designation "zaddik." Traditionally, the term *zaddik* referred to a righteous person; and a folk belief was prevalent that every generation contained thirty-six hidden *zaddikim,* whose deeds sustained the world and hastened the final redemption. According to the multivalent symbolism of classical Kabbalah, the *zaddik* signified one of the ten emanating divine potencies (*sefirot*) that sustained the lower worlds by infusing them with divine vitality.[25] Hasidism's theorists fused the social and esoteric denotations together, proclaiming the new zaddik to be both a living saint who sustained his fellow Jews and a human embodiment of one of the most axial *sefirot.* R. Jacob Joseph of Połonne occasionally used the title "zaddik" in this way, while R. Elimelekh of Leżajsk (d. 1786) applied the term more consistently.[26] The first zaddik to be explicitly identified as such may have been R. Jehiel Michael of Złoczów, following his death in 1781.[27]

Hasidism presents a lucid example of how a new social formation can convert the meanings of ideological elements.[28] Application of the term "zaddik" to the new mystical leader was but one way that Kabbalistic concepts were transmuted into useable social referents by this new cadre of innovative mystics. They also began assigning palpable and accessible meanings to other esoteric concepts of relatively old provenance whose potential for activation into the wider sociopolitical arena had not yet been fully realized.[29] In homiletic sermons delivered at the ceremonial third meal of the Sabbath, which disciples diligently memorized and transcribed later that night, audiences were informed that the *sefirot* could be influenced by a zaddik to the benefit of his community, thanks to a parallel *sefirotic* structure within the human psyche.[30] Other times, the *sefirot* were depicted as storehouses of divine vitality that could be mined by a zaddik.[31] Precisely how one was supposed to conceive of the *sefirot* was less important than the assertion that a zaddik could exert a tangible, positive influence upon them.

This cosmic intervention was possible, they learned, because of the zaddik's unique ability to cleave to the godhead, vaguely construed, in a prophetic-like state of communion known as *devekut.*[32] But *devekut* marked only the first phase of the zaddik's mission. Moshe Idel explains that "the zaddikim did not conceive of ecstasy as their ultimate goal; rather, they had an additional spiritual aim: the drawing down of the divine effluence for the benefit of the community."[33] Upon his achievement of this supreme connectedness, the zaddik caused the divine flow to emanate from the *sefirot* and translated it into the satisfaction of human needs.[34] The crystallization of that second, theurgical phase, during which the zaddik acted as his community's benefactor, marked Hasidism's evolution into a full-fledged social movement.[35] The refinement of the "zaddik idea" thus engendered a claim that average Jews, unable to achieve *devekut* themselves, could still accrue the spiritual and material gains of *devekut* by "cleaving" to their zaddik.[36]

The zaddik's singular attainments also equipped him to redeem the divine sparks that, according to the sixteenth-century doctrine of Lurianic Kabbalah, suffused the world.[37] This immanentist belief lent itself to the mildly antinomian inference that if "divine sparks" were scattered throughout the material realm, then materiality itself could be embraced, consecrated, and redeemed. Thus was born the notion of "worship through corporeality" (*avodah be-gashmiyut*). The zaddik's singular ability to achieve *devekut* enabled him and those who cleaved to him to recover holiness from profane yet legal acts and entities like eating, drinking alcohol, coitus, non-Jewish folktales, folksongs, and dances. Sometimes "worship through corporeality" was framed as an imperative: the only way to liberate oneself from matter was to cooperate with it in order to unlock its spiritual potential.[38] Such ideas bear an affinity with Sabbateanism, as contemporaneous critics were quick to point out; and the possible connections between the clandestine messianic movement and Hasidism have yet to be exhausted.[39] But, more important from an institutional standpoint, "worship through corporeality" provided an ideological bridge between the zaddik's mystical and communal roles. According to its logic, the zaddik had to "descend" from his spiritual level in order to redeem wayward members of his flock. He was even obliged to enter the profane and frequently nasty sphere of communal politics to elevate the divine sparks that resided there.[40]

From the perspective of social and cultural history, the emergence of "worship through corporeality" was a watershed, for it saved Hasidism from a quietist retreat from society by sacralizing the zaddik's worldly endeavors and requiring struggle and activity.[41] As we shall see, even the rank-and-file were encouraged to attempt to moderate forms of worship through corporeality, for example by being mindful of the spiritual benefits to be derived from their daily business pursuits (tuition for their sons' Torah studies, dowries to attract scholarly sons-in-law, etc.). Although zaddikim began issuing warnings against its more antinomian applications, worship through corporeality was probably a more formative concept for the average Hasid than even *devekut*, for it was both attainable and applicable to quotidian reality.[42] And as we behold the manifold sociopolitical and socioreligious projects of the zaddikim, it will become evident that worship through corporeality was paramount for them, as well.

These conceptual innovations drew power not only from their application in the social arena but also from the manner in which they were framed within the quietly audacious Hasidic homiletic sermon. The manner in which the term "zaddik" itself was invoked in those sermons was the most daring of all: biblical heroes and contemporary Hasidic leaders alike were described as "zaddikim" and thus subtly but unmistakably equated. The pioneering Hasidic theorist R. Jacob Joseph of Połonne, for example, illustrated the importance of attaching oneself to a contemporary zaddik by invoking the example of the Israelites' cleaving (*devekut*) to Moses and the contemporary zaddik's responsibility for bringing the masses to repentance through the examples of Moses and Abraham.[43] Owing to the centrality of "worship through corporeality," the sins of biblical characters exerted a special fascination. R. Jacob Joseph found justification for the occasional sins of the contemporary zaddik in the sins of Moses and King David. Jacob's scandalous kiss of beautiful Rachel upon their first meeting (Genesis 29), which medieval commentators have struggled to explain away,[44] was painted by R. Levi Isaac of Berdyczów as a zaddik's redemption of the holy spark embedded in physical beauty.[45]

The socioreligious motivation informing such parallelism should not be missed: if the ancients were zaddikim, and there was a tacit understanding that the homilies' authors were also zaddikim, a mutual identification was implied. Latter-day zaddikim were frequently claimed to embody biblical archetypes like the priest, king, and prophet.[46] The parallelism worked the other way, as well, enabling latter-day zaddikim to render the ancients as thinly disguised representations of themselves.

Not surprisingly this daring exegetical finesse, arguably a form of self-iconography, was decried by contemporaneous critics as a violation of the hallowed conception of the "decline of generations," according to which later generations were necessarily inferior to earlier ones. In response, Hasidic apologists were forced to get creative. It was argued that Hasidic sages were greater than many earlier ones because the Besht had "ascended the heights to become the disciple of Ahijah the Shilonite who had heard the Torah from Moses our teacher himself." Another apologist claimed that latter-day zaddikim possessed the reincarnated souls of the ancients; thus they do not technically belong to the "generations in decline."[47] Latter-day zaddikim, according to these claims, transcended human history and so eluded its rules.

Having arrogated the spiritual rank of ancient priests, kings, prophets, and sages, zaddikim claimed the ability to purify defiled souls, heal with their blessings, and discern the "clean" from the "unclean"; assume a royal bearing; attain prophetic states and act as intercessors before God; and serve as the only true interpreters of Torah.[48] They could even ostensibly avert punitive heavenly decrees like epidemics, famine, anti-Jewish violence, and so on.[49] Such claims translated into extraordinary authority over their followers' personal religious lives, which engendered a considerable loss of spiritual autonomy for the latter. R. Abraham Joshua Heschel of Opatów taught that if pious thoughts happened to occur to a businessman, inspiring him to study a little, pray, or give charity, those holy thoughts should be understood as having derived from his zaddik.[50] R. Elimelekh of Leżajsk warned that although one might attain love, rapturous prayer, and proper Torah study on his own, the only way to be certain his exhilaration did not derive from an idolatrous source was to attach himself to a zaddik. Furthermore, "whosoever wishes to receive divine blessedness from the zaddik must be in accord with the zaddik, in which case he is blessed with much blessedness. But if he is not in accord with the zaddik, then it is obviously impossible for him to be blessed with the zaddik's divine blessedness."[51] R. Nahman of Bratslav went so far as to admonish each follower to "cast off from himself all prior learning, and to remove his mind from it as if he has no thoughts except what he receives from the zaddik." As long as there remained even a remnant of his own thinking, he was not in a state of perfection.[52] Such moments compel us to read Hasidic homiletic literature as more than just mystical ethics. In asserting the zaddik's absolute authority as "natural" or "right," Hasidic discourse must be understood as ideology: an instrument by which a new cadre of socioreligious leaders sought to appropriate or preserve power and legitimacy.[53]

Hasidic ideology may have been based on ancient typologies, but it lent sanction to the zaddik's ongoing amalgamation and subordination of every major contemporary spiritual leadership role in east European Jewish society, including that of rabbi, *ba'al shem,* old-style mystic (*hasid*), preacher (*maggid*), and, to a certain extent, Messiah. Zaddikim were thus anything but other-worldly spiritual adepts, for their vocations lay squarely within the earthly realm as judges and teachers, healers and miracle workers, moralists and personal advisors, and temporary redeemers.[54] They established courts to which pilgrims would travel with written requests for supernatural interventions, services for which they were compensated with a "redemption fee" (*pidyon*).[55] In the eyes of initiates, the assumption of communal responsibilities and lucrative miracle enterprises by men who would have been content to soar permanently in the upper realms was not, however, self-serving or ambitious. Descending from his lofty state of *devekut* in order to attend to the undisguised material needs of his fellow Jews formed an obligatory "exit rite," the zaddik's grim responsibility to return to regular life after immersion within the divine. Worldly duties, even if financially compensated, drew the zaddik away from his sublime *devekut* and were thus rendered in a spirit of generosity and self-sacrifice.[56]

By contrast, old-style mystics who studied and practiced Kabbalah in seclusion without troubling to lead their communities *as mystics* were purportedly selfish elitists consumed with their own spiritual quests. The term "hasidism" had previously referred to the exclusivist practice of Kabbalistic prayer and study within cliques of the wealthy and highborn.[57] Now, an entire corpus of homiletic literature sanctioning the new zaddik's role as mystic for the masses by grafting biblical verses onto the zaddik doctrine began to crop up across eastern Europe. A passage in one such work, *Zava'at ha-Ribash* (Żółkiew, 1793), attributed to the Great Maggid, contrasts the old- and new-style mystics:

> "The *zaddik* flourishes like a palm tree; he grows like a cedar in Lebanon" (Psalms 92:12)—for behold, there are two types of *zaddikim,* and they are both complete *zaddikim.* But the difference between them is that the first one is always in communion with the Holy One, Blessed Be He, and performs the divine service that is expected of him; but he is only a *zaddik* for himself and not for his fellow man. Which is to say, his righteousness does not influence

others. And he is to be compared with a cedar tree—as our Rabbis of blessed memory said—which does not bear fruit (*Ta'anit* 25b). For he is only a *zaddik* with respect to himself, and does not bear fruit in order to return others to good and increase and multiply *zaddikim* in the world. This type works on his own behalf, so that his own reward will grow and increase. But the second zaddik is to be compared with a palm tree, which bears fruit. And he "flourishes like a palm tree," which is to say, he produces good out of evil [i.e., causes sinners to repent],[58] and causes good to thrive and spread in the world . . . and his reward is exponential compared with that of the first aforementioned *zaddik*. Nevertheless, both of them are complete *zaddikim*.[59]

Psalms 92:12, we learn, instructs us that the elitist type of zaddikim merely grows like cedars; while the popular type flourishes like palm trees. The passage thus grants a conciliatory nod to the old-style mystic, who is admittedly still a zaddik but appears to be self-centered compared to the activist zaddik. The latter gains manifold reward by inspiring mass repentance, or "producing good out of evil," another ingenious application of "worship through corporeality."

This favorable comparison, decidedly more ideological than mystical or ethical, would be repeated by subsequent zaddikim in an apparent attempt to justify their assumption of public roles as mystics.[60] By the end of the eighteenth century, the new-style zaddikim were realizing the passage's sociopolitical blueprint by commandeering communal institutions and expanding their influence over great swaths of Jewish eastern Europe. To accomplish this, they reached across social lines, attracting poor and rich alike while drawing male scions of the Jewish elite into their leadership ranks. Before that point, they seem little different from leaders of the multitude of contemporaneous non-Jewish movements of spiritual awakening (Pietists, Old Believers, etc.). But they soon distinguished themselves through the scope and durability of their sociopolitical authority.[61] The new, attenuated Hasidism embraced progressively larger circles of disciples and followers of zaddikim, who called themselves "Hasidim." Only with the appearance of these leaders, disciples, and followers, who for a time referred to themselves collectively as "Men of Silk," may one properly speak of a movement, for it was only at this point that the social possibilities inherent in concepts like *devekut* and "worship through corporeality" were realized. The new ideology was so relentlessly promoted and widely received that zaddikim emerged as east European Jewry's new supracommunal leaders at a time when the Council of Four Lands had been formally dissolved (1764) and the rabbinate was in decline. Only the northwestern part of historic Lithuania, domain of the renowned talmudist and old-style hasid R. Elijah the Vilna Gaon, managed for the most part to resist Hasidism's east European conquest.

Scholarly Explanations for the Rise of Hasidism

Research on Hasidism during its crucial maturation phase usually inhabits a more theoretical plane.[62] Hasidism's profound success is often attributed to the allure of its popular mystical doctrine.[63] Yet several intellectual historians have begun to question the sufficiency of doctrine as an explanation for Hasidism's triumph in the social realm. Immanuel Etkes argues that Hasidic homiletic literature served to merely to ratify existing Hasidic leadership institutions, and that what mattered most was not a zaddik's particular doctrine but his "personal charisma."[64] Mendel Piekarz appears even more suspicious of explanations derived from Hasidic doctrine, which he characterizes as a mystical mosaic that was largely derivative of earlier Kabbalah. Piekarz explains, "what was decisive for the spiritual orientation of the movement was not the mosaic of mystical ideas inherited from past generations of kabbalists . . . rather, it was the endeavour to realize the aim of inner spirituality through a new socio-religious movement whose ideology was influenced to some extent by kabbalistic ideas." Piekarz directs our gaze toward the "social institution of zaddikism."[65]

If doctrine was secondary to personalities and institutions, as these intellectual historians seem to insist, a reorientation along the lines of social and cultural historical inquiry is vitally important. While decontexualized ideological analyses may illustrate how zaddikim justified their authority to their devotees, they only bring us to the brink of the actualization of their ideas in the social sphere. To proceed further, it is necessary to shift our focus onto the mechanics of Hasidism's ascendancy, inquiring what zaddikim and their cohorts *did* as opposed to what they said. To this end, several historians have already contributed valuable studies of a narrower scope.[66] Of considerably less value, however, are the majority of more comprehensive social historical analyses, for they tend to operate on the problematic assumption that Hasidism arose as a reaction to some sort of crisis. Their predominately negative explanations have the effect of riveting the reader's attention away from the movement's vital, affirmative features and onto external problems like violence, poverty, discrimination, the erosion of autonomy, or the alleged crisis of modernity.

Simon Dubnow, who laid the foundation for modern historical study of the movement, attributes Hasidism's mass reception to the Chmielnicki massacres of 1648, the absence of Jewish civil rights, and the increase in Jewish poverty.[67] Raphael Mahler, in consonance with his Marxist leanings, blames burdensome Jewish taxes and devastating restrictions against Jewish innkeeping and alcohol production. As their poverty deepened, he argues, Polish Jews sought refuge in religious ecstasy and zaddikim.[68] Benzion Dinur argues that a secondary intelligentsia composed of preachers (*maggidim*), schoolteachers, kosher slaughterers, and cantors became so disenchanted with the current Jewish leadership that they joined fledgling Hasidic circles as a means toward gaining leadership positions for themselves.[69] Jacob Katz argues that an allegedly potent and threatening Enlightenment in eastern Europe sent traditional

Jews floundering toward the insular, ecstatic movement.[70] Finally, Chone Shmeruk offers the more convincing but by no means unproblematic explanation that Hasidism filled a vacuum created by the abolition in 1764 of the supracommunal Jewish self-government, the Council of Four Lands, in addition to the diminished effectiveness of local kahals (organs of local government).[71]

There are several reasons to suspect "crisis" as a catalyst for this burst of religious creativity. To begin with, it seems that crises tend more to generate cultural responses that are conservative and reactionary rather than spiritually innovative or revolutionary. In the case of diasporic Jewish history, moreover, the currency of crisis is rather cheap: one does not have look far to discover something of a crisis in any and every period. Finally, the specific crisis explanations proposed either do not withstand scrutiny or appear inadequate. The massacres of 1648 are easily dispensed with, for they occurred over a century before the advent of Hasidism, and the Jewish populations in affected towns were replenished fairly quickly.[72] Nor can the absence of Jewish civil rights have provoked a crisis, for this had eternally defined the Jewish condition in the Polish lands. What is more, certain rights were actually gained by Jews in postpartition Poland. In the tsarist empire, Jews of the first two merchant guilds were able to elect municipal officials in many towns of the Pale of Settlement after 1804.[73] Jews in Austrian Poland (Galicia), beginning in 1782, obtained partial emancipation as a result of the Toleration Patents of Joseph II.[74] Finally, Jews in temporarily Prussian-dominated regions saw their occupational opportunities broaden and their legal position in Warsaw improve considerably after 1802.[75]

Allegations of increased Polish Jewish poverty and misery driving the desperate masses into the arms of zaddikim are tempting, until we inquire whether standards of living really had declined. Gershon Hundert contends that "the middle decades of the eighteenth century saw the beginnings of a general economic recovery from the nadir reached at the turn of the century."[76] Even Raphael Mahler, who takes pains to elaborate the mass devastation wrought by anti-Jewish economic decrees, admits that Jewish occupational and residential opportunities improved considerably by the beginning of the nineteenth century.[77] Anecdotal observations by contemporaries corroborate these assessments. In 1815, the English tourist Robert Johnston proclaimed: "the whole retail trade of Lithuania and Poland is carried on by the Jews."[78] J. T. James, an English traveler in 1813–14, found Polish Jews to be the only people in a state of activity, "exercising almost all professions, and engaged in almost every branch of trade; millers, farmers, whitesmiths,[79] saddlers, drivers, ostlers,[80] innkeepers, etc." Their "constant bustle made them appear more abundant in number than they really were."[81] True, Jews seemed to be "rather viewed as profitable objects of taxation than in any more honorable light, and they suffered accordingly the most enormous exactions" at the hands of the government. Yet they were, as far as James could tell, "an industrious and persevering people, and of a nature that, notwithstanding the oppressive hand of government, seem everywhere to thrive; some, indeed, have amassed large fortunes in spite of all the difficulties, and settling in one or other of the Jewish towns, live in a state of considerable opulence and luxury."[82] In James's view, many Jews were able to successfully cope and even prosper.

The impotent rage that informs Polish anti-Jewish tracts only affirms those observations. In 1789, and again in 1815, Stanisław Staszic complained that the Jews had conquered all branches of trade to the impediment of Polish townsmen, had turned the peasants into drunks by dominating the liquor trade, and were, disgracefully, the only vital economic element in the kingdom.[83] In 1834, Antoni Ostrowski protested: "there is no trade in Poland other than Jewish trade; there is no petty trade, save Jewish; there is no industrial movement, save Jewish (despite certain exceptions to this rule). Who is an arms purveyor? The Jew. Who during wartime feeds and clothes the army? The Jew."[84] Wawrzyniec Surowiecki, a more moderate social critic, remarked in 1810 that "in nearly all localities Poland has salvaged her trade and industry thanks to the Jews."[85] Such hyperbole was probably intended to spur Polish audiences into increased economic activity. But it was rooted in a common perception of Jewish commercial prowess, if not predominance. As we shall observe further on, a thin stratum of Jews did in fact emerge as the region's premier entrepreneurs in banking, military purveying, and industrialization.

All this is not to deny that broad segments of Polish Jewry endured considerable economic pain and uncertainty. The last quarter of the eighteenth century saw a series of campaigns to abolish Jews from villages and the liquor trade, which detonated an urban Jewish population explosion. The resultant overpopulation, a creature of the various regimes' own making, was eventually treated with a most debilitating expedient—the institution of ghetto-like residence restrictions (rewiry), commencing in 1809, in what would amount to 12–15 percent of Central Poland's towns and cities.[86] Additional policies impacted the Jewish masses in particular—increased poll taxes; a kosher meat tax (6 grosz per pound, the cost of one pound of nonkosher meat!); licenses to engage in trade that were conditional upon the applicant's assets; and other trade, retail, craft, and labor restrictions.[87] A British tourist from the period described "most" of Warsaw's Jews as "extremely poor."[88] The zaddikim unquestionably offered the worst victims hope and consolation. But the mistaken assumption is that they appealed principally to those sectors. To the contrary, we will discover a full socioeconomic range of supplicants.

The conception of Hasidism as a product of a disgruntled secondary intelligentsia rebelling against the Jewish establishment on behalf of the masses has already confronted considerable doubt. A posthumously published manuscript composed in 1942 reveals that Ignacy Schiper discerned a relationship between Polish zaddikim and mercantile elites, and thus rejected the idea of Hasidism as an intercessory force for the disenfranchised masses.[89] Shmuel Ettinger suspected the notion that members of the Besht's immediate circle were wandering preachers or other members of a secondary intelligentsia.[90] Yeshayahu Shahar, after comparing Hasidic and non-Hasidic moralistic literature, has found significantly less social criticism in the former.[91] Finally, Moshe Rosman's archival analyses prove conclusively that Hasidism's founder resided tax-free in a kahal-owned house in Międzybóż, refrained from local conflicts, and was embraced by local elites.[92] Ada Rapoport-Albert remarks pointedly, "the picture of a spiritually ambitious, egalitarian, 'democratic' Hasidism, however attractive to the modern eye, does not square with one solid historical fact."[93]

As for the possible crisis that the Enlightenment entailed, scholars tend now to downplay the transformative power of the Enlightenment compared with the effects of emancipation.[94] Arnold Eisen argues:

> the role of *Enlightenment* per se—intellectual and ideological upheaval—has not been as predominant among Jews (and, I suspect, others too) in their negotiation of modernity as we might think. But *Emancipation*—by which I mean the assumption of new sorts of selfhood by Jews in a radically altered social and economic order—has, in contrast, been decisive.[95]

Neither extensive emancipation nor acculturation prevailed in eastern Europe during this period, and one may doubt the potency of a less personal and life-changing, not to mention comparatively weak, Jewish Enlightenment (Haskalah). We might allow for a certain amount of anxiety on the part of eastern European Jews who traveled westward on business and gained exposure to secular currents. But Enlightenment ideology without the realistic promise of emancipation was bound to be a hard sell. We would do well to heed Micha Yosef Berdychevski's lone dissent back in 1899: Hasidism was not born out of the crisis of Jewish Enlightenment, nor was it even aware of it in its inception.[96]

Did the abolition of the Council of Four Lands create a need for new forms of supracommunal leadership, as Chone Shmeruk suggests? This is a more plausible negative explanation; yet the actual magnitude of the leadership vacuum is unclear. Scholars have begun to downplay the effectiveness of the Council of Four Lands by the time it was abolished and demonstrate that Jewish communal life remained basically intact after its demise.[97] Artur Eisenbach finds that several illegal supracommunal gatherings occurred immediately after its abolition. Eventually, supracommunal activity was reinstated by the Polish government for fiscal reasons, and Jewish communities were required to appoint syndics (*shtadlanim*). After the partitions, only Prussia succeeded in seriously diminishing Jewish supra-communal autonomy. Hasidism might accordingly be expected to thrive in Prussian Poland, but it did not. Instead, the movement reached its creative and organizational zenith in regions like Central Poland, where officials had already restored a great deal of Jewish autonomy by requiring the appointment of community and district representatives for tax collection, censuses, and licensing.[98] Supracommunal conferences were held in both Central Poland and Galicia, another flourishing center of Hasidism.[99] Rather than precipitate a crisis, the abolition of the Council of Four Lands seems, at most, to have destabilized the old supracommunal leadership.

We would do better to focus on the weakened state of Jewish communal leadership on the local level. In a separate study, Shmeruk argues that by the eighteenth century, east European kahals proved increasingly ineffective in preventing ruinous encroachments on Jewish leases of noble-owned taverns, mills, and entire villages by fellow Jews. Such leases, known as *arrendas*, were a mainstay of the Polish Jewish economy. Hasidic leaders proved better able to regulate *arrenda* competition through moral rebukes, threats of magical retribution, and communal compulsion. They furthermore proved more adept than kahals at raising funds to ransom *arrenda* holders held captive by noble owners as a result of their inability to meet payments (recall the aforementioned letter by R. Zusya).[100] Gershon Hundert has argued, similarly, that the pre-Hasidic institutions of Jewish communal autonomy, "so much celebrated in certain older schools of historiography, provided, in fact, only the illusion of independent decision-making, and frequently served interests outside of the (Jewish) community."[101] Increasingly by the eighteenth century, "elections could be cancelled, rabbis' fees could be established, elders could be demoted, and generally all activities could be, and were, closely supervised by the [non-Jewish] town owners."[102] Interference in Jewish communal elections by profit-conscious Polish town owners had become common. Some scholars argue that awarding the office of town rabbi to the highest bidder had transformed the rabbinate into just another *arrenda* to be leased from the nobility.[103] According to Hundert, as soon as it became apparent that Jewish lay and religious leaders were serving the interests of the Polish nobility rather than the Jewish community, the way was open for novel forms of leadership that could claim to be "entirely free of political and economic interference."[104] Zaddikim could present themselves as untainted representatives of Jewish agency.[105]

Comparative religious theories that posit similarities between Hasidic and surrounding Christian practice may also hold some promise. Christian influences on Hasidism were seized upon by the eighteenth-century Hasidic opponent R. David of Maków in recalling a conversation between a Hasid and a skeptical traveler from Lublin. When the latter complained that the zaddik Jacob Isaac of Lublin had succeeded in nothing but causing poultry prices to escalate, the offended Hasid asked, "Why do you say such things about the *Rebbe*? Do people not pay him heed, are distinguished people not drawn to his door to seek well-being?" The traveler retorted: "This is nothing new. Do not several hundred magnates and nobles go to seek the divinities of the places Częstochowa, Kobylańska and Kalwaria?" The comparison to Christian pilgrims was too much for the Hasid, who let out a scream, produced a knife, and ripped the blasphemer's clothes.[106] T. Ysander and Yaffe Eliach were the first modern scholars to venture a comparison between Hasidism and Christian mystical revivalist movements in eastern Europe.[107] Hundert, in a preliminary manner, draws attention to similarities between Hasidism and eighteenth-century spiritual movements like Pietism, Quietism, Wesleyanism, Jansenism, the Great Awakening, and the Old Believers. Rather than posit any Hasidic imitation of Christian movements, however, Hundert describes "the appearance of a similar *geist* at a similar *zeit* among both Jews and Christians." These movements were not a reaction to the Enlightenment but rather shared *with* the Enlightenment "the emboldening of the individual to independence of thought and feeling in matters of the spirit."[108] This *Zeitgeist*, Hundert concludes, was fueled by the spread of the printing press.[109]

Several of these environmental and phenomenological factors were undoubtedly conducive to the flourishing enterprises of Hasidism's founding geniuses. The most significant were probably the widespread debasement of local rabbinical authority and the increase of religious individualism that attended the spread of printing, not to mention the allure of Hasidic concepts themselves. But these new realities and ideas did not in any direct sense foster Hasidism's formation into a mass movement, nor did they ensure its enduring success and fixity. The key to Hasidism's advent as a mass movement, we will find, resided within the movement's institutional architecture.

The Approach of This Study

The sources that have nourished the historiography of Hasidism are divided linguistically between Jewish and non-Jewish languages, with scholars tending to draw upon one category to the exclusion of the other. This division has occasioned a conspicuous polarization in the field between "internal" studies based on Hebrew and Yiddish sources—homiletic literature, Hasidic tales and eye-witness testimony, anti-Hasidic polemics, correspondence, and so on—and "external" studies based on sources in non-Jewish languages—predominately Polish, Russian, and German archival documents. The former afford an internal Jewish perspective, albeit one that is refracted through divergent ideological dispositions. They richly depict inner Hasidic life and doctrine, yet usually fail to acknowledge its historical context. In the case of the latter, the reverse tends to occur: outside, non-Jewish perspectives are provided, and governmental policies toward Hasidism are illuminated, but the movement's inner dynamics are usually missed.

Moshe Rosman's biography of the Besht, *Founder of Hasidism*, composed of chapters based on internal sources and others based on external ones, is the first work to begin to overcome this bifurcation. Rosman's broader palette enables him to contextualize the incipient movement and finally and decisively overturn the dubious conception of the Besht as folk hero and social revolutionary by grounding the enigmatic leader in his historical milieu.[110] Gershon Hundert has similarly employed internal and external sources, offering up a mélange of explanations for Hasidism's preliminary transition into a movement. Based on internal sources, he points to the de-emphasis of asceticism and even Torah study in favor of "the pursuit of the experience of the presence of God, including in the human community;" and based on external sources, he highlights factors like the preponderance of youth in the region and the role of the printing press.[111] These insights into Hasidism's origins cannot, however, be automatically applied to the generation of disciples that forged Hasidism into an organized, multivalent, trans-regional movement.[112] This study extends an integrated multilingual analysis to the emergence of Hasidism "proper"—a mass movement that produced a cultural sea change in Jewish Eastern Europe.

The first obstacle to approaching Hasidism in this manner is the questionable reliability of Hasidic sources, for Hasidim seldom recorded their day-to-day experiences in writing.[113] They have proven assiduous custodians of memory by orally preserving recollections about zaddikim, but their recollections were only transcribed and published during the latter half of the nineteenth century in an apparent attempt to compete with the newly emergent modern Jewish literature.[114] Such material is hagiography—sacred biography whose primary function is to inspire piety by recounting the miraculous deeds of zaddikim. Its potential as a historical source has generated considerable controversy, most recently between Moshe Rosman and Immanuel Etkes. Rosman in effect disqualifies the classic hagiography *Shivhei Ha-Besht* as a legitimate historical source, admitting only its heuristic value.[115] His objections are worth noting, for they may apply to Hasidic hagiographical sources in general. The tales in *Shivhei Ha-Besht*, Rosman argues, were subject to the corruption inherent in oral transmission over the span of many decades. Second, they were possibly deliberately altered through selective emphasis in an effort to address evolving contemporary anxieties. Third, Rosman feels that the book is intrinsically compromised by the pious agendas of its printer and compiler.[116]

To Rosman's concerns, we may add the disconcerting fact that Hasidic leaders themselves doubted the veracity of certain hagiographic accounts. According to one account, the zaddik Abraham Joshua Heschel of Opatów "used to tell tall tales"; while either R. Levi Isaac of Berdyczów or the Seer of Lublin "(I do not remember if it was told in the name of the Berdyczówer or the Lubliner)" claimed to know "the Lurianic secret of small exaggerations; therefore, he was able to tell the tall tales effectively."[117] The zaddik R. Mordecai of Neskhiż is said to have proclaimed that he did not listen to any of the accounts of deeds of zaddikim, "for many such tales are fabrications and full of errors, except for tales about the Besht, may his memory be for a blessing. For even if such a tale did not reflect an actual occurrence it was in any case in the Besht's power to do anything."[118] Skepticism within the Hasidic camp should considerably deepen our own.

Compounding the problematic nature of hagiography is the increasing awareness that certain accounts bear an uncanny resemblance to earlier Jewish tales and contemporaneous non-Jewish folktales. Some echo tales of medieval German Pietists and even the messianic pretender Shabbetai Zvi.[119] Parallels exist between the earlier tales of the Safed mystic R. Isaac Luria in *Shivhei ha-Ari* and certain tales in *Shivhei ha-Besht*; while other tales in the latter are adaptations of tales about earlier ba'alei shem.[120] Versions or motifs of Hasidic tales have been located in classical Jewish literature.[121] Motifs, plots, and even characters of certain Hasidic tales have turned up in Polish and Ukrainian folk culture, as well.[122] One pioneering study demonstrates that certain tales told by Hasidic storytellers originated among the Ukrainian peasantry.[123] An incarnation of the Christian version of the "Gregorius Legend" of incest and repentance has been identified in a Hasidic tale attributed to the son-in-law of the nineteenth-century zaddik Israel of Ruzhin.[124] And parallels have even been observed between a series of tales about the wanderings of the brothers Zusya and Elimelekh, from which "The Horses" was derived, and Polish accounts of the legendary wanderings of Jesus and St. Peter.[125] Not all such Hasidic versions were necessarily permutations of their counterparts.[126] But the resemblances cast doubt on their historicity.

Nevertheless, such instances of demonstrated fabrication and imitation are rather limited. And notwithstanding the possible corruptions and alterations alluded to here, hagiography can be shown to retain a great deal of reliable information. First, as David Assaf occasionally demonstrates in his biographical study of the mid-nineteenth-century zaddik Israel of Ruzhin, elements of hagiographical accounts can be verified through corroboration and sound historical reasoning.[127] Second, hagiographers had to contend with multiple living witnesses, including relatives and descendants dedicated to preserving a "true" record of a zaddik's life. This may explain why they were often moved to record trustworthy members of oral transmission chains, a form of Hasidic footnoting that bespeaks a desire for legitimacy.[128] Recitations of Hasidic tales by professional raconteurs during the Third Meal of the Sabbath, moreover, received fixed ritual status, a sacralization of storytelling that may have discouraged overt fabrication.[129]

As for Rosman's most compelling objection, that Hasidic hagiography was created to serve unabashedly pious and didactic agendas, it is important to acknowledge an equally strong compulsion to faithfully record a Zaddik's every action and utterance. This latter imperative explains why hagiographers disclose so many mundane and even potentially embarrassing details that fail to forward the objective of edifying the Zaddik. One can sense their struggle as they recount, for example, the repeated dependence of Zaddikim on their female patron Temerel Sonenberg-Bergson, which runs against the society's patriarchal grain. As we will see, in such cases hagiographers are willing to mitigate but not extirpate unflattering accounts in order to preserve the greater part of something that can only be termed the historical record.[130] Hasidic hagiographical accounts, when unaltered by Buber and company, are more accurately understood as sites of tension than straightforward evangelical forms.

The following passage, depicting the dedication of a *bet midrash* (study house) in Płock by the newly minted zaddik Alexsander Zusya Kahana will help to illustrate the complexity of Hasidic narratives:

> In 1834, on Hannukah, our rabbi [Alexsander Zusya Kahana] of blessed memory dedicated the new *bet midrash* in Płock, which was built by the wealthy and generous Reb Mordecai Katriel Danziger, peace be upon him. And in his dedication speech, our rabbi inspired the community assembled there to establish fixed times for [studying] Torah. And afterward our rabbi blessed the entire community, and in particular blessed the aforementioned generous man

[Danziger], proclaiming that Torah study will never be removed from the new *bet midrash*. And this blessing of our rabbi, the zaddik, of blessed memory, was fulfilled. For before the new *bet midrash* was built, the center for Torah study had been in the big *bet midrash*, and now the study center was the new bet *midrash*. And according to the testimony of elders—which they themselves remember and which their fathers told them—ever since the new *bet midrash* was built and down to today [1939], for over a hundred years, Torah study has not ceased in this *bet midrash* for an instant.[131]

How much is legendary, and how much historical? Its late date of publication—quite poignantly, 1939—is worrisome. Its claim of unceasing Torah study in the new Hasidic-sponsored bet midrash appears polemical, for it is meant to contrast favorably with the older non-Hasidic bet midrash, and may additionally serve to assuage contemporary concerns about the erosion of tradition.

Yet elements of the account are eminently plausible. The date of R. Kahana's dedication fits the schema of the Hasidic conquest in Płock: R. Kahana was appointed town rabbi in 1829 over the objections of both Maskilim and powerful supporters of a rival Hasidic candidate; yet those opponents had conceded by this date. The ceremony's occurrence on Hannukah, when the ancient Temple was rededicated, may be a product of poetic license, but is feasible nonetheless. The narrator supplies details and names and, however vaguely, "footnotes" local elders and their fathers, all of which demonstrates a concern for accuracy and credibility. The contention about unrelenting Torah study may be hyperbolic, but the sense it conveys affirms what we know about the intellectual focus of Hasidism's Przysucha school (see chapter 1). More important, the narrator describes what we will find to be a rather typical attempt to extend Hasidic control over local study and worship through the domination or construction of local buildings and institutions (see chapter 2). At the same time, he discloses the very *limits* of Hasidic control by referring to "the community assembled there" rather than the town's entire Jewish population, and by acknowledging the continued functioning of the big *bet midrash* (which archival sources in chapter 2 confirm as non-Hasidic domain).[132] He divulges additional phenomena that we will come to recognize as typical components of a Hasidic takeover: the assistance of a wealthy patrons like Danziger (see chapter 3); the assumption of power by a well-pedigreed Hasid like R. Kahana (see chapter 4);[133] and R. Kahana's grassroots popularity in spite of the favoritism he demonstrates toward wealthy patrons (see chapter 5). Finally, the crossgenerational transmission of this account is, itself, testament to the Hasidic genius for promotion and publicity (see chapter 6).[134] Płock Hasidim, we gather from this account, appointed an emergent zaddik as town rabbi and constructed a thriving Hasidic bet midrash; yet they proved unable to fully "Hasidicize" the town's population or dominate its central institutions. They prevailed, but only to a limited degree. Hagiography can thus be sifted for elements that appear extraneous to the goal of edifying the zaddik—transmission chains, dates, specified actors, mundane or embarrassing details, and so on—and sometimes find external corroboration.

There is, on the other hand, good reason to also question the Rankean hierarchy that always prefers contemporaneous, written sources. As Gwyn Prins has pointed out, "documentary sources are not as unintentionally, unselfconsciously bequeathed to us as one might think," while "long-term memory, especially in individuals who have entered that phase which psychologists call 'life review,' can be remarkably precise."[135] An openness to memory is vital if we are ever to hope to recover the experiences of Jewish society's less powerful members. This is particularly true with respect to women, who formed a considerable proportion of Hasidism's constituency and could prove instrumental behind the scenes, but were omitted from the historical record.[136] At the same time, a healthy dose of skepticism should unquestionably be applied to all non-Hasidic, contemporaneous sources, for they are products of the power struggles of the age. The first group of Jewish opponents, Mitnaggdim, usually represented a segment of the rabbinic or scholarly elite that was rapidly losing ground to the populist zaddikim. The next major Jewish opposition group, comprising proponents of integration and Enlightenment-based reform who, for the sake of convenience, may be labeled "Maskilim" (Enlightened), opposed Hasidism's perceived obscurantism.[137] Then there are the multiple archival sources. Thanks to the renewed accessibility of east European archives following the events of 1989, a bounty of hitherto unknown or insufficiently analyzed records about Hasidism from a non-Jewish perspective is now available. But official observations were usually based on the observations of anti-Hasidic informants, while officials themselves all too often revealed anti-Hasidic biases. If these limits are kept in mind, archival sources can revolutionize our understanding of Hasidism by providing an insight into how individual zaddikim coped with the distinct challenges presented by the new regions into which they expanded.

This book focuses on Hasidism's spread into "Central Poland," a relatively economically advanced, semiautonomous entity that was partitioned, conquered, and ruled indirectly by several regimes—Prussian, Austrian, French (the Duchy of Warsaw), and Russian (the Congress Kingdom of Poland). As the setting of eastern Europe's nascent industrial revolution, Central Poland encompassed the region's most urbanized, industrialized areas, on the one hand, and rural expanses with scattered, less developed small towns and villages, on the other. Central Poland's Jewish communities consequently encompassed a broader social spectrum than was found in other formerly Polish lands where Hasidism flourished, like the Ukraine, Belarus, and Galicia. Zaddikim whose formative careers were in Central Poland, referred to as "Polish zaddikim," garnered a following along the entire social spectrum, from the wealthiest, most educated, and cosmopolitan Jews residing in Poland's economic nerve centers to the most impoverished "shtetl" Jews. Their versatility alone should dispel notions about zaddikim as obscurantist social revolutionaries, and compel us to revise the portrayal of Hasidism as a predominantly demotic, small-town, folk phenomenon.[138]

How to explain "Polish Hasidism's" upsurge during that period in at least a preliminary way? If we had the ability to travel back in time and ask a Polish Hasid what drew him to his master, we would probably hear about the zaddik's commanding presence—his piercing yet transcendent gaze, his holy aura, and the inspirational effect of his sermons, blessings, and divine worship. This is probably what certain historians mean when they invoke the term "charisma." One eyewitness, for example, attests to the charisma of R. Jacob Isaac, the Seer of Lublin—his "wondrous feats animated by a holy spirit, his exalted spiritual level, and his spectacular, self-abnegating worship amidst flames of fire."[139] Such performances enhanced the zaddik's credibility: surely such an inspired figure must also possess the power to heal the sick, bestow fertility, ensure success in business, and exorcise demons. Confidence in the charismatic leader was bolstered by his simple yet profound teachings, which scholars are able to access indirectly through Hasidism's impressive cannon of homiletic literature, and which were reportedly all the more impressive when delivered by the zaddik himself. The premier accomplishment of such spiritual supermen was their inducement of intense spiritual experiences among devotees.

Nevertheless, something lay behind the zaddik's charisma, miracles, and skillful hermeneutics. It seems that whether they are disparaged or romanticized, religious revivalists are constantly underestimated in terms of their potential for accruing secular authority through organization, fundraising, and cutting-edge marketing. Against all expectations, revivalists seem to rather thrive on the opportunities presented by modernizing economies. The organizational acumen of a mid-nineteenth-century Ukrainian and Galician zaddik was recently explored in detail by David Assaf.[140] We will find that in Central Poland as well, at an earlier stage than that explored in Assaf's book, zaddikim were exceptionally well-organized, financed, and promoted. Their sociopolitical projects, like their doctrines, engendered a brilliant combination of elitism and popular appeal which I have termed "populism." Beginning in the late eighteenth century, they began to alter communal and regional politics, governmental policy toward Jews, and economic trends, in addition to Jewish culture. Hasidic institution building may thus be said to have constituted the ultimate "worship through corporeality."

Chapter 1 here highlights the regional distinctiveness of Polish Hasidism and attempts to quantify its regional expansion. Chapter 2 concerns the mechanics of Polish Hasidism's political ascendancy by reconstructing conquests of local institutions. Chapter 3 uncovers Polish Hasidism's vast patronage network within the Jewish mercantile elite. Chapter 4 considers the significance of familial ties between zaddikim and the rabbinic elite. Chapter 5 evaluates the movement's profound grassroots appeal. And Chapter 6 focuses on Hasidic marketing and propaganda campaigns, from cutting-edge printing ventures to the dissemination of oral and nonverbal media. Zaddikim, like many leaders of cultural and religious revivals, successfully tapped into their region's vital folkways. Yet, when gathered together, these various strands reveal the movement as inclined decidedly toward the elite. This study thus seeks to place Hasidism's popular component in perspective.

As most enduring movements amass various types of power to propagate their creed, practice, and lifestyle, highlighting the facets of Polish Hasidic power has been set as our paramount task. Such an emphasis may demystify the zaddikim to a degree. Yet the reader will gain manifold recompense by glimpsing the complexity of their personalities and activities. Hagiography often performs a disservice by smoothing over the hero's persona to the point of abstraction. A more candid portrayal reveals how motivations like ambition, acquisitiveness, vindictiveness, spiritual inspiration, and compassion could coexist in a *single* individual. Recognizing Hasidism's power dimension is additionally risky, in that its followers might be misconstrued as having been somehow duped. It is important to recognize that Hasidim were not passive agents being acted upon. Their allegiance yielded a sense of empowerment and control over the unknown, not to mention an exhilarating communal solidarity; while certain Hasidic pioneers in banking, trade, and industry could determine matters as weighty as leadership succession. The latter group might seem least likely to have been inclined toward a movement that promoted insularity, mystical piety, and spiritual submission; yet were Hasidism really restricted to simple, déclassé Jews, as was once assumed, its survival would have been improbable in a society as hierarchical as that of east European Jewry. To the contrary, it will be shown that Polish Hasidism was conveyed upon the modest wave of economic modernization that began to sweep the region at the end of the eighteenth century.

Notwithstanding the movement's theological ingenuity and emotional richness, the homiletic handiwork and charisma of early zaddikim fail to wholly satisfy the question of how, precisely, they became communal and supracommunal leaders. The following chapters tell the story of a group of mystical elites who, backed by a sizeable segment of the emerging Jewish bourgeoisie, mobilized the Jewish masses to consent to and actively support their authority at the expense of fellow elites, while nevertheless managing to preserve the existing social hierarchy. Their silk garments did not, therefore, only signify zealous compliance with the inscrutable biblical injunction against mixing wool and linen. They also announced an earthly grandeur.

I

Hasidism in Central Poland, 1754–1830

And I asked the Messiah, "When will the master come?" And he
answered me, "Once your teaching [Torah] will have spread throughout the world."
                        —R. Israel ben Eliezer, the Ba'al Shem Tov,
                                              "The Holy Epistle"

Borne by the Besht's disciples and descendants, Hasidism expanded
northward from its origins in Podolia through Volhynia and into
historical Lithuania during the second half of the eighteenth century, coalescing in towns such as Karlin and Witebsk and flowing
westward into Galicia, where an important center formed in the
town of Leżajsk.[1] The Besht's illustrious great-grandson R. Nahman
carried Hasidism southeastward into the Bratslav (Bracław) Palati-
nate and established a court, while a few of the Besht's disciples, including the pioneering Hasidic theorist R. Jacob Joseph of Połonne,
resided in Bessarabia for a time. Several traversed the Carpathian
mountains and settled in Hungary.[2] During the Besht's lifetime, disciples of his preeminent successor, R. Dov Ber the "Great Maggid"
of Międzyrzecz, made inroads in Central Poland. Hasidism thus arrived in Central Poland a good deal earlier than is usually supposed,
even penetrating Warsaw before the end of the eighteenth century.[3]
The brothers R. Samuel Shmelke (1726–78) and R. Phineas Horowitz (1730–1805), disciples of the Great Maggid who had become
Hasidic during their youth, became rabbis in Ryczywół (1754) and
Witków (1760).[4] When R. Samuel Shmelke left Central Poland in
1772 to assume the prestigious Nikolsburg post, several of his disciples emerged as the pillars of Polish Hasidism: R. Levi Isaac of Żelechów (later, of Berdyczów), R. Israel, "the Maggid" of Kozienice,

and R. Jacob Isaac, "the Seer" of Lublin. Disciples of the latter, including R. Jacob Isaac, "the Holy Jew" of Przysucha, R. Simha Bunem of Przysucha, and R. Meir of Opatów/Stopnica, established thriving courts in Central Poland during the first decades of the nineteenth century. As those leaders spent their formative years in Central Poland, historians refer to them as "Polish" zaddikim.

The historiography of Polish Hasidism is still in its beginning stages. David Assaf has drawn attention to this lacuna in his pioneering bibliographical survey:

> The period of Hasidism's origins has received something which its period of peak expansion has been denied: a scholarly treatment that is quantitatively and qualitatively rich, comprehensive and multi-faceted from historical, social, ideological, and spiritual, perspectives, and enhanced by textual and bibliographic analyses. Polish Hasidism, the arena for the movement's principle developments during the nineteenth century, still lacks the most basic systematic sketch of its full historical, biographical and chronological picture through a survey and analysis of its ideological and spiritual growth in all its factions, courts, and abounding variety.[5]

How can it be that the arena for the movement's "principle developments" during its "period of peak expansion" was so neglected by historians? Assaf alludes to certain "ideological and social motivations that led [secular] scholars of Hasidism to concentrate principally on Hasidism's first generations, as well as [secular scholars'] hostile condemnations and undisguised derision toward nineteenth-century Hasidism." Their attitude contrasts completely with that of Orthodox Hasidic historians, who "prefer for opposite reasons to deal with later Hasidism."[6] While he prefers not to explore this fascinating and unsettling paradox, Assaf does define its consequence: most of what has been written on nineteenth-century Polish Hasidism is composed by Orthodox Hasidic historians and based almost entirely on hagiography.[7]

There are relatively few exceptions. Zvi Rabinowicz and Avraham Rubinstein compiled somewhat more diverse and reliable sources, yet did not integrate them into larger theoretical constructs.[8] Aaron Aescoly, on the other hand, produced a grand synthesis of Polish Hasidism that highlights colorful personalities and intrigues but rarely introduces new evidence.[9] Raphael Mahler's archival-based work is perhaps most recognizable as history; yet a reexamination of Mahler's sources reveals him as given to hasty and ideologically motivated pronouncements.[10] Fortunately, however, there has been a surge of recent scholarly interest in early Polish Hasidism. Intellectual historians have begun to distill the doctrines of R. Jacob Isaac, "the Seer of Lublin," R. Israel, "the Maggid of Kozienice," R. Simha Bunem of Przysucha, and the latter's Izbica/Radzyń offshoot.[11] Social historians have meanwhile begun to examine the intercessory (shtadlanut) activities of Polish zaddikim, their publishing endeavors, and the movement's geographic spread.[12] Marcin Wodziński has published new archival sources related to the subject.[13] And Ignacy Schiper's recently discovered prewar manuscript has enriched our understanding of Polish

Hasidism considerably, not the least through its transcriptions of sources destroyed during the razing of the Warsaw ghetto.[14]

These studies yield a series of colorful vignettes about pioneering Polish zaddikim, as follows.

The first zaddik of Central Poland to achieve major celebrity status, R. Levi Isaac of Żelechów (later, of Berdyczów, 1740–1810), was a disciple of the Great Maggid of Międzyrzecz and, from 1761, a disciple of R. Samuel Shmelke. He succeeded the latter as rabbi of Żelechów four years later. R. Levi Isaac's tenure was tempestuous, and he was eventually forced to leave town. After another tumultuous term in Pińsk, beginning in 1772, he became rabbi of Berdyczów (the Ukraine) in 1785, where he remained the rest of his life. R. Levi Isaac's passionate advocacy of common Jews earned him the moniker *Darbarimdiger* (the Merciful One). His discourses collected in *Kedushat Levi* (Sławuta, 1788) reveal him as one of Hasidism's most thought-provoking theorists. After R. Levi Isaac's departure from the region, Polish Hasidism came to revolve around three courts, Kozienice, Lublin, and Przysucha—although R. Levi Isaac continued to exert an influence over Polish Jewish affairs.

The first major Polish Hasidic center, in Kozienice, was founded by R. Israel Hopstein, known as the "Maggid of Kozienice" (1733/7–1815), a disciple of the Great Maggid of Międzyrzecz. Upon the latter's death, he transferred his allegiance to R. Elimelekh of Leżajsk, the Galician leader who set the emergent "zaddik" vocation on a theoretical foundation. The Maggid of Kozienice became permanently employed as a preacher (*maggid*) in the town of Kozienice, and his soaring fame attracted the attention of members of the Polish aristocracy. Hagiography depicts him as physically frail but spiritually mighty. His teachings, conveyed in *Avodat Yisrael* (Josefów, 1842), display his mastery of normative legalistic methods (*halakha*) and classical Kabbalah. Upon his death, part of his following went over to his son Moses Eliakim Briya (1757–1828); however, his most prominent disciples eventually established their own courts (e.g., Isaac Meir Alter of Ger [1789–1866]).

A second Polish Hasidic center emerged in the city of Lublin, around the court of R. Jacob Isaac Horowitz, the "Seer of Lublin" (1745–1815), another disciple of R. Elimelekh of Leżajsk's. The Seer was born in 1745 in Jozefów,[15] and raised in Tarnograd. He studied in Łańcut under R. Moses Zvi Meisels, and he became a disciple of the zaddik Samuel Shmelke in Ryczywół, Sieniawa, and Nikolsburg, and then a disciple of R. Elimelekh of Leżajsk. During his master's lifetime, the Seer revolted and formed his own court in Łańcut (Galicia), and eventually settled in Lublin, a city renowned for its giants of Talmudic interpretation. Despite initial opposition, the Lublin kahal eventually endorsed his prayer house, which was something of a watershed in Hasidic history. The Seer promoted a miracle-centered approach to Hasidism, stressing the zaddik's obligation to magically provide for his followers' material needs. Although that doctrine appealed to society's lower echelons, the Seer proved equally successful at attracting scions of the rabbinic elite. This had a great deal to do with the efforts of his recruiter, R. David Biderman of Lelów (1746–1813), who brought in future stars like R. Jacob Isaac, "the Holy Jew" of Przysucha, R. Simha Bunem of Przysucha, R. Isaac of Warka, and the renowned physician Hayyim David Bernard to the Lublin court. The Seer died in 1815 after falling from his window on the eve of Simhat Torah, an event that gave rise to a great deal of unkind speculation among Hasidic opponents.[16] In Central Poland, his doctrine of "material zaddikism" was sustained by his disciple R. Meir of Opatów/Stopnica (1760–1831), whose discourses appeared later in *Or Le-Shamayim* (Lublin, 1909).

Among the Seer's more innovative and distinctive disciples was R. Jacob Isaac Rabinowicz, "the Holy Jew" of Przysucha (1765–1814). Born in Przedbórz to a family of illustrious lineage, R. Jacob Isaac studied under several rabbinic luminaries and was eventually assigned the moniker "Holy Jew" perhaps to differentiate him from his teacher of the same name. He was entrusted with the education of the Seer's scholarly followers but broke away and formed his own court in Przysucha, an episode that would find dramatic expression in Martin Buber's novel *Gog and Magog*. The Holy Jew's somewhat elitist, Talmud-centered approach formed a counterpoint to Lublin Hasidism. He introduced a rigorous curriculum, demanded of his disciples uncompromising self-scrutiny, and conceived his role as less miracle worker than spiritual guide, (working miracles, he once claimed, was nothing compared to the difficulty involved in becoming a "good Jew"). Most controversially, the Holy Jew counseled followers to delay their prayers until after they had achieved a state of mental preparedness. His discourses appeared later in works like *Nifla'ot Ha-Yehudi* (Piotroków, 1908). The Holy Jew's sons reverted to miracle working and only succeeded in attracting a portion of their father's following.[17]

The main inheritor of the Przysucha method was the Holy Jew's preeminent disciple, R. Simha Bunem (1765–1827), author of the discourses in *Kol Simha* (Breslau, 1859). Remarkably cosmopolitan for a Hasidic leader, he had studied in the Matesdorf and Nikolsburg Yeshivas, mastered several non-Jewish languages, traded in Leipzig and Danzig (where he had indulged in dubious activities like card playing [gambling?] and attended theater performances), and had been one of the first Jews in the region to earn a pharmaceutical license. Despite those secular predilections, R. Simha Bunem denounced governmental efforts to modernize Jewish education and transform occupational norms in his capacity as delegate to the Jewish Committee's advisory chamber in the Congress Kingdom of Poland. His combination of scholarly Hasidism and worldliness made him the most popular zaddik of his day; but it also aroused controversy. At the famous Ustila (Uściług) wedding, the elder zaddik Abraham Joshua Heschel of Opatów/Międzyboż presided over deliberations to possibly ban the Przysucha school because of its disregard for prescribed times of prayer and its alleged Sabbatean tendencies. R. Simha Bunem was exonerated, thanks to attestations by several star disciples, as well as an attestation by his rival, the Holy Jew's son R. Yerahmiel Zvi.[18] Upon R. Simha Bunem's death, part of his following passed to his son R. Abraham Moses, including the future zaddik Isaac Kalish of Warka (1779–1848), Polish Jewry's premier intercessor (*shtadlan*).[19] But the larger part of R. Simha Bunem's following went over to his disciple, the fiery Menahem Mendel of Kotsk (Kock) (1787–1859). The Przysucha approach was sustained in the courts of Kotsk, Gur (Góra Kalwaria), Warka, Aleksander (Aleksandrów Łódzki), Izbica, and Biała.

The Qualitative Dimension: The Question of "Polish" Hasidism

In a series of intriguing theoretical articles, David Assaf has problematized the entire project of delineating schools of Hasidic doctrine by geographical region. Followers of a given zaddik, he argues, could live anywhere in eastern Europe, marry across geopolitical borders, and visit zaddikim from other regions; while zaddikim themselves were not constrained by official borders when dispatching emissaries. Assaf also cautions historians against stereotyping Hasidism by region: Lithuanian and Belarusan schools of Hasidism were not necessarily more scholarly or elitist, nor were Ukrainian and Galician schools of Hasidism any more folksy or popular. Hasidism's basic features (zaddikim, disciples, courts, etc.) transcended any geographical divisions or distinctions. As for Hasidism in Central Poland, Assaf speculates that it is more accurate to speak of "Hasidism *in* Poland" than "Polish Hasidism." The ideologies within Polish Hasidism seem so varied as to elude common categorization, while Polish Hasidic practices seem to fundamentally resemble those of Hasidim in other regions.[20]

Assaf's caveats help scholars avoid the facile, politically motivated stereotypes generated by Hasidic regional rivals, which have too often been accepted uncritically. They appear well founded if confined to Hasidism's ideological tenets and basic practices. Indeed, the intellectual historian who would undertake to distinguish a "Polish" Hasidic doctrine must contend with the quite divergent Hasidic doctrines that arose within Central Poland. At the same time, the ways Hasidism was "performed" transcended regional and temporal boundaries. Both considerations militate against an unequivocally "Polish" Hasidism, as the following analysis of Polish Hasidic texts and testimonies will demonstrate.

As already noted, Polish Hasidism became divided between the Lublin school, which promoted a materially oriented Hasidism, and the Przysucha school, which demanded rigorous character scrutiny and Talmudic study.[21] The Lublin school's more "material" form of zaddikism is borne out in the Seer of Lublin's interpretation of Leviticus 1:2, which commands the Israelites to sacrifice from their cattle to expiate their sins:

> "When any man among you offers something up, he shall bring his offering from the cattle" (Leviticus 1:2): the verse teaches us that if we desire Israel to be brought to repentance, the only aim should be to fulfill all their needs; then they will be good.
>
> First, because we need this—just as at the beginning of creation God provided sustenance for Adam and subsequent creatures.

In addition, so that by this they will come to know God's mercy and recognize his favors and wonders, and their hearts will burn for their Creator, blessed be He.

And in addition, because the words of the zaddik who draws down the divine bounty are heeded; and he is then able to teach them the ways of God. And for this reason we say "If any man from among you offers something up to God," meaning that if [the zaddik] wants to actually "offer up" [i.e., bring near] one of you to God, I advise him *from what* he can offer them up to God: *"from the cattle,"* namely, that [the zaddik] should draw down *material and animalistic things.* And this is done in a general sense, for all types of material things. And afterwards the divine bounty, which contains all types of bounty—children, life, sustenance, from which all other needs and good things derive—is distributed amidst the people.[22]

Rather than accept the verse as a simple commandment to the high priest to offer up the Israelites' cattle as a sacrifice to God, the Seer imposes a miracle-oriented message upon it. The zaddik is the equivalent of a latter-day high priest; only instead of burnt sacrifices, he "offers up" his followers to God by means of material incentives (i.e., "cattle"). The ideological impetus is unmistakable: the Seer has subtly inserted himself, whom everyone recognizes as the quintessential miracle-working zaddik, into Leviticus 1:2. We are then afforded a glimpse at the process by which the Seer qua high priest works his miracles: he draws down a general "divine bounty," which contains the recognizable categories of children, life, and sustenance, which then branch out into more specific personal benefits for each pilgrim.[23]

A markedly different sensibility informs the Przysucha school of Hasidism, which conceived the zaddik more as a guide for those wishing to achieve mystical inwardness within a modern, urbanized reality:[24]

"The Man has become like one of us, knowing good and evil . . ." (Genesis 3:22). Indeed, the correct interpretation seems to be that the most principle aspect of all creation is Man. For the Creator created the world in His wisdom, and created Man in order that he would apprehend [*yitbonen*] His creations and behold the extent of His boundless, inestimable wisdom, and then praise, glorify, extol, and exalt the One who created all this.

And before the sin [of eating from the Tree of Knowledge], Adam apprehended it constantly, and his wisdom and soul were one. For every part of his soul apprehended the wisdom of the exalted God; and thus he had no knowledge [*yediyah*]. For the entire essence of his soul was clothed in this apprehension constantly.

But after the sin, although Adam could occasionally apprehend the greatness of God, he could no longer do so constantly. And thus he required knowledge [*yediyah*] of his apprehension, so that he could know when he apprehended. And this is the meaning of "The

Man has become like one of us," which is to say, like "another one" *with respect to himself,* so that he can know when he apprehends.[25]

Before Adam sinned, he was in a permanent state of *hitbonenut*—a constant, transcendent apprehension of God devoid of any self-consciousness. As punishment for eating of the Tree of Knowledge, Adam was now only able to attain *hitbonenut* temporarily. As consolation, however, he received *yediyah*—a rationalistic, self-conscious kind of knowledge that was inferior but still vital, for it allowed him to stand outside of himself to detect when he had achieved *hitbonenut.* By implication, the latter-day mystic, too, should retain a degree of self-consciousness and rootedness in reality by nurturing yediyah rather than losing himself completely in ecstatic devotion. Leaders of the Przysucha school placed a premium on restrained, "rationalistic" mysticism. Interestingly enough, a permutation of this teaching found its way into Martin Buber's twentieth-century existentialist treatise *I and Thou.*[26]

Thus far, Assaf's preference for the designation "Hasidism in Poland," as opposed to "Polish Hasidism," appears justified. Although the ideologies of both schools arguably entailed reactions to the region's rising urbanization— the former in its embrace of materialism, the latter in its more earthbound and rationalistic mysticism—they appear too distinct to warrant common classification. In fact, Lublin Hasidism may be said to share more in common with one of the many miracle-centered doctrines of Hasidic dynasties across the border, while Przysucha Hasidism seems to bear more of a resemblance to rationalistic Lubavitcher Hasidism, located in what is present-day Belarus. In the realm of ideology, Hasidism's cross-regional similarities indeed seem to have outweighed differences.[27]

Assaf's theory appears further justified when applied to Hasidism's basic experiential features. In the few testimonies of charismatic performances by zaddikim, distinctions between Lublin and Przysucha in the practical realm virtually vanish; yet they appear equally indistinguishable from Hasidism in other eras and regions. The zaddik's arresting performance seems to have been regionally nonspecific. A Lublin Hasid provides an uncharacteristically levelheaded account of the Seer's grandiloquent worship, carefully distinguishing between the Seer's preparatory phase and his actual performance of a blessing:

> Once I celebrated the holiday of Sukkot in the holy community of Lublin with that man of God, our Rabbi Jacob Isaac, of blessed memory. And prior to the *hallel* service he went to the Sukkah to perform the blessing upon the brandishing of the palm branch and the four species. And all the visitors followed him into the Sukkah; and I, too, was among them. And before performing the blessing, the zaddik quaked and cowered with terrific frenzy and enormous gesticulations for about an hour. And the people who were present watched this intently, for they considered it to be the principle act. And they thought that they were achieving a state of great awe, and they, too, were rocking with what seemed to be great trembling and

quaking. But I sat on the bench and did not try to cleave to that "principle" act. Instead, I waited until the cessation of the frenzy and cowering. And only then did I arise and intently observe (the Seer's) performance of the blessing itself. And you cannot imagine the exalted level he achieved at the time of the actual blessing![28]

A devotee of R. Simha Bunem of Przysucha describes a similar type of performance:

And by the way, I should mention that one time I was in the holy community of Łęczna on the holiday of Shavuot. And behold, at the evening meal at the table, the *admor* of blessed memory [R. Simha Bunem] delivered a teaching in the name of the Jew [R. Jacob Isaac, the Holy Jew of Przysucha], of blessed memory, who said, "on Shavuot eve we do not speak words of Torah, for upright practice [*derekh erez*] takes precedence over Torah. And it is not an upright practice to speak words of Torah when we are to "receive" the Torah tomorrow."[29] These are the words of the Rabbi, the Holy Jew [of Przysucha], of blessed memory. And [R. Simha Bunem] concluded, "But what do we do tonight to prepare ourselves to receive the Torah in fear and trembling and quaking and awe?" And in the middle of saying this, he was seized by fear and trembling and quaking and awe. And all of his limbs and joints shook, and they knocked against each other, until he had to grab onto the table, but nothing helped, until our whole group was scared and had to take him away from the table. And they carried him to his special room and placed him on his bed. And he lay there until the fear subsided. And then he came back and sat down at the table. I actually saw this when I was with him.[30]

It is no great surprise that the ecstatic performances of the Lublin and Przysucha zaddikim were so similar. They were the hallmark of Hasidic inspirational display, undoubtedly modeled on accounts of pioneering Hasidic leaders appearing in *Shivhei Ha-Besht* that circulated orally long before its publication in 1814.[31] The Besht's "terrible gestures" during his prayers and ascents are detailed several times there; while the Great Maggid, according to one account, "began to tremble and he gripped the table that was there and the table too began to shake with him. . . ."[32] The resemblance between R. Simha Bunem's episode and this latter account would not have been lost on his audience.

From a very different perspective, that of Ukrainian Maskil Abraham Gottlober, supraregional similarities between Galician and Ukrainian Hasidism were so striking that he regarded Hasidim from each respective region as virtually interchangeable:

Indeed, it seemed to me as if the people whom I saw there [Galicia] were the same people I had seen in my native region [the Ukraine], except that their dialect differed somewhat from that of the Hasidim in our region. Their words were the words of our Hasidim. The Hasidim of our region shout "Oy ve, Tateh!," while those in Galicia shout "Oy vei Tateh!" Both sweep away every seed of mind and knowledge with a broom of fanaticism. Nothing but praises of the zaddikim are in their mouths all day long, extolling and sanctifying them. Only the names of zaddikim are different: theirs are not the names of our zaddikim.[33]

Although Gottlober's chief purpose was to underscore the unanimous Hasidic scorn for Haskalah in each region, he conveys the sense that Galician and Ukrainian Hasidim looked the same, sounded the same, and possessed a similar mentality.

It is thus reasonable to conclude with Assaf that in terms of both doctrine and basic practices, Polish Hasidism lacked significant regional distinctiveness. However, when we move beyond those parameters, the "Polish" inflection of Hasidism in the region under discussion becomes quite pronounced. This "Polishness" derived from Central Poland's unique historical context. As the eighteenth century came to a close, the Polish-Lithuanian Commonwealth was gradually deprived of autonomy through a series of partitions (1772, 1793, 1795) that divvied the country up between neighboring Russia, Prussia, and Austria. From 1807 to 1813, a degree of Polish autonomy was restored in Central Poland under the auspices of the Napoleonic "Duchy of Warsaw," a French protectorate that suffered exactions on a colossal scale. After Napoleon's demise, a semiautonomous entity with reduced borders passed into the hands of Tsar Alexander I during the Congress of Vienna and was renamed the "Congress Kingdom of Poland." It became a constitutional monarchy under the indirect rule of the tsar, who was considered its "king." This anomalous status was retained down to the rebirth of Poland in 1918; however, in the interim, Polish autonomy was progressively degraded in retaliation for the uprisings of 1830 and 1863.

Internal Jewish autonomy was curtailed during this period, as well. As discussed in the introduction, Jewish political autonomy had been considerably eroded by the time that Hasidism emerged as a movement. The Council of Four Lands, which had been in decline during the eighteenth century, was finally dissolved in 1764 for fiscal reasons, while local and regional kahals were enfeebled by enormous debt burdens.[34] The various new regimes—Prussian, Austrian, French, and Russian—sought to liquidate medieval corporate vestiges and were accordingly less and less content to leave their Jewish subjects to their own devices. Unable to fathom what was undoubtedly the most expedient integrationist measure, emancipation, officials of those regimes began proposing measures to solve the "Jewish question" through coerced acculturation, occupational change, and secular education. A small vanguard of acculturated Jewish social reformers, whom we may loosely label "Maskilim," embraced these programs and proposed initiatives of their own.[35] But the masses of Jews regarded such measures as threatening to their traditional way of life. They were determined to evade, stall, limit, or thwart them by any means, and the zaddikim emerged as their champions.

The zaddikim proved by and large successful, thanks to an unmistakable ambivalence on the part of officials toward those very modernizing initiatives. Officials in the increasingly reactionary regimes that ruled the Polish lands by the nineteenth century, including even the Napoleonic Duchy of Warsaw, appeared uncertain about how forcefully Jews should really be encouraged to adopt the language and culture of the conquered Poles. Napoleon's "Infamous Decrees" (1808) against France's own Jewish citizens signaled to Duchy of Warsaw officials that Jews were untrustworthy. In the minds of many Russian, Prussian, and Austrian authorities, moreover, it was downright dangerous to expose Jews to Enlightenment-inspired secular education, with its Western liberalism, "freethinking," and anticlericalism that ran counter to the idea of absolutist monarchy. The various regimes and their accommodationist Polish administrators were, in the end, too nervous about the risks entailed in Enlightenment-based reforms, no matter how much lip service they paid them. Polish zaddikim and their patrons discovered that such officials could be negotiated with, lobbied, and bribed to inhibit the initiatives of Maskilim. They appealed to the venality and conservatism of the authorities while aggressively promoting Hasidism within Jewish society.

For all their insularity, however, Hasidic communities were still deeply affected by the reorganization of political authority entailed in the partitions of Poland.[36] In the Ukraine, Belarus, and Galicia—formerly Polish-ruled territories now under the direct reign of absolutist Russia and Austria—zaddikim came to resemble their absolutist monarchs, a tendency that Arthur Green has termed "royalism."[37] R. Barukh of Międzybóż (d. 1811) established his own court, employed a jester, rode a horse-drawn carriage in regal display, and claimed his preeminence as a zaddik on the basis of his direct hereditary descent from the Besht. His experience of direct tsarist rule in Międzybóż during the last nineteen years of his life undoubtedly encouraged these excesses.[38] R. Mordecai of Chernobyl (1770–1837), who had experienced absolutism since the age of twenty-five, seems also to have drawn inspiration from the royal pomp of tsarism. Each one of his eight sons established his own court, foreshadowing later dynastic norms. The first conscious, deliberate institutionalization of a dynasty occurred within Lubavitcher Hasidism, after 1813.[39] R. Israel of Ruzhin (1797–1851) exceeded everyone in royalism: laying emphasis on his hereditary descent from the Great Maggid, residing in palaces, and employing orchestras to accompany his stately processions.[40] According to David Assaf, it now became "customary for the position of "zaddik" to pass automatically to a son, to the degree that the phenomenon began to arouse concern and to constitute a problem even in the Hasidic view."[41] Indeed, the number of Ukrainian, Belarusan, and Galician zaddikim who established enduring, hereditary lines in the late eighteenth and early nineteenth centuries, several of which evolved into Hasidism's most famous dynasties, is considerable.[42]

Central Poland, in contrast, possessed neither a consistent nor a direct "royalist" model. Polish Hasidism developed under constitutional regimes, excluding areas temporarily under Prussian or Austrian rule. Those experiments with constitutionalism, however limited their scope, were remarkable in the geopolitical region. The last days of the Polish Commonwealth witnessed the Constitution of the Third of May, which treaded cautiously in a liberal direction. Under Napoleon's rule in the Duchy of Warsaw, a constitution was drawn up that similarly avoided structural changes like emancipation of the peasantry and the Jews, but did introduce new liberties.[43] The Congress Kingdom, a constitutional monarchy under the indirect rule of Tsar Alexander I, also had a relatively modern and liberal profile and engendered additional gains for Jews. The Polish Parliament (Sejm), administrative council, viceroy, justice system, and constitution all served to slightly diminish the authority of the king (i.e., the tsar). Moreover, at least ten of the sixteen ministers serving the Kingdom between 1815 and 1830, as well as senators and other high state officials, were members of Masonic lodges.[44] And although liberties prescribed by the constitution of November 27, 1815, were increasingly ignored after a honeymoon period of several years, and no fundamental changes in Jewish status would be accorded until 1861–62,[45] certain laws of the Congress Kingdom were more liberal than even those of the Napoleonic Duchy of Warsaw.[46] Finally, as we shall see, wealthy Jews could gain exemption from debilitating legislation.

During the period under discussion, a group of Republicans had arisen in Warsaw who demanded civic rights for all on the French model and tried to put a utopian spin on Central Poland's vestiges of absolutism. Hugo Kołłątaj hoped that Napoleon would create a world in which every country would be a homeland for every inhabitant on the globe. Stanisław Staszic, notwithstanding his anti-Jewish rantings, envisaged "an epoch in which all peoples would be united under one scepter and law." After Napoleon's fall, Staszic assigned the universalizing mission to Tsar Alexander I.[47] Concerned as he was to revitalize Polish society, Staszic viewed nationalism with "a measure of exasperation, as being all too handy a shield for the protection of 'egotism.' "[48] The Warsaw republicans may have balked at the idea of emancipating the Jews, but their economic liberalism benefited the Jewish community. They linked their vision to economic prosperity: the important thing now that Poland had been partitioned, according to Staszic, was triumph in the economic field through practical education and investment. His scheme more or less came to fruition under Finance Minister Drucki-Lubecki, although the Jewish role was perhaps more central than Staszic would have liked.[49] The new economics-driven liberalism was summed up by Wawrzyniec Surowiecki in 1810: Polish citizens should be given the ability to grow rich and production allowed to increase under the protection of a caring government that respected the rights of citizens and was, in turn, worthy of their respect.[50] Even Jewish business acumen should be harnessed for the nation's benefit.[51] According to the historian Jerzy Jedicki, "the spirit of the age of 'enlightened liberalism' still reigned in Warsaw and Vilna several years after the Congress of Vienna, before the Holy Alliance stripped the whole country of its liberties."[52]

The rise of economic liberalism and Central Poland's incipient industrial revolution shaped Jewish society, which now possessed plutocrats on a grand scale. This impacted Hasidism in the region. While some wealthy members of Warsaw's Jewish mercantile and protobanking elite chose the path of acculturation and assimilation, particularly those immigrating from western and central Europe, many native-born notables became patrons of zaddikim. The zaddikim, for their part, were not merely recipients of the money of the bourgeoisie; they were in many regards products of the bourgeoisie. Raphael Mahler has already noted the unusual degree of appreciation for economic initiative permeating the teachings of Polish Hasidism—teachings that often associate wealth with divine favor.[53] R. Simha Bunem of Przysucha allegedly went so far as to warn that every poor person will one day have to justify being poor.[54] Audiences were more than once assured that they could fulfill the Torah by engaging in trade, so long as they were honest and had it in mind to support scholars or zaddikim with their profits.[55] This emphasis on economic productivity may not confirm a distinctly "Polish" Hasidic doctrine, but it does show an unmistakable regional inflection.

Even more striking is the way the enterprising environment appears to have affected ideas about who could become a zaddik. Elsewhere, a successful candidate tended to be someone who was perceived as untainted by mundane or worldly pursuits—a scholar, mystic, son of a zaddik, and so on. But in Central Poland there appeared, in addition to those types, prominent zaddikim who had been full-time merchants before assuming their more lucrative spiritual roles. Oral traditions and eyewitness accounts repeatedly acclaim R. Simha Bunem of Przysucha's success as a lumber and grain merchant and, eventually, a pharmacist.[56] His signature as an agent appears on a kosher meat tax (korobka) lease for the town of Siedlce in 1812.[57] He was somewhat sympathetic to scientific pursuits, as well, to judge by his admiration for his brother-in-law, a medical doctor, which appeared in the first edition of the book Asarah L'Meah (and was censored out of subsequent editions!).[58] That a merchant became the most popular Polish zaddik of his day bespeaks the spirit of the region. Additional Polish zaddikim, including R. Menahem Mendel of Kotsk (Kock), R. Isaac Meir Alter of Gur (Góra Kalwaria), and R. Isaac of Warka, also tried their hands at trade.[59] Not surprisingly, they proved adept business advisors to their devotees.[60] Their worldliness and intimate contacts with wealthy elites produced a more urban, cosmopolitan, and politically savvy Hasidism.

As merchants, those zaddikim had needed to possess a grasp of the language of the land in order to communicate with non-Jewish customers, suppliers, and partners. According to one tradition,

> [t]he rabbi R. Bunem of Przysucha, of blessed memory, was a merchant before he became a rabbi. And once he went to the market to purchase some goods. And he bargained with one farmer, and the farmer wanted more money than he was willing to give. And the farmer said to the holy rabbi R. Bunem, of blessed memory, in Po-

lish: *Poprawić!* [Improve!]. And his intention was to "improve" on the price. But when the holy R. Bunem of blessed memory went home, he took those words to heart, and thought: even a farmer had appealed to him to improve, i.e., to improve his ways. If so, the time had obviously come to fully repent.[61]

The narrator wished to illustrate R. Simha Bunem's ability to extract a spiritual concept from a Polish phrase uttered during a business transaction, exemplifying "worship through corporeality." But, however inadvertently, the tale also illustrates the future zaddik's embeddedness in the non-Jewish world.[62] Even Polish zaddikim who had never been merchants betrayed a certain facility for the Polish language, signaling a degree of immersion in the non-Jewish world. The Maggid of Kozienice was known to appropriate Polish maxims and derive numerical significance (*gematriya*) from Polish words.[63] Non-Jews sought his healing remedies, and members of the Polish aristocracy visited him.[64] Mitnaggdim charged that the Maggid of Kozienice and R. Levi Isaac of Berdyczów dared to insert Polish phrases into their prayers (customarily read in Hebrew) for added effect.[65] Hasidic tradition corroborates R. Levi Isaac's use of Polish phrases: on Yom Kippur in the city of Lemberg (Lwów/L'viv), in order to threaten the guardian angel of the Polish nation, R. Levi Isaac cried out the Polish words "Ja ciebie nauczę!" ("I'll teach you!") during the *mussaf* prayer. Even his admirers were scandalized until they were privy to his esoteric purpose.[66] Interestingly enough, Maskilim of this region also distinguished themselves by frequently employing Polish rather than Hebrew in their polemical and apologetic writings.[67]

Constitutionalism, industrialization, and familiarity with Polish among Hasidism's leaders facilitated a greater degree of political activism. R. Levi Isaac joined the Jewish delegation to the so-called "Great Sejm," which was convened from 1788 to 1792.[68] The Maggid of Kozienice was initially included in a delegation on behalf of all of Polish Jewry in 1811.[69] Several Polish zaddikim took an unusually keen interest in the Napoleonic Wars, attempting to enlist their supernatural powers to influence the outcome of Napoleon's invasion of Russia in 1812.[70] R. Simha Bunem, on the strength of his grasp of Polish, German, and Latin, was selected as a delegate to the advisory chamber of the Jewish Committee of the Congress Kingdom in 1825.[71] The zaddik Isaac of Warka succeeded him and went on to become Polish Jewry's leading intercessor (*shtadlan*). By capitalizing on legislative inconsistencies and constitutional guarantees, R. Isaac persuaded tsarist officials to reverse a ban on *eruvim* (1835), make Jewish prisoners less vulnerable to army conscription and less compelled to violate religious observances (1841), relax civil divorce requirements in favor of Jewish law (1842), contravene the army recruitment decree for Polish Jews (1843), and appoint official inspectors at kosher butcher stalls (1845). His much-publicized failure to persuade Sir Moses Montefiore to combat a tsarist decree outlawing traditional Jewish modes of dress (1846) should only be viewed in light of those other successes. R. Isaac resisted the Jewish Committee's measures to transform educational and occupational norms, but supported efforts to attract Jews to agriculture. As a result of his readiness to engage in political activism, communities across Central Poland accepted him as their advocate and representative, regardless of their inclinations toward Hasidism.[72] It is difficult to imagine such a record of activism in the autocratic states that bordered Poland.

Polish Hasidism seems also to reflect the individualism inherent in industrializing societies. The movement was afflicted by a persistent cycle in which rebellious disciples appropriated part of their masters' following during the latter's lifetime, only to be subjected to the same fate by their own star disciples. The Seer of Lublin broke away from his reclusive Galician master, R. Elimelekh of Leżajsk, and took many of his master's followers with him to Łańcut, and finally, Lublin.[73] But he, in turn, experienced the same treachery when his prominent disciple, R. Jacob Isaac, the Holy Jew, broke away and established his own flourishing court in Przysucha.[74] The cycle of rebellion reasserted itself when R. Mordecai Leiner of Izbica deserted the reclusive R. Menahem Mendel of Kotsk and established his own thriving court.[75] That such acts were perceived as seditious probably had to do with the conduct of the breakaway disciples: they did not merely continue their master's method in a new setting but established new schools of Hasidism that openly contradicted the methods of their masters.[76]

The region's social realities appear to have also impacted patterns of succession. Transmissions of power between deceased masters and their prominent disciples consistently won out over father–son successions. Upon the death of the Maggid of Kozienice, according to one hagiographical chronicle, some disciples did go over to his son R. Moses Eliakim Briya on the direct order of the Seer of Lublin; but the most prominent eventually defected.[77] The Seer of Lublin's preeminent disciples, including R. Meir of Stopnica/Opatów, R. Simon Deutch of Żelechów/Radzyń, R. Menahem Mendel of Rymanów, and R. Naphtali Zvi of Ropszyce, each established thriving courts upon their master's death, in contrast to the Seer of Lublin's sons. The "Holy Jew" of Przysucha's major successor was not one of his sons but rather his disciple R. Simha Bunem of Przysucha.[78] After the death of R. Isaac of Warka, his eldest son, Jacob David, established the Mszczonów (Amshinów) line. However, most Warka Hasidim transferred their allegiance to R. Isaac's colleague/disciple Feivel Danziger of Grójec (d. 1849), founder of the Aleksander (Aleksandrów) dynasty.[79]

The conflicts that bedeviled some of these transmissions seem more frequent than those of other regions. The events following R. Simha Bunem of Przysucha's death in 1827 are among the better documented. After R. Simha Bunem's death, his son R. Abraham Moshe set up court in Przysucha, while his disciple R. Menahem Mendel established a court in Tomaszów. R. Abraham entreated R. Menahem Mendel in a letter to return to Przysucha after learning that he had been harassed there two days earlier. Addressing R. Menahem Mendel, rather presumptuously, in the familiar form, he promised that "their anger has abated and those enemies have been transformed into loved ones. So my friend, if your desire still burns to approach as before please do come back." Playing on the aspiring zaddik's name, he added, "Perhaps our consolation [*nahmoteynu*] will come from Menahem!"[80] R. Menahem Mendel, however, continued to consolidate his reign from his court in Tomaszów. In a letter to R. Isaac Meir, the future zaddik of Gur, whom he addresses with the formal "you," R. Menahem Mendel seems to anxiously seek R. Isaac Meir's endorsement:

> I cannot restrain myself and keep silent, because my heart trembles
> that I have not received a letter from you since about three months,
> and my spirit is very sorrowful from sitting in loneliness, and from
> misfortunes of loved ones which my heart could not fathom. And
> just as I was faithfully with you in Warsaw, so am I now. Of all the
> remnants of Przysucha, followers of the *admor* [R. Simha Bunem],
> his soul in Heaven, of all the youth who seek strength of heart to
> illuminate their darkness, those who remain faithful and those who
> remain empty, to you alone I send condolences in a letter, because
> of your stature.[81]

R. Isaac Meir's failure to write for three months suggests an initial ambivalence. But he eventually overcame it, became R. Menahem Mendel's disciple, and, perhaps according to a prearrangement, inherited R. Menahem Mendel's disciples upon the latter's death.

A police report from April 17, 1859, describes the impact of the succession on his neighborhood in Warsaw:

> With the death of the rabbi of the city of Kotsk [Kock], where a
> stream of Jews known as Chusetów [Hasidim] continually arrived;
> all of this stream since a certain time has filled Warsaw with Jewish
> Chuseci [Hasidim] from the provinces, known for their uncleanliness, desiring to hold their old, usually numerically large gatherings
> in Kotsk. Owing to the death of the rabbi there, they have gathered
> in Warsaw as a meeting point for similar aims, and appointed as
> their rabbi a certain Itche Majer [Isaac Meir], residing at Krochmal
> Street number 1015. And in this place they gather sometimes in
> numbers reaching several thousands, holding a variety of absurdities
> supposedly related to religion, to such a degree that every Jewish
> resident in Warsaw is increasingly indignant, either owing to their
> antiquated superstitions, or their indescribable uncleanliness.[82]

Multitudes of Hasidim from Kotsk, whose hygiene suggests considerable poverty, converged upon R. Isaac Meir's Warsaw residence. But the unwanted police attention and protests by more acculturated Jews, in addition to a possible desire to shield younger followers from Warsaw's cosmopolitan influences, induced his move to the small town of Góra Kalwaria later that year.[83]

Low-level wrangling sometimes gave way to open quarrels. This occurred between followers of the Seer of Lublin and those of the Holy Jew; between followers of R. Simha Bunem and those of R. Meir of Opatów/Stopnica; and between followers of R. Menahem Mendel of Kotsk and those of R. Yerahmiel, son of the Holy Jew of Przysucha. Succession conflicts even entailed violent acts leveled against competing camps and their zaddikim. A band of Kotsker Hasidim is said to have attacked R. Yerahmiel and cut off his beard when he was staying at an inn in Tomaszów.[84] Nevertheless, it all held together without a resort to the hereditary transitions that were becoming the established norm elsewhere. David Assaf attributes the failure of many father–son successions in Central Poland to Hasidism's late arrival on the scene, which allegedly placed it in an earlier phase of sociohistorical development.[85] But the Central Polish context holds a more propitious explanation. As we will see in chapter 3, the region's powerful Jewish plutocracy was emboldened to play a more active role in the cultivation of zaddikim. These self-made men and women seemed less sympathetic toward father–son succession. They may have also been more exposed to popular theories propounded by Polish thinkers like Kołłątaj and Staszic, who openly criticized the hereditary nobility while extolling Christian townspeople as the source of the nation's vitality.[86]

These are, broadly speaking, some of the ways the Central Polish context did shape modern Judaism's most self-consciously inward-looking movement. Hasidism seems, after all, to have engendered something of a template upon which regionally distinctive institutional and cultural expressions could emerge. In subsequent chapters we will continue contextualizing Hasidism, which is usually abstracted out of its historical context for the sake of analysis, by appraising the impact of government officials and their initiatives, the rise of industrialization and banking, the consequences of constitutionalism, the influence of Polish folk culture, and the spread of the printing press. The ability of Polish zaddikim to resist or co-opt these forces determined their degree of success in conquering what was eastern Europe's most urbanized, industrialized, and variegated region.

The Rise of Polish Hasidism: Quantitative Impressions

Based on more than forty years of research on Hasidism, Simon Dubnow declared that by the nineteenth century the Hasidic movement "had conquered . . . most of the [Jewish] communities in Central Poland."[87] Like many of his claims about Hasidism, however, Dubnow's geographical assertions have been subjected to reexamination and revision.[88] The most recent and seemingly rigorous revision was published by Marcin Wodziński. Hasidism, he reasons in his monograph, *Oświecenie żydowskie w Królestwie Polskim wobec chasydyzmu*, was numerically unthreatening to many Polish Maskilim;[89] hence their neutral, indifferent, and occasionally positive dispositions toward the movement. Wodziński admits there were exceptions; but he deems the obsessive anti-Hasidism of the Polish Maskil Abraham Stern unique, a product of the influence of the Galician Maskil Joseph Perl, and shrugs off the anti-Hasidic references in the writings of the Polish Maskil Abraham Buchner, owing to their relative infrequency.[90] Having dispensed with these exceptions, and having observed the far more strident opposition to Hasidism expressed (again, with notable exceptions) by Galician and Ukrainian Maskilim,[91] Wodziński has been moved to drastically lower the estimated numbers of Hasidim in Central Poland. In a recent article incorporated into the English translation of his monograph, Wodziński undertook a breathtaking revision of Hasidic demography. He attempted to show that during the period up to 1815, which encompassed the careers of such Hasidic icons as the Seer of Lublin and the Maggid of Kozienice, the number of adherents to the Hasidic movement in Central Poland was so negligible that it is best described as "marginal." From 1815 to 1830, an interval that included the reigns of Simha Bunem of Przysucha and Meir of Opatów, Hasidic devotees allegedly still did not approach even 10 percent of the Congress Kingdom's Jewish population.[92] Wodziński thus proposes a depiction of Polish Jewish culture that is virtually the obverse of that of Raphael Mahler, who saw Polish Maskilim, rather than Hasidim, as marginal and numerically insignificant.[93]

Wodziński is undoubtedly correct to admonish historians against anachronistically applying late nineteenth-century perceptions of Hasidism's numerical triumph to earlier periods. Yet the magnitude of his revision is unwarranted. In the first place, the moderate stances of certain Polish Maskilim can be explained without devaluing Hasidism's numerical strength so radically during a period that is, after all, regarded as its golden age. Polish Hasidism's distinctive qualitative features, discussed earlier, form an important part of an explanation: the region's relatively worldly and politically savvy zaddikim were merely less alarming to Maskilim. Years later, Jacob Tugenhold would candidly differentiate between Polish zaddikim and their Ukrainian counterparts, observing that "in the Kingdom of Poland there are some of these fanatical leaders, but as they lead a pious existence and are less intrusive, they are far less harmful" than Ukrainian zaddikim.[94] Other Maskilim made similar observations.[95] They would, in any case, have had difficulty depicting representatives of the rationalistic Przysucha school and its prominent offshoots as grotesque purveyors of superstition and backwardness. In addition to the character of Hasidic leadership, it may be surmised that the familial and business ties among prominent patrons of Hasidism and Haskalah within the Warsaw mercantile elite helped prevent Haskalah attacks from reaching the level of those in other regions.[96] Finally, as government clerks (as opposed to Maskilim in other regions, who were usually tutors and teachers), many Polish Maskilim were in a position to directly influence governmental Jewish policy at a fundamental level. With the exception of the uncompromisingly idealistic Stern, they tended to put their energy towards achieving concrete institutional reforms and innovations by advocating in Polish language publications rather than lampooning zaddikim before Jewish audiences. They were for a brief period rather successful, installing their representatives in kahal posts and governmental censorship or advisory committees, and founding Jewish hospitals, orphanages, educational institutions like elementary schools and the Warsaw Rabbinical School, and a congregation for Warsaw's modernizing Jews.[97]

The low governmental estimates upon which Wodziński largely relies do pose a dilemma, however, for they bear an appearance of objectivity and are in remote instances corroborated by local Jewish sources, yet diverge widely from what one might reasonably have expected during Hasidism's heyday. But their accuracy is impugned by several prominent considerations. First among these considerations is the impressive record of Hasidic communal conquests during the first two decades of the nineteenth century. Zaddikim served in the capacity of *av bet din* (town rabbi)in various communities, some of them quite important, including Ostrowiec, Nowy Dwór, Nowe Miasto, Opatów, Ryczywół, Żelechów, Stopnica, Płock, Gowarczów, Ruda, and Warka. In addition, rank-and-file Hasidim were known to push out the local *av bet din* of a given town and usurp the position for a Hasidic candidate.[98] The phenomenon was sufficiently recurrent to elicit stipulations in rabbinical contracts that the new rabbi promise not to introduce Hasidic innovations.[99] Hasidim were members of the bodies that functioned as Warsaw's Jewish community governing board; they won official authorization of their separate prayer houses (as in Lublin), dominated local study houses (as in Kozienice and Żelechów), and erected synagogues (as in Praga and Warka). Zaddikim appointed their own communal functionaries in towns like Janów Zamoyski, Sierpc, and Gołąb; and two zaddikim were appointed consecutively as regional representatives to the most influential Jewish body of the day, the advisory board of the Congress Kingdom of Poland's Jewish Committee. In view of the considerable anti-Hasidic controversies of the day, the Hasidic affiliation of those successful candidates was not merely incidental.[100] It simply strains credulity to imagine a tiny minority imposing its will on Jewish communities known to so jealously guard their autonomy and resist innovation.

A second factor that casts doubt on the low official estimates is the scale of Hasidic book production, importation, and smuggling during the period in question. The printing of Hasidic books proceeded, despite the region's uniquely strict anti-Hasidic censorship and the paucity of printing presses in Central Poland. At present, it is sufficient to note the sudden publication of six Hasidic titles during a short reprieve from censorship in the honeymoon period following the establishment of the Congress Kingdom (1816–18).[101] Where printing failed to keep pace with demand, Hasidim resorted to importation and smuggling. The government repeatedly complained about the importation and smuggling of large quantities of Hasidic books into Central Poland during the second or third decade of the nineteenth century.[102] These facts attest to a healthy appetite for Hasidic homiletic literature, meaning a sizeable Hasidic reading public. A related factor is the publication in Warsaw of the two classic works of anti-Hasidic literature, *Sefer Viku'ah* and *Zemir Arizim* (both appearing in 1798). As we will see in chapter 5, their main targets are Polish zaddikim like R. Levi Isaac, the Seer of Lublin, and the Maggid of Kozienice. It seems highly unlikely that leaders of a numerically insignificant group would have aroused the profound ire evinced in these works.

A third countervailing consideration is the impact of Hasidism on Jewish demography. The direction of population growth in several key towns coincided with the arrivals and departures of zaddikim. The Jewish population in Kozienice, for example, swelled from 1,368 in 1765 to 2,107 in 1790 during the Maggid's rise to prominence. Lublin's Jewish population nearly doubled during the Seer's ascendancy, from 1,578 in 1790 to 2,973 by 1810.[103] Populations of towns where zaddikim departed between those same years, in contrast, declined markedly: in Ryczywół (which lost 36.7 percent), Żelechów (20.4 percent), and, most impressively, Wieniawa (70.7 percent).[104] A negligible Hasidic presence would not have occasioned such profound demographic shifts. Where Hasidism prevailed slightly later, a similar pattern is found. Opatów's Jewish population amounted to only 597 in 1787. After just three years, it jumped to 972, probably owing to the arrival of the zaddik Moses Leib of Sasów, and had reached 1,377 after the tenure of the zaddik Abraham Joshua Heschel and his successor, the zaddik Meir of Opatów/Stopnica (1827). The latter's presence in Stopnica seems to explain why the town's population of 366 Jews in 1790 tripled to 1,014 by 1827.[105]

These data reflect only permanent Jewish settlement; they do not capture the pilgrims who swelled local Jewish populations on Sabbaths, holidays, weddings, and other special occasions, creating a distinct impression of safety in numbers. During a wedding in Żelechów in around 1805, attended by Polish zaddikim, the town was flooded with "their great disciples and disciples of those disciples and many Hasidim from far and near without number. . . . All the houses of the city were not enough for them, and they nearly had to sleep outside."[106] "One hundred guests and followers" attended the Sabbath service presided over by the Maggid of Kozienice that preceded a week-long wedding celebration in 1806.[107] A Polish nobleman who visited the Maggid around 1814 described throngs of local Jews proclaiming the Maggid's wisdom and "baskets of contributions for the saint" rolling in from all the surrounding lands.[108] A pilgrimage to Lelów on the holiday of Sukkot prior to 1815 included enough musicians to form an orchestra that was "heard throughout the town."[109] According to a Haskalah satire from the same year, on the holiday of Shemini Azeret "the whole city [of Lublin, i.e., about 3,000 Jews] from young to old— men, women, and children—congregated at the door of the Seer's tent, to celebrate the joy of Torah with him."[110] In 1825, the Opatów police complained that on major holidays as many as six hundred Hasidic pilgrims arrived from all over the region, swamping a town whose Jewish population was normally about thirteen hundred.[111] With the exception of the latter, the foregoing accounts relate to the pre-1815 period.

A consideration of how official figures were derived reinforces suspicions about their prima facie reliability. To begin with, we should recall the well-known East European Jewish tendency to dodge official census takers, whose task engendered the expectation of increased taxation and military recruitment. Controlling for this factor has become axiomatic among Jewish historians.[112] If basic population data were so difficult to come by, we can only imagine how problematic gathering data on an internal Jewish phenomenon like Hasidism would have been. That Hasidism even registered on the official radar screen is thus suggestive of a much larger presence. Moreover, the figures that were finally derived were only as accurate as their predominately non-Hasidic sources allowed them to be, which is hardly encouraging. In fact, officials openly admitted to having difficulty ascertaining the numbers of Hasidim in their jurisdiction.

It is possible to identify several prominent groups of Hasidic adherents that would have been statistically invisible. Officials would have missed the numerous casual, sporadic adherents of zaddikim—those who undertook pilgrimages from time to time but did not label themselves Hasidim.[113] In addition, they would have missed the many adolescents who became Hasidim independently of their parents or parents-in-law. Yet Hundert has attributed the movement's very success to the rising numbers of young people in late eighteenth-century Jewish communities.[114] Adolescents were known to sneak away to Hasidic gatherings without the knowledge of their parents and guardians and would not have readily volunteered their affiliation.[115] Finally, historians must contend with the exclusion of women in official estimates, which may be said to constitute their most serious flaw. As Joan Wallach Scott has written, "recent research has shown not that women were inactive or absent from events that made history, but that they have been systematically left out of the official record."[116] Certain Mitnaggdim identified women as the primary victims of the zaddikim,[117] as did several Maskilim.[118] Maverick female allegiance was so pervasive that Jewish communal officials complained about wives diminishing the local treasury by bringing donations to zaddikim without their husbands' knowledge.[119] Yet Polish officials appeared ignorant and not overly concerned about Hasidic women. The question of independent female allegiance was finally raised during the Kingdom-wide investigation of 1824, when officials asked the zaddik Meir of Opatów/Stopnica whether wives of non-Hasidim were accepted as members of Hasidic communities.[120] They were apparently satisfied with his patently false denial. That Hasidic letters and petitions to the government were composed and signed only by men deepens the likelihood that female adherents were overlooked.[121] And the fact that female involvement rarely translated into enfranchisement within the movement, not to mention leadership, also lowered their profile.[122]

The most extensive governmental survey of the Hasidic presence, concerning the province of Podlasie in northeastern Poland, appeared in 1823 (see table 1.1).

Wodziński has published these admittedly unimpressive figures several times, sometimes without qualifying phrases like "approximately" or "up to," and without the officials' admissions of their incapacity to report numbers with any precision or certainty.[123] But such qualifiers are instructive. The Podlasie figures certainly do not merit the description "relatively objective."[124] At best, they reflect a growing awareness of Hasidism outside of the Jewish community based on interrogations of local Jews, converts to Christianity, and in only two cases for certain, Siedlce and Parczew, a Hasid. (In Parczew, local Hasidim only corroborated official estimates with respect to *one* of the town's two prominent Hasidic groups.[125]) Even in those rare cases where local Jewish and non-Jewish sources roughly match up, the question remains: who was counted?

TABLE 1.1 Official Perceptions of Hasidism in Podlasie, 1823

Town in Podlasie *województwo*	Estimated Hasidim in 1823
Siedlce	30
Parczew	'up to 40'
Łuków	'approximately 20'
Żelechów	'up to 60'
Stężyća	0
Stoczek	0
Garwolin	0
Łaskarzew	0
Macijowice	0
Parysów	0
Osieck	0
Adamów	0
Węgrów	'up to 30 families (it is not possible to establish this for sure)'
Kosów	'up to 10 (it is not possible to establish this for sure)'
Sokołów	100
Biała	'15 individuals gather together in a separate rented house for services'
Terespol	'up to 5, who also have a rented house for services'

When we recall the Podlasie region's statistically invisible casual adherents, adolescents, and independent female devotees, we have reason to doubt whether instances of corroboration say anything conclusive. The Podlasie table inadvertently reveals a related problem as well: only the Węgrów official seems to have taken notice of entire families. In contrast, estimates in Biała, Terespol, and probably Siedlce[126] were confined to active members of Hasidic prayer quorums consisting exclusively of adult men. As Raphael Mahler has estimated the size of a late eighteenth-century east European Jewish family as 4.4 people, we should at least quadruple an ample segment of the Podlasie Hasidim to allow for heads of households and their presumably Hasidic families.[127] This more nuanced reading needs to be applied consistently to all official estimates, rather than selectively, for officials apparently seldom considered entire families.[128]

Before delving into the full scope of available general estimates, including several which were overlooked by Wodziński, it should be reiterated that the estimates in question were almost unanimously delivered by ambivalent or hostile outside observers whose minimal acquaintance with Hasidism meant that they could not have been aware of many of the movement's cells. We can find solace only in the fact that the diversity of dispositions among outsiders affords a degree of corroboration. Mitnaggdim and Maskilim would possibly not tend to influence each other excessively, while non-Jewish observers, although influenced by Maskilim, were at least divided over the seriousness of the Hasidic threat. Their agreement on certain issues is worthy of consideration.

Mitnaggdim (literally, "opponents") were probably the most familiar with

Hasidism at the local level, because they were more geographically dispersed than the urban-oriented Maskilim. In 1798, R. Israel Loebel furnished a sense of the movement's growing proportions with his claim that zaddikim were fleeing prohibitions enacted by the Russian and Austrian governments and "have now crossed into another part of Poland," managing even to gain support among the wealthy and powerful in Warsaw.[129] That same year, R. David of Maków described "herds and herds of Hasidim" coming "hither and thither to find shelter under [the Seer of Lublin's] shade."[130] In 1814, the Warsaw traditionalists resolved to enlist the aid of "the great zaddikim, whose influence, they felt, could deliver the masses from heresy and skepticism."[131] In 1818, the Mitnaggdim in the town of Olkusz acknowledged that Hasidim "are found in every city in the district" and that they even included numbers of rabbis.[132]

Maskilim would have had less direct contact with Hasidism in smaller towns and villages but a better grasp of the urban situation. The Maskil Mendel Lefin Satanower complained of a sizeable presence of Hasidim in the Polish capital in 1791:

> There is also a considerable niche in Warsaw, which is often visited
> by the chiefs, who are from time to time themselves of good blood.
> A short time ago one of their Rabbi—*Grand Pensionaires* (the zaddik
> Levi Isaac of Berdyczów),[133] after leaving his District rabbinical post
> where he incited several disputes, came here from deep in the
> Ukraine with the Jewish delegates (to the Great Sejm).[134] But as his
> playing at St. Simon on his pillar was of no avail here, either, he
> cleared out. Nevertheless, he still made his adversaries feel the dan-
> gerous effects of his displeasure.[135]

According to Lefin, although the zaddik felt compelled to abandon the capital, he proved influential enough to punish the detractors. In 1797, the Maskil Jacques Calmanson appeared more alarmist, warning that zaddikim "lure one community, which upon recovering health simultaneously infects another." He worried that Hasidism "has increased substantially in recent years and that the zaddikim were poised to become despots throughout the Polish lands if the government did not thwart their spread immediately."[136] Calmanson apparently considered the messianic movement of Jacob Frank even more threatening; however, it is unclear whether he saw the threat as quantitatively or qualitatively more grave.[137]

By the turn of the nineteenth century, according to the Maskil Abraham Gottlober, "the hand of Hasidism had already attacked in Wołhyń, Podolia, and all the land of Poland and Russia, apart from the district of Lithuania, until one could not dare to publicly oppose them."[138] The author of the anonymous play *Di genarte velt* proclaimed in 1815 that Hasidism had "multiplied, spread, and infested the whole world; wherever there is a town, there are zaddikim [*rebbes*]."[139] In 1818, Abraham Stern counseled Congress Kingdom officials that rumors about the power of zaddikim had done their work: "From this noise, each gullible and, especially, female person proceeds to this Ringleader."[140] The Maskil Jacob Samuel Bik asserted in 1829 that the zaddikim led "hundreds of thousands of Israel," without, however, providing specific geographic details.[141] The problem in many of these cases is surely a tendency to exaggerate for rhetorical effect; but agreement among such diverse observers suggests a palpable basis.

Hasidism loomed as a prominent phenomenon in the eyes of several non-Jewish observers. In 1791, a proposed bill on the reform of Polish Jewry read before the Four-Year Sejm mentioned "all of their sects," a phrase that may testify to the strength of Hasidism in prepartition Poland.[142] The commissioner of Olkusz reported in 1818 that "the sect of so-called Hasidim (Hussytów) is found in every city where Jews reside."[143] That same year the commissioner of Płock echoed the claim: "they are so numerous that in nearly every town in this *woiewódstwo* (district) they have prayer houses."[144] Wodziński notes that explicit references in official documents do not emerge until after the deaths of the Seer of Lublin, the Maggid of Kozienice, and the Holy Jew of Przysucha (c. 1815) and takes this as proof that Hasidism was a peripheral phenomenon before then. But it may say more about the Maskilim themselves. Judging by their institutional successes, which did not occur until the 1820s, it was only by that period that they felt emboldened to assume a more activist stance, which included imposing Hasidism upon the official consciousness.

According to the uneven estimates of several independent non-Jewish observers, the movement had mushroomed by the second decade of the nineteenth century. Jan Radomiński's scathing proposal for Jewish reform from 1820 proclaimed: "This sect has spread now into every province of our country."[145] Radomiński reappraised their size at "a few tens of thousands" four years later. But if he meant only adult men, the adjusted figure could still amount to over one hundred thousand.[146] Additional hints emerge in accounts by Christian missionaries, who in 1823 were persuaded by a Warsaw cantor that if he should become a Christian "thousands would follow him."[147] Missionaries depicted Hasidim as forming a majority in towns like Przysucha and Zamość during this period.[148] True, one author of a letter to the Committee on Internal Affairs and Police from between 1827 and 1834 regarded Hasidim as "not more than one-twentieth of the Israelite people in the Kingdom" (i.e., about 18,850). But he hedged his unconvincing estimate by allowing that "for some time their numbers of adherents have been increasing considerably."[149]

In the end, it is a question not merely of what official numbers say but also of how to read them. Although the impressionistic nature of the available sources makes it impossible to calculate the popularity of Hasidism in Central Poland with any great precision, the sense from all quarters—Jewish and non-Jewish—is of a considerable but not overwhelming Hasidic presence in Central Poland by the early decades of the nineteenth century. Consciousness of factors like statistically invisible female and adolescent male adherents, Hasidic families, repeated conquests of communal offices by Hasidim, a sizeable Hasidic reading public, population shifts that mirror the movements of zaddikim, substantial pilgrimages, questionable official sources, and outright admissions of unreliability—all of these encourage the conclusion that before 1830, Polish Hasidism quite generously exceeded 10 percent of the Jewish population.

So how many Hasidim, loosely defined, were there in Congress Poland? On July 8, 1824, the Przysucha Hasid R. Alexsander Zusya Kahana, whose eminent fair-mindedness and esteem in the eyes of non-Hasidim and non-Jews is underscored in Hasidic hagiography, composed a letter to the Committee on Religious Denominations depicting Hasidim as constituting "almost one-third of the Jews" of the Kingdom. R. Kahana was the one source who would have possessed a detailed knowledge about Hasidic cells throughout the Kingdom. Officials took his estimate seriously enough to suspend their ban against Hasidic gatherings and launch an inquiry into the movement.[150] With nearly 377,000 Jews in the Congress Kingdom of Poland,[151] R. Kahana's estimate of 30 percent translates into 113,100 Hasidim by 1824. This is not unlikely, considering Radomiński's adjusted figure cited earlier. But assuming R. Kahana was attempting to make his movement appear less marginal, as Wodziński believes (although this is by no means a foregone conclusion), and that the true figure was only two-thirds that amount, the total might be more like 75,325, or about 20 percent of the Jewish population.[152] This range accords better with the totality of available testimonies, not to mention common sense.

The next way to evaluate Dubnow's assertion that Hasidism conquered "most of the communities" of Central Poland is to locate where, precisely, Hasidim were found. Basing themselves upon the itineraries of celebrity zaddikim, Simon Dubnow, Ignacy Schiper, and others have provided a preliminary picture. Wodziński is probably correct to question their assumptions about the strength of Hasidic groups based on the detection of one zaddik or several Hasidim in a given locale.[153] But indications of a presence do help clarify Polish Hasidism's hazy geographic beginnings. Ryczywół, where R. Samuel Shmelke was appointed rabbi in 1754, was probably the location of the first community.[154] R. Samuel Shmelke subsequently brought Hasidism to Lubartów.[155] In the 1770s, zaddikim seized the reins of leadership in Opatów and Żelechów; in the 1780s, Nowy Dwór; and by the end of the eighteenth century they were firmly entrenched in Praga, Lelów, Przysucha,[156] Kozienice, Warsaw, Czechów/Wieniawa, and Lublin.[157] Others add Witków (near Zamość), where R. Samuel Shmelke's brother Phineas was rabbi in around 1760; Ostrowiec and Nowe Miasto Korczyn (before 1786);[158] Magnuszew (before 1809); Siedlce (before 1815); Opoczno (before 1825);[159] Brzeziny, where the pioneering Polish zaddik Fishele (Ephraim) Shapiro ("Fishele Strykover," 1743–1825), whose father was a disciple of R. Jacob Joseph of Połonne, resided during his second marriage; Włodawa (1800); and Radoszyce (1815).[160]

Primary sources help fill out the picture. *Shivhei ha-Besht* mentions several of the Besht's followers in Chmielnik.[161] Hasidic correspondence includes a letter written by the Maggid of Kozienice to his mentor in Przysucha in 1761;[162] and a letter of recommendation written by the Maggid of Kozienice on behalf of his disciple to the rabbi of Końskowola, from 1811.[163] R. Joseph Levenstein's correspondence with Dubnow asserts early Hasidic influence in Bartinik and Przasnysz before 1787; and Czechów by the end of the eighteenth century.[164] In 1796, according to his endorsement of R. Zvi Hirsch Pińsker's *Zemah le-Avraham*, the zaddik Levi Isaac of Berdyczów was "compelled to spend a fine Sabbath in the holy city of Płońsk."[165] The first Hasidic book to appear in Central Poland—the popular conduct manual, entitled *Alfa Beta*, by Zvi Hirsch of Nadworna—was printed in Nowy Dwór in 1799. Anti-Hasidic tracts attest to Hasidic settlement in Grodzisk, Bielsk, Stryków, Janów, Krasnystaw, Czechanów, and Sierpc by 1798; and Maków by 1809.[166] The "Great Wedding," attended by the Seer of Lublin, was held in Żarnowiec in 1801.[167] According to Moses Wassercug's memoir, the Hasidim in Sierpc drove out the town rabbi before 1803.[168] A Hasidic wedding held in Warka in 1806 was presided over by the zaddik Israel of Kozienice.[169] In 1812, the Seer of Lublin appointed a kosher slaughterer in the town of Gołąb.[170]

Archival and missionary reports further fill out the picture. An ample Hasidic presence in Płock is revealed in a petition signed by ten representatives of a Hasidic community, in existence since 1808.[171] The Wodzisław community forced its new rabbi to swear to avoid relations with the "new Hasidim" in 1812;[172] but Hasidism seems to have nonetheless penetrated the community by 1816.[173] Around 1815, a quorum of Hasidim resided in Częstochowa.[174] The zaddik R. Meir of Stopnica (Stavniz) and Opatów (Apt) was rabbi of Stopnica in 1814, and formally stepped down in favor of his son in 1817.[175] Hasidim and Mitnaggdim quarreled openly in Olkusz that same year, at which point the authorities also learned of a Hasidic "prophet" in Stopnica.[176] In 1823, the government identified a rabbi of Żelechów, who had recently moved to Radzyń, as one of the two main Hasidic leaders in Poland (the other residing in Przysucha).[177] That year, missionaries encountered Hasidim in Warsaw and Wyszogród.[178]

The available sources produce the following maps of Hasidic presence in Central Polish towns during two phases, 1815 and 1823 (see maps on pages 50 and 51). As early as the end of the eighteenth century, the Hasidic presence in Central Poland stretched westward in what is roughly a crescent shape whose outer points consist of Lelów and Sierpc. Dubnow's characterization of the conquest of "most of the communities" of Central Poland is more accurate with respect to the Kingdom's eastern half, at least by the second decade of the nineteenth century.[179]

The spread of Hasidism was not unidirectional. A back-flow from Central Poland toward eastern regions is seen in the itineraries of R. Levi Isaac of Żelechów (Central Poland), Pińsk (historic Lithuania), and then Berdyczów (Ukraine); or of R. Abraham Joshua Heschel of Opatów (Central Poland), Jassy (Moldavia), and then Międzyboż (Ukraine).[180] The memoirist Gottlober recalls how during his childhood in Czernichów, Ukraine, around 1823, a Hasidic emissary from Central Poland began to go "day after day to the *bet midrash* to pray—not with the public, for he began his prayer after the worshipers finished their public prayer—with great and terrible shouts."[181]

In only isolated instances did Hasidism flow westward from Central Poland, but it could not take root. Two ideological adversaries, the Maskil Mendel Lefin of Satanów and the zaddik R. Nahman of Bratslav provide essentially corroborating accounts of the limits of the westward expansion. Lefin confidently proclaimed that, in contrast to historical Lithuania, Great Poland (i.e.,

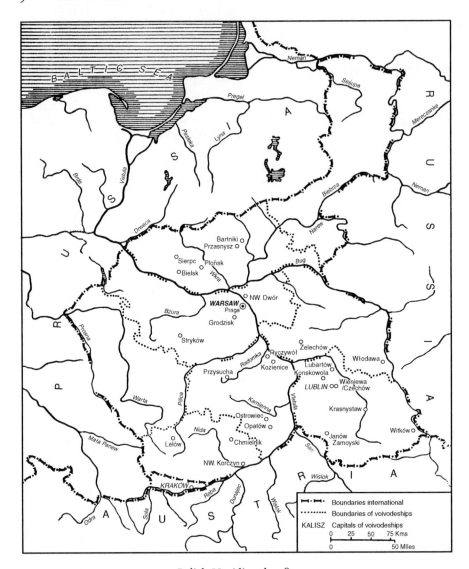

Polish Hasidism by 1800

the northwestern region) was "not yet entirely infected by Hasidism"; while the preeminent mystical text the *Zohar*, whose popularity would purportedly mean easy reception for Hasidism, still lodged in obscurity in Germany. The zaddik Nahman of Bratslav, with characteristic candor, corroborates those western boundaries.

> In this land [i.e., eastern Europe] . . . ba'alei shem are esteemed. And in truth, there have been some authentic ba'alei shem and zaddikim. But nowadays fraudulent ba'alei shem have proliferated. And

Polish Hasidism by 1823

as a rule, anyone who wishes and desires to go into it . . . succeeds
even if he is a fraud and really knows nothing except that it is based
on his rapture: how he bestirs himself and revels in it. It also de-
pends on where he sets up the venture. If he starts in a place where
they believe in it, or if he begins with women—for they are prone to
believe in everything—then he succeeds. And after that, it is possible that those who are far from believing in such a thing will also
come to believe in him . . . on account of his having "succeeded."

> But there is another land where such an endeavor is not esteemed
> at all, for example the German lands, where they do not have any
> belief in ba'alei shem. And there is no success or foothold for one
> who wishes to engage in it there. And such is also the case with the
> exploits and renown of the zaddikim in this land; whereas in an-
> other land they do not enjoy the same prestige.[182]

R. Nahman implies that the east European Jewish disposition was more receptive to miracle working, both fraudulent and authentic. Whether west European
Jewish women were less "prone to believe in everything," however, he does
not say.

A few zaddikim did slip across the east-west divide, perhaps as early as
1758.[183] In 1773, as noted, R. Samuel Shmelke accepted the Nikolsburg (Mik-
ulov) rabbinate, while his brother R. Phineas accepted the rabbinate of
Frankfurt-am-Main. Several Polish zaddikim, including the Seer of Lublin and
the Maggid of Kozienice, were for a certain time disciples of R. Samuel
Shmelke while he was in Nikolsburg. In 1774, R. Samuel Shmelke was elected
by a majority of twenty-three to the office of Rabbi of the Province of Moravia.
His election drew substantial local opposition, and his rivals sought to restrict
his jurisdiction to religious and educational matters alone. But the Empress
Maria Theresa sided with R. Samuel Shmelke, confirming his election and
inauguration on January 21 and May 27, 1775. The empress defended R. Samuel Shmelke again on June 17, 1776, this time against accusations of corruption. One wonders if the persistent opposition did not have something to do
with his adherence to Hasidism.[184]

There is much promise in Gershon Hundert's suggestion that an inward-
looking movement like Hasidism was more attractive in eastern Europe because, "while Jews elsewhere could persuade themselves that the modern middle classes were permeable or penetrable," there could be no such thinking in
eastern and east central Europe.[185] Western European Jews were increasingly
preferring western universities to the Yeshivas of eastern Europe, while their
east European counterparts continued to regard such institutions as nests of
heresy and apostasy.[186] The differing attitudes probably derived from differing
sociopolitical conditions. The emancipation of western European Jews offered
the opportunity to promote themselves from pariah status to at least that of
parvenu by embracing secular education and entering the professions. Hasidism, with its premium on insularity, took root where emancipatory initiatives
did not.

A more mundane determinant of the course of Hasidic expansion, also
raised by Hundert, was demography: Jews comprised 70 percent, 80 percent,
and even 90 percent of many town populations as one traveled southeastward.[187] While population density in and of itself cannot suffice as an explanation for Hasidism's spread, it would have been a prime consideration for
aspiring populist leaders in search of new territory. That may be why Hasidism
initially spread within Podolia and Volhynia (the Ukraine) and, only after those
regions had been claimed by first-generation zaddikim, began a northward and

westward climb as star disciples sought to carve out their own domains. R. Samuel Shmelke was exceptional in moving so far westward, for most aspiring zaddikim would have been primarily interested in areas where the most Jews resided. It would have been obvious to them, as it was even to tourists of this period, that Jewish populations generally dwindled the further west one traveled. Within Central Poland, zaddikim accordingly concentrated their efforts on the region's eastern half, where Jewish population was densest. Hasidism's western borders were thus determined by demographically driven decisions in addition to external factors like emancipation.

2

Anatomy of a Hasidic Conquest

. . . that small and intellectually meager town, a town which the Hasidim conquered and then converted or abolished all the old customs, a town whose synagogue was closed and locked during all six months of Winter . . . and the liturgy was mixed and muddled with every other liturgy, the doings of the new Hasidim, and even the synagogue was looted and the old liturgy completely abolished from there by force—upon my arrival in that town, I too was dragged into the custom of the town's inhabitants and forced to pray in the bet midrash according to the liturgy of drunks: the Sefarad liturgy.

—Abraham Gottlober,
Zikhronot u-Masa'ot

Scholars of Polish Hasidism frequently note the ideological fissure that divided the Lublin and Przysucha schools in the beginning of the nineteenth century.[1] As noted, R. Jacob Isaac, the "Holy Jew," and his disciple R. Simha Bunem not only deserted their master the Seer of Lublin and established a court at Przysucha but also instituted a wholly new approach to Hasidism that privileged Talmudic study over miracle working. Their renewed emphasis on the Talmud was undoubtedly motivated in part by doctrinal concerns. However, a powerful motivation seems also to have been political expedience. According to firsthand testimony, R. Simha Bunem prevailed upon his disciples to leave off their studies of *Zohar* and *Midrash* and return to Talmudic studies so that they could more successfully compete for rabbinic posts throughout the region. "Is it not fitting," he chided them, "that spiritual descendants of the Besht break into [rabbinical] posts throughout the Ashkenazic lands?"[2]

This tradition reflects a decidedly conservative approach to communal transformation, one that engendered a quite limited impact on existing political structures. Rather than supplant local organs of Jewish self-government—the kahals—with newly fashioned institutions, zaddikim preferred to stack kahal offices with their own devotees.[3] They similarly infiltrated many of the local confraternities.[4] Zaddikim thus superimposed Hasidism upon the remnants of east European Jewish political autonomy in a manner similar to the "imperial method" of conquering empires: co-opting elites and institutions without troubling to alter existing structures. While the "Hasidic court" may be considered one type of innovation, it was much less formal at this stage than by the middle of the century.[5] A second type of innovation, the Hasidic prayer house, was equally informal, and probably intended as a temporary expedient until the communal *bet midrash* (study house) or main synagogue became Hasidic domain. Hasidism's essentially conservative approach to social change suggests that it is inappropriate to deem it a sect or social antistructure.[6] To be sure, Hasidism entailed liminal activities like pilgrimages and ritual revelry during Sabbaths, holiday gatherings, and weddings, and formed something of a subculture. But its members sought chiefly to appropriate the existing socioreligious infrastructure, not to undermine or supplant it.

The memoirist Abraham Gottlober delineates the following three stages of the Hasidic usurpation of communal infrastructures:

> [The Hasidim] introduced a new combination of Ashkenazic and Sephardic customs, quit the various communities for no reason other than to form special, small houses of prayer, which they called by the name *"kloyz"* (1). And gradually, as their power increased, they brought their customs also into the main *bet midrash* (2). And only in small, poor towns did they become strong enough to conquer even the main synagogue (3).[7]

What, precisely, did Gottlober mean by *kloyz* and *bet midrash? Kloyz* originally applied to a small room where elitist, old-style hasidim engaged primarily in Kabbalistic study, not prayer. It was often attached to a *shtibl*, where prayer sessions took place according to the liturgy of the sixteenth-century Safed Kabbalistic circle of the aforementioned R. Isaac Luria.[8] Although both the *kloyz* and the *bet midrash* were chiefly spaces for study, the *kloyz* was independent and privately funded, while the *bet midrash* was supported by communal funds.[9] By Gottlober's day, however, the meanings of *shtibl* and *kloyz* were conflated to denote a Hasidic space for study and prayer.[10]

Establishing a separate prayer house was, according to Gottlober, only a prelude to a more thoroughgoing Hasidic colonization via the *bet midrash* and synagogue. But non-Hasidim also established unofficial, regular spaces for worship. Polish officials took a dim view of them and actually sealed up the prayer house of a congregation of acculturated ("German") Jews at 616 Danielowiczówska Street in 1809, only agreeing to reopen it in 1815 after a protracted effort by five prominent acculturated Jews.[11] Two years later, Minister Stanisław Staszic launched an inquiry into "prayer services in private houses," seeking to clarify "if the Constitution ensures all faiths freedom of such religious ceremonies," and "if the Treasury has not enacted any law for collection of a fee for this, and accordingly should it be granted an exemption agreement"?[12] Officials identified over one hundred prayer houses in Warsaw alone by 1826.[13] But both Hasidic and non-Hasidic prayer houses proved too numerous and clandestine for government regulation, particularly in Warsaw, which lacked a synagogue in this period.

The second arena to be conquered, the *bet midrash*, continued to refer to a public prayer and study hall throughout Hasidism's ascendancy. The Maskil Abraham Stern explained the term at the request of the Commission on Denominations in 1832. A *bet midrash* was a "house of religious study, where every Israelite is free to attend at any time and read books having to do with the Israelite religion." It was devoted "not only to the celebration of daily services, but also has this other purpose: that every single Israelite wishing to read books on religious knowledge comes there for that purpose at any time." The *bet midrash* was more versatile and open to all (presumably male) Jews than the third arena, the synagogue, which was "devoted exclusively to celebration of daily prayer services."[14] Hasidim occasionally erected their own synagogues. The wealthy Warsaw merchants Berek and Temerel Sonnenberg-Bergson founded the first Hasidic synagogue in the Praga suburb of Warsaw in 1807.[15] One finds reference to the "synagogue of the Hasidim of the Rabbi of Lublin" in Warsaw, and a synagogue allegedly constructed by the Maggid in Kozienice.[16] The latter laid the cornerstone of a new synagogue in Warka in 1810.[17] But the Hasidic synagogue was less common than the Hasidic *bet midrash* or *kloyz/ shtibl*.[18] Moreover, the term "synagogue" is often applied loosely.[19]

Zaddikim attained the second and third phases by dispatching cantors to impose Hasidic modes of worship. Gottlober explains that

in order to disseminate the Hasidic system it was essential to
change the old liturgy that was used by all the Jews in the towns,
that is the Ashkenazic liturgy, into the *Sfarad* liturgy. . . . And not
only the liturgy was essential, but also the melodies of the prayer
and their delivery before the public (the *fartrag*).[20]

The inveterate Mitnagged R. David of Maków provides a colorful description of the incursions: "they begin to shout many great shouts with strange utterances in the middle of the Eighteen Benedictions, like *bam, bam, bam, ee, ee, ee, noy, noy, noy, gei, gei, gei, um, um, um*."[21] The most flamboyant won the most esteem: "he who raises his voice in prayer to a roar [*sha'on*] is called by the name 'genius' [*ga'on*] . . . he who claps hand against hand [*kaf*] is called by the name Hasid and *rav*!"[22] The Maskil Abraham Stern affirms that "in order to spread the reputation of this novelty among the Israelites and appear in an impressive form, [the Besht] and his disciples began to distinguish themselves from other Israelites by celebrating daily services with unusual clapping, most indecent leaping, and the strangest shouts, while substituting a rather different liturgy accepted by some kind of Spanish [*sic*] Jews," that is, the Sfarad liturgy.[23]

Hasidic testimony proudly substantiates those descriptions. R. Levi Isaac of Berdyczów "would run from corner to corner and dance with great and quite terrible fervor."[24] According to another tradition, "it was his custom during prayer to pray with fear and trembling. And he could not stand in one place owing to his holy awe. 'And when one placed him in one corner, he would then be found in another corner.' (Babylonian Talmud, Berakhot 31a)."[25] As for those who were present at the time of his prayer, "their hair would stand on their heads, and their hearts would melt, and all their crookedness would be removed on account of his voice."[26] But this mode of worship probably did not derive from pious enthusiasm alone. Liturgical and stylistic innovations served as territorial markers that could be planted in community after community by the zaddik's phalanx of worshipers. In addition, theorists of religion have identified ritual as a vital instrument for constructing power relations—less heavy-handed than military or economic compulsion, yet all the more effective, given its claims to divine legitimacy. Hasidic liturgical and ritual innovation thus probably also served to impose a new hierarchy of ritual specialists.[27]

To Gottlober's three phases of conquest, we may add a forth: appointments or assumptions of communal offices by zaddikim throughout their informal jurisdictions. Appointments of Hasidic ritual slaughters have attracted scholarly attention, owing to their economic ramifications.[28] In *Shivhei Ha-Besht*, the Besht's appointments and dismissals of ritual slaughters are the first indications of his sociopolitical authority.[29] Gottlober, as we have seen, stresses cantorial appointments. On the recommendation of R. Levi Isaac of Berdyczów, Gottlober's father was appointed cantor of Starokonstantynów over the objections of the Mitnaggdim.[30] But in terms of spiritual authority, neither vocation approaches that which the following Hasidic tradition alludes to:

> The holy zaddik R. Joseph Kizes traveled to Lublin. And [the Seer of Lublin] said to him, "Welcome, Rabbi of Janów [Zamoyski]." And eight days had not passed before a delegation from Janów Zamoyski came to ask his advice about whom to take on as rabbi. And he answered them, "Indeed, your rabbi is already with me." And he presented him to them.[31]

Assuming the reliability of this somewhat late tradition, Polish zaddikim were appointing town rabbis—previously the most powerful religious functionaries. Occasionally, zaddikim themselves assumed rabbinical offices, as in the towns of Żelechów, Stopnica, and Opatów. Some served as supracommunal judges, as reflected in the following tradition concerning the activities of the Seer of Lublin at the "Great Wedding" of Żarnowiec in 1801.

> And afterwards, when the zaddikim had gone one by one into [the Seer of Lublin's] tent, and the crowd filled his tent, one packed against another, the various litigants set their complaints before him, and they included many claims and quarrels. And until sunset he rendered just legal decisions; and [R. Solomon of Radomsko] was amazed, and loved him very much.[32]

This, too, is of late provenance; but the assumption of supracommunal judicial roles by zaddikim is corroborated in at least one non-Hasidic source.[33] Such accounts suggest a power shift of great magnitude.[34]

Not surprisingly, Hasidim were confronted by formidable opponents—Jewish and non-Jewish—at every turn. Among Hasidism's Jewish opponents, the traditionalist-oriented Mitnaggdim decried the separate Hasidic prayer quorums on the grounds that they employed ritual modifications supposely reserved for the elite.[35] Separate spaces for worship also undermined the local pecking order, manifested in preferred seating assignments and ritual honors in the synagogue.[36] The establishment of a prayer house could sometimes provoke expulsion from a town, as in the case of R. Jacob Joseph of Połonne's dismissal and expulsion from Shargorod (the Ukraine) in 1748.[37] However, as the nineteenth century progressed, Mitnaggdim increasingly seemed reluctant warriors. Some even began joining forces with Hasidim against Maskilim, whose integrationist programs were suspected by both groups as encouraging secularization and Christianization. Maskilim, for their part, were less concerned about Hasidic religious innovation than about the barrier Hasidism seemed to pose to modernization and emancipation. In comparison to Mitnaggdim, Maskilim became bolder and more threatening by the second decade of the nineteenth century, as they won authorities over to their cause.

Certain Polish officials attempted to hinder Hasidism after they became persuaded, usually by Maskilim, that it was inhibiting Jewish social reforms. Some additionally believed that its adherents posed a social menace. Indeed, one is occasionally moved to empathize with bewildered local police, confronted as they were by Hasidic revelry and unregulated influxes into their towns. Nevertheless, certain officials tolerated or defended the Hasidic right to worship. Perhaps here is the place to caution that historians often fail to appreciate the spectrum of attitudes among Polish bureaucrats. Raphael Mahler's description of a "heavy, dull-witted bureaucratic apparatus" persecuting relatively helpless Hasidim yet proving too inept to suppress Hasidism is not justified in many documents that will be brought to light here. We will find a variety of attitudes among Polish bureaucrats, ranging from animosity to impartiality to even sympathy. At the same time, certain Hasidim will be revealed as much more savvy and resourceful than Mahler would allow. Materials from the Polish archives, largely inaccessible from World War II until the revolutionary events of 1989, enable us to revisit known anti-Hasidic investigations, discover new ones, and integrate them with sources in Jewish languages.[38] Bearing in mind Gottlober's schematization, let us now survey the phases of Hasidic conquest in ten Central Poland towns.[39]

First Phase: Hasidic Prayer Houses in Płock, Przysucha, Wodzisław, and Lublin

By the first decades of the nineteenth century, Hasidim in Central Poland were making bold incursions into local religious life. During the same period, however, Maskilim also began to gain ground. The Jewish community in Płock possessed 731 members by 1800, but almost tripled during the Prussian occupation (1794–1807) to 1,932. This was largely the result of an influx of Jews from Prussia, where acculturation and its ideological dimension, Haskalah, had gained substantial ground. Their impact was soon felt. Around 1796, the Płock kahal hired a secretary with a facility for Polish and German, Moses Wassercug. In his memoir we catch a glimpse of the acculturation process in Płock: an esteemed Jewish merchant (*sar ha-yehudim*) named "Itzikel" invited Wassercug to attend a comedy at the local Polish theater and, despite his reservations about being seen in such a place, Wassercug allowed himself to be persuaded.[40] The rabbi of Płock from 1798 to 1805, R. Judah Leib Margaliot, had espoused Enlightenment ideals,[41] and his flirtation with rationalism included criticisms of *ba'alei shem*.[42]

The potential for cultural warfare in this town was high. With the establishment of a prayer house in 1808, Płock constituted the northwesternmost point of Hasidic convergence. In 1818, the district commissioner Florian Kobyliński (1774/7–1843) was induced by Maskilim to promulgate a district-wide ban against Hasidic prayer houses, and initiated an anti-Hasidic campaign that lasted through December.[43] In the ensuing battle, the Płock Hasidim employed every means at their disposal: bribery, behind-the-scenes influence, relentless requests, and a refined petition invoking constitutional arguments. This case is particularly germane to the question of "Polish" Hasidism, for it illustrates the readiness of the region's Hasidim to engage in political activism by appealing to the kingdom's professed constitutionalism.

Brigadier General Kobyliński had led a unit of Napoleon's legionnaires and lost both his legs as a result of injuries sustained during the French retreat of 1812. The tsar, who was usually forgiving toward Poles who fought for Napoleon, appointed him commissioner of the Płock *wojewódstwo* (district) in 1815.[44] In his new post, the general waged a campaign against Hasidism. His first charge was that several clandestine prayer gatherings were being held in private homes. He was determined to ban these gatherings, on the grounds that they were not held within designated public buildings, they encouraged the formation of sects, which bred dissent and hatred, they detracted from synagogue attendance and thus obstructed the delivery of government decrees, and they involved unregulated "income or secret, hidden contributions, or certain donations which results in the diminishing of general funds intended for the head of the public synagogue, and creates the opportunity for abuse under the pretense of Religious practice."[45] This list of rationales, based for the most part on a professed concern to guard synagogue prerogatives, was followed by a reminder of "the tendency of the Jewish nation toward negligence." Here the commissioner's reproach reached its highest pitch: "Are we to allow rituals performed in honor of the Highest Being to be celebrated in private homes, sordid and defiled, when there are public places dedicated to worship in honor of GOD, and out of this consideration, at least safe from the usual Jewish uncleanliness?"[46] It clearly had not occurred to Kobyliński that unsanitary conditions in the Jewish Quarter might be attributed to a decree on November 8,

1811, which had crammed the nearly two thousand Jews of Płock into a ghetto consisting of eight streets.[47] In any case, his low opinion of Jews was openly acknowledged. The commissioner next described the Hasidim, who were "known by the name 'Men of Silk' [*Kitajcy*], and notorious for their scandals." They unnecessarily isolated themselves from other Jews, simply because they wished to engage in lengthier services. Instead, they should simply oblige the rabbi to extend services, which was by no means against the dogma of the religion.[48] On receiving this petition, an official from the Commission on Denominations and Public Enlightenment in Warsaw who signed his comments "N"[49] requested further clarification.[50]

After Kobyliński's first report, several Men of Silk approached him and requested not to be prohibited from gathering in private homes for prayer services. Not having received word from the central government concerning whether the Men of Silk were to be respected as a separate sect, Kobyliński did not know how to answer them. In his next communication, he informed Warsaw that "it is known that certain Men of Silk differ themselves in their rituals from other Jewish *Men of Silk* [emphasis in the original], and they live with them in mutual hatred," a reference to the division between the Przysucha and Lublin schools. The Men of Silk had grown so numerous that they possessed prayer houses in nearly every town in the *wojewódstwo*. Moreover, "even despite the great official prohibition, Men of Silk have been able to continue to separate themselves from traditional Jews through payments to lower police officials,"[51] that is, through bribery. The time had come to investigate this confession and its general spirit. Did they have harmful laws? Could they be tolerated, considering their hatred of traditional Jews?[52] Kobyliński intimated that the Commission on Denominations and Public Enlightenment in Warsaw was competent to answer such questions itself, "because the chiefs of this sect are found there (i.e., in Warsaw)." The presence of zaddikim in the capital was thus common knowledge.[53]

The Hasidic petition enclosed with Kobyliński's report, the first extant document of its kind, requests "the support of peaceful secondary houses of Prayer for the Supplicants, in Płock, the fifth day of May, 1818." It reads:

> By the local synagogue are to be found two prayer houses—a main one and a second, smaller one. In spite of this, we the undersigned under the name Men of Silk maintain a third, similar School for engaging more in other prayers and spiritual learning, which has peacefully existed already for ten years. And its existence is protected by the local Police, according to the copy of the annex attached here. Whereas it has been formed upon good religious principles and perfect spiritual, religious knowledge by especially good people, the existence of the said School, which is not only fundamentally useful, but also not harmful; whereas we, the undersigned have carried out every public obligation and burden, both Spiritual and Governmental, and all public proclamations, only differing by devoting ourselves longer in other Services and spiritual learning, for which we

need separate Schools; whereas in the main and smaller Synagogue the general Jewish population—among them Artisans, Merchants, etc.—gather to hold services of short duration and we cannot manage our own devotions in such a short amount of time; and whereas on the second day of this month, the supervisor of the local police arrived and prohibited our conducting Prayer and Study in this School, we accordingly place ourselves in this petition to the *województwo* Commission under the highest protection and humbly request for the utmost grace, by dint of constitutionally guaranteed general tolerance and protection, to peacefully maintain our existing Schools. And because our Religion obligates us to pray publicly everyday, for this reason we request the most speedy gracious resolution, in the hand of Szaie Michel, professing the deepest respect.[54]

The petition is signed by ten Hasidim on behalf of the Hasidic community of Płock, suggestive of a substantial community.[55] Their prayer house had existed already for ten years, that is, since 1808.[56] This rare exposition of a Hasidic perspective, presumably through a hired scribe, emphasizes their separate liturgy, their distinct types of learning, and the duration of their services. The Hasidim evidently hoped to appear more pious than other Jews, something for which the government officials surely could not fault them. But most significant is their appeal to "constitutionally guaranteed general tolerance and protection," an insistence that the government live up to its own rules.

In August, Kobyliński had still not received a reply from the central government; so he announced that, until otherwise advised, he had prohibited Hasidic gatherings in private homes.[57] By September, he appeared agitated, complaining "as the Men of Silk reside in many cities in the *województwo*, they constantly present requests to the *województwo* Commission on this matter; which for lack of a final decision from the Government we have no means of addressing."[58] When Viceroy Józef Zajączek did finally respond on November 10, 1818, it could not have been what Kobyliński had hoped for: "As there are *ceremonial* differences between Men of Silk and Jews of the Mosaic persuasion, according to absolute tolerance we understand that Men of Silk may be left free to hold their services in homes, and not necessarily in Synagogues."[59] The viceroy had sided with the Hasidim on the professed basis of constitutionally guaranteed religious tolerance.

Two notes signed by "N," one scrawled in the margins of Zajączek's decree and the second rendered in more polite language, advanced counterarguments based on a report by "a Jew who desires the good of his fellow believers," probably a Maskil.[60] "N" argued that the desire for longer services was not sufficient reason for separate services, and raised objections that bear an unmistakable Haskalah stamp: "if they are permitted to have separate services, this could generate many different Sects amongst Jews, which would hinder all means of their enlightenment. Then, even Rabbinical Schools such as the one in Warsaw will not effect the enlightenment of this people."[61] This fear of a Hasidic threat to the hypothetical Rabbinical School in Warsaw, whose plan had only been formulated earlier that year, was not unfounded, for when the Rabbinical School finally opened eight years later, the politically activist zaddik Isaac of Warka led a veritable crusade against it.[62] Nevertheless, Zajączek decreed that notwithstanding "various eccentricities and superstitions that accompany the ceremonies of their persuasion" the Hasidim were only guilty of longer synagogue services and stricter religious observance. They in no way opposed the obligations to the laws and regulations of the land, and were accordingly entitled to "the enjoyment of the liberty and freedom of every other confession in our land." They were not to be obstructed in conducting their services.[63] "N" reiterated the decree to Kobyliński.[64]

The Hasidic appeal to a constitutional principle seems to have prevailed. But the idea that this was the sole rationalization, seeing as it was furnished by members of a regime who by now so frequently ignored and repealed features of its constitution (see the example of censorship in chapter 6), requires a measure of skepticism. Moreover, as a proponent of Enlightenment and Jewish acculturation, Zajączek should have been expected to be much more receptive to Kobyliński's Enlightenment-based arguments. Finally, the short duration of the ordeal is surprising: it took only six months to reopen the Hasidic prayer houses in the district, whereas it took six *years* (1809–15) for acculturated Jews to gain permission to reopen their progressive congregation on Danielowiczówska Street.[65] On the basis of these considerations, we may surmise that Hasidism's powerful patrons in the capital, among them a major creditor of Zajączek and Nowosilców (see chapter 3), played a behind-the-scenes role.[66]

Kobyliński sought at least to diminish the impact of the decree. He grumbled to the Commission on Denominations that his banning of Hasidic worship did not limit tolerance, for he wished only to prevent the creation of sects and schisms in Judaism and prevent harm to Jewish customs. He saw no reason why the Men of Silk could not hold their services in the regular synagogue, but if the Men of Silk were allowed to hold separate services, at least let them choose one single house for their services (at present they gathered in several different houses). Kobyliński, of course, accepted the Viceroy's decree, but hoped that the central government might reconsider.[67] "N" replied that if the gathering in several different houses was truly a police matter, Kobyliński should formally present this subject to the Commission.[68] Kobyliński then adopted a new tactic, proposing broader reform measures for the Jews of the Kingdom. Although he did not mention Hasidim in his proposal from May 13, 1824, there is little doubt whom he had in mind when he impugned Jewish "lack of enlightenment, and superstitions," their living in "the dirtiest state of dark fanaticism, causing moral sickness," and their obstinate refusal to "gain familiarity with the Language of the Land." Invoking the reigning dissent in the Płock Jewish community, Kobyliński argued that the only recourse against the dark fanaticism was to abolish the rabbinate in its present form. The Jews should elect a rabbi for life, who would thereby be independent enough to oppose their fanaticism; and the government should appoint assistant rabbis who "are experienced in both Jewish knowledge and literature, and in other science and knowledge."[69] Again, one detects Maskilic influence.

Staszic's reply was blunt: "Putting the aforementioned project into effect would not only be dangerous, but moreover produce harmful results." Instead of facilitating a rapprochement between the government and Jews of the land, Staszic predicted, a great divide would form between government appointees and superstitious rabbis. (Indeed, something to that effect did occur during the mid-nineteenth century as a result of the tsarist policy of appointing "state rabbis" alongside "spiritual rabbis.")[70] Staszic then revealed his own plan to establish a Rabbinical School, which would form a "Department of Jewish Religious Knowledge" at a university and determine the "true Jewish religious books," meaning those that imparted knowledge about religion and morality. It would prescribe the books from which the Jewish public might sing and read at times of prayer, but proscribe Talmudic study, in order to "root out the harmful influence of the Talmud on Jewish enlightenment."[71] Proper books were to be written in either Polish or Hebrew, and not in that "language of perverted German," which could only mean Yiddish.[72] While no such Jewish studies department was created, the Rabbinical School opened several years later. Both Staszic and Kobyliński were thus positively inclined toward the promotion of Enlightenment among the Jews, despite what Mahler has claimed.[73]

In 1829, the Hasidim of Płock attempted to install R. Alexander Zusya Kahana as av bet din.[74] That his nomination provoked a fresh controversy in the town is not surprising; but the nature of the controversy, alluded to in a letter from R. Isaac Meir Alter, the future zaddik of Gur, to the influential local rationalistically oriented Mitnagged R. Solomon Posner, is unexpected:[75]

> I beseech His Eminence to grant a small thing on behalf of my
> friend, the great Rabbi, av bet din of Płock, who is in a dispute with
> "wicked people" [anshei belial][76] in his city. For they informed on
> him, saying that there are divisive sects amidst our people, and that
> he is not fit to be av bet din. And he very much needs His Holiness,
> may he live, to write a letter there, so that, God forbid, there will be
> no division among our people.[77]

A recent analysis of archival sources by Marcin Wodziński encourages the conclusion that the "wicked people" alluded to in the letter were neither Mitnaggdim nor Maskilim (hagiography claims the latter)[78] but rather local elites who sought to appoint a different Hasidic candidate, R. Abraham Rafael Landau of Ciechanów, in R. Kahana's place. The supreme irony is that R. Landau was not only Hasidic but a Przysucha Hasid who merely enjoyed more intimate ties with members of the local Płock oligarchy.[79] The struggle over the Płock rabbinate was by this time an inner Hasidic one.

Hasidic hagiography dismisses the controversy as brief and frivolous (lo le-shem shamayim), ascribing it to R. Kahana's refusal to kowtow to certain local power brokers. His great teachings and deeds, we learn, swiftly won his opponents over. The challenger, R. Landau, remains unnamed in such accounts, probably out of deference to this future zaddik.[80] Of course, if the controversy had occurred during R. Simha Bunem's lifetime, it would have indeed been brief, for both sides would have instantly done the zaddik's bidding. But the event occurred two years after his death, when his succession remained unresolved: some adherents, including R. Kahana, elected to follow R. Simha Bunem's son R. Abraham Moses, while others chose his disciple R. Menahem Mendel of Kotsk. In seeking the intervention of a prominent Mitnagged rather than a Hasidic figure, R. Isaac Meir signaled the dawning of a new era of accommodation between Hasidim and Mitnaggdim. In spite of the factionalization, escalation, and redressive action against them, Hasidim were steadily reintegrating themselves into Jewish society.[81]

Hasidim seem also to have established a separate prayer house in Wodzisław, a stronghold of Mitnaggdim. Wodzisław's rabbi had previously been R. Avigdor of Pińsk, the renowned Mitnagged who replaced the zaddik Levi Isaac of Berdyczów as rabbi of Pińsk in 1786, and whose petitions to Tsar Paul prompted the second imprisonment of the zaddik Shneur Zalman of Liady in 1800.[82] But the town was also the birthplace of the future zaddik R. Simha Bunem of Przysucha, whose father Zvi was the famed "Maggid of Wodzisław."[83] By 1816, the new rabbi of Wodzisław, Saul Spiro, was fighting his dismissal from the post for reasons that seem to have been connected to Hasidism. Spiro's rabbinical contract from 1812 had expressly warned him not to tolerate Hasidism. After praising Spiro for having forgone profit and temporal happiness to accept a paltry rabbinical salary of 9 złoties per week, the authors of his contract admonished him to follow the example of his parents and rabbinical predecessors in the town with respect to prayer services in the synagogue and *bet midrash*, and not to permit any assembly of Jews who celebrated services with any alterations "like the recently emerging Husidów/: newly emergent Sect:/."[84] Spiro thus embarked upon his stormy tenure in Wodzisław with the understanding that Hasidic rite was not to be tolerated.

Despite an insufficient salary, according to his complaint to the Polish authorities in 1816, Spiro let himself be persuaded by the community to turn down another offer and remain in Wodzisław in lifelong tenure. He soon had cause to regret that decision, as he was not paid a total of 824 złoties of that salary. Kahal members "who autocratically opposed the will of the majority" attempted to dismiss Spiro to avoid paying him. This prompted an inquiry, during which one hundred members of the community voted against his dismissal.[85] But Spiro's conflicts with the kahal did not end there, for a new matter now came to his attention. In spite of the strong wording in his own contract against tolerating separate prayer services with liturgical innovations, Spiro learned that an old document that had been concealed from him until now actually permitted separate prayer services to one of his enemies in the kahal, Moses Rubinowicz.[86] What irked Spiro was the fact that Rubinowicz was actively attempting to prevent other Jews, most likely Hasidim, from doing the same under the severest threats of excommunication. He had apparently gone so far as to pronounce unauthorized bans against the separate worshipers.[87] Spiro, declaring himself to be "foremost responsible for the abolition of dissent," protested both Rubinowicz's private prayer services and his banning of others who did the same. In retaliation, the kahal called again for his dismissal.[88] Spiro now protested his dismissal on the basis of (1) his dignity, described in the attached rabbinical contract from 1812; (2) the justice of his refusal to bow to Rubinowicz's demands; (3) the absence of reasons to violate his contract; and (4) his large numbers of supporters, in contrast to the small, autocratic clique seeking to remove him. Spiro went on to request his return to office, an annulment of the bans of excommunication pronounced by the kahal against the new separate worshipers, the removal of the autocrats who stripped him of his honor and title, and payment of his 824 złoties.[89]

Although the outcome of this process is not recorded, the nature of the conflict itself is instructive. Rubinowicz's own separate services, in contrast to the newer ones, allude to the persistence of old-style hasidism in Wodzisław. Although members of certain guilds (butchers, tailors, etc.) also held separate services, Rubinowicz was a member of the communal elite, who, like many old-style hasidim by the second decade of the nineteenth century, occupied important kahal posts.[90] Rubinowicz was attempting to resist a new Hasidic incursion. As in most cases of Mitnaggdic protest, it was not prayer innovations or separate gatherings per se that would have offended Rubinowicz, but their adoption by non-elites. Threatened with dismissal for the second time, Spiro took the drastic measure of informing the non-Jewish authorities about Rubinowicz's hypocritical actions. If the identification of Rubinowicz as an old-style hasid is correct, the challenge to his exclusive right to separate worship by a town rabbi who was neither a Hasid nor Mitnagged indicates a new weakening of Mitnaggdim.

A third dispute over the establishment of Hasidic prayer houses occurred in Przysucha. In 1776, the town became the possession of the widow Urszula Dembińska, whose economic initiatives caused the local population to flourish.[91] Przysucha consisted of three contiguous market squares—Jewish, Polish, and German.[92] The number of Jewish-owned homes steadily increased from seventy-six (in 1775) to eighty-five (in 1777) to ninety-two (1790).[93] A letter composed in Przysucha to the Maggid of Kozienice by R. Abraham of Przysucha, who allegedly had taught the Maggid Kabbalah and introduced him to famous Hasidim, suggests that the town may have possessed a Hasidic cell as early as 1761.[94] The minute book of the Przysucha Holy Society (Hevra Kadishah) was signed by both R. Abraham and the future zaddik R. Simha Bunem in 1793.[95] Around this time, the "Holy Jew" left the court of the Seer of Lublin and settled in Przysucha. The deaths of three major zaddikim from 1814 to 1815—the Holy Jew, the Maggid of Kozienice, and the Seer of Lublin—thrust Pryzsucha and its new zaddik, R. Simha Bunem, into the spotlight.

According to the Parczew police chief in 1823, local members of the "Jewish Sect Hussytów," who were praying in private homes, "have a Rabbi in the City of Przysucha on the Wisła [sic], upon whose opinions they rely, and to whom they go for business advice."[96] The complaint sparked a statewide anti-Hasidic investigation in 1824 (see chapter 3). A report from later that year divided Hasidim into two inimical groups, followers of R. Simon Deutch, recently established in Radzyń,[97] and those of Rabbi Simha Bunem of Przysucha. The town of Parczew was home to about twenty boisterous devotees of R. Simha Bunem, whom a Parczew official portrayed in the following terms:

They do not attend synagogue, but rather choose to celebrate services in rented houses, where sometimes throughout the entire night
they make a great noise and celebrate services, with various songs,
jumps, dances. It has frequently been seen that they played in this
same place chosen for prayer service, games in which different
drinks are drunk and songs are sung. And they fly out into the
street singing, jumping and producing various shouts, which the
mayor of the city cannot tolerate, and are punished by the police for
disturbing the peace at night.[98]

The complaint reflects the self-assurance of Przysucha Hasidim far away from
their zaddik's domicile.[99] They quite audaciously established what James C.
Scott has termed an unauthorized "space for a dissident subculture."[100]

We can only imagine the scene at the Przysucha headquarters. According
to a report from 1824, "every district except Augustów is more or less infected
with them, and the city of Przysucha, in the Sandomierz district, is their main
abode.[101] The author of a related decree felt compelled to specify that "their
Rabbis residing in Przysucha, under the strictest threat, are forbidden to collect
fees and provide advice or opinions."[102] Ludwig Hoff, a Christian missionary
who encountered Przysucha Hasidim firsthand in 1825, observed that the
greater part of the Jews in the town were followers of R. Simha Bunem ("a
blind rabbi"). When Hoff attempted to proselytize among them, the Hasidim
tried to prevent others from listening to him. Hoff then "followed them, and,
reproving their prejudices, told them once more what was my intention in
visiting them. I offered Tracts, but they would not take them; and rage sparkled
in their eyes."[103] The next day, Hoff and his fellow missionaries were "exposed
to the fury of the Hasidim. A number of them entered the room with proud
and angry looks. They addressed us, scolding and blaspheming." The Hasidim
even dared to offer their own superstitious interpretations of Scripture.[104] Several days later, two Hasidim came to argue on the coming of Messiah, but "as
they were tipsy, I spake to them of their wickedness, and shewed them out of
our rooms."[105]

Hoff also encountered a lapsed Maskil in Przysucha, who was taking up
the doctrine of the Hasidim. The young man, who had formerly attended the
Enlightenment-oriented schools in Breslau (Wrocław), had returned to Przysucha to study the doctrines of Hasidism. When Hoff expressed his sorrow that
he had exchanged a valuable study for so destructive a doctrine, the former
Maskil acknowledged this to be the case but confessed that being dependent
on his parents, he had no opportunity to pursue his former studies. Afterward,
he brought a German book to the missionaries to exchange for a copy of the
Prophets and promised to thenceforth study the Word of God, and other useful
things.[106] The missionaries left a week later for Koński, where initially they
found the Jews more liberal than in Przysucha. But they were soon visited by
more Hasidim, whose "confusion of ideas, which I have always found among
this sect, I found with these men also."[107]

The predominance of Przysucha Hasidism is also borne out in the national political arena, where R. Simha Bunem exercised considerable influence within the parameters of power extended to the Kingdom's Jews. When delegates were chosen for the advisory chamber of the Jewish Committee of the Congress Kingdom in 1825, the Sandomierz *województwo* elected to send the traditionalist merchant Jacob Mintz of Ostrowiec and R. Simha Bunem. Both proved to be thorns in the side of the Jewish Committee, condemning its plans to transform Jewish educational and occupational norms.[108] R. Simha Bunem's prominence was also such that it aroused the envy of other zaddikim, according to a follower of the Gur offshoot of the Przysucha school:

> In those days, when the way of Przysucha Hasidism spread more and more among the small towns of the Polish State, and many of the young Torah wonders gathered in the Hasidic community of Przysucha, the spirit of enmity and jealousy prevailed among the opponents of the holy Rabbi Bunem, may his memory be for a blessing. And they produced much propaganda, in order to spread various libels about the way of Przysucha Hasidism, and befoul them in the eyes of all the zaddikim in the Land of Poland and His Majesty the Tsar. And the Satan of Unwarranted Hatred, who dances among us, assisted them; and their work came to fruition. And they cast the fruit of severe hatred among all the Hasidic cells against Przysucha Hasidim.[109]

As mentioned in chapter 1, concern over questionable practices like delayed prayer and antinomianism fueled the opposition to Przysucha that culminated in the deliberations at the Ustila (Uściług) wedding. Additional sources cite the "rationalism" (*yesodei ha-iyun ha-sikhli*) of the Przysucha Hasidim, who lacked "feeling of the heart," and even failed to display "respect and honor before their elders."[110] But according to this citation, the opposition was principally animated by envy over the school's extraordinary popularity.

In 1794, a Hasidic prayer house also appeared in Lublin, a city renowned for its traditional rabbinic luminaries. Archival records indicate a large building on Szeroka Street facing the Lublin palace, called Besmedresz de Hasydem. It had been dedicated by a certain "Icek Szternfeld, a local Rabbi," and is described as "established in a Mosaic man's chamber, able to hold 180 people."[111] Regional court records confirm that Icek Szternfeld was none other than the zaddik Jacob Isaac, the Seer of Lublin, who sometimes used Szternfeld as a surname in official documents.[112] The Seer was a former disciple of R. Elimelekh of Leżajsk, who had broken away and formed a court in Łańcut, then Rozwód, and then Wieniawa and Czechów, adjacent to Lublin. Wieniawa, a small, poor town that had been skipped over by the new main roads to Warsaw, would seem an odd choice of venue.[113] But notwithstanding the mystical reasons supplied in Hasidic traditions, the Seer probably intended all along to use the nondescript town as a stepping stone for entry into Lublin.[114] Still, he faced considerable opposition within the city. According to Alexander Tsederbaum's mid-nineteenth-century narrative, "thousands of people traveled to the Holy One of Lublin from near and far, and also in the city he had followers, but also many opponents and rebels."[115] Among those opponents was the powerful Mitnagged R. Azriel Horowitz of Lublin, known as the "Iron Head."[116]

Resistance to the Seer's socioreligious innovations might be expected in a city that had been home to the famous Lublin Yeshiva (est. 1567) and the pioneering Talmudists R. Shalom Shakhna and R. Meir of Lublin (Maharam). Hasidic tradition acknowledges the lengthy struggle that preceded the Seer's acceptance: "From the beginning, the Mitnaggdim were against the Rabbi [Jacob Isaac "The Seer"] in Lublin." However, the tradition continues, "after his being there seven years in Lublin, and they saw that all his deeds accorded with the Holy Name, the communal leaders [parnasim] and the righteous rabbinical court sent a letter to the Rabbi, accepting him as head of a synagogue in their city."[117] Although the basic story seems plausible enough, the idea that the Seer's holy deeds were the sole rationale for his acceptance seems suspect. Moreover, details of this account are inaccurate: the Seer was not installed as the head of any synagogue, and the duration of the struggle, seven years, is undoubtedly meant to parallel the duration of the biblical Jacob's labors. Another Hasidic tradition refers to R. Saul Margaliot's ban upon private prayer gatherings that had taken effect a decade earlier, in 1783. True to form, exception was made for an old-style hasid, R. Joseph Te'omim, av bet din of Ostrowiec.[118] But one day the kahal was inspired to amend its record book (pinkas) to allow the Seer's private prayer gatherings:

> When [R. Meir Halevi of Ostowice] was in Lublin, he wanted to see the pinkas of the Lublin kahal, for it is a valuable and ancient thing. And they brought it to him, and he opened the pinkas. And he saw there this deed: concerning the decree in Lublin from a previous judgement of the great R. Saul Margaliot, may his memory be for a blessing (son of the Meir Netivim),[119] av bet din of this community, that one may not pray in separate prayer quorums; but rather only in the Great Synagogue. But owing to an amendment of the synagogue, because of the holy man and zaddik the rabbi R. Jacob Isaac Halevi Horowitz, may his memory be for a blessing, they permitted, during a gathering of the heads of the kahal, worship with [the Seer] in his own synagogue in a set quorum.[120]

As in the prior tradition, the reversal is attributed to the Seer's holiness.

However, a letter from 1803 signed by kahal lay elites (significantly, no mention is made of "the righteous rabbinical court")[121] attributes the reversal to more mundane considerations. The wall of "the chief holy bet midrash" had collapsed, preventing many Jews from praying publicly during the "period of terrible ice" (i.e., winter). As spaces for worship were now urgently needed, it was necessary to grant official recognition to the Seer's prayer house, "a stone house which he built anew behind his own house to be a house of prayer for all who come through the gates of our city to pray evening and morning, on Sabbaths and new [moons] and festivals to sanctify God . . . in the liturgy of the Holy Ari [R. Isaac Luria]." The Seer's prayer house was to operate henceforth "without any thought of subversion from us and our offspring and their eternal generations."[122] Lublin notables thus sanctioned the Seer's Besmedresz de Hasydem with a full understanding that the general public would participate in its Lurianic services, thereby gaining access to formerly privileged rite. However, even the explanation supplied in this most reliable of the available testimony raises certain questions. For had the damage to the "chief holy *bet midrash*" been the sole reason for this concession, would their permission not have been only temporary, that is, until the renovation of the old *bet midrash* was completed? Their permanent sanction of the Besmedresz de Hasydem heralded something greater: a formal toleration of Hasidism in the city. How, then, may their reversal be better explained? One possibility relates to the sorry state of the Lublin kahal finances, in deep disarray as a result of mounting indebtedness over the past two centuries.[123] Hasidim might have easily offered to help finance the renovation of the old, poorly maintained *bet midrash* in exchange for formal recognition. We may surmise that the Seer's own extraordinary prosperity, reflected in his sizeable estate in 1815, played at least some role in his ultimate acceptance.[124] All told, his struggle for acceptance had lasted nine years.

The Hasidic ascendancy in Lublin proceeded no further than this official sanction of the Seer's prayer house, however. Neither the main *bet midrash* nor the rabbinical office succumbed to Hasidism.[125] A state of equilibrium seems rather to have prevailed. On August 12, 1822, Minister Stanisław Grabowski of the Commission on Denominations sent a letter of inquiry to the local government in Lublin concerning "the existence of services and schools (probably meaning "shuls," or prayerhouses) in private homes, despite there being places established for these purposes." Grabowski wished to establish whether "such prayer houses in private homes may be exempt from the tax which since a long time ago has been collected for the Treasury from flour, bread, meat, fish, etc."[126] Two years later, officials were alerted to the specific phenomenon of Hasidim praying in homes as part of the Kingdom-wide investigation against Hasidism in 1824.[127] A copy of Zajączek's decree was filed, stating that members of "the Jewish sect Hassydymów" do not base themselves on a harmful principle, nor do they behave contrary to good customs; but "rather only isolate themselves from other Jews, wishing to have separate Synagogues which they are permitted to maintain at this time, and which are not forbidden."[128] Members of the sect were not to be persecuted, but were to be allowed to gather for religious services in private homes.[129] The absence of denunciations by Jewish informants suggests a *modus vivendi* between Hasidim and Mitnaggdim in Lublin, not to mention a weak local Haskalah. Absent denunciations by fellow Jews, local Polish authorities tended not to probe internal Jewish religious matters.

Second Phase: The *Bet Midrash* in Kozienice

The memoirs of the Countess Anna Potocka contain an aside about an astrologer in the palace of Stanisław Poniatowski, castellan of Cracow and father of the future king of Poland, who informed his curious hosts that "he was travelling in the interest of science; he wanted to interview a famous rabbi who lived at Kozienice, a little town not far from Wołczyn."[130] While details of the account are questionable, the famous rabbi could have only been R. Israel, the Maggid of Kozienice. If the identification of Poniatowski—who was castellan of Cracow until his death in 1762—is accurate, R. Israel's fame would have already been established during his mid-to late twenties.[131] But assuming the identification is mistaken, the account still constitutes one among several indications that the Maggid was known at the highest levels of Polish society.

In this period, Kozienice contained the largest concentration of Jews in the Radom *wojewódstwo*.[132] An article in *Dziennik Handlowy* from 1791 depicts Jewish life in the town as secure and prosperous. Other religious minorities besides Jews resided there, including sixteen Evangelicals. And a clear division of occupations between Jews and non-Jews indicates coexistence. The former dominated trades like soapmaking, tailoring, stocking production, coppersmithing, goldsmithing, and tinsmithing, and had allegedly "completely taken over" stores, market stalls, flea markets, slaughterhouses, and alcohol distilleries. Many worked as porters, as well. Christians, on the other hand, tended to be shoemakers, saddlemakers, wheelmakers, coopers, bakers, cabinet makers, carpenters, embroiderers, well-diggers, grave-diggers, and stove-setters.[133] Despite two fires in 1767 (destroying 15 Jewish houses)[134] and 1782 (destroying 105 Jewish houses), the Jewish population approached 1,240 by 1787, comprising 54.9 percent of the general population.[135] Hasidic tradition holds that after the second fire, in 1784, the Maggid rebuilt an entire street and donated the houses to the poor.[136] On an inventory of Jewish property in Kozienice in 1784, one of the twenty-nine houses still standing after the fire is registered as belonging to him.[137]

Kozienice emerged as the first of the three major centers of Polish Hasidism, followed by Lublin and Przysucha. A series of hostile testimonies from 1773 appears in the tract *Shever Posh'im*.[138] Notwithstanding their transparent attempt to discredit Hasidism, the testimonies inadvertently reveal the weakening of normative kahal and rabbinical authority in the face of the Hasidic ascendancy. According to the first testimony, the Maggid warned several distinguished members of the community that they had better acquiesce to the Hasidic practice of inserting the *keter* prayer into the *kedushah* portion of the *mussaf* liturgy.[139] He reminded his opponents that another zaddik, R. Levi Isaac of Berdyczów, had burned down the town of Żelechów, "so watch out, and protect your wife and children. If you say "We will sanctify Thy Name" instead of "keter" it will really be a sanctification of God's Name!" implying that they would bring martyrdom upon themselves.[140] While details of this testimony are untenable,[141] the gist is that the Maggid was behaving boldly and defiantly by 1773.

The second set of testimonies addresses the Maggid's decision to rule questionable meat kosher; this pitted him against communal officials. R. Joseph, who was "appointed over the ritual slaughters," delivered the first testimony. He had learned that the ritual slaughterer had killed a cow belonging to a non-Jew without his supervision, and had confronted the ritual slaughterer: "How dare you slaughter and make it kosher? This is a sick cow belonging to a gentile; and the butchers have an agreement with the gentile that if it stays with him it will become non-kosher, and so they won't have to pay him. A sick cow belonging to a gentile is forbidden until she can steadily walk four cubits." The slaughterer replied that the Maggid had sanctioned his act. R. Joseph went straight to this usurper and showed him a passage in the *Siftei Kohen*[142] that proved that the cow was nonkosher. The Maggid remained unperturbed: "If it came forth from my mouth, it is kosher. Perhaps there is a soul in the cow, and so God desires that Jews eat the meat in order to rectify the soul."[143] R. Joseph could only reply, "I have no dealings with mystery lore." The cow was subsequently sold as kosher. Alas, on Sabbath eve it was shown that the organ was pierced, indicating that the cow was not kosher and that a "great damage" had been done.[144] The Maggid's casual esoteric justification had caused a serious dietary transgression.[145] But perhaps equally grievous in the eyes of the authorities, he had encroached on the supervision of kosher slaughtering, both threatening the local hierarchy and diminishing the kahal's revenue.[146]

The cantor of Kozienice then confronted the Maggid, but immediately had cause to regret it. The Maggid called him "Evil One," and claimed that Satan stood at his right hand. When the cantor attempted to reply, the Maggid said, "Leave, impure one. You are banned and defiled in this world and the next. You're still wearing your shoes? Take off your shoes." One of the Hasidim cried, "Let us distance ourselves from him!" As the cantor again tried to respond on his own behalf, the Maggid repeated, "You are banned, etc. And you will force me to pray that you be disqualified from cleansing on Yom Kippur [the Day of Atonement]!"[147] The Hasidim in Kozienice thus placed their opponent under ban, just as prominent Mitnaggdim in Vilna and Brody had done to Hasidim the prior year. At this point, the rabbi of Kozienice and kahal intervened. But instead of backing down, the Maggid hurled threats at the rabbi and the entire kahal, ordering them to beg him and his Hasidim for forgiveness in the communal *bet midrash*. He gave them until the recitation of the words "Come in Peace," the last verse of *Lekha Dodi* recited on Sabbath eve, after which he warned there would be no remedy. The messenger was so shaken that he begged the rabbi's forgiveness before delivering the message. The rabbi was shocked: "Perhaps you are mistaken. Perhaps he said that he and his congregation will come to *me* to ask forgiveness? Therefore, go to the Maggid and ask him again." But the messenger was ordered to return to the rabbi with the same words, because "I'm waiting until "Come in Peace." If the rabbi and kahal come and ask forgiveness, all is well. If not, it's too late."[148]

Is such behavior conceivable for a leader of movement under siege? One would expect the Maggid to be more circumspect so shortly after the first wave of anti-Hasidic bans, especially considering the strategy of restraint that was urged by the Great Maggid of Międzyrzecz and adopted by disciples like R. Menahem Mendel of Witebsk and R. Schneur Zalman of Liady.[149] The audacity of the Maggid of Kozienice becomes more comprehensible, however, when we recall that he and his Hasidim were holding their services in the *bet midrash*, an indication that they had already attained Gottlober's second stage of ascendancy. It is further illuminated by the Jewish political situation in Kozienice, where one of the inter-elite power struggles so typical of east European Jewish communities during this period was occurring.[150] Three years before the foregoing testimony, the former rabbi of Kozienice, Oszyja Józefowicz, initiated a lawsuit against the kahal for 3,000 złoties. R. Oszyja was a powerful and unscrupulous man who had been accused in 1756 of assault and theft in a tavern while serving as town rabbi. At that time, the kahal elders and gentile authorities had sided with R. Oszyja, who had emerged victorious. But in 1770, R. Oszyja, described now as the "former rabbi," was embroiled in conflict with the kahal, his former protectors. The conflict was eventually resolved through a financial arrangement whereby the kahal repaid R. Oszyja 3,300 złoties (i.e., 300 złoties more than the original claim) on the condition that he pay 2,500 złoties to an orphan whom he had wronged.[151] In the resolution, the kahal condemned R. Oszyja's efforts to install his "relatives and friends" as rabbis and judges.[152] By warning the rabbi and kahal to ask his forgiveness or "it's too late," the Maggid may have been implicitly threatening to side with the powerful R. Oszyja, who for the past four years had been attempting to install his son Solomon as rabbi of Kozienice against their will. Indeed, it is possible to speculate that the Maggid and R. Oszyja did reach an understanding, for in 1792 R. Oszyja secured an agreement that left the town's top rabbinical post to his son Solomon upon his death, over the kahal's objection.[153] As late as 1816, the Kozienice rabbi is recorded as Szlomo Szyjowicze (i.e., Solomon, son of [O]szyja), eighty-six years old.[154]

The Maggid would certainly have been in a position to determine such an appointment, for he was by then the most powerful Jewish figure in Kozienice, allegedly constructing a synagogue of several stories.[155] The well-known Mitnagged R. David of Maków alludes to the Maggid's influence in 1798, warning his readers about "frivolous women . . . [who] during times of distress flock to build houses for themselves in Kozienice or Neskhiż (Nesuhoyezhe), and lose their wealth for nothing."[156] More extensive testimony appears in the memoirs of Leon Dembowski (1789–1878), a young member of Prince Adam Jerzy Czartoryski's court. A nobleman named Skowroński had been robbed of 11,000 ducats on his return trip from Danzig (Gdańsk). After several years, when the loss was already forgotten, Skowroński received a letter from "the famous Magiet, rabbi in Kozienice, considered a saint by Jews." The letter reported that the money had been recovered and could be reclaimed under the conditions that the thief is forgiven, that Skowroński be contented with on 10,000 ducats (the rest having been squandered by the thief), and that he not inquire of the rabbi how he discovered the thief. The money was returned under these conditions. Prince Czartoryski, whose palace was located near the Maggid's court, decided to visit him "to thank him on behalf of his friend." Several versions of this event circulated among the Polish peasantry.[157]

In Dembowski's account of the visit, we are first treated to a description of the town itself, which, apart from Długa Street, the large market square, and

the royal palace, "consisted of dirty, narrow, wooden houses, and muddy for-
mations of streets upon which transport was maintained with the help of
coaches."[158] The prince and his retinue arrived at the residence of the Maggid,
"whose house was found amidst the dirty streets." They immediately encountered local Jews, ecstatic over their distinguished visitors: "the first group
shouted, the second sang, and others danced. Jew-boys and little brats cried
from happiness." [159] Finally, the noble travelers beheld the Maggid himself:

> Amid this noisy tumult we entered the Magiet's residence, straight
> through a hall and into a big room, where behind a partition-wall lay
> the saint on a pyramid of bedding. He was an old little guy [staru-
> szek] of about ninety years of age, dressed completely in white, with
> a beard as white as snow reaching all the way down to his belt. His
> face was full of tiny, narrow wrinkles.[160]

The Prince and his court were disappointed, however. Czartoryski began to
speak to the Maggid in Polish; and receiving no answer, tried German. Still
receiving no response, the field marshal in the retinue tried to speak to the
Maggid in Hebrew, which "he knew very well," but to no avail.

Seeing that not a word could be extracted from the enigmatic saint, the
Prince and his entourage retired to the inn for lunch. On the way out, the same
enthusiastic crowd of Jews converged, exclaiming, "Our Magiet, what a wise
man!" The bewildered memoirist was not sure if such "stubborn silence" qual-
ifies as wisdom. But at the same time, he admitted, the Maggid was charitable:
"from all the surrounding lands baskets of contributions for the saint rolled
in. He received it all, and on a given Friday distributed whatever came in among
the poor. Besides monetary donations, they consumed from 80 to 200 [quarts]
of dry goods each week."[161] By 1814, the probable date of the event, the Maggid
had accumulated throngs of admirers and generous donors.[162]

Kozienice remained a Hasidic center after the Maggid's death, at which
point his son Moses Eliyakim Briyah succeeded him. Although hereditary succession was rarely accepted in Polish Hasidism during this period, several of
the Maggid's disciples temporarily complied with the Seer of Lublin's order to
pass their allegiance on to their deceased master's son.[163] On March 26, 1824,
when the central government instructed the district commissioners to attempt
through "knowledge and persuasion to return [Hasidim] from their errors,"
the instruction to the Sandomierz commissioner contained an addendum expressly condemning the rabbis of Przysucha (i.e., R. Simha Bunem) and Kozienice (R. Moses Eliyakim Briyah) on the grounds that they, "under some
pretext, gather contributions or give advice and prophetic opinions for which
Jewish folk, particularly masses of sectarians, frequently gather."[164] Two years
later, on September 29, 1826, the Christian missionary W. F. Becker referred
to Kozienice as "a chief seat of the Chasidim, where they have a famous
rabbi."[165] Both sources reflect the movement's continued predominance in Kozienice.

Third Phase: Invasion of the Synagogue of Olkusz

In 1817, at least five Hasidim—Michał Friedman, Isaac Rosenheim, Joachim Nayman, Solomon Hayman, and Jonas Rosenheim—invaded the main synagogue in Olkusz and most likely attempted to impose liturgical innovations. A brawl erupted in the synagogue, eliciting a formal complaint by the Mitnaggdim and prompting a governmental inquiry.[166] Yet the ensuing investigation succeeded only in exposing the weakness of the Mitnaggdim and the clout of the Hasidim. When called before the district authorities, the Mitnaggdim shrank from their initial complaints and, despite their enemies' designs on the town synagogue, assured officials that Hasidism was both harmless and widely accepted.

The Jewish community of Olkusz, whose members were primarily involved in the exportation of silver and lead from the town's mines, consisted of only 162 members in 1765.[167] But the town grew in influence after a jurisdictional dispute with Kazimierz in 1779, at which point the Olkusz kahal emerged with a domain consisting of the towns Czarnowice, Wielka Wieś, Każniowce, Rudawa, and Młynek.[168] Hasidism is mentioned in the memoirs of the nobleman Stanisław Wodzicki, who spearheaded the notorious Olkusz blood libel of 1787.[169] King Stanisław Augustus himself, perhaps at the request of his Jewish military suppliers, intervened and condemned the blood libel in no uncertain terms.[170] But as late as 1840, Wodzicki continued to nurse "the deepest conviction that although the blood of an animal is forbidden in Mosaic Law, known through the removal of the veins in kosher meat, there exists one sect, Chassydymów [Hasidim], who despite that law hunger for the blood of Christian children for their ceremonies."[171]

The first dependable testimony appeared in 1817, in the wake of the synagogue brawl. Jacob Brull lodged a formal complaint against members of a sect called "Michałki," who included Friedman and his colleagues. The name "Michałki," bearing the additional meaning of "fools" in old Polish, was derived from the name of one of the Hasidim, Michał Friedman. According to Brull, the five men instigated the fistfight by forming a new religion "that is causing division among the inhabitants of Olkusz of the Jewish faith." As only the Jewish religion itself was acknowledged as tolerated by the constitution of the Kingdom, and as Jews could not abide the formation of new sects, Brull requested protection against his oppressors.[172] This time, it was Mitnaggdim who were invoking the Kingdom's constitution.

The court asked the Commission of the Cracow *wojewódstwa* to determine if the formation of such new sects was indeed a violation of the constitution, as Brull and his colleagues maintained.[173] The district commissioner ordered an investigation in Olkusz to establish: (1) whether the Michałki sect actually exists; (2) how long it has existed; (3) whether many people belong to it; (4) how far its branches reach; (5) who founded it; (6) to what extent does it differ from the Jewish religion; and (7) what its purpose is and whether it contains morally harmful principles.[174] Several months later, the Olkusz commissioner informed the district commissioner that he would have to delay his inquiry into the aforementioned sects; however, he wished to mention that "there is a similar Sect called Hussytów [i.e., Hasidism] that is found in every town where Jews reside, and is merely *strictioris observantia*."[175] The Olksuz comissioner's next report contained the startling discovery that "no Michałki Sect exists at all—only Hasuty [i.e., Hasidim], who only differ from other Jews in their use of distinct books for Prayer, with which they pray in separate places." According to the Jew Ziskind Rosenheim, they had been prohibited by the past regime; however, this could not be substantiated. In addition, Rosenheim asserted that a leader of the sect resided in Stopnica and was conducting himself like a prophet, attracting less enlightened Jews and commanding them to "purchase redemption from him, under the rubric of donations."[176] The commissioner concluded that there was no reason to obstruct the Hasidim.

The proceedings from which his conclusion derived are appended to the report.[177] On October 29, 1818, Jacob Brull was interrogated, as follows.

(1) Do you persist in your petition to the Olkusz Police Court on December 6, 1817 to the protocols that in the town of Olkusz is found a separate Sect of Jews under the specific name Michałki, and do you insist that this Sect and its followers exist?

Answer: My petition to the Olkusz Police Court on December 6, 1817, raised in the protocols is acknowledged and insisted upon.

(2) What proof do you have that this Sect exists in Olkusz, and does it exist in other cities, and what is more, how does it differ from your ancient Religion, and do the Rabbis not scorn those who belong to the Michałki Sect, and command you to disconnect yourselves from this Sect if you do belong to it?

Answer: That this Sect is found here in Olkusz is proven by other Jews who reside here, because they celebrate one type of service and we another. But I called them Michał because the oldest one of them who lives in Olkusz is named Michał Friedman. But they have always called themselves Hussyty, and are found in every city in the district. The main difference between our ancient Religion and the Hussyty is that they recite the prayer *Twiles Swert*[178] and we according to ancient custom and rites *Twiles Aschkenas*.[179] Our Rabbis do not have any objection to this Sect, within which several themselves are to be found.

(3) Do the ceremonies of these Michałki members, or Hussytów as they are called by you, not entail something which might be contrary to the laws of the State? Or harmful to your Religion?

At this point, Brull requested a few days to prepare his answer. On November 2, he returned and pleaded that he knew little more about the Hasidim beyond their use of different prayer books. He appealed to the Commission to call Meir Blumberg of Pilica, "who is better informed about this." The Commission then asked Brull if he had anything to add or to change, to which Brull replied: "I would only like to add that you will not arrive at the truth about this Sect from Rabbis who belong to it. But it would be better to call the local Jew Ziskind Rosenheim, who does not belong to this Sect—because he is better informed than I." Brull did not want the Commission to hear the Hasidic side of the story.

They next called upon Joshua Landau, rabbi of Pilica since 1806,[180] who was questioned because "no Rabbi exists in the town of Olkusz," owing to the departure of the former rabbi, Samuel Unger, to Pilica.[181] The vacancy in the Olkusz rabbinate suggests that even more may have been at stake in this struggle than the synagogue liturgy. The Commission asked R. Landau: "Does the Sect called Michałki or Hussety actually exist among Jews?" to which he replied:

> Of any Sect called Michałki we are not informed, and if there is I never heard of it. I only know that among us Jews there are certain Jews whom we call Hussety. They use books called *Twiles Swert* in their prayers, which have certain changes and additions, corrected by ancient, enlightened men. But such Jews do not differentiate themselves insofar as Religion and Laws of the great State—for other laws would not be tolerated. These Jews are, I believe, less enlightened. That is why they pray in separate Schools. And this causes them to have certain changes and additions, as I related above. And in order not to disturb others, they pray in separate places.

R. Landau downplayed the differences between Hasidism and the normative Jewish community, limiting them to acceptable liturgical variations and differing degrees of "enlightenment," a curious concern for a small-town rabbi.

The final subject of the interrogation was Ziskind Rosenheim, whom Brull had recommended as a reliable source on Hasidism. The Commission asked, "Is it known that the Sect called Michałki or Hussety actually exists among Jews, how do they differ from your religion, and are many people in your congregation found among them?" Rosenheim supplied the only potentially damaging testimony:

> Of any Sect called Michałki I do not know. I only know that among us Jews there are certain Jews whom they call Hassety. Jakub Brull, out of hatred called them Michałki because he is involved in a law suit with Michał Friedman, who belongs to the Hassyty. This Sect Hassyty was prohibited by the previous Austrian government's *Majiers—Cesarz* decree;[182] no one was even allowed to let a Hassyt spend the night with them. But the Elders here lost the decree. And truthfully may I say that this Hassytic Sect is harmful to our community, as some of these Hassytów act as Prophets. There is one in Stopnica—whose name I do not know—who attracts less enlight-

ened Jews and commands them to pay redemption money under the rubric of donations.[183]

The "prophet" was undoubtedly the zaddik R. Meir of Stopnica (Stavniz) and Opatów (Apt), who was the official rabbi of Stopnica in 1816.[184]

The reserve of these Mitnaggdim may well astonish those who are conversant in Mitnaggdic accounts of the late eighteenth century (note the contrast with the Kozienice testimony!). Liturgical differences had merely prompted Hasidim to found separate prayer houses "in order not to disturb others"— hardly an incriminating claim. No mention was made of the five Hasidim who entered the synagogue and assaulted Brull, who himself acknowledged that "our Rabbis do not have any objection to this Sect, within which several themselves are to be found." Landau assured the authorities that the Hasidim most certainly do not oppose the laws of the State. And Rosenheim undermined the credibility of his potentially damaging allegations by referencing an Austrian decree that had somehow been lost and a prophet in Stopnica whom he could not even identify. Perhaps the Mitnaggdim decided upon further reflection that involving the non-Jewish authorities was going too far; or perhaps fear of a Hasidic reprisal dampened their resolve. Be that as it may, these timid allegations and retreats further indicate a general weakening of Mitnaggdic determination, a pattern already established in the cases of Lublin, Wodzisław, and Kozienice. This impression is strengthened by Landau and Rosenheim's attempts to depict Hasidim as "less enlightened," a resort to Haskalah terminology that reflects that movement's growing influence. The authorities were forced to conclude that "it appears that there is some sect Hussytów among Jews"; but it remained unclear when they had appeared and what they stood for.[185] After a few additional official exchanges, the matter was dropped.[186] It is unknown whether the Hasidim henceforth dominated the synagogue services.

Fourth Phase: Conquest of the Rabbinate in Stopnica, Opatów, and Żelechów

Who was the supposed "prophet" referred to by Rosenheim? R. Meir Rothenberg of Stopnica (Stavniz) and Opatów (Apt) was born in Pacanów in 1760 and raised in Stopnica, where the Jewish population was calculated at 563 in 1765.[187] He joined the inner circle of the Seer of Lublin and became a fierce opponent of the breakaway Przysucha disciples. Among the "young Torah wonders" that R. Simha Bunem of Przysucha had wooed away from R. Meir was R. Isaac Meir Alter, the future zaddik of Gur.[188] Unable to contain his irritation over this latest triumph by the former merchant and pharmacist, R. Meir wrote R. Simha Bunem a letter in which he taunted him that "achievements and high spiritual levels will come to me from Torah study, not through mercantile pursuits and Danzig theaters." R. Simha Bunem is said to have replied, not without irony, that humility is even more important than Torah study.[189]

In 1809, R. Meir replaced the zaddik Abraham Joshua Heschel as rabbi of Opatów when the latter left to become rabbi of Jassy.[190] Six years later, R. Meir accepted the rabbinical post in Stopnica, his prior home. On August 17, 1816, the Stopnica rabbi was still recorded by Polish officials as "Majer Rothenberg, a native of Pacanów, fifty-seven years old and elected by the Jewish Community for the second year."[191] However, on January 17 of the next year, R. Meir abruptly turned the post over to his son, R. Israel. In a petition to the High District Committee of the Cracow wojewódstwa, the elders of the Stopnica kahal requested the required confirmation, in lieu of the required fee, for their election "together with all of its synagogue last year, 1816, of the Jew Israel Moses Rothenberg [i.e., R. Meir's son], inhabitant of your City, as Rabbi in this Stopnica kahal."[192] In their original explanation, dated September 27, 1816, the kahal lay elites begged R. Meir's pardon because, notwithstanding his election to the rabbinate, they were convinced that he was having difficulties teaching and praying owing to his "ill health." They were sure, however, that they would be able to continue to make frequent use of his much-needed assistance in the synagogue. In his place, they nominated and elected R. Meir's son Israel as rabbi, deeming him "sufficiently trained for such religious responsibilities and for matters of private custom." Authority was conferred on R. Meir's son with the understanding that "in times of need [R. Meir] will provide his sweet, renowned assistance and advise him. And his son will be content with this honor every time."[193] R. Meir thus retained ultimate rabbinical authority, while his son was to serve in his place only by proxy.

Their unusual request prompted an official inquiry. On February 9, 1817, the kahal elders were ordered to appear before the Stopnica district commissioner at 9:00 the next morning. The commissioner asked the elders whether it was, indeed, their unanimous wish that Israel Rothenberg, son of Meir Rothenberg, be elected; and whether he was "qualified for such seniority, and how old is he?" The elders affirmed that it was their unanimous wish; that Israel was thirty years old; that he had been acting as rabbi of the synagogue since October 5, 1816; and that his age was no impediment to assuming a position of such seniority. After the sixteen elders signed the agreement, R. Israel signed his statement of acceptance, and his father explained his resignation:

> In conclusion, mindful of this election, the Jew Meir Rothenberg, fa-
> ther of Israel Rothenberg, until now regarded by the Stopnica Syna-
> gogue as rabbi, declares voluntarily in the presence of the gathered
> residents of the Mosaic faith- that owing to his weak health, and out
> of goodwill to his son Israel Rothenberg, the senior rabbi of the
> Stopnica Synagogue completely resigns—and to bestow the honor
> on his son Israel Rothenberg, he steps down.[194]

It is doubtful that the fifty-seven-year-old zaddik was in "weak health," for he lived an additional feisty fifteen years, until 1831. Nor is "good will to his son" a very convincing reason. It is more likely that the death of the Seer of Lublin a year and a half earlier had opened the way for R. Meir's emergence as the Seer's main successor. His consolidation of power during this critical phase probably made him too busy for local rabbinical functions, which is why his son had been performing those functions since October of the prior year. The authority of town rabbi, of course, paled in comparison to that of a zaddik. Still, R. Meir retained authority over local spiritual matters in Stopnica through his son. The scheme received several confirmations, and a fee of 40 złoties to the Commissioner garnered the official stamp.[195]

R. Meir eventually resumed the rabbinical post in Opatów, which was another setting of Hasidism's triumph at the highest level. Opatów was for well over a century the domain of the powerful Landau family, but the rise of Hasidism had spelled the end of their dominance.[196] The Opatów Eternal Light Society accepted seven-year-old Israel, the future Maggid of Kozienice, as a member in 1744.[197] As early as 1762, R. Jacob Emden charged that the alleged heretic and ignoramus R. Nahman of Kosów, a member of the Besht's inner circle, "corrupted a holy community when he was sent to Opatów."[198] By the end of the eighteenth century, Opatów possessed a prayer house called Havruta Kadisha, one of whose members opened a *shtibl* in his home across the street.[199] Sometime before 1790, the zaddik Moses Leib of Sasów opened his own Hasidic prayer house in the town.[200] Details of the transition from a separate prayer house to usurpation of the rabbinate are murky. R. Aryeh Leib ben Ze'ev Wolf Harif, appointed town rabbi on January 5, 1777, was a teacher of the Holy Jew of Przysucha, although there is no evidence that he was Hasidic.[201] The decisive year was 1800, when the zaddik Abraham Joshua Heschel was appointed rabbi of Opatów. The zaddik's rabbinical contract announces his great lineage (*yihus*) and incorruptible character, and bears forty-nine signatures. Included is the signature of another powerful local Hasid, R. Aaron of Opatów—compiler of the classic collection of teachings attributed to the Besht entitled *Keter Shem Tov.*[202]

As mentioned earlier, R. Meir of Stopnica succeeded R. Abraham Joshua Heschel as rabbi of Opatów in 1809, then assumed the Stopnica rabbinate in 1815, but eventually returned to Opatów. He appears in government documents from 1824 as the Opatów town rabbi in connection with the anti-Hasidic investigation conducted that year. On July 2, a special subcommittee led by Stanisław Staszic summoned several Hasidic leaders to Warsaw for interrogation. R. Meir attempted to elude the summons in a letter cowritten with his rival R. Simha Bunem of Przysucha, requesting a written questionnaire instead.[203] R. Simha Bunem was able to persuade the subcommittee of his weak health and old age in a subsequent letter, and at least avoid a protracted interrogation.[204] But R. Meir, despite a second letter pleading ill health, was summoned before the subcommittee.[205] The interrogation and its favorable outcome will be described in the next chapter.

R. Meir's involvement with the authorities did not end there. R. Meir wrote to the wealthy Warsaw merchant/industrialist Jacob Bergson later that year concerning continued intrusions of his prayer services by the Opatów police, and Bergson protested to Staszic. The latter agreed that Hasidic services in private homes had been deemed permissible as a result of the investigation concluded that year, but denied that this decision applied to "free gatherings of Jews from *different locales*," that is, Hasidic pilgrimages.[206] Additional officials read Bergson's complaint and requested clarification.[207] On February 13, 1825, R. Meir appeared before the Opatów commissioner and, during the ensuing interview, complained that local police were continually entering private houses and demanding passports from out-of-town Jews. In order to avoid "future unpleasantness," he had written Bergson asking him to quickly send Zając-czek's decree to Opatów so that he could publicize it locally. For despite decreed tolerance for Hasidic worship, the Opatów police "came twice into the chamber of my residence when services were being held, asking if any out-of-town Jews were there, and told me that such a large number of people may not gather together." They had not conducted themselves impolitely, but nonetheless "caused a certain amount of anxiety."

At the interview's end, the commissioner was curious to know why R. Meir claimed the title "Chief of the Hasidim." R. Meir's reply reflects the reordering of authority in Polish Jewish society that was underway in Hasidic areas: "There are Rabbis who are not chiefs of the Sect of the Hasidim, because they do not belong to this Sect—I however, in spite of being Rabbi of the city of Opatów, being also a disciple of this Sect and its principles—am considered a chief more universally than they."[208] The combined roles as zaddik and town rabbi denoted, in R. Meir's mind, supreme authority. That Opatów was now rivaling Przysucha as the capital of Polish Hasidism can be gathered from the reaction of the Opatów police to Bergson's intervention. They complained that, decree of toleration or not, they had to constantly check the passports of the Jewish pilgrims at R. Meir's house because "a great number" of them were from out of town. Jacob Bergson had misinterpreted the decree of toleration as a criticism of the police. When, in fact, the police had entered the prayer houses—which they could hardly ascertain to be places of prayer anyhow—they had only requested that "those out-of-town Jews behave politely, quietly and peacefully." Finally, they were not disturbing Hasidic gatherings per se, but rather investigating suspected smugglers. The whole situation was in any case unbearable: "In a city as populated with Jews and as open as Opatów, passport control is difficult. For on every Sabbath approximately two hundred—and on bigger holidays between five hundred and six hundred—out-of-town Jews are arriving from everywhere."[209] The out-of-town Jews did not register with the local police, but rather pressed into the Jewish quarter at all times of night. Such "huge numbers of Jews roaming in carriages and on foot" undoubtedly contained suspicious characters and smugglers.[210] We might sympathize with the police, trying as they were to maintain some semblance of order, as was their duty. Their conduct certainly does not merit Mahler's description of "persecution," despite their presumption that criminals were to be found among the pilgrims.[211] R. Meir must have been aware of the delicacy of this situation himself, for he prudently withdrew his complaint.[212]

The town of Żelechów was a well-known setting for Polish Hasidism's most advanced stage of communal conquest. R. Levi Isaac of Berdyczów, author of *Kedushat Levi* (Sławuta, 1798),[213] served as rabbi of Żelechów from 1765 until his expulsion ten years later, in 1775. His term was tumultuous, despite (or perhaps as a result of) his efforts to establish a synagogue, implement ritual reforms (*takkanot*), and organize study fellowships for tailors, bakers, and simple merchants.[214] The choleric zaddik encountered opposition from Mitnaggdim and zaddikim alike.[215] In Hasidic testimony, he occasionally appears somewhat unbalanced. According to the zaddik Yizhak Isaac Judah Jehiel Safrin of Komarno, R. Levi Isaac's quarrels "used to depress him beyond measure. And in the year 1773, owing to his terrible loss of heart, he fell from his lofty level . . . and prayed rapidly from his little prayer book, and went a little out of his mind, as is known," a remarkable admission for a Hasidic source![216] The testimony of R. Abraham of Pinczów also raises questions about R. Levi Isaac's stability:

> The Holy Maggid of Kozienice, his disciple, helped him a great deal and said that the celestial beings had surely not caused him to fall from his lofty level, God forbid, but that in heaven above there was also an accusation that he [R. Levi Isaac] had provoked the supernal angels that year, and that because of this it was impossible to help him.[217]

R. Levi Isaac eventually "returned to his great level in brilliant light"; however, when R. Abraham was with him in 1794, he admitted to being depressed again.[218] These attestations provide an intriguing perspective on the zaddik's personality and high-profile controversies.

One of those controversies derived from an incident in the Żelechów *bet midrash* in 1773, and involved the Maggid of Kozienice. It undoubtedly contributed to his dismissal from the Żelechów rabbinate two years later. According to hostile testimony, the Hasidim marched around with the Torah on Shemini Azeret eve (which non-Hasidim only do on Simhat Torah eve) and then proceeded to mock a learned and distinguished rabbi. The Maggid stood on a table and "screamed all sorts of mockery and epitaphs and bad numerical combinations [*gematriyot*] against this rabbi, who is not of their sect—words that should not even be put in writing, etc." The Maggid and R. Levi Isaac then ordered the sexton to cry "A gentile does not bless an *etrog*," and everyone responded "True!" and again began to curse the rabbi. The sexton announced, "A gentile doesn't blow *shofar*." And they all again responded, "True!" The next morning, during the carrying of the Torah, the Maggid, R. Levi Isaac, and their Hasidim announced, "All is good for one who prays *Keter*. And upon whomever impedes the recitation of '*Keter*' shall be invoked all bans and curses, etc." And everyone replied, "True!"[219]

Before we proceed with the consequences attending these provocations, it is important to note that Mordecai Wilensky expressed reservations about identifying the "Maggid" as R. Israel of Kozienice, on the grounds that his physical frailty—as portrayed in hagiographical accounts—would have made traveling to Żelechów and standing on a table difficult for him. But Wilensky was unable to suggest a viable alternative and, even more important, failed to consider that the thirty-seven-year-old Maggid may not have been as physically frail at this point in his life. Assuming, with historian Abraham Rubinstein, the accuracy of these identifications, we are privy to more Hasidic boldness shortly on the heels of the first wave of anti-Hasidic bans.[220] The incident is reminiscent of the Kozienice episode cited earlier; however, the insults hurled at a respected local scholar made it even more incendiary.

The Hasidim were soon reminded that their conquest of Żelechów was unconsolidated, for R. Levi Isaac was forced to depart in 1775. His departure generated a demographic loss of about three hundred Jews in the town.[221] Hasidic tradition maintains that a fire raged in Żelechów as a result of his expulsion, and Mitnaggdic testimony also connects the fire to R. Levi Isaac's displeasure.[222] But the fire seems to have actually occurred a few years earlier.[223] In any case, the expulsion shook the Hasidic world. The zaddik Elimelekh of Leżajsk tried to downplay it:

> Why do you imagine that this is in any way novel? Things of this
> kind transpired from the earliest times. We find that Nimrod cast
> our father Abraham, peace be upon him, into the fiery furnace from
> which he escaped in safety. . . . [Just as the biblical Abraham was
> tested], so, too, all the zaddikim who have opponents [*Mitnaggdim*]
> will be justified. These rise against them, speaking falsehoods and
> determined to quarrel. Yet our eyes see how righteous the zaddikim
> are, for their prayers are answered just as the prayers of the righ-
> teous were in ancient times.[224]

R. Levi Isaac's trials were no different from those of the biblical forefather, and his prayers were no less potent.

The setback was in any case only temporary. Less than ten years later, at the wedding of the grandson of the Seer of Lublin to the daughter of R. Avigdor, rabbi of Żelechów, a rabbinical appointment occurred that proves that Żele-chów did not revert permanently to non-Hasidic leadership and that R. Levi Isaac's influence over the town did not even cease. Abraham Zusman wit-nessed the wedding in c. 1805, and is adamant about the accuracy of his ac-count: "even though this event was almost sixty years ago, and now it is 1864, praise God that I remember most of it as well as if it were yesterday. And everything that I have written is true and sure." His detailed, rhapsodic account begins as follows.

> When I was sevn or eight years old, there was a great wedding in
> Żelechów. For the holy Rabbi Jacob Isaac [the Seer] of Lublin . . .
> married his dear grandson Moteli (as he was called at that time)
> with the daughter of the princely rabbi R. Avigdor of Żelechów.[225]
> . . . And there at the wedding was the holy, old *maggid*, our pure
> rabbi Israel of Kozienice . . . and also the aforementioned Rabbi of
> Lublin, and also their great disciples and disciples of those disciples
> and many Hasidim from far and near without number. And all the
> houses of the city were not enough for them, and they nearly had to
> sleep outside. And the wedding was on Friday, the evening of the

Sabbath. And during the preceding week their great disciples (with many of their own Hasidim) had come to Żelechów. And I cannot remember their specific names, except for the zaddik, our rabbi Jacob Simon, because the aforementioned holy ones made him at this time rabbi of Żelechów on the condition that the genius rabbi, man of God, our rabbi Levi Isaac of Berdyczów agreed to it, for the Żelechów rabbinate had belonged to him. And the aforementioned holy ones wrote and signed the rabbinical contract and sent it to Berdyczów and asked him to agree with them and forgive him the rabbinate and sign the rabbinical contract himself, and he did so. And [R. Jacob Simon] remained rabbi of Żelechów many years.[226]

For reasons unknown, R. Avigdor, the father of the bride, was being replaced as rabbi of Żelechów by R. Jacob Simon (known as R. Simon Deutch), a disciple of the Seer of Lublin and vocal opponent of Przysucha Hasidism.[227] The Maggid and the Seer felt compelled to attain R. Levi Isaac's consent, even though he now resided in the Ukrainian city of Berdyczów, for the Żelechów rabbinate was still considered his by right.

The second part of Zusman's account evokes the vast popularity of the zaddikim in Żelechów, as well as the exalted social position of many of their devotees:

And on the fourth day before the wedding our rabbi of Lublin came to Żelechów, and all the great ones and many Hasidim, and all the great ones of the city went out to call on him in carriages and on foot. And in the evening they arrived to the city with him in great joy and surrounded him with their carriages. In the stores that stood in the center of the market were many great torches, and there were candles lit in all the windows of the houses. And it is not possible to imagine or describe the joy that existed then in the whole city, what's more in writing. And on the next day the aforementioned old, holy Maggid of Kozienice came, and they also paid him all of the respect they had given to (the rabbi of Lublin) on the previous day.[228]

The self-confident display reminds us of how misleading it is to characterize Polish Jewry in general as a besieged "minority," a depiction found in older historiographical schools. Jews formed a sizeable majority in towns throughout eastern regions.[229] According to figures compiled in 1787, the Jews of Żelechów amounted to 70.7 percent of the population and owned almost half the houses of the town.[230]Hasidic sympathizers and adherents apparently formed the greater part of that population according to this account, which makes the official estimate of "up to sixty" Hasidim (see chapter 1, table 1.1) so improbable.

At the wedding, the zaddikim made their grand entrances. R. Jacob Simon was accorded the honor of escorting the Maggid, who proceeded to perform the ceremony with the Seer.

And on Friday afternoon there was a *huppa* [wedding canopy] in front of the synagogue. And I remember that on that same day it was muddy outside, and they placed boards on the ground from the holy Maggid's house until the entrance of the synagogue. And I saw with my own eyes that the holy Maggid walked on the boards and the aforementioned rabbi, Zaddik Jacob Simon, walked beside him in the mud and held onto the holy Maggid's right hand. And another great one walked on the other side and held the holy Maggid's left hand. The holy Maggid made the betrothal and marriage blessings. And our holy rabbi of Lublin read the betrothal agreement. (The holy Maggid was a short man and older than our holy Rabbi of Lublin). At the third meal of the holy Sabbath, the two holy ones did not eat together in one house, but rather each one ate in his own lodging. And where they prayed on Sabbath eve and morning, I do not remember now. And before the afternoon prayer of the Sabbath, the holy Maggid of Kozienice came to the synagogue and preached on the podium. And our holy Rabbi of Lublin was also there in the synagogue, and heard the sermon.[231]

The fact that these events occurred in the main synagogue, not to mention the rabbinical appointment of the future zaddik Simon Deutch, suggests a full reassertion of Hasidic control in Żelechów. Continued Hasidic prominence, at least before 1823, is affirmed in a police report from that year, which divides Hasidim into two adversarial groups: adherents of R. Simon Deutch, who had by now moved to Radzyń, and those of the R. Simha Bunem of Przysucha.[232]

Polish Bureaucrats and Fellow Christians

As Jewish self-governing institutions were under the ultimate jurisdiction of the state during these acquisitions, Hasidim required above all the acquiescence of government officials. Those officials occupied one of two distinct social strata. The clerks at the highest level were usually members of the aristocracy (Stanisław Staszic, an ex-priest and townsman, was an exception), while the lower levels consisted of landless petty nobles, intellectuals, and merchants. In the Duchy of Warsaw, most members of the administration were Polish, and included many former soldiers who had fought for Napoleon. When Duke Constantine took charge in 1815, he appointed increasing numbers of German immigrants and allegedly filled posts with his favorites without considering qualifications or morals.[233] According to a contemporaneous satire, a government clerk now required the following qualities.

First of all, he must be a member of a Masonic lodge; after that, he must be long known by everyone for his meanness or his servility; finally, he must know how to cheat, steal from the treasury and fleece people. Must a clerk be conscientious? On the contrary, conscience and religion are obstacles for a clerk. And when a religious conscience is found in a clerk, he is, in the midst of clerks, like a *bonifrater* among lunatics who turns everything upside-down.[234]

Other contemporary writers are more benevolent, however, describing town clerks as knowledgeable of administrative necessities and working in harmony with local populations.[235]

In several of the Hasidic investigations mentioned earlier, officials are revealed as genuinely concerned about Jews being exploited by charlatans, threats to public order, and the constitutional right of Judaism to function untroubled by sectarianism. Usually, it was fellow Jews, either Mitnaggdim or Maskilim, who sparked local officials' concerns about Hasidism. Only where public disorder was evident—as in Parczew and Opatów—did the police move against Hasidim on their own initiative. It does not appear that Hasidim, as Jews, were singled out by those officials. This conclusion is reinforced by comparing anti-Hasidic investigations to the treatment of Christian miracle workers. In 1806, for example, a widow named Marianna Zawistowska beheld a vision inside "a wooden figurine of Beloved Christ" and set up a votive candle in her home. Two pious widows, several travelers, and Zawistowska's own children witnessed the miraculous healing of pilgrims before the figurine. As a result, the local priest took the figurine to the church and placed it upon the altar, and pilgrims began to stream in from all over. The authorities then swiftly decreed that the figurine be "removed from the altar and concealed in a closed closet, sealed up with three seals."[236] They proved no more tolerant of this impromptu Christian pilgrimage than of Hasidic ones.[237]

In 1810, reports of miracles began to proliferate. Two nine-year-old children saw trees moving, a shining cap, and burning lamps.[238] Twenty sightings, mostly of the Virgin Mary, are enumerated in an attached report.[239] On October 22 of that year, the prefect in Warsaw took action against a lessee of a liquor distillery who had been collecting donations at a miracle site in the town of Sanniki. According to the Warsaw prefect, "dark folk from different locales gathered and did not fail to chip in monetary donations approaching the sum of 1,200 złoties."[240] Such gatherings of "gullible folk," motivated by "greed for profit and fanaticism," must be abolished, the prefect commanded. The 1,200 złoties would be used to compensate the local church and farmers whose grain crops were damaged by the gathering.[241] Gorski, the minister of internal affairs, ordered that the 1,200 złoties be handed over to the provost of the Sanniki church, who was instructed to compensate those he deemed deserving.[242] These Christian cases place official treatment of Hasidism in perspective: official concerns about fanaticism, exploitation of gullible folk, and disruptions of public order applied in both cases. If anything, zaddikim ultimately enjoyed better treatment than Christian miracle workers.

Conclusion

The foregoing cases afford a new perspective on Polish zaddikim like Levi Isaac of Żelechów, the Maggid of Kozienice, the Seer of Lublin, Simha Bunem of Przysucha, Meir of Opatów/Stopnica, and Alexander Zusya Kahana. In contrast to their hagiographical depictions, which place emphasis on their miracles and piety, and collections of their homiletic discourses, which exhibit their exegetical finesse, the foregoing sources reveal these zaddikim as deft organizers and power brokers who methodically dispatched emissaries to set up prayer houses, recruit locals, and make daring sorties into public spaces of worship while they, themselves, usurped kahal prerogatives, controlled appointments, and assumed important rabbinical posts. What has been argued here is that we must read episodes like the Seer of Lublin's move to Wieniawa, R. Meir's vacating the Stopnica post for his son, the Hasidic invasion of the Olkusz synagogue, and similar acts as part of a sociopolitical program. Zaddikim like the Maggid of Kozienice and R. Levi Isaac sometimes astonish with their brazen challenges to the scholars and normative religious functionaries who attempted to hinder their advance. Other zaddikim, like R. Jacob Isaac of Lublin and R. Meir of Stopnica/ Opatów, appear more tactful but no less effectual. True to the dictates of "worship through corporeality," each seems to have deliberately "Hasidicized" local communal offices and institutions, causing each of the towns surveyed here to succumb at one level or another. These were not men focused exclusively upon attaining *devekut* and drawing down divine effluence.

One can imagine how Hasidism began to impact everyday reality at the local level. At first, certain members of the community would have become conspicuous through their absence during synagogue services, and their conduct in their separate prayer houses would have begun to attract attention. When they made their way out of the prayer houses and into the main *bet midrash* and synagogue, they provoked violence, official complaints, and occasionally governmental interference. Nevertheless, they must have begun to seem invincible by the turn of the nineteenth century as those residing near the residence of a zaddik or the site of a grand Hasidic wedding witnessed pilgrimages and celebrations on a colossal scale. On such occasions, the streets of a town were teeming with Hasidim from distant locales. In certain towns, Hasidim maintained only a separate prayer house; in other towns, they established a presence in the main *bet midrash*; in still other towns, the struggle pertained to the main synagogue; and in several cases, it concerned the rabbinate itself. In each case, regardless of the stature of their adversaries, the outcome nearly always favored a Hasidic advance. The cases surveyed here are snapshots of this social and cultural transformation.

Their success proceeded in the face of an evolving opposition. The accepting attitude of Mitnaggdim in Lublin, challenges to old-style hasidim in Wodzisław, and the timidity of the Olkusz Mitnaggdim reveal a deterioration of Mitnaggdic resistance by the first decades of the nineteenth century. But more effective adversaries with more programmatically driven objections, Mas-kilim, had by that time appeared on the scene, and the old official complaints were now accompanied by allegations about Hasidism's threat to Enlighten-ment projects. It is quite strange that advocates of Enlightenment in the central government would continue to decide in favor of Hasidism and against the Jewish Enlightenment reformers and local and regional Polish officials. To make sense of this curious pattern, it is necessary to visit the situation in Warsaw, the cradle of eastern Europe's industrial revolution.

3

Warsaw and the Patrons of Polish Hasidism

There is also a considerable niche in Warsaw, which is often visited
by their chiefs.

—Mendel Lefin Satanower, Essai d'un
plan de reforme ayant pour objet
d'éclairer la Nation Juive en Pologne
et de redresser par la ses mœurs

The Polish zaddikim and Hasidic foot soldiers who infiltrated study
houses, synagogues, and kahals during this period of growth and expansion were not acting alone, but were backed by a cadre of influential Jewish merchants in the capital city of Warsaw. As patrons
who subsidized, protected, and promoted the movement, these
grands notables formed an absolutely vital component of Polish Hasidism's success formula. All the merriment, religious ecstasy, com-
forting advice, inspiring sermons, and putative miracles ultimately
rested upon a sturdy foundation of patronage. Members of the Jewish mercantile elite ensured the movement's longevity, for it was
they who facilitated Hasidic victories over apparently more sophisti-
cated foes, and it was they who stabilized Hasidic society. The irony
of this formidable patronage network should not be missed, for it
implies that eastern Europe's industrial revolution, rather than im-
peding or undermining a doggedly antimodernist movement like
Hasidism, enabled its financial and political sponsorship on an unprecedented scale. It also adds a twist to the story of the region's
modernization, which was pioneered, it turns out, by devotees of the
very movement blamed repeatedly for "Jewish backwardness and superstition."

The central role of representatives of the Jewish mercantile elite in transforming Polish Hasidism into a thriving mass movement has largely escaped notice in both Hasidic and more general Polish Jewish historiographies, each of which seems prisoner to a certain economic determinism that assumes a necessary connection between wealth and assimilation. Historians of Hasidism, following the pioneering endeavors of Simon Dubnow, tend to depict zaddikim as heroes of the allegedly impoverished, uneducated, economically backward masses.[1] Complementing this older view, economic historians still generally accept Artur Eisenbach's characterization of Polish Jewish mercantile elites as assimilationists, bearers of Enlightenment, and advocates for emancipation and social reform.[2] Few seem able to fathom a convergence between economic modernization and a retrograde movement like Hasidism.[3] As this chapter will show, however, the zaddikim were not only warmly received by sectors of the emergent Polish Jewish bourgeoisie but were financed, promoted, and protected by its premier members. Advocates in such quarters helped ensure that government-sponsored projects for Jewish educational, occupational, and sartorial reforms would make little headway in Central Poland, while Hasidism would spread almost unhindered.

Recently, a very different contribution to Hasidic history, composed in the Warsaw ghetto by Ignacy Schiper during "October of the ghastly year 1942" (as indicated in its foreword), was discovered. Schiper, a pioneering Polish Jewish historian, managed to bury sections of his manuscript in sealed casks before his fatal deportation to Majdanek. Published under the title *Toward a History of Hasidism in Poland*,[4] his hitherto lost work turns out to have constituted a first step away from Simon Dubnow's depiction of Hasidism as a popular folk movement:

> Members of the Jewish plutocracy in Warsaw therefore cooperated with the general populace in the matter of Hasidism. This factor is highly significant, and is deserving of emphasis! . . . Would such cooperation between the rich and the "common folk" have been possible had Hasidism been an intercessory force for the disenfranchised masses, continuing the operations of the ancient "people's tribune"?[5] It is clear that the "class" character of Hasidism is, upon confrontation with the facts in Warsaw, a hypothesis that rests on an exceedingly frail basis.[6]

While Schiper was careful to acknowledge Hasidism's popular features, he insisted that authors like Dubnow had vastly overemphasized its demotic, folk dimension.[7] Had his work been extant in the immediate postwar years, it would have undoubtedly spawned a counterschool of Hasidic social history. However, even without the benefit of Schiper's research, several scholars have suspected the Dubnow depiction and tentatively posited a connection between Hasidism and the mercantile elite. Moshe Rosman, as noted, was able to actually prove such a connection with respect to the Besht.[8] Still, it seems only proper to think in terms of a Schiper school of Hasidic social history, in contradistinction to a Dubnow school.[9]

Proponents of the Schiper school will, in addition, find themselves at odds with Artur Eisenbach's emancipation narrative, which assumes a neat causal relationship between economic success, acculturation, and the acquisition of individual rights and privileges. Although his thesis holds true in the case of many acculturated and assimilated Jewish notables arriving from the West, like Samuel Kronenberg, Nathan Gluecksberg, and Jacob Epstein, the cultural profile of the Polish Jewish mercantile elite was in fact far more diverse. The almost exclusive focus on the small vanguard of merchants of western and central European origin by Eisenbach and other historians has had the effect of distorting the prevailing east European Jewish mentality during this period. In actuality, most Jews in the formerly Polish lands did not think that they wanted integration or emancipation beyond basic economic and residence rights, but were rather content with their relative social and cultural isolation.[10] As a result of this mentality, in marked contrast to the case of Berlin and its generously endowed Haskalah, Poland's native Jewish bourgeoisie often championed Hasidism.[11] The following analysis is meant to ensure that Hasidic patrons like Hayyim Feivel Wolberg of Kamieniec-Podolski, Joseph Mandelsberg of Kuzmir (Kazimierz Dolny), Moses Halfan Lipschutz, and, above all, members of the Bergson family assume their rightful place within the pantheon of Polish Jewish entrepreneurs. This "other" Jewish plutocracy, whose members preferred the courts of zaddikim to those of the nobility, allows us to delve beneath Hasidism's folksy visage.

The Rise of the Warsaw Jewish Mercantile Elite

As mentioned in chapter 1, the area referred to as Central Poland was partitioned, conquered, or ruled indirectly in the late eighteenth and early nineteenth centuries by several regimes—Prussian, Austrian, French (the Duchy of Warsaw), and Russian (the Congress Kingdom of Poland). As paradoxical as it may seem, the attendant wars and insurrections proved beneficial to the region's long-term economic development. Destruction of life and property remained relatively minimal, while the hunger of Polish and occupying armies alike for ammunition, horses, uniform fabric, meat, and other provisions created ample investment opportunities. Army purveying involved the greatest commercial transactions of the day, and allowed several individuals to accumulate sufficient capital to expand their activities into banking and industry.[12] These inititatives fueled eastern Europe's incipient industrial revolution.

Those who availed themselves of the new opportunities were less likely to be noblemen or Christian merchants. To the chagrin of Polish reformers like Stanisław Staszic, Hugo Kołłątaj, and Piotr Świtowski, most Polish noblemen with substantial means proved unwilling to think beyond the increasingly frail grain export trade and unable to overcome the age-old prejudice that other mercantile endeavors were innately shameful and dishonest.[13] Few were willing to exchange the pomp and extravagance of the old noble family lifestyle for the thrift and industriousness demanded of a merchant.[14] Nor were Christian townspeople psychologically or economically prepared to become industrial pioneers. Those with sufficient wealth preferred to imitate the patterns of conduct and culture set by the upper nobility, the magnates. The wealthiest townspeople tended to purchase noble status and were thus absorbed into that leisurely sector.[15] Meanwhile, Polish towns had been in decline for over two centuries, owing to international trade through the port town of Danzig (Gdańsk), which flooded the Commonwealth with cheap imports and overwhelmed domestic markets. Christian town inhabitants, furthermore, suffered from legal and political handicaps, and the nobility, in an attempt to eliminate competition, actually forbade them to export anything but cattle and oxen. Instead, the nobility privileged Jewish intermediaries, whose exclusion from the corporate structures of the towns rendered them politically unthreatening.[16] The convenience of having at its disposal a group of disenfranchised middlemen—something of a captive service sector—helps explain why the nobility so adamantly resisted proposals for Jewish emancipation.

Ironically, this marginalized middleman status enabled many Jews to develop precisely the types of skills that would prove vital during the process of economic modernization.[17] Thus, although the sum of their disabilities far outweighed those of the Christian townspeople, many Jews were better positioned to fill the economic vacuum. Polish Jews had for centuries energetically pursued international trade in an auxiliary manner, which yielded valuable experience and networks of personal contacts.[18] The records of the Leipzig trade fairs reflect an accelerated involvement of Jews in the international trade by the end of the eighteenth century relative to their Polish Christian counterparts. In 1775, 413 Polish merchants attending the Leipzig fairs were Jewish, compared with 68 non-Jews. By 1796, a full 791 were Jewish, while the number of non-Jewish merchants from Poland had declined to 60.[19] To a great extent, it was the rising demand for army supplies during this tumultuous period that enticed growing numbers of Jews into international trade.[20] Several Jews could thus assume leading roles in the region's budding industrialization, banking, and trade expansion.[21]

While it may be premature to declare a revolution in the Jewish economic situation by the end of the eighteenth century without knowing the precise sources of Jewish capital, Jews unquestionably figured prominently in the modest industrialization that fueled the region's wars and insurrections. Some established textile factories, tanneries, slaughterhouses, and other relatively self-sufficient enterprises, which would have allowed them to become less dependent upon loans from Christian townspeople and noblemen than in preceding centuries.[22] Some began to move from the periphery of international trade— where Jews had traditionally dealt more in secondary items like linen, hemp, flax, wax, tallow, skins, and handicrafts—into larger scale trade in cattle, horses, grain, leather, cloth, and other military provisions.[23] Increased economic self-sufficiency and involvement in international trade coincided with a momentous development in Polish economic history: the collapse of the nobility-dominated grain trade.[24] Contemporaneous Polish social commentaries rather predictably reflect envy and resentment against individual Jewish gains.[25]

The capital city of Warsaw lay at the epicenter of the east European eco-nomic transformation.[26] Harro Harring, a memoirist of German origin, went so far as to compare Warsaw in the 1830s to some of the finest cities of Europe, including Vienna and Lyons, although Warsaw possessed "neither the gaiety of the former, nor the trading bustle of the latter."[27] To be sure, Harring's sketch impresses upon the reader what was really meant by a Polish city in the early nineteenth century: Warsaw was surrounded by "mean mud walls" which could not possibly "answer the purpose of fortification"; while the main streets "through which the Grand Duke Constantine daily drives" were little more than roads, "being paved only on the sloping part next to the foot-path. In some places this pavement is of free-stone."[28] However, from the perspective of the Ukrainian zaddik Nahman of Bratslav, Warsaw conjured up visions of adven-ture, speculation, and worldliness—things the pious must eschew.[29] Humble as it may have seemed from a western standpoint, it was eastern Europe's fulcrum of progress.

Foreign observers were convinced that most of Warsaw's merchants were Jewish. In 1815, according to the British traveler Robert Johnston, "the present population of Warsaw is estimated at fifty thousand individuals, of whom twenty thousand are Jews, and who seem to manage all the trade of the city."[30] Municipal authorities were so alarmed over the prospect of Jews conquering Warsaw's trade and depriving its Christian inhabitants of their livelihoods—thereby turning the city into a "Jewish settlement"—that they instituted a sys-tem of daily ticket payments for entrance into the city for all but ninety-six "tolerated" Jewish merchants.[31] Fears of the Jewish economic specter occasion-ally still resonate in Polish historiography.[32] Against these alarmist views, how-ever, the 1792 census conveys that only one-quarter of Warsaw's Jewish pop-ulation was involved in commerce (an estimate that would have, however, excluded statistically invisible and exceedingly humble endeavors like ped-dling).[33] Either way, it is clear that Jews formed a surrogate middle class for the region. The failure of social reformers to integrate this productive element through emancipation ensured that the Polish middle class would remain weak at a time when societies were in essence defined by their middle classes.

What is remarkable is that most Jews were not supposed to be living in Warsaw at all. They were officially banished from Warsaw by the 1527 decree of *de non tolerandis Judaeis*. Nevertheless, Jews were allowed to reside in sur-rounding towns and noble-owned *jurydyki* inside Warsaw, which eventually served as stepping stones for Jewish migration.[34] Most important was the Praga suburb, where formal permission for Jewish residence was extended in 1775. Despite repeated expulsions from Warsaw (1768, 1776, 1784, and 1790), anti-Jewish violence, and a burdensome system of ticket payments for sojourners, the Warsaw Jewish community rose from 2,519 members in 1765 to 9, 200 members by 1800. In his memoirs (1777–1779), N. William Wraxall describes Warsaw as "crowded with Jews, who form a considerable proportion of the inhabitants . . . From time to time they are plundered, exiled, imprisoned, and massacred; yet, under such accumulated vexations, they continually multiply, and are here found in far greater numbers than even at Amsterdam."[35] The

Prussian occupiers legalized Jewish settlement in Warsaw in 1802; and the Duchy of Warsaw confirmed its legality in 1808. By 1810, Warsaw's Jewish population had shot up to 14,600. This was consistent with an overall trend of Jewish urbanization following their expulsion from the countryside.[36]

Hasidic Contacts with the Mercantile Elite in Warsaw

Maskilim were all too aware of Hasidism's financial support by the Jewish mercantile elite. Mendel Lefin condemned "their numerous courts composed of rich pilgrims who visit them from many places,"[37] while Abraham Stern charged that zaddikim constantly endeavor "to beguile and ensnare" the young and unlearned, "particularly the wealthy and those of the female sex."[38] One Haskalah satire quips "Both rich and poor flock to them / And they're taken for a ride,"[39] and another has a zaddik counsel his son:

> Honor the wealthy. Seek the well-being of officials like city and town council members, kahal leaders, tax lessees, military recruiters, agents of nobles, lessees of the kosher meat tax, guildmasters, quartering commissioners,[40] and the like. . . . For all of these will prepare your throne; and you will accumulate much wealth and great honor, and be like an honored citizen.[41]

Non-Hasidic communal leaders were acutely aware of financial support of zaddikim by rich merchants' wives: "matters have reached the point that women abscond with their husbands' wealth" to give it to zaddikim, which created "difficulties in collecting taxes for the treasury."[42]

Of course, such complaints ignored the fact that informal public support of Jewish spiritual leaders had been in practice since late antiquity, and that unsalaried, old-style hasidic scholars with no formal rabbinical post, like the Vilna Gaon or members of the Brody *kloyz* enjoyed financial support and authority during this period.[43] It is, moreover, necessary to acknowledge that Maskilim gained patrons of their own among the acculturated merchant vanguard.[44] Wealthy recruits in fact formed an indispensable part of any new spiritual movement, providing not only financial support but prestige as well. To invoke a more extreme example, a group of Polish Jews informed a Christian missionary in 1824 that "if some of the rich Jews would become Christians . . . they were all ready to follow"; while a second group promised, "if any of the rich Jews would make a beginning they would all be baptized."[45] One can well imagine how the support of wealthy Jews advanced less radical departures from Jewish tradition.

There was, however, an important difference in the case of Haskalah patronage. Unlike zaddikim or old-style hasidic scholars, Maskilim continued to earn a regular income through normative types of employment like tutoring and teaching, or, in the case of Central Poland, as government clerks, even as they received financial support from wealthy patrons. This distinction has to do with the very nature of charismatic leadership, for, as Max Weber has explained, "what is despised, so long as the genuinely charismatic type is adhered to, is traditional or rational every-day economizing, the attainment of a regular income by continuous economic activity devoted to this end." Strictly voluntary support by gifts represented the only type of support deemed acceptable by charismatic leaders who felt, much like the Polish upper nobility, demeaned by normative modes of employment.[46]

Patronage of zaddikim was also rooted in the custom of paying *ba'alei shem* for their magical services, which, it must be emphasized, was more than a folk phenomenon. In the eighteenth century, Moses Kadainer, "a wealthy person among men, the intimate of the nobleman," and members of the elitist Katzenellenbogen family availed themselves of *ba'al shem* services, while an extremely rich family of Słuck summoned the Besht to drive demons from their house.[47] With zaddikim, the difference was largely one of status: even the wealthiest dared not summon them in a similar way. Apart from occasional trips to scattered adherents, the zaddik usually sat in his "court," to which rich and poor pilgrims alike would flock.[48] His court was sustained by considerable donations by prosperous individuals, including members of the most illustrious families, alongside payments by pilgrims for specific services.[49] By the beginning of the nineteenth century, members of the Warsaw mercantile elite had emerged as full-fledged patrons of zaddikim. According to hagiographical accounts, Joseph Mandelsberg of Kuzmir sponsored the Maggid of Kozienice, as did Moses Halfan Lipschutz, until he was financially ruined.[50] Hayyim Feivel Wolberg of Kamieniec-Podolsk, known as Feivele Kamienitzer, supported the Maggid of Kozienice, the Seer of Lublin, and, most passionately, the Holy Jew of Przysucha. But the most prominent Hasidic patrons were members of the Bergson line: Szmul Zbytkower, his son Berek, his son's wife Temerel, and their son Jacob.[51]

The sources attesting to Hasidism's penetration into Warsaw during the eighteenth century are many and varied. In the summer of 1781, the famous Hasidic-Mitnaggdic disputation between the zaddik Levi Isaac of Berdyczów and R. Abraham Katzenellenbogen was held in the Praga suburb. The Maskil Mendel Lefin alluded to R. Levi Isaac's visit to Warsaw as a member of the Jewish delegation to the Great Sejm (1788–92) in Warsaw.[52] In 1791, he bemoaned "a considerable niche in Warsaw which is visited by its leaders, who are themselves from time to time of noble [*bonne*] blood."[53] The Mitnagged R. Israel Loebel described R. Levi Isaac's scandalous methods of prayer in the Łazienki spa in Warsaw and claimed that he bungled biblical interpretations at a Sabbath meal in Praga.[54] Warsaw's assistant rabbi, R. Isaac Benjamin Wolf (d. 1802), was an ardent Hasid.[55] There are indications of a Hasidic presence in Warsaw as early as 1768 (in *Shivhei ha-Besht*), in 1785 (minute book of the Praga Burial Society), and in 1789 (in an unpublished manuscript).[56] Sources from the early nineteenth century reflect a more entrenched Hasidic presence in Warsaw. As mentioned in chapter 2, the Płock commissioner Floryan Kobyliński commented that the "the chiefs of this sect are found there."[57] In 1823, Christian missionaries met a Hasidic cantor and a "schoolmaster of the Chasidim," and learned the next year that Warsaw Hasidim were spreading rumors that "the house of the missionaries was full of evil spirits which take possession of the Jews who enter it." A potential convert in Warsaw complained to the missionaries that "the superstitious Hasidim under whom I work" continually vexed him regarding his weekly visits to them.[58] Finally, by 1827, the zaddik Isaac Meir Alter of Gur made so bold as to request official sanction for his Hasidic prayer houses in Warsaw.[59]

Notwithstanding his legendary image as advocate of the poor, R. Levi Isaac remained a darling of the Warsaw mercantile elite. Whenever he traveled to Warsaw during the last quarter of the eighteenth century, he resided in the homes of such notables as Hirsch Danziger.[60] According to one tradition, Danziger's son Feivel of Gritsa (Grojec) once mimicked R. Levi Isaac's flamboyant prayer style, to the horror of his older sister, who feared the zaddik would be offended. But the zaddik graciously interpreted it as a sign of Feivel's future greatness (indeed, Feivel was to become the famous zaddik of Aleksander).[61] R. Levi Isaac's aforementioned disputation, held in Szmul Zbytkower's Praga prayer house, was itself highly significant, in that Zbytkower, Central Poland's preeminent merchant, thereby enabled R. Levi Isaac to showcase the tenets of the new movement. His alleged defeat did nothing to abate its spread.[62]

The Maggid of Kozienice was another intimate of Warsaw notables. Although he is described by Hasidic tradition as the son of a poor bookbinder, his father Shabbatai was in fact an officer of the Eternal Light society in Opatów, a relatively exclusive society with substantial membership fees.[63] The society was led by a member of the most powerful family in Opatów, Moses Landau.[64] As he grew, the Maggid studied in the Ryczywół Yeshiva with Joseph Mandelsberg of Kuzmir, who went on to become one of the richest merchants in Poland through a salt monopoly and timber exports via Danzig. It was probably during those years that they became disciples of the zaddik Samuel Shmelke, then rabbi of Ryczywół. Joseph later became one of the Maggid's most important patrons.[65] The Maggid occasionally solicited assistance from such wealthy followers on behalf of Hasidim who had fallen on bad times.[66] According to R. David of Maków, the Maggid also enlisted "the wealthy in the city of Warsaw" to prevent the publication of his anti-Hasidic tract.[67] In 1811, he was invited to take part in a distinguished delegation of Warsaw notables to Napoleon on behalf of Polish Jewry, although his advanced age and physical weakness prevented him from making the journey.[68]

The extent of those connections is evidenced by the marriage alliances formed between zaddikim and the wealthiest merchants. Hirsch Danziger married his daughter to the son of the zaddik Levi Isaac of Berdyczów[69] and married his son to the daughter of the zaddik Simha Bunem of Przysucha.[70] Feivel Kamienitzer married his granddaughter to the future zaddik Abraham Mordecai Alter of Gur (Góra Kalwaria).[71] Moses Halfan Lipschutz secured matches for his daughters with the future zaddikim Menahem Mendel of Kotsk (Kock) and Isaac Meir Alter of Gur.[72] Jacob Moses Mushkat, a wealthy book publisher, married his son to the daughter of the zaddik R. Isaac of Radzywił.[73] Berek and Temerel Sonnenberg-Bergson secured a match between their daughter and Issachar Berish Horowitz, grandson of the zaddik Samuel Shmelke

Horowitz.[74] Where ambivalence over such matches is detected, it is usually on the part of the zaddikim rather than the merchants. Among Jewish traditionalist intellectuals and mystics, matches concluded with those whose status depended on wealth alone were frowned upon.[75]

The Bergsons

In 1908, the hard-nosed Zionist Max Nordau disparaged the ideas of the famed philosopher Henri Bergson by proclaiming: "Bergson inherited these fantasies from his ancestors, who were fanatic and fantastic 'wonder-rabbis' in Poland."[76] The assertion contains a grain of truth—members of the Bergson family were Polish Hasidism's preeminent patrons. None approached the wealth and influence of that family, whose progenitors were Szmul Zbytkower, his son Berek Sonnenberg-Bergson, and the latter's wife Temerel. A recent study asserts, "at the end of the eighteenth century and during the nineteenth as well, there was one family most renowned for its wealth: that of Szmul Zbytkower and his son after him, Berek Szmul."[77] An entire district in Praga became Szmul's namesake. "If you are anything of a Warsavian, then you surely know what Szmulewizna means," writes Nahum Sokolow in his panegyric on the Bergson family. "It belonged to Szmul Zbytkower."[78] One-fifth of all the banks in Central Poland were founded by Szmul's descendants and their spouses.[79] Szmul was merely favorably disposed toward Hasidism, while Berek and Temerel served as the movement's foremost sponsors and advocates at every turn.

Born in 1727 in the village Zbytki to his father Avigdor Jacob, a poor innkeeper, Szmul began his climb by trading in various consumer goods and attending trade fairs.[80] He settled in the Warsaw suburb of Praga around the age of twenty-five (i.e., 1752), and acquired his fortune by provisioning both the Polish and Russian armies with horses, grain, leather, cloth, and other goods during the struggles accompanying the partitions of Poland.[81] He is listed on a register of Warsaw army purveyors for the years 1764–94 as *faktor* of the royal court and supplier for the Polish army since the 1770s, and supplier of the Russian army in 1773–75 and 1793.[82] In 1771, the Prussian King Frederick appointed Szmul *komisant*; and in 1787 Frederick William conferred the titles *hof-factor* (Court Jew) *und commissarius* upon him.[83] Catherine dubbed him "General Supplier of the Russian Army" in 1775.[84] An underground newssheet from Warsaw from January 10, 1782, notes that "Famous Szmul" failed to receive a lucrative contract during the Russo-Turkish War.[85] Nonetheless, in 1790, General Wodzicki admitted: "without the care of the army supplier Szmul, the Cracow storehouse would not have been in a proper state to send a transport to the standing cavalry." The Russian government owed him around 80,000 rubles and 9,000 ducats for his services during the years 1792–94, about half of which he recovered by obtaining King Stanislaw August's help through his third wife, Judyta, whose linguistic attainments and business savvy would continually prove indispensable.[86] Thanks to her machinations, he became the king's manager and advisor.[87] When the king visited the army camp in Praga in July of 1792 he also paid Szmul a visit, an episode that inspired the following doggerel verse:

> The King took an oath, made Polish valor famous
> Glanced at the camp from the window, then went to Szmul,
> He who justified the confidence of the whole nation,
> Saddened every wise man, amazed every fool.[88]

Consorting with the major supplier of Poland's occupying armies was an unpopular, yet no doubt necessary, move on the part of the king. As for Szmul, his double dealings and varied connections yielded houses and entire estates. He became the first Polish Jew to own real estate.[89] The designation "court Jew" is quite appropriate in his case.[90] Yet Szmul's supplies to the Russian army and the Confederacy of Targowica during the Kościuszko insurrection left him vulnerable to charges of espionage and treachery, and led to the destruction of his tannery and confiscation of his other property. Although he was cleared of those charges by the court of the Insurrection, several historians strove to clear his name again.[91]

Leaving aside the thorny question of loyalty during the partition period, Szmul's army contracts enabled him to expand his enterprises into the textile industry, the cattle and leather trade, kosher slaughtering, coin minting, and beer brewing. He opened a tannery and a mine in Praga, a brickyard in Warsaw, and one of the first banks in the region.[92] In Sokolow's estimation, "Reb Shmul, a Jew with beard and sideburns, in a long silk coat with a *gartl*, engrossed in business affairs in Praga, provided a livelihood for many Jews."[93] Szmul is often lauded for his great deeds of charity.[94] He allegedly used his wealth to save Jews and bury corpses during the 1794 Praga massacre, ransoming living Jews out of a jug filled with gold, and paying for the proper burial of corpses out of a jug filled with silver.[95] Scholarly accounts are less glowing, however, painting him as an ignoramus who accumulated his wealth in a ruthless fashion.[96] In 1773, the hated minister of finance, Poniński, appointed Szmul as head of a reified Council of Lands through which to tax Polish Jewry. His first act in that capacity was to extract 18,000 złoties from the fifty-eight signatories, the burden of which was borne by Warsaw Jewry.[97] Szmul's success in persuading King Stanisław Augustus to establish a much-needed cemetery in Praga proved a mixed blessing, as well.[98] No burials were permitted without the explicit permission of Szmul and his burial society, and burial fees, including a special tax for the wealthy and other arbitrary exactions, went directly to him. Complaints directed to the Polish and Russian authorities were ineffectual, for they referred the matter to the Warsaw rabbinical court, which predictably decided in Szmul's favor.[99]

Szmul's relationship to Hasidism has long been debated.[100] Several factors argue for a very positive inclination. As mentioned, he arranged the famous disputation in 1781, which he must have known would provide a platform for the controversial new movement. Moreover, Szmul held private prayer services in his home that were attended by at least one Hasid, Raphael, meaning that the liturgy was probably Hasidic. Visitors to his home also allegedly included "great rabbis and zaddikim."[101] Finally, his sons Berek, Abba (or Abel), and Isaac Szmul became Hasidic.[102] But Szmul's relationship to Hasidism was complicated by the fact that Judyta, his third wife, was a secular-educated German Jewish woman with a low tolerance for Polish Jewish religious customs. Several of Judyta's children converted to Christianity after Szmul's death.[103] Hasidic tradition, moreover, appears ambivalent about Szmul, describing the repair (*tikkun*) of his flawed soul by the Maggid of Kozienice after a protracted struggle.[104] Perhaps Szmul constitutes a reminder that even during the period of controversy between Hasidim, Mitnaggdim, and Maskilim, one can still speak of sympathies as opposed to outright allegiances.

Szmul's son Berek Sonnenberg[105] (1764–1822) was a less ambiguous supporter of Hasidism,[106] although he is occasionally portrayed as a renaissance man.[107] His synthesis of Hasidism and worldliness found expression in his employment of a court painter to produce portraits of zaddikim.[108] Secular proclivities aside, the zaddikim must have been enormously gratified to possess a patron of Berek's stature. Having sustained his father's financial empire through army supplying, operating a prosperous firm on 308 Orla Street, and winning monopolistic leases on state salt, tobacco, and the kosher meat tax (*korobka*), Berek rapidly emerged as a plutocrat in his own right.[109] There has been disagreement among historians over whether the period of the Duchy of Warsaw (1807–12) was a time of unequivocal ruin or whether seeds of economic development were sown in the midst of crisis.[110] But the government's tremendous debt burden and military budget unquestionably led to an increased reliance upon individual merchants like Berek for loans and army supplies, which redounded to their advantage.[111]

Berek augmented his inheritance through daring and initiative. In 1806, despite conditions of great peril (Napoleon's armies were, after all, poised to conquer Central Poland), he transported a herd of six hundred cattle to Danzig to set up a trading venture.[112] The next year, he obtained a government contract to procure meat and leather for the Prussian army. At that very time, he was also transporting horses to the Russians and Austrians, and supplying Napoleon's army and its Polish legions led by Zajączek and Poniatowski.[113] The following year, *Gazeta Warszawska* announced that as the contract with "the *citizen* of Jewish persuasion, Berek Szmul of Warsaw" for supplying meat to the Storehouses of the Bydgoski Department would soon terminate, the contract was now up for auction to the lowest bidder.[114] Berek did not let the contract slip away. Meat supplies for Polish units stationed in Warsaw and Praga yielded him 85,575 złoties in December 1810; 69,534 złoties in January 1811; and 77,753 złoties in February 1811. Next to Berek, the largest monthly sum acquired by any meat supplier was Jacob Eyzenberg's comparatively modest 17, 629 złoties, earned by supplying the Lublin army unit in February 1811.[115]

By then, Berek had maneuvered himself into an extremely advantageous position vis-à-vis the government. An alarmist letter dated April 5, 1811, from the office of the minister of war complained that Berek had raised his price of meat supplies for the Warsaw and Płock units above the price stipulated in the original contract, and that he threatened to cease the supplies if the increase was not forthcoming. The War Ministry worried that "the Army is in peril of having insufficient provisions." Although obligations to army suppliers had reached 552,946 złoties for one month's requirements, and such costs could not possibly be met, "army suppliers, despite the mentioned prices, do not cease to claim their appropriateness; and there will soon be absolutely no means in the Treasury to pacify them and ensure the flow of further provisions."[116] The Treasury Ministry responded that as Berek's services were indispensable, his demands would have to be met. For despite several hundreds of thousands of złoties still owed to him by the Treasury, only he was in a position to regularly supply meat for the army. "There is no other way to ensure Provisions for the army, for the flow of funds into the Treasury diminishes more and more," the report confessed.[117] The quandary was really of the government's own making, however, for the military consumed an astonishing 66 percent of the state's budget. The new finance minister Tadeusz Matuszewic immediately downsized the military upon his appointment in 1811.[118]

Berek also consistently won the lease on the government salt monopoly, which was one of its major sources of income. In 1807, Berek obtained the lease on the Wieliczka salt mine with a wealthy Cracow merchant. By 1812, his Salt Works Company was the general supplier of Central Poland.[119] Upon the creation of the Congress Kingdom, Berek and five other merchants obtained a five-year lease. Meanwhile, he had obtained the salt monopoly in the Free City of Cracow that same year.[120] Berek then obtained an eleven-year lease jointly with Ignacy Neumark in 1821. But the reformist minister of finances Drucki-Lubecki stepped in and annulled it, having calculated that the current system was incurring losses of 1,411,735 złoties per year. He brushed aside Berek's protests as "arrogant," and resolved to restrict the monopoly to the transport of salt.[121] After protracted bidding, Berek emerged with the transport lease.[122]

Crucial to the rise of Hasidism was the fact that such ventures brought Berek into contact with the region's most influential leaders. According to the Polish reformer Antoni Ostrowski, some French officials even maintained that were it not for Berek's assistance, preparations for Napoleon's expedition against Moscow in 1812 would have been impossible. If accurate, this claim would reveal Berek as a pivotal figure in modern European history. In any case, Ostrowski also scoffed that "the French *Ordinators* greatly esteemed Pani Szmulowa of Praga (i.e., Judyta) and famous Berek; as 'Their Majesties' also casually associated with many dukes, counts, and senators."[123] Berek's credit operations, in fact, won him the protection of both Viceroy Józef Zajączek and Senator N. N. Nowosilców in both private and public struggles. When Lubecki canceled Berek's salt lease in 1821, Zajączek interceded with the tsar on Berek's behalf. In the ensuing bidding war over the salt transport monopoly, Nowosilców arrested Berek's rival (and brother-in-law!) S. A. Fraenkel on charges of bankruptcy.[124] Berek's connections also came in handy in 1821, when the Polish authorities interpreted his appeal for money to rebuild a synagogue in Jerusalem as a scheme to rebuild the Kingdom of Israel. Nowosilców intervened and recommended that the Grand Duke Constantine drop the matter.[125]

Berek's contacts in such high circles help explain governmental moderation with respect to the Jewish community as a whole, including possibly Nowosilców's liberal proposal for reforming anti-Jewish legislation.[126] In times of crisis, Berek utilized his influence with these ministers for the community's perceived benefit. By intervening with Zajączek, he was able to delay and effectively annul the Napoleonic military draft decree. The historian Szymon Askenazy can scarcely control his fury over the episode, for by avoiding army service, the "kahal diplomats and Hasidic politicians" (rather than Napoleon) were to blame for preventing Jewish emancipation.[127] In 1812, when a decree was issued to abolish Jews from the liquor trade within two years' time, the zaddikim intervened in heaven to reverse the decree while Berek did his part on earth and, with Nowosilców's aid, the prohibition was softened.[128] During a series of blood libel accusations in 1816, Berek headed a deputation to St. Petersburg and, with Nowosilców's letter of recommendation in hand, procured a forceful official denial of the charge.[129] Nowosilców intervened at Berek's behest in 1819 when the government contrived again to abolish Jews from the liquor trade and force Jews to send their children to public schools and abandon their traditional dress, the latter being particularly distressing for Hasidim.[130]

Hasidic sources occasionally disclose Berek's ties with zaddikim. Sometimes his example was invoked in their sermons: R. Isaac of Warka once quipped that relating a zaddik's miracles and wonders is as superfluous as stating that Berek, "the mighty tycoon in this country" owns a commonplace object like a noodle board.[131] One rather garbled tradition describes how the Seer of Lublin employed his clairvoyant powers to locate Berek and his wife during the chaotic days following the Praga massacre of 1794:

> [R. Ephraim Zalman Margaliot's] daughter was the bride of the revered leader Berki Berkson, son of the renowned Szmul Zbytkower. And after the massacre by the Russian forces in Praga, naught was known of [Berek's] health or existence. The Hasid Moses Yatshis went to [R. Ephraim] and suggested that he go to the rabbi Itsikel the Lancuter [i.e., the Seer of Lublin]. . . . The holy one walked to the window and said, "Your daughter now goes about in such and such colored clothes. And she is preparing noodles. And she is rocking the cradle of her son with one of her legs." He noted the hour and day. And when his daughter returned, she said that this was so. So R. Zalman gave a plot of land next to the *Parnas Bet Midrash*, which he possessed in Lublin, to the Rabbi [the Seer] of Lublin.[132]

The account is marred by a major inaccuracy: by 1794, Berek was married to Temerel, not Margaliot's daughter. But it does seem to reflect a bond of sorts, however vague.

The nature of this bond is clarified in more probable accounts, which describe how the Seer of Lublin sometimes functioned in a "human resources" capacity for Berek's enterprises. The Seer once instructed an impoverished follower, R. Mordecai Rakower, to seek employment as an agent for Berek's salt works; and Berek obligingly hired him. Berek thus collaborated in a demonstration of "material zaddikism," the doctrine according to which a zaddik assumed responsibility for the physical sustenance of his community.[133] A similar role is revealed in a letter from the Seer to one of Berek's employees:

> Concerning the matter upon which you asked advice from me. I considered the matter on the evening following the holy Sabbath, after the *havdalah* service. And behold, the present situation is good for both of you. And the opposite, God forbid, is not good for you and not good for them. Therefore, your sweet command: do not depart.[134]

The Seer thus forbade his follower to resign from Berek's company.

The future zaddik R. Simha Bunem of Przysucha played a more central role in Berek's enterprises. He was Berek's employee for a time, serving as an agent in his lumber concern:

> Once he [R. Simha Bunem] went to Danzig with the lumber of the wealthy Temerel's [husband] Berki of Warsaw, and the rate for lumber declined significantly, until it was necessary to go home with a loss of capital. And there was almost no money left to transport the lumber there. And he sat in Danzig for several weeks, and did not sell the lumber. And once, when he was sitting in his hotel, he began to weep, and said "Master of the Universe, behold: the house of the Egyptian was blessed because of Joseph. So is it not fitting that my master should be blessed because of me? For if I am not to be likened to Joseph the zaddik, nevertheless my master Berki is not to be likened to the Egyptian." And when he finished his prayer and appeal, an agent came to the hotel with a merchant and asked if he had more lumber. For the rate had increased, because word had gone out from afar that there was a need for lumber. And he began to bargain.[135]

If the partnership between biblical opposites had prospered, so might the partnership between the future zaddik and his future patron.

Documentary sources complement these accounts, by revealing how Berek employed his wealth and influence to promote Hasidism. In 1807, he and his wife Temerel built a Hasidic synagogue and *bet midrash* in Praga.[136] He donated 100 thalers toward books for the *bet midrash* in 1815.[137] But Berek's most outspoken promotion of Hasidism occurred in 1814 as elder of what was, in effect, Warsaw's "kahal."[138] That year, the Warsaw traditionalists met to discuss ways of combating a group of Maskilim who were criticizing abuses by representatives of this self-governing body and calling for its abolition. During the meeting, Berek arose and proclaimed that it would only be possible to combat those heretics with the aid of the great zaddikim, who enjoyed the support of the masses. Owing to opposition by the Mitnagged R. Solomon Eiger, no immediate decision was reached. But shortly thereafter, the representatives resolved to heed Berek's suggestion and directly invite various zaddikim to Warsaw, signaling a major triumph for Hasidism.[139] This episode marks one of the earliest indications of the crystallization of an alliance between Hasidim and Mitnaggdim against Maskilim, their new common enemy. However, such alliances were not consistent as yet.[140]

Berek's allegiance to Hasidism complicated his efforts to gain exceptional rights, particularly the right to purchase property in parts of Warsaw where Jews were not formally allowed to settle.[141] During the period of the Duchy of Warsaw only Jews who demonstrated both wealth and acculturation could purchase property, and a Hasidic patron like Berek could hardly appear sufficiently acculturated.[142] According to A. N. Frenk, his petition for the right to purchase houses throughout Warsaw in 1809 was denied when the interior minister saw that he had refused to shave his beard and side-locks or alter his traditional dress. Nevertheless, the interventions of the minister of law and Minister of the Army Józef Poniatowski and a letter reminding Napoleon of his substantial debts to Berek eventually secured a reversal.[143] Archival sources verify parts of Frenk's account. On August 11, 1810, the Saxon king—as duke of Warsaw— did confer upon Berek "the same exclusive rights as were granted to several other Jews," in addition to "freedom of dress and other features that distinguish [them] as people of the Mosaic persuasion" for himself and his children.[144] This last qualification should be highlighted, for it proves that Berek won certain exceptional privileges without having to alter his Hasidic demeanor. In the end, wealth rather than acculturation proved decisive in gaining exemption from restrictive decrees.[145]

Such privileges did not yet include the right to purchase houses anywhere in Warsaw. This was the topic of a petition the following year on Judyta and Berek's behalf by Salamon Muskat, an owner of a vodka distillery who had himself received the right to own property outside the Jewish quarter.[146] Muskat stressed the wealth that Judyta and Berek brought to the treasury, their moral virtue, and the fact that they had been granted ownership of the house at 1808—ski street[147] by the Prussian regime in Warsaw and the former Warsaw municipality. In light of these considerations, Muskat begged the Most Beloved Lord to "deign to bestow his grace upon the Most Noble Jews Szmul's Widow and Berek Szmulowicz."[148] Significantly, he omitted the usual claims about the subjects' conformity in habits and dress with the rest of the Polish inhabitants, for he could make no such claim about his Hasidic friend.[149] Berek and Judyta seem nonetheless to have prevailed, for they acquired the right to acquire property throughout Warsaw.[150] Again, wealth was decisive, not acculturation.

The transformation of the Duchy of Warsaw into the Congress Kingdom spelled the end of many of Berek's privileges. On November 27, 1815, he made so bold as to request "full civic freedom" from the newly established Congress Kingdom regime, mentioning his father Szmul's extensive privileges and reminding the regime that he had just donated more than 600,000 złoties to the Treasury.[151] He also referenced his unsurpassed services to the country "despite ties to my religion."[152] Nevertheless, the authorities rejected Berek's request as they rejected all such requests.[153] Nowosilców's intervention was ineffective this time.[154] Berek then sought permission to at least acquire land, the sin qua non of status. He had previously acquired land on lease and freehold (a type of perpetual lease), and had gained the right to acquire property outright in the Prussian areas of Poland and within the Warsaw city limits.[155] In 1821, the Rada Administracyina discussed, in Nowosilców's presence, Berek's request for permission to acquire real estate from the lord of Matuszewiczów Kicki. The governor was inclined to grant the permission, but asked the minister of the interior and police to determine whether it was really possible for the regime to permit such a "stark exception."[156] Berek loaned 200,000 złoties to the government in 1822 in an apparent attempt to smooth over any resistance; but the process was cut short by his death later that year.[157]

According to his will, attested in 1818 by the future zaddik Alexander Zusya Kahana, Berek's successors agreed to donate 20,000 złoties to "Christian institutions," 2,500 złoties to the Institute of the Deaf, 10,000 złoties to build a Jewish hospital, and 150,000 złoties to a fund for the poor.[158] One-tenth of his estate was placed in the hands of the executors Feivel Kamienitzer and Berek's son Jacob to distribute to the poor and support "people reading Books of Law," that is, yeshiva students.[159] Another one-tenth was set aside to pay Berek's debts. Books and other property were to be divided among his children, but the main beneficiary was to be his wife Temerel.[160] The inscription on Berek's majestic tomb, which survived the ravages of World War II and may be viewed to this day, stresses the wondrous "generosity of his heart."[161] Indeed, his record for charitable giving is impressive.[162] His obituary in the Polish newspaper *Kurjer Warszawski* on November 19, 1822, describes him as "the wealthiest Israelite in Warsaw and without a doubt in the whole Kingdom of Poland," and "an entrepreneur who earned millions as a Lessee and Army Supplier."[163] To his list of legacies we may add Central Poland's burgeoning Hasidic movement.

A Patroness of Polish Hasidism

Many of Berek's acts of benefice for the Hasidic community occurred at the behest of his wife, Temerel, who, according to historian Avraham Rubinstein, "brought Hasidism to her husband's house."[164] The essayist Nahum Sokolow proclaims that Berek would have been forgotten were it not for his wife: "The loveliness of a flower, the modesty of a dove, a soul with wings of gold, and fruitful as an olive tree . . . Temerel was a sort of mother Rachel in Warsaw Jewish legend. One hears less of Berek: he was her prince consort."[165] Even Hasidic hagiographies, hardly known for recognizing the public endeavors of women, make such observations as "all of Berek's deeds were nothing compared to the good deeds of his famous wife of the good name the zaddika ha-

Berek and Temerel Sonnenberg-Bergson

Hasida Mrs. Temerel, whose acts are known and praised in all of Israel." Temerel cared for every poor person and beggar, and "supported openly and secretly all the zaddikim and Hasidim in Poland, visited many times their holy courts, and distributed money like ashes."[166] Another Hasidic tradition reflects the type of anxiety we are more inclined to expect:

> In the city of Warsaw there was a certain woman named Temerel.
> And her property and possessions amounted to a million. And she
> performed even the commandments which women are exempt
> from, for she wore a *tallit katan* [fringed garment]. And when the
> boy Ezekiel [Panet] heard this, he was baffled and asked the rabbis:
> "How can it be? Does not the Torah state 'a man's garment shall not
> be worn by a woman'?" And the great ones saw this, and marveled
> at the pure idea of the small boy.[167]

Even this ambivalent recollection discloses Temerel's prominence in the traditional community, however.

Little is known about Temerel's origins, other than that her father was the "learned and exceedingly wealthy" Abraham of Opoczna.[168] Temerel was briefly married at a young age to a Warsaw merchant named Jacob Jacobson, with whom she bore her son Hirsch. In 1787, after her husband Jacob had passed away, she married the twenty-three-year-old Berek. Their extravagant wedding, which occurred in chilly February under the open sky, was attended by King Stanisław August himself.[169] Berek's testament extols Temerel's abilities as both businesswoman and wife:

> I have long known her to be a clever and just wife, always my bulwark, guarding my person and property. She acted with all her

strength for my own good and grace, so much that I cannot express
the wisdom with which she built my House, and extended her open
hand to the poor and downtrodden. She always delighted in leading
my children on a good and just path of God and Man. Praise God
that it was the Lord's pleasure that fortune was achieved by her
hand, in everything toward which she turned it.[170]

Berek then expressed confidence not only that Temerel would employ his fortune for Godly purposes but also that his substantial debts would be paid off
if placed in her care.[171] Temerel proved equal to the task of sustaining Berek's
business enterprises, including the salt company. Even Berek's legal dispute
with Ignacy Neumark over the salt monopoly lease was resolved in Temerel's
favor.[172] She also founded a bank that would circulate about 20 million złoties
from 1830 to 1837.[173]

Temerel acquired that which her late husband could not: permission from
the new regime to purchase real estate. As early as 1810, during the period of
the Duchy of Warsaw, she had owned a house at 1076 Królewska Street, one
of the streets technically forbidden to Jews, and was among the sixty Warsaw
Jews exempted from the ghetto residence laws.[174] On July 17, 1827, she attempted to purchase the estate of the nobleman Jerzy de Hesse Darmstadt.[175]
After five months' deliberation, it was announced that the tsar had granted
"the Jewish widow Temerle Berkowey Sonnenberg" permission to acquire the
estate. Temerel was subjected to the same restrictions as the Jewish property
owners Joseph Redlich and Jacob Epstein, namely, "that the management of
the acquired property must be entrusted to People of the Christian Faith."[176]
Having Jews actually manage estates, meaning the Christian peasants residing
on them, was regarded as too incendiary. Nevertheless, Temerel received rights
that had been granted to only two other Jews in the Congress Kingdom.[177]

Equally impressive was Temerel's attainment of status within the patriarchal Hasidic community. Historians have begun to recognize that European
women were not completely excluded from public life if they had substantial
incomes to apply toward patronage. A study about female patrons among the
Polish nobility documents the extensive influence of the eighteenth-century
Polish noblewoman Barbara Radziwiłł.[178] Temerel's biography proves that an
early nineteenth-century Polish Jewish woman with financial wherewithal
might attain considerable clout in Hasidic society by funding places of worship
and sponsoring zaddikim. As mentioned earlier, she cofounded a Hasidic synagogue and study house with Berek in 1807 (according to Schiper, they were
really built at her bidding).[179] She also established one of the 101 "hidden synagogues" officially registered in Warsaw in 1826, most likely a Hasidic prayer
house.[180] On a more modest scale, Hasidic tradition recalls how Temerel
bought a Torah scroll prepared by the future zaddik Feivel of Grojec, who
allegedly used the proceeds (1,600 ducats) to marry off several female or-
phans.[181]

There is a fair amount of Hasidic lore about Temerel's financial support
of zaddikim. When R. Simha Bunem and his disciples were at the Carlsbad

baths and their money began to run low, Temerel appeared like an angel with cash in hand and, the narrator makes sure to inform us, took care of their laundry as well.[182] When R. Simha Bunem began to reign as zaddik after the death of the Holy Jew of Przysucha, Temerel "anointed" him with an astronomical monetary gift.[183] Also prominent are tales that feature future zaddikim miraculously refusing her financial assistance in spite of their poverty. Temerel sent gifts to the future zaddik R. Meir Alter of Gór Kalwarja when he was in desperate straits, but he refused her aid.[184] A similar story is told regarding R. Menahem Mendel of Kotsk, who spat at the thought of receiving financial help.[185] Upon the Seer's death, Temerel allegedly attempted to bribe the Lublin officials into placing his tombstone beside that of the renowned talmudist R. Shalom Shakhna.[186]

The most fascinating accounts concern Temerel's employment of Hasidim and potential zaddikim in her various business enterprises. Many are hagiographic; yet one may surmise that authors of such accounts would be disinclined to exaggerate, let alone even mention, such instances of female authority over future zaddikim. Temerel employed many Hasidim from Lublin, where she visited once a year.[187] Among the up-and-coming zaddikim employed by Temerel was R. Simha Bunem of Przysucha.[188] According to one tale, after R. Simha Bunem was ruined financially he went to Warsaw and, being rather too accustomed to comfort, stayed in a posh hotel until his money ran out completely. He began to weep and pray, until Temerel appeared and offered to hire him as an agent in her liquor distillery. Realizing that the "gates of fortune have opened for me again," R. Simha Bunem allegedly held out until Temerel returned and offered him a full partnership (which sounded more acceptable to Hasidic audiences).[189] Wearing "German" clothes and armed with the knowledge of several foreign languages, the future zaddik traveled to the Leipzig trade fairs as Temerel's agent.[190]

The future zaddik Isaac of Warka had fallen into serious debt when Temerel hired him to manage her properties.[191] R. Isaac leased the government tobacco monopoly in Żarki,[192] and managed Temerel's holdings in Ruda. According to one amusing account, several traveling Hasidim unwittingly wandered onto a field belonging to Polish farmers, who dragged them to the nobleman of the town to have them arrested. The "nobleman," found poring over a volume of Talmud "like an angel," was none other than R. Isaac himself.[193] Temerel transformed Ruda when it came into her possession by replacing the Polish nobles who had lived there with her own clerks, including R. Simha Bunem:

> For many years, the *admor* R. Simha Bunem of Przysucha resided in Ruda, serving as a bookkeeper, before he was crowned as Rabbi of Hasidim. Together with him was the businesswoman Temerel and several of the greatest Hasidim. They only dedicated a few hours to clerical duties and managing the rich holdings. Temerel did not even demand this. They dedicated the remaining hours of the day and night to Torah and service. From her profits, the wealthy

woman established a house of study, whose doors were open day
and night. And wealthy Temerel believed in all her heart that,
through the merit of this house of study, and through the merit of
her great Hasidic clerks, she was becoming rich, and was proceed-
ing without sorrows and complications. The Rabbi of Przysucha
ended his tenure at Ruda, and in his place came the old *admor* of
Warka, before he was crowned as Rabbi. He, too, did not abandon
his work in the town of Ruda until Hasidim came and filled Ruda
and distracted him from his work. When the Rabbi of Warka left
Ruda, Temerel also abandoned the great holdings, selling them to
Count Jankowski, the Pole.[194]

The account contains minor inaccuracies, for Temerel did not receive permission to purchase land outright until 1827, the year of R. Simha Bunem's death,
and would have acquired Ruda in another manner (perhaps on freehold). But
such discrepancies aside, it emerges that Temerel helped cultivate a new type
of merchant-zaddik whose worldliness helped the dissemination of Hasidism
in more economically developed areas.[195]

Temerel's efforts earned her the masculine honorific "Reb" on the order
of the Seer of Lublin. A character in Joseph Perl's anti-Hasidic satire *Revealer
of Secrets* recalls hearing, from tavern regulars, the reason why the Hasidim
called Temerel—by order of the zaddik of Lublin—"Reb Temerel." How was
it fitting to call a woman "Reb"? A complicated, sophistic explanation, based
on a misreading of the *Zohar*, was supplied. (The real-life Temerel was not
amused: she attempted to suppress Perl's satire, offering 3 złoties for every
copy so that she could burn them.)[196] The great zaddikim also honored Temerel
by attending the weddings of her children. The Maggid of Kozienice attended
both the wedding of her daughter and Issachar, grandson of the zaddik Samuel
Shmelke Horowitz;[197] and the wedding of her son Jacob in the town of Warka.
During the former wedding, the Maggid had to delay his sermon because,
although the spirit of the zaddik Samuel Shmelke had arrived to witness the
event, the spirit of Szmul Zbytkower was tardy.[198] The minute book of Warka
describes the latter wedding:

> In 1806 the celebrated Temerl of Warsaw held her child's wedding
> in Warka. The wedding was attended by the Maggid of Kozienice,
> Reb Israel Hapstein. The Maggid spent two Sabbaths in Warka, the
> Sabbaths of the weekly Torah readings *Yitro* and *Mishpatim*. On the
> first Sabbath, he was joined by one hundred guests and followers.
> Great feasts were held daily, at which Austrian whiskey was served.
> The Maggid preached words of Torah at these meals, the likes of
> which had never been heard. During his visit he gave countless ser-
> mons. The scribe added that he entered all of these facts into the
> minute-book owing to the "dearness of the matter," and to ensure its
> eternal remembrance. According to oral tradition, the Maggid urged
> in his sermons that a synagogue be built in town.[199]

In 1810, four years later, the Maggid laid the cornerstone to the new synagogue. The synagogue was tall, built of wood, and topped with an "oriental-style" dome-shaped roof.[200]

Temerel was regarded as a protector and benefactor by most Polish Jews, both Hasidic and non-Hasidic. One Mitnagged who received her charity dubbed her "the Polish Hasidah."[201] In 1818, she donated 53,970 rubles to the Warsaw communal charity.[202] Upon her death in 1830, Temerel bequeathed a sum of 300,000 złoties to an organization that cared for the Warsaw poor.[203] The epitaph on her tombstone, which still stands in Warsaw's Jewish cemetery, announces:

> In this Land, a life that was mighty among princes
> To her nation she was a protector against oppression—a helper during distress.
> To the poor she was a mother
> She was a virtuous woman, powerful and famous.[204]

Early nineteenth-century Polish Hasidism thus enjoyed the sponsorship of one of Polish Jewry's most beloved and admired figures.

The 1824 Investigation

The benefits of ties to members of a Jewish plutocracy with friends in "high places" were realized during the period's anti-Hasidic investigations. The final arbiters in those investigations were Viceroy Zajączek and Minister Staszic, advocates of Enlightenment who ultimately desired Jewish integration, although they differed over the extent to which Jewish autonomy should be curtailed (with Staszic favoring more radical measures).[205] They were possibly even willing to consider emancipation if Jews would first reform their occupations, manners, and dress. One would naturally expect them to rule against representatives of a movement that so vociferously opposed these innovations. Yet more mundane considerations seem to have intruded. During the first anti-Hasidic campaign in Płock in 1818, Berek Sonnenberg Bergson had been Zajączek's creditor, as well as a ready source of cash for the Treasury. Minister Stanisław Staszic, a former priest and committed social reformer, was more difficult to influence; but the Institute of the Deaf, founded by none other than Staszic himself, received 2,500 złoties from Berek's estate in 1822. Although the donation was somewhat coerced, the Bergsons' acquiescence paid dividends during Staszic's anti-Hasidic investigation two years later.[206] These factors, in addition to direct interventions by members of the Jewish mercantile elite, help elucidate official policy toward Hasidism.

The anti-Hasidic investigations of 1824 are best known through Raphael Mahler's archival-based description. However, Mahler neglected most of the earlier memory-based accounts; while new documents have come to light. Admittedly, the former accounts are garbled, as R. Joseph Levenstein's letter to Dubnow, written seventy years after the events, demonstrates.

In the year 1825 [sic], the following heads of the Hasidim had to appear before the government in Warsaw to discuss the use of Sfarad liturgy: the holy Rabbi, the zaddik and man of God, Meir of Apta [Opatów], author of the book *Or le-Shamayim;*[207] the Rabbi, zaddik Moses of Kozienice, author of the book *Kol Be'er Moshe;*[208] the wise Rabbi, R. Simha Bunem of Przysucha, author of *Kol Simha.*[209] And with the help of the wealthy Reb Berek [sic] and his wife Temerel of Warsaw, the Hasidim won their case.[210]

The passage's numerous inaccuracies include the date of the investigation, the alleged appearance of R. Moses of Kozienice in Warsaw, the assistance of Berek (who was deceased at the time!), and the claim that Hasidic liturgy was a prime concern of the government's. Nevertheless, such memory-based accounts do supply information that is missing in archival documents. Temerel, as a woman, could not act in an official capacity, and thus does not appear in official documents. Yet every anecdotal version of events, no matter how tradition-minded its author, credits Temerel with the Hasidic victory. Secular-oriented authors tend to concur.[211]

Hasidic recollections produce the following scenario. When the government's curiosity about Hasidism was aroused, an apostate and former Hasid, Ezekiel Stanisław Hoga, defended Hasidism by downplaying its distinctiveness. The Mitnaggdim in the Synagogue Council supplied the government with vague information and denied that Hasidism was harmful.[212] But Maskilim charged that Hasidism bred fanaticism and willful unemployment, and impeded secular education. As a result, the government contemplated restricting Hasidic prayer houses and confiscating Hasidic books. Hoga informed Temerel, who rushed to Zajączek (occasionally confused with his successor Paskiewicz) and prevailed on him not to impose a decree against Hasidism. She urged Zajączek to inquire about Hasidism from Hasidim themselves, whereupon Zajączek proposed a disputation. One author claims that the disputation, presided over by Staszic, occurred in Zajaczek's palace on July 18, 1824.[213] The Maskilim were allegedly represented by Antoni Eisenbaum, future director of the modern Rabbinical School. On the Hasidic side, R. Meir of Stopnica/Opatów did not know Polish, while R. Simha Bunem of Przysucha did not wish to attend; so the Hasidim were represented by none other than the apostate Hoga.[214] On August 30, 1824, Staszic concluded that Hasidic gatherings should not meet with any hindrance. The Hasidim celebrated with a feast in Temerel's house. True to Hasidic expectations of feminine modesty, Temerel (in one account incorrectly described as wife of Michael Bergson) refused to take credit for her intercession, but rather credited the prayers of the zaddikim.[215]

The claim about Hoga's decisive role in the victory in Hasidic sources is nothing short of astounding. Hoga had been a follower of the Seer of Lublin in his youth, but became permanently disillusioned after he tested the Seer's clairvoyance by slipping him a note that proclaimed him the Messiah, and the "Seer" fell for the ruse.[216] Hoga defected and became a Maskil. In 1818, he appears in a government memo instructing officials on the significance of "poles and ropes" around unwalled cities (i.e., *eruvim*).[217] He advised them that the poles and ropes were an expression of superstition and should be removed.[218] As a member of the Warsaw Synagogue Council from 1821 to 1824, Hoga continued his Enlightenment-based criticisms of certain Jewish practices.[219] Several times he complained that rabbis failed to study anything other than holy writings and commentaries, and called on the government to promote enlightened rabbis who could pass qualifying exams.[220] In 1824, he submitted a memo denouncing child-age unregistered marriage, which he claimed was even occurring among the Jewish poor.[221] He also authored Polish-language textbooks on religion and prayer in an attempt to inculcate Jewish youth with the language of the land.[222] Hoga converted to Christianity in 1825, that is, one year *after* the investigation, and gained employment as Staszic's secretary.[223] A Christian missionary noted in his journal that the faith of one Jew in particular "is greatly shaken by the conversion of Hoga."[224] This was an odd choice of a champion of Hasidism.

Nevertheless, the Maskil Jacob Tugenhold insisted upon Hoga's decent character and deep knowledge of Judaism, in contrast to other converts he knew.[225] Hoga justified Tugenhold's praise when, several years later, he wrote a pamphlet defending portions of the Talmud and refuting the Blood Libel, and later wrote another pamphlet defending Jewish practice and condemning efforts to convert Jews by vilifying Judaism.[226] According to one tradition, he was Berek's source for discovering planned government decrees against the Jews; however, this is undercut by the fact that Berek died three years before Hoga's conversion.[227] But how to explain his sympathetic treatment in a Hasidic tradition that was hardly forgiving toward apostates? Near the end of his life, Hoga appears to have returned to Judaism in London and expressed deep contrition over his apostasy.[228] This may have encouraged Hasidic storytellers to cast him as the "righteous apostate."

In archival documents, Hoga's involvement in the investigation appears more modest: he submitted a measured report about Hasidism to the government during the 1818 investigation (in contrast to a scathing report by Abraham Stern), which was cited during the 1824 investigation.[229] As a protege of Minister Staszic and a member of the Warsaw Synagogue Council in 1824, Hoga was probably consulted a second time, and may have refuted some of the more flagrant allegations against Hasidism. As for Temerel, her role during the investigation is not reflected in government documents at all. But her son Jacob figures prominently, and eventually served as an interpreter during the interrogations.[230] Jacob was one of the three members on the Synagogue Supervisory Board in the crucial year 1824, a body that functioned as Warsaw's kahal.[231] It was more likely Jacob, not Hoga, who alerted Hasidim about the impending decree.

On September 29, 1823, in response to Colonel Dulfus's complaint about "the creation of a Hussite [*sic*] sect by Jewish youths in the town of Parczew," the Commission on Denominations[232] requested that the Synagogue Supervisory Board supply a detailed report on the alleged sect.[233] Several months later, the Board issued the innocuous statement that "Hussites" are actually Hasidim, members of an old sect that consisted of Jews who are more devout and sometimes even sing and jump during their prayers.[234] Probably after consulting Maskilim, however, the Commission on Denominations became persuaded that Hasidic leaders kept their followers subservient and in a state of darkness and superstition.[235] On March 15, 1824, Zajączek issued a decree against "Rabbis residing in Przysucha," strictly forbidding them to "collect fees and give advice or opinions," and prohibiting all "hidden Hasidic prayer gatherings in private homes."[236] In Warsaw, the corrupt assistant to the chief of police, Joseph Birnbaum, spread the rumor that because Hasidism had been deemed harmful all adherents must have their beards and side-locks shorn. He procured a vast collection of bribes from Hasidim seeking to dodge the nonexistent decree.[237]

Archival documents now at our disposal reveal the maneuverings of members of the Hasidic mercantile and rabbinic elite to reverse the March 15 decree. On May 9, the wealthy merchant Feivel Kamienitzer Wolberg and the well-respected future zaddik Abraham Zusya Kahana sent letters to the Commission on Denominations and Viceroy Zajączek requesting that they reconsider the decree against the Hasidim, "who, we are convinced, are the most virtuous of the Jews."[238] The government agreed to reconsider.[239] On July 8, a special subcommittee was established under the direction of Stanisław Staszic to determine whether or not "the Jewish sect Hasidim have harmful principles which are contrary to good customs."[240] Staszic asked a Hasidic deputation to appear before the commission in Warsaw, to be composed of R. Simon Rudenberg of Chęcin, R. Moses of Kozienice, R. Simha Bunem of Przysucha, R. Meir of Stopnica/Opatów, and Feivel Kamienitzer. Only the latter three would actually appear.[241]

On August 4, 1824, the seventy-two-year-old Feivel Kamienitzer stood before the commission. He introduced himself as having become Hasidic thirty years ago (1794), at which time his father had persuaded him that the Hasidim were the most virtuous Jews. Feivel replied to twenty-eight questions about the Hasidic movement. He maintained that Hasidism was not distinct from Judaism; that its members did not consider Christians to be idol worshipers; that Hasidism was not closed and secret; that non-Hasidic rabbis were not considered inferior; that neither sons nor wives of non-Hasidim were excluded from praying with Hasidim; that donations to zaddikim were strictly voluntary; that poor pilgrims were not compelled to pay a fee (*pidyon*); that Hasidim could indeed serve in the army; that followers did not have to jump and dance during prayer; that defectors from Hasidism were not punished; and that members were not forcibly recruited.[242] In response to one question that is particularly pertinent to the subject at hand, "Why are you not farmers and factory owners?" Feivel replied, "We are free to be farmers and factory owners, but for the most part we are elderly and weak." A more sincere answer to the question was supplied by the zaddik Meir of Opatów/ Stopnica, the next to be questioned. With Jacob Bergson and Hersz Sztamm serving as his interpreters, R. Meir replied: "Many of us work in factories; and this Jew Jacob Bergson maintains a factory, and Hersz Sztamm is their commissioner, and many of them have workers who are Hasidic or children of Hasidim."[243] R. Meir no doubt wished to stress the economic "usefulness" of Hasidim.

Regardless of the dubious quality of some of these answers, particularly those concerning donations to zaddikim, the Commission was satisfied. The government decided not to persecute Hasidim, who should be free to praise God provided that they refrain from dancing, shouting, drinking, and nocturnal gatherings. Staszic concluded with suggestions for the reform of Polish Jewry, including the establishment of a rabbinic school for training enlightened rabbis.[244] Zajączek then decreed, as he had six years previously, that Hasidim do not have principles opposed to good customs, and that they should not be obstructed when holding their services in private homes.[245] These interrogations have been remembered by Hasidic tradition in a manner more flattering to its leaders, that is, as a "disputation." Yet memory and history do agree about the instrumentality of Jewish mercantile elites in securing Hasidism's exoneration.

Conclusion

According to a homily in *Zot Zikharon*, composed by the Seer of Lublin, the patron's intercessions on behalf of the zaddik are merely illusory. Certain Jews do appear able to defend zaddikim from the Gentiles "because they work amongst them, know their ways, and are able to intercede with the governmental officials on their behalf." Those Jews also appear able to sustain the zaddikim through money accrued from their business transactions. However, the Seer explains, it is actually the merits of the zaddikim that bring those Jews success in their intercessions and business transactions in the first place. So although it appears to the patrons that they are defending and sustaining the zaddikim, the opposite is really the case. Why, then, do the zaddikim continue to let the patrons enjoy their false sense of importance? It increases their fear of God and brings them nearer to the zaddikim.[246]

One wonders how the wealthy members of the Seer's audience reacted to these less-than-edifying addresses. What was it about Hasidism that attracted their support? In a typical patron-client relationship, the patron supplies economic aid and legal protection against authorities, while the client provides loyalty, good will, political support, and adds to the name and fame of his patron. The patron is superior in his ability to grant goods and services.[247] Yet as the Seer's sermon illustrates, a different hierarchy prevailed in the Hasidic world. The largest contributors may have accrued benefits like preferred seating at the zaddik's Sabbath table or prayer house, public recognition, small gifts, and greater personal attention from the zaddik.[248] Berek and Temerel even groomed future zaddikim and influenced succession decisions. But the majority of wealthy patrons were merely preferred customers who, in the end, submitted spiritually to the zaddik and faithfully carried out his instructions.

Some may have attended Hasidic gatherings for business purposes. In a forgotten chapter on Hasidism written in 1889, Klemens Junosza explains, "even wealthy merchants had opportunities at such [Hasidic] gatherings with their co-religionists, upon whose fidelity and brotherly friendship they could count, to conclude contracts with the intention of increasing the profits from their goods."[249] Magic and superstition also may have come into play. According to Junosza, "the weak-minded rich were influenced by the fear that only through the help of multiple donations to 'zaddikim' could they be free from the threat of future misfortune."[250] R. Israel Loebel, an eighteenth-century Mitnagged, reports that "every *arrendar*, before receiving the contract, travels to [the zaddik] and asks him to pray that he will enjoy the nobleman's favor."[251] The zaddik Abraham Joshua Heschel of Apt [Opatów] seems to corroborate these assertions by promising that upon receiving a businessman's contributions, "the zaddik prays on his behalf, recommends him to the Holy One Blessed be He, and draws upon him Mercy and Lovingkindness in all his business affairs and needs. . . ."[252]

According to the Mitnagged R. David of Maków, the zaddik business advisers encouraged Hasidic debtors to default on their loans, announcing that they were owed the same amount from a prior reincarnation.[253] R. Israel Loebel accused Hasidic merchants of cheating non-Jews, and warned that such practices would surely intensify anti-Jewish sentiment and endanger the entire Jewish community.[254] But if such accusations were valid, evidence would probably appear in governmental records. We ought to consider the possibility that Polish zaddikim, some having been merchants themselves, proved extremely adept business advisers. R. Simha Bunem may have been justified in boasting, "I am among the merchants during their business, and everything that I say turns out to be so. And this is not the case with the other merchants, even in their own business affairs, for I have a business sense."[255]

Another prominent motivation was the attainment of honor. The historian Aaron Ze'ev Aescoly speculates that the Bergson family was "wealthy and hated," owing to Szmul's authoritarian and corrupt behavior, which compelled them to support the new Hasidim to spite the old "aristocratic" families who snubbed them.[256] Szmul does indeed appear to have been stigmatized as a nouveau riche boor. The Praga burial society denied him membership, a decision that inspired Szmul to establish his own burial society and methodically destroy theirs.[257] Notables of humble origins like Szmul might have attained honor more easily within the new movement, which was eager for wealthy recruits. Schiper has suggested, alternatively, that when the half-sisters of Szmul's sons Berek and Ajzyk converted to Christianity, the brothers felt compelled to support Hasidism in order to dispel any doubts about their own piety. But this does not explain Szmul's sympathies toward the movement.[258] In Temerel's case, a protofeminist sensibility may well have come into play: she could garner honor within a traditional patriarchal community through her patronage of activities. Still, it should be noted that Hasidic patrons like Feivel Kamienitzer, Moses Halfan Lifshutz, and Joseph Mandelsberg of Kuzmir did not lack for familial prestige or honor within mainstream traditional circles.[259]

Many wealthy merchants would have been attracted to the teachings of the Polish zaddikim, which assume a more positive stance toward the attainment of wealth. Notwithstanding the sentiments about merchants cited earlier, the Seer of Lublin taught:

> When a merchant travels on business, he should say to himself: "I am traveling for business so that I will have money to serve God by paying for my sons' tuition, so that my sons will be Talmudic scholars, engaging in Torah and *mizvot* for the sake of Heaven; and so that I can marry my daughters to Talmudic scholars, and sanctify the Sabbath, and give charity." . . . And in this way, he connects his business to God.[260]

By invoking the Hasidic concept of worship through corporeality (*avodah be-gashmiyut*), the Seer reassured busy merchants in his audience that they could transform business trips into paths to holiness. The Maggid of Kozienice promised vicarious mystical attainment to merchants who attached themselves to him:

> There are zaddikim who cleave to God and serve him; yet even so, they occasionally descend from their level and speak with lesser people in order to elevate them and attach them, also, to God and his service. And even merchants, whose work is not always for the sake of God, by cleaving to zaddikim are removed and raised to God.[261]

Most merchants, consumed by practical concerns, could not "cleave" to God by themselves. Not to worry: by "cleaving" to the zaddik through visits to his court and generous donations, they could bask in divine glory by proxy. Female merchants, with even fewer avenues to spirituality, would be even more enticed by the notion of vicarious communion with God.[262] The exoneration of economic pursuit was embodied in the career of R. Simha Bunem of Przysucha who, as a former merchant himself, could reassure his devotees that the cutthroat modern city did not have to prevent one from experiencing God's grandeur.[263]

Such considerations, important as they are, do not however suffice as comprehensive explanations for Hasidism's appeal among Central Poland's economic elites. To complete the picture, it is necessary to widen our scope to include the historical milieu. The failure of emancipation in eastern Europe during an incipient industrial revolution, a subject of deep interest to social historians, has been all but ignored by scholars of Hasidism; yet herein lies a key to Hasidism's appeal. That failure produced the absurd phenomenon of spectacularly wealthy Jewish merchants with almost no civil rights, not to speak of prestige, within Polish society. The result was that the class level of the Polish Jewish notable was drastically out of sync with what Max Weber would term his "status level."[264] A Jewish notable who took pains to appear acculturated might gain admittance to a Masonic lodge or sponsor a salon attended by enlightened officers and noblemen, but even the most basic rights of citizenship failed to follow until he or she finally converted to Christianity. Some indeed chose this route.[265] But for many, Hasidic courts offered subcultures within which they could enjoy status commensurate with their material success without having to renounce Jewish customs and traditions. In historic Lithuania, support of the great regional and supraregional yeshivas of the Mitnaggdim may have fulfilled a similar function.[266]

Why, then, did some choose acculturation and Haskalah, while others preferred Hasidism? A key indicator is geographic origin. Most members of the assimilationist group derived from Prussia, Silesia, and Moravia, having been lured by prospects of profits from military supplying during the Napoleonic wars.[267] In contrast, Hasidic notables tended to derive from eastern European locales like Zbytki,[268] Kamieniec-Podolski,[269] and Kazimierz-Dolny.[270] It comes as little surprise that the latter group, who had not yet tasted emancipation, should find it easier to renounce a radical integrationist option in favor of the relative honor and influence that Hasidic society accorded them. In the absence of emancipation, they had little difficulty rejecting the uncertain prospect of becoming "Poles of the Mosaic Persuasion," and were rather easily enticed by the vital Hasidic subculture or the less dazzling Mitnaggdic alternative. This helps explain why most Jews in the Polish lands chose not to emulate the pattern of integration found in western Europe, an issue that has long confounded historians. Only the bestowal of rights of residence, political enfranchisement, entry into the professions and universities, and other concrete gains could have persuaded most Polish Jewish notables and thousands of less prosperous merchants that it was possible to fully enter Polish society. Only emancipation could have lured most of them away from their Hasidic subculture. This seems to have occurred to an extent in the 1860s in the wake of Tsar Alexander II's partial emancipatory measures. But for now, leaders of the various regimes in Central Poland were too concerned not to alienate the Polish nobility, whose support they still cherished.

4

Yihus

The Social Composition of Hasidic Leadership

> In religion, the holy man who makes himself to all appearances
> poorer than the meanest beggar may, and in fact often does, come
> from a wealthy or aristocratic, or at least highly educated stratum of
> the social structure. St. Francis, for example, was the son of a rich
> merchant; Gautama was a prince.
>
> —Victor Turner, *Dramas, Fields and*
> *Metaphors: Symbolic Action in*
> *Human Society*

At least in the case of the Bergson family, Hasidic courts provided
something more than settings where wealthy merchants could garner status and honor. They also formed arenas within which they
could discreetly exercise power. We may never know the full extent
to which Berek, Temerel, and Jacob determined matters as weighty
as Hasidic succession, but their grooming, employment, and financ-
ing of up-and-coming Polish zaddikim ensured an extensive influence over such processes. Polish Hasidic succession patterns bear
this out: while hereditary succession did occasionally occur, master-
disciple transmissions were far more frequent and enduring during
the pre-1862 era. The Bergsons and other plutocrats evidently preferred to hand-pick talented disciples who had proven their mettle in
the marketplace rather than automatically promote sons of zaddikim. To this end, they employed such disciples in their enterprises,
provided them with the financial wherewithal to begin acting as zaddikim themselves, protected them against rivals and governmental
bans as their fame began to soar, and ensured that their own promising disciples would succeed them upon their deaths.

According to Max Weber, charismatic leadership is inherently unstable, for it not only possesses antinomian and antiinstitutional predispositions but also lacks a provision for leadership succession. For a charismatic movement to survive the death of the charismatic leader it has to undergo what Weber terms "routinization," becoming either traditionalized, rationalized, or both.[1] As mentioned earlier, zaddikim in the Ukraine, Belarus, and Galicia—territories directly under absolutist Russian and Austrian rule—began to emulate the conduct of their monarchs, which included basing succession claims on hereditary credentials.[2] The list of zaddikim whose progeny set into motion enduring hereditary lines is impressive: R. Jehiel Michael of Złoczów (d. c. 1781), R. David Halevi of Stepan (d. 1810), R. Abraham Abba-Joseph of Soroca, R. Mordecai of Neskhiż (d. 1800), R. Samuel Ginzberg of David-Gorodok, R. Meir of Przemyśł (d. 1773), R. Shabbetai of Raszków (d. 1745), R. Phineas Shapiro of Korzec (d. 1791), R. Zvi Hirsch of Kamenka (d. 1781), R. Dov Ber of Międzyrzecz (d. 1772), R. Menahem Nahum of Chernobyl (d. 1798), R. Aaron Perlov "the Great" of Karlin (d. 1772), R. Solomon of Karlin (d. 1792), R. Mordecai of Lachowicze (d. 1810), R. Schneur Zalman of Liady (d. 1813), R. Menahem Mendel of Kosów (d. 1825), R. Isaac Eizik Eichenstein of Safrin (d. 1800).[3] Several of these progenitors' lines evolved into the premier dynasties of the nineteenth and twentieth centuries, including Chernobyl, Karlin, Ruzhyn, and Lubavitch. Among Weber's "routinizing" solutions, historians of Hasidism thus point to hereditary succession.[4]

But this was by no means a binding scenario. Polish Hasidic successions during the first half of the nineteenth century seem rather to have been determined by another of Weber's scenarios—selection by members of the original charismatic leader's "staff," particularly patrons.[5] As a result, select disciples could compete successfully with sons of zaddikim. The hereditary-based claims of the latter were further undermined in the absence of the direct, consistent monarchical model that prevailed in other regions. The master-disciple succession pattern accordingly predominated in Central Poland until the tsarist regime effectively emancipated the Jewish mercantile elite in 1862 in an effort to stave off potential support of the impending Polish Insurrection and then, in response to the Insurrection, dissolved the Congress Kingdom's constitution and Russified its administration. The resulting absorption of much of the Polish Jewish mercantile elite into the bourgeoisie and exposure to direct monarchical rule brought Polish Hasidic succession tendencies in line with those of neighboring regions, allowing sons of Polish zaddikim to establish more viable dynasties.[6]

The involvement of the Jewish mercantile elite during the period in question sheds further doubt on the presumed folk nature of Hasidism; however, it still does not resolve the question of who the main beneficiaries were. Did these Jewish notables facilitate upward mobility for gifted and charismatic young men of any and all social backgrounds, thereby upsetting the east European Jewish social order? Or, notwithstanding their reluctance to automatically sponsor sons of zaddikim, did they still favor scions of the very rabbinical elite that had always shaped public spirituality? This chapter tests the elitism of Hasidic leadership through a Jewish aristocratic concept known as *yihus*, meaning roughly "noble lineage." If few zaddikim could boast distinguished ancestors and living relatives, if their teachings reflected a disapproval of kinship as a central leadership criterion, and most significantly, if that disapproval impacted their actual marital and matchmaking behavior, then the folksy/obscurantist image constructed in hagiography and anti-Hasidic literature would seem to retain validity. However, we will find instead that *yihus* remained a central feature of the east European Jewish social context throughout the rise of Hasidism. Most early zaddikim accordingly possessed *yihus* to begin with, sanctioned it in sermons, and allowed it to inform their matchmaking practices. Those few who were not highborn nearly always married off their children with *yihus* in mind. Therefore, while zaddikim are usually defined as "charismatic" leaders, it is possible to be more precise: zaddikim tended to be charismatic scions of the old Jewish aristocracy.[7] This tendency was radicalized by zaddikim residing in absolutist monarchies in their adoption of hereditary succession and outright dynasties, while Polish zaddikim, in contrast, preserved the more fluid aristocratic leadership of pre-Hasidic and early Hasidic leadership. Yet both cases argue for a populist, as opposed to popular, designation.

As writers on early Hasidism tended until the end of the twentieth century to uncritically accept hagiographic and polemical portrayals of zaddikim, they tended to assume that early zaddikim lacked *yihus* themselves and repudiated its value. In 1926, Chaim Zytlowski gave his American audience a democratic Hasidism: "There is no doubt that Chassidism exerted a powerful influence for democracy wherever it became established. Old caste distinctions between learned and ignorant, between the poor and the rich, vanished away."[8] Joseph Weiss's description was less edifying: "a smell of money-grubbing rises from the grubbing of these poor wretches for a living."[9] Simon Dubnow's grand narrative had convinced an entire generation of historians and social commentators to represent zaddikim as members of an impoverished, uneducated, and economically backward sector.[10] Zaddikim were depicted variously as members of a disenchanted secondary intelligentsia, a "religious elite itself arising out of the mass of the people" who set aside the "existing 'aristocracy' of spiritual possession," or "lowly folk" deriving from "plebeian origins."[11] The rustic image even resonates within some of the more important recent treatments of Hasidism.[12]

As a matter of fact, the two main founders of Hasidism, the Besht and the Great Maggid of Międzyrzecz, apparently did derive from humble backgrounds. The Besht, according to *Shivhei ha-Besht*, agreed to marry above his station on the curious condition that the father of the bride simply write " '*Mar* [Mr.] Israel, son of *Mar* Eliezer' " on the engagement contract. When the bride's brother, R. Gershon of Kuty, discovered the contract, he was "amazed that his father, who was a famous man, could make a match with a person of low rank, and, moreover, with someone whose background and family lines were unknown."[13] The tale presents an incognito Besht who does not wish to flaunt his scholarly and familial credentials. But in the absence of evidence to the contrary, even after he "revealed" himself at age thirty-six, it appears more likely that he really did lack *yihus*.[14] Latter-day attempts to link his family to the biblical house of David are without merit.[15] According to Moshe Rosman, the Besht was posthumously made to resemble a nineteenth-century pedigreed zaddik by hagiographers, and was only found in the company of *yihus*-possessors later in his career.[16] Elhanan Reiner's research corroborates these assertions, establishing that the Besht initially belonged to a publicly funded *bet midrash* rather than a *kloyz*, the latter being established and attended by members of prominent families.[17] The Great Maggid, for his part, signed a certificate of ordination for a kosher slaughterer from 1767 and a book appro-bation issued in 1765 as "Dov Ber, son of Rabbi Abraham of blessed memory" without attributing any post or title to his father.[18] He signed a letter discovered in the Stolin *geniza* the same way.[19] Biographies only mention Abraham's pov-erty, and remain curiously silent about any scholarly or other attainments.[20] Thus it does, indeed, seem that both the movement's primary inspirational figure and organizational genius derived from humble origins. However, this does not justify accepting their social profiles as prototypical.[21]

Several studies concede the relevance of *yihus* during the rise of Hasidism. Immanuel Etkes observes that success in practical mysticism came to confer *yihus* among *ba'alei shem*, several of whom were considered full members of the elite. As amulets and magical knowledge were passed from father to son or grandfather to grandson, *yihus* was sustained within the profession.[22] Isaac Levitats illustrates the continued nepotism that allowed certain families to re-tain control of communal leadership and local confraternities through the ex-ample of the admission to the Holy Society in Łiożno of the future zaddik Shneur Zalman of Liady at the age of three.[23] Bedřich Nosek notes the sense of importance that the zaddik Samuel Shmelke Horowitz attached to his fa-milial descent.[24]

On the closely related issue of Hasidic succession, Shmuel Ettinger and Stephen Sharot conclude that early Hasidim preferred master-disciple succes-sion to the father-son option embraced by later schools.[25] However, Ada Rapoport-Albert has problematized the entire notion of "succession" by argu-ing that calculated formal transmissions of leadership did not occur during the movement's early stages. The Great Maggid was not appointed successor to the Besht, but merely "came to be regarded as the greatest Hasidic leader of his time, just as the Besht had been regarded before him." The Great Maggid then allowed his disciples to establish their own circles during his lifetime, which ensured a smooth and geographically distributed leadership transition upon his death.[26] Yet as Nehemia Polen points out, there still remains the vital question of when and why formal hereditary succession and self-conscious dynasties did emerge. In an attempt to explain that development, Polen cites hagiographic depictions of the key role of wives and mothers of zaddikim, arguing that it was they who pushed their husbands and sons to establish dynasties.[27] According to Rosman, Hasidism's initial transition to hereditary succession occurred in the Belarusan "Lubavitcher" dynasty as a result of a contest between two rival successors to R. Schneur Zalman of Liady—his star disciple R. Aaron of Starosielce, and his son R. Dov Ber of Lubavitch (Lyubavichi).[28] The latter presented himself as the sole legitimate source for his father's teachings on account of heredity.[29] After that, according to Anne Berger-Sofer, "the position of rebbe has always remained in the family, with each new rebbe being a descendant of Schneur Zalman."[30] More specifically, "the offspring of Dov Ber's daughters were continually drawn back into the lineage in order to contribute potential leaders to the group and to keep Dov Ber's gene pool." This gave the zaddik absolute control over his male family members, who were all potential successors.[31]

Yihus similarly became radicalized among Galician and Ukrainian zaddikim. According to Joseph Salmon, it was a predominant source of authority for the Galician zaddik Naftali Zvi of Ropczyce, despite his stated ambivalence about his illustrious descent.[32] The zaddik Israel of Ruzhin's accession at so young an age and without scholarly qualifications marked the triumph of the principle of hereditary succession within Ukrainian Hasidism. David Assaf describes how the dyslexic and uneducated zaddik assumed leadership at the age of sixteen primarily on the strength of his distinguished *yihus*.[33] At this point, Hasidism reached its "advanced stage," characterized by the dynasty and the court.[34] The period after 1825 saw the emergence of famous families of zaddikim, the institutionalization of Hasidic courts, the predominance of hereditary succession, and the creation of dynastic subdivisions by sons of the same departed zaddikim. "Victory for sons of zaddikim," Assaf contends, was virtually absolute by that time.[35] However, we will observe here the exceptional path taken by Polish zaddikim, who retained their predecessors' more measured, if still elitist, regard for *yihus*.

Pre-Hasidic Attitudes toward *Yihus*

Gauging the influence of *yihus* in Jewish society before the rise of Hasidism is complicated by the often vague and inconsistent applications of the term. Scholars studying societies of early medieval Geonic times, where hereditary succession was practiced less ambiguously, tend to understand *yihus* in its restricted sense of "lineage."[36] In contrast, those studying societies where leadership came to be based more on merit apply *yihus* more broadly.[37] A definition that begins to reveal the nuances of *yihus* as understood in eastern Europe is offered by Mark Zborowski and Elizabeth Herzog: "it relates to family background and position, but cannot be called pedigree since it can be acquired currently as well as by inheritance, and does not necessarily require transmission 'by blood.' "[38] This is a good starting point in that it reveals how east European *yihus* could mean something more than lineage and could be attained as well as inherited. *Yihus* may be more precisely defined as prestige grounded in the scholarly, mystical-magical, political and, to a lesser extent, economic achievements of one's ancestors and living relatives. It transcended mere lineage because it was conferred on a person by virtue of his own attainments or those of living brothers, brothers-in-law, cousins, sons, sons-in-law, and so on. When a Jewish male became accomplished, most commonly as a

Torah scholar, his prestige radiated throughout his entire family and improved not only his own marriage prospects but those of his unwed family members and progeny. They now had a better chance of securing matches with other *yihus* possessors, wedding prestige with prestige.[39] Exceptional rabbinical families whose scholarly achievements, political influence, and wealth spanned several generations became identifiable through adopted surnames like Horowitz, Shapiro, Landau, and Margaliot. Such families claimed a supreme form of *yihus* and were able to dominate local and regional kahals, and supracommunal bodies like the Council of Four Lands and the Lithuanian Council.[40] They constructed networks of lay and rabbinical offices across eastern Europe, and individual members sustained the networks by bequeathing rabbinical offices to their sons.[41] Importantly, hereditary succession in communal self-government was also practiced in non-Jewish Polish municipalities.[42] Both groups were probably influenced by patterns of behavior among the Polish nobility, which consolidated its position through the inheritance of land, exclusive legal privileges, and titles.[43] However, in the case of Jewish families, prestige derived from less tangible—most commonly, scholarly—achievements of forebears and living family members, and this required infusions of new talent from generation to generation. Sons of the elite enjoyed educational advantages and were subject to greater familial expectations, and thus had a decent chance of sustaining their *yihus*. But in the absence of achievement a family's *yihus* dwindled.

A tension runs through rabbinic literature on the subject, but the balance in the Mishnah, Gemara, and Midrashim is decidedly tilted toward genealogical purity and the maintenance of lineage distinctions.[44] Ideally, however, one possessed both *yihus* and merit.[45] Hereditary leadership continued to predominate in Jewish communities of medieval Germany.[46] The tendency probably spread to Poland with the first Jewish settlers, who included prominent German pietists (*hasidei Ashkenaz*).[47] But increasingly, as Tosafist predilections took hold, sons-in-law were chosen for scholarly as much as hereditary qualifications.[48] *Yihus* thus began to evolve into the paradoxical conception of family status that might be inherited or acquired. Judging by the tension between the preference for hereditary versus unalloyed scholarly credentials that pervades commentaries and responsa from the early modern period, the paradox was incompletely resolved.[49] According to Jacob Katz, a purely genealogical "sacred-biological" conception of *yihus* that stigmatized families containing a bastard (*mamzer*), prostitute, apostate, or excommunicate continued to coexist with the more capacious notion of *yihus* as something derived from familial relations or ancestors who had combined worldly attainments like political (kahal) appointment, access to secular rulers, and economic prosperity—with Torah scholarship. But this latter understanding tended to predominate.[50]

How did this play out in the social sphere? Although Jewish society offered some opportunity for upward mobility, communal leadership frequently congealed into oligarchies.[51] Jewish self-government was democratic in only a narrow sense of requiring implicit public sanction.[52] In the marriage market, women lacking in *yihus* had to depend upon economic attributes and skills, physical beauty, and a reputation for chastity.[53] Poor young men could with extraordinary perseverance master Talmudic learning and become sought after by wealthy unlettered heads of families.[54] However, the educational system seems to have been designed to preserve social stratification rather than diminish it by ensuring failure for the majority of economically disadvantaged students.[55] As a result, rabbis and wealthy lay leaders were usually connected to each other by ancestry or marriage.[56] By the eighteenth century, members of the Landau family included rabbis in at least twenty communities, elders of the regions of Cracow-Sandomierz and Lwów, and lay leaders of a number of communities. In addition to their lineage, learning, and wealth, the Landaus enjoyed special access to the magnate town owners, and could thus monopolize local communal leadership and check challenges to their authority.[57] Israel Rubinowicz, a Jewish latifundium manager, secured rabbinical posts for his son-in-law and his son-in-law's own son over trenchant opposition, and obtained a three-year exemption from all taxes—Polish and Jewish—for his son.[58] The latter cases demonstrate how familial status was also contingent upon the visible support of Polish noblemen.

The preoccupation with *yihus* is also manifest in autobiographies. R. Phineas Katzenellenbogen (b. 1691), a member of the rabbinic elite who resided in Poland during his childhood, privileges the scholarly dimension of *yihus*.[59] Nearly every name in his autobiography is festooned with rabbinic heraldry.[60] Katzenellenbogen recalls that as a child, when he was unable to explain a certain passage, his father shamed him by reciting each scholar in his ancestral line.[61] When he reached a marriageable age, he appraised matches by the scholars in their families and considered marriage little more than a means for attaching himself a great family.[62] He proudly married off his own daughter to a "son of a great one in Israel in Torah and prestige."[63] The wine merchant Ber of Bolechów (1723–1805) also privileged scholarship over other *yihus* determinants. His own match, a widow, was "beautiful, clever, accomplished and of a good family; her brothers are distinguished scholars."[64] An associate of Ber earned his esteem for having married all of his children into "families of Rabbis and other notable people."[65] Ber recalled the marriage of one of his sons to the "daughter of the excellent scholar R. Joseph" and proceeded to delineate R. Joseph's distinguished *yihus*.[66] The prospective in-laws, for their part, visibly appreciated Ber's wealth.[67] The Maskil Solomon Maimon (c. 1753–1800) felt embittered by the manner in which *yihus* determined his unhappy union. Although Maimon's fame as a scholar had "already provoked the attention of the most prominent and wealthy people of the town," a widow of modest economic means named Madam Rissa managed to win him as her son-in-law with the aid of the chief rabbi, who highlighted "the high ancestry of the bride (her grandfather, father and uncle having been learned men, and chief rabbis)" among her attractions.[68]

Social criticism of the day reflects less discomfort over the premium placed on *yihus* than with the corruptions or excesses associated with it. R. Eliezer ("the Roke'ah") complained that the rich virtually purchased the *yihus* of ancient families by obtaining their progeny as sons-in-law, an unnatural union between Torah, wealth, communal leadership and *yihus*.[69] R. Ephraim of Łęczyce appears most concerned with undue pride among *yihus* possessors: those "who it seems have a slight advantage over their friend, or greater wealth, or greater *yihus*; who claim wealthy men or scholars as their relatives; or who possess some of those advantages themselves" were prone to distance themselves from their fellow man and "turn up their noses" at the poor and oppressed.[70] Neither critic felt moved to assail *yihus* as such. Some actually feared the demise of *yihus* as the premier factor during matchmaking procedures. The zaddik Samuel Shmelke recalls the advice of his eminent grandfather, R. Meir of Tykocin:

> Be very, very careful to make matches for the sake of heaven for your children, according to the words of the sages: "always sell [everything you have and marry your daughter to a scholar]."[71] For the vast majority of matchmaking arrangements in these generations, owing to our many sins, are based upon the desire for wealth. And the woman is purchased with coins and money, or for the sake of rabbinical office, or for other motives. Indeed, God forbid that this must be mentioned at all. For the foundation and great principle in the eyes of the Lord and men is to arrange matches with the *yihus* possessors in Israel.[72]

Yihus, rather than wealth or rabbinical office, was to be the paramount consideration during matchmaking procedures.

Early Hasidic Attitudes toward *Yihus*

With the advent of Hasidism, *yihus* retained its importance for Mitnaggdim and Hasidim alike, although they differed over what exactly constituted it. Mitnaggdim clung to the old determinants, favoring spiritual leaders who were descendants of scholars and had developed into scholars and/or mystics themselves. Hasidim modified this classical formula by privileging descendants of scholars, merchants, or zaddikim who could "perform" *devekut* through inspiring modes of worship, preaching, and teaching. The primacy of Torah learning as a determinant of *yihus* ceased among Hasidim, for scholarship was now as much a means for achieving *devekut* as a tool with which to derive ritual and legal rulings.[73] Nevertheless, the tension between the purely genealogical, "sacred-biological" conception or the more meritocratic understanding continued to endure among Mitnaggdim and early Hasidim alike.

Among Mitnaggdim, R. Elijah ben Solomon, the Vilna Gaon (1729–97) represented the former stance, depicting *yihus* as a prerequisite for divine grace: whereas the son of a zaddik is "saved from evil," the son of an evil person will surely fall victim to evil even if he, himself, is a zaddik.[74] The views of his preeminent disciple, R. Hayyim of Volozhin (1749–1821) are situated at the other end of the spectrum:

sons of the poor do more good deeds in Volozhin than sons of the rich, because their fathers could not offer much tuition money for good teachers [*melamdim*], and their deeds remained only potential deeds. And here, through their own persistence, they go from potentiality to action. But as for the rich, that which was potential was already realized by means of good teachers.[75]

R. Hayyim valued the resilience of pious "sons of the poor" who were able to succeed through their own efforts. When boys of humble backgrounds attained propitious matches, R. Hayyim assumed it was destined from on high, which amounted to an endorsement of the more fluid conception of *yihus*.[76]

Early Hasidic teachings on *yihus* oscillate within the same parameters. The Besht, like all early leaders, was certainly impressed by those with great *yihus* and actively sought to draw them into his movement. According to one tradition:

> For the Besht, may he be always remembered, said that three families have been pure generation after generation, "which He made with Abraham, swore to Isaac, and confirmed with Jacob":[77] 1) the Margaliot family; 2) Shapiro; and 3) Horowitz. And because of this, the Besht loved the Rabbi *Meir Netivim*, the genius, our teacher Meir Margaliot, and the holy R. Phinehas Shapiro from Ostróg, and the holy R. Zvi Hirsch Horowitz, *av bet din* of Zborów and Czortków, who were his students.[78]

Other traditions corroborate this inclination. That the Besht admired the Horowitz family is attested in his reaction to R. Isaac Horowitz's initial opposition to him: "What can I do? He is of a stock whose descendants are heard when they weep before the Lord."[79] The Besht recruited the Margaliot brothers while working as a kosher slaughterer.[80] *Shivhei ha-Besht* similarly portrays the Besht as cherishing the value of *yihus*.[81]

Yet according to a tale in *Shivhei ha-Besht* that must have vexed many a nineteenth-century Hasidic reader, he refused to be guided by *yihus* when it came to his own son, Zvi Hirsch. He ostensibly denied Zvi Hirsch a soul that would have yielded him greatness without effort, an assertion that implies that granting such a soul would have demeaned the value of individual struggle. Yet the gamble had not paid off. Zvi Hirsch nearly slept through the Besht's last living hours. When roused by several disciples and brought to the deathbed, he asked his father to teach him something; but alas, he could not grasp it. The Besht limited himself to teaching Zvi Hirsch a single name, and a way to remember it.[82] A teaching in *Keter Shem Tov* (1794–95) also appears more circumscribed:

> The man who, even though he possesses self-importance and pride and he knows that he is a great scholar, a possessor of *yihus* and good qualities, a zaddik, God-fearing, pleasant, and delightful; and yet owing to his virtuousness he deems it inappropriate to befriend

or heed any man lest they cause him to become arrogant, for he reasons that his pious duty is to be humble—if so, he will succeed in
becoming humble. And this is illustrated in a parable: one who sits
on a cart and falls asleep while the owner of the cart takes him up a
high mountain; and afterwards, when he has come straight up the
mountain and the sleeping man awakens, and they tell him that he
is on the mountain, he does not believe it, because he does not see
any evidence. Yet it will be revealed as he descends the mountain
down the other side. And likewise is the man who was *born* on this
mountain, which is high, etc. He will not be able to discern [his true
level] until he accustoms himself to the quality of humility [i.e. "descending"], by which he shall know the greatness of the Creator and
his own lowliness.[83]

Only by descending the "mountain" of his pride will the highborn scholar
perceive his true station in the grand scheme of things by recognizing his
lowliness compared with the greatness of God.[84] Such moments suggest that
although the founder of Hasidism was impressed by *yihus*, which he himself
lacked, he was concerned lest his highborn disciples succumb to arrogance.
The Besht repudiated a nakedly sacred-biological conception in favor of a quasi-
meritocratic one.

This more measured stance predominated among his first-generation disciples. R. Jacob Joseph of Połonne's *Toldot Ya'akov Yosef*, Hasidism's first theoretical work, contrasts those who are humble like Moses with "notables and
yihus calculators" like the rebel Korah and his followers.[85] R. Jacob Joseph offers
a taxonomy according to the biblical forefathers. Isaac represents the highborn
students who rely on the natural process of reward and punishment, only
earning rewards that are precisely equal to their attributes, especially their
yihus. Isaac-types thus derive their reward from God's "Severe Justice" (*Din*)
attribute. Abraham represents a second, higher category, composed of those
who lack *yihus* and must rely on God's compassion. Abraham-types draw their
reward from God's "Lovingkindness" (*Hesed*) attribute. A third category comprises those who combine *yihus* with merit, represented by Jacob. These draw
strength from both "Severe Justice" and "Lovingkindness," and apparently constitute the ideal.[86] The Great Maggid of Międzyrzecz promoted a similarly moderate stance, arguing, for example, that sons of evildoers could reverse their
nature and become full-fledged zaddikim.[87]

Hasidism's preeminent theorist of the next generation, R. Elimelekh of
Leżajsk (1717–86), was even more forceful in promoting a more meritocratic
understanding of *yihus.*[88] R. Elimelekh, we should recall, was the master of
major Polish zaddikim like the Maggid of Kozienice and the Seer of Lublin.
According to a frequently cited teaching, sons of zaddikim often became zaddikim by dint of their upbringing, yet sons of common parents who managed
to also become zaddikim were less likely to "fall from their sacred rank, for
they have nothing to rely on, and they stay humble and perpetually watch
themselves with open eyes." Those who already possessed *yihus* were in greater

danger of falling from their rank because they were less self-reliant and more prone to "diverge from the true path and become haughty."[89] A lowborn zaddik, he taught elsewhere, was someone who had returned to Earth by means of reincarnation and accordingly possessed an advantage over the zaddik with yihus because "he had already been in heaven, and heard everything that will occur in the future of the world, and accordingly has the ability to bestow advice. But one who is a zaddik owing to ancestral merit is not on this level."[90] Those who lacked the aid of ancestral merit should therefore "serve God in earnest," and heavenly assistance would come regardless of family background.[91] The son's bond with his father gradually weakened, in any case, for the zaddik became his true kinsman.[92]

R. Elimelekh was chiefly concerned about undue pride in yihus. He interprets the verse "forget your people and your father's house and let the king be aroused by your beauty" (Psalms 45:11) as an injunction to forget about yihus:

> if you reach such a level that you forget from which "people" you
> are, and from which "father's house" you are descended then you
> will arouse the "king"—King of the Universe—"by your beauty."
> And this is the meaning of: "a lamb according to the house of their
> fathers," meaning that they will be humble in their yihus.[93]

Familial status was nonetheless valuable as long as it was accompanied by proper humility. It "helps one to serve his Creator so that their merit stands him and his seed in good stead but does not gratify him and make him proud." It can inspire him to "always worry and think 'when will I reach the place of my ancestors, so that I will be a zaddik like them?' "[94] And it is a "great thing, and stands a man in good stead when he wants to serve God, for it will be his heavenly assistance in accomplishing a good deed perfectly. And this is only because he did not bring the virtue of yihus to another [evil] side, accordingly it positions him serve the Creator."[95] Yihus possessors were merely warned of the pitfalls of pride, as in pre-Hasidic times.

During this generation, however, the sacred-biological conception began to take hold among those who stood to gain the most: descendants of the Besht. Historians in search of the roots of Hasidism's dynastic impulse would do well to begin here. R. Barukh of Międzybóż (1753–1811), who regarded himself as the Besht's sole legitimate heir, emphasized yihus to an extreme degree.[96] A collection of traditions about R. Barukh has an aging R. Jacob Joseph of Połonne counsel him, "Borukhl, I heard from your grandfather the Besht that you will be his successor. . . . Can you take snuff like the Besht? For the Besht, when he wanted to go to the upper worlds, would take snuff."[97] R. Barukh taught that the biblical Abraham's son Isaac achieved prominence equal to his own without the effort that Abraham had expended.[98] According to Gottlober, R. Barukh publicly mocked the folksy zaddik Aryeh, "the Grandfather of Szpola," on the grounds that he lacked yihus.[99] During R. Barukh's quarrel with R. Levi Isaac of Berdyczów and R. Shneur Zalman of Liady, the zaddik Asher of Stolin sided with R. Barukh, lest the Besht's "holy seed cease, God forbid."[100]

But this did not amount to an endorsement of his exclusive claims to hereditary entitlement, which represented a departure from earlier norms in the region.

Another prominent descendant of the Besht, R. Nahman of Bratslav, appears more conflicted but, in the end, nearly as entitled as R. Barukh. R. Nahman apparently felt burdened by his link to the Besht once his mission crystallized, being painfully aware that "the world thinks that it is because I am the [great-]grandson of the Besht that I have attained this eminence."[101] Once he dramatically refused to visit the Besht's grave, retorting "if my grandfather wants to see me let him come here"; however, he did promise to visit the Besht's grave upon his return.[102] R. Nathan Shternharz of Nemirów, his preeminent disciple, recalls R. Nahman's insistence that "even were he not of the godly seed of the Baal Shem Tov, may his memory be for a blessing, but even from the lowliest Jewish family, he still would have attained what he did by dint of the magnitude of the extraordinary labor and effort he expended in his divine service."[103] Additional protestations appear in R. Nathan's testimony.[104]

Nevertheless, they are belied by R. Nahman's conduct. During his pilgrimage to the Land of Israel, he invoked his *yihus* whenever he was in danger.[105] His alleged descent from the House of David even persuaded him of his messianic role.[106] R. Nahman did caution his disciples that pride in *yihus* may impede one's prayer.[107] But his preference for sons over disciples was unambiguous:

> There is a distinction between a son and a disciple. For the son who is a disciple is on an additional level compared to the disciple alone, because the son is entirely drawn from the father, from his head to his feet and does not possess anything which is not drawn from the mind of the father. As a result, his attainment as a son is on a higher level than his attainment as a disciple.[108]

The aspect of "son" was unquestionably superior. In *Sefer ha-Midot* (Mohilev, 1811), R. Nahman's sacred-biological conception is made explicit: "1) A *yihus* possessor is not susceptible to the potency of a curse; 2) Even a righteous woman, if she lacks *yihus*, gives birth to unworthy sons; 3) It is difficult for the Holy One Blessed Be He to disregard or hinder great *yihus* possessors."[109] Such pronouncements place R. Nahman at the extreme of the spectrum.

The attitudes of most zaddikim in absolutist monarchies of the nineteenth century advanced along this latter trajectory. The nineteenth-century Galician zaddik Zvi Elimelekh Shapiro of Dinów taught:

> A great thing derives from the names they attribute to a man, in addition to his principle name. From this is known one's family *yihus* for generations to come, because members of generations are called by the names of their fathers, and likewise the sons of sons for generations. And it is also known after several generations that he is from a certain house, for example the families Rapoport, Horowitz, and Shapiro.[110]

In accordance with this belief, R. Zvi Elimelekh changed his own family name from Langsam to Shapiro.[111] Still, the Galician zaddik, R. Naftali Zvi of Ropczyce, doubted R. Zvi Elimelekh's ability to sustain a dynasty precisely because he lacked sufficiently distinguished lineage.[112] Another nineteenth-century Galician zaddik taught that the appointment of a deceased zaddik's son permitted his followers' service of God to proceed uninterrupted. With the appointment of the zaddik's son "it is as if the zaddik is not dead, i.e., he has not departed from this world. For the power of the father is in the son. And when the son does his service, it is accepted before God as if the father himself continues his service without pause."[113] R. Israel of Ruzhyn made even stronger pronouncements about the primacy of *yihus*.[114] Appointing the zaddik's son was coming to be seen as a spiritual imperative so paramount as to overshadow shortcomings in the scholarly arena.[115] Dynastic succession soon elevated *yihus* to a level unseen for centuries.[116]

Maskilim in those regions derided this radicalization of *yihus*. Joseph Perl composed the following dialogue between two Hasidim: "Wouldn't it be better for him to match himself up with the son of our holy rebbe? Even though he don't walk the straight and narrow, at least he's the son of a real zaddik and he's sure to be promoted soon. But this sinner, son of the fake rebbe, has no *yihus* at all, and he'll certainly always remain a total sinner."[117] Heredity purportedly trumped moral rectitude. The Ukrainian Maskil Isaac Ber Levinsohn's satire *Emek Rafa'im*, composed in the late 1820s or early 1830s, has a zaddik counsel his son about how to ingratiate himself with the wealthy and powerful in order to become a zaddik like himself.[118] The episode is not so far-fetched: Hasidic tradition records the Ukrainian zaddik Mordecai of Chernobyl advising his eldest son Aaron: "you too can travel and go from town to town, receiving *kvitlach*, and you will be able to make a living."[119] Maskilic mockery would erupt with more fierceness in 1873, when R. Asher II of Karlin was succeeded by his four-year-old son.[120]

Zaddikim in Central Poland, in contrast, retained the more moderate stance of prior generations. True, the inheritance of rabbinical posts, which had become the norm by this time, did not cease.[121] R. Samuel Shmelke, for his part, insisted that the zaddik's familial bonds conducted his holiness throughout his entire kinship network.[122] Nevertheless, the region's contextual distinctiveness appears to have helped preserve the older attitudes toward *yihus*. R. Levi Isaac insisted: "it is not fitting for a man to exult in anything other than that for which he himself labored, and toiled, and achieved. And the opposite is the case regarding a thing for which he has not labored, such as the *yihus* of his fathers. Exultation is not appropriate here, for what is its value?"[123] The Maggid of Kozienice cited the following teaching in R. Levi Isaac's name:

> If a man from good and honest stock walks on an pure path, this is nothing to marvel at, for "the Torah returns to its lodging." . . . But if a man from a lowly family does well in the eyes of God and man, then he will be praised more than the son of a respected family in leaving the ways of his father and inclining toward good.[124]

R. Levi Isaac still nourished a respect for *yihus*, for example praising R. Nahman of Bratslav "for his own merit as well as for that of his holy ancestors."[125] But his teachings betray the prior generation's ambivalence.

Not surprisingly, the Maggid of Kozienice, one of the rare zaddikim of his generation to lack *yihus* himself, also tried to downplay its significance. According to one tale, a member of the Landau family mocked the Maggid for his undistinguished lineage, but the Maggid shamed him with his erudition.[126] According to another tradition, the Maggid ironically proclaimed his pride in his "ancestry" because he derived, like all Jews, from the biblical forefathers Abraham, Isaac, and Jacob.[127] The Maggid taught that one's deeds effectively transformed one's *yihus* for better or for worse:

> When a man does something good in the eyes of God, he arouses the root of his soul through his father and his father's father, and brightens everyone in the light of its holiness. And when, God forbid, the man is blemished in his deeds in a certain matter, this is enough to blemish his root through his father and his father's father.[128]

Still, the Maggid, too, expressed his regard for *yihus* in his correspondence with *yihus* possessors.[129]

The Seer of Lublin insisted that disciples were a zaddik's spiritual sons.[130] The biblical Phineas was a spiritual "son" of Aaron the Priest, that is, his disciple.[131] Like R. Elimelekh, he warned that *yihus* contained the potential for good and evil. Sometimes it happens that a person "derives from a great zaddik, a priestly family, Hasidim and their stalk, but the person himself is not of that ilk; and sometimes the reverse occurs." Hence "return every man to his family" (Leviticus 25:10) should be interpreted as meaning "return to his ancestors' lofty level."[132] However, "Go forth from your country, homeland, and father's house" (Genesis 12:1) implies that one must refrain from relying on his father's house and "not think about *yihus* and kinship at all." The verse's continuation, "I will make your name great," means "new *yihus* will begin from you."[133] There are two types of hearts—the heart of Moses, which is humble and full of repentance, and the heart of Korah, who "dwelled on his *yihus*, being the 'son of Yizhar,' etc."[134] The name Korah itself "derives from 'bald' (*Kere'ah*), for he who is bald, i.e., lacking good qualities, thinks only of his father's *yihus*." Korah's impertinence suggests, paradoxically, that he did not have true *yihus*.[135] The Seer exhibited what he deemed the proper balance between *yihus* and merit when he arranged the future zaddik Isaac Eizik Jehiel of Safrin's marriage. In persuading the prospective bride's father, R. Abraham Mordecai Horowitz, to marry his daughter Gitel to Isaac Eizik, he conceded, "True, you do actually have greater *yihus* than the Rabbi (Alexander Sender) of Komarno," the boy's father. Yet assured him that "the groom will one day illuminate the world."[136] However, we would be remiss not to mention that Isaac Eizik's *yihus* was also rather exalted: R. Yom Tov Lipman Heller, author of *Ha-Tosafot Yom Tov*, was his maternal great grandfather, and the Galician zaddik Zvi Hirsch of Żydaczów was his uncle.

Yihus and Reality: The Lineage and Marriage Alliances
of Polish Zaddikim

But were their actions consistent with their ideological pronouncements? It
turns out that during the first generations of Hasidism, most zaddikim were
in practice a lot closer together. Whether or not they professed a preference for
self-made disciples, most were themselves scions of the most illustrious Jewish
families in eastern Europe or individual communal leaders, and sought to
ensure their children and grandchildren's elite membership. The humble backgrounds of the Besht and the Great Maggid should not blind us to the social
profile of nearly every zaddik of the first several generations. During the rise
of Hasidism, members of Jewish society's lower echelons rose to positions of
leadership with no greater frequency or ease than they did in the parent society.
Those few zaddikim from modest backgrounds, like the Besht and the Great
Maggid, nearly always sought and secured a higher social credit rating through
their marriage strategies. Almost nobody challenged *yihus* in practice, for it
yielded prestige, legitimacy, and charisma in the absence of a formal hierarchy
like that of the Church.

An analysis of the available genealogical records underscores the elitism
of early Hasidic leadership. Among fifty prominent early zaddikim of all
regions, three categories of *yihus* are discernible:[137]

1. *Yihus azmo,* or honorary *yihus.* With the rise of Hasidism, *yihus azmo*
   belonged to the rare mystical leader who overcame the stigma of low
   birth by acquiring a substantial following. He usually cemented his
   newfound acceptance within the elite through marriage strategies.
2. Aristocratic family *yihus* owing to one's membership in a prominent
   rabbinical family whose surname had been retained for generations.[138] Such rabbinical surnames existed long before the mass surname adoptions of the late eighteenth century.[139]
3. *Yihus* derived from a prominent scholar, rabbinical or lay office
   holder, or wealthy forebear who lacked an aristocratic surname. Zaddikim from this category had parents and grandparents in spiritual
   leadership positions like *av bet din* (head of the local rabbinical court).

Among fifty major zaddikim from the first three generations, forty-four
(88%) possessed *yihus.* Eighteen were members of aristocratic families with
recognizable surnames, while an additional twenty-two possessed familial distinction on a more individual basis (e.g., a father who was *av bet din*). Only six
may have initially lacked *yihus.* When marrying off their children, nearly all
sustained or attained their *yihus* through grooms and brides whose fathers
inhabited rabbinical or lay offices or were recognized zaddikim.[140] In nearly
every case, the six zaddikim who lacked *yihus* enhanced their social credit rating
through auspicious matches for their children (see appendix A). The social
equilibrium was reestablished fairly quickly.

Polish zaddikim, unlike zaddikim in absolutist lands, usually did not or could not implement hereditary succession throughout the first half of the nineteenth century. Father-son transmissions simply failed to compete successfully with those between masters and disciples. This does not mean, however, that *yihus* was not a major, defining characteristic of Polish Hasidic leadership. The only major early Polish zaddikim who lacked normative *yihus*, R. Israel "the Maggid" of Kozienice and R. David Biderman of Lelów, were sure to acquire it through marriage strategies (see table 4.1). The Maggid of Kozienice and R. David of Lelów were exceptional in their lack of familial credentials, yet quite typical in their marital strategies.

More Polish zaddikim belonged to the second category, *yihus* derived from membership in a family with a recognizable aristocratic surname. Members of this supreme category organized marriage alliances with other aristocratic families and individuals. The first zaddikim of the Horowitz family were the brothers R. Samuel Shmelke and R. Phineas Horowitz, the pioneers of Polish Hasidism. They fortified their noble lineage through careful matchmaking practices.[141] Another renowned Polish zaddik of the Horowitz clan was R. Jacob Isaac, the Seer of Lublin.[142] He, too, sustained his hereditary credentials through auspicious unions.[143] R. Fishele (Ephraim) of Brzeziny and Stryków, known as "Fishele Strykover," (1743–1822) belonged to the Shapiro family. He forged a controversial but auspicious marriage alliance with the famous Maskil-turned-Hasid, Dr. David Hayyim Bernard of Piotroków.[144] R. Jacob Isaac, the "Holy Jew" of Przysucha (1766–1813) was a member of the Rabinowicz family.[145] His marriage and those of his sons were auspicious.[146] The Zak family produced the zaddik R. Moses Leib of Opatów (later of Sasów, 1745–1807), whose matchmaking patterns were consistent with those of his colleagues.[147] R. Moses bequeathed his Sasów rabbinical post to his son R. Yekutiel Shmelke.[148]

TABLE 4.1 "Self-Made" Zaddikim in Central Poland

Zaddik	Marriage Strategies for Children
R. Israel "the Maggid" of Kozienice, son of Shabbatai, son of Zvi; and Perl; married Raizel	Moses Eliakum Bryah m. Beilah, d. of R. Aryeh Leib Hakohen of Annipol, author of *Or ha-Ganuz*. 2nd m: d. of Zaddik Eleazar Weissblum, son of Zaddik Elimelekh of Leżajsk
	Perl m. Zaddik Avi Ezra Zelig Shapiro of Mogielnica, son of R. Moses Isaac Shapiro, descendant of Nathan Nata Shpira, author of *Megale Amukot*.
	(Daughter) m. R. Ezekiel Halevy, son of R. Ariel Judah, *av bet din* of Zwolin
R. David Biderman of Lelów, son of Rachel and Solomon Zvi; married Hannah, d. of Jacob of Negnevicze.[a]	Moses Biderman of Jerusalem m. Rebecca Rachel, d. of Zaddik Jacob Isaac, the "Holy Jew" of Przysucha
	Nehemia m. d. of Mordecai of Stopnica, brother of Zaddik Meir of Opatów/Stopnica
	Avigdor's wife is unknown.

[a]Closest approximation to Hebrew spelling.

The third category of *yihus*, descent from a scholar, rabbinical office holder, or possessor of wealth absent an aristocratic surname, was the largest category for Polish zaddikim. Among the most prominent was R. Levi Isaac of Berdyczów. His father, R. Meir, was *av bet din* of Gusaków, and according to several hagiographers, the sixteenth generation of his family to obtain an *av bet din* position (probably in various locales). His grandfather was R. Moses, *av bet din* of Zamość, son of R. Zvi Hirsch, *av bet din* of Lemberg. R. Levi Isaac's mother, Sosha Sarah, was granddaughter of R. Moses Margaliot and a descendant of R. Samuel Eliezer Edels, "the Maharsha." R. Levi Isaac was married to Pearl, daughter of a rich contractor named Israel Perez, also of distinguished lineage.[149] R. Levi Isaac married at least several of his children with *yihus* very much in mind.[150] R. Abraham Joshua Heschel of Opatów also came from a long, distinguished line of rabbis, including the Maharam of Padua and R. Saul Wahl. His father, R. Samuel, was *av bet din* of Zamigród, and then of Nowe Miasto Korczyn. R. Abraham Joshua Heschel married Hayyah Sarah, daughter of the wealthy Jacob of Torczyn, a disciple of Elimelekh of Leżajsk.[151] Their offspring married accordingly.[152] The zaddik Meir Rotenberg[153] of Opatów/Stopnica was son of R. Samuel Halevi, a descendant of R. Isaiah Horowitz, author of *Shnei Luhot Ha-Brit*; and Mirel Miriam, a descendant of R. Shabbetai Cohen, "Ha-Shakh." R. Meir married the daughter of R. Reuven Horowitz, *av bet din* of Żarnowiec, a disciple of R. Elimelekh of Leżajsk; and/or the daughter of R. Joseph David Zeidman. He forged auspicious unions for his children.[154] R. Simha Bunem of Przysucha was the son of Sarah and R. Zvi, "the Maggid of Włodzysław," author of *Arez Zvi* (Prague, 1786) and *Asarah l'Me'ah* (Berlin, 1801). He wed Rebbeca, daughter of the wealthy Moses Orverger-Kazov of Będzin. The marriage of their son R. Abraham Moses joined them to the the Holy Jew of Przysucha's family.[155]

The pattern held true for the next wave of Polish zaddikim from this third category. R. Isaac Kalish of Warka was son of Yuta and R. Simon of Zluszyn, known as "Simon the Merciful," a descendant of R. Mordecai Jaffe (1530–1615).[156] R. Isaac married Rachel, daughter of Meir of Żarki, and one of their daughters' marriages connected their family to that of R. Abraham Moses of Przysucha.[157] R. Menahem Mendel of Kotzk was the son of Judah Leibush Morgenstern, a poor glazier who nevertheless possessed distinguished *yihus*: he was son of R. Mendel of Karów, who was son-in-law of the famed R. David Halperin, *av bet din* of Ostróg and Zasław (one of the Besht's disciples), who was son of R. Israel Halperin, *av bet din* of Ostróg. R. Menahem Mendel married Glickel, daughter of R. Isaac Eizik Noy, who bore him R. David of Kotsk. R. Menahem Mendel's second wife was Hayyah, daughter of Moses Lipshitz Halperin of Warsaw, whose sister married R. Isaac Meir Alter of Gur. Their son Benjamin was married to the daughter of R. Abraham Mordecai Alter of Gur, while their daughters were married to *avei bet din*.[158]

In the final analysis, the marital behavior of those leaders is even more important than the ideals they professed. These genealogical analyses correct misconceptions about the social profile of the Polish Hasidic leadership, which turns out to have been as elitist as that of its network of patrons in Warsaw.

Even the most vocal critics of abuses associated with *yihus* did not depart from oligarchic practices themselves, but pursued marriage strategies aimed at enhancing their *yihus*. If, under the influence of the Jewish mercantile elite and the regime's quasi-liberal character, they rarely instituted hereditary succession throughout the first half of the nineteenth century, *yihus* remained a cherished ideal. As a result, in spite of their struggle with the old rabbinic elite, Polish zaddikim essentially preserved its core social hierarchy and values. This was representative of the Hasidic movement as a whole. Social upstarts like the Besht and R. Dov Ber of Międzyrzecz were not permitted to become the norm.

The Fate of *Yihus* in Eastern Europe

Concerns about the cultural backgrounds of prospective spouses intensified during the Hasidic-Mitnaggdic conflicts of the late eighteenth century following pronouncements against marrying Hasidim at the Fair of Zelwa in 1781. But these concerns tended to subside by the mid-nineteenth century, along with the waning of the Hasidic-Mitnaggdic conflict discussed in chapter 2. The fact that two nineteenth-century memoirists from non-Hasidic families— Abraham Gottlober and Ezekiel Kotik—were betrothed to Hasidic women illustrates the rapprochement. Gottlober's father, neither Hasidic nor Mitnaggdic, married him to Judith, daughter of a wealthy Ruzhiner Hasid named Nahman Leib of Czernichów.[159] Ezekiel Kotik's situation was more awkward, for his father was a Hasid while his grandfather, the ultimate authority, was a Mitnagged. The latter rejected each of the father's proposed matches with girls from Hasidic families. Finally, a Hasidic rabbi who was revered as a scholar proposed a match to Ezekiel's grandfather, who responded:

> My Ezekiel is a very good boy. His mother is a possessor of great
> *yihus*, for she is one of the grandchildren of R. Hayyim of Volozhyn,
> and I do not want to disgrace that *yihus*. I can, indeed, trust the
> Rabbi that if the match is made with you—and you are a great
> scholar—it is apparently well and also suits me. But in spite of all
> this, I need to know more about your wife's family.[160]

After a recitation of "all of the *yihus*, detail after detail," Ezekiel's grandfather was finally reconciled to the match.

By the nineteenth century, arranged marriages came increasingly under fire by Maskilim.[161] The Maskil Mordecai Aaron Guenzburg depicted the arranged marriage as "a set of transactions in which each family tries to maximize its three basic sources of 'capital': learning, ancestry, and money."[162] During his own matchmaking process, tragedy struck: a relative of his father's converted to "Islam," likely a euphemism for Christianity. His *yihus* ruined, Guenzburg was "sold into bondage to a family of wealthy but vulgar tailors."[163] Increasingly, as well, a new factor—the degree of the candidate's loyalty to tradition—became an issue.[164] A father of a Jewish socialist had to actually move to another town in order to secure matches for his other children.[165] Interestingly enough, Jewish socialists developed their own version of *yihus*, deriving from a relative's fame as a revolutionary.[166] In cases where arranged marriages did continue to occur, the consent of the couple was now increasingly sought.[167] But in smaller towns and villages in particular, the primacy of *yihus* endured into the twentieth century:

> In those days seeking a wife did not mean looking for a girl. It meant searching for a family, for *yihus*—pedigree, or caste, if you will. The girl was really the last thing to be considered. Of prime importance were not only her immediate forebears, but those of generations back, as well as uncles, aunts and kinfolk of all kinds, no matter how distantly related. Everything that happened in, and everybody who was connected with, a family was important in the matter of marriage. Although affluence and influence were considerations of importance, *yihus* usually involved learning and scholarship. The more scholars a family boasted, the greater was its standing.[168]

A deeply engrained, constitutive feature of traditional society was not easily displaced. Ethnographic studies of small-town Jewish communities illustrate the enduring force of *yihus* all the way down to the destruction of European Jewry.[169] *Yihus* remains particularly resonant in today's Hasidic communities.

5

Charlatans or "Lovers of Israel"?

Evaluating Hasidic Populism

Behold, I heard from my Lord and father, the genius, zaddik (Eleazar Hakohen of Pułtusk) of blessed memory, how splendid it was there at the godly table. For those who gathered in (R. Abraham Joshua Heschel of Opatów's) shade were seated at the pure table dressed in white. But when the holy attendant was walking with a dish of food for everyone, and bumped into one of them with the dish of gravy, he accidentally spilled a little gravy on the white clothes of an elderly man and stained his garment. And the elder fixed a terrible gaze on the attendant. And when our holy Rabbi (Abraham Joshua Heschel) saw it, he said jokingly, "Why is your anger aroused against the attendant who did this to you? He spilled the gravy on you because he saw a stain on your character!"

—Joshua Hakohen of Sochaczew, "Ez Avot," in *Hiddushei Maharakh*

The 1813 event described in this tale exemplifies the hall of mirrors that is early Hasidism's social visage. Rather than chastising the servant for staining the elder's white garment, the zaddik endows his clumsiness with allegorical significance and chastises the haughty elder instead. As in Buber's tale "The Horses," cited at the beginning of this book, there occurs a delightfully ironic inversion of social ranks. At the Hasidic court, according to Chaim Zytlowski's fecund imagination, "[t]he meanest beggar might enter the most sumptuous room and lie with his muddy boots upon the sofa, and, without let or hindrance, order the rich man about, as though he were his own brother. It is not to be wondered at, therefore, that the new doctrine gained instant victory over the old order of things." But such notions are quickly dispelled when we recall that the 1813 episode was orchestrated by a zaddik who was, himself, ensconced in the elite. Why, we must ask, were these zaddikim forever pretending to subvert the very social hierarchy that sustained them? Considering the political astuteness witnessed in earlier chapters, it would seem they had discovered that the mere appearance of solidarity with commoners had tremendous resonance. But their folksy leadership style could have also been inspired by something more than political expediency. In this chapter, I will make the case that Polish zaddikim were additionally motivated by a genuine sympathy for the masses which, however, fell short of a willingness to grant them greater access to sociopolitical power.

The struggles attending the initial rise of Hasidism are best understood as an internecine elite conflict in which the populism of the zaddikim prevailed over the unconcealed exclusivism of old-style hasidim, the most prominent of Mitnaggdim. The impact of Hasidic populism on the old order was indeed dramatic, although not quite in the way that Zytlowski and others conceived it. In one sense, zaddikim did contribute to the leveling of the old order. Jewish spiritual authority had previously been divided between a normative, official leadership composed of rabbis, judges, *shtadlanim* (lobbyists), and kosher slaughterers on the one hand and a more popular, informal leadership composed of *maggidim* (preachers) and *ba'alei shem*. The latter were for the most part itinerant—communities only placed members of those professions on their payroll inconsistently.[1] This meant that the religious head of the local kahal, or *av bet din*, commanded a secure and distant station compared to itinerant preachers and *ba'alei shem*, who were dependent on their popular reception. Excepting the rare cases where they attained celebrity, their prestige and political influence were weak. Zaddikim collapsed this popular/normative distinction by appropriating the functions of rabbis, judges, lobbyists, *maggidim,* and *ba'alei shem* alike. Although they tolerated the continued existence of those offices, they subordinated them to their own authority. Thus, while zaddikim did conflate the old hierarchy, they imposed themselves above it and thus created a new stratification.

The blurring of the boundary between official and popular religious leadership can be observed in the case of zaddikim themselves. Many had served in traditional formal or informal capacities before achieving their new status. Some had been *maggidim,* while others had served as town rabbis. This was particularly true of the first generations of Polish zaddikim. Yet there is little to suggest that a zaddik who happened to be a preacher by vocation, such as R. Israel "the Maggid" of Kozienice, was any less influential than a zaddik who was a town rabbi, like R. Levi Isaac of Berdyczów. True, as mentioned in chapter 2, R. Meir of Stopnica/Opatów might proclaim himself "Chief of the Hasidim" on the grounds that he claimed both the title of zaddik and that of Rabbi of Opatów. But there is no evidence that this preeminence was recognized by any but his own devotees. Each of these leaders was first and foremost a zaddik who happened to exercise traditional functions. It was as zaddikim that they possessed supreme spiritual authority.

Jacob Katz describes the consequences for the rabbinate:

> Although the authority of the rabbi in his own designated field was apparently preserved, in fact his status had contracted and his influence had declined. A role reversal had occurred. In the traditional period, it was the halakhic scholar who represented the ultimate goal of religion—the observance of the precepts as prescribed—while the preacher, the teacher of *agada* and ethics, was his assistant. Now the situation was reversed. The goal was to achieve a certain standard of Hasidic piety, a standard embodied by the zaddik, who helped his followers achieve it. The halakhist rabbi had dropped to the rank of a mere aid.[2]

The town rabbi ceased to be the final spiritual arbiter and became more of a functionary whose duties were confined to determining minutia of Jewish Law. Often he was the appointee of a zaddik who, as Katz reminds us, might be a mere *maggid*. According to Alexander Tsederbaum, writing in 1867, zaddikim appointed not only rabbis but judges, slaughterers, cantors, teachers, beadles, and even bathhouse attendants throughout their scattered domains.[3] As for itinerant religious functionaries, whose authority was even less secure, zaddikim toured their territories whenever the spirit moved them, preaching and setting up their own miracle enterprises. We know that zaddikim in the Ukraine, at least, secured exclusive *maggidut* contracts in the towns that constituted their domains.[4] *Ba'alei shem* and *maggidim* accordingly took on an increasingly harried aspect as the nineteenth century advanced.

This conflation and subversion of traditional roles could not but elicit the most truculent opposition on the part of non-Hasidic elites. For nearly everyone else, however, it meant unprecedented accessibility to powerful spiritual luminaries. Those who were denied access to the yeshiva and old-style *kloyz* and would have had difficulty gaining audience with one of the towering Talmudic authorities obtained a newfound spiritual immediacy at the zaddik's court. It was not only that a paragon of piety worshiped, preached, dined, and danced in their presence. Even the most bilious testimonies admit that the zaddik was willing, however briefly, to privately address any petitioner's pressing spiritual and material concerns, regardless of status. Women experiencing difficulty conceiving, young people tormented by depression, small-scale merchants in need of business advice, and the most destitute Jews were all granted audience with scions of the rabbinic and mercantile elite who were ready to employ magic or theurgy on their behalf. The *pidyon* probably seemed a small price to pay for their ministrations.

Hasidism accordingly presents an exception to what Peter Burke has described as the increased tendency of the eighteenth century European upper classes to withdraw from popular culture, as "clergy, nobility and bourgeoisie alike were coming to internalize the ethos of self-control and order" and reject the language and culture of ordinary people.[5] The engagement of zaddikim in popular religion is, to be certain, also distinct from the detached rediscovery of folk culture by nineteenth-century university-educated ethnographers, who found its artifacts quaint, exotic, and fascinating.[6] Zaddikim, whether of the early or later generations,[7] embraced folk religion and magic wholeheartedly, as did many other members of the east European Jewish elite. As a cadre of miracle workers graced with education, *yihus*, wealth, decorum, and political prowess who often favored theurgical prayer over more blatant magical practices, they rendered popular religiosity more palatable to fellow elites, particularly those exposed to the waves of science and Enlightenment that were beginning to sweep Polish cities. Thus, while Immanuel Etkes asserts that zaddikim mitigated the practice of magic by substituting prayers for charms and spells, it seems more likely that they actually elevated the prestige of magic by refining and further professionalizing the tawdry business of miracle-working.[8]

The importance of the popular dimension of Hasidism, as argued throughout this book, was greatly overemphasized by proponents of the "Dubnow School." However, it would be equally misguided to try to disregard the movement's folk appeal, which needs rather to be placed in proper perspective. This may be approached from several different vantage points. First, we will compare zaddikim to their *ba'al shem* competitors to discern any significant differences among the former in terms of practices and social status. Second, we will test the degree to which the motivations behind popular religious practices of zaddikim transcended political opportunism by evaluating contemporaneous accusations of charlatanism together with claims that they were champions of the common folk. And third, we will test the boundaries of Hasidic popular religion through the rationalistic Przysucha school, whose reticence concerning magic and miracles is well known. In each of these cases, Polish zaddikim emerge as both stewards of popular religion and guardians of social hierarchy, aspirations that were not at all mutually exclusive.

Ba'alei shem and Zaddikim of the Early Nineteenth Century: A Comparison

Shortly after the formation of the Congress Kingdom in 1815, police were vexed by a proliferation of reports of miracle enterprises.[9] Such enterprises were seen as nothing more than attempts by charlatans to manipulate the naive masses, and the police were usually quick to bring the culprits to justice. The phenomenon was widespread in both Christian and Jewish society; however, the police discovered that the case of the Jews was more complicated. There appeared to be two different breeds of Jewish miracle workers: "Kabbalists" (i.e., *ba'alei shem*) and "prophets" (i.e., zaddikim). While the former were easily intimidated and controlled, the latter proved well connected and required more delicate handling. Police treatment of *ba'alei shem* accordingly stood in sharp contrast to that of zaddikim, despite the similarity of their activities.

Historians have tended to neglect *ba'alei shem* after the rise of Hasidism, which creates the impression that their vocation was appropriated completely by zaddikim. Yet *ba'alei shem* were witnessed continuously throughout the nineteenth century. In 1826, the Christian missionary E. Henderson denounced Jews who "arrogate to themselves the title—*ba'alei ha-shem*, "Possessors of the Name"; pretending that they have received the true mystery and signification of the incommunicable name of Jehovah, by which is conceded to them the power of working miracles."[10] Abraham Gottlober (1810–99) encountered *ba'alei shem* in Starokonstantynów (the Ukraine) during his childhood. A local *ba'al shem* named Abraham Jacob charged Gottlober with the task of hand-copying esoteric books and manuscripts for him. One day, Starokonstantynów was graced with a visit by a more renowned *ba'al shem* from Lemberg, Berish, who possessed a book with the names of "one hundred demons, each with its sign and the wonders which one could effect through it, and by means of the charms written there."[11] Notwithstanding threats of demonic persecution, Gottlober copied the book. After his marriage in 1823, he and a young Ruzhiner Hasid put the book to use by attempting a magical shortening of a journey (*kefizat ha-derekh*).[12] They hung amulets around their necks, raced hither and thither, descended upon the *bet midrash*, terrified a small boy, and finally stood still, too exhausted to continue. Gottlober recalls, "I was a prisoner in my house for many days after that, and could not exit or enter, for my legs were swollen and the pain was enormous."[13] The book's ineffectiveness pushed Gottlober further along the path to Haskalah.

The Maskil Chaim Aronson recalls how in Vilna, in 1841, his friend Eliezer cynically proposed that they travel throughout eastern Europe together; "he would be a miracle-worker, and I would be his collector and assistant." Eliezer proposed:

> You will tell them that I am the son of the renowned Kabbalist and Rabbi of the holy city of Doikloik;[14] that I have been acclaimed by all the great Rabbis of Lithuania and Zamot[15] as a very holy person who has driven out many *dybbuks* and cured many epileptics; that I can adjure demons and spirits; that in a certain city I raised the dead who had been in their graves for ten years; and have also made barren women fertile. Indeed, who has not heard of the famous miracle-worker Rabbi Eliezer of Doikloik? You will then see that the idiots will send me their barren wives and their sick women, with gifts of money.[16]

Some nineteenth-century *ba'alei shem* were thus conscious pranksters and charlatans, in apparent contrast to those of prior centuries.[17]

Complaints against *ba'alei shem* appeared in late nineteenth-century integrationist-oriented publications. In 1872, a German Jewish memoirist from the western Polish city of Leszno recorded their exploits.[18] And in 1896, the Polish journalist Henryk Lew lamented, "*ba'alei shem* not only contribute to the dissemination of superstitions, but also take advantage of people in every possible way," extracting money from ill or barren Jews.[19] Significantly, Lew drew a clear distinction between *ba'alei shem* and zaddikim, asserting that the former were "even more harmful than zaddikim" because they worked primarily as unlicensed doctors.[20] Lew seemingly considered zaddikim less threatening because they did not confine themselves to amateur medicine. It is important to note, as well, that non-Jewish society claimed its own informal healers. In 1884, for example, a Polish shepherd operating as a medicine man in the Opoczyn church was discovered by authorities.[21]

The distinctions between *ba'alei shem* and zaddikim thus far seem to relate primarily to self-image. The former were more modest in claiming only specific magical abilities deriving from charms, names, spells, and physical remedies that might, in theory, be accessed by anyone who could read charm books. Of course, piety and purification rites were prerequisites to applying their prescriptions, as Etkes has pointed out.[22] But Berish's threats against Gottlober, should he dare to copy his book of charms, amounts to an acknowledgement of their wide accessibility. Moreover, even this more renowned *ba'al shem* relied on books of charms rather than the innate prophetic powers claimed by the Besht and, later, zaddikim (remote vision, prognostication, ability to hear decrees, ability to heal through ecstatic prayer, etc.).[23] Perhaps the absence of claims to native exceptionalism among *ba'alei shem* invited imposters like Eliezer.

Notwithstanding this underlying difference, however, the services provided by both types of practitioners in the popular religious realm were often outwardly indistinguishable. This may be witnessed in cases involving what was considered the premier mental health issue of the day: demonic possession. A principle function of *ba'alei shem* and zaddikim alike was to exorcise dybbuks—demons created out of the souls of Jews who had sinned so deeply that they could neither transmigrate, nor enter Gehennah (the purgatorial Hell), and had to wander on earth as demons.[24] What we find in such cases is a tendency to employ a blend of theurgical and magical formulae like the chanting of psalms, blowing of *shofars*, composition of amulets, and uttering of divine names. It appears that zaddikim preferred the age-old methods of *ba'alei shem* during such crisis situations.

By the seventeenth century, dybbuks were reportedly increasingly seeking refuge in the bodies of young Jews.[25] According to nineteenth-century Polish ethnographic studies and Hebrew accounts alike, they could enter their victims when a doorway lacked a *mezzuzah* (doorway parchment) or a perfunctory blessing was forgotten. They preyed upon children when they yawned, men who did not wear ritual fringes, women without aprons, women who read secular books, and ordinarily pious individuals who sinned, forgot to say their prayers, failed to give alms, or made a false oath.[26] Demonic possession was a socially acceptable way to express anxiety among unmarried women and pre-Bar Mitzvah boys, that is, those poised on the threshold of adulthood and who thus inhabited a social "no man's-land."[27] The possessed were expected to indulge in normally unacceptable conduct like speaking non-Jewish languages, professing an inability to utter the name of God, blaspheming, mocking religious services, and most embarrassingly of all, recounting everybody's sins.[28]

Jewish demoniacal beliefs were nourished by the surrounding Polish culture. According to Tobias Hakohen, "[o]ne cannot find a land where people engage more in matters of spirits, amulets, spells, names and dreams than in the aforementioned land" (i.e., eighteenth-century Poland).[29] Polish demonic lore was, however, much richer than its relatively narrow and formulaic Jewish counterpart, with non-Jewish demons appearing in greater variety (devils, spirits, goblins, hobgoblins, ghosts, spooks, and phantoms);[30] residing more often in natural settings like forests, bodies of water, swamps, and the ground; and using millers, shepherds, carpenters, beekeepers, and hunters as spies in order to stalk their victims.[31] One might be possessed by as many as five demons at once, as in the case of an unfortunate Lublin man.[32] Those most susceptible were drunks, one who yawned while passing though the forest, and one who doubted religious belief, cursed, or blasphemed.[33] The Christian possessed were unable to stay in church during the sacraments, unwilling to recite psalms, suddenly familiar with foreign languages and lofty subjects, able to prophesy, and endowed with super-human strength.[34]

Non-Jewish demons were extremely physical and violent. They were called "breakers of the ill" because they beat the possessed in addition to shaking and contorting them. One demon flung a Tarnów girl against a wall; another pelted priests and ministers with pitch and manure and stuffed the head of a fourteen-year-old boy into a hot oven; and others forced their victims to commit crimes ranging from theft to murder.[35] They often tried to exit through the eyes or stomach in order to injure the possessed.[36] A Polish miracle diary kept from 1705 and 1720 includes four exorcisms, that is, about one every four years.[37] Such exorcisms could be more violent than the possessions themselves, involving beating or flagellating the possessed and flinging excruciating holy water on them.[38] Exorcists were supposed to be elderly priests, pure in faith and deeds, who recited specific prayers and verses of proven effectiveness.[39] Nevertheless, victims would seek help from whomever they could, including sorcerers and Jewish miracle workers.[40] A Polish nobleman approached the zaddik of Bełz for help with a possessed son; but the zaddik referred them to a small-town priest (upon whom the demon was then transferred).[41] A peasant from Olesk was persuaded that his mentally ill son was possessed by a "Jewish demon" (dybbuk), but sued to prevent having to pay for the ba'al shem's expensive and ineffective amulets.[42]

In contrast to their non-Jewish counterparts, most ba'alei shem and zaddikim followed the more docile prescriptions of the Safed Kabbalist Hayyim Vital, who prescribed prayers with special mystical concentration (yihudim), placing a finger on the pulse of the possessed, reciting biblical verses and Names, blowing the shofar, placing amulets on the possessed, and bargaining with the dybbuk by invoking threats of excommunication and promises to pray on its behalf. However, the Maggid of Kozienice was not beyond beating the dybbuk out of male victims with his cane;[43] while the late nineteenth-century zaddik Samuel Abba of Żychlin struck a possessed girl in the face with a lulov until she bled.[44] Their divergences from Vital's script suggest external influence. After the dybbuk departed, usually through the left toe of the possessed, the former victim behaved like a renewed person, forgot the whole incident, and seemed surprised by the presence of bystanders. Most important, the erstwhile victim now reacquired the ability to pray, signaling his or her return to normative Jewish society.⁴⁵

Jewish exorcists had to possess knowledge of holy names, and were exclusively *ba'alei shem* before the emergence of Hasidism.⁴⁶ The first public act performed by the Besht himself was an exorcism; however, the demon's departure of his own will, without the customary threats and bargaining, signaled that here was a *ba'al shem* of an entirely new order.⁴⁷ Gedaliya Nigal argues that only zaddikim who possessed the requisite knowledge of Names performed exorcisms.⁴⁸ This would mean that *ba'alei shem* could be considered superior exorcists owing to their arsenals of time-worn techniques and theurgically potent names. Nor were qualified zaddikim necessarily successful. The Maggid of Kozinice expelled a dybbuk from the daughter of R. Reuven of Grodzisk; she had begun speaking an "alien language" and had lost the ability to recite the name of God. Yet, in spite of an amulet that the Maggid composed for her, the dybbuk came back and prevented her from going to synagogue during the High Holy Days until Yom Kippur, at which time she created a spectacle with her "mocking and derision by laughing, giddiness, and speaking a foreign tongue, God forbid." Later, the dybbuk explained that he had been able to return to her because a portion of the Maggid's amulet had been inadvertently erased.⁴⁹ However, those who dared to express skepticism about the ability of zaddikim to exorcise demons were said to be destined to transmigrate in the form of a spirit.⁵⁰ In conclusion, the example of exorcisms serves to illustrate how difficult it is to differentiate between the *ba'al shem* and zaddik on the basis of the content of their popular religious services.

Distinctions do, however, materialize on the social plane. The social status of *ba'alei shem* appears to have become markedly inferior by the turn of the nineteenth century, in contrast to the exalted social level of most zaddikim demonstrated in the previous chapter. One no longer finds the *ba'al shem*-rabbis or scholars of prior centuries like R. Elijah of Chelm, R. Elijah of Luanez, R. Joel Halpern, R. Naftali Katz of Poznań, R. Hirsch Fraenkel, R. Binyamin Binush, and R. Joel II.⁵¹ Instead, we are confronted with a ragtag group of small-time miracle workers, occasionally unscrupulous, whose demeanor implies a deprofessionalization of the vocation by this time.

The social distinctions between early nineteenth-century *ba'alei shem* and zaddikim and the ensuing consequences are illuminated in a police report from 1818. Bearing the sarcastic title "Prophets of the Mosaic Persuasion," the file contains back-to-back investigations into the enterprises of a *ba'al shem* and a zaddik in Warsaw. The first report describes an exorcism by a *ba'al shem* in the market square, and is transcribed in full in appendix 2. To summarize, a Jew from Wyszogród arrived in Warsaw with his twelve-year-old son who was "ill with something like convulsions," intending to check him into the Jewish Hospital. After unsuccessful treatment, the father proceeded to a *ba'al shem* ("Kabbalist") who had just arrived from Białystok. The *ba'al shem* examined the boy and declared that he was possessed by a dybbuk.⁵²

In a section marked "omit" because it was deemed irrelevant to the case, the informant is revealed as a Maskil:

I was with this boy on [the] eve of the departure of the spirit, which was September 7, 1818. Glancing at me, he asked: "Is he also a Jew? Why do I not recognize his clothes?" I answered him, that it is so. The boy said, "If you are a Jew, show me your *Cyces*. . . ." I told him, Silence! Again, he asked further: "Why does he shave his beard if he is a Jew?" I gave him the answer: that this is the custom among German Jews. "But that is against the commandment that the beard may not be shaved!" cried the boy. Here, everyone was silent, and I was not a little bit confused, for every eye turned toward me.

Through the Maskil's eyes, we are privy to the interweaving of religion and magic in a popular religious ritual: the *ba'al shem* invokes names of angels like spells, blows a *shofar*, chants psalms, hurls bans of excommunication, and even allows the dybbuk to rest on the Sabbath. Reinforcing religious observance is thus a central motivation, although the Maskil is quick to remind police of the *ba'al shem*'s economic motivation. By the performance's conclusion, the broken taboo that had caused the dybbuk to be created in the first place—conversion to Christianity—is redressed through the redemption of the dybbuk's soul, while the young victim's renewed ability to pray signals his return to tradition. The Maskil is the only unredeemed, liminal figure at the performance's conclusion, for it is *his* faithfulness to the tradition that is now in question. Only in the second half of the nineteenth century would testimony in a similar skeptical vein begin to appear.[53]

Another of the *ba'al shem*'s endeavors is described at the end of the report. In this case, the *ba'al shem* claimed that a demon had sought completion inside the body of a woman through sexual intercourse rather than possession:

There is a Jewish midwife here in Warsaw, whose married daughter has been ill for several years. For this reason, she stays with her mother. This woman took this same Kabbalist into her apartment in order to heal her daughter. The Kabbalist declared that the cause of her daughter's illness is that she used to sleep at night with an evil spirit, and even claimed that her youngest of three children was produced by this spirit. Nevertheless, she continued to live with her husband at the same time. Furthermore, he said that if the mother of the children is to get healthy, these children must die. It is easy to imagine how these children are now afflicted by their parents, and how costly bad beliefs must be for them.[54]

This incident depicts "the incubus and the succubus," an outgrowth of legends in the *Midrash* and *Zohar* regarding the propagation of demons through sexual union with sleeping humans.[55] The case was particularly serious, for the *ba'al shem* advised the mother to have her daughter's children killed. Despite its drastic ramifications, however, this case did not preoccupy the Polish authorities as much as the exorcism, perhaps because it was not witnessed directly.

In their reactions, the police reflected an enlightened worldview, echoing concerns about "the exploitation of the gullibility of the Jewish population" and the "harmful consequences" of such behavior.[56] During the ensuing investigation, the *ba'al shem* was identified as one Berek Baruchowicz, assistant rabbi of Białystok. In order to prevent "further similar perversity," it was suggested that he receive strict admonishment, be expelled from the country, and return to Białystok.[57] The possessed boy, identified as Zusman, son of Lewek Samsonowicz, was sent to a Warsaw doctor who "most conscientiously examined Zusman's state of health and aforementioned malady." The boy was then taken to the Jewish Hospital, while the father was taken back home to Wyszogród. Berek Baruchowicz, after a stern rebuke, was ordered to leave Warsaw. He departed for Białystok a week later.[58]

The Polish authorities, like their Russian counterparts, were more interested in apprehending those they considered sorcerers than the victims of possession, who they viewed in light of the emerging field of psychiatry.[59] The final report of D. Rudnicki and A. Kerslij from September 15, 1818, is laced with sarcasm and humor. Upon carefully examining the father and son three times at their residence at 1421 Zielna Street, it was determined that Zusman had "confused thoughts owing to a strong nervous disorder." The *ba'al shem* had taken advantage of the boy's genuine disorder, which had elicited a "double effect: the appearance of exceedingly stupid Jews, and . . . an occasion for an equally dark fanatic [i.e., the *ba'al shem*] to conduct a laughable ceremony aimed at expelling an imaginary evil spirit from the sick boy." The *ba'al shem* had exploited the boy's crisis of illness in order to deepen the belief of the Jewish rabble in the existence of demons, and had permanently deformed the boy's small left toe—the point of departure for the demon.[60] They recommended:

> 1) That the young Zusman, being poor and sick, will end his escapades receiving treatment in the Jewish Hospital; 2) The Rabbi, however, who dared to confirm Jews in their stupidity and harmful beliefs through methodical, careless treatment of the ill—it is best that he be given a passport in order to return to the place from whence he came, so that in this holy, secluded spot he will first of all expel the same stupid demon from *himself*.[61]

Thus ended the Warsaw exploits of Berek Baruchowicz, the *ba'al shem* from Białystok.

Conveniently enough, the file also contains an investigation into the activities of the zaddik Moses of Kozienice, son and successor of R. Israel, the Maggid of Kozienice. The brevity of the investigation is, itself, telling. On January 30, 1819, the following report appeared:

> We have received information that several days ago there arrived in this city the Jew Moses of Kozienice, son of some famous, deceased prophet there [i.e., the Maggid]. Allegedly not being able to enter the unclean city, he remained behind the customs house on the road to Wola,[62] at the residence of a certain daughter of Melekh the Military Supplier, where crowds of Jewish folk assemble and collect considerable donations for him in return for blessings. The Police commis-

sion (K.R.W.R.P.P.), with the goal of preventing further swindling by the alleged prophet, has acknowledged the need to call upon the Warsaw municipality (KSP.MiP.MSW) to utilize all this information to stop the abuse immediately, using prudent methods. The Police Commission has deemed it proper to call the Jew Moses to present his accounts from his collection of considerable donations from the naive people.[63]

The police restraint in this case contrasts sharply with their swift prosecution and banishment of the *ba'al shem*. They still opposed the exploitation of gullible Jews via their "considerable donations" to the alleged prophet, yet for some reason they urged "prudent methods" in putting an end to R. Moses' activities. The police appear above all concerned about financial considerations, demanding that R. Moses present his "accounts" from the donations, presumably for taxation.

Why the different treatment? First, R. Moses was not so audacious as to set up his operation in a major thoroughfare in Warsaw, but rather remained behind the customs house on the road to Wola. In light of the willingness of other Polish zaddikim to visit "unclean" Warsaw, as well as the sanction of "worship through corporeality," we may conclude that discreetness, rather than fear of contamination, motivated his choice of location. We are also privy to a detail about R. Moses' temporary residence: the house of the daughter of a military supplier named Melekh. This connection with a military supplier, possibly a person of wealth and influence, could further explain the zaddik's lenient treatment. In any case, when R. Moses' operation was exposed, he proved ready to withdraw to his home base. It was next reported that "Israel [*sic*] Moses of Kozienice" left Warsaw and returned to Kozienice of his own accord, without punishment or rebuke.[64] As in the case of the zaddik Meir of Stopnica/Opatów in 1825 and the investigations of 1818 and 1824 (chapters 2 and 3), the authorities felt compelled to adopt a policy of prudence and leniency. We may conclude that the most important qualities that distinguished zaddikim included discreetness, savvy, operational agility, and an effective patronage network, attributes that would seem to have derived from their more exalted social status. As for their *ba'al shem* competitors, it seems that their inferior status by the nineteenth century influenced many historians to anachronistically project that status upon *ba'alei shem* from prior centuries.[65]

Zaddikim in the Eyes of Mitnaggdim, Maskilim, Non-Jews, and Hasidim

Recognition of the differences between *ba'alei shem* and zaddikim allows us to better understand the relative silence of Mitnaggdim and Maskilim over the former and their near obsession over the latter. It seems likely that suspicions over zaddikim were aroused in part because of their higher social status: why would *shayne yidn* (elites) bother with commoners, if not from malevolent motives like greed, vanity, and lust for power? An additional reason for their singling out of zaddikim seems to have been the superior scale, organization, and stability of their popular religious enterprises, which alarmed both those who were vested in the kahal hegemony and those who sought to modernize Jewish society. The inferior status and lack of organizational élan among *ba'alei shem* made them much less threatening.

Such attitudes render the testimony of Mitnaggdim and Maskilim problematic, but not useless. Neutral or sympathetic concessions do occasionally crop up; and several non-Hasidic witnesses actually went so far as to describe zaddikim as champions of the common people ("lovers of Israel") who employed folk remedies to alleviate their desperate plight. Hasidic claims are no less problematic, suffering as they do from positive hyperbole. A Hasid, by definition, was blinded by love for his zaddik, although he might exhibit ambivalence toward rival zaddikim. Not surprisingly, certain Hasidic testimonies depict their leaders' ministrations to the common people as completely altruistic, and deny any possible opportunism. However, occasionally there appears testimony that inadvertently highlights the elitist proclivities of zaddikim by illustrating, for example, the favoritism shown toward scions of elites. At the same time, there are Hasidic testimonies in which zaddikim reveal their sincere belief in magic and miracles. Thus, although variant testimonies can be irreconcilable, it is still possible to extract their nonpolemical elements and distill a net impression about the motivations informing Hasidic popular religion.

Three waves of traditionalist opposition arose in response to the burgeoning movement. The first occurred in 1772, a reaction to the establishment of a Hasidic prayer house in Vilna. The second, in 1781, followed the publication of the first Hasidic book, *Toldot Ya'akov Yosef* (Korzec, 1780). The third, sparked by the publication of *Tanya* (Sławuta, 1796) by R. Shneur Zalman of Liady, extended into the nineteenth century.[66] In the numerous bans and screeds accompanying these waves of opposition, one finds strenuous objections to Hasidic concepts like worship through corporeality. According to R. David of Maków, zaddikim taught that even fantasies about gentile women during prayer could be uplifted, which he charged was tantamount to bringing an idol into a holy place: "Who can restrain himself and not shout 'Hoy!' over the abomination and heresy of introducing an idol into the Supernal Palace. But when the 'strange thought' of some Gentile woman whose name is Kaszka or Margarita (their profane names) appears, he has to raise *them* into the Supernal Sanctity!"[67] Thus, while the Besht argued that "straying thoughts" during prayer could be consecrated, Mitnaggdim considered them abominations to be scrupulously avoided.[68] Additional objections related to the social consequences of Hasidic concepts. These included separate prayer houses in which prayer liturgy, times, and methods were altered and decorum was dispensed with; changes in ritual slaughter; neglect of Torah study and disrespect for scholars; merrymaking and antinomian—even Sabbatean—beliefs; bizarre behavior and dress; and greed and exploitation of fellow Jews.[69] In the case of Polish zaddikim, at least, accusations of greed and exploitation predominated.

The third phase of the Hasidic-Mitnaggdic controversy saw the composition of several classics of anti-Hasidic literature, including R. Israel Loebel of Słuck's *Sefer Viku'ah* (Warsaw, 1798) and R. David of Maków's *Zemir Arizim* (Warsaw, 1798), in addition to *Shever Posh'im*, which was unpublished until recently.[70] The tracts were written in a stylistic form called *melizah*—a mosaic of biblical verses and rabbinic dicta cited out of context, often eliciting the opposite effect intended in their sources. The reader who recognized the original contexts of the verses was jolted by their new, ironic application. The biblical and rabbinic raw material not only lent a veneer of mock-holiness to the subject being vilified, but additionally enabled the author to show off his learnedness and dexterity.[71]

Perhaps because both anti-Hasidic classics were published in Warsaw, Polish zaddikim were most frequently lampooned in these tracts. Both R. David and R. Israel personally encountered them. R. David of Maków seems to have been best acquainted with R. Levi Isaac of Berdyczów, recalling how Polish Hasidim delayed their afternoon prayer until after the appearance of the stars, and the evening prayer until close to midnight, "as I saw in Żelechów," when R. Levi Isaac served as rabbi there.[72] R. Levi Isaac is also known to have visited R. David's town of Maków, where a devotee by the name of R. Lizer resided.[73] R. Israel Loebel encountered the Maggid of Kozienice and the Seer of Lublin in the winter of 1797 by posing as a petitioner. The unsuspecting zaddikim promised to ensure that his prayers were answered, but the joke was on them: not even the "Seer" perceived that R. Israel Loebel's prayers were for their destruction![74]

Remaining as faithful as possible to R. David's *melizah* style, departing only from his rhymes, we behold the following grotesque depiction of R. Levi Isaac's visit to a small town:

> The Rabbi, Hasid, *av bet din* of the holy community of Żelechów,
> who is full of Torah, to him applies the law of first born;[75] he, too,
> behaves unseemly. Descending upon the town with his quorum of
> Hasidim, he saunters in, "like a vision of horses is their appearance,
> and like horsemen they gallop" [Joel 2:4]; "Before them the land was
> like the Garden of Eden, and after them, a desolate wilderness, and
> nothing escapes them" [Joel 2:3]. The *gabbai*[76] roars aloud, "Set on
> the pot, set it on, and also pour water into it" [Ez. 24:4]. One person
> brings the light, and one brings the wood and the fire, and the third
> arranges the great layout[77] to throw them a feast, "the shoulder and
> broad tail" [I Sam. 9:24].[78] "And the fire of the layout[79] burning in it
> shall not be extinguished" [Lev. 6:6], "the bonfire is of much fire
> and wood . . . like a stream of brimstone, he kindles it" [Is. 30:33].[80]

R. Levi Isaac was "full of Torah," an admission that should be underscored; but this only rendered his boorish behavior more repellent: he and his hordes would roll into a given town and proceed to eat up everything in sight.

The host, ashamed to refuse a zaddik's demands, impoverished his household to supply the feast:

"And the poor man had nothing except one small lamb which he bought . . ." [II Sam., 12:3] for his bread and the bread of his household, to sustain his life. And because shame clouds his vision, he does not have pity on his flock, and does not have mercy on his offspring, and he acts like "a [brutal] raven to his son" [Talmud Yerushalmi, Kiddushin 1:7], as is the custom of the newly arrived guest. And when he cooked the meat and the *gabbai* arrived with fork in-hand, "and he stuck it into the pan, or kettle, or cauldron, or pot; all that the fork brought up, he took" [I Sam. 2:14] for his meal, "piece by piece, take it out" [Ez. 24:6], cooked or half-cooked. And "when you were in the flesh-pots" [Ex. 27:3] "and the flesh is half consumed" [Num. 12:12], he ate it, and after a minute "stamped the remainder with his feet" [Dan. 7:7], "every choice piece, thigh and shoulder" [Ez. 24:4], they ate more than enough. And it is permissible "to trip over their feet" [Ez. 34:19] to bring it before the Rabbi.[81]

The Hasidim feasted away at their poor host's expense, only pausing to bring the choice pieces to the zaddik.

Next, we encounter R. Levi Isaac himself, a drunken glutton who gorged himself at his poor host's expense:

The rabbi "sits upon his stately bed, and a table prepared before it" [Ez. 23:41], before his crowd, roaring from all the happy and joyous men and women. And the Rabbi says to the host: "Serve me, and I will eat from your game, that my soul will bless you" [Gen. 27:25]. The rabbi "blesses . . . with a loud voice, rising early in the morning, it shall be reckoned a curse to him" [Prov. 27:14]. And after he blessed the leg, lying like a lion at its prey, his teeth gnashing, and ate the meat and soup "like the vegetable garden" [Deut. 11:11],[82] until there were barely any remains, "he ate until his mind wandered" [B.T. Ber. 44a]. The host stands around, his teeth menacing, "and a lean, meager portion" [Michah 6:10]. "Sparks of fire leap out" [Job 41:11], "covering his upper lip" [Lev. 13:46]. "Smoke pours out his nostrils" [Job 41:12] "like the smoke of a furnace" [Ex. 19:18]. "And a flame goes out of his mouth" [Job 41:13], [R. Levi Isaac] drank and exhausted the remaining cups. "In his neck resides strength" [Job 41:14], "he drinks up a river" [Job 40:23], and it will rush no longer. "A flame goes out of his mouth [Job 41:13], "and terror dances before him" [Job 41:14]. And afterward he lies on his bed and takes his afternoon nap until midnight.[83]

Having watched helplessly as the zaddik ate his fill, drank rivers of alcohol, and fell asleep, the host noticed that he himself had been denied a satisfying portion.

His despair only increased the next day, when he awoke to find his house left desolate:

"And it came to pass in the morning that his spirit was troubled"
[Gen. 41:8], that is, the host; all that remains is "like an abyss without fish" [Berakhot 9b]. And without food and provision, there is
neither prophet nor vision! And rising with singing and chanting,
all raise their voices in lamentation and despair. And he answers
like an echo, "How I remain alone!" [Lamentations 1:1]. "He made
me like an empty vessel, swallowed me . . . and filled his belly with
my delicacies [Jer. 51:34]. "This is the portion of his spoil, and the
fate of his plunder" [Is. 17:4].[84]

When the food and drink were gone, zaddik and followers were gone. What,
possibly, could the attraction have been for such Hasidic sympathizers, aside
from their hesitancy to refuse an alleged zaddik? Some clues appear in
R. David's biblical admonitions against accepting false prophecy and medical
remedies: "Israel shall know it: the prophet is a . . . crazy man of spirit" (Hosea
9:7), his rubbish "is like an open tomb" (Jer. 5:16) "but he cannot heal you, nor
cure you of your wound" (Hosea 5:13), "and the helper shall stumble, and the
helped shall fall" (Is. 31:3).[85] The masses were sacrificing their possessions for
the zaddik's prophecies and cures.

R. David then turns to R. Israel, the Maggid of Kozienice, who had recently
enlisted "the wealthy in the city of Warsaw" to suppress this very tract.[86] He is
initially defensive over publicly condemning the Maggid, who is considered a
Talmudic scholar, arguing that the Maggid's sins and blasphemy are such that
they require a public rebuke.[87] Besides, the Maggid's many activities as zaddik
surely precluded Torah study:

And first of all, I will ask them to answer: how can it be that his
"Torah and faith" [Sotah, 21a], keeps him from sleeping? Does he
not need to make space between the supernal cleaning and between
the chapters to heal the sick and bless the women, to take *pidyon
nefesh*, and to prescribe remedies according to Kabbalah, helping
barren women, slaying evil with the breath of his lips, prescribing
penitence to sinners, ascents of the soul, traveling through the Garden of Eden "in partnership with heaven" [Berakhot 34a], and all his
other needs; praying for rain and for "those who go down to the
sea" and traverse the deserts [Is. 42:10–11], and over many evils and
sorrows—after troubling with all these things, he is of course disinclined to study one hour in a month or all year.[88]

How could the Maggid possibly find time to study, consumed as he was with
cures, blessings, curses, ascents, and prayers on behalf of his pilgrims?[89]

R. David appears particularly exercised over the Maggid's appeal among
women:

And the frivolous women, they "have perfected your beauty" [Ez. 27:
4], "with your eye-shadow" [Jer. 4:30], they gave you glory, joining

hands with you. You spread your wings over them to bless them with a hundred blessings, kept and arranged from birth, and from stomach, and from pregnancy, "from thence, from the shepherd, the Stone of Israel" [Gen. 49:24], and they say in heaven, there is none like the Lord, and on earth "who is like you" [Deut. 33:29] Israel. For they came to you "stricken and smitten" [Is. 53:4] with their sins and horrors, and you said "see, I have removed your sins and dressed you in festive costume." And when the poor who had hit rock bottom came to you, you said, "you shall once again 'bring forth boughs like a plant' " [Job 14:9] and bless God, who crowned Israel with glory. By promising every barren woman with a mouth full of "behold, you are pregnant" "and it is reversed through His stratagems" [Job 37:12]; and promising marvels and wonders through "the report of his power and his graceful speech" [Job 41:4]; all the women gave valuables and "broke the golden earrings from their ears" [Ex. 32:2].[90]

The Maggid was offering barren women, no matter how sinful, vain promises in return for their *pidyonot*. The final Job verses, referring to divine power in their original context, mock the Maggid's "stratagems" and "graceful speech" and the rumors of his "miracles." The Exodus verse implies that his *pidyonot* smack of idolatry.

R. David's most venomous attacks are reserved for the Seer of Lublin. Unlike R. Levi Isaac and the Maggid of Kozienice, the Seer is a total ignoramus, in R. David's estimation—a "king of hypocrites"[91] who "was never a Talmudic scholar and never will be":[92]

Around him gather herds and herds of Hasidim . . . he is late for the afternoon prayer. During the Days of Awe[93] all the Hasidim come, hither and thither to find shelter under his shade, and witness his magnitude, "and not for nothing does the starling go [with the raven], but because he is of his kind" [Baba Kama, 92b]. He chases bribes, with the soothsayers and wizards. In claiming, "I am a doctor" like smoke to the eyes, you are craftsman like vinegar to teeth.[94]

The Seer is only popular, the Baba Kama citation suggests, among ignoramuses. This can be refuted by mentioning disciples like the Holy Jew and R. Simha Bunem; however, it should be reiterated that the Seer did once admit that he had little time to devote scholarship.[95] In any case, the charge of ineffectual prophesying and healing for the sake of money ("bribes") resurfaces here. This perceived greed made the communalism among his followers reek of hypocrisy: as the Seer enriched himself, his Hasidim were like " 'partners sharing [courtyard] entrances' [Eruvin 71b], i.e., several, one like the other, money or clothes: the turbans and the veils, or booty; the gauze and linen, the tiaras and ornaments [Is. 3:18–22]."[96] And the Seer's loud, flamboyant prayers formed the sole basis for his claim to the titles of "Genius, Hasid, and Rabbi."[97]

To sum up, the charges against Polish zaddikim included profligacy, drunkenness, gluttony, neglect of Torah study and mocking scholars, excessive and inappropriate dealings with women, communal living, flamboyant and delayed perfunctory prayer, fake miracles, prophesies and cures, use of special knives for slaughtering, and, worst of all, charlatanism. Yet certain of these charges should not be accepted at face value. Concerning Hasidic slaughtering, for example, which is actually permitted by Jewish law (halakha), Chone Shmeruk points out its detrimental effect on the community revenues while Shaul Stampfer emphasizes the separation from the normative community its practice engendered.[98] As for the accusation of mocking of scholars, Adam Teller argues that what was most objectionable was its social ramifications: Mitnaggdim were usually old-style hasidim, who did not occupy an official rabbinical post but wielded "a new kind of spiritual authority based on seclusion and study." Such old-style hasidim, the most famous being R. Elijah, the Vilna Gaon, could not suffer Hasidism's devaluation of their ascetic, scholarly-based authority.[99]

It should also be observed that by this phase of the conflict many old-style hasidim now occupied kahal posts as preachers (*maggidim*), judges, and rabbis of important towns.[100] They were not representatives of the "establishment" in any formal or exclusive capacity, but had, according to Ya'akov Hasdai, become "integrated into the traditional leadership, cooperating and strengthening the *kehilah's* authority."[101] R. David of Maków and R. Israel Loebel of Słuck each served in a formal capacity as *maggidim* and judges in their respective towns.[102] R. David additionally managed to secure the Maków rabbinical post for his son.[103] In light of their vested interests in the normative communal structure, it is not surprising that they were most of all concerned about the spectacular popularity of the feasts, miracles, prophesies, and folk remedies of zaddikim. As mentioned earlier, they did not revile *ba'alei shem*, who might easily be accused of similar abuses on a lesser scale. Their silence over the latter suggests they were less troubled by the practice of folk religion per se than its performance on a grand, institutionalized scale by mystic-magicians among the elite who would encroach upon traditional prerogatives, draw masses of Jews outside of the kahal's orbit, and infiltrate and commandeer increasing numbers of kahals. That certain Polish zaddikim were recognized Torah scholars only rendered them all the more threatening.

Mitnaggdim did not, however, accuse zaddikim of promoting backwardness and superstition, for they do not seem to have rejected the efficacy of folk religion themselves. The idea of Hasidism as an impediment to the spread of rationalism, Enlightenment-based reform, and by extension, emancipation, was promoted by a new power-seeking group: acculturated Jews who may be loosely labeled Maskilim.[104] While several of their accusations, such as the exploitation of ostensibly naive women and young men through revelry and miracle working, recall those of Mitnaggdim, Maskilim distinguished themselves by denouncing miracle working in principle. Their proposed solutions were, moreover, steeped in innovation—only when Jews attained secular education, mastered non-Jewish languages, and conformed to the sartorial norms of non-Jewish society would they merit emancipation. Being more open to religious innovation themselves, Maskilim were apparently less worried by Hasidic deviations from religious traditions. What they found most objectionable was their alleged obscurantism, which poisoned the Jewish populace with ignorance and superstition. As a newly emergent group themselves, Maskilim may have needed that caricature of Hasidism against which to define their mission.[105]

Mendel Lefin of Satanów, a Galician zaddik who spent some time in Central Poland, saw in zaddikim only untrammeled greed and a penchant for intemperance, which they satisfied by enticing popular support through the cynical employment of fake miracles. In his *Essai d'un plan de Réforme* (1791), composed in Warsaw, Lefin charges that re-printings of the Kabbalistic classic the *Zohar* had "given birth to a new sect which makes zeal and faith the base-principle of religion," rather than reason.[106] Members of the sect "believe prophecy and monetary donations effect miracles, which they attribute to the leaders of their sect like an article of faith."[107] The new sect was almost universal in the Polish-Lithuanian Commonwealth because "it always recruits young people, whose credulity and age make them easy to ensnare."[108] Zaddikim encouraged followers to "engage as much as possible in singing their praises, to shore up their universal renown."[109] Another important cause of their success was their recruitment of the wealthy:

> This is why they pretend to serve their proselytes, and are enriched considerably by their donations. These faithful disciples have frequent occasions to convince themselves more and more of the great merit of their Masters, by beholding their numerous courts composed of rich pilgrims who visit them from many places, as well as by the elegance of their tables laden with silver vessels and with the most exquisite dishes of meat. Just as these great men know how to ennoble themselves through these earthly pleasures, they are believed to obtain the remission of sins more surely than the ancient laws that command tears and lamentations. This is the real mystery of the Dignity of these High Priests and of the new world of these higher luminaries.[110]

Their ostentatious display and "rich pilgrims" generated greater and greater followings, for visitors interpreted wealth a as sign of greatness and accepted their Epicureanism as being justified on religious grounds. In another tract, Lefin brings similar charges, claiming that zaddikim

> dress and sleep in expensive fine silks from the monies drawn from donations from the *pidyonot*, enjoying the galloping horse and a dancing chariot with a turtle wagon, with kitchen servants traveling after them, and who adorn their daughters and their wives with precious jewels and pearls, who make their secular times the sacred times of others, and their minds are comfortable with fattened [foods] and old wine that neither they nor their ancestors ever used.[111]

Occasionally, Lefin evinces religious concerns, as well. Hasidic feasting and licentiousness occurred in the synagogue itself, and Hasidic mourners wore a casual and joyous demeanor, standing by the synagogue doorway smoking tobacco in their Sabbath clothing or trotting to rhymed songs in a manner appropriate for joyous occasions.[112]

But Lefin's major preoccupation is greed. He concludes that zaddikim were little more than charlatans (*ramaim*). They imposed obligations on the public collectively and took from the public coffers.[113] The *pidyon* (lit. "redemption money") was only redeemed "through the distillers of [alcoholic] spirits and through the artisans and sellers of cloaks and expensive foxes," that is, through their conspicuous consumption.[114] They "endear the people with all kinds of language of affection and cajolery . . . asking how they are doing, inquiring after their well-being in order to turn them into faithful lovers, to obligate them to recognize their goodness, and to be their disciples, with all their hearts and money, in the future."[115] The smooth persuasion sometimes degenerated into outright extortion:

> They promise an individual man or even entire communities that they see an edict about to befall them, and they [the zaddikim] have already begun to pray for them [the communities] with all of their might and they [the communities] allowed them to accept their offerings [*pidyoneihem*] from the Heavens. Thus they [the Hasidim] send their agents and spies in order to find out the answers [to the edict], to allocate the paths of repentance for them [the communities] and to examine their means [*tahbulot*] of making a living, in order to use them for their own pleasure and the pleasure of their acquaintances.[116]

As Lefin's accounts are vague and generalized, however, one wonders how much direct experience he had with Hasidism. It appears that he based his claims on rumors concerning the extravagant court of Barukh of Międzybóż.

The Polish Maskil Jacques Calmanson, whose tract on Jewish reform was published in Warsaw (1797), also underscores the alleged exploitation of the ignorant masses by charlatans who passed for prophets and healers. However, in contrast to Lefin's emphasis on their opulence, Calmanson identifies Kabbalistic "knowledge" as the tool of their deception and exploitation:

> This sect, which continues to exist, rejects all true teachings. It treats ignorance like a distinction, which was previously a fault and rejected by them [i.e., the Jews], and which is today considered attractive; and at the very least, laziness is cultivated like a virtue. They know only one teaching, Kabbalah, which possesses neither sense nor utility. The contemplative life is prescribed as the proper life for which a man is created. They publicly renounce greed but privately do not adhere to this confession. For them, all property is commu-

nal, and several people always enforce the rules, and are even graced with the more-pompous-than-appropriate title "infallible."

Furthermore, this knowledge of Kabbalah, the depth of knowledge and utilization of which their elders are pompously praised, and whose secrets they carefully, and cleverly conceal from the masses for their profit—in order not only to preserve their irreversible tyrannical power, which they hold over their followers' minds and is the sole principle and mainstay of their authority, but in addition to this, in order to appear to have a right to the possessions of newly arriving followers I say, this Kabbalistic knowledge is for these reasons alone kept secret. Considering these two motives, it is astonishing to recount how skillfully they manipulate their simpleton visitors with senseless fervor. But on the other hand, one must pity the lack of enlightenment, as opposed to good and nonsuperstitious belief, among their unenlightened and gullible people, who believe that with this insane blindness they act completely in order to serve God, while at the same time all of their toil is sacrificed to the eccentricity of several cunning zealots, who stand to become despots if the Government fails to consider the means to thwart their spread immediately.[117]

Calmanson's account is useful in that it raises the appeal of Kabbalah as a reason for Hasidism's popularity, and affirms that Hasidim continued to live communally. However, his sweeping generalizations suggest that his information, too, was secondhand.

Several Maskilim recorded their impressions about Hasidism within the Congress Kingdom, and these are of particular value to this discussion. The Galician Maskil Samson Halevi Bloch (1784–1845) wrote a satire against the Seer of Lublin in 1815 so scandalous that the Mitnagged Ephraim Dinard felt compelled to censor portions when he printed it in 1904.[118] The narrator of the satire, an enlightened merchant from Białystok, poses as a supplicant at the Lublin court and plies the Hasidim with alcohol in order to discover the details of the Seer's ultimately fatal fall from a window in 1814. The narrator learns that the accident occurred during a *Shemini Azeret* celebration at the Lublin court. The Seer had declared that all present "should drink profusely that day" and preached that, as the Temple and altar are no longer available to expiate sins, one must offer wine libations to the zaddik instead: "And today I am the altar, and I will expiate your sins. So those who know this should come and donate wine to the altar."[119] He then sold the donated wine back to visitors or drank it himself, "and it rose in his throat and he vomited, until no one could sit near him."[120] The drunken Seer then proclaimed he was experiencing the spirit of prophecy and retreated to his bedroom, a "little upper chamber with walls (see II Kings, 4:10), with glass windows around it (see I Kings 6:4), with an open window in its loft, facing the entrance to the rubbish heap, where the people would go to take care of their bodily needs, covered with human mud, filth, and excrement."[122] What follows is one of the crudest passages that ever dripped from the pen of a Maskil—a *melizah*-enhanced description of the Seer's ultimately fatal drunken plunge onto the rubbish heap.

The uncensored version reads:

> And he fell on his bed, like one who lies upon the top of a mast [see Prov. 23:34], until he had to relieve himself. So he climbed upon the window of his balcony and held his genitals and poured his water upon the ground. Before he finished relieving himself, the flesh still in his hand [see Num. 11:33], he staggered like a drunken man [see Ps. 107:27] and fell completely from the high open window down to the ground, upon the excrement. And he lay there without speech or words [see Ps. 19:4], only a "small voice" was heard [I Kings 19:12], and "no one knows his grave" [Deut 34:6].
>
> And when it was evening, the departure of the Hasidim, and two guards came there to relieve themselves, they lifted their eyes and saw that the rabbi lay like a prophet with his nose in the ground [see Daniel 10:9], and that the window was open. And they "turned to each other in amazement" [Is. 13:8], and "they were afraid to come near him" [Ex. 34:30], for they said "the spirit of prophecy seizes him, and let us hear what God is saying to him." "And they waited until it was late" [Judges 3:25], and he did not stir, and no vision was discerned. And they approached him and turned him and saw that his [sign of the] covenant[121] was faithful to him [see Ps. 78: 37], for it was in his hand. And they shouted: "Oh, a miracle has been bestowed upon the house of Israel." And they took him and dragged him to the room, and bathed and anointed him and changed his dress [his excrement-covered clothes] [see II Sam. 12: 20]. And a report was heard in the city of Lublin [see Genesis 45:16] that Rabbi Itzikel Lancuter is among the prophets. And he did not know of his fall or ascent [Gen. 19:33], for the heat of the wine burned within him [Esther 1:12], and his face was like fire flaring up, and his countenance like burnished copper [Ezekiel 1:4 and 40:3]. And a trance fell upon him, and he slept from evening until the afternoon feast of the next day.[122]

David Assaf argues that this satire's assertions, with their vulgar liquid motifs and sexual innuendos, merely serve to demonstrate how adherents of an opposing camp projected their obscene fantasies about Hasidism onto the Seer's fall.[123] Indeed, much of the satire appears too absurd to be of much use to the historian. Nonetheless, Bloch's claims about Hasidic revelry, monetary gain, prophetic presumptions, and undue veneration of the zaddik do match those of other testimonies.

Abraham Stern's comparatively measured report to officials seems more reliable, however.[124] Written on September 29, 1818, and copied and recirculated in 1823, Stern's "Information Concerning the Sect of the Hasidim" helped fuel the anti-Hasidic investigations of 1824. A brief history of the origins of

Hasidism is followed by an uncharacteristically specific and detailed exposition of the movement's development in the Kingdom of Poland.

> After the death of the aforementioned Israel Ba'al Shem, his disciples spread into various locales, and each made it known in his locale that he had inherited the secret of miracle working; taught and demanded that everyone coming to him with a certain request must first give a *pidyon*, which means a ransom for one's soul, upon which he may already be sure that his request was granted a favorable outcome. Each of them would attempt to beguile and ensnare the younger and less sensible, particularly wealthy, part of the Israelites, and the female sex.—The most urgent consideration therefore was to have their partisans everywhere in cities and towns, and for each one to have a little school for holding services, according to their custom, with clapping, jumping and other indecorousness; and by such means in particular to be able to draw young people to their society and their meetings.—When one of these Ringleaders[125] died, several of his partisans or disciples arose in his place, declared themselves leaders, and in promoting the same course as their Ringleaders, bred superstition and advanced deceitfulness to the highest level.
>
> The state and method of Hasidim at present is such.—That they spread a rumor among the Israelite populace that in such or such city is found this or that Israelite who by virtue of being inspired by the holy spirit sees everything; that through the connection of his soul with God his utterance can change one's fortune in the world. To reinforce their claims, they spread the word about his fictitious miracles. From this noise, each gullible and, especially, female person proceeds to this Ringleader personally or through a messenger in writing, with a variety of questions, for example if it is better to enter into this or that kind of trade? If one should stay in a marriage or get a divorce? Some requests are, for example, about fertility, good fortune in trade, healing the ill, rescue from some misfortune, recovery of stolen items, exorcism of a demon or evil spirit from a person, receiving a favorable response to a petition to the authorities, winning a court case. In the last two cases, some even personally take or send the paper upon which a petition or other document is to be written so that this holy ringleader will bless the paper.—In every case a *pidyon*, or ransom of the soul, must be given to the Ringleaders.—The Hasidim see to it that whatever their Ringleader utters will occur, by stipulating that the petitioners must believe in the Hasidim and their Ringleaders without the slightest doubt. Each of these common petitioners receives an assurance from the Ringleader of the Hasidim, and after this does not occur and the deceived person grumbles, the Hasidim are then able to explain evasively that the petitioner surely could not have believed in their

Ringleaders, or that the petitioner had become more of a sinner than he had been initially [i.e., at the time of his request].

The swindling and superstition is so extensive that Hasidim and those who are hoodwinked by them engage in the unprecedented act of bringing their written requests to the graves of deceased, saintly Ringleaders.—In those places, the son of the deceased or another who succeeded him in leadership becomes, in such cases, a mediator between the dead and the petitioner, and grants the hearing; but this must be preceded by a *pidyon*, or ransom of the soul. Such Hasidic Ringleaders have multiplied in Poland at present, each with his own partisans in various places, and certain Hasidim consider one or another to be on a higher level of saintliness. And although all the Hasidim have similar deceptive intentions for the spread of superstitions, and all aim for darkness, nevertheless hatred and quarrels often occur between these same Ringleaders, each maintaining that the other is a vile swindler.

In every city or town where several Hasidim are found, each strives to have a place for holding separate services and, most principally, for frequent licentious rendezvous. This serves as a most effective means of enticing youth.—This is a place for incubating different degenerate superstitions and immoral deeds, and where idleness becomes the norm. They frequently hold rendezvous, but especially on Saturday before sundown—*Suda Szlyszys*, which means Saturday's third feast, at which time they eat, drink and sing songs, and their Ringleader imparts groundless, harmful superstitions through lectures with an absurd message. After this, they hold evening services and feast again.—*Milawe Małke* means sending off the Queen, which carries the allegorical meaning of seeing off the departing Sabbath—drink, sing, and jump, which commonly lasts until midnight, and often throughout the entire night.—The Hasidim try to claim that this conduct is a way to commune with God.

The most important rendezvous and gatherings are visits to the Hasidic Ringleaders of the highest level; they gather together and travel from even the remotest locales on a Holiday or Sabbath; the richest travel by carriage, and the poor make the journey on foot. Often it happens that young people, without the knowledge of their Parents and even against their express will, steal away with a *pidyon*, or redemption for the soul, either their own or of someone who cannot be present, writing the name of the petitioner and object of the request on a note.—There, everything becomes strange, for mystical and Kabbalistic sermons assume a solemn form.[126] Each word that the Ringleader utters by means of his inspired saintly soul (according to their claims) is meaningful, for it is also pronounced in Heaven. A substantial part of the young people remains there for several Sundays and achieves more idleness and superstition.—This is the sum of conduct and knowledge aimed for during the Hasidic

rendezvous and gatherings, at which, apart from their religious and
mystical knowledge, they do not inculcate the youth with any other
knowledge or skill, even the reading of a scientific book; rather nothing is considered relevant to Religion if it is written in another language and alphabet, but is considered a religious offense. The Israelite people in Poland generally regret that these charlatans and
deceivers with every passing day advance so much superstition and
that, as a result, they spread harm and endeavor to avert the Youth
from enlightenment; but they are not able to summon the strength
to remedy this evil.

Raphael Mahler claims that "this banal essay . . . contains nothing new compared with the polemical writings of the Mitnaggdim but is inferior to them
because of its superficial historical description and its hollow generalizations."[127] He admits that a portion of the report identifies petitioners' concerns,
but dismisses its utility because of the author's inaccuracies about Hasidic
liturgy and doctrine.[128]

Yet despite minor inaccuracies, Stern's report enhances themes mentioned
in other Haskalah testimonies, including the use of merrymaking, prophecy,
Kabbalah, and obscurantism in general for financial gain. We are reminded of
the considerable proportion of women and young men among the zaddik's
petitioners, as well as wealthy Jews, and are privy to a wide variety of petitioners'
requests (healing, fertility, business advice, exorcism, etc.). But more than that,
Stern outlines the *pidyon* system, including the way it functioned during visits
to a deceased zaddik's grave by means of his successor. Such tomb pilgrimages
had become routine by this phase, and even descendants of priests (*kohanim*)
apparently participated. According to R. Levi Isaac of Berdyczów, "tombs of the
Zaddikim do not cause bodily defilement, because the bodies of zaddikim are
so purified that their bodies [in addition to their souls] desired to uphold the
Torah and the commandments."[129]

We also gain insights that are absent in Hasidic sources. We learn that
zaddikim employed a form of insurance: their prophesies would fail if a petitioner did not have sufficient faith in them. Occasionally discordant relations
with other zaddikim, corroborated in Hasidic sources, are noted as well. Separate prayer houses allowed Hasidim to sing, drink, and dance in an unre-
strained fashion, presumably because they were free of many of the social
strictures of the synagogue. On the Sabbath and other holidays, Stern charges,
young people were wont to steal away and remain at the court for several weeks,
a form of adolescent rebellion that sound plausible. Stern concludes by condemning the Hasidic rejection of scientific books, or any book not written in
Hebrew or Yiddish, as obstructing Jewish Enlightenment. Indeed, the Hasidic
condemnation of secular literature is well known, and probably entailed a resistance to integration and acculturation. The report's last claim—that "the
Israelite people in Poland generally regret that these charlatans and deceivers"
on the grounds that they "avert the Youth from enlightenment" may be wishful
thinking at this early stage; but the admission that "they are not able to sum-

mon the strength to remedy this evil" accurately conveys the weakness of Haskalah. For all its alleged backwardness, we may conclude, Hasidism was continuing to predominate.

Not all Maskilim were as negatively inclined toward Hasidism, however. The most famous voice of moderation was the Galician Maskil Jacob Samuel Bik. Repulsed by his colleagues' fanatical anti-Hasidism, Bik maintained that certain zaddikim evinced a great "love of Israel" by caring for poor fellow Jews.[130] The Vilna Maskil, Samuel Joseph Fuenn, was impressed by the Lubavitcher zaddik during the latter's visit to Vilna in 1835, although his skepticism won out in the end.[131] The Ukrainian Maskil, Eliezer Zvi Hakohen Zweifel, composed a conciliatory tract on Hasidism.[132] And certain Polish Maskilim proved moderate, as well. Jacob Tugenhold defended Hasidism before the Commission on Denominations in 1824 on the grounds that they displayed an admirable brotherly unity. He contrasted Hasidim favorably with "zealous Talmudists," or Mitnaggdim, who he felt were more stubborn in resisting reform.[133] In 1831, Tugenhold rejected the designation of Hasidism as a sect on the grounds that the Hasidim did not "renounce a single existent law and precept, such as the Divine Old Testament, nor the Talmud and other later works, and they take the Israelite Religion extremely seriously." Hasidim, he argued, were merely attempting to be better Jews: "The obligation of every Hasid is: to comply with every such law and precept more scrupulously than appears to be required," writes Tugenhold.[134]

Occasionally, Polish Maskilim were won over. Dr. Hayyim David Bernhard was a physician from Działoszyce who was educated in Berlin. In 1793, he returned to Poland and participated in the Kosciuszko uprising, was eventually appointed General Józef Zajączek's physician, and subsequently became medical inspector for the Duchy of Warsaw.[135] Bernhard then experienced a spiritual crisis that compelled him to approach the zaddik David of Lelów. The latter introduced him to the Seer of Lublin, who converted him to Hasidism. Bernhard grew his beard and side-locks long, and although he never quite mastered Yiddish, became both head of the local hospital and a wonder-working Hasid in the town of Piotroków. He served as the Seer's physician in the wake of the tragic fall satirized by Bloch. Eventually, Bernhard began accepting his own petitions and *pidyonot* from Hasidim.[136] While we have no direct evidence of Bernhard's interventions with his former employers on behalf of Hasidim, we should probably add him to our list of highly placed patrons and protectors.

It is also worthwhile to examine non-Jewish accounts of Hasidism in Central Poland, which are in many ways similar to those of Maskilim. This is hardly surprisingly, considering that the latter constituted their main source of information. However, one must be even more cautious with their accounts, which can be even more distorted. In 1818, General Wincenty Krasiński (1782–1858) noted a Masonic-like movement among the Jews that had arisen when "Israel Hirszowicz, Rabbi of Międzyborz in Poland, founded a new sect, after the doctrine of Moses Maimonides, a Jew of Alexandria in Egypt."[137] A similar misrepresentation appears in the novel *Levi and Sarah* (1821), by the famous romantic author Julian Ursyn Niemcewicz (1758–1841), explaining that a rabbi

named Israel Bael Achem claimed to have access to esoteric knowledge discovered by a Jew named Laryl in Maimonides' library in Egypt in 1575.[138]

Niemcewicz believed that his country's Jews needed to break free of the
stultifying influence of the traditional rabbis in order to achieve cultural emancipation, and regarded Hasidism as the cause of Jewish obscurantism. His
information was likely derived from Solomon Maimon, Calmanson, Hoga, and
others whom he considered models for Polish Jewry.[139] In his serialized novel
Levi and Sarah, the protagonist Abraham portrays Hasidism as a sect consumed with gratifying sensual desires and guided by bizarre beliefs. Hasidim,
according to Abraham, "entice our youth by their fantastic representations as
well as by their debauched lives, and plunge them into an ever deeper abyss."
Abraham decides to visit the supreme rabbi of the Hasidim in order to expose
his trickery. The rabbi receives him graciously, blesses him, and then initiates
him into his mysteries. "Oh, with what pain my heart filled at the sad state of
a people devoted to the madness of these fanatics," laments Abraham. The
rabbi was not an absolute charlatan, for he "in fact believed that he was the
lord over angels and spirits." Nevertheless, Abraham is determined to reveal
his insanity to the whole world.[140] He proceeds to play the same practical joke
on the rabbi that Stanisław Ezekiel Hoga played on the Seer of Lublin (see
chapter 3), and the story is no doubt based on that event. Abraham writes a
letter ordering the rabbi to undertake preparations for the coming of the Messiah the following year, and slips it into the pocket of his white silk ceremonial
gown. The rabbi discovers the letter and announces the coming of the Messiah.
Fearing a messianic crisis, Abraham reveals his ruse but is obliged to seek
refuge from Hasidic wrath in enlightened Berlin. Although marred by bias and
factual errors, the diatribe is interesting because of its sympathetic allowance
that zaddikim were not charlatans. They believed in their own powers.

More helpful is a report by another author, a "Polish official," probably
from 1824.[141] The author actually criticizes Maskilim as "freethinkers" who are
more dangerous to the government than Hasidim (there are grounds for attributing this report to Jacob Tugenhold, as he expressed similar sentiments
elsewhere and was, technically, a "Polish official"). The author advises the government *not* to destroy Hasidism, because it serves as a check against the
increase of these freethinkers. Certain inaccuracies aside, the author seems to
have taken the trouble to investigate Hasidic custom and doctrine. Entitled
Comments concerning the Jewish Sect Hasidism, the essay commences with the
following explanation.

> The Jewish people is divided, according to changes which occurred
> in the past century, into three sects, namely: 1) Ordinary Jews, 2)
> Freethinkers and 3) Hasidim.—each of these sects hates the other
> two; but the last is the least tolerated by the first two, because they
> both believe that if not for the Hasidim, all those who are [Hasidic]
> followers would belong to their group, and that they would be more
> popular than the other.[142]

Abraham Stern

"Ordinary Jews" were no doubt Mitnaggdim, while "Freethinkers" were Maskilim. Both coveted Hasidic membership, another indication of its substantial size.

What follows is a more sympathetic description of Polish Hasidism than is found in other non-Hasidic writings:

> Followers of the Hasidic sect are rather superstitious; however their superstition did not originate with them, but rather they inherited it from their Jewish great-grandfathers. But being more fervent in everything than typical Jews, certain developments occurred among them, for example believing that both an evil and a good spirit can reside in society with people, and allowing many absurdities to result from such beliefs, such as: the charming of spirits, the invocation of ghosts,[143] requesting intercessions with God on their behalf from the deceased, the wearing of *kemajów*[144] [several words and imagined names of angels, written on parchment], healing of the ill through magical means, etc.[145]

Thus far, the description might just as well apply to *ba'alei shem*. Indeed, the author is aware that magical practice pre-existed Hasidism. What is new is its scale, as well as Hasidism's ecstatic dancing during prayer and excessive devotion toward zaddikim.

> All of this from time immemorial existed among Jews, but became more widespread among [the Hasidim]. According to the opinion of Hasidim, they imitate the piety of ancient Jews; the ancient patriarchs were none other than good Hasidim; and David, King[146] of Israel, who [according to the claims of holy texts] danced with the Ark of the Covenant, had the same saintly rapture as the Maggid of Kozienice, a leader of this sect who died several years ago, who was accustomed to dance during prayer. They selected chiefs among themselves whose piety they honored so much that they blindly believed everything they said; they honored them as diviners of the future who, by virtue of intercession with God, could reverse all evil and obtain all good; they rely on their advice for everything, and their commands are like heavenly decrees; they hold them to be fluent in Kabbalistic science, which is not true, for they have very little conception of it; for that science exists only in books which no one is able to understand, and you do not find anyone today who possesses them [!].[147]

This last assertion is, of course, untrue: teachings by Polish zaddikim like the Maggid of Kozienice reveal fluency in a whole array of Kabbalistic works.[148]

What follows, however, is a fair-minded, if critical, assessment of the tenor of Hasidic leadership and society.

> These chiefs are not deceivers, but rather deceived, for they are usually blessed with vivid imaginations, and by dint of their popularity, which they possess through their followers, and by completely evading every enlightened thing and plunging into mysticism, they believe themselves to be enraptured, and that they are inspired by the spirit of prophesy. They fulfill every Jewish precept, differing only in opinions and certain customs, although among themselves they have much fluency in Talmud, yet still do not have respect for ordinary rabbis, considering them to be hypocrites without piety. According to them, one who occupies himself with stories of miracles achieved by their chiefs has greater merit than one who submerges himself in profound Talmudic disputes. The basic difference between this sect and other Jews is: that it places as much stock in fulfilling religious precepts as in pious reflection. . . .
>
> The Lord God only demands one's heart, [Hasidism's] adherents say, recognizing that not everything depends on fulfilling commandments, but rather on purity of intention and love for God. Be happy, humble, immerse yourself every day in a stream or river, give charity, share everything communally with the society, pray fervently with an inspired spirit, with a trembling body and with all your strength, gather around the chief for *shabbos*,[149] listen to his teach-

ing, sing hymns, eat and drink well and enjoy the company; these are the most important virtues for them. Being haughty, sad, and not immersing yourself in water after the previous night causes impurity; all these they regard as great offenses. They consider as adherents those who are held to be sinners by other Jews, claiming that merely wanting to improve oneself is sufficient for becoming good, that repentance does not require fasting or affliction, but rather sincere and fervent prayer. Prayer is for them the most important obligation. Some spend all day in prayer, some do not pray at all for several days, rationalizing that lacking pure thoughts and not being prepared for prayer, they prefer not to pray at all.[150]

Although the author derides their superstitions, criticizes their blind faith, misrepresents their grasp of Kabbalah, and deems them harmful fanatics, he remains surprisingly optimistic about members of the "sect." Hasidim are not ignorant, but prefer to emphasize prayer, piety, and storytelling over Talmudic erudition. Hasidic life is innocent and even charming: adherents stress the importance of a cheerful disposition, humility, communal living, ritual immersion, participation in gatherings on the Sabbath, storytelling, and fervent prayer. They accept sinners who have been cast off by the normative community, because the only important thing is to demonstrate a willingness to repent. Zaddikim are most guilty of "completely evading every enlightened thing and plunging into mysticism," an accusation that was at least untrue of several zaddikim.[151] But the author insists that they are not charlatans, for like Niemcewicz he believes they are "not deceivers, but rather deceived" in thinking that they possessed certain powers.

The report concludes with a recommendation that, like the report of the Warsaw police who encountered R. Moses of Kozienice, counsels prudent treatment of zaddikim. But the justification is astonishing: persecuting Hasidism "might lead to an increase in the number of free-thinking Jews." Instead, the government is urged to

> use its powerful infrastructure for establishing equilibrium between the other two Jewish sects as a tool to achieve its goals, but must only keep a watchful eye upon the progress of the [Hasidic] chiefs, must be prudent with them so that they will, in turn, promote the Government's viewpoint. As for the enthusiasm of these fanatics, although it is harmful now, by sensibly dealing with them, they can become the most powerful means for abolishing each obstacle which the Government now faces in promoting Jewish reforms.[152]

The government would do best to try to win over these popular leaders to the cause of reform.

Testimony of a different order is provided by British missionaries who traveled through east central Europe during the first decades of the nineteenth century. The London Society for Promoting Christianity among the Jews sponsored missionaries in Central Poland beginning in 1814. Three years later, a

member of the society, Lewis Way, traveled to Russia and the Congress Kingdom and nearly transformed the political condition of Polish Jewry, for in talks
with Tsar Alexander I and other high authorities he argued that Jewish assimilation and conversion would surely occur if the Jews were granted full civil
rights and their oppression was ended.[153] His arguments were timely, for they
occurred one year after the introduction of Senator Nowosilców's draft bill for
partial Jewish emancipation and coincided with the tsar's temporarily liberal
domestic policy. Although Polish officials like Kajetan Kozmian, Stanisław
Staszic, and Adam Czartoryski helped thwart Nowosilców's bill, and although
the tsar's liberalism ultimately proved too shallow for any concrete emancipatory legislation, Way's missionary program was permitted to continue.[154]

The results were rather meager—one study claims that between 1821 and
1854, only 361 Polish Jews were baptized; while a more recent study roughly
doubles that figure.[155] But the missionaries performed an indispensable service
as amateur anthropologists and ethnographers. On March 1, 1823, the missionaries Hoff, Becker, Wendl, and McCaul met a teacher of the Hasidim in
the Congress Kingdom, who "disputed violently, and brought forward many
foolish things from the Talmud, which he gave out as great wisdom, saying
the Talmud was wiser than we and our Messiah."[156] They would continually
encounter their most vociferous opposition in Polish Hasidim, who took it
upon themselves to defend the Jewish traditional way of life against any who
would threaten it. To be sure, isolated Hasidim appeared curious. But Hasidic
resistance in general was so noisome that missionary testimonies actually lack
the typical allegations of economic exploitation by zaddikim, so preoccupied
were they with the impediment zaddikim and their followers seemed to entail
to the spread of imputed Christian truths.

In Wyszogród, their informal disputations lasted from May 15 through
June 1:

> The next day they began to bring forth their objections; especially
> two Jews of the Hasidim defended the Jewish principles. H. being
> somewhat restored, argued with one, and W. with the other; both
> were surrounded by many Jews. H. soon perceived that his oppo-
> nent is not a man who seeks the truth, for he began very soon to
> injure both ourselves and our cause, and therefore H. was obliged to
> break off and bid him go; but W. could speak in a reasonable way
> with his opponent. . . .

> Sunday, eighteenth (Pentecost). . . . In the evening the Hasid Tuchal,
> and other Hasidim, came and staid with us till very late in the night,
> by which we were much fatigued indeed. Though he was a little
> more reasonable than yesterday; however, he did not blush to call
> again darkness light, and light darkness. . . .

The missionaries seemed to nearly get through to a Hasid named Tuchal:

Wednesday, 21st. A Hasid told H. that he should consider him as one of his brethren, if he only would not insist upon Jesus being the Messiah. When H. had given him the reasons why Jesus is his all in all, he seemed to know no answer to this. H. had afterwards a conversation with him on the nature of sin, by which the heart of the Hasid seemed to be touched.

Sunday, June 1st. Tuchal the Hasid returned the New Testament which we had lent him; but, like the Pharisees of old, he has become still more perverted by seeing the great deeds of Jesus, and thus he continued to fight against the Holy One of Israel. After H. had several times rebuked him concerning blasphemy, he told him to leave the room. May the Lord have mercy on this blind young man.

Although Tuchal had proved more open to listening and debating them, it did not have the desired effect; in fact, it seems to have accomplished the reverse.

The encounter with the Jews of Terespol proved no more gratifying. On October 29, 1824, a curious episode is recorded. A "rabbi and a Hasid" came to dispute with McCaul and Hoff, and the missionaries were sure they had bested the two. But they were suddenly interrupted by an old rabbi with a white beard, and those present were "immediately afraid, and all stood back." The missionaries were surprised to find that "he, however, appeared to be equally afraid of the others." They begged everyone to be silent, and began explaining a chapter in scripture. Nevertheless, each still appeared to be afraid of the other. It is possible that the missionaries were witnessing Hasidic-Mitnaggdic tension in Terespol. In any event, another old Hasid came to them that evening and engaged them in another disputation, but he was "a sad instance of what the Hasid fanaticism can do when planted in the desperately wicked heart of man."[157]

At this point, McCaul and Hoff relate an incident that they heard about in Warsaw, undoubtedly involving R. Simha Bunem of Przysucha:

A Hasid had a lawsuit with a nobleman, and knowing that he had been guilty of fraud, he was afraid of losing it. He, therefore, went to a celebrated blind rabbi [i.e., R. Simha Bunem][158] to request that he would pray for the death of the nobleman, for the Hasidim believe that whatever their rabbi prays for must happen. The rabbi took his money, and promised to do so; in the mean time the nobleman left the country, and during his absence his wife died. The Hasid now returned to the rabbi to complain that he had not fulfilled his promise. The rabbi defended himself by saying, "You must not blame me; I sent the angel of death to fulfil his office, but he not finding the husband at home, took away the wife." The Hasid went away, perfectly satisfied with this answer.[159]

Here was a clear opportunity to raise economic objections against zaddikim. But this macabre rumor about R. Simha Bunem only confirmed them in their belief about the absurd "enthusiasm of this sect."[160]

Two weeks later, the missionaries had further reason to despise the Hasidim when a zaddik, probably R. Abraham Joshua Heschel (now of Międzybóż), issued a ban against any Jew having contact with them. Apparently, they had enjoyed success with a certain Hasid's son:

> When Meyersohn's father found that his son was really lost to Judaism, he went to a certain Hasid Rabbi at M—, and prevailed on him to thunder out an anathema against all who should have any thing to do with missionaries, or who should receive their books. This was done privately, for it is forbidden in all the European states; and if it could be proved against him, the Rabbi would be liable to a criminal process. The young man told us further, that this anathema had been made known in all the synagogues throughout the country, and we have reason to think that this account was true, from the treatment which we everywhere met with from the Jews, especially as they seemed afraid to touch our books.[161]

Legal or not, R. Abraham Joshua Heschel's anathema had spoiled the entire region, for "this hostile feeling continued the whole way to the Polish fortress, that is, wherever Hasidim had any influence." The missionaries returned to the Central Poland, where matters appeared to be reversed.[162]

But this perception does not constitute proof of the weakness of Hasidism in Central Poland, as was recently argued, for the missionaries encountered plenty of Hasidic resistance back in that region, as well. In Warka, a Jewish woman warned Becker that "the Hasidim were chiefly against me."[163] More frustration followed when McCaul and his colleagues arrived in Ostrów and visited the Hasidic town rabbi on the Sabbath:

> We found an old man so deaf that we could not carry on a regular conversation: he was reading in the book of Zohar when we entered. In the next room were three Jews lying on a bed, one was singing and clapping his hands and feet, making the most barbarous noise. This is what the Hasidim call the joy of the Sabbath (*Shabbat Simha*). They came out soon after we entered. One, the rabbi's son-in-law, when he saw the Prophets and New Testament which we had brought for the rabbi, said, "Wares that are hawked at a house for sale are never good." To the rabbi he said, "It stinks; fui, fui; throw it on the earth;" and then again to us, "Go to the synagogue and darshan, (preach), perhaps you may pick up some crazy fellows." I replied, that if it were our intention to pick up crazy fellows, we need not go so far; but we had come to speak to them concerning Messiah out of Tnach, the law, the prophets, and the Hagiographa. "That book is not Tnach," said he. "Well then, bring your own." Here the

man who had been singing, began again to sing, and jump about
the room, hoping to silence us by his noise. We cried out that he
profaned the Sabbath (Mehallel ha-Shabbat), and the rabbi put him
out of the room.[164]

In the presence of several members of the local elite—the elder reading the
Zohar, the rabbi, the rabbi's son-in-law—the missionaries were mocked and
drowned out by the singing and jumping of a Hasid who, by his behavior and
initial deference to the rabbi, appears more déclassé. Perhaps constrained by
his sense of decency (singing and jumping are, in fact, permitted on the Sabbath), the rabbi sent the noisy dissenter away. McCaul then began to preach
about sin and repentance, to which one of the Jews replied, "A man might
commit sins, and yet be a saint, (he meant a Hasid). Thus David, who had
committed adultery, says, (Psalm 66:2), 'Preserve my soul, for I am holy.' "
After this antinomian retort, several Hasidim began to taunt the missionaries,
and the dissenter returned: "The dancer now danced in again, and sung most
barbarously; he also pushed against us, and as the other laughed, we thought
it best to go. Afterwards, two came to our lodging, but one was very abusive."[165]
The missionaries now found that the local Jews would no longer come to them.

Once, a Warsaw Hasid appeared primed for conversion. On April 11, 1823,
Becker met "the Chanter, or Vorsinger of the Hasidim," and was assured by
the gregarious cantor that should he become a Christian, thousands would
follow him. Becker believed him, "because the Hasidim think very highly of
their superiors, so that I believe, if one of their great men should profess the
Christian religion, a multitude would follow him."[166] The cantor visited the
missionaries several more times that week, and Becker "admonished him
again to prayer."[167] Yet two years after his tantalizing receptivity, the Hasid was
still stalling:

> The vorsinger of the Hasidim, who two years ago often visited me,
> came to-day again. He assured me again of his faith in the Lord Je-
> sus, but still pleaded his worldly engagements, (being a military fac-
> tor besides,) as hindering him from confessing his faith publicly. He
> said, he always thought of the Lord Jesus in his prayers, and when
> repeating the words, "Hear, O Israel, the Lord our God, &c." he al-
> ways applied "our God" to him.[168]

It is doubtful, however, that the Hasidic cantor/military supplier ever took the
final step, for his conversion would have been duly noted.

A year later, the missionary E. Henderson published his travel diary. In a
section on Hasidism, he allowed that accusations of gross immorality brought
against members of the sect by the Mitnagged R. Israel Loebel had been called
into question in Gregoire's Histoire des Sectes Religieuses.[169] Nevertheless, Henderson had been informed "by one, who has had the best opportunities of
investigating the subject, that their morals are most obnoxious, and that the
representations that have been given of them are by no means exaggerated."[170]

Hasidim were an antisocial element: they were "not only at enmity with all the other Jews, but form the bitterest and most bigoted enemies of the Christian religion." Henderson then describes them:

> To their Rabbins, whom they honour with the name of *zaddiks*, or "Righteous," they pay almost divine homage. The extravagance of their gestures during their public service, entitles them to the appellation of the "Jewish Jumpers." Working themselves up into ecstasies, they break out into fits of laughter, clap their hands, jump up and down the synagogue in the most frantic manner; and turning their faces towards heaven, they clench their fists, and, as it were, dare the Almighty to withhold from them the objects of their requests.[171]

Henderson's entry concludes with a dire warning about increasing Hasidic numbers: "This sect has increased of late years, that in Russian Poland[172] and European Turkey,[173] it is reported to exceed in number that of the Rabbinists in these parts."[174]

Hasidim themselves might readily own up to some of Henderson's accusations, considering their rather different convictions about what "enlightenment" entailed (decorum was low on the list). Attempting to appreciate their perspective is, in any case, essential to weighing the merits of the accusations mounted by Mitnaggdim, Maskilim, and Christians. Of course, the positive bias that animates Hasidic testimony presents its own hazards, for absolute devotion to zaddikim was considered a virtue, and no Hasid would think to accuse them of charlatanism or willful obscurantism. This positive bias is integral to any religious perspective, which, according to Clifford Geertz, differs from today's scientific perspective in that "rather than detachment, its watchword is commitment; rather than analysis, encounter."[175] Nevertheless, Hasidic recollections are not necessarily any more biased or exaggerated than those of their enemies. Moreover, they provide an intimacy that is lacking in skeptical reports.

A comparison of non-Hasidic and Hasidic testimonies will illustrate this latter point. The Maskil Solomon Maimon (1754–1800) personally encountered R. Dov Ber, the "Great Maggid" of Międzyrzecz. His well-known description reads:

> Accordingly on Sabbath I went to this solemn meal, and found there a large number of respectable men who had gathered from various quarters. At length the awe-inspiring great man appeared, clothed in white satin. Even his shoes and snuff-box were white, this being among the Kabbalists the colour of grace. He gave every newcomer his greeting. We sat down to table and during the meal a solemn silence reigned. After the meal was over, the superior struck up a solemn inspiring melody, held his hand for some time upon his brow, and then began to call out, "Z—of H—, M—or R—," and so on. Every newcomer was thus called by his own name and the name

of his residence, which excited no little astonishment. Each recited, as he was called, some verse of the Holy Scriptures. Thereupon the superior began to deliver a sermon for which the verses recited served as a text, so that although they were disconnected verses taken from different parts of the Holy Scriptures they were combined with as much skill as if they had formed a single whole. What was still more extraordinary, every one of the newcomers believed that he discovered, in that part of the sermon which was founded on his verse, something that had special reference to the facts of this own spiritual life. At this we were of course greatly astonished.[176]

In the presence of "a large number of respectable men," the Great Maggid displayed his phenomenal memory and penetrating psychological insight by manipulating verses *melizah*-style.

Yet Maimon's description misses the phenomenological dimension captured by the Great Maggid's disciple, the future zaddik R. Ze'ev Wolf of Żytomir:[177]

Once I heard the Maggid say to us: "I will teach you the way Torah is best taught, not to feel oneself at all, but to be like a listening ear that hears the world of sound speaking but does not speak itself." And as soon as he would [begin to] listen to the words themselves, he would immediately stop. Several times I myself saw that when he opened his mouth to speak words of Torah, he looked as if he was not of this world at all, and the divine Presence spoke out of his throat. And sometimes, even in the midst of saying something, in the middle of a word, he would stop and wait for a while.[178]

The Great Maggid's display of *devekut* was what inspired initiates, not his skillful *melizah*.[179] A similar description is found in Polish Hasidic testimony about the zaddik Simha Bunem of Przysucha, who would draw down his lectures from the heavenly spheres. "Know that it is not as you assume, that when I am quiet while teaching I am considering what I will say afterward," R. Simha Bunem confided to a disciple. "Rather, when I pause to think, I am in a different place. Only in returning from there do I speak of those things which I say during class."[180] Such testimonies impart greater insight into the attractions of zaddikim.

The same may be said concerning their other conduct. R. David of Maków, we recall, depicted the zaddik Levi Isaac of Berdyczów as nothing more than a glutton who enjoyed his meals at the expense of his gullible hosts. But R. Isaac of Neskhiż (Nesuhoyezhe), a latter-day zaddik who married R. Levi Isaac's granddaughter and boarded with him for several years, puts a different spin on his culinary predilections:

Once I saw him before the eve of Yom Kippur, when he was sitting at his meal, and beautiful sounds came out of his mouth. And after that, only two tears, no more, flowed from his eyes. After that, they

placed stuffed fish [*memuleh*] before him, called *oksen*. And he said
"fulfill [*maleh*] all our wishes."[181] And after that, they placed the dish
of gravy before him, called in Yiddish *yohel*,[182] and began to call out
"Israel awaits [*yahel*] God."[183] And he once again was very, very
happy, and worshiped in tremendous joy.[184]

By identifying the symbolic correspondence between foods and sacred verses,
R. Levi Isaac transformed the act of eating into a holy act, demonstrating worship through corporeality.[185]

Hasidic testimony also affords insight into the motivations behind the
movement's popular dimension. We recall how in testimony by Maskilim in
particular, it is suggested that zaddikim were exploiting the naive masses by
cynically charging money for magic, miracles, blessings, and cures that they
knew to be ineffectual. Hasidic testimony inadvertently refutes this charge of
charlatanism by showing that their belief in magic was, as far as one can tell,
quite sincere. This is demonstrated throughout the secret mystical diary of the
zaddik Isaac Eizik Jehiel Safrin of Komarno (1806–74), which was not published until 1944. R. Isaac Eizik reports, for example, that his own birth was
decreed by the Seer of Lublin, who also predicted the death of R. Isaac Eizik's
father.[186] The zaddik Isaac of Neskhiz recalls the Seer's (or "Lubliner's,")
visit to his father, R. Mordecai of Neskhiz (1748–1800), during which the zaddikim
demonstrated their sincere belief in magic. The account's reliability is helped
by the fact that it admits to the failure of the Seer's celebrated clairvoyance.

> Our master told us several times, including in the presence of the
> Sasanowizer [Rebbe], that the Lubliner heard a decree from heaven
> that there is none as godly as Mordecai [of Neskhiz], son of Gitel.
> And he inquired after him, and they said that he was in Neskhiz. And
> he came to Neskhiz; and the entire town went out to greet him and
> pay their respects. The great R. Mordecai himself was also among
> those who greeted him, but did not reveal who he was. And by mi-
> raculous means, he hid himself so that the Lubliner would not rec-
> ognize him at all. And he bid him "Shalom," and he answered "Sha-
> lom" from within the crowd, and he did not perceive him. And
> coming into the town, by the house of the Rabbi the Neskhizer, he
> asked where the rabbi lives. And the Neskhizer answered him, "I re-
> side here." And the Lubliner marveled a great deal, and said "This is
> a remarkable thing to turn your hat around and prevent me from
> sensing your eminence."[187]

The continuation of the testimony involves another failure of the Seer's
clairvoyance, but is even more significant in its acknowledgment of genuine
magical belief.

> And at the time of the Lubliner's departure, the Neskhizer sat with
> the Lubliner in his carriage. And our master [R. Isaac, the narrator]
> said that they sat him on their laps. And his brother, the Koweler

[Rebbe], and his brother-in-law R. Meir Feivel [son-in-law of the Nesk-hiżer] sat across from them in the carriage. And by the village of Do-roticz,[188] they descended from the carriage, and the Lubliner re-quested of the Neskhiżer "Let us walk alone together, without anyone behind us." And so it was. And I walked beside my father, of blessed memory, as I was a child. And I heard the Lubliner ask my father, "What should I do, for there is a controversy in my city? Per-haps this is because of my practice of revealing the esoteric, and be-cause of this I am embroiled in controversy." And my father an-swered him, "Behold, there is no doubt that what you do is for the sake of heaven, and you cannot desist, for it is in service of the Blessed Creator." But he told him, "So did you build some building there?" And he answered, "No. I only put a new roof on my house, with shingles." And my father answered, "If so, this is what you must do. Remove a certain row of shingles, and the controversy will be eradicated." And during this conversation, the Lubliner saw me with them, and said, "Did I not stipulate that no one shall come with us?" And my father answered, "And what of it? Is he not just a boy?" Thus they spoke. But I understood their words well.[189]

In a rare disclosure during a "private" conversation, the Seer momentarily doubted the wisdom of his "practice of revealing the esoteric," which seemed to form the root of his controversy in Lublin. R. Mordecai, with complete sincerity, disclosed a magical palliative. The controversy was, incidentally, fa-vorably resolved in 1803 (see chapter 2). But, most important, for our purpose here, we learn that zaddikim, too, shared in the widespread magical beliefs.

Followers seem to have felt empowered, not exploited, by their contact with zaddikim. Israel Zinger recalls the impact of the Seer of Lublin on a young man named Berish at the "Great Wedding" in Żarnowiec in 1801:

Once, the "Seer" came to the great sala [banquet room]. And there were many people there. And when he came, he sat at a small table which was there. And afterward, he stood on his feet and hinted that the young man R. Berish [of Oświęcin] should prepare his pipe. And [R. Berish] walked over to him with great difficulty and took the pipe from him, and went to the kitchen and took an ember, and lit the pipe with it, and walked back and gave him the pipe. And as soon as [the Seer] took the pipe from his hand, R. Berish felt all feeling rush out of him. And afterward, the Holy Rabbi began to speak with him about something. Suddenly, all feeling returned to him. For he had received from him knowledge of divestment of corporeality. And from then on, whenever he wished, he could divest himself of cor-poreality.[190]

The testimony depicts the impact of the Seer's charisma. It seems unnecessary to question whether R. Berish really felt the empowering sensation that was reported.

Hasidim occasionally responded directly to accusations of charlatanism. The Polish zaddik R. Samuel Shmelke of Nikolsburg argued that Hasidim were attacked merely for making Lurianic worship accessible to all. While residing in Sieniawa in 1772, shortly before his departure for Nikolsburg, he wrote to the Brody kahal opposing their anti-Hasidic ban.[191] R. Samuel Shmelke perceived a double standard, for the Brody ban permitted "worshipers in the first *shtibel* next to the *kloyz*," known as "famous ones," to pray from the Lurianic prayer book while forbidding the rest of the community to do so.[192] He proclaimed, "God-fearers, even if they are not 'famous,' are entitled to perform services of the heart with all their strength, and to be as strict as possible in matters of their dress and their yoke [i.e., divine service]."[193] He would not suffer the Brody authorities to "distinguish between the famous and those who are not famous, between the young and old."[194] They should be ashamed for supporting the Vilna ban issued earlier that year: "Will such wise men (may those like you increase in Israel) add to the sin of the discipline imposed by members of the holy community of Vilna, may God protect them, as if 'we live by her mouth' (Ketubot 12b)?"[195] Instead, they should have praised the fervent prayer and study habits of Hasidim precisely because of their inclusiveness:

> To the contrary, all those who have come under the influence of the Hasidim, and redirect their souls to service of the heart, i.e. prayer, and engage in Torah study every free moment, without delay and worries about time considerations, who stretch a tent over all of our Israelite brethren in this bitter exile, there are among them penitents and complete zaddikim, distinguished lovers of Torah and its study. And if, indeed, they prolong prayer with all their strength and jump and dance, did not the preeminent singer King David, of blessed memory, jump and "leap about before God" [II Sam 6:14], and "Mikhal, Saul's daughter looked" [. . . and despised him for it. II Sam 6:16]?[196] And R. Akiva, "if someone placed him in one corner . . ." [he would find him later in another] "on account of his many genuflections and prostrations" [Berakhot 31a].[197]

If Hasidic devotion was indecorous, could not the same be said of King David and R. Akiva? The important thing was that the Hasidim were willing to "stretch their tent over all of our Israelite brethren," i.e., to embrace all Jews irrespective of social rank.

Herein lay the source of the ideological slippage occurring in old-style hasidism, whose adherents formed the core of the Mitnaggdim. It became increasingly hard to defend the privileged status of Kabbalistic rite when its new accessibility was proving so inspirational for so many Jews. Leaders like R. Samuel could point out that by making esoteric rite more available, zaddikim had kindled mass repentance. Redirecting souls to "service of the heart" surely took precedence over preserving the exclusiveness of Kabbalah. R. Samuel warned, "you had better take care that the flock does not disperse, and that the people not become divided in half. Rather, examine the deeds of the Hasidim and their details and particulars and intentions—perhaps you will find good in them, and [see] that their hearts are sincere." In attempting to hold back the present revival through religious snobbery, he argued, the Brody kahal, not Hasidism, was provoking a schism. R. Samuel's populist argument contained enormous force.

To what extent was this antielitist claim valid? It is possible to gauge the extent of Hasidic inclusiveness by examining testimony concerning two marginalized groups: youth and women. One category involves the use of metoposcopy by zaddikim to predict the futures of young children.[198] R. Isaac Eizik Jehiel of Safrin records the following recollection by his mother:

> On the third day of my circumcision, one of the disciples of our lordly teacher the Besht lodged in my native city, Sambor. And many residents of the city were with him, including women with their children, as it is the accepted custom with zaddikim of our generation to bless Israel, great and small alike, with love of the spirit of Israel, the holy people. And among the visitors was my mother, who entered with me so that the zaddik would bless me. And when he placed his hand on my head, he gave a great shout, and cried in Yiddish, " 'Hoy! This small one has a great and awesome mind and a wonderful soul!" And my mother was completely shocked by this exclamation, and he said to her, "Fear not, for this boy will be a great light."[199]

When, at the age of six (in 1812), R. Isaac Eizik attended a Passover meal with the Seer of Lublin, there occurred a similar episode. The Seer took the bone from his plate and extended it to R. Isaac Eizik, withdrawing it three times until he "gazed with his holy spirit down to the root of my soul, and then he gave it to me in awe and fear, as was his holy manner." R. Isaac Eizik understood his intention: "Just as the letter *lamed* extends above every letter, so I would one day extend above all people, because I reach out to the Name of three *yuds*."[200]

Another episode is recorded about the "Great Wedding," involving the future Polish zaddik Solomon Hakohen of Radomsko at the age of six:[201]

> And on the holy Sabbath, everyone wanted to say "Good Sabbath" to the Rabbi of Lublin, may his memory be for a blessing. And the youth Solomon also ran up to him to tell him "Good Sabbath." And the Rabbi of Lublin . . . took him and held his hand and asked him, "Whose son are you?" And he answered that he was the son of R. Dov Zvi of Wlochy,[202] who is among the guests. And the Rabbi called to [R. Dov Zvi] and told him to keep an eye on his young son, for he will be a great light for many days to come.[203]

The accessibility granted to children in these cases is impressive. However, the selection of these particular children for future greatness was not incidental. In both cases, the children possessed great *yihus*: R. Yom Tov Lipman Heller was Isaac Eizik's maternal great-grandfather, and the Galician zaddik Zvi

Hirsch of Żydaczów was his uncle; while Solomon was a member of the Rabinowicz family and a descendant of Nathan Nata, the Ba'al Amukkot. Such *yihus* indeed presaged their future renown. But we are forced to wonder whether future greatness was also detected in children of more humble backgrounds.

Another category of testimonies that provides insights into Hasidic inclusiveness relates to Hasidic pilgrimages. According to Arthur Green, such pilgrimages were an outgrowth of the notion of the zaddik as *axis mundi*, a being who stands at the center of the cosmos: "the place where the zaddik dwells, be it the miserable Polish town that it is, becomes the new Temple, the place of pilgrimage."[204] Disregarding the unedifying description of Polish towns, Green's observation about the purported redemption of the Polish landscape through pilgrimage is fascinating in that it reveals yet another variation on the principle of "worship through corporeality." Jewish youth had additional reasons for embarking on pilgrimages. Victor Turner has discerned an inherent "rite of passage, even an initiatory ritual character about pilgrimage," which he attributes to its inherent dangers.[205] Basing himself on the Polish sociologist F. Znaniecki, who probably observed Christian pilgrimages to Częstochowa, Turner further discerns a "communitas" aspect to pilgrimages, wherein normal social structures are radically simplified and equalized.[206] Pilgrimages formed antistructural communities that temporarily dissolved structured divisions and liberated participants from their status roles, which for Jewish youth meant temporary acceptance in the adult world.[207]

In addition, particular adolescent concerns like relief from spiritual despondency inspired such journeys. After his marriage at the age of sixteen, Isaac Eizik Jehiel of Safrin became unmotivated in his studies and depressed. Following a period of brief recovery, he fell again and finally understood that he needed to travel to the court of a zaddik, "who would draw the light of the Blessed One upon me, for I already had a clear vessel. And I traveled to Międzybóż to my teacher and rabbi, the holy rabbi, man of God, R. Abraham Joshua Heschel. And during this time my daughter, the modest, righteous, pious Hinda Sarah, may she live, was born to me."[208] If R. Isaac Eizik appeared untroubled by the possibility that his wife would conceive in his absence, it was because mending the spirit took precedence over everything else. Maimon's accusation that "young people forsook parents, wives and children, and went *en masse* to visit these leaders" may contain an element of truth.[209]

Young people were also likely drawn by the fun and excitement of pilgrimages. R. Isaac Szmulewicz[210] describes the Hasidic procession to the court of R. David of Lelów on a major holiday, en route to the Seer's court in Lublin:

> Several days before the holiday of Shavuot [Pentecost], the Hasidim
> of R. David gathered in the town of Lelów. One Persian mile [*parsah*]
> outside of Lelów, everyone gathered together in a single group.
> From there, they went on foot to Lelów. Among them were musi-
> cians, who played very well. And when they came to the town next
> to Lelów, they began play like an orchestra, until they were heard

throughout the town. With this song, they came to the court of R. Dudel [David] with sounds of joy and thanksgiving, a festive crowd, and they did not stop playing until the holy R. David awoke and came to the courtyard with lit candles, for when they came there it was night. When he entered the crowd, he began to preach Torah. His face was glowing like a fiery torch, from the innovative interpretations which he revealed to them with sparks of fire, a divine flame. Thus it continued for several hours, several times, up until dawn. After that, he bade them "Farewell," they drank a toast, and escorted him to his home with singing and joyful shouts. The next day they prayed together. And after the prayer service, they sat down for a meal with R. Dudel. And after that, they traveled in company to the Rabbi of Lublin for the holiday of Shavuot. The coins which they had for the journey were given by everyone together, each according to his ability, and R. David was the treasurer, depositing and withdrawing.[211]

While the description of pageantry seems to confirm anti-Hasidic suspicions about libertinism, it is vital to note that the zaddik's Torah interpretations formed the festivities' centerpiece. This component is often lacking in anti-Hasidic descriptions. But the last line forces us to also acknowledge a barely concealed social hierarchy: when the Hasidim continued on to Lublin, they pooled their resources and appointed R. David as their treasurer. The Seer of Lublin therefore appears at the top of the ladder, followed by R. David—a sort of underzaddik (owing, perhaps, to his lack of *yihus*)—followed by the rank-and-file. "Communitas" succumbed to hierarchy.

The journey of the future zaddik Eleazar Hakohen of Pułtusk (1791–1881) from Warsaw to R. Abraham Joshua Heschel's court in Międzybóż in 1813, at the age of twenty-four, also illustrates the fragility of pilgrimage egalitarianism. It is conveyed in scintillating detail by his son Joshua:

And behold, my father and teacher [R. Eleazar], of blessed memory, desired in his youth to travel to the Rabbi, great genius, illuminated lamp of piety and distinction and of a chain of *yihus*, our holy teacher Abraham Joshua Heschel, may his memory be for a blessing, *av bet din* of the holy community of Opatów [and now, of Międzybóż]. And this journey occurred without the knowledge of [R. Eleazar's] father. And he joined up with a certain Hasid, and they traveled together to Międzybóż. And when they came upon the middle of the road, not far from Międzybóż, it was Thursday. And some farmers chased after them, and they did not know if they were night bandits or road watchmen, and they did not have papers. And God in His great mercy helped them, and let them escape.

In this first part of the testimony the initiatory and communitas elements of pilgrimages stressed by Turner predominate. R. Eleazar undertook the journey without his father's knowledge and became fast friends with an anonymous

Hasid. Their comradery must have grown as they braved the dangers of the journey together, fleeing bandits or guards (it did not matter which, since they lacked passports).

The two managed to escape and find shelter in a small-town inn. The narrator admits his inability to recall the name of the town, an admission that seems to enhance his credibility as an informant.

> And in the middle of the night they came to a townlet, but I forget the name of the town. And they went into an inn to be refreshed a bit from the road and give their spirits repose. And on account of their fear and alarm from being chased by the farmers, and particularly owing to the fact that [R. Eleazar] was not accustomed to travel such a long way, he fell on the bed exhausted and weary, and all his limbs and bones were extremely heavy. And the heat got to him, and his ideas and distressed thoughts were confused. And when the man who was traveling with him perceived [R. Eleazar's] great pain, he took wine with arrack[212] and doused his body with it from foot to head, and covered him in a blanket. And God saw him through, and warmed his whole body, and he slept deeply, and he perspired in his sleep and was completely restored.

Apparently because of R. Eleazar's sheltered upbringing, being "not accustomed to travel such a long way," he was quite traumatized by this first adventure. His companion had to resort to a folk remedy to revive him. We now have a hint as to the social distinction between the two pilgrims.

The social distinction between them continued to manifest itself:

> And in the morning, the day of the holy Sabbath eve [Friday], his former strength returned. And he told the man, in the form of a command, to go immediately to the post office and hire a carriage there, and pay whatever it costs and not to worry about the money, for it was another three Persian miles [parsaot] to Międzybóż. And he said to [R. Eleazar] that his heart feared to travel in the simple cart, for what if Satan danced among them and prevented them from arriving at their destination before the holy Sabbath, and they would have to spend the Sabbath in the middle of the road, God forbid? And when this man went to the post office, after [R. Eleazar] commanded him to do so, it happened that there were not any horses there at the post office. And an agent came to their inn with a farmer, and told [R. Eleazar] that this farmer had good horses and a good cart, and accepted upon himself that they would travel to Międzybóż in three hours. And when they saw that they did not have any alternative, they hired this farmer.

Upon recovering, R. Eleazar commanded, rather than requested, his companion to hire a carriage, instructing him not worry about the cost. When his colleague tried to demur, R. Eleazar commanded him a second time. The egalitarianism thus vanished in a time of stress.

Now the pair faced the terrifying prospect of failing to reach the zaddik's court before sundown on Friday. The initiation rite intensified:

> And when they had not traveled far from the town, they heard the voice of someone pursuing them. And when the farmer heard the voice of the pursuers, he beat his horses many times so that they would run with all their might. And they ran swiftly for an hour. And after that, the cart traveled at a normal pace. And [R. Eleazar] asked, "What was this fright and this beating the horses? Perhaps you feared in your heart that they were murderers, or guardsmen of the Government, may it be exalted?" And he answered that there was an old law enacted by the Government, may it be exalted, that when someone wanted to travel on a private road the owner of the cart had to go with him and announce that he was traveling with the cart on his road. "And if he gave me permission, I could travel or pay him a sum of money for every mile according to a rate. Therefore, when I turned off the King's road and traveled on this road, because this road is a short-cut, and the owner [of the road] saw that I was traveling without his permission and had not paid him the rate of money; so he chased after us with several of his companions in order to detain us and take us to the mayor of the village. And now that I have come back onto the King's road, I am no longer afraid of them. And therefore, have no fear. And you can sit on the cart in peace, without any fear or dread."

Having eluded danger and the law a second time, the two pilgrims finally arrived at the zaddik's court.

The reception accorded to R. Eleazar by the zaddik further undermines the sense of communitas and reveals his social distinction:

> And in the afternoon the honored guests came to Międzybóż and rested a little at the inn. And afterward they went to greet the rabbi. And the rabbi received [R. Eleazar] with a nice welcoming expression, because he knew him from before. And he ordered him to dine at his holy table with him for the holy Sabbath meals.[213]

R. Eleazar alone was welcomed by the zaddik and invited to dine at his table. Although he had played the humble pilgrim, he was now treated like a promising scholar with *yihus* (it was undoubtedly also on the strength of those qualities that R. Abraham Joshua Heschel "knew him from before"). R. Eleazar's companion, on the other hand, behaved more like his squire. We hear no more about him.

Indications of stratification resurfaced during R. Eleazar's visit with R. Simha Bunem of Przysucha in Warsaw:

> And the Rabbi, genius, zaddik, of blessed memory told me that one day, our rabbi [Simha Bunem] of Przysucha came to Warsaw for the

common good. And when the rabbi, zaddik, Foundation of the World, R. Isaac of Warka, of blessed memory, and also the zaddik Jacob of Radzymin, of blessed memory, and the remaining great ones of Israel heard, they streamed toward him to hear words of his wisdom and the wisdom of God which surrounded him, to instruct the ways of God and His Torah; and also the Rabbi, genius, zaddik was among the visitors . . . and they studied and ate bread before God. And after the meal which our rabbi from Przysucha gave, while he rested his spirit in his inner chamber, the rabbi, genius, zaddik [R. Eleazar] of blessed memory called on him in his room. And when he came into his room, he paid him due respect, and ordered the attendant to bring a chair for His Honor, and he sat on the chair by his bed.

Of all the "great ones of Israel" streaming toward the zaddik to hear his wisdom, only R. Eleazar was permitted to call upon the zaddik in his room, where he was accorded "due respect." The continuation of the episode reveals the source of R. Eleazar's special treatment—his exalted *yihus*:

And after several minutes he called him by his name twice: "Eleazar, Eleazar," affectionately, and said the following: "If the wealthy of Warsaw do not honor me as is befitting, they are justified, for I am a simple man, etc. etc. However, why and for what possible reason do they not honor the holy and pure Rabbi . . . Meir of Apt [Opatów]? Is he not an eminent scholar, and more?" Then he said to him, "Know, my son, that the learning of your father-in-law the rabbi, true genius . . . Jacob of Leszno, of blessed memory, reached a portion of the secret of Jewish Law, owing to the fact that he pushed himself to aim for the truth, according to the saying of the sages, "Teaching I reached and found."[214] And after several minutes, he turned his holy face toward the wall and slept a little, for fifteen minutes, and then awoke. And the rabbi, genius, zaddik of blessed memory continued to sit on the chair, for it was not his manner to leave such a great man and prince of God without words of farewell.

This first part of the testimony contains several unanticipated phenomena, including the continued lack of acceptance of the Polish zaddikim by certain members of the traditionalist Warsaw mercantile elite, and R. Simha Bunem's impassioned defense of his arch-rival, R. Meir of Opatów/Stopnica. But even more striking is R. Simha Bunem's praise of R. Eleazar's deceased father-in-law, R. Jacob of Leszno, suggesting that it was owing to him that R. Eleazar was graced with a special audience. In addition, R. Eleazar's father Ze'ev Leipziger was a wealthy Warsaw merchant. Perhaps R. Simha Bunem wished that his complaint would be conveyed to R. Eleazar's father.

Even greater privileges than this were to derive from R. Eleazar's *yihus*. In the next part of the testimony, the zaddik ends his messianic prediction by commanding that R. Eleazar assume leadership:

And when (R. Simha Bunem) saw that the Rabbi, genius, zaddik of blessed memory continued to sit, he said to him the following: 'Eleazar, know that after many days, according to the rebuke of Isaiah the prophet, in the future messianic times: "For behold, the Master, Lord of hosts, takes away from Jerusalem and Judah the stay and the staff, . . . and the elder, the captain of fifty and the honorable man . . . And I will make youngsters their princes, and babes shall rule over them. And the people shall be oppressed, every one by another, and every one by his neighbor. The child shall behave himself proudly against the elder, and the base against the honorable" [Is. 3:1–5]. When it is the end of days, all will know that the Messiah will come, and they will envy the Hasidim, who have already found shelter under the zaddikim of their time, and the elders who have found shelter under his shade and streamed towards him to drink thirstily his words—this is how it will be in the last generations. And if there is an elder among them who is not such an "honorable man"? On account of his having taken shelter with me. . . . ' And he seized his lapel and said, " 'You have clothing, be our ruler!' "[Is. 3:6].

And every single person who hears my words, which I heard from the mouth of the first elders, will find repair for his soul's needs. And may this story remain with the Hasidim like pure gold and pearls more precious than all jewels.[215]

R. Simha Bunem's fervent messianic belief and intimation that even a dishonorable man will be saved in the end of days by virtue of having been a follower of a zaddik are rendered with great candor. So, too, is his opinion of R. Eleazar, who is commanded to become a zaddik himself. While it might not constitute a formal appointment, the pronouncement furnished R. Eleazar with a clear sanction to lead. For our purposes, its great value resides in the way it reveals the opportunities accorded a young Hasid with *yihus*. Those groomed for leadership had more than raw talent.

The limits of Hasidic inclusiveness are also manifest in testimonies involving Hasidic women. Zaddikim offered women a new sense of spiritual immediacy through face-to-face audiences; yet it is vital to note that women attained few concrete social and spiritual gains beyond increased access to male leaders. They could almost never hope to become spiritual leaders themselves.[216] As a matter of fact, women were not even permitted to be schoolteachers during this period.[217] Many Hasidic women continued to be the main breadwinners in their families, but there is no evidence that this improved their status.[218] The case of Temerel Bergson was exceptional, for her wealth and initiative were unusual by any standard. In Galician Hasidism, the status of women seems to have actually declined during this period. When the zaddik Menahem Mendel of Rymanów arrived in that town in 1807, his first act was to forbid "the licentious clothing styles of the nations of the world," particularly the jewelry and embroidered clothing worn by women. When a woman from a "large city" who had married a local homeowner dared to show up on the street in "arrogant clothing and finery," R. Menahem Mendel ordered the youths of the city to call her by a certain "word."[219] In 1815, R. Menahem Mendel ordered his disciple R. Naftali Zvi of Ropczyce to issue decrees that forbade the Jewish women of Ropczyce to braid their hair, wear sandals or "German" clothes, or even appear in public without an escort.[220]

The position of women in Polish Hasidism appears more mixed. In the teachings of Polish zaddikim, women were no longer associated with the demonic realm, as they had been in earlier Hasidic sermons.[221] The Maskil Joseph Perl charged that the Maggid of Kozienice's daughter Perele was partner to her father's deception by selling home remedies to Hasidic pilgrims, and several sources claim that Perele adopted religious customs normally reserved for men.[222] The Maggid of Kozienice himself attracted a great deal of criticism for his famous decision to clear a Staszów woman of her *agunah* (forbidden) status so that she might remarry.[223] The Seer of Lublin appears to have been lenient in matters pertaining to women, at least with regard to his own conduct. He once astonished his disciples by publicly escorting a woman; and when they questioned his immodest display, he explained that the act of escorting women contains a deep mystical secret, adding that they should not, however, try it themselves.[224] Upon the death of his wife Tehilla Shprinza, the elderly Seer married a young maiden from Lemberg named Beila.[225] Before the wedding, he was assailed by complaints that his fiancé was walking around in dyed clothing, according to the latest fashion. In response, the Seer walked to the window, wiped away the drops, looked out, and said "Does not such-and-such woman walk around in dyed clothing? This is nothing." The narrator of the tale emphasized, however, that Beila only did this in Lemberg.[226] Yet the Seer's last will and testament discloses his generous gifts of jewelry to Beila, which she might certainly have worn in Lublin.[227]

Polish Hasidism appears increasingly reactionary on this score by the second decade of the nineteenth century, notwithstanding Temerel's prodigious role. During the interrogations of the anti-Hasidic investigation of 1824, the zaddik Meir of Opatów/Stopnica was asked if wives of non-Hasidim were accepted as members. He responded, "They are free to come to our 'schools,' but women are not usually Hasidic. Moreover, women and children are under the authority of the father. If it is against the father's will to be Hasidic, they are not to be accepted."[228] In fact, R. Meir's answer was not accurate, for we know that women constituted a large proportion of Hasidic adherents and would visit zaddikim without their husbands' permission.[229] But the sentiment informing his reply is instructive. In this period Polish zaddikim, like their Galician predecessors, also began to issue restrictions against women walking around "with their flesh exposed" on the grounds that it invited divine wrath.[230] Access to the blessings and counsel of zaddikim thus came at a price.

Women who possessed *yihus* did enjoy a degree of favoritism, however, as witnessed during the encounter of the mother of R. Eleazar of Pułtusk with the Maggid of Kozienice:

The *gaon*, zaddik [R. Eleazar], of blessed memory told me: my
mother, the righteous Rabbanit, woman of valor among women . . .
Breindel, of blessed memory, once traveled on a journey, and traveled through the town of Kozienice with another woman, and I do
not remember who this other woman was, if she was her daughter
or sister. And when they came to the aforementioned town, they
wished to go to the house of the Maggid, the rabbi, true, holy, exalted *gaon* Israel [of Kozienice], of blessed memory, to receive a
blessing from him. And when they came to the outer room, the attendant said to them, "What is your request, where are you from?"
And they answered him "We are from the town of Leszno, in the
country of Prussia, daughters of the true genius, R. Jacob, *av bet din*
of Leszno." And he asked them what was their request, and they answered him that they wanted to receive a blessing from the zaddik,
Foundation of the World. And the attendant said that a few minutes
ago he had gone to pour his heart out before his Creator in the *bet
midrash*, to pray the morning service.[231]

The women made sure to mention their familial relationship to R. Jacob of
Leszno, who was revered in the Hasidic world.
    The identification of their *yihus* paid off:

And when the Rabbi, the Maggid, of blessed memory, was not too
far from his house, he saw that two women were walking to his
room. And he said to the attendant who was walking with him, "Go
back and ask the women who they are and what is their request."
And the attendant did so. And the attendant answered the holy rabbi
that those women were daughters of the true genius R. Jacob of
Leszno. And when he heard this, the rabbi, the holy Maggid, went
with his prayer shawl and phylacteries under his arm back to his
house and asked my mother and teacher, of blessed memory, "What
can I do for you?" And they said to him, "We came to the abode of
the zaddik, and we will not depart without a blessing." And the
Maggid, of blessed memory, placed his holy hand above their heads
and blessed them.[232]

Upon learning that the female petitioners were "daughters of the true genius,
R. Jacob, *av bet din* of Leszno," the Maggid put off his prayer and returned to
his house to inquire what he could do for them. Had they not possessed illustrious familial descent, we may suppose, the Maggid would not have been so
accommodating. Some members of "Israel" were loved more than others.

Evolving Attitudes Toward Miracles: The Case of Przysucha

Anti-Hasidic witnesses consistently fail to mention a crucial development in
Polish Hasidism at the beginning of the nineteenth century: the deemphasis

of miracle working by zaddikim of the Przysucha school. Perhaps Jacob Tugenhold had this school in mind when he claimed that Polish zaddikim were
"far less harmful" than their Ukrainian counterparts.[233] In any case, flamboyant
prophecy, healing, and other miracles had fallen out of vogue in these quarters.
R. Jacob Isaac, the "Holy Jew" of Przysucha, is famous for having asked rhe-
torically, "Is it such a great thing to be a miracle worker? Anyone who has
attained a basic level can invert heaven and earth. But to be a *good Jew*—that
is difficult."[234] Scholars have sometimes deduced from this tradition that zaddikim of the Przysucha school preferred more rationalistic pursuits like Talmudic study to the complete exclusion of magical and miraculous endeavors.[235]
However, as Mendel Piekarz has observed, one never finds an outright repu-
diation of magic and miracles in the Przysucha School. The Holy Jew and his
successor R. Simha Bunem continued to receive *pidyonot*, distribute advice,
prophesy, and render magical services, albeit more discreetly.[236] Their ambivalence helps establish the baseline of Hasidism's popular religious dimension.

There may be several explanations for the school's neutralization of miracle working. The "Holy Jew" and his followers represented a cadre of young
scholars who were disenchanted by the Seer of Lublin's preoccupation with
the material needs of his popular following, which, according to his own admission in a book endorsement (*haskamah*), left him little time for scholarship
and teaching.[237] This anti-intellectualism apparently disappointed the Holy Jew,
who initiated the great defection. It was no less problematic for R. Simha Bunem, whose Talmudic expertise was complemented by a grasp of secular
knowledge and non-Jewish languages, and whose training as a pharmacist and
experience as a merchant in Danzig, Breslau, and Leipzig predisposed him to
value sound advice over miracles.[238] R. Simha Bunem's attitude is borne out
in the quasi-autobiographical accounts in *Ramata'im Zofim* (Warsaw, 1885)
attributed to his scribe, R. Samuel Sieniawa (c. 1796–1874).[239] The accounts
comprise R. Simha Bunem's formative years, from his troubled school years
around 1775 through his initiation as a disciple of the Seer of Lublin.[240] In light
of the rarity of autobiographies of zaddikim, they are a boon to historians.[241]

R. Samuel was seventeen years old when he first encountered R. Simha
Bunem. At this meeting, R. Simha Bunem predicted the birth of his son
Joshua, our first indication that the worldly zaddik did not completely eschew
popular religion.[242] He could not, however, ward off his own blindness near
the end of his life; so he enlisted R. Samuel as his personal assistant. R. Samuel
enthusiastically recalls the first time that he "wrote the letter as he instructed
me, in his holy tongue, letter for letter."[243] Such service was a holy task:

> Once he said to me "Everything that you do in serving me, even the
> small things, do for the sake of the *mizvah* (good deed)." And be-
> cause I was always with him, and I would recite my lessons in his
> presence, the perceptive will understand that it was the greatest
> thing out of all the Torah and good qualities, for no one is equal to
> one who "is commanded and fulfills, etc.".[244] For through this, one
> reaches spirituality and holy cleaving from above to below.[245]

R. Samuel's duties and absolute submission were a preeminent means for achieving *devekut*.

R. Samuel had his work cut out for him, however. The young R. Simha Bunem emerges in these accounts as a complex religious personality, enduring alienation and rejection while seeking to balance his secular and religious strivings. As a pious scion of the elite he was, to be sure, accorded preferential treatment by some. But others disapproved of his secular proclivities and antinomian conduct. This was not ideal material for Hasidic sacred biography. But R. Samuel alighted on a brilliant solution for portraying this worldliness in a manner acceptable to his conservative readers: he loosely modeled the young Simha Bunem on the incognito Besht, whose own questionable conduct during his youth is described in *Shivhei Ha-Besht*. Of course, this approach had its limits, for unlike the Besht, R. Simha Bunem rarely displayed his miracle-working abilities. R. Samuel's solution to this second dilemma was to attempt to persuade his readers that R. Simha Bunem's rather commonplace or dubious feats were actually miracles. *Ramata'im Zofim* may thus be read as an updated *Shivhei ha-Besht*.

R. Simha Bunem's unremarkable performance at school fit in well with the Besht's famous disinclination toward conventional educational modes:

> Once His Holiness, the *admor* of Przysucha, of blessed memory, told me that when he was about ten years old, when he studied with the schoolteacher in Wodzisław and could not do as the schoolteacher demanded, the schoolteacher was furious with him and said to him in great anger, "Go away, for you will not be a scholar through the methods of the schoolteachers." And he dismissed him. And these words penetrated into his heart, and his heart broke as he sobbed profusely. And he walked to the river nearby. And he cried and cried until he felt comforted, and went back into town. And there was a homeowner who was distinguished and extremely acute, who taught a daily class in the *bet midrash*, by the name of R. Abba, of blessed memory. And he approached him, and asked him to read something for him. And he gave him the passage "*Le'odi Torah*, etc.," in the [Talmudic] volume *Baba Kama*.[246] And it came time to recite it before him, and he knew in his heart that he did not know anything. And when he came before him, he wept profusely. And [R. Abba's] heart warmed to him, and he began to assist him, and practically studied with him, and [Simha Bunem] grasped it very well. So when he fully understood that passage, [R. Abba] began to ask him about inconsistencies and questions, until he was amazed by his acute mind. And he was astonished, and saw that his capacity was amazing, and that he was a great prodigy; and so he began to study with him in the *bet midrash*. And afterward, he studied in the great yeshivas in Hungary, and with the genius R. Mordecai Benet of Nikolsburg.[247] And then a fire burned within him, and he would constantly hide himself in the attics, where he would recite songs

and praises. And he would hope for and anticipate the time when he would be able to lay *tefillin*.[248]

Like the Besht, the young Simha Bunem could not conform to the normative educational regimen. When he was tested in a less conventional yet more rigorous way, however, his extraordinary talent gleamed through.

Eventually, he began to blossom intellectually in the more individualistic yeshiva world and impress leaders of the normative community.

> Once he told of how he left the country of Hungary, where he stud-
> ied with the true genius Jeremiah of the holy community of Mates-
> dorf, for his father the Maggid [of Wodzisław] of blessed memory
> had brought him there to study.[249] And on his way home, he passed
> through the city of Lesko, in the country of His Majesty the Kai-
> ser.[250] And the great, famous rabbi and holy, pure genius Menahem
> Mendel ben Jacob, of blessed memory, who was the son-in-law of
> the great, holy genius R. Isaac Horowitz, *av bet din* of Hamburg,
> was there. And the aforementioned rabbi [Menahem Mendel] was
> the father of the holy Rabbi . . . Naftali, the rabbi of the holy commu-
> nity of Ropczyce, in the country of His Majesty the Kaiser.[251] And
> when he came to the holy community of Lesko, he went to the rabbi
> of the city, as is the manner of all yeshiva students. And when he
> beheld his face, [R. Simha Bunem] found favor in his eyes, and he
> invited him to his Sabbath table. And they ate together as one; and
> afterward, he departed in peace and affection. And it is known that
> [R. Menahem Mendel's] habit was to always eat alone, and there
> were never any youngsters with him on the holy Sabbath, for he was
> holy and awesome, as is known. And in spite of this, he asked him
> to dine with him! For obviously he saw what will come of this young
> man. And in the eyes of [R. Simha Bunem] this was such a won-
> drous thing that he remembered it for a long time. And the percep-
> tive will understand how great are the deeds of zaddikim![252]

The reason for the favoritism is unclear. Was it due to Simha Bunem's intellectual prowess? His *yihus*? His personality alone? Whatever the reason,
R. Samuel insists that we regard it as miraculous.

Another set of accounts invites parallels to *Shivhei Ha-Besht*, as well: like
the Besht, R. Simha Bunem could discern that meat of questionable ritual
purity was kosher.[253]

> And [R. Simha Bunem] said that he could sense, even during his
> distant childhood, that he had attained such a great level that he
> would be able to eat in places where Hasidim do not eat, such as
> villages and the like.[254]
> And once, when he journeyed to Lublin with other Hasidim, he
> ate meat in a village. And this did not appear to the Hasidim to be
> God-fearing. But when he came with them to greet the rabbi [Jacob

Isaac, the Seer of Lublin] there, the rabbi of blessed memory placed his hand on [R. Simha Bunem's] stomach and said, "Your flesh (i.e., meat) is holy flesh"![255]

His dietary laxity extended to foods considered exotic, and therefore of uncertain status, as well. This was probably owing to his comparative worldliness:

> Once he told us about the great zaddik R. Moses of Przeworsk,[256] of blessed memory, who was known to the whole world as manifestly possessing the holy spirit, and of whom all the world—even those who were not Hasidic—was in awe on account of his great righteousness: "And the rabbi R. Elimelekh [of Leżajsk] of blessed memory traveled to him. And the aforementioned rabbi R. Moses the Great was in the holy community of Mogielnica. And R. Jacob, son of the aforementioned R. Elimelekh of Leżajsk [was there].[257] So the Hasidim traveled there, and I, too, was among the visitors. And they made a morning feast on his behalf, and on behalf of the various renowned people. But the rabbi R. Moses did not generally eat any meat, except on the Sabbath, and so the meal was dairy. And he ordered them to prepare him a vegetarian dish called *kraut*. And when he sat there at the table with the important Hasidic people, and they brought the vegetables to the table, he said, 'Who can eat the vegetables with me?' And they replied that they could not eat the vegetables. And they did not want to eat it, because they were ever cautious about this, and said, 'Not everyone can eat this dish' [because of its uncertain status]. And R. Moses got up from the table and walked up and down the room and asked each person to eat the dish with him. And when he was asking, he found me among the Hasidim at the end, for I had not pushed my way up to the front. And when he saw me, he took me by the hand and walked with me to his seat at his table. And he said to me, 'Sit with me and eat the vegetables with me, for you are permitted to eat this dish.' And he ate the dish with me in the same bowl, and everyone was astonished by this." And this occurred during his youth.[258]

Eating meat in places where dietary standards were more relaxed, or in the latter case, exotic foods, was perceived by some as impious. Indeed, there is a palpable suggestion of antinomianism here. But R. Simha Bunem was always exonerated by zaddikim of the stature of the Seer of Lublin and R. Moses of Przeworsk, the reader is assured.

The young Simha Bunem further resembled the incognito Besht in exhibiting "non-Jewish" behavior.[259] By R. Simha Bunem's day, this meant dressing in a Western manner and studying secular subjects. The most striking parallelism appears in the later collection *Si'ah Sarfei Kodesh* (Counsel of the Holy Seraphs):

> I heard that before the holy R. Simha Bunem, of blessed memory, of Przysucha revealed himself, he was a bookkeeper for the *Konsu-*

mpcja [Kosher Meat Tax] in the town of Siedlce.[260] And he shared an apartment with the rabbi, the Hasid, R. Kalman of blessed memory, and used to behave and dress like a commoner. Once on the eve of the holy Sabbath, when R. Kalman of blessed memory came back from the prayer house, the rabbi R. Simha Bunem of blessed memory remained in his room [after prayer] and did not go to the dining room. And when R. Kalman's wife tired of waiting for [R. Simha Bunem] to come, she went herself and opened the door to his room. And she looked, and behold, the holy rabbi R. Simha Bunem of blessed memory was dressed in white silk and wrapped in a prayer shawl, and this was wondrous in her eyes. And she told her husband about the wondrous thing she had seen. But her husband rebuked her never to look in there again.[261]

R. Simha Bunem was to all appearances a "commoner," not a gentle and pious Torah scholar—the ideal Jewish masculine-type.[262] His splendor was revealed only to R. Kalman's wife, an accidental witness. Similarly, the Besht, according to *Shivhei Ha-Besht*, "changed into clothes like those worn by simpletons: a short fur coat and a broad belt. And he changed his demeanor and manner of speech." Only on the Sabbath would the Besht surreptitiously don white garments and pray with extraordinary attachment. Once, a guest who was sleeping in the Besht's home on the Sabbath awoke to find a fire blazing around the Besht as he prayed, and this was also "wondrous in his eyes." But the Besht rebuked him "not to look at what he was not supposed to see."[263]

In *Ramata'im Zofim*, a great zaddik like R. Moses Hayyim Ephraim of Suzylków, grandson of the Besht, could see through the young Simha Bunem's disguise.

And once he related how the holy rabbi R. [Moses Hayyim] Ephraim of the holy community of Sudzylków[264]—author of the book *Degel Mahane Ephraim* [Berdyczów, 1808], brother of the great rabbi R. Barukh of Międzybóż, and grandson of the Besht, may his merit defend us—this zaddik was in the holy community of Lemberg. And he spent the Sabbath with the great zaddik R. Leib the Whisperer [*di memeles*] there, brother-in-law of the holy Rabbi of Lublin, may his soul rest in peace. And he was wealthy and a great host, as everyone knows. And [R. Simha Bunem] of Przysucha of blessed memory was at this time in Lemberg for business purposes (to earn his pharmaceutical license from the *Rada Lekarstwo* [Medical Board]. And the director, when he saw the greatness of his medical wisdom without any teacher or textbook owing to lack of money, gave [R. Simha Bunem] six Reichsteller to buy the course book which he needed for this business. And he bought a *Zohar* book [instead], for a local bookseller appeared before him just as he was going out of there.)

Here we should pause to point out a minor discrepancy: the detail about R. Simha Bunem earning a pharmaceutical license in Lemberg in parentheses, probably inserted by the editor. It is inaccurate, considering that Jews were not allowed to obtain pharmaceutical licenses in Galicia until 1832, five years after R. Simha Bunem's death. Aaron Marcus was probably correct in asserting that he earned the license in Danzig.[265]

Regardless of the precise purpose of his visit to Lemberg, R. Simha Bunem was not dressed as a proper Hasid. This bothered his host, notwithstanding the editor's gracious rationalization:

> And when [R. Simha Bunem] heard about this zaddik [R. Moses Hay-yim Ephraim], and he went before the zaddik in German clothes, for he did not have time on Sabbath afternoon to change his clothes, [R. Moses Hayyim Ephraim] greeted him and told him to go to the aforementioned homeowner R. Leib the Whisperer, to seek permission to eat with him on the holy Sabbath. But when he came before the aforementioned rabbi R. Leib, he did not want to receive him (because they [the other Hasidim] did not know him. And the Hasidim would shame him,[266] and he would feel badly on account of this guest). And [R. Simha Bunem] protested: do you not receive all guests throughout the city, even vagrants and beggars, on every holy Sabbath? And why am I considered less than them? And [R. Simha Bunem] wanted to pay him, but he did not accept. And he said to himself, "I will do this: I will put a piece of bread the size of an olive in my sleeve. And I will sit in the doorway of the house so they will not see me. And in any case, I will be with the zaddik [Moses Hayyim Ephraim] within the walls of the house."

R. Moses Hayyim Ephraim, a true zaddik, was not fooled by the young Simha Bunem's secular disguise. He quickly identified him, showed him great respect, shared his own food with him, and regaled him with homilies and drinks throughout the night.

> "And when [R. Moses Hayyim Ephraim] came to make the blessing over the wine, he looked here and there and did not find me. And he walked away from the table to seek me within the crowd, and inquired, and found me sitting by the stove. And I said to him, 'Good Sabbath.' And he took me by the hand and walked me to the table in front of everyone. And then the Rabbi [Moses Hayyim Ephraim] made the blessing over the wine according to his custom. And after the blessing, he poured wine into the cup and gave it to me to bless. And when I received the cup, after the blessing over the wine, I drank the cup of wine and said to the aforementioned holy Rabbi, 'I already discharged my obligation for the blessing through the Rabbi's blessing.' And afterward, he took me by the hand and sat me with him, and let me eat from his plate, from each thing. And

he said, 'If the homeowner [R. Leib] does not want to feed you, I can give to whomever I please from my own plate.' And after the meal, I excused myself. And the aforementioned zaddik said to me that he would like for me to spend the night of this holy Sabbath with him, in his room. And he ordered his attendant to prepare him a big goblet of liquor for the night. And that they should prepare pillows and cushions well for me, and that I would reside with him. Then he taught on the verse 'And he called his name Esau' [Gen. 25:25] that everyone called him thus.[267] For the word 'calling' is related to the word 'drawing.' For everyone is drawn to lies, but not everyone understands truth."[268] And when he recalled these things, the well-known wealthy R. Izik Rapoport of Lemberg was there with him.[269]

Like the Besht, R. Simha Bunem was treated as an outcast during this incognito period. Only a zaddik like R. Mosese Hayyim Ephraim detected his hidden greatness. Such instances of recognition occurred during the Besht's incognito phase, as well.[270]

This loose conformity to earlier typologies in *Shivhei Ha-Besht* does not necessarily negate the historical value of these testimonies. First, it is likely that R. Simha Bunem sought deliberately to model himself on the Besht by staging scenes similar to those from *Shivhei Ha-Besht*.[271] But one also detects the interpretive hand of the hagiographer, whose delicate task was to present events in a form that was acceptable to his traditional audience without, however, sacrificing precious details about a zaddik's life. The incognito claim enabled hagiographers to contend with widely known flaws or shortcomings. The Besht's hagiographer could justify his uncouth appearance and lack of normative learning, *yihus,* and wealth by depicting it as a temporary concealment, in addition to invoking the familiar leitmotif of "secret zaddikim"—undetected holy men who were believed to be present in every generation.[272] The incognito model also allowed the Besht's hagiographer to appeal to several distinct audiences at once. Educated elites were reassured that their ranks had not been infiltrated by a commoner, for, appearances aside, the Besht had been holy and refined all along. Members of the lower strata were also reassured, for although he was a picture of pious perfection, it helped to be reminded that he was once considered an ignoramus, a commoner, or as "un-Jewish" as them. R. Samuel seems to have absorbed this lesson well. He could explain away his latter-day zaddik's unconventional intellectual development and controversial secular pursuits as a disguise, invoke the by now classic model of the incognito Besht, and achieve the multifaceted appeal that constitutes the touchstone of effective populism.

However, as mentioned, R. Samuel was constrained by R. Simha Bunem's ambivalence toward miracles. His solution was to construe anything that appeared out of the ordinary in his master's biography as a miracle. In contrast to the exorcisms and a host of other types of miracles that animate the tales in *Shivhei ha-Besht*, the feats in *Ramata'im Zofim* thus appear extremely mundane. A miracle is barely implied in the following description of R. Simha Bunem's exploits as a pharmacist during the Napoleonic Wars:

Once on Yom Kippur eve he related that when he was a merchant [pharmacist] and there was at that time a great war, the French established a huge camp in Prussia.[273] And there was an expert doctor with them. [The account now shifts to First person.] "And I prayed the *kol nidre* prayer of Yom Kippur at the lectern. And during the hour of silent prayer, may God not exact vengeance, messengers of the doctor came up to me in the synagogue with a [receipt] he wrote for a certain higher officer of the army; and it was very urgent. And they waited until I finished the silent prayer. And they approached me at the ark and gave me the [receipt]. And I read it, and responded that after the prayer service I will be with the Chief of Staff. And they went away and did not come again, and I concluded my prayers. But when I went home, I found the aforementioned doctor and his children sitting in my house and crying that I should have mercy on them and not go to the aforementioned officer, so that he will know who put him in mortal danger. For [the doctor] had intentionally given me the receipt in order to obstruct me in my prayer. And the Holy One, Blessed be He confused his heart, and he wrote a certain poisonous prescription upon it! And as is known, during a time of war this made him subject to the death penalty. And the doctor confessed, and sanctified the name of Heaven before the multitudes, for the entire city had gathered there. And I was quite callous and had no mercy on him. But the other people had mercy on him and requested it of me, and I did not so much as look at them either. The crowd, who wanted to donate a large sum of money to the kahal as a redemption for his soul—but I did not want to accept it—advised him to gather all the homeowners of the city and donate money to the kahal; and they would run to them and request their presence. 'And if not, then he will not have mercy on you no matter what; for you sought to distract him from his prayer.' And thus he did. And he gathered all the homeowners and fell on the ground before them. And the delegation requested that I show him mercy, particularly since he says that he will never again oppress another son of Israel. And I said, 'For your sake, I will do this and have mercy on him. And do not take anything from him, God forbid.' " All this he recalled on Yom Kippur eve, in order to publicize the matter, and the wonders of those of pure inclination and the providence of the Holy One, Blessed be He.[274]

The miracle, the doctor's accidental prescription of poison, is attributed to divine retribution for obstructing R. Simha Bunem's Yom Kippur prayers. God, rather than the zaddik, is the author of this miracle. The most one can say about this highly unlikely incident is that R. Simha Bunem enjoyed a special divine favor, and that the typical hierarchy between a doctor and a pharmacist was in this case inverted.

Miracles are equally elusive in the series of accounts concerning R. Simha Bunem's discipleship with the Seer of Lublin:

> Once he recalled how he used to always travel to Kozienice, and he still did not know the Rabbi of Lublin, of blessed memory. For he had not yet become famous, for he had just come to Lublin from Łańcut on account of the Rabbi, Hasid R. Jamshi of Lublin, of blessed memory. And the holy rabbi R. Phineas of [Ma]gniewszów,[275] of blessed memory, who is famous, was there with the rabbi, the holy Maggid [of Kozienice]. And he said to him, "Know that the root of your soul is with the Rabbi of Lublin," of blessed memory. "And when I heard this, after I departed from the holy rabbi, the Maggid, of blessed memory after the holy Sabbath, I set my face toward Lublin. And I was there with him on the holy Sabbath, and he taught Torah on the eve of the holy Sabbath." And [R. Simha Bunem] said: "I did not understand anything that the rabbi of blessed memory said. But this much I understood well: that the upper world, the World to Come, was here in this world with this rabbi. And after the blessing after the meal, when the rabbi got up from the table to leave, he passed before me and both his holy hands fell upon me, and [he] said in these words, '[Bunem, Dear], join yourself to me, and you will have a holy spirit from the World of *Azilut*,[276] and all the world will run to you!' and other similar blessings; but I cannot recall those other things exactly.[277]
>
> "And once, before Rosh Hashanna, he ordered all those gathered to introduce themselves before him. And though I barely could, I introduced myself too. And the Rabbi said, 'The *shofar* blast is wisdom, etc.'[278] And for this, R. Bunem shall blow it." And I entered before him, and he taught me the special intention of the *shofar* blast. And after that, he said to me, 'Take the *shofar* and "intend" it.' And I said, 'I will never be able to blow it.' And he was angry with me. And I replied, 'Even Moses our Rabbi, peace be with him, spoke this way before God, saying "Tell me what is Your Name, etc." [Ex. 3:13]; "I am that which I am, etc." [Ex. 3:15]; And he said, "I am not an eloquent man." [Ex. 4:10].'[279] Witness and comprehend the powers of zaddikim![280]
>
> Once he related how the holy rabbi the Rabbi of Lublin, of blessed memory, said to him that he must study a certain Law with him, so that he will be his disciple. And the Rabbi, of blessed memory, walked to the chest of books and randomly selected a book. And the book was the *Shulhan Arukh*, "Even ha-Ezer." And he opened the *Shulhan Arukh* randomly, and the Rabbi found the law of Seven Blessings,[281] and when we should say, "joy in His chamber."[282] And

he studied these laws with him in his chamber. And after he finished with it, the Rabbi of blessed memory said, with his holy mouth, "Now you are my disciple, and I am your Rabbi," several times. And he concluded: "And we, too, have a nice, fond memory, for your name is 'Simha Bunem,' and there is truly "joy [simha] in his chamber!" And they departed in peace. And who can grasp the secret of holy ones? For the Holy One, Blessed be He, undoubtedly provided these opportunities for [the Seer's] own good, so that there will be a fond memory of him. And it is possible that this was the year of [the Seer's] death,[283] and the purpose was to sustain him according to the saying, "A man shall only depart while speaking of Jewish Law, so that by this he will be remembered."[284]

R. Simha Bunem admits that when he met the Seer of Lublin, he could not understand him; and the miracle appears to be his ability to detect the Seer's greatness notwithstanding. When R. Simha Bunem was commanded by the Seer to blow the *shofar*, he failed to do so. Here, the miracle is apparently R. Simha Bunem's clever invocation of the failings of Moses. When the Seer opened the *Shulhan Arukh* randomly, he hit upon a law that lent itself to a nice pun. Yet the miracle is again attributed to God rather than the zaddik.

Seldom has Hasidic hagiography revealed so flawed and ordinary a hero. He did not excel in a conventional sense in primary school, he played fast and loose with dietary laws, dressed in non-Jewish attire, and pursued secular training. He proved almost unwilling to forgive the doctor who obstructed his Yom Kippur prayers, revealing himself as stubborn and vengeful. But the most striking feature of *Ramata'im Zofim* is the extremely ordinary nature of the miracles. We are expected to marvel at the most simple things: R. Simha Bunem's atypical intellectual development, his invitations to dine with the reclusive R. Menahem Mendel of Lesko and the zaddik Moses Hayyim Ephraim of Sudzylków, his daring to eat questionable foods, and his witty repartees with the Seer of Lublin after failing in the holy task assigned to him. True, this all occurred during R. Simha Bunem's incognito phase. But even after he was "revealed" as a zaddik, he seldom showcased his supernatural powers. Extravagant miracle claims were rarely made, and deliveries of health, fertility, and material sustenance were usually rendered indirectly. Prayers were the principle theurgical tool: according to one witness cited in *Ramata'im Zofim*, the Rabbi of Łęczna, Przysucha zaddikim proclaimed that their prayers could "bear fruit below" and "achieve repairs and unifications above."[285] But even those events that we might recognize as miracles seem steeped in the mundane. According to a twice-repeated account, R. Simha Bunem once perceived "from heaven" that a *pidyon* of 3 rubles had derived from a dishonest business transaction, and would cause him to be punished. The zaddik returned the money to the original donor and rebuked him.[286] The business world, rather than the demonic realm, is its focus.

The Rabbi of Łęczna attempts to explain the Przysucha position on miracle working: "the way of the *admor* of Przysucha of blessed memory was to not pay heed to miracles, even his own. Nevertheless, I heard from his holy mouth that it [i.e., miracle working] is the mark of a zaddik."[287] We are to ignore, then, the zaddik's defining characteristic. The paradox is probably meant to be left unresolved, for only such ambiguity could accommodate emergent rationalistic trends in Central Poland without diminishing popular devotion to the Przysucha zaddikim. Popular religion was thereby rendered in a spirit that was more acceptable to an increasingly urbanized and worldly Jewish youth. As a result, Przysucha Hasidism attracted some of the next generation's most talented scholars and founders of major Polish Hasidic courts, while at the same time continuing to draw a mass following.

Conclusion

R. Simha Bunem was a product of a transitional age, and a symbol of Polish Jewry's simultaneous economic advancement and social retreat. He belied contemporary caricatures of Polish zaddikim by casting his magical services in a rationalistic mold, which was eminently compatible with the rationalistic form of Prysucha Hasidism's teachings. To be sure, all zaddikim invested their folk remedies, blessings, divination, exorcisms, and other conventions of popular religion with a certain amount of discretion and decorum, certainly a great deal more than contemporary *ba'alei shem*. But Przysucha zaddikim went furthest in dignifying and professionalizing their popular religious enterprises. They thereby represent an extreme case of the impressive adaptability of Polish zaddikim to the region's increasingly urbanized landscape and diverse Jewish population.

Such savvy should not lead us to assume that Polish zaddikim were guided solely by political expedience or more base motivations, however. They seem in many cases to have sold magical services that they believed they could really render. In describing them as "not deceivers, but rather deceived, for . . . they believe themselves to be enraptured, and that they are inspired by the spirit of prophecy," the anonymous report cited earlier may have been more generous than other non-Hasidic testimonies. But we still should not dismiss the power of suggestion and the psychological force of charisma within a community of believers. If credulous petitioners had not conceived children, regained their health, prospered in business ventures, and felt empowered despite their unemancipated status, a zaddik's popularity could not have been sustained. When it comes to the potency of hope, faith, and a sensation of empowerment, the historian must withhold judgment. At the same time, perhaps we ought also to be open to the possibility that deception did occur. It may well be that zaddikim sometimes knowingly manipulated followers—through the employment of spies (as Solomon Maimon charged), deliberately obscure Kabbalistic exegesis (as Jacques Calmanson charged), or rationalizations for failed predictions (as Abraham Stern charged). But it may be that they did so for reasons other than filling their coffers and expanding their popular bases. Occasional deception provided hope: a pilgrim whose business affairs were inexplicably improved thanks to his zaddik's inside information, or who received a placebo for an ailment, still gained a sense of empowerment where the alternative was anxiety and despair. The zaddikim probably sensed that the rabbinic elite had failed the Jewish masses, and strove to encourage and console them through popular religious forms.

This heightened concern for the "common person" should not, however, be mistaken for inclusiveness. True, Polish zaddikim received all petitioners, regardless of class, gender, or prior sinful conduct. In particular, they supplied restless and moody youth with rites of passage, spiritual succor, and release for pent-up emotions; and they offered women new avenues to spirituality by addressing their fertility concerns, granting face-to-face interviews, and elevating their souls vicariously through their own *devekut*—all occurring outside of the women's galley in the synagogue. But they cultivated folk religion on their own terms, preserving the social hierarchy by selectively grooming successors among sons of wealthy or scholarly followers. Only members of lower classes who proved exceptionally promising could earn similar favor. It may be concluded that Polish zaddikim empowered non-elites by dispensing popular religious services indiscriminately, but never empowered them in a sociopolitical sense.

6

Sermons, Stories, and Songs

Marketing Hasidism

Believe me, there are among them such zaddikim as are capable of
virtually raising the dead through the potency of their prayer. I have
seen it with my own eyes, not simply heard it by rumor, how on
many occasions they brought to them invalids for whom there was
no hope. And yet by means of their pure prayer, these people were
restored to perfectly good health as before.

—Zechariah Mendel of Jarosław, letter to
his uncle, printed in the appendix to
Elimelekh of Leżajsk, *No'am Elimelekh*

As we have seen, Hasidism emanated from scions of the Jewish
elite and yet penetrated the most diverse reaches of the Jewish populace. The "incognito" device discussed in the previous chapter was
but one way that a broad appeal was achieved. In other instances,
zaddikim crafted sermons that invoked Kabbalistic symbols that, ar-
cane as they might be, were comprehensible on one level for the un-
initiated and on another level for initiates. The ten emanations of
God, or *sefirot*, were particularly well suited to a multitiered purpose
because they signified the potencies of the godhead by means of recognizable human traits (wisdom, mercy, might, glory, etc.). The imputed confluence between each divine potency and its human no-
menclature invited listeners to recognize a correspondence between
their own psyches and an otherwise remote theosophical structure.
In Hasidism, according to Gershom Scholem, "almost all the Kabbalistic ideas are now placed in relation to values particular to the
individual life."[1]

This occasional "psychologization" of Kabbalah may be illustrated through a discourse by the Seer of Lublin:

When the human quality of mercy [*hesed*] is restored, the same effect is produced above, so that God does not favor Israel's enemies,
nor love them, nor show them a merry countenance.

And so it is with the opposite quality, might [*gevurah*]: one
should only anger and despise evil people. This ensures that there
will not be any severe judgment [*din*] on Israel, God forbid, and that
severe judgment will only be visited upon Israel's enemies.

And so it is with the attribute of glory [*tiferet*], that one will not
intentionally glorify himself. Rather, he should glorify only the Holy
One, Blessed be He, so that He will in turn glorify us. This ensures
that the enemies of Israel will not have any reason to glorify themselves.[2]

This exemplary passage would make sense to most Jews. They need not visu-
alize the specific upper *sefirot* signified by "mercy," "might," and "glory." They
need only recognize those attributes within themselves and understand that
their application somehow aroused supernal entities for the betterment of Jews
or their oppressors. Kabbalistic initiates in the audience, on the other hand,
could sate their curiosity about the inner workings of the universe by visual-
izing the precise divine potencies and their corollary, interactive process. Other
Polish Zaddikim delivered similar multitiered discourses on the *sefirot*.[3]

But it was not always possible to achieve comprehensive appeal at one
stroke. More often, zaddikim tailored their didactic modes to the capacities of
specific audiences, and did it so effectively that their dissemination of Hasidism may be considered a type of marketing or propaganda. The emissaries
who descended upon various communities, preaching, worshiping, and chanting in the Hasidic fashion, represented the movement's preliminary outreach
efforts. But the maturation of Hasidism into a mass movement saw a refinement, expansion, and intensification of publicity campaigns utilizing printed
homiletic sermons, oral and written folktales, and songs and dances. Although
there was some overlap (Hasidism was surely experienced as an interplay of
various genres), specific genres were expected to resonate more among groups
possessing certain linguistic abilities or limitations. Hebrew homiletic literature, written in the learned idiom of rabbinic exegesis, was directed more at
the elite; printed wonder tales in Hebrew and Yiddish translation reached a
wider readership consisting of both elites and literate nonelites; and oral and
nonverbal media, like folktales, songs, and dance carried Hasidism to the semiliterate and illiterate masses, including most women. This sociolinguistic dimension enables us to more fully comprehend the potentially misleading social
inversions in "The Horses" and other tales that were disseminated among
semiliterate and illiterate groups in their original oral forms. Similar praise of
the disenfranchised at the expense of elites is notably lacking in Hasidic homiletic literature, and this should come as no surprise: such biting social criticism would not have earned a very enthusiastic response in what I will argue
was a predominately elite Hebrew readership. This disparity of message, which

cannot have been accidental, illustrates how different strata of Jewish society experienced Hasidism in different, sociolinguistically determined ways.

"Preaching to the Thousands and Ten Thousands": Hasidic Printing

According to Abraham Joshua Heschel, "this great movement is essentially an oral movement, one that cannot be preserved in written form. It is ultimately a living movement. It is not contained fully in any of its books."[4] Ze'ev Gries, the preeminent historian of Hasidic printing, similarly warns that the Hasidic experience "was not essentially literary but rather a direct, immediate, personal experience of relationship with the Hasidic leader and his community of followers."[5] While these scholars are no doubt correct to emphasize the oral nature of the movement, they nonetheless fail to account for the veritable explosion of Hasidic literary output by the end of the eighteenth century and the concomitant sizeable Hasidic reading public. The pioneering historian Majer Bałaban, for example, identified Hasidism as the single most important force behind the acceleration of Polish Jewish book production during this period.[6] The record of Hasidic printing, usually facilitated by non-Hasidic and non-Jewish printers driven solely by considerations of profit, reflects extraordinary consumer demand. Where barriers to Hasidic book production proved insurmountable, as in the case of Central Poland during the early nineteenth century, the importation and smuggling of Hasidic books from other regions merely intensified. And whenever censorship was temporarily relaxed, Polish Hasidim swiftly resumed their publishing endeavors.

How to explain the prodigious literary output of this avowedly oral movement? We will begin this section with a full accounting of printing during the movement's rise, followed by a look at the motivations behind printing expressed in rabbinic endorsements (haskamot). We will then describe the Hasidic reading public, and conclude with a discussion of the evidence of Hasidic reading in Central Poland in particular. It will become evident that although books assumed a secondary importance in comparison to the direct delivery of sermons from the lips of the zaddik, it was what we might call a "close second." Hasidic books played a vital role in elevating the "zaddik idea" among the traditional elite, which indirectly raised its status among the masses.

The majority of Hasidic books fall under the rubric of *mussar* (ethics)[7] and may be subcategorized as homiletic works, conduct literature, epistles, and hagiography.[8] Homiletic works are best described as anthologies of mystically inspired biblical exegesis. As they are by far the most prominent type of Hasidic book, scholars of Hasidism usually depend on them to distill the Hasidic message. Yet Ze'ev Gries has introduced a great deal of skepticism about what these books can really teach us about the movement. According to Gries, the fact that the first such book, *Toldot Ya'akov Yosef,* did not appear until 1780, rather long after the emergence of Hasidism, proves their low priority. Moreover, he argues, most Hasidic books comprised secondhand accounts: previously oral Yiddish sermons delivered during the Sabbath Third Meal that were subsequently translated into Hebrew and written down by disciples (rather than the masters themselves). They were seldom printed until years after their authorship, often after the zaddik's death. Gries concludes that "early Hasidism did not consider the book an important tool for the dissemination of Hasidic ideas or the construction of a distinctive community ethos; both of these functions were performed chiefly by the circulation of oral traditions."[9] Hasidic literature is only of use to the historian because "the oral traditions of early Hasidism are no longer retrievable in their original form, and . . . our only access to them is through the literary adaptations and translations within which they have been preserved."[10] Gries's skepticism about the relevance of Hasidic printing—a subject to which he has ironically devoted the larger part of his career—is quite a gadfly, for the majority of scholarship on Hasidism is based on its printed homiletic literature.

In a more crude and polemical manner, the inveterate early twentieth-century Mitnagged Ephraim Dinard made a similar argument, noting that "jumbled and crazy Hasidic and Kabbalistic books were only printed forty or fifty years after the rise of Hasidism."[11] Like Gries, Dinard ascribed this delay to the movement's low estimation for printed works in general, albeit in absurdly exaggerated terms: "those books did not merit study by anybody, and the small numbers of them were left to wallow in the darkness of the repositories of huge libraries, and no one saw them. And most Hasidim did not even hear of their titles, and no one perceived them aside from the bibliographer." He concluded:

> it is difficult to find a Hasid who knows the Hasidic teachings from books. And as for the Hasid who believes in truth—although there are but few of them—it is enough for him to look at the face of his rabbi, for there he will behold a symbol of truth, the Torah, and God. And this is more important for him than that which is in a book, printed on paper.[12]

Although Dinard was obviously given to hyperbole and naked derision, his core assertions seem to accord with those of Gries.

If such claims about the low priority of printed teachings are stripped of their excesses and restricted to Hasidism's earliest period, they are arguably valid. But the undoubtedly lengthy process of transcription and circulation of manuscripts that preceded an immense output of Hasidic books beginning in 1780, the numerous endorsements (*haskamot*) that accompanied the books, as well as the inexhaustible efforts to import or smuggle them in when censorship proved effective, all cry out for explanation. Would such energy be invested in an enterprise that was only of marginal importance? It is more plausible that the Hasidic attitude toward printing evolved in tandem with the movement's sociopolitical aims. These evolving objectives explain why printed collections of Hasidic teachings did not appear until 1780 and then began to proliferate so dramatically. That date marks the transition from a manuscript culture, which was necessarily highly restricted, to a more accessible print culture. It therefore also marks the realization of an agenda to disseminate the zaddik-idea throughout eastern Europe's entire Hebrew readership.[13]

According to Meir Wunder, Hasidic teachings were entirely oral in the first stage owing to a fear that the zaddik's holy words would be compromised in print.[14] Wunder cites the well-known tale in *Shivhei Ha-Besht*, in which the Besht saw a demon walking with a manuscript containing his teachings. The Besht "gathered all his followers and asked them, 'Who among you is writing down my teachings?' " The man admitted it and he brought the manuscript to the Besht. The Besht examined it and said, 'There is not even a single word here that is mine.' "[15] The Besht's disavowal extended to Hasidic printing in general, and suggests an insipient movement struggling to retain its "pure" form by remaining oral. We should add that, according to a recently discovered manuscript, an eighteenth-century *ba'al shem* named Hillel similarly decried printed manuals of mystical practices as bastardization.[16] However, this mind-set was ironically repudiated through the printing of Besht's tale itself in 1815.

Wunder then discerns a second stage during which the teachings of zaddikim were written down for the sake of pilgrims who lived in distant locales "so that what the zaddik said on the Sabbaths which they missed would not also be missed."[17] Several Hasidic masters were willing to pay dearly for copies of *Toldot Ya'akov Yosef*, and R. Jacob Joseph himself (d. 1782) professed a positive inclination toward the written word.[18] R. Dov Ber, the "Great Maggid" of Międzyrzecz (d. 1772), actually demanded an explanation from his disciple R. Solomon of Łuck when he refrained from recording his teachings. R. Solomon protested that he saw how other disciples distorted his teachings when committing them to writing, but the Great Maggid replied, "Nevertheless, in whatever form they are written they are all for the better, for they are testimony to the worship of God, Blessed be He." The Great Maggid then revealed the immortalizing function of books: "Is what King David sought such an insignificant thing in your eyes: 'I will dwell in Your tents forever [*olamim*]' (Psalms 61:5); that is, in *both* worlds [*olamim*]?"[19] The implication was that after his death the Great Maggid could simultaneously dwell in heaven and on earth, the latter in the form of a book. R. Elimelekh of Leżajsk (d. 1786) eventually expressed the wish that his teachings be printed after his death, as well.[20] This transitional stage, probably occurring in the 1770s, was followed by a third, in which publishing the zaddik's teachings now became the norm and certain zaddikim literally authored their books.[21]

It is difficult to say more on the subject without a full accounting of early Hasidic printing ventures. As it stands, it is not known how many Hasidic titles were printed during the movement's rise, which ones were printed most frequently, when and where they were printed, who authored them, and who endorsed them.[22] The list in appendix 3 attempts a comprehensive record of works by Hasidic authors through 1815, including their various editions and endorsers. The sheer volume of works on the list is impressive. By the end of 1815, according to appendix 3, a total of sixty-eight titles had been printed in what amounted to 165 editions. R. Dov Ber of Międzyrzecz's disciples thus oversaw a spectacular literary revival. We can thus state with certainty that sweeping generalizations about the ancillary role of printing in Hasidism are untenable.

The second thing to note is what was generally read. The most frequently printed titles by the end of 1815, according to appendix 3, were *The Tanya* (eleven); *Maggid Devarov le-Ya'akov* (eight); *Zava'at ha-Ribash* (eight), *Alfa Beta* (seven), *No'am Elimelekh* (seven); *Hilkhot Talmud Torah* (six) and *Or ha-Me'ir* (six). This list reveals a great deal about the popularity and influence of specific titles. Although many of these seven titles are already assumed to have been important during the movement's ascension, the reception of Zvi Hirsch of Nadvorna's *Alfa Beta* is rather unexpected. This concise, alphabetized conduct manual, printed seven times by 1815, had a popularity that was way out of proportion with the scholarly consideration it has received (only Gries, grounded as he is in Hasidic bibliography, devotes attention to it).[23] Even more vexing, however, is the absence of several books that have attracted a disproportionate amount of scholarly attention. This absence raises disquieting questions about scholarly priorities, which appear quite arbitrary from a bibliographical perspective. For example, how representative of the early Hasidic ethos, we might reasonably ask, was a book like Menahem Mendel of Witebsk's *Pri ha-Arez*, printed only once during the movement's entire formative phase yet frequently invoked in essays on Hasidism?[24]

The list in appendix 3 also disputes assumptions about geographical distribution. Hayyim Lieberman has contributed to the issue by proving that few presses that produced these books were owned or run by Hasidim.[25] Yet Lieberman is surely wrong in claiming that Polish and Galician Hasidism were too marginal before 1837 to warrant bibliographical scrutiny.[26] A mere glance at the geographic distribution of Hasidic printing up to 1815 corrects this profound oversight (see table 6.1). The presses in Żółkiew and Lemberg, both in Galicia, actually yielded the greatest number of Hasidic titles through 1815. Competition from Galician printers was moreover keenly felt in the Korzec, located in the Ukraine and part of the Polish Commonwealth until the second partition. In 1787, Johann Anton Krieger, owner of the Korzec press, persuaded the statesman Tadeusz Czacki to transfer the border point for stamping books further away from Galicia so that it would be more difficult to import Galician books.[27]

TABLE 6.1 Hasidic Titles per City, through 1815

Żółkiew—27	Kopyś—6	Dubno—2	Grodno—1
Lemberg—22	Sławuta—6	Sudzylków—2	Podberezce—1
Korzec—20	Russia/Poland	Międzyrzecz—2	Minkowce—1
Połonne—10	(unknown)—5	Poryck—2	Warsaw—1
Szklów—9	Mezirów—4	Mięzyboż—2	
Ostróg—8	Mohylów—4	Łaszczów—2	
Berdyczów—7	Żytomir—4	Nowy Dwór—1	

Source: Appendix 3, this volume.

The third column of appendix 3, which delineates authors of *haskamot* (rabbinic endorsements) to Hasidic books, is most pertinent to the subject of popularization. Prominent rabbinic figures whose ties to the Hasidic movement were tenuous or nonexistent, including even old-style hasidim (e.g., members of the Ostróg *kloyz*), occasionally authored such endorsements. Even if such endorsers were unaware that a given book was Hasidic, their casual neglect would suggest a waning of Mitnaggdic hostility in some quarters as early as the 1790s.[28] Also intriguing is the fact that Polish zaddikim were the most frequent endorsers of early Hasidic books: R. Levi Isaac of Berdyczów (twelve), R. Abraham Joshua Heschel (six), R. Israel "the Maggid" of Kozienice (five), and R. Jacob Isaac "the Seer" of Lublin (five). This is one strong indication of the value of printed Hasidic works in Central Poland.

Haskamot originally arose as an attempt to protect printers against encroachments by their competitors, as well as to prevent unsupervised printing, dangerous anti-Christian sentiments, and the spread of Sabbateanism.[29] But by the end of the eighteenth century, *haskamot* seem primarily to have served to encourage consumption of the book and provide copyright protection. The publisher of the first Hasidic book, *Toldot Ya'akov Yosef,* ascribed its lack of *haskamot* to "printing troubles."[30] It is, however, doubtful that the lack of *haskamot* sparked the first anti-Hasidic controversy, as has been argued, for other early Hasidic books without *haskamot* were not similarly condemned.[31] R. Solomon of Łuck, who published *Maggid Devarov le-Ya'akov* (Korzec, 1781) nine years after the death of the Great Maggid, apologized that "the printing work of this holy book was very hurried due to a rumor of a decree by our lord, the King [Stanisław August] and his ministers, God have mercy, in crushing the printing." As a result of this perceived time constraint, he "had no free time to acquire *haskamot* and *heremot* of the geniuses of our time."[32] Notwithstanding these publishers' explanations, it is to be noted that most authors whose works consistently lacked *haskamot* were well established at the time of printing (additional examples include R. Levy Isaac of Berdyczów, R. Dov Ber of Lubavitch, and R. Shabbetai of Raszków). This suggests that the publishers were confident enough about sales to not feel compelled to undertake the arduous task of collecting *haskamot*. Only Maskilim, such as Naphtali Ullman, rejected rabbinical *haskamot* on principle.[33]

On the opposite end of the spectrum are Hasidic books that are festooned with *haskamot*. The most extraordinary number appear in *Or Pnei Moshe*, by R. Moses of Przeworsk (thirty-four), *No'am Elimelekh*, by R. Elimelekh of Leżajsk (fourteen), *No'am Meggedim*, by Eliezer Horowitz of Tarnogród (eleven), and R. Schneur Zalman of Liady's *Tanya* (eleven).[34] The cases of the more obscure *No'am Meggedim* and *Or Pnei Moshe* require explanation. In the former, it was the publisher, R. Moses of Sambor,[35] who attracted endorsements more than the author himself: the Seer of Lublin for example claims that but for the request of R. Moses of Sambor he would have refused to write the approbation at all.[36] The author is much less frequently praised.[37] As for R. Moses of Przeworsk, also a lesser known figure who received an astonishing thirty-four endorsements, it pays to examine the bodies of several of his colorful *haskamot.* R. Zvi Menahem Mendel and R. Israel Abraham, sons of the zaddik Meshullam Zusya of Annipol (d. 1800), relayed their father's first encounter with him:

> "While wandering here and there, I [R. Zusya] stayed in the holy community of Przeworsk, and the lodgings were insufficient in my opinion. A little boy came and said to me 'Does the master wish to lodge? Come with me.' And he led me to the old rabbi (he who possessed wisdom, our teacher R. Moses Sofer, may he be remembered, of Przeworsk). And I saw him to be a learned man. The form and image standing before me was like the form of an angel of God's legions." And because he is the writer of this holy book, a flame shoots out of the letters. All this we heard from his holy mouth. And when God merited us to meet the same zaddik face to face, we understood and recognized the greatness of his righteousness and memory and pure mind.[38]

The Seer of Lublin was also proud to have known R. Moses, and also felt compelled to acquaint the potential readership with his holy, scholarly mien:

> Even though it is not my way to behave pompously by giving an endorsement to a book, I departed from my custom this time. For I knew my lord the rabbi, the luminous lamp, our teacher M. Moses Sofer, scribe of Moses' Torah, of the holy community of Przeworsk, who left behind a blessing. And his modesty was to such a degree that it was not known that he was a scholar. And I knew him, for when I was in my youth I accepted his authority and drank his pleasant waters. And I knew that all his affairs were only for the sake of heaven and gratification of his Creator, blessed be He. And he had attained such a level that the deceased genius, our teacher R. Moses Alsheikh,[39] of blessed memory, revealed himself to him. (And this was in his youth.) And I heard many pleasing things from him myself.[40]

The endorsers emphasized R. Moses' living presence, angelic bearing, and oral teachings. He had even merited a visit by an apparition of a sixteenth-century sage.[41] But the acknowledgment that "it was not known that R. Moses was a scholar" could hold the key to his inordinate numbers of *haskamot*: he required extra promotion.

Each basic component of Hasidic *haskamot* exalts the endeavor of printing, and thus militates against any presumed irrelevance of Hasidic printing. Introductions to *haskamot* extolled the endorser, proclaiming him through formulaic honorifics;[42] followed by his name, his father's name, or his surname; followed by his titles (*av bet din, maggid mesharim*); followed by the "holy community" over which he presently presided, and sometimes communities he had served in previously.[43] The body of the *haskamah* praised the author and publisher, referring to the author's prior work,[44] or great *yihus*.[45] Endorsers made biblical wordplays on the names of the author, publisher, or editor,[46] and likened publishers to angels.[47] The Seer of Lublin apologized in his frequent endorsements, "it is not my way to behave in greatness and magnificence" by composing *haskamot*, but always explained that he was willing to make an exception for the author or publisher in question.[48] At times, endorsers professed humble reticence: "Who am I to dare to write an approbation to such a great work? But how can I refuse the request of so great a man [i.e., the publisher]?"[49] One endorser confessed that he lacked experience in esoteric lore.[50] Several protested that "the famous need no attestation" before attesting to their greatness.[51]

The endorsers' descriptions of their meetings with the publishers disclose the great effort exerted by publishers in collecting *haskamot*. While passing through Lemberg, R. Levi Isaac was waylaid by Asher Zelig, "a bundle full of the writings from his respected late father [R. Benjamin of Złoczów] in his hands, seeking my endorsement."[52] Fourteen years later, according to R. Levi Isaac's encomium to *Degel Mahane Ephraim*,

> While I was passing through the holy community of Stopnica, there came before me the famous *hasid*, our holy teacher R. Jacob Jehiel, may his light endure, (son of the same famous zaddik the late rabbi, genius, our teacher R. Moses Hayyim Ephraim . . . of Sudzylków, grandson of the holy man of God, Israel, rabbi of all the sons of the Diaspora, of whom the light from his teachings shines from one end of the world to the other, our holy teacher Israel Ba'al Shem Tov, may his memory be for a blessing). And he took out before me a bundle of documents in which R. Ephraim [of Sudzylków] was the preacher from the beginning of the teachings until the end.[53]

Zaddikim like R. Levi Isaac, approached during their regional tours and meetings with fellow zaddikim (in this case, R. Meir of Stopnica), would claim that they had seen "two or three berries" (Isaiah 17:6) of the work, that is, read a few scattered portions, and that what they had read was "sweeter than honey and the honeycomb" (Psalms 19:11), or "set upon sockets of fine gold" (Song of Songs 5:15). One endorser admitted that he had not seen the work at all.[54] These may have constituted attempts to evade responsibility for any controversial or heretical teachings that might turn up later.

But why bother to print at all when, in the words of the Seer of Lublin, "I did not consider writings as anything at all, because I myself heard the Rav from his holy mouth"?[55] As stated earlier, written teachings were secondary to direct, oral delivery. But several bodies of *haskamot* furnish strong reasons for undertaking the arduous process. Three out of the four *haskamot* to *Amtahat Benyamin* profess an aesthetic objective ("the goal of beauty").[56] The approbation of Mordecai b. Phineas of Korzec to *Or ha-Me'ir* proclaims the desire "to enact [Ze'ev Wolf's] words 'with an iron and lead pen' in beautiful and splendid print, and on beautiful and pleasing paper."[57] The Ostróg *dayanim* complained that *Shivhei ha-Besht* had been printed previously "only [sic] in the community of Żółkiew[58] but was not pleasing to look at." They applauded the present publishers for "giving consideration to learning and teaching the form of beauty through ornate letters."[59] A second motivation was quality control. The zaddik Meshullam Zusya of Annipol explained that although it was not the author's intention or custom to publish writings, "these booklets have spread in the midst of all Israel in numerous copies by sundry copyists, and, as a result of the many transcriptions, the copyists' errors have multiplied exceedingly; thus he felt compelled to bring these booklets to the printing press."[60] R. Nathan Shternharz furnishes a similar justification in his introduction to R. Nahman of Bratslav's *Sippurei Ma'asiyot*.[61]

The most consistent rationale for printing, however, was the desire "to merit the multitudes" by granting them access to great teachings.[62] These expressions reveal grand popularizing ambitions. R. Meir of Zelwa proclaimed, for example: "it is already known that the endeavor of printing is as if one is preaching to the thousands and the ten-thousands."[63] The verse "and the spring will be dispersed outward" (Proverbs 5:16) was invoked as an image for the dissemination of printed teachings. Printing would "multiply and increase Torah and awe";[64] and meant that "the said work will be spread throughout the land."[65] The maxim of R. Moses Alsheikh, "that which departs from the heart [of the teacher] penetrates the heart [of the student]," was reapplied to author and reader.[66] For R. Levi Isaac of Berdyczów, a printed Hasidic work could kindle hope and widespread repentance. He graced the opening pages to R. Menahem Nahum of Chernobyl's classic *Me'or Einayim* with an elaborate homily, part of which reads:

> And it is today that we have found hope, and our spirits have beheld love, for God has illuminated the pure heart of the venerable, great rabbi, the famous, old Hasid, man of God, our teacher R. Menahem Nahum from the holy community of Chernobyl, may they "disperse the fountain" [Proverbs 5:16] of his wisdom beyond his throne. And my heart rejoiced very much when I heard, for "a good rumor fattens the bones" [Proverbs 15:30]. And what's more, in seeing his writings the writing of holy God, that all his sayings are sayings of the living Lord, to awaken a person's soul to ascend upward, to arouse their hearts to serve God, blessed be He. And I anticipated and hoped to God that every reader of this holy work will say, "Behold, this is an innovation!" and it will refresh him "like cold water on his tired soul" [Proverbs 25:25]. And accordingly I said: "I shall arise and give an endorsement, so that this pure work will be printed very quickly."[67]

This rousing endorsement assigns a printed anthology a pivotal role in helping readers endure the long exile. Occasionally, printers even evinced a messianic expectation.[68]

Appreciation for a zaddik's written teachings understandably intensified after his death. The majority of early Hasidic books were, in fact, printed postmortem; and *haskamot* often doubled as eulogies. Printing the zaddik's teachings caused his lips "to murmur in his grave,"[69] and helped to "celebrate the merit of the zaddik's soul."[70] One endorser allowed that the living zaddik would have turned many away from sin through his oral teachings, "but what can we do, for his light has passed beyond this world? Let this be our consolation, that he left a blessing behind him." The book was "a stone of sapphire, hewn from his oral teachings."[71] His oral teachings were preferred, but the book became a deceased zaddik's surrogate. Books also constituted a form of bequest, for many were printed by the sons, grandsons, or sons-in-law of deceased zaddikim (see table 6.2).

Endorsers unfailingly noted the familial relationship between publisher and author, citing "the son will honor the father" (Malakhai 1:6). According to an endorsement to *Mivasser Zeddek*, R. Issachar Dov mi-Geza Zvi, "at the time of his old age, because his eyes were dimming, would dictate his teachings, and authored a nice book with innovative *halakhic* decisions and fine explanations of astonishing acuteness and expertise."[72] After R. Issachar's death,

"the son will honor the father," there now arises his son, the wonderful, noble rabbi, our teacher Judah Leib, may his light endure, "the son will honor the father," after his death, to establish the words of his father, and wishes to set his words in print so that his

TABLE 6.2 Sons, Sons-in-Law, or Grandsons of the Author as Publishers

Title	Author	Publisher
No'am Elimelekh	Elimelekh of Leżajsk	Eleazar (son), Zechariah Mendel
Kedushat Levi	Levi Isaac of Berdyczów	Joseph b. Meir (grandson)
Me'ir Netuvim	Meir Margaliot of Ostróg	Nahman of Połonne (son), Bezalel of Ostróg (son)
Sod Yakhin u-Voaz	Meir Margaliot of Ostróg	Bezalel of Ostróg (son)
Or Pnei Moshe	Moses of Przeworsk	Menahem Nahum of Annipol (son-in-law)
Divre Moshe	Moses Shoham of Dolina	Samuel Shoham (son)
Or ha-Hokhma	Uriel Feivel of Krasnopol	Menahem Mendel (son)
Degel Mahane Ephraim	Moses Hayyim Ephraim of Sudzylków	Jacob Jehiel (son)
Ahavat Dodim	Benjamin of Złoczów	Asher Zelig (son)
Hilkhat Binyamin	Benjamin of Złoczów	Asher Zelig (son)
Amtahat Binyamin	Benjamin of Złoczów	Asher Zelig (son)
Mivasser Zedek	Issachar Dov Ber mi geza Zvi	Judah Leib (son)
Bat Eyni	Issachar Dov Ber mi geza Zvi	Judah Leib (son)
Alfa Beta	Zvi Hirsch of Nadworna	David Aryeh (son)[a]
Toldot Ya'akov Yosef	Jacob Joseph of Połonne	Abraham Dov Urbach (son-in-law)

[a]David Aryeh published his father's book in Berdyczew after several editions had already appeared. But according to Ze'ev Gries, his edition "has proved to offer no significant improvements on any of the earlier editions." See Gries, "The Hasidic Managing Editor," 143, no. 6.

"spring will be dispersed abroad" (Proverbs 5:16), and "his lips will murmur in the grave."[73]

A *haskamah* to *Kol Aryeh* announces:

> Behold, well known is the immense degree of respect accorded the Rabbi, the great light, rebuker of all of us, who was loved by the whole world while he was alive. And now the great, holy rabbi, of a chain of *yihus*, our teacher Israel (son of our teacher, Rabbi Jehiel Michael . . . grandson of acute, great light, R. Isaac, *maggid mesharim* of the holy community of Drohobycz), arises to publish mysteries and print his holy, pure book, which lay in the archives of the Rabbi, great light, acute *av bet din* of the holy community of Linitz [Illi-niec], for twenty years.[74]

In this way a son or grandson gained custody over his father's teachings, which undoubtedly heightened the movement's hereditary tendencies.

To reiterate what has been argued thus far, the sheer mass of Hasidic books and the rationalizations for their publication in *haskamot* suggest that the deemphasis of the role of the written or printed word in Hasidism is only appropriate to the very beginning stage of the movement, that is, during the reign of the Besht. The Great Maggid's reign entailed a gestation period during which he encouraged disciples to transcribe his teachings, probably with an eye toward creating a full-scale movement. To that end, his disciples oversaw a frenzied publishing enterprise from 1780 on. *Haskamot* composed by fellow zaddikim and other distinguished spiritual leaders extolled the book as a vital means of disseminating a zaddik's teachings that was second only to his direct, oral delivery and yet superior in its geographic reach. After his death, of course, they were an irreplaceable repository of his teachings and a legacy for his descendants. It should be reiterated that *haskamot* also professed functions of advertising[75] and copyright.[76] But these only give further emphasis to the grav-ity of the enterprise.[77]

Ze'ev Gries has posed another series of questions vital to the subject at hand: "What is the significance and influence of the sermon in its written form? Did it affect Jewish daily life or the weltanschauung of the everyday Jew, or only of the elite among the literate Jews? Since Jewish life is affected mainly through rituals and customs, which shape Jewish consciousness, did homiletic literature serve as a vehicle for this purpose?"[78] Concerning Hasidic homiletic literature, Gries wonders about "precisely who initiated this enterprise, and whose interests it was designed to serve."[79] The question of the printed Hasidic sermon's relevance for the everyday Jew strikes at the heart of the problematic relationship between the purportedly oral movement and its robust printing enterprises. A key to Hasidic readership resides in the languages of its books.

Surprisingly enough, given assertions by historians and literary critics about the movement's communication ethos,[80] Hasidic titles seldom appeared in the Yiddish vernacular during the first half of the nineteenth century (see table 6.3). Only four Hasidic titles were printed in the vernacular and thus

TABLE 6.3 Hasidic Books in Yiddish, through 1850

Author	Title	Comments
Israel Jaffee, re: R. Israel Ba'al Shem Tov	*Shivhei ha-Besht* (Ostróg 1815; Korzec 1816; Nowy Dwór 1816; Warsaw, 1816; Żółkiew 1816,1817; Sudzylków 1830; Lemberg 1840,1840, 1840; Żółkiew 1840; Jassy 1843)	Yiddish translations. Also translated into Polish before 1819; and into Ladino in Salonica, 1860.
Nahman of Bratslav, Nathan Shternharz	*Sippurei Ma'asiyot* (Ostróg 1815; Lemberg 1820)	Ostróg edition is bilingual, while Lemberg edition is in Yiddish only.
Schneur Zalman of Liady	*Seder Birkhot ha-Nehenin* (Sudzylków [?] 1820; Józefów 1847)	Yiddish translations.
Dov Ber of Lubavitch	*Pokeah Ivrim* (n.p. 1805 [?]; Szkłów 1832, 1832, 1832, 1832, 1833; Warsaw 1845; Lemberg 1849)	Original in Yiddish.

Sources: Vinograd, *Thesaurus of the Hebrew Book*; Yehoshua Mondshein, *Sifrei ha-Halakha Shel Admor ha-Zaken*; Naftali Loewenthal, "Hebrew and the Habad Communication Ethos"; Lieberman, "Le-She'elat Yahas ha-Hasidut le-Lashon Yiddish."

rendered accessible to most women and many men. The vast majority were published exclusively in Hebrew, placing them out of their reach. This was quite intentional, for the original sermons were delivered in Yiddish.[81]

What are these Hasidic authors and scribes telling us by usually selecting Hebrew over Yiddish? The Hebrew language, like Latin, functioned to distinguish the intellectual elite by excluding commoners and women, both of whom rarely had the opportunity to master Hebrew. According to Shaul Stampfer, "Hebrew was an elite language up to the end of the nineteenth century, and the aura and status of the language contributed to its survival. In many respects, traditional Jewish society in Eastern Europe fitted the pattern of a closed semiliterate society."[82] If the Holy Language served to elevate a book's status, it admittedly elevated it out of the reach of most Jewish men, and virtually all Jewish women.[83] The English missionaries discovered this only after they arrived in Poland with thousands of Hebrew copies of the Old and New Testaments. They soon realized that few Jews could read them. In 1821, McCaul had collected a small group of Warsaw Jews inclined toward conversion, but complained, "None of them, except the teacher, understands the Hebrew, therefore the Testaments I have are quite useless to them."[84]

In his urgent appeal to his readers back home to support a Yiddish ("Judeo-Polish") translation of the New Testament, McCaul summed up Hebrew literacy in the following way.

> It is generally calculated that there are in the Russian dominions
> two millions and a half of Jews: out of these, at the very highest cal-
> culation, there are only 500,000 who understand Hebrew enough to

be able to read the whole Bible, especially the Prophets, so that there are four-fifths of the Jewish population to whom our exertions cannot extend, as they cannot translate the passages which we adduce out of the prophets. Of these there are two-fifths, a million of souls, all the Jewish women, and many, many poor Jews, who do not know one word of Hebrew, who have never read one single verse in that blessed book which maketh wise unto salvation, and who are to the full as ignorant of the most common histories of the Bible as the Hottentots. How are we to approach these people? Whence are we to draw our arguments? By what means are we to overcome their blind prejudices? Only, only by giving them the Old Testament in the only language which they understand [i.e., Yiddish].[85]

According to McCaul's breakdown, only 20 percent (five hundred thousand) of Russian and Polish Jews were fully literate in Hebrew. At the other end of the spectrum lay the completely illiterate, amounting to 40 percent (one million) of the population.

Next, McCaul addressed those with a low to intermediate grasp of Hebrew, comprising another 40 percent (one million):

The other two-fifths of the unlearned understand some Hebrew; they have learnt the five books of Moses, some of the Psalms, and a very few portions of the Prophets. To this class belong almost all the schoolmasters. . . . It is in vain that your Missionaries attempt to show that [Rashi's] explanations are contrary to grammar and to the Bible. They have learned no grammar, and do not know the root, the tense, or the mood, or hardly even whether a word be a substantive, and adjective, or a verb. If we quote another verse of the Bible, to shew that it contradicts Rashi's commentary, either they cannot translate it, and will not accept our translation, or they know Rashi's commentary upon this verse also, and so the argument goes on *ad infinitum*.[86]

It is noteworthy that McCaul considered "almost all the schoolmasters" as belonging to this category of semiliterates who remained ignorant of grammar, a theme stressed by Maskilim, as well. Nor was he very impressed with the fully literate group:

In the learned class, estimated at 500,000, or one-fifth of the whole population, who by dint of reading can translate, this Jewish [i.e., Yiddish] translation would not be useless, as they have received their first instructions from the schoolmasters of the preceding class, and are, in general, as ignorant of grammar as the preceding class; or if they do know any thing of it, they study only the accentuation; and when they come to a difficult passage they are almost as much at a loss, as the former class of Jews.[87]

McCaul's use of grammar as a standard for linguistic mastery may reflect a Western bias. But he also refers to numerous members of the semiliterate category who could not even translate biblical verses. His breakdown of degrees of Hebrew literacy is corroborated in other missionary accounts, which should shatter any romantic notions about past Jewish literacy.[88] We may conclude that most Hasidic books were inaccessible to a sizeable majority of east European Jewry.

When disciples and descendants of zaddikim began publishing their masters' teachings, they were accordingly not aiming at the average Jew. This was true even of Habad Hasidism, notwithstanding its presumed premium on accessibility. The two Yiddish books published by Habad in the first half of the nineteenth century hardly compare to the vast majority of Habad books written in Hebrew. Naftali Loewenthal has argued that "through these teachings, the sacred tongue [i.e., Hebrew] became a vehicle to impart overt intimations of 'holiness' to those for whom encounter with Hebrew texts was a natural part of everyday life."[89] But only a thin, elite stratum could truly claim Hebrew texts as a "natural part of everyday life."

If most Hasidic literature was out of reach for the ordinary Jew, then is it really fair to characterize it as propaganda? Without trying to deny the works' spectacular spiritual insights, there is good reason to regard it in this way. A Jewish movement could only succeed during this period through a Hebrew medium. The language cast an aura of holiness around teachings, bolstering Hasidism's prestige in the eyes of the Jewish populace even as it limited its readership. Some who purchased a given book would not even read it, as R. Nahman of Bratslav himself observed, but were merely collectors.[90] Jews with an intermediate level of Hebrew proficiency might access simplified works like *Alfa Beta*, and preachers might repeat teachings from Hasidic books before wider audiences. But Hasidic books were primarily aimed at advanced yeshiva students, rabbis, and well-educated merchants, that is, society's intellectual and spiritual role models.

In light of the foregoing considerations, the publishing record of Polish Hasidism represents somewhat of an enigma. Table 6.4 indicates how seldom Hasidic books were printed in Central Poland through the first half of the nineteenth century.

According to Gries, the meager literary output by Polish zaddikim is unproblematic: it merely reflects a Hasidic preference for actual deeds over published ideals.[91] Yet there are overwhelming indications that Polish zaddikim valued printed teachings to an unusual degree. As mentioned earlier, R. Levi Isaac of Berdyczów, the Maggid of Kozienice, the Seer of Lublin, and R. Abraham Joshua Heschel were the most frequent book endorsers of all zaddikim. The Maggid of Kozienice and R. Abraham Joshua Heschel, moreover, were ardent bibliophiles who endorsed non-Hasidic books and presided over new printings of legal, mystical, and Hasidic classics.[92] Even a governmental report from 1823 mentions a book as the cornerstone of Polish Hasidic belief and practice:

TABLE 6.4 Hasidic Books Printed in Central Poland, through 1850

Author/Book	City/Date
Zvi Hirsch of Nadworna, *Alfa Beta*	Nowy Dwór, 1799
Dov Ber Scheersohn of Lubavitch, *Pokeah Ivrim*	Warsaw, 1805
Dov Ber of Iliniec, *Shivhei ha-Besht*[a]	Nowy Dwór, 1816
Dov Ber of Iliniec, *Shivhei ha-Besht*[b]	Warsaw, 1816
Dov Ber of Iliniec, *Shivhei ha-Besht* (Yiddish version)	Hrubieszów, 1817
Elimelekh of Leżajsk, *No'am Elimelekh*	Hrubieszów, 1817
Menahem Nahum of Chernobyl, *Me'or Einayim*	Hrubieszów, 1818
Elimelekh of Leżajsk, *No'am Elimelekh*	Hrubieszów, 1818
Levi Isaac of Berdyczów, *Kedushat Levi*	Hrubieszów, 1818
Hanokh Henokh ben Tovayah Hakohen, *Yesod Emunah ve-Midot Anavah*	Warsaw, 1821
Israel of Kozienice, *Avodat Yisrael*	Józefów, 1842
Zecharia Mendel of Jarosław, *Darkhei Zeddek*	Warsaw, 1844
Moses Wartman, *Divrei Torah*	Warsaw, 1845
Zecharia Mendel of Jarosław, *Darkhei Zeddek*	Warsaw, 1845
Elimelekh of Leżajsk, *Iggeret ha-Kodesh*	Warsaw, 1850

[a]Hayyim Dov Friedberg refers to this as *Sippurei Ba'al Shem Tov.* See *Toldot ha-Defus ha-Ivri be-Polaniyah* (Tel Aviv: n.p., 1950), 82.
[b]Dauber, *Antonio's Devils*, 252.

Source: Vinograd, *Thesaurus of the Hebrew Book*; Shatzky, *Geschichte fun Yidn in Varshe* III:356; Szaja Friszman, *Drukarnie hebrajskie na Mazowszu od ich założenia do roku 1831.*

Husydymy literally fulfill the precepts of Mosaic and Talmudic law, [the latter] issued by later rabbis. This sect emerged eighty years ago. Rabbi Sról of Międzybóż set down its rules, as is declared in the work entitled: *Cewues Rywusz* [i.e., *Zava'at ha-Ribash*], which was written by him—the theme of this work was supposed to have been derived from the Davidic psalms 149 and 150. The aforementioned psalms recommend praising God through dancing and other Instruments, from which it therefore arose that Husydymy most of all dance and sing during their Prayers.[93]

Finally, the Maggid of Kozienice, the Seer of Lublin, Levi Isaac of Berdyczów, and R. Abraham Joshua Heschel of Opatów were among the few zaddikim who authored their own manuscripts rather than relying on disciples' transcriptions.[94]

Why, then, did Polish zaddikim print so few works? Historians of print culture have overlooked the significance of the distinctive Central Polish context, in particular its especially severe official constraints on Hasidic publishing in comparison to other regions during the early nineteenth century. In tsarist Russia, censorship was not established effectively until 1826; and even then, the government proved unable to cope with the multiplicity of Hebrew presses in small towns across the Pale of Settlement. Only in 1836, in reaction to a series of denunciations against Hasidic books leveled by Maskilim, did D. N. Bludov introduce a far-reaching censorship law that effected closer supervision over Jewish books.[95] In the Habsburg Empire, at the end of 1818, the government attempted to ban and confiscate thirty-six Hasidic and mystical books appearing on lists compiled by the Maskilim Joseph Perl and Peter Beer.[96] Nevertheless, in Raphael Mahler's words, "the Galician administration was simply too weak to successfully carry out its crusade against Hasidic and Kabbalistic literature."[97]

In Central Poland, in contrast, the suppression of Hasidic printing proved far more effective. The first reason is that there were few Hebrew presses to begin with. By the middle of the eighteenth century, the state of printing in the Polish Commonwealth was so undeveloped that Hebrew presses only functioned in Żółkiew, Lublin, and Cracow, compelling Polish Jews to import vast quantities of Hebrew books.[98] In 1787, the editor of the Polish newspaper *Dziennik Handlowy* decried this state of affairs on the grounds that it transported vast amounts of money abroad. He recommended that Polish Jews be encouraged to set up their own presses, and that the government increase the tax on official stamps required on imported books so as stimulate domestic printing. Polish lawmakers reacted to this editorial by merely making the importing of books more difficult. Several international Jewish booksellers had their products confiscated.[99] However, the new regulations helped a limited number of Hebrew book printers, including the Christian printer Johann Anton Krieger, owner of the Korzec press (until 1787) and the Nowy Dwór press (from 1780 until its dissolution in 1816).[100] Krieger and Lazer Isaac of Krotoszyn, his Jewish partner/manager of the Nowy Dwór press, attempted to corner the Jewish book market and curtail foreign book imports.[101] Although their lobbying efforts were unsuccessful, their business flourished until 1791, at which point they were accused of selling books without the required government stamp. The Kościuszko insurrection (1794–95) further curtailed Hebrew book production.[102]

Upon the formation of the Congress Kingdom in 1815, according to Natalia Gąsiorowska, there were only four presses printing Hebrew books, compared to an impressive twenty-eight in the Ukraine, five in present-day Belarus, and four in present-day Lithuania.[103] Gąsiorowska is probably referring to the Polish presses in Nowy Dwór,[104] Hrubieszów,[105] and two Warsaw presses[106] (the Lublin press having closed in 1719).[107] A fifth was established by Isaiah Wax in Józefów, 1822, after extensive wrangling with government officials.[108] Jacob Tugenhold protested that printers of Hebrew books outside of the Congress Kingdom were able to "dispose of their abundant printings year after year for what is believed to be several hundreds of thousands of złoties."[109] Congress Kingdom authorities did implement a tariff on certain Hebrew books, but for some strange reason did not see fit to apply it to imports from the eastern regions (*Kresy*), including the Ukraine and historical Lithuania, where presses were flourishing in step with the advancing Hasidic movement.[110] Polish Hasidim thus strove mightily to import or smuggle in books. One report asserted that "the books used by the Hasidim are . . . printed in Lithuania, and from there, after succumbing to the appropriate censorship inspection, are dispersed throughout the Polish Kingdom."[111] Hasidic books, the report continues, were also frequently smuggled into Central Poland: "besides these religious works there are others which are concealed [from the authorities] and scattered throughout the country."[112] These reports suggest that Polish Hasidim were bringing in large quantities of Hasidic books by both licit and illicit means.

Even more important than the limited number of presses in Central Poland, however, was the Kingdom's rigid and effective censorship. This is illustrated in table 6.4, according to which most Polish Hasidic printings occurred during the first years of the Congress Kingdom, suddenly ceased after 1821, and then resumed again in 1842. This pattern may be easily explained: when the onerous censorship that had been in effect throughout the Prussian and Napoleonic regimes temporarily relented during the advent of the Congress Kingdom in 1815, a spate of Hasidic books appeared for a few years because publishers of Hasidic books could take advantage the freedom of press temporarily ensured by article 16 of the new Constitution. But censorship was gradually reasserted in line with the increasingly reactionary nature of the regime. On May 22, 1819, Zajączek introduced three new articles that effectively reversed article 16's provision for freedom of the press.[113] The new articles paralyzed Polish printing in general and Hebrew printing in particular.

Harro Harring describes the result for all publishers. "With regard to liberty of the press, it is almost unnecessary to observe that no such thing exists in Poland, and literature is at its lowest possible ebb." Apart from the poet Adam Mickiewicz, who, "in spite of the narrow boundaries within which he is circumscribed, rises like a proud cedar in the desert, whose summit the sun lights before his rays descend to the plain," most poetic talent and philosophic and scientific inquiry was "checked in the bud."[114] Bookselling was "confined chiefly to school books and French novels, which the bookseller [Nathan] Glucksberg circulated very extensively." Article 16 [115] was thus "a downright irony":

> But we are told "the press is free!" O violent truth, what a declaration! The press in Poland free! When scarce a book dare be printed, and when the printing of anything approaching truth is out of the question! The press is free indeed! While hundreds and thousands were daily put under arrest, for some expression of their thoughts and feelings, not by writing, but orally, and with fear and hesitation!
>
> The press said to be free! When a German whose name has escaped me, a literary man, who was employed as a librarian by one of the magnates, was condemned to serve for life as a common soldier, in a regiment of Lithuanian infantry; because, in a public house he read some paragraphs of the Polish Constitution to two of his friends, and toasted the articles!
>
> The press free! When the editors of the severely restricted Journals did not dare to insert the most harmless word without incurring the risk of being arrested and imprisoned in the fort without any hope of deliverance!
>
> The press free, truly! When scarcely a press dared be established, for to say nothing of a book, no one would venture to print a

single page without trembling for some malignant interpretation of a phrase, every word of which, before being committed to paper, had undergone the most serious consideration.

This Article (16) is really a satire which does much credit to its author.—Honour to the talent for ridicule of this Great Unknown![116]

Arrests, imprisonment, impressments into the military—this was the lot of those who dared to freely express ideas in print. Polish printers had to navigate a veritable obstacle course.

Printers of Jewish books were subjected to even more intense scrutiny. According to a file in the State Archives in Kielce, official attention was first drawn to Jewish books in 1817. On September 24, Minister Staszic requested information about the state of Jewish printing presses in Cracow, a protectorate of Russia, Prussia, and Austria. Staszic inquired about their number, precise locations, condition, approximately how many sheets of paper they printed per year, and what types of writings they printed. He wished to know whether the Cracow *wojewódstwo* "can supply enough Jewish books needed for its entire *wojewódstwo*, and whether its printing output is on the same scale as foreign printing enterprises."[117] The Cracow *wojewódstwo* replied that no such printing presses existed there.[118] This was almost true: only four Hebrew books had appeared in Cracow during this period.[119] Staszic may have been searching for a way to diminish Jewish book imports.

The next year, the government began to crack down on Jewish books imported by subscriptions to foreign presses. On November 22, the foreign printers Hersz Srulowicz and Chaim Ickowicz were caught in Warsaw distributing preordered books. Officials concluded that such books were one of the major causes of "Jewish darkness," for they offended even the Jewish religion with their "immoral superstition and professions of hatred toward other peoples' faiths, passed from generation to generation." Now, to the officials' dismay, uncensored Jewish books were entering the country in abundant numbers from foreign presses, owing to the collapse of printing presses in the Congress Kingdom.[120] The authorities confiscated the books, and ordered that other such foreign books be confiscated and returned to their bearers only after their contents had been examined.

On August 2, 1820, Staszic attempted to subject Polish Jewish books to the severest scrutiny. No Jewish book was to be printed or sold in the land, or imported from abroad through sale or subscription, without the express permission of the Commission on Religious Denominations and Public Enlightenment. Every Jewish book was to be perused by the Commission and, if possible, in two copies. It was now forbidden to print Jewish books "in the common, corrupt language [i.e., Yiddish] in this land, but rather in Hebrew and, as much as possible, in German or Polish letters, or in the language of the land, Polish." Every Jewish book and written work imported from abroad was, as before, to be first dispatched to the Commission in Warsaw. But the same would now be required of subscription books. If, upon perusal of the books or subscription collections, the Commission permitted them in their original form, the final products were to be exact copies of the original, which would be "closed tightly and sealed in a box and sent—at the cost of the owner—to Warsaw, where upon examination of that [original] copy and none other, the stamp of the Commission . . . will be affixed to it, and it will be given back to the owner." Censors who discovered imported Jewish books that were "harmful to faith" were to immediately seal them up.[121] Staszic's decree signaled the end of a brief freedom of the press, and crippled Polish Jewish printing for the next two decades. During the five-year window preceding this clampdown, six Hasidic books had been printed. A seventh squeezed through in 1821, right before the activities of the Jewish Censorship Committee commenced.

There are additional indications that Jewish books were singled out for suppression. The government acceded to a request by the senate of Cracow to ease the arduous process through which its residents had to export books to the Congress Kingdom—except with regard to Jewish books. In 1822, the notorious Ludwik Chiarni, author of an anti-Talmud diatribe, was appointed chairman of a newly formed Committee for the Censorship of Jewish Books.[122] The official attitude toward Jewish books worsened after 1823, when the reactionary Stanisiław Grabowski became head of the Commission on Denominations and Public Enlightenment. Grabowski complained about the ease with which Jewish books were brought over from Russia, accusing Jewish books of promoting intolerance and hatred of Catholics, the monarchy, and the Christian regime. He sought a double censorship of Jewish books entering from Russia, that is, censorship on both ends. This, along with several other schemes, was never actually implemented, however.[123]

In such a climate, Hasidic books stood no chance at all. On April 3, 1823, Grabowski proclaimed that Kabbalistic books "spread darkness and superstition and instill anti-social maxims."[124] However, the key to the blackout in Polish Hasidic printing from 1822 to 1842 resides in the composition of the Committee for the Censorship of Jewish Books. Stansiław Ezekiel Hoge, preconversion, was appointed to the planned Censorship Committee in 1818.[125] Two years later, Chiarni was appointed as well. Finally, on January 2, 1822, the activities of the Censorship Committee commenced, with Chiarni presiding over a staff consisting of Adam Chmielewski, Abraham Stern, Jacob Tugenhold, and B. Herzfeld (in place of Hoga, who left to work as a translator of Hebrew books into Polish). Chiarni, however, rapidly became exasperated by his predominately Jewish staff and resigned. Adam Chmielewski, a professor of Greek and Hebrew at Warsaw University, assumed the Committee chairmanship. He was more an overseer than an active chair.[126]

Whence the anti-Hasidism? It did not stem from the secretary of the Committee, Jacob Tugenhold. To be sure, Tugenhold was hated by his fellow Jews, who accused him of fraud, issued bans against him, and once forced him to seek the protection of the mayor of Praga.[127] Yet Tugenhold's attitude toward Hasidism was not unequivocally negative, as we have seen.[128] Abraham Stern (1762–1842), however, constituted an entirely different case. In his proposal for a rabbinical school presented in 1816, Stern had argued that part of the director's role would be to wage war against Hasidism "to the bitter end."[129]

He was extremely active in the Censorship Committee, and served as its chairman beginning in 1832.[130] According to Jacob Shatzky, Stern was "liberal towards learned and enlightened works, but vigilantly sifted out Hasidic works."[131] Table 6.4 affirms that assessment. Stern's paramount role in suppressing Hasidic publishing is reinforced by the fact that the printing of Hasidic books in Central Poland resumed in 1842, the very year of his death.[132] Polish Hasidic book production was not meager for want of consumer demand. It was paralyzed because the Congress Kingdom, a relatively compact and manageable entity, had as its Jewish censor a zealous anti-Hasidic Maskil.

Crossover Genres: Printed Tales

Having seen the great effort the Hebrew-reading elite invested in producing and procuring printed homiletic literature, it is now time to consider the motivations informing a more socially transcendent printed genre, the folk tale collection. The Maskil Abraham Gottlober distinguished between the two genres in the following way.

> And at the same time as the wise counselors of the Hasidim promoted their system and instruction by means of their books (such as the book *Likkutei Amarim* of the aforementioned Maggid [of Międzyrzecz], the book *Toldot Ya'akov Yosef* of the Preacher [*sic*] of Połonne, and approximately fifty years [*sic*] after them, the book *Kedushat Levi* of the Rabbi of Berdyczów, the book *No'am Elimelekh* of R. Elimelekh of Leżajsk, the book *Me'or Eynayim* of R. Nahum of Chernobyl, the book *Or ha-Me'ir* of R. Ze'ev of Żytomir, the book *Toldot Aharon* of the Maggid of Żytomir, and many others like them), the charlatans of the day endeavored to publicize fabricated tales in order to ensnare the masses, who are not savvy about books and studies. And the tales from the deceptive books misled many people, until, after some time, the daring of the charlatans grew and the evildoers did not shrink from inscribing their wonder tales in a book and thereby place them "before all their people"[133] in the book *Shivhei ha-Besht*, printed several times in the Holy Language and in the language of Ashkenazic Jewry [Yiddish], in Hebrew letters and in Rashi and German[134] script in Międzybóż, Berdyczów and the many additional printings of those days, without anyone waking up and paying attention and inquiring as to what he printed and about what he was printing, and everyone acted according to his fancy. And the more they printed, the more people among them told wonder tales orally, until all the heaps of written wonders in their books were considered as nothing compared to them.[135]

While Gottlober is usually a reliable observer, here he appears to fall prey to typical Haskalah assumptions about producers and consumers of popular culture. First, he errs in deeming producers of homiletic literature "wise counselors of the Hasidim" as distinct from the "charlatans of the day" who published popular collections of tales. As a matter of fact, producers of both types of literature were cut from the same stripe, merely differing in the scope of their marketing ambitions (producers of homiletic literature, because of the sacred texts they were working with, could not vastly expand their readership through Yiddish translations). Nor does Gottlober's assertion about readers of "wonder tales" withstand scrutiny. The multiple Hebrew editions of Hasidic tales reflect their consumption by a sizeable segment of the male elite, while only their Yiddish versions could have been designed to "ensnare the masses." Hasidic tales could be read by anyone who possessed literacy in a Jewish language, that is, a spectrum of Jewish society that included elites and "masses."

In spite of their wide accessibility, only two printed collections of Hasidic tales appeared during the first half of the nineteenth century: *Shivhei ha-Besht* and *Sippurei Ma'asiyot* (tales of R. Nahman of Bratslav). The accounts in *Shivhei ha-Besht* were circulated orally in the Yiddish vernacular for many years, were afterward gathered in variant Hebrew manuscript versions (the urtext is still unknown), and only then printed in Hebrew and Yiddish versions (Kopys, 1814, in Hebrew; Ostróg, 1815, in Yiddish).[136] The printing of *Sippurei Ma'asiyot* followed a similar course. The tales were delivered orally in Yiddish between 1806 and 1810, were circulated in manuscripts, and were then published in 1815 in a bilingual edition with Hebrew above and Yiddish below (Ostróg, 1815). The placement of the Yiddish version at the bottom of each page may have affirmed a linguistic hierarchy, but it opened up the tales to much wider audiences.

Shivhei ha-Besht and *Sippurei Ma'asiyot* were popular throughout eastern and east central Europe, including in the region of Central Poland (see table 6.4). Nevertheless, no other compilation of Hasidic tales would appear until 1863. Historians of Hasidism term this lengthy hiatus a "fifty years' silence." Joseph Dan, in his pioneering work *The Hasidic Tale*, posits three reasons for it: (1) the overwhelming influence of *Shivhei ha-Besht*; (2) censorship; and (3) the satires of *Shivhei ha-Besht* in the wake of its initial printings.[137] Ze'ev Gries's explanation for the "fifty years' silence" accords with his general view of Hasidic printing: the absence of new printed tales merely reflects the movement's limited appreciation for Hasidic literature.[138] But these explanations fail to account for the continuous reprintings of *Shivhei ha-Besht* and *Sippurei Ma'asiyot* throughout the "fifty years' silence." Reprintings occurred despite the mockery they elicited from certain circles. Maskilim, most prominently Joseph Perl, frequently made sport of both books.[139] When a Polish translation allegedly appeared around 1819, Hasidim were exposed to the ridicule of their Polish landlords. One Hasid recalls how a nobleman held up a copy and bellowed, "Jews! Have you read this 'holy' book?" The nobleman walked up to him holding the book and "mocked him and laughed at him."[140] Nevertheless, *Shivhei ha-Besht* reached twenty-one printings in Hebrew and Yiddish during the first half of the nineteenth century alone, while *Sippurei Ma'asiyot* was also reprinted several times.

There is also a problem with the very conception of a "fifty years' silence," in that it implies too close a contextual relationship between *Shivhei ha-Besht* and *Sippurei Ma'asiyot* on the one hand and collections that began to appear in the late nineteenth century on the other. We should rather accept the former for what they are: exceptional works surrounding extraordinary personalities, written down and printed by unusually devoted disciples at a unique juncture: the death or impending death of nearly every major third-generation zaddik (c. 1815). This crisis apparently created a desperate compulsion to publicize Hasidism as widely as possible, as seen particularly in the case of *Shivhei ha-Besht* (immediately after the initial printing, it came out in Yiddish in Korzec, 1816; Nowy Dwór, 1816; Warsaw, 1816; Żółkiew, 1816, 1817; and in Hebrew in Berdyczów, 1815, and Laszczów, 1815). The depth of that sense of crisis would only be equaled in the late nineteenth century, which saw a wave of new tale collections printed in response to the seemingly invincible rise of modern secular Jewish literature.[141]

Content-wise, there is little relationship between *Shivhei ha-Besht* and *Sippurei Ma'asiyot*. The tales of *Shivhei ha-Besht*, like the majority of Hasidic tales, praise the deeds of specific zaddikim and purport to be historical. The tales in *Sippurei Ma'asiyot*, on the other hand, constitute oblique parables that transcend time and space, and are seldom explicitly Hasidic.[142] But *Shivhei ha-Besht* and *Sippurei Ma'asiyot* do have a formal similarity owing to their shared popularizing agenda. Producers of both collections were venturing into territory that was infrequently charted: the publication of folk tales for mass consumption. Both thus felt compelled to justify their publications. Israel Jaffee, printer of *Shivhei ha-Besht*, invoked the Besht's teaching that "when one relates the praises of the zaddikim it is as if he concentrates on the secrets of Ezekiel's chariot vision [*Ma'aseh Merkavah*]."[143] He next cited the classic collection *Shivhei ha-Ari* as a precedent for printing tales.[144] Finally, he claimed he had printed the tales to avoid a proliferation of errors and corruptions through frequent hand copies.[145] Similarly, R. Nathan Shternharz felt compelled to explain that the many faulty manuscript copies of the tales necessitated an authoritative printed version of *Sippurei Ma'asiyot*. Moreover, R. Nahman of Bratslav himself had requested that the tales be printed, even specifying that it should appear "in the Holy Language on top, and at bottom in this language [i.e., Yiddish]." If the enemies of Bratslav Hasidism mocked the tales and remained ignorant of their deeper meanings, so be it, for "we are obligated to do [R. Nahman's] bidding."[146] The apologies reveal the controversy engendered in printing tales. Typically—although there were exceptions—Jewish literature deemed worthy of printing fell into three categories: classical (including Kabbalistic) texts and commentaries; rabbinic responsa; and moralistic literature. Tales were occasionally printed, as Jaffee himself pointed out, but this was unusual.[147] Complete Yiddish translations or versions of Hebrew originals required additional boldness. By violating Jewish society's linguistically preserved borders, *Shivhei ha-Besht* and *Sippurei Ma'asiyot* demonstrated the prominence of the popularizing motive by this stage. Notwithstanding the occasional variants between Hebrew and Yiddish versions, their availability in both languages granted elite and popular audiences unusual shared access to a single literature.

Oral Tales, Songs, and Dance

The Hasidic wonder tales in *Shivhei ha-Besht* are a mere sampling of thousands of oral wonder tales circulating from the beginning of the Hasidic movement down to the present day. As Gottlober noted, oral tales both preceded *Shivhei ha-Besht* and proliferated independently throughout its many printings. *Shivhei ha-Besht* did not, and could not, set these stories in stone. The oral versions refracted Hasidic ideology among women and uneducated men in ways that Hebrew texts could not. Their recitation was, in fact, elevated to a spiritual imperative. R. Moses Hayyim Ephraim of Sudzylków invoked the example of his grandfather, the Besht, who "would tell wonder tales and speak of secular matters and serve God through them . . . namely, he would clothe his pure wisdom in them."[148] R. Nahman of Bratslav claimed that the Besht, his great-grandfather, was able to "effect mystical unifications through a wonder tale. When he saw that a supernal channel was broken, and it was not possible to repair it through prayer, he would fix and connect them by means of a wonder tale."[149]

Oral tales were not confined to circulation among the "masses." The tales recited by household guests during R. Nahman's childhood in Międzybóż proved critical to his own spiritual formation:

> [R. Nahman of Bratslav's] own principle motivation to worship God
> actually derived from tales about zaddikim. And he told us how all
> the zaddikim would frequent the house of his father and mother,
> the zaddikim of blessed memory, for all the zaddikim could be
> found in the community of Międzybóż, for it had been the home-
> town of the Besht, of blessed memory. And the majority lodged in
> the house of his father, of blessed memory. And [R. Nahman] heard
> many tales about zaddikim. And his principle enthusiasm for God
> derived from this, until he attained that which he attained.[150]

Storytelling was a favorite pastime of R. Nahman's family and their celebrity guests, and proved transformative for this scion of the Hasidic elite.

Still, the evidence suggests that oral tales were foremost a means of directly reaching the functionally illiterate masses. Most obviously, oral tales did not require the barest literacy or textual competence. Another indicator is their ethos of simple piety. In one tale, the Besht praises the dull-witted son of a villager who blows a whistle to express himself during Yom Kippur prayers; in another, he deems a hose-maker who recites psalms while he works "the cornerstone which will uphold the Temple until the Messiah comes." As in "The Horses," praise of the pious poor often comes at the expense of haughty merchants and scholars in these tales. One of R. Elimelekh's scholarly disciples begins to follow a crude coach driver around after seeing that he is favored by the zaddik; but the coach driver ejects him on the grounds that he is unworthy of the company of common people. The zaddik Samuel Shmelke proclaims that "more than the poor man needs the rich man, the rich is in need of the poor."[151] As discussed earlier, this motif of social inversion can be misleading if taken at face value. But it can provide valuable insight into the tales' target audience: the very work-a-day Jews they exalt. It is no accident that such egalitarian fantasy is virtually absent in Hasidic homiletic literature, published in Hebrew and intended for elite consumption. There, it should be recalled, the common folk are mere "men of matter" who can attain spiritual heights only by cleaving to "men of form."[152] It is thus possible to speak of several overlapping Hasidisms experienced by different sociolinguistic groups.

Zaddikim were well aware of the fact that by clothing profound ethical lessons in tales they could disseminate their message among a much broader audience. They were also aware that oral tales offered a more subtle means of inspiring widespread repentance than the rebuking sermons of prior centuries, which were increasingly out of vogue. The zaddik Kalonymous Kalman Epstein of Cracow insisted that only "wonder tales and secular talk" could stir a sinner to repentance, because they spared him the shame involved in more direct methods.[153] R. Nahman argued similarly that tales, in contrast to jarring rebukes, gently roused a sinner from his sleep-like state without overwhelming him. He elaborated a more ethereal explanation, as well: tales hid their holy kernels from lurking demons and smuggled their holy kernels to those already in the clutches of demons, for they touched listeners on a primordial level where demons cannot dwell.[154]

Hasidic dance and music professed a similarly serious mystical function. Dancing was an integral feature at all Hasidic gatherings, because it was conceived as an instrument for defeating depression, drawing down joy from the *sefirot*, and achieving spiritual fervor, ascents of the soul, and supernal rectification.[155] As with storytelling, anyone (at least any male) could enjoy it. For similar reasons, music, as well, became a vital part of Hasidism, prompting one early twentieth-century researcher/observer to remark that "without the songs, it is impossible to even conceive of Hasidic rite. One might give up the "Torah" of the [zaddik's] table, but never the songs."[156] Polish Hasidism in particular was known for its illustrious musical tradition. Polish zaddikim, whose melodies lay somewhere between Habad melancholy and the light, fluttering melodies of Galician Hasidism, were among Hasidism's renowned composers. The Seer of Lublin founded a style redolent of the joyful, major-key, Beshtian variety. His original composition "Melodies of Angels" became a staple on the Sabbath eve in several Galician dynasties, and he sacralized the singing of Hasidic melodies at the Third Meal of the Sabbath.[157] Musical performance, as well, reached an apogee in Central Poland. R. Meir of Opatów/Stopnica, who preached that the divine bounty was drawn upon the Jewish People by means of "worship in song, and joy, and a good-heartedness," was one of Hasidism's premier cantors.[158] R. Abraham Moses of Przysucha, who "knew how to play according to the rules of music," according to one tradition, would accompany his midnight devotions (*tikun hazot*) with his violin.[159] When R. Levi Isaac of Berdyczów sang, "everyone immediately forgot the whole world and was suspended in a world of melody and song. And the spirits of the listeners were drawn after the voice of the singer like oil to a wick."[160] Several rank-and-file Hasidim earned renown as singers, too. R. Hirsch of Parysów, for example, a pipe-smoking cantor who lived to the ripe age of ninety-four, was a favorite of the zaddikim of Lublin, Kotsk, Ger, and Aleksander.[161] Musical performance and composition were refined at the Polish courts throughout the nineteenth century, with each dynasty developing its distinctive melodies and repertoires by the late nineteenth century.[162] Thus, in contrast to their publication endeavors, which were by necessity comparatively meager, Polish zaddikim fostered a magnificent, if more ephemeral, musical revival.

Music was believed to possess theurgical potency. At a performance witnessed by the zaddik Isaac Meir Alter of Gur, the Maggid of Kozienice rectified Szmul Zbytkower's soul through a melody:

> "And once on the holy Sabbath . . . the Maggid himself began to chant a beautiful, lovely melody, and those present had never heard such a melody and could not even assist him with their voices. And after the service, when the Maggid greeted the worshipers, he explained, 'it is now three years since the aforementioned Reb Szmul Zbytkower died. And several angels of destruction prosecuted him on account of his sins. But the good, defending angel who was created out of the great aforementioned deed [during the Praga massacre] made a great noise and shouted "Does not this great incident—saving many souls of the Children of Israel—outweigh everything? It is fitting that he go immediately to the Garden of Eden." And the Supernal Tribunal issued the verdict that, in truth, he deserves an important place in the Garden of Eden on account of this deed, but it is impossible to elevate him immediately without the purification of his enormous blemishes. And this continued for three years. And now the angels conducted him to his place in the Garden of Eden. And as they walked him, they sang this new melody which you heard from me.' And after that, the Maggid concluded that even though the cleansing continued for three years, nevertheless an additional blemish was found on his 'garment.' " And our Rabbi [Isaac Meir Alter] said that apparently there was an adulterous matter among his sins, and that is why purification was so difficult.[163]

Music even had the power to exonerate the controversial Szmul Zbytkower, whose transgressions, we have seen, were not limited to adultery.

In composing their stories, songs, and dances, many zaddikim drew liberally upon parallel expressional modes from the non-Jewish milieu. This is ironic in light of the sacred and occasionally theurgical functions Hasidim attributed to them. But these external borrowings constituted a means of negotiating with a dominant culture adopted by many Diaspora and colonized groups. The semiotician Yuri Lotman's description of this prevalent cultural hybridization and its rationale has been summarized as follows.

First, a text arrives from the outside; it appears in its original form, in its own language, its strangeness is intact; it is not considered a threat or a problem because it is presumed to be superior and therefore will offer a positive contribution.

Second, a transformation at both ends begins to occur—that is, the imported text and the receiving culture begin to restructure each other. The foreign text is idealized because it offers the local culture the opportunity to break with the past. Here the foreign text is imbued with salvific qualities. However, there also emerges a counter-tendency in which the foreign text is linked to a submerged element in the receiving culture; the foreign thus activates a dormant component, and is therefore interpreted as an organic continuation or a rehabilitation of the familiar culture.

Third, there emerges a tendency to *deprecate the source from which the text originated, and to emphasize that the true potential of the text is only realized by being integrated into the receiving culture.* Reception has not only led to transformation but is also a form of transcendence. Before, it was crude and particularistic; now it has the grace of fullness and universality.

Fourth, after the imported text has been fully assimilated, its distinctive presence has been dissolved, and has led to the production of a new model. Now that the receiver has internalized the text and restructured its own axioms and values, the local becomes producer of new and original texts.

Fifth, the receiver is now a transmitter.[164]

Lotman's third axiom looms particularly large in Hasidic homiletic literature.

As detailed in the introduction to this book, motifs, plots, and even characters of some Hasidic tales have been shown to derive from local or regional non-Jewish Polish and Ukrainian folk tales.[165] The Besht's rationale immediately recalls Lotman's third axiom: "The leader of the generation is able to elevate the common sayings and stories of peoples of his time, linking the material with the spiritual."[161] His grandson R. Moses Hayyim Ephraim of Sudzylków likewise explained:

Sometimes the zaddik sits among several people and speaks with them about some worldly matters and [listens to] stories which appear to be trivial. But actually, that zaddik sitting there is mentally cleaving to God. And even though that which is said is worldly and trivial, he contemplates and sees spiritual things and holy things in it. And thus in all the folk tales of the world that they tell him, and in all those matters which they discuss with him, he always sees holy matters within those very words.[167]

The Besht's great-grandson, R. Nahman of Bratslav, similarly taught that non-Jewish folk tales contain "many hidden and extremely exalted things." They had been corrupted by non-Jewish storytellers, but the zaddik was able to locate the "extremely lofty things concealed in the tales told by the rest of the world."[168] According to these generations of the Besht's line, non-Jewish folk tales merely required rectification by the zaddik.

The same tendencies obtained in Hasidic music.[169] Musical borrowings were conscious and deliberate, no doubt encouraged by the Besht's proclamation that "in all the *lieder* that the nations of the world sing, there is an aspect of fear and love [of God], extending from above down to all the lower levels."[170] Perhaps the most famous proponent of this type of borrowing was R. Isaac Eizik Taub Kalev (1751–1821).[171] The Hungarian zaddik was wandering through a field one Friday afternoon before the Sabbath eve when he heard the following shepherd's song.

> Rose, Rose, how far away you are!
> Forest, Forest, how vast you are!
> If only Rose were not so far away,
> You, Forest, would not be so vast!
> Who will guide me out of the Forest
> And unite me with my rose?

The next day, in honor of the Sabbath, the zaddik restored the song to its holy source:

> God, God, how far away You are!
> Exile, Exile, how long you are!
> If only God were not so far away,
> You, Exile, would not be so long!
> Who will guide me out of the exile
> And unite me with God?[172]

The zaddik's followers were free to enjoy the Jewish interpolation, even in a non-Jewish language.[173] In one rather extreme case, lyrics were preserved in their entirety and an inner Jewish meaning was merely implied through articulation in a religious context: R. Meir of Przemyślany was known to sit by his window smoking his pipe, singing the popular folksong: "Oy, you are stupid, stupid! / Why do you go to the trade-fair? / You don't buy, you don't sell / You only pick quarrels!" R. Meir had transformed a rebuke against those who interfere with market activities into a rebuke against those who waste their time quarreling rather than improving their character.[174] When a non-Jewish song was "redeemed" through a Jewish alteration, no matter how subtle, it could enter the Hasidic repertoire.

Hasidism's opponents were appalled by these borrowings. An early detractor was the Mitnagged R. Israel Loebel, who complained that Hasidim "always sing during the Rabbi's gatherings . . . ; and if that were not enough, sing in every language. . . ."[175] Abraham Gottlober recalls the Polish folk dances at Hasidic weddings:

> Afterwards, the wedding musicians played a Polonaise, and the groom was called to approach the bride and take her hand through a shawl or handkerchief, and he danced with her without touching her with his hand. But before turning her once, everyone approached and linked hands, and the musicians switched to a different Polonaise which gave rise to jumping and skipping, and everyone danced and spun in a circle with all their might, with the exception of the bride, who sat on a chair.[176]

Gottlober was shocked to find that "zaddikim embraced the bride while they danced with her, in front of everyone!" The wedding jesters, he recalls, could not resist a jibe against the zaddikim who, in contrast to the groom, are supposedly "not controlled by the Evil Impulse, and do not fear it, and thus take the bride's hand in their bare hands and dance with her".[177] The latter-day Mitnagged Ephraim Dinnard also balked at Hasidism's assimilation of folk culture:

> Hasidic "solidarity" is seen only on days of drinking and joy, in their imbibing of wine and dancing, and in their dancing like rams, each man grabbing his neighbor's neck, and chanting and singing, "The Rabbi ordered us to be joyful." Anyone who has been in a Russian village at a peasants' gathering on Sunday in a tavern, where they drink beer and spend the whole day smoking their pipes and gladdening their hearts with wine, waiting to tell tales, has seen such "solidarity." And this is what I have seen of Hasidic solidarity in their gatherings in the native villages of their holy ones.[178]

Like Gottlober, Dinard cites the incorporation of Slavic folk culture as proof of the movement's indecency and lowbrow appeal. In doing so, both critics betray a priggishness that seems to have been lacking among zaddikim.

Given the sacred and theurgical functions attributed to these cultural expressions, it is indeed curious that conscious borrowings from "foreign" folk culture were tolerated at all, let alone embraced as popularizing vehicles. But the concept of "worship through corporeality," the notion that under the aegis of zaddikim one could sanctify non-Jewish folktales, songs, and dances by engaging them with a holy intention, was a compelling rationale. If divinity permeated and sustained all foreign entities, then they could, in the Besht's words, be "elevated" and "linked to the spiritual" by the zaddik and his followers. Worship in corporeality enabled Hasidim, in Lotman's terms to "deprecate the source from which the text originated" by conceiving the story, lyrics, and so on as outwardly profane, and to "emphasize that the true potential of the text is only realized by being integrated into the receiving culture" by conceiving the Jewish version as its redemption.

Conclusion

Scholars who study subaltern groups have noticed that indigenous peoples frequently appropriated and transformed the language, cultural norms, and Christian signifiers of European colonizers without surrendering or subsuming their own cultures.[179] Certain subaltern societies in South America, for example, absorbed features of Christianity selectively while preserving or creating their own narrative symbolism, performance criteria, and churches, even their own line of prophets.[180] The Hasidic importation of dominant cultural forms was not as extensive, for zaddikim eschewed overtly Christian ideology and signifiers while continuing to cultivate a more insular elite Hebrew literature through sizeable printing initiatives. But they did permit the surrounding culture to bear a controlled influence in the popular realm, effectively harnessing it instead of vainly attempting to apply the elite culture's rigid insularity on a mass level. This was not acculturation or assimilation, but appropriation, for non-Jewish structures were made to accommodate a Jewish content, and they arguably inoculated Jews against the dominant culture. But appropriation still constitutes a form of hybridization. And as it occurred on a local or regional level, the various Hasidic permutations necessarily took on a local or regional inflection. As a result, regionally distinct varieties of Hasidic popular culture began to emerge. In the case of Central Poland, Hasidic popular culture acquired a distinctly Polish coloring.[181]

This appropriation on the level of popular culture proved ingenious from a popularizing perspective. Most work-a-day Jews responded exuberantly to the importation of elements of surrounding cultural expressions. When folk tales were Hasidicized by replacing their heroes with zaddikim and installing a religious moral, forbidden fruit was rendered fit for consumption and one could enjoy a taste of the attractions of non-Jewish culture without remorse. This practice succeeded particularly among the lower and middling strata, who were less insulated from Slavic popular culture on a daily basis. As for traditional scholarly elites, who would have required a more elaborate justification for this contentious use of the surrounding culture, they had only to attend the zaddik's sermons delivered at the Third Meal of the Sabbath or dip into the movement's vast ideological fund—its rapidly expanding canon of Hebrew homiletic literature. More often than not, they too were won over by validations rooted in "worship through corporeality." On the strength of this preeminent concept, Hasidism was borne to the furthest reaches of Jewish society.

Conclusion

The Besht once compared the outside observer of Hasidism to a
deaf man who happens upon a group of blissfully dancing Jews. Unable to hear the music, the man assumes that the dancers are complete lunatics.[1] The message for critics of Hasidism is clear: lacking
insight into the movement's mysteries, they see only lunacy. How
could they possibly understand that by cleaving to each other in lov-
ing unity the dancers are elevating divine sparks and achieving ascents of the soul! The allegory anticipates the criticisms of Mitnaggdim, Maskilim, and pioneering Jewish historians alike.
Nonetheless, it can also be invoked to illuminate the perils of sympathetic revisionism, for many outsiders have been too easily
charmed by the dancers' blissful brotherhood and have tended to accept it at face value.

What has been argued here is that awareness that the dancers
were at the same time achieving an ambitious sociopolitical conquest enables us to delight in their dance without becoming too
mesmerized. They offered their fellow Jews an alluring subculture
as an alternative to an enfeebled rabbinate or a Christian society that
continued to disenfranchise them. They appeared worldly enough to
appeal to the region's burgeoning protoindustrialist class, folksy
enough to attract members of impoverished or rural segments of
Polish Jewry, and intellectually innovative enough to draw the most
talented scions of the rabbinical elite. Their broad appeal enabled
them to infiltrate towns and cities, set up separate prayer houses,
penetrate local study houses and synagogues, and appoint disciples,
devotees, and sympathizers to kahal posts. Wherever Mitnaggdim,
Maskilim, or Polish officials challenged them, they emerged at least
partly victorious, thanks to their own political savvy and, in large

part, their patrons among the mercantile elite. The latter probably proved so receptive to Polish zaddikim because they could offer them honor commensurate with their material success, and, in many cases, acceptance into the Jewish aristocracy.

The tour de force of the Polish zaddikim was their achievement of grassroots support despite their elitist orientation. Like *ba'alei shem,* they proved obliging practitioners of magic, yet brought refinement and prestige to the enterprise. They boosted their popularity further by disseminating the zaddik-idea in print and in oral or nonverbal media. Their readiness to selectively appropriate elements of the surrounding folk culture and indulge fantasies of social inversions proved particularly prescient. Yet even as they catered to all Jews, "great and small," the Polish zaddikim were careful to groom only male scions of the rabbinic elite for actual leadership. So unobtrusively did they preserve hierarchy that even the most humble followers could feel part of a movement. This does not make the Polish zaddikim charlatans, for they seem to have performed their magical and theurgical services in earnest. But it does suggest that their "love of Israel" was not as undiscriminating as their defenders claimed.

The recontextualization of Hasidism forces us to assess the limits of intellectual histories and relinquish certain impressions conveyed by older historiographical schools. The rise of Polish Hasidism is not only explicable through the appeal of spiritual doctrines and their charismatic delivery, for these were sustained by activities in more mundane spheres. The movement's ascendancy was so methodical, organized, and well funded and publicized that a description of zaddikim must also acknowledge their political acumen, lucrative connections, and *yihus.* It is, moreover, quite misleading to portray Hasidism as a movement of simple, déclassé Jews, revolutionary egalitarianism, romantic antibourgeois idealism, spiritual autonomy, and other projections of latter-day concerns informing works composed by the Dubnow school. The Men of Silk were aptly named, for they long remained shrouded in mystery.

Contemporaneous testimonies, both internal and external, instead reveal Polish Hasidism as a blend of spiritual innovation and conservative populism—a combination that proved too potent for even the most determined adversaries. Mitnaggdim were worn down, losing their will to fight what they came to realize was really just another brand of traditionalism. Maskilim were more formidable, as they shared goals of acculturation and integration with several of the powerful non-Jewish authorities. But in the absence of emancipation, Polish zaddikim could overcome even adversaries such as these by offering Jews a sense of agency. In the final analysis, the rise of Polish Hasidism was thus as much about empowerment as it was about power.

An appreciation of the movement's populist character helps us better comprehend the apparently self-destructive promotion of anti-establishment sentiments by zaddikim, who were by-and-large members of the Jewish aristocracy, through tales like "The Horses." If such tales appear from our perspective to invite social upheaval, this was not the effect in their socially stratified traditional setting. They did not fire the ambitions of déclassé Jews beyond a desire to closely associate with the new *yihus*-enhanced, miracle working zaddikim, who seemed to value their simple piety and empathize with their plight. Accessibility to spiritual elites marked, by itself, a significant innovation in this period, and the egalitarian assertions in many tales may have had the added function of quelling doubts about the appropriateness of such inter-class intimacy. In any case, it was not until the late nineteenth century that a disenfranchised East European Jew could imagine something as lofty as social revolution. In the meantime, the accessibility and empathy of the zaddikim earned enough popular consent to enable the zadikkim to triumph over their fellow elites.

Yihus and Marriage Strategies of Early Zaddikim outside Central Poland

Examples through 1815

The following represents a large sampling of the *yihus* of early Hasidic leaders outside of Central Poland, drawing upon the sources from which we derived the figures presented near the end of chapter 4. Together, these lists present the familial ties and marriage strategies of fifty early zaddikim.

YIHUS AZMO

The most prominent member of this category was the Besht, son of Eliezer of Tłuste and Sarah.[1] The Besht married Hannah, daughter of R. Ephraim, *av bet din* of Brody. The resistance by R. Gershon of Kuty, Hannah's brother, illustrates the inherent difficulty of such a social climb.[2] Upon his social promotion, the Besht consolidated his standing though shrewd matchmaking practices for his children. He married his disappointing son Zvi Hirsch of Pińsk to Malka, daughter of Samuel Hasid and Nahama. Although precise information about Samuel is lacking, he might be identified as Samuel Hasid of Pińsk (d. 1757), a member of the Brody *kloyz*.[3] In any event, the name "Hasid" denotes an old-style mystic who was probably a member of the Besht's elite circle. Samuel married another of his daughters to R. Jacob Joseph of Połonne. For his daughter Adel, the Besht secured a match with R. Jehiel Michael Ashkenazy, son of R. Barukh and Shifra Ashkenazy. The dedication of an entire section of the Hasidic classic *Degel Mahane Ephraim* to R. Jehiel Michael's teachings suggests he was a scholar of stature.

R. Zvi Hirsch and Malka had three sons. The first, R. Israel the Silent, is a mysterious figure known through legends.[4] Their other sons were R. Dov Ber of Ulanów and R. Aaron of Titów,[5] both zaddikim. R. Dov Ber of Ulanów was an in-law of the zaddik R. Zusya of Annipol. His daughter Simah married R. Moses Zvi, son of R. Abraham Dov Urbach, R. Jacob Joseph of Połonne's son-in-law; and Zvi Menahem of Annipol, son of R. Zusya of Annipol. R. Aaron of Titów married two of his children into the Chernobyl (Czarnobyl) dynasty (his daughter, Simha Husha, to R. Aaron of Chernobyl in her second marriage; then to the zaddik R. Barukh of Międzyboż;[6] and his son, R. Naftali Zvi of Skwira, to the daughter of R. Mordecai of Chernobyl).[7] The wife of R. Aaron's other son Abraham is unknown.

More famous are several of the descendants of the Besht's daughter, Adel, and R. Jehiel Michael Ashkenazy. R. Moses Hayyim Ephraim was matched with Esther, daughter of Gershon of Kuty, the Besht's brother-in-law. One of their children, Ethel, married David Horowitz, of another aristocratic family. The matches of their other children, Jacob Jehiel, Isaac of Kałusz, and Joseph are unknown.[8] Another son of Adel and R. Jehiel Michael, R. Barukh of Międzyboż, was married first to the daughter of the wealthy Tuvia Kazkish of Ostróg. His second marriage was, as noted, to the daughter of R. Aaron Titów.[9] R. Barukh had no sons through which to pass on his legacy. However, his daughter Adel was matched with R. Jacob Phineas Urbach, another son of R. Abraham Dov, R. Jacob Joseph of Połonne 's son-in-law. Hanna was married to R. Isaac of Drohobycz/ Kałusz, son of R. Joseph of Jampol, son of the Besht's prominent disciple R. Jehiel Michael of Złoczów. R. Barukh married his third daughter, Raizel, to R. Dov Ber of Tulczyn, rabbi of Czarny Ostróg and son of the zaddik Solomon of Karlin. A third son was known as Israel the Dead (*Toyter*).

Adel and R. Jehiel Michael's only daughter, Feige, was married to Simha, son of the Besht's disciple R. Nahman of Horodenka. The latter descended from the R. Judah Loewe, the Maharal of Prague, and purportedly Rashi.[10] His son Simha was not known to be a scholar; apparently he was married for his *yihus* alone. The child of this union, the famous R. Nahman of Bratslav, was married first to Sosha, the daughter of a lessee of villages named Ephraim Ber of Zaslaw. Immediately after the death of R. Nahman's wife Sosha, he arranged a second marriage to the daughter of a rich community leader in Brody, Ezekiel Trachtenburg. R. Nahman hoped that the messiah would come from the union between his daughter Sarah and Isaac, son of the wealthy Leib Dubrowner.[11]

While it is difficult to know how many marriages were arranged by the Besht himself, we may assume he influenced the matches that occurred during his lifetime. His interest in his grandchildren, as portrayed in his letter to Gershon that described the progress of young Moses Hayyim Ephraim, was keen.[12] Eventually, R. Moses became R. Gershon's son-in-law. In the foregoing marriages in the Besht's family, *yihus* appears to be a major factor in the majority of cases. Four of the matches were probably motivated by wealth, and three according to the groom's scholarly ability. What emerges is an attempt by the Besht and his descendants to consolidate their *yihus*, hence their social position.

Another extraordinary zaddik who probably acquired *yihus* was R. Dov Ber of Międzyrzecz. As discussed, the evidence for his father Abraham's purported greatness, a claim intended to ease the concerns of later generations of Hasidim, is scanty. Little is known about Abraham, "a poor Hebrew teacher,"[13] and his wife, Havah. R. Dov Ber was quite a student, meriting a teacher as great as R. Joshua Falk, author of the Talmudic work *Pene Yehoshuah* (Żółkiew, 1742).[14] His scholarly diligence earned him a father-in-law named R. Shalom Shakhna, *av bet din* of Tulczyn. Despite his unaided rise into the elite, however, he unabashedly requested two communal leaders to "arrange for my son, may he have a long life, to marry the daughter of the rabbi, our teacher, Feivel, the author of the book *Mishnat Hakhamim*." Thus a match was arranged between Abraham the Angel and Henya, daughter of R. Meshullam Feibush Halevi Horowitz of Krzemieniec.[15] R. Dov Ber's offspring would now be Horowitzes, although even that distinction would pale in comparison to R. Dov Ber's own celebrity as a Hasidic leader, organizer, and thinker.

R. Abraham the Angel did not become a zaddik himself. He was in no way a rightful heir, an idea that came into existence at a later stage of the movement.[16] R. Abraham's sons' marriages nevertheless reflect a continued effort to consolidate the family's social status, although both R. Dov Ber and R. Abraham passed away when the sons were young. At least one son, R. Shalom Shakhna of Probst,[17] was raised in the house of the zaddik Solomon of Karlin. He married Hava, daughter of Malkha and Abraham of Korostyszów, a son-in-law of the zaddik Nahum of Chernobyl (Czarnobyl), *rosh yeshivah* and *rosh medinah* in Korostyszów. They bore R. Israel, founder of the Ruzhiner dynasty. R. Abraham the Angel's other son, R. Israel Hayyim of Ludmir (Wladymir, Volhynia), was matched with a daughter of the zaddik Solomon of Karlin in his first marriage, and a daughter of his father's disciple R. Gedaliya Rabinowitz of Iliniec in his second marriage.

Several other zaddikim appear to have also hearkened from humble backgrounds and achieved *yihus azmo*. R. Aryeh Leib Sarah's, of whom we know little else, was the son of Joseph, a Hebrew teacher, and Sarah, whose name he inherited.[18] His tombstone lacks any mention of distinguished forebears. R. Aryeh Leib had no children through whom we might measure his attitude about *yihus*.

Another zaddik who may belong to this category of self-made men is R. Hayyim Haykl of Amdur (Indura). The precise identity of his father, Samuel, is a mystery. R. David of Maków, a ferocious enemy of R. Hayyim, asserted that R. Hayyim's father-in-law was "known as a great ignoramus" who made his living cooking gruel for small change.[19] If this is accurate, and R. Hayyim did not marry the daughter of a prominent man, it suggests that he himself lacked *yihus*. In 1768, R. Hayyim's name appears in the Indura communal register as a "simple member" of the burial society, which was, however, the most prestigious society in any community.[20] He has also been described as the town cantor in his youth, a position of some distinction.[21] In any event, his son Samuel filled his place in Indura, and married the daughter of R. Aaron "the Silent" of Żelechów,[22] a disciple of R. Elimelekh of Leżajsk and R. Uziel Meisels.[23] The match of R. Hayyim's son Dov Ber is unknown. R. Hayyim's daughter married R. Nathan of Maków, a disciple of R. Jacob Isaac, the Seer of Lublin.

Another possible case of *yihus azmo* is that of R. Aaron Perlów "the Great" of Karlin. "Perlów" is a calque of the name "Margaliot."[24] This is not proof of *yihus*, though, for R. Aaron seems to have had no forebears by that name. Some assert Aaron's descent from King David, rabbis, and "hidden zaddikim," without substantiation.[25] Upon his order, R. Aaron's tombstone bore the inscription: "Here is buried an anonymous man [*ish ploni*], born of an anonymous woman, one who was an anonymous man, son of an anonymous man."[26] We cannot know whether it was out of actual humility. R. Aaron was the son of Jacob, a beadle in a *bet midrash* in the small town of Janów, another indication of humble descent.[27]

The identity of Aaron's wife is unknown. His daughter Hayya Sarah married the zaddik Mordecai of Chernobyl. Another daughter, Ribla, married first a certain R. Israel, and then R. Shalom Shakhna, father of the zaddik Menahem Mendel of Lubavitch (Lyubaviche). Another daughter married R. Aaron of Łachowce (son of the zaddik Mordecai of Łachowce), a disciple of R. Solomon of Karlin. R. Aaron's son Jacob married the daughter of a certain R. Abraham Karliner. The wife of Aaron's most famous son, Asher of Karlin-Stolin, Feige-Batyah, was the widow of R. Aaron "the Silent" of Zelechów.[28] R. Asher filled his father's position as rabbi of Stolin, and many of his father's followers attached themselves to him upon his father's death at age thirty-six. If R. Aaron of Karlin indeed lacked *yihus*, his children appear to have achieved aristocratic membership.

R. Solomon of Karlin, son of Meir Halevi (or Nahum) Gottlieb of Karlin, was a disciple of R. Aaron the Great of Karlin. Although R. Solomon's father sometimes used the surname Gottlieb, R. Solomon and his offspring do not appear to have used it. His son, R. Dov of Tulczyn married the daughter of R. Barukh of Międzyboż; while his other son, R. Moses of Ludmir, married the daughter of R. Leib Kohen- a *maggid* in Annipol and author of *Or ha-Ganuz*- and succeeded his father in Ludmir. R. Solomon's daughter Yuta married R. Israel Hayyim of Ludmir, son of R. Abraham "the Angel," son of R. Dov Ber of Międzyrzecz. Another daughter married Dov Moses, grandson of the author of *Ha-Hakham Zvi* (Amsterdam, 1702).

A possible exception to this pattern is R. Aryeh Judah Leib, the Grandfather of Szpola. His father, Barukh Gerundi, originally from Bohemia, was a tax collector for a nobleman of the Potocki family. His mother Rachel's background cannot be identified. R. Barukh of Międzybóz, the quintessential *yihus* possessor, publicly derided R. Aryeh for his lack of *yihus*.[29] R. Aryeh refused or was unable to serve as rabbi in a formal capacity, or be called "rebbe"; and he stipulated that his sons refuse those roles.[30] Legend has it that R. Aryeh was ordered by his master, R. Phineas Shapiro of Korzec, to marry the daughter of a kosher slaughterer in Mydowdików.[31] This seems plausible, as R. Aryeh would likely be matched with the daughter of someone of similarly humble stature. We do not know how R. Aryeh married his sons Jacob and Barukh Gad (or Jacob, Abraham, and Pesah),[32] but the very lack of information about their spouses might imply that R. Aryeh refused to use their marriages for social advancement. On his tombstone, only his name and date of death were written.[33] R. Aryeh's refusal or failure to achieve social advancement was unique for a zaddik of his renown.[34]

ARISTOCRATIC FAMILY *YIHUS*

In addition to those identified in chapter 4, a Horowitz among the early Hasidim was R. Aaron of Starosielce, disciple of R. Shneur Zalman of Liady. R. Aaron's father was Moses Horowitz of Starosielce, a seventh-generation descendant of R. Isaiah Horowitz, author of *Shnei Luhot Ha-Brit*.[35] This distinguished lineage bears upon his controversy with R. Dov Ber, son of R. Shneur Zalman, for it exposes the struggle as inter-elite rather than merely between a disciple and son of a zaddik. Regarding the marriages of R. Aaron and his children, however, the sources are silent. All that is known is that his son R. Hayyim Raphael succeeded him as rabbi of Starosielce.

Another aristocratic family that was a source of zaddikim was the Shapiro family, which claimed descent from Rashi.[36] The family derived its name from the German city Speyer, in memory of martyrs of that city from the Crusades (1096) and Black Death (1348) massacres. Perhaps the most famous Shapiro was R. Nathan Nata (b. 1585), author of the first extensive numerical interpretation of the Scriptures, *Megale Amukot* (Cracow, 1637). The first Hasidic leader from this family was R. Phineas Shapiro of Korzec.[37] R. Phineas's father, R. Abraham Abba of Szklów, was a Lithuanian scholar and an itinerant preacher. His grandfather, known as R. Phineas Shapiro the Elder, was a well-known *maggid* in Reisen and Szklów.[38] His mother, Sarah Rachel Sheindel, was a descendant of R. Eliezer bar Nathan, known as "Raban" (c. 1090–1170). R. Phineas first married Treina, daughter of Jonah Weill of Sławuta, descendant of many other prominent scholars bearing the name "Weill."[39] His second marriage was to a woman named Yuta. R. Phineas was exceedingly proud of his family, signing his letters "Shapiro" and ordering that his tombstone be engraved with that name.[40]

R. Phineas's marriage strategies for his children were as follows: (1) R. Judah Meir, *av bet din* of Szepetówka, married Sarah, daughter of the zaddik Jacob Samson of Szepetówka, a descendant of R. Samson of Ostropole; (2) R. Moses, *av bet din* of Sławuta, married Rachel, daughter of Isaac, a rabbinical judge in Prague, son of Saul, *av bet din* of Cracow. Rachel was sister of the zaddik Gedaliya of Iliniec, another disciple of R. Dov Ber and, allegedly, a descendant of Rashi; (3) Jacob Samson of Zasław married the daughter of R. Dov, rabbi of Zasław, whose position Jacob Samson inherited; (4) Ezekiel of Ostróg married the daughter of a certain Joseph of Połonne;⁴¹ (5) Elijah married the daughter of a certain Joseph of Wanisnowiec;⁴² (6) Rezel (or Sarah) Sheindel married R. Samuel, *av bet din* of Koniów, Kolinblat,⁴³ and Zwenigorodka.⁴⁴

Another prominent zaddik from the Shapiro family was R. Mordecai of Neskhiż.⁴⁵ Like R. Phineas, his lineage is traced to the author of *Megalleh Amukot*. R. Mordecai's father, R. Dov Ber, was a scribe of the *vaad* of Tulczyn and *av bet din* of Leszniów and Neskhiż; his mother was named Gitel. R. Mordecai married Reiza, daughter of R. Joseph Katzenellenbogen, *av bet din* of Leszniów, son-in-law of R. Jacob, *av bet din* and *rosh yeshivah* in Ludmir. R. Mordecai served as *av bet din* of Ludmir, Neskhiż, and Kowel. R. Mordecai married, a second time, the daughter of the zaddik Samuel Ginzberg of David-Gorodok. Regarding his marriage strategies for his children, we know: (1) Joseph Katzenellenbogen of Ustilla married the daughter of R. Judah Meir Shapiro of Szepetówka, son of R. Phineas of Korzec;⁴⁶ and then the daughter of R. Jacob Joseph "Rav Yevi" of Ostróg; (2) Isaac of Neskhiż married the daughter of Michael of Kaszówka, son-in-law of R. Moses Halevi Ephrati, *rosh yeshivah* of Berdyczów and Batoshin,⁴⁷ and then married the daughter of the zaddik Levi Isaac of Berdyczów; (3) the wife of R. Jacob Aryeh Shapiro, rabbi in Kobla, is unknown; (4) Zartel married R. Meir Shraga Feivel, rabbi of Zaslaw and Rzeszów; (5) another daughter married a certain Joseph of Leszno.

The third family the Besht purportedly admired was the Margaliot family. Deriving its name from *margalit* (pearl), this family traced its descent to Rashi. R. Jacob, rabbi of Regensburg (d. between 1499 and 1512) is the earliest identifiable member. One distinguished member of this line was R. Ephraim Zalman Margaliot (1760–1828), who authored many standard books and responsa.⁴⁸ The most prominent Margaliot among the Hasidim was R. Meir Margaliot of Ostróg, author of *Meir Netivim* (Połonne, 1791–92) and *Sod Yakhin u-Voaz* (Ostróg, 1794). His grandfather was rabbi of Jazlowice (Czech lands);⁴⁹ and was succeeded by his son, R. Zvi Hirsch. R. Meir's mother, Shaynzya, was sister of R. Aryeh Leib Urbach, *av bet din* of Stanisław, and daughter of R. Mordecai Merdosh of Krzemieniec, *av bet din* of Jazłowiec and Bomberg (German lands). R. Meir himself served as rabbi of Horodenka, before filling his father's place in Jazłowiec. He then garnered rabbinical appointments over the entire Lwów and Ostróg districts.

His first marriage was to Hayya, daughter of a certain Hayyim Katz of Horodenka. His second was to Reizel, daughter of his uncle R. Aryeh Leib Urbach, *av bet din* of Stanisław. Reizel was widow of R. Meshullam Zalman Ashkenazi, *av bet din* of Pomerania. R. Meir's son Bezalel, who succeeded him in Ostróg, married the daughter of a certain Joshua Rishower. He then wed the daughter of R. Hayyim Hakohen Rapoport, author of *Zekher Ha-Hayyim* (Lemberg, 1865).⁵⁰ One of R. Meir's daughters married R. Naftali Herz, *av bet din* of Shargoród. Another daughter married Simha, son of Nahman Katz Rapoport. Meir's daughter Hayya, of his second marriage, married the wealthy Judah Leib of Pińsk. R. Meir's son Saul, *av bet din* Zabaraż, Agafin,⁵¹ Komarno, and the entire Lublin district, was son-in-law of the *kazin* (leader or judge) Saul, brother of the well-known scribe R. Abraham Parnas, and son of Hayyim of Lublin. We do not know the matches of the other sons, R. Joseph Nahman, *av bet din* of Połonne, R. Naftali Mordecai, *av bet din* of Remelów,⁵² and Solomon Dov Ber.

In addition to the Horowitz, Shapiro, and Margaliot families, we find prominent zaddikim of the first generations from old and prestigious families such as Leiper,

Ginzberg, Hager, Rabinowitz, Heller, and Weissblum.[53] From the Leiper family came the zaddik Meir of Przemyślany (1780–1850), an early disciple of the Besht and son of Jacob "the Innocent" of Przemyślany. His forebears are described as "fifty generations of possessors of holy spirits from him, to R. Jacob Mervish of Korvil, author of the responsa *Min Shamaim*."[54] R. Meir's son Aaron Aryeh Leib married a certain Yenta; while the wives of Meir's other sons, David of Kałusz and Pesah Hasid, are unknown. A member of the Ginzberg family who became an early Hasidic zaddik was R. Samuel Ginzberg of David-Gorodok/Kosówka. R. Samuel was son of Michael Ginzsburg of Kosów. He married the daughter of R. Aaron, *av bet din* of Turobin. R. Samuel married his daughter to the zaddik Mordecai Shapiro of Neskhiż, as noted earlier.[55] The spouse of his son Ze'ev, who succeeded him, was the granddaughter of the zaddik Levi Isaac of Berdyczów. His son Jehiel Michael of Kosówka married the daughter of R. Moses Ephrati of Berdyczów, son of R. Eliezer, *rosh yeshiva* of Pińsk. In his second marriage, Jehiel Michael was son-in-law of R. Judah Meir of Szepetówka.

Another aristocratic family that provided a major zaddik early on was the Hager family, of R. Menahem Mendel Hager of Kosów (1769–1826).[56] His father was R. Jacob Kopel Hasid Hager of Kolomyja. R. Menahem Mendel was married young to Sheina Rachel, daughter of his uncle, Samuel Simha Zimmel Kook of Kosów. They had two sons and a daughter, each of whom was provided with a distinguished spouse. David of Zabłotów married Pessi Leah, daughter of the zaddik Moses Leib of Sasów. Another son, R. Hayyim Hager of Kuty, married Zipporah, daughter of Judah Meir Shapiro of Szepetówka, son of the zaddik Phineas Shapiro of Korzec. Their daughter Sarah Leah married Israel Abraham of Annipol, who may have been the son of the zaddik Meshullam Zusya of Annipol (of the same name). After their divorce, Sarah Leah wed R. Gershon Ashkenazi, *av bet din* of Kolomaja.

The Rabinowitz family provided early zaddikim, as well. R. Gedaliya of Iliniec (1738–1804), son of R. Isaac of Iliniec, a rabbinical judge in Połonne, allegedly descended from Rashi. His sister Rachel married R. Moses Shapiro of Sławuta, son of the zaddik Phineas of Korzec. R. Gedaliya himself married the daughter of a certain Moses of Chartorier. We do not know the wife of his son Samuel Judah Leib. His other son, Isaac Joel, married Miriam Simah, daughter of a certain R. Jacob of Lubartów. Among his daughters, two unquestionably advantageous matches can be discerned: one married R. Elijah Dov, son of Moses, *av bet din* of Iwanice and disciple of the Besht; and another married the zaddik Aaron of Chernobyl, son of R. Mordecai of Chernobyl. Of the other daughters, one married a certain Jacob Kugal; Hasia married a certain Zvi ben Joseph of Kamenki, and the match of a third, Hanna, is unknown.

Another zaddik who was a member of an aristocratic family was R. Meshullam Feibush Heller (1740–95), author of *Derekh Emet* (Lwow, 1830) and *Yosher Divrei Emet* (Munkacs, 1905). R. Meshullam Feibush was a descendant of R. Yom Tov Lipman Heller, and son of R. Aaron Moses Heller, *av bet din* of Sniatyn. He married, first, the daughter of R. Mordecai Halpern, *av bet din* of Brzeżany. From this union was born Moses Aaron. In his second marriage, he wed Yentl, daughter of R. Abraham Hayyim Shorr, author of *Zon Kedoshim* (Wandsbeck, 1729). The children of this marriage were R. Barukh Isaac, *av bet din* of Zwiniacz, and Samson of Jezierzany.[57] The latter married Sheindel Leah, daughter of R. Joseph Joska Halevi Horowitz, *av bet din* in Jassy and son of R. Mordecai of Krzemieniec.

The Weissblum family, of R. Elimelekh of Leżajsk and R. Zusya of Annipol (d. 1790), is another such family. Their father, Eleazar Lipman, was a wealthy man of noble descent (from Rashi and, it is claimed, R. Yohanan "Ha Sandlar.") Their paternal grandfather, Abraham of Tykocin, had married the daughter of Eliezer Lipman Halpern of Tarnogród. R. Elimelekh married Shprinza, who possessed "a *yihus* written in golden letters," which included her father R. Aaron Rokeah, brother of R. Eleazar, *av bet din* of Amsterdam. One of her brothers, R. Moses, was *av bet din* of Będzin. R. Elimelekh, a critic of reliance upon one's *yihus*, nevertheless groomed his son R. Eliezer for leadership.[58] Upon his death, however, most of R. Elimelekh's followers switched allegiance to one of his disciples, and not his son.[59]

R. Elimelekh married his son R. Eleazar to the daughter of R. Israel Zvi Hirsch Lipiner, *av bet din* and *maggid* of Grodzisk, grandson of R. Leibush Dominiz of Grodzisk. In his second marriage, R. Eleazar wed the daughter of a wealthy "Naggid" of Sieniawa. Another son, R. Eliezer Lipa, married the daughter of R. Samuel "the Melamed" of Sieniawa, whose precise identity and descent are unknown. R. Elimelekh's third son, R. Jacob, who became *av bet din* of Mogielnica, married the daughter of a miracle worker or minor zaddik, R. Reuben of Grodzisk.[60] Of R. Elimelekh's daughters, one (Meirush/ Meirel) married the zaddik Elijah of Biało Czerkiów, son of Jacob Yokel of Łańcut. Another married R. Israel, *av bet din* of Grodzisk.[61]

R. Elimelekh's brother, R. Zusya Weissblum, and his wife Hendel pursued similar strategies for their sons Israel Abraham Abba of Czarny Ostróg and Zvi Menahem Mendel. Israel Abraham married Zizah Hiyyah, daughter of the zaddik Ze'ev Wolf of Czarny Ostróg, and was Ze'ev Wolf's successor. In another marriage, he may have wed Sarah Leah, daughter of R. Hayyim Hager of Kosów, son of the zaddik Menahem Mendel of Kosów (see earlier). Zvi Menahem Mendel was married first to the daughter of a certain Moses Ibenezer, and second to Simah, daughter of the zaddik Dov of Ulanów, grandson of the Besht through the latter's son, Zvi Hirsch. R. Zusya's daughter was matched with a certain Menahem Mendel of Annipol.

The Polish zaddik Uziel Meisels of Neustadt/Nowe Miasto Korczyn was son of Zvi Hirsch of Siemiatycze (known as "Zvi Hirsch Natal's), son of R. Isaac of Włodowa and the daughter of R. Nafthali Herz, *av bet din* and *rosh medinah* of Wien[62] in Lithuania, who descended from Rashi; and Dreisel, daughter of R. Abraham Nata, *av bet din* of Wysznice in Lithuania, author of *Nata Sha'ashu'im* (Amsterdam, 1735), a descendant of R. Moses Isserles. He married the daughter of the wealthy R. Solomon Meir of Żelechów. His son Israel of Kolbuszowa married the daughter of R. Isaac b. Isaiah, *av bet din* and *rosh medinah* of Kolbuszowa. His wealthy son Zvi Hirsch's wife is unknown. R. Uziel's daughter married R. Kalonymous Kalman b. Judah Leibush of Nowe Miasto Korczyn, grandson of the *av bet din* and *rosh medinah* of Cracow.

YIHUS ABSENT AN ARISTOCRATIC FAMILY

The famous R. Jacob Joseph of Połonne's father, Zvi Hakohen Katz, was a descendent of R. Samson of Ostropol and R. Yom Tov Lipman Heller. R. Jacob Joseph married a daughter of Samuel Hasid and Nehama (whose other daughter married the Besht's son, Zvi Hirsch). We do not know to whom R. Jacob Joseph married his son and successor in Raszków, R. Abraham Samson, but he married his daughter to R. Abraham Dov Urbach, son of R. Abraham HaKohen Urbach.[63] R. Abraham Dov published Jacob Joseph's masterpiece, *Toledot Ya'akov Yosef* (Korzec, 1780) and succeeded him as rabbi of Połonne. He married his son, Moshe Zvi, to Simah, the daughter of Zvi Hirsch, son of the Besht.

Another major disciple of the Besht, R. Jehiel Michael of Złoczów, was the son of R. Isaac of Drohobycz, a disciple of the Besht and official *maggid* in Ostróg, Drohobycz, and Karków.[64] His father, R. Joseph Wirnik of Pistyn, was known as "Joseph the Honest." His grandfather, R. Moses of Pistyn, *av bet din* of Świerze, was a famous martyr. His other grandfather was R. Isaac Hayyot, *av bet din* of Prague. The family ultimately claimed descent from Rashi.[65] R. Jehiel Michael married Sarah, daughter of a certain Moses. Their first-born son, R. Isaac of Radziwiłów, was married to the daughter of the zaddik Moses Shoham of Dolina, son of Dan and disciple of the Besht. In his second marriage, R. Isaac wedded the daughter of R. Zvi Hirsch of Nadworna, and succeeded him as rabbi there. Another son, R. Mordecai of Krzemieniec, married the daughter of Eliezer, a children's teacher in Kowsów,[66] son of R. Ephraim Fischel, who is mentioned in the approbation to the book *Zikharon Shmuel* and was the descendant of many famous rabbis.[67] R. Jehiel Michael's son Moses married the daughter of R. David, *av bet din* of Grabowiec. The wife of another son, R. Benjamin Ze'ev Wolf of Zabaraż, cannot be identified. Finally, R. Jehiel Michael married his daughter Miriam to David Halevi of Stephan, a disciple of the Besht and grandson of the author of *Turei Zahav* (Żółkiew, 1754).

The biography of R. Menahem Nahum of Chernobyl (Czarnobyl, 1730–98) is difficult to reconstruct.[68] His grandfather was R. Nahum "Ha Gaon," *av bet din* of Norinsk (Gurinsk). The father of R. Nahum "Ha Gaon" was allegedly R. Nathan Nata Katzenellenbogen, son of R. Nahum Katzenellenbogen, son of R. Meir Katzenellenbogen, son of the legendary Saul Wahl. But this may be a fabrication.[69] R. Menahem's father Zvi succeeded his father in Norinsk. One of R. Zvi's brothers, R. Aryeh Leib, was a friend and colleague of the Besht. For his son Menahem Nahum, R. Zvi procured a match with Simha Sarah Shapiro, granddaughter of R. Isaac Shapiro, *av bet din* of Kowno and Lublin, son of R. Nathan Nata Shapiro, author of *Mavoh Sha'arim* (1575) and descendant of R. Nathan Nata Shapiro, the Megale Amukot.

R. Menahem Nahum is sometimes considered the first zaddik to institute hereditary succession, transmitting his office to his son Mordecai upon his own death in 1798 (however, R. Jehiel Michael of Złoczów may have done so first).[70] R. Mordecai first married Hayya Sarah, R. Aaron of Karlin's daughter. According to legend, the Great Maggid himself acted as matchmaker for the pair.[71] In his second marriage, R. Mordecai married Feigela, the daughter of R. David Leikes of Bar, a disciple of the Besht. Of R. Menahem Nahum and Simha Sarah's other children, it is known that one daughter, Malka, married Abraham, son of R. Zvi Hirsch and *rosh yeshivah* and *rosh medinah* of Korostyszów; and that another daughter married R. Leib, *av bet din* of Bendery (Bessarabia). The spouse of their other son, Moses, is unknown to us. The manner in which R. Menahem Nahum, a possessor of *yihus*, consolidated his family's *yihus* in at least two of his children's marriages should be taken into account when one considers his legendary profile of a humble, impoverished teacher of children.[72]

R. Shneur Zalman of Liady, author of the *Tanya* (Sławuta, 1796), and son of R. Barukh, has been traced back to Judah Loewe, the Maharal of Prague.[73] R. Barukh's wife Rebecca, although her father's name is not extant, may have been remarkable herself, for Shneur Zalman occasionally signed his name as "son of Rebecca."[74] R. Barukh and Rebecca bore, in addition to Shneur Zalman: (1) R. Judah Leib of Janowiec, author of *Sha'arit Yehudah* (Vilna, 1841); (2) R. Mordecai Posner, rabbi of Orsha (Witebsk), (3) R. Moses, *av bet din* of Ajewa,[75] Bijów,[76] Lijefli,[77] and Rudnya (near Lubavitch), and (4) Sarah, who married Israel Kozak, subject of at least one tale.[78] They married R. Shneur Zalman to Sterna, daughter of a rich businessman named Judah Leib Seigel of Witebsk and Biała.

R. Shneur Zalman and Sterna had three sons—Dov Ber, Moses, and Hayyim Abraham—and three daughters: Deborah Leah, Frieda, and Rachel. His successor, R. Dov Ber of Lubavitch, married Shayna, daughter of a children's teacher who was one of Shneur Zalman's Hasidim. Moses married the daughter of a certain Zvi Hirsch of

Ulla,[79] and later stunned the Hasidic world by converting to Christianity.[80] R. Hayyim Abraham's spouse cannot be identified. R. Shneur Zalman married his daughter Deborah Leah (mother of the "Zemah Zedek") to Shalom Shakhnah, son of Noah (father-in-law of Issachar Ber, official *maggid* in Lubavitch); Frieda to a certain Eliezer, son of Mordecai; and Rachel to Abraham Shaynas of Szklów, son of Zvi, a prominent man in Szklów who opposed the Hasidim. Although Schneur Zalman came from noble lineage and married well, it is more difficult to evaluate the marriage patterns of his children. Their chances in the marriage market may have been hurt by the conversion of their brother Moses.

Several lesser known zaddikim and other prominent disciples of the Besht, R. Dov Ber of Międzyrzecz, and R. Phineas of Korzec fall into this category. R. Abraham Abba Joseph of Sorocko was the son of Shemariah, official maggid of Korzec. His better known son, Shemariah Weingarten of Lubaszewo (d. 1847), married a daughter of the zaddik David Halevi of Stepan. R. Abraham Hayyim of Złoczów (1750–1816) was son of Gedaliya, *av bet din* of Żółkiew, son of R. Benjamin Wolf, also *av bet din* of Żółkiew. In his first marriage, he wed the daughter of the zaddik Phineas Horowitz. After the union was childless, R. Abraham divorced her and married the daughter of R. Issachar Dov Ber, *av bet din* of Złoczów and author of *Bat Eyni* (Dubno, 1781) and *Mevasser Zeddek* (Lemberg, 1850). He succeeded his father-in-law as rabbi of Złoczów. This union was childless as well. R. Abraham raised the son of one of these wives, whose name was Joseph Azriel, son of R. Hayyim Aryeh Leibush, *av bet din* of Gologory. R. Jacob Samson of Szepetówka was the son of R. Isaac, rabbi of Sławuta, and a descendant of R. Samson of Ostropol. R. Jacob Samson married the daughter of R. Hayyim Jacob, *av bet din* of Połonne and grandson of R. Joel Sirkes, "the Bach" (1561–1640). He married his daughter, Sarah, to R. Judah Meir of Szepetówka, son of the zaddik Phineas Shapiro of Korzec. The wife of his son Joshua, who died during R. Jacob Samson's lifetime, is unknown.

APPENDIX 2

An Exorcism in Warsaw, 1818

A SHORT DESCRIPTION OF THE FANATICAL WORKS OF A JEWISH
KABBALIST HERE IN WARSAW FROM BIALYSTOK DURING THE
PAST MONTH.

Two months ago, a certain Jew from Wyszogród arrived here with his twelve-year-old son, ill with something like convulsions, with the intention of checking him into the Jewish Hospital and healing him. But as after a certain amount of time the illness did not leave him, the father of this boy proceeded to a Kabbalist who had just arrived from Białystok, with the question: could he not perhaps help him with something? The Kabbalist looked over the boy and declared that the illness was possession by an evil spirit. The soul of some Jew, who converted to Christianity and for this was sentenced after death to eternal wandering around the world, could find no rest in the grave. The joker undertook the task of expelling that evil spirit by the power of placing a curse (Cherem), invoking the names of angels, trumpeting, and so on. For this operation he assigned a day when a multitude of Jewish folk gathered,[1] so that they would be witnesses to the miracles of this holy man. The Kabbalist had the following conversation with the spirit.*

> KABBALIST Who are you, from where were you taken, and why did you enter this boy, who is not yet subject to sin?
>
> SPIRIT (answered nothing to this).
>
> KABBALIST Are you going to answer me? Or shall I curse you in the name of *Tac, Tacyock, Tartarach, etc.* (in this place was mentioned may more similarly unclear words, for the names of righteous Angels.)[2]
>
> SPIRIT What do you want of me?

---

* The sick boy always answered for the spirit, but the Kabbalist insisted that this same spirit spoke, and bystanders were so blinded, that they claimed that the boy's lips and tongue did not move during the time of this conversation.

KABBALIST   That you depart from this boy.

SPIRIT   And where can I go?

KABBALIST   Go to the forest and enter some tree.

SPIRIT   I won't go there, for I would never be free of torment.

KABBALIST   But I command you, and if you are not willing to leave, I will use other means against you. (Here he turns to the people) Give me the trumpet![3] (They give it to him) (Trumpet blasts).

At this harsh melody, the boy fell into convulsions and began to move his chest, snorting. The Kabbalists, seeing this, ordered the bystanders to chant a psalm, and immediately the convulsions stopped, upon which he declared that "the spirit wanted to exit through the throat and strangle the boy." As this operation was undertaken on Friday and close to the Sabbath, on which even spirits rest, his miracle was postponed until Sunday. The very first act of the Kabbalist on Sunday was, for more comfortable battle with the spirit, to order the sick boy to another home. There he bound up the head and hand of the Possessed with parchment with names (Szemot) written on it.[4] On his stomach, however, he placed his Cherem, written on half a sheet of paper, and his questioning began thus:

KABBALIST   And now do you finally want to leave?

SPIRIT   I will leave, but I will enter into one of the greatest Magnates[5] and tell him that Jews ordered me to possess him, and tell him to do some harm to you.

KABBALIST   You will not dare. Look, I am collecting money for you, in order to redeem your soul. (Each of the spectators had to give something.) And I will collect even more, but depart!

SPIRIT   For this, I will go into an unsealed barrel (i.e., a Jew without a *gartel*).[6]

KABBALIST   (To the spectators) For the love of God, fasten your belts! (Everyone does so. Here, the boy begins to undergo convulsions again and starts to snort. The Kabbalist ordered a psalm to be sung, after which the convulsions ceased. This fanatic declared again "that the spirit wanted to exit through the throat and strangle the boy."[c] He said further:)

KABBALIST   I command you not to harm this boy in any way. Depart through the small toe of the left foot. (began again to chant spells).

SPIRIT   I will leave, but allow me to do this at the same time I entered.

KABBALIST   And when did you enter?

SPIRIT   On Tuesday, between nine and ten o'clock at night.

To this the Rabbi consented, and postponed the operation until Tuesday. When the appointed time arrived, the spirit requested an extension until the time of night when angels praise God.[7] And to this the Kabbalist consented, and ordered him to enter into a hen, which when Jews pray upon it and slaughter it, the spirit would be liberated from pain.[8] At the same time, however, he, that is the Kabbalist, would intercede for him through prayers to God. At 12:30 at night, the spectators supposedly heard a bang and scream, and at that time, as the Kabbalist claimed, the spirit departed.

The next day, when the Kabbalist approached the boy, he asked him who is this? He answered him: this is a Rabbi. The boy gave him his hand, and said that this was the first time he ever saw him. After that, he ordered him to pray, which he did. Before [the exorcism], however, he did not even want to hear holiness; he even recoiled from pronouncing the word Adonai.

[section marked "omit"]:
I was with this boy on the eve of the departure of the spirit, which was September 7, 1818. Glancing at me, he asked: "Is he also a Jew? Why do I not recognize his clothes?" I answered him, that it is so. The boy said, "If you are a Jew, show me your *Cyces*."[9] These are threads that a Jew binds to his Clothes, wearing them in the form of a shawl.

He was told, Silence! Again, he asked further: "Why does he shave his beard if he is a Jew?" He was answered: that this is the custom among German Jews. "But that is against the commandment that the beard may not be shaved!" cried the boy. Here, everyone was silent, and I was not a little bit confused, for every eye turned toward me. He was asked, what happened to him? "My head, bones, and everything hurts me," he answered. I noticed then that his vision was good enough, the boy was happy and smiled often and spoke very sensibly. After the departure of the spirit, they say, he had neither convulsions nor anything, but the little toe of his left foot was crooked, which the Kabbalist forbade him to show for a long time.

APPENDIX 3

Works by Hasidic Authors, through 1815

The following is a comprehensive list of works produced by Hasidic authors during the first three generations of Hasidism. While several are not technically "Hasidic" works, in that they do not contain explicitly Hasidic ideas, they are included in order to illustrate the full range of literary output by leaders of the movement.[1] Main Sources: Yeshayahu Vinograd, *Thesaurus of the Hebrew Book*; and *Ha-sefer Ha-Ivri* (CD-Rom).

Author	Title	Endorsers
Aaron b. Zvi Hirsch of Opatów (d. c1800)	*Oneg Shabbat* (Lwów, 1793)	—
	Or ha-Ganuz le-zaddikim (Żółkiew 1800)[2]	Israel of Kozienice, Moses Zvi Hirsch Meisels of Żółkiew
Aryeh Judah Leib of Połonne (d.1769)	*Kol Aryeh* (Korzec 1798)	Levi Isaac of Berdyczów, Asher Zvi of Ostróg, Mordecai b. Phineas of Korzec
Benjamin of Złoczów (d.1791)	*Ahavat Dodim* (Lemberg 1793)	Zvi Hirsch Rosens of Lemberg, Samuel b. Moses Phineas of Tarnopol, Joseph Ginzberg of Żelechów, Issachar Berish mi Geza Zvi of Złoczów, Levi Isaac of Berdyczów, Eliezer Halevi Ish Horowitz of Złoczów, Aryeh

		Leib of Białystok, Simon Ashkenazi of Dobromyl, Solomon Isaac Halpern of Bar
	Hilkat Binyamin (Lemberg 1794)	Levi Isaac of Berdyczów, Eleazar Horowitz of Żelechów
	Amtahat Binyamin (Minkowice 1796)	Levi Isaac of Berdyczów, Reuben Aaron of Słabkowice, Judah Leib of Mohilev, Jacob Zvi of Usicze
Joseph b. Abraham Blokh (1724–1790)	*Ginze Yosef* (Lemberg 1792)	Zvi Hirsch of Różaniec, Alexander Sender Margaliot of Brody, Meir b. Zvi Hirsch Kristinapoler, Levi Isaac of Berdyczów, Jacob Samson of Szepetówka, Issachar Ber mi-Geza Zvi, Aryeh Leib b. Shalom of Zabarazh, Joseph Ginzberg d'Mitkarei Dan, Eliezer Lipman Halpern, Mordecai b. Zvi Hirsch, Samuel Sheindliger, Abraham Moses b. H.Z., Meshullam Zusya of Annipol
Dov Ber of Lubavitch (1773–1828)	*Derekh Hayyim* (Kopys 1799)[3]	—
	Sha'ar ha-Teshuva veha-Tefilla (Kopys 1799, 1809)	—
	Lehavin Inyan ha-Hishtathut al Kevre zaddikim (Szklów 1813)	—
	Pokeah Ivrim (Warsaw, 1805)[4]	—
Dov Ber of Międzyrzecz (1704–72)	*Maggid Devarov le-Ya'akov* (Korzec 1781, 1784; Lemberg 1792, Ostróg 1794; Lemberg 1797; Korzec 1797; Żółkiew 1804; Berdyczów 1808)	Solomon of Łuck (editorial apology, Korzec 1781), Asher Zvi, Maggid Mesharim of Ostróg (1794), Levi Isaac of Berdyczów (Berdyczów 1808)
	Or Torah (Korzec 1804)	Asher Zvi of Ostróg, Mordecai b. Phineas of Korzec
Elimelekh of Leżajsk (1717–86)	*No'am Elimelekh* (Szklów, nd,[5] Lemberg 1788, 1788;[6] Szklów 1790; Sławuta 1794; Połonne 1804, 1814)	Ze'ev Wolf of Leżajsk, Samuel of Przeworsk, Issachar Ber mi Geza Zvi, Eliezer Horowitz of Tarnogród, Abraham Moses of Przeworsk, Jacob Joseph of Ostróg (Lemberg 1788), Jacob Samson of Szepetówka, Meshullam Zusya of Annipol, Aryeh Leib of Białystok (Sławuta, 1794), Abra-

		ham Dov Urbach of Połonne, Bezalel Margaliot of Ostróg (1804), Jacob Zvi b. Judah Leib of Nakowice (?), Joseph Hayyim b. Jacob, Solomon b. Meir of Połonne (1814)
	Iggeret ha-Kodesh (Lemberg 1785; Żółkiew 1800; Russia/Poland 1810; Berdyczów 1815	—
David Halpern of Ostróg (d.1765)	*Darkhei Zion* (Połonne 1798)	—
Hayyim b. Solomon Tyrer of Czernowice (c1760–1816)	*Sidduro Shel Shabbat* (Mohilów 1813; Żółkiew 1815)	—
Meshullam Feibush Heller (1740–1795)	*Likkutim Yekarim* (Lemberg 1792; Meżyrów 1794, 1798; Żółkiew 1800)[7]	Joseph Gelerntner of Zamość, Issachar Dov Ber mi Geza Zvi, Hayyim of Zabarazh (Lemberg 1792), David b. Israel Lekish of Bar, Abraham Moses of Rohilov (?) (1794), Joseph Gelerntner (1800)
Eliezer Horowitz of Tarnogród (1740–1806)	*No'am Meggedim u-khevod ha-Torah* (Lemberg 1807, 1815)	Jacob Orenstein of Lemberg, Meir Kristanoplerof Brody, Ephraim Zalman Margaliot of Brody, Israel of Kozienice, Jacob Isaac of Lublin, Abraham Joshua Heschel of Opatów, Abraham Hayyim of Złoczów, Mordecai of Korzec, Simon Oder Berg, Moses Teitelbaum of Sieniawa, Moses Berin Blum of Konstantynów (Lemberg 1807)
Israel Baal Shem Tov or attributions to (1700–60)	*Zava'at ha-Ribash* (Żółkiew 1793, 1794, 1795, 1796; Lemberg 1797, Korzec 1797;[8] 1800; Russia/Poland 1803; Berdyczów 1815).	Israel of Kozienice (Lemberg, 1800)
	Keter Shem Tov (Żółkiew 1794, 1794, 1795; Korzec 1797).	Menaham Mendel of Łuck/Solomon of Karlin/Abraham Moses of Przeworsk (Żółkiew 1794?)
	Sefer Katan (Żytomir 1805)	Michael b. Jacob Kopel of Żytomir, Isaac Eizik b. Bezalel of Żytomir
	Shivhei ha-Besht (Kopys 1814; Berdyczów 1815; Laszczów	Moses b. Israel of Kopys (Kopys 1814), Bezalel Margaliot of Ostróg, Meir Halevi of Zelwa, 5

	1815; Ostróg 1815 (Yiddish).	Ostróg *Dayanim*, Israel Shalom of Lubartów (Berdyczów 1815), Mordecai Ziskind of Laszczów, Abraham Jacob b. Maharam of Tyszowce, 5 Ostróg *Dayanim*[9]
Israel, son of Levi Isaac of Berdyczów (unknown)	*Likkutei Moharin and Toldot Yizhak ben Levi* (Berdyczów 1811)	—
Issachar Dov Ber mi geza Zvi (d.1810)	*Bat Eyni* (Dubno 1798)	Ze'ev Wolf of Dubno, Samuel ha-Naggid Falkon Peled of Tarnopol, 5 Dubno *Dayyanim*[10] (Dubno 1798)
	Mevasser Zedek (Dubno 1798)	Ze'ev Wolf of Dubno, 5 Dubno Dayyanim (Dubno 1798)
Jacob Joseph of Połonne (d.1782)	*Toldot Ya'akov Yosef* (Korzec 1780, 1783; Szklów 1797[11])	Hanokh Henokh b. Samuel Shik of Szklów, Zvi Hirsch b. Maharam of Szklów, Jacob b. Yerahmiel Katz of Szklów, Samuel b. Aryeh Leib of Szklów, Aaron b. Jacob of Szklów (1797)
	Ben Porat Yosef (Korzec 1781)	—
	Zafnat Paneah (Korzec 1782; Lemberg 1782)	—
Jacob Joseph of Ostróg (1738–91)	*Mora Mikdash* (Korzec 1782, Lemberg 1797)	—
	Rav Yevi (Sławuta 1792, Ostróg 1808)	Ze'ev Wolf of Dubno, Levi Isaac of Berdyczów, Asher Zvi b. David, Ostróg *Kloyz* (5),[13] (1792), Hayyim Kohen Rapoport (1808)
	Nahalat Shimon (Połonne 1815)[12]	—
Levi Isaac of Berdyczów (1740–1810)	*Kedushat Levi* (Sławuta 1798; Żółkiew 1806; Berdyczów 1810/11)[14]	Abraham Joshua Heschel of Opatów, Aaron of Żytomir (1815?) (1798), Jacob Orenstein of Lemberg, Levi Isaac of Berdyczów (?)(1806)
	Sefer ha-Zekhirot[15] (Mezyrów 1794; Żółkiew 1800;[16] Międzyboż 1812)	—
Meir b. Levi Isaac of Berdyczów (d.1806)	*Keter Torah* (Mezyrów 1803); II (Żytomir 1803, 1807)	—

Meir Margaliot of Ostróg (1700–90)	Meir Netivim: Or Olam (Połonne 1791; Korzec 1791; Połonne 1795)	Levi Isaac of Berdyczów, Ostróg Kloyz (5),[17] Isaac Joseph of Połonne, Meshullam Zusya of Annipol/Joseph of Kamienice, Abraham Joshua Heschel of Zamigrod, Jacob Israel of Konstantynów (1791)
	Ha-Derekh Tov ve-Yashar (Połonne, 1795)	—
	Sod Yakhin u-Voaz (Ostróg 1794; Połonne 1813)	Levi Isaac of Berdyczów, Meshullam Zusya of Annipol, Hayyim of Krasny, Israel of Kozienice, Aryeh Leib of Opatów, Hanina Lipman Meisels, Asher Zvi b. David of Ostróg, Ostróg Kloyz (5),[18] Israel b Ezekiel Urbach (1794)
Uziel Meisels of Neustadt[19] (1744–86)	Tiferet ha-Zvi (Żółkiew 1803)	—
Meir of Przemyślany (1728–71)	Darkhei Yesharim (Żółkiew 1794, Żytomir 1805, Russia/Poland 1805[20])	Isaac Eizik of Żytomir, Michael b. Jacob Kopel of Żytomir (Żytomir 1805)
Menahem Mendel of Witebsk (1730–88)	Pri ha-Arez (Kopys 1814)	Moses b. Israel of Kopys
	Iggeret ha-Kodesh (Mezyrów 1794, Żółkiew 1799)	David b. Israel Lekish (1794), Abraham Hakohen of Lemberg (1799)
Menahem Nahum of Chernobyl (1730–98)	Me'or Einayim (Sławuta 1798; Połonne 1810)	Jacob Samson of Szepetówka, Aryeh Leib of Zabarazh, Levi Isaac of Berdyczów, Meshullam Zusya of Annipol, Asher Zvi of Ostróg, Judah Leib Hakohen (1798)
	Yismah Lev (Sławuta 1798; Żółkiew 1800)	Moses Zvi Hirsch Meisels, Jacob Samson of Szepetówka (?), Moses Zvi Meisels (1800)
Moses of Przeworsk (d.1805)	Or Pnei Moshe (Międzyrzecz 1809; Międzybóż 1810; Międzyrzecz 1810)	Levi Isaac of Berdyczów, Israel of Kozienice, Zvi Ari of Alik, Zvi Menahem Mendel of Annipol/Israel Abraham of Czarna Ostrów (sons of Zusya of Annipol), Jacob Isaac of Lublin, Abraham Joshua Heschel of Opatów, Menahem Mendel of Rymanów, Ephraim Zalman Margaliot of Brody, Jacob Orenstein of Lem-

berg, Simha of Bobrka (1809 and Międzyrzecz 1810), Hayyim b. Solomon Tirer of Botoshani, Asher Zvi of Ostróg, Mordecai b. Jehiel Michael, Bezalel b. Meir Margaliot, Abraham Hayyim b. Gedaliya Moses of Złoczów, Nahman Zvi Halevi Epstein, Joseph Halpern of Radzyn, Mordecai b. Phineas of Korzec, Joshua Heschel of Tarnopol, Moses Eliezer b. Aaron of Chotynicze, Isaac Frankel of Rashstein,[21] Menahem Mendel b. Jacob Kopel of Kossów, Issachar Dov b. Abraham, Solomon Halpern of Radzyn, Simon b. Nafthali Herz of Czortyków, Zvi Aryeh b. Abraham Landau, Hayyim Jacob b. Abraham Dukla, Platiel Isaac b. Nafthali Hakohen of Senatyn, Nafthali Horowitz of Ropszyce, David Halpern Weingarten of Leżajsk, Jacob b. Jacob Moses Leiberbaum of Kalisz, Joshua of Dynów, Moses b. Aaron Blum of Kasentin[22] (Międzyrzecz 1810)[23]

Moses Hayyim Ephraim of Sudzylków (1748–1800)	*Degel Mahane Ephraim* (Berdyczów 1808, Korzec 1810, Berdyczów 1815)	Levi Isaac of Berdyczów, Israel of Kozienice, Jacob Isaac of Lublin, Abraham Joshua Heschel Opatów, Menahem Mendel of Łuck, Hayyim Botoshani (Berdyczów 1808 and 1810), Isaac Abraham Eliezer Horowitz, Menahem Mendel of Lesko (1810)
Moses Shokham of Dolina (eighteenth c.)	*Divre Moshe* (Połonne 1801; Międzybóż 1801)	Abraham Joshua Heschel of Opatów, Isaac of Złoczów(Połonne 1801)
Nahman of Bratslav (1772–1810)	*Likkutei Moharan* (Ostróg 1808;[24] Mohilów 1811;[25] Ostróg 1815)[26]	Abraham Hayyim of Złoczów, Meir of Brody, Ephraim Zalman Margaliot of Brody (composed in 1808, but not printed until 1821).
		Jacob Isaac of Lublin, Israel of Kozienice (composed in 1808; but not printed until Lemberg, 1906).[29]
	Sefer ha-Midot (Mohilów 1811)	—

	Kizur Likkutei Mo-haran (Mohilów 1811)	—
	Likkutei Ezot (Dubno 1813)	—
	Sippurei Ma'asiyot (Ostróg, 1815)[27]	—
	Shemot ha-zaddikim (Mohilów 1811)[28]	—
Shabbetai of Rasz-ków (1655–1745)	*Sefer Klalot Tikkun ve-Alyot ha-Olamot* (Lemberg 1778)[30]	—
	Seder Tefilla mi-Kol ha-Shana (Korzec 1794,[31] 1797[32])	Meshullam Zusya of Annipol, Joseph Moses of Międzyrzecz, Judah Leib Segal of Szydlów, Pesah b. Samuel of Zwoleń
Shneur Zalman of Liady (1745–1813)	*Hilkhot Talmud Torah* (Szklów 1794; Żołkiew 1795;[33] Lemberg 1798;[34] Sławuta 1798;[35] Lemberg 1799); Sudzyłków 1799(?)[36]	Hanokh Henokh b. Samuel Shik,[42] Zvi Hirsch b. Maharam (1794), Moses Leib of Sasów (Sudzyłków and Lemberg, 1799), Joseph b. Jacob Isaac Hokh Gelerntner (Lemberg, 1799)
	Tanya: Likkutei Ammarim (Sławuta 1796; Żółkiew 1799, 1805, 1805, 1805; Szklów 1806, 1806; Sudzyłków 1814 (?);[37] Kopys 1814; Szklów 1814,1814)	Judah Leib Hakohen, Meshullam Zusya of Annipol (Sławuta 1796), Moses Zvi Hirsch Meisels of Żółkiew, Isaac Halevi of Lemberg, Isaac Samson b. Pesah Eleazar Halevi Segal (Żółkiew 1799), Barukh b. Judah of Szklów, Moses b. Israel of Kopys, Zvi Hirsch b. Jacob of Smolin (Szklów, 1806), Dov Ber of Lubavitch/ Hayyim Abraham/ Moses (Szklów 1814)
	Luah Birhkot ha-Nehenim (Szkłów 1800;[38] Żółkiew 1801; Korzec1801; n.p. 1801;[39] Lemberg 1803	Abraham Hayyim b. Gedaliya of Złoczów, Meshullam Hakohen Zeddek of Lemberg (Żółkiew, 1801)
	Shulhan Arukh, Hoshen Mishpat (Szklów, 1814)[40]	Copyright in Introduction, signed by Dov Ber, Hayyim Abraham, and Moses, sons of author
	Shealot ve-Teshuvot (Kopys, 1815)	—
	Siddur (Szkłów 1803)[41]	—
Simha b. Joshua Haas of Złoczów(1711–68)	*Lev Simha* (Żółkiew 1757)	Hayyim Kohen Rapoport of Lemberg, Joseph b. Israel, Moses Menahem Mendel b. Shakhna,

		Zvi Hirsch b. Ze'ev of Żółkiew, Israel b. Ze'ev of Zamość
	Netiah Shel Simha (Żółkiew 1763)	Abraham Mordecai Halpern of Żółkiew, Isaac Halevi Ish Horwitz of Brody, Zvi Hirsch b. Ze'ev of Żółkiew, Naftali Herz b. Avigdor of Żelechów, Moses Phineas Nahman of Lemberg
	Ahavat Ziyon (Grodno 1790)	—
Uriel Feivel of Krasnopol (d.1808)	*Or ha-Hokhma* (Laszczów 1815)	Meir of Brody, Jacob Orenstein of Lemberg, Ephraim Zalman Margaliot, Jacob Isaac of Lublin, Zvi Aryeh of Alik, Israel Ashkenazi of Ahowniów,[43] Mordecai Ziskind of Leszów (dated 1808!), Aryeh Leib of Olszyc, Aryeh Leib of Sieniawa, (rabbi of) Tartaków (signature) (Laszców, 1815?)
Zechariah Mendel of Jarosław	*Darkhei Zeddek* (Lemberg 1796; Minkowice 1797; Lemberg 1801; Żółkiew 1810; Połonne 1810)	—
Ze'ev Wolf of Żytomir	*Or ha-Meir* (Korzec 1798, 1798, 1806, 1813; Poryck 1815, 1815)	Judah Leib of Szydlowiec, Joseph of Konstantynów, Levi Isaac of Berdyczów, Asher Zvi of Ostróg, Mordecai b. Phineas of Korzec (Korzec 1798), Judah Leib b. Joseph Segal, Joseph b. Moses of Konstantynów (1806) Israel Dov Ber b. David Halevi of Stefan, Mordecai b. Phineas of Korzec (1815)
Zvi Hirsch of Nadvorna (d. 1801)	*Alfa Beta* (Russia/Poland 1790; Ostróg 1794; Żółkiew 1794; Podbierezce 1796; Nowy Dwór 1799; Lemberg 1800; Russia/Poland 1800	—

Notes

INTRODUCTION

1. Martin Buber, *Tales of the Hasidim: Early Masters*, tr. Olga Marx (New York: Schocken Books, 1958), vol. 1, 240.

2. See Steven Aschheim, *Brothers and Strangers: The East European Jew in German and German Jewish Consciousness, 1800–1923* (Madison: University of Wisconsin Press, 1982), chap. 6, esp. p. 125. On a similar use of Hasidism by other western European intellectuals, see Michael Lowy, *Redemption and Utopia: Jewish Libertarian Thought in Central Europe*, tr. Hope Heaney (Stanford, Calif.: Stanford University Press, 1992).

3. Joseph Dan, "A Bow to Frumkian Hasidism," *Modern Judaism* 11 (1991), 175–193. This objective was shared with Eastern European writers like I.L. Perets and S. Ansky, and may be traced back to Michael Frumkin-Rodkinson, who beginning in 1863 tapped into the "growing market for Hasidic nostalgia among the increasing number of Jews who were detached from their Hasidic roots. . . ." (185).

4. Dan, "A Bow to Frumkian Hasidism," 187.

5. Actually Eleazar would only have leased land or owned it on freehold. In Galicia (Austrian Poland), Jews were not allowed to own land outright until February 18, 1860. See Artur Eisenbach, *Emancipation of the Jews in Poland*, ed. Antony Polonsky and tr. Janina Dorosz (Oxford: Blackwell, 1991).

6. See the letter in Abraham Joshua Heschel, "Umbakante Dokumenten Zu der Geschichte fon Hasidut: Vegen dem Hasidut-Arkhiv fun Yivo," *Yivo Bleter* 36 (1952), 126. On the success of Hasidic leaders in ransoming such prisoners, see Chone Shmeruk, "Ha-Hasidut be-Askei Ha-Hakirut," *Zion* 35 (1970), 182–92.

7. Author of *No'am Elimelekh* (Lemberg, 1788). On education as an agent of stratification, see Shaul Stampfer, "*Heder* Study, Knowledge of Torah, and the Maintenance of Social Stratification in Traditional East European Jewish Society," *Studies in Jewish Education* 3 (1988), 271–89.

8. Buber, *Tales of the Hasidim: Early Masters* (NY: Schocken, 1975), vol. 1, 263; and see 308–309. Similar tales are included in Jiri Langer's *Nine Gates to the Chassidic Mysteries,* tr. Stephen Jolly (New York: David McKay, 1961), e.g., 181–2.

9. According to an oft-cited parable of R. Jacob Joseph, the king's minister must disguise himself as one of the commoners with whom the wayward prince had been associating in order to persuade the prince to return to the king.

10. On Sabbateanism and Frankism in eastern Europe, see Bernard Weinryb, *The Jews of Poland to 1800* (Philadelpia: Jewish Publication Society, 1983), 236–61.

11. Moshe Rosman, *Founder of Hasidism* (Berkeley: University of California Press, 1996), 15.

12. Immanuel Etkes, *Ba'al Ha-Shem: Ha-Besht—Magiyah, Mystikah, Hanhagah,* chap. 1, esp. 33–53. Translation: *The Besht: Magically Mystic, and Leader,* tr. Saadya Sternberg (Waltham, MA: Brandeis University Press, 2005), 14–24.

13. Rosman, *Founder of Hasidism,* 18; Dan Ben-Amos and Jerome Mintz, eds., *In Praise of the Ba'al Shem Tov* (Bloomington: Indiana University Press, 1970), 173–4, no. 152: "When the Besht came to the holy community of Medzhibozh, he was not regarded as an important man by Hasidism—that is to say, by Rabbi Ze'ev Kotses and Rabbi David Forkes—because he was called the Besht, the master of a good name. This name was not considered proper for a pious man." On the skepticism encountered by Hillel Ba'al Shem, see Yohanan Petrovsky-Shtern, "The Master of an Evil Name: Hillel Ba'al Shem and His *Sefer Ha-Heshek,*" *AJS Review* 28:2 (2004), 237.

14. Etkes, *The Besht: Magician, Mystic, and Leader,* 47.

15. Rosman, *Founder of Hasidism,* chapter 11; and Etkes, "The Historical Besht: Reconstruction or Deconstruction?" *Polin* 12 (1999), 304; idem., *The Besht: Magician, Mystic, and Leader,* 78 and 97–112.

16. For a detailed overview of the Besht's theological innovations, see Etkes, *The Besht: Magician, Mystic, and Leader,* chapter 4 (esp. 122).

17. Ada Rapoport-Albert, "Hasidism after 1772: Structural Continuity and Change," in Ada Rapoport-Albert, ed., *Hasidism Reappraised* (London: Littman Library of Jewish Civilization, 1997); Gershon Hundert, *Jews in Poland-Lithuania in the Eighteenth Century: A Genealogy of Modernity* (Berkeley: University of California Press, 2004), 160–76.

18. Rapoport-Albert, "Hasidism after 1772," 85.

19. R. Jacob Joseph of Połonne, for example, demonized rabbis as elitist. Samuel Dresner, *The Zaddik: The Doctrine According to the Writings of Rabbi Yaakov Yosef of Polonoy* (London: Abelard-Schuman, 1964), 75–110.

20. Isaiah Shahar, *Bikoret ha-hevrah ve-hanhagat ha-zibor be-sifrut ha-mussar ve-ha-derush be-Polin be-meah ha-18* (Jerusalem: Merkaz Dinur, 1992).

21. Ze'ev Gries, "The Hasidic Conduct (*Hanhagot*) Literature from the Mid–Eighteenth Century to the 1830s" (in Hebrew), *Zion* 46 (1981), 198–236; David Fishman, *Russia's First Modern Jews: The Jews of Shklov* (New York: New York University Press, 1995), 7–8.

22. On the first major publicist and populizer of Kabbalah—Nehemia Hayyon, a Sabbatean whose works appeared in the early eighteenth century—see Elisheva Carlebach, *The Pursuit of Heresy: Rabbi Moses Hagiz and the Sabbatean Controversies* (New York: Columbia University Press, 1990), esp. pp. 94–104.

23. On efforts to suppress all Kabbalah during the century following Sabbateanism, see Israel Halpern, "Va'ad Arba Arzot be-Polin ve-ha-Sefer ha-Ivri," in *Yehudim ve-Yahadut be-Mizrah-Eiropa* (Jerusalem: Magnes, 1968), 87.

24. Mendel Piekarz, "Hasidism as a Socio-Religious Movement on the Evidence of *Devekut*," in Rapoport-Albert, *Hasidism Reappraised*, 225–48; Huridert, *Jews in Poland-Lithuania*, 118–130.

25. *Zohar* 1, 245b; Gershom Scholem, "Zaddik," in *On the Mystical Shape of the Godhead* (New York: Schocken Books, 1991). Scholem writes: "The mystical symbol of the Kabbalah and its earthly representative . . . were here fused into one image." See also Rachel Elior, "Between *Yesh* and *Ayin*: the Doctrine of the Zaddik in the Works of Jacob Isaac, the Seer of Lublin," in Ada Rapoport-Albert and Steven Zipperstein, eds., *Jewish History: Essays in Honor of Chimen Abramsky* (London: Halban, 1988), 393–456; and Etkes, "The Zaddik," 165.

26. Etkes, "The Zaddik," 165.

27. See Mor Altshuler, "The First Tzaddik of Hasidism: The Zlotchover Maggid and His Circle," *Jewish Studies Quarterly* 11 (2004), 177. The Polish zaddik Uziel Meisels referred to him as a "zaddik."

28. Stuart Hall terms this process "articulation." See, ed. David Morley and Kuan-Hsing Chen, eds., *Stuart Hall: Critical Dialogues in Cultural Studies* (London: Routledge, 1996), 142–3.

29. Followers of Shabbetai Zvi invoked Kabbalah to justify his messianic claims and antinomian excesses, but this did not ensure longevity within the normative communities.

30. Scholem claims: "almost all the Kabbalistic ideas are now placed in relation to values particular to the individual life. . . . Hasidism is "Kabbalism turned ethos . . . a system whereby personality takes the place of doctrine." See *Major Trends in Jewish Mysticism* (New York: Schocken Books, 1974), 341, 342, 344. "According to the Hasidic sources I am familiar with," writes Moshe Idel, "Kabbalah is preeminently a paradigm of the human psyche and man's activities rather than a theosophical system." See Idel, *Kabbalah: New Perspectives* (New Haven: Yale University Press, 1988), 132.

31. This use of *sefirot* has been overlooked in scholarly literature. For examples, see R. Jacob Isaac Horowitz of Lublin, *Zot Zikharon* (Tel Aviv, 1987), 36–8; 70; 151–2; 155–6; 189; 217; 267; 275.

32. On *devekut*, see Gershom Scholem, "*Devekut*, or Communion with God," in Gershon Hundert, ed., *Essential Papers on Hasidism: Origins to the Present* (New York: New York University Press, 1991), 275–98; Ada Rapoport-Albert's revision, "The Zaddik as a Focal Point of Divine Worship," in Hundert, *Essential Papers on Hasidism*, 299–329; Elimelekh of Leżajsk, *No'am Elimelekh*, ed. Gedalyah Nigal (Jerusalem: Mosad Ha-Rav Kook, 1978), introduction, 97–9; Piekarz, "Hasidism as a Socio-Religious Movement on the Evidence of *Devekut*," 225–48; Miles Krassen, *Uniter of Heaven and Earth: Rabbi Meshullam Feibush Heller of Zabarazh and the Rise of Hasidism in Eastern Galicia* (Albany: State University of New York Press, 1998), 43–93. On the prophetic aspect of *devekut*, see Benzion Dinur, "The Messianic-Prophetic Role of the Baal Shem Tov," in Marc Saperstein, ed., *Essential Papers on Messianic Movements and Personalities in Jewish History* (New York: New York University, 1992), 377–88 (esp. 385).

33. Moshe Idel, *Hasidism: Between Ecstasy and Magic* (Albany: State University of New York Press, 1995), 1. On "drawing down," see also 189–207.

34. Elior, "Between *Yesh* and *Ayin*," 427.

35. Rachel Elior, "Bein 'hitpashtut ha-gashmiyut' le-bein 'hitpashtut ha-ahavah gam be-gashmiyut,' " in Israel Bartal, Ezra Mendelsohn, and Chava Turnianski, eds., *K'minhag Ashkenaz ve-Polin: Sefer yovel le-Chone Shmeruk* (Jerusalem: Merkaz Zalman Shazar, 1993), 229. Elior depicts the zaddik's role as (1) converting materiality, or *yesh*,

into spiritual nothingness, or *ayin*; and (2) reversing the process by drawing down the divine *shefa*.

36. See, for example, Joseph Weiss, "The Saddik—Altering the Divine Will," in David Goldstein, ed., *Studies in Eastern European Jewish Mysticism* (London: Littman Library of Jewish Civilization, 1985), 183–93; and Ada Rapoport-Albert, "God and the Zaddik as Two Focal Points of Hasidic Worship," in Hundert, *Essential Papers on Hasidism*, 318.

37. Certain biblical verses allow for such an interpretation; for example, Isaiah 6: 3, "the whole earth is full of His glory." On the disputed centrality of Lurianic ideas in early Hasidism, see Idel, *Hasidism*; and Rachel Elior's persuasive rejoinder, "Hasidism—Historical Continuity and Spiritual Change," in Peter Schafer and Joseph Dan, eds., *Gershom Scholem's "Major Trends in Jewish Mysticism" Fifty Years After: Proceedings of the Sixth International Conference on the History of Jewish Mysticism* (Tubingen: Mohr, 1993), 315–7.

38. Rivka Shatz-Uffenheimer, *Hasidism as Mysticism: Quietistic Elements in Eighteenth Century Hasidic Thought*, tr. Jonathan Chipman (Jerusalem: Magnes, 1993), 52–4; 108–10; Louis Jacobs, "The Uplifting of Sparks in Later Jewish Mysticism," in Arthur Green, ed., *Jewish Spirituality: From the Sixteenth-Century Revival to the Present* (New York: Crossroad, 1987), esp. 115–25. Most recently, see Immanuel Ekes, *The Besht: Magician, Mystic, and Leader*, 134–147.

39. For a summary of scholarly views on the ties between Sabbateanism and early Hasidism, see Hundert, *Jews in Poland-Lithuania*, 182–5. As is well known, this derived from the more starkly antinomian approach of radical Sabbateans, some of whom argued that engaging in outright sin could redeem sparks entrapped within the demonic realm. For texts propounding "worship through corporeality," the English reader should consult Norman Lamm, ed., *The Religious Thought of Hasidism: Texts and Commentary* (New York: Yeshiva University Press, 1999), 312–8, 323–36.

40. R. Nahman of Bratslav went so far as to elevate his own political persecution to a desirable spiritual principle. Arthur Green, *Tormented Master: The Life and Spiritual Quest of Rabbi Nahman of Bratslav* (Woodstock, Vt.: Jewish Lights, 1992), esp. 114.

41. Elior considers "worship through corporeality" the sine qua non of the zaddik-idea. See "Bein 'hitpashtut ha-gashmiyut' le-bein 'hitpashtut ha-ahavah gam be-gashmiyut,' " 209–41. See also Shatz-Uffenheimer, *Hasidism as Mysticism*, 108–10.

42. See, for example, the warning cited in Miles Krassen, *Uniter of Heaven and Earth: Rabbi Meshullam Feibush Heller of Zabarazh and the Rise of Hasidism in Eastern Galicia* (Albany: State University of New York Press, 1998), 179.

43. Jacob Joseph of Połonne, *Zafanat Pa'ane'ah*, 128; Jacob Joseph of Połonne, *Toldot Ya'akov Yosef*, parshat Aharei; parshat Bo, p. 157b; parshat Ki Tissa, sec. 3. Passages cited in Lamm, *The Religious Thought of Hasidism*, 307, 313, 299, and 297.

44. See, for example, Abraham Ibn Ezra, *The Commentary of Ibn Ezra on the Pentateuch*, tr. Jay Shachter (Hoboken, N.J: Ktav, 1986), 281; A. M. Silberman, ed., *Chumash with Targum Onkelos, Haphtaroth and Rashi's Commentary* (Jerusalem, 1983), 135; David Rosin, ed., *Perush Ha-Torah Asher Katav Rashbam* (Jerusalem, 1970), 35; Joseph Bechor Shor, *Perush L'Humishei Torah*, (Jerusalem: Makor), 1978) 43; Yaakov Gellis, *Tosafot Shalem*, "Mifal Tosafot" (Jerusalem, 1982), 134; Nahmanides, *Perushe Ha-Torah* (Jerusalem: Mossad Ha-Rav Kuk, 1969), 163; Bahya, *Sefer Rabeinu Bahya al Ha-Torah* (Jerusalem, 1992), 186.

45. See Levi Isaac of Berdyczów, *Kedushat Levi Ha-Shalem* (Jerusalem, 1993), parshat *Veyatzei*, 53. Jacob is especially suited to this task because of his symbolic association with Tiferet (beauty), one of the ten *sefirot*.

46. Arthur Green, "Typologies of Leadership and the Hasidic Zaddiq," in Green, *Jewish Spirituality* vol. 2 (New York: Crossroad, 1987), 127–56.

47. Quoted in Louis Jacobs, "Hasidism and the Dogma of the Decline of the Generations," in Rapoport-Albert, *Hasidism Reappraised*, 212–3.

48. Green, "Typologies of Leadership."

49. Weiss, "The Saddik—Altering the Divine Will," 183–93; Rapoport-Albert, "God and the Zaddik as the Two Focal Points of Hasidic Worship," 321.

50. Abraham Joshua Heschel of Opatów, *Ohev Yisrael*, parshat *Pinhas*, 193. The term "home owner" (*ba'al bayit*) is used to denote a businessman of means.

51. Elimelekh of Leżajsk, *No'am Elimelekh*, p. 173; p. 26. On Exodus 6:12, R. Elimelekh explains that Moses' doubts concerning his leadership ability resulted from certain Israelites taking it upon themselves to be ascetics and worship God without a leader, under the misapprehension that they could bring the exodus themselves (p. 183).

52. R. Nahman of Bratslav, *Likkutei Moharan* 1:123. See also translation in Lamm, *The Religious Thought of Hasidism*, 312.

53. On ideology, see Catherine Bell, *Ritual Theory, Ritual Practice* (New York: Oxford University Press, 1992), 190–2.

54. Certain zaddikim tended to favor the functions of rabbis, serving as *av bet din* or rendering occasional *halakhic* decisions, while others were more like ba'alei shem.

55. Joseph Weiss, "A Circle of Pneumatics in Pre-Hasidism," in *Studies in Eastern Jewish Mysticism*, 27–42.

56. On this "exit rite," see Idel, *Hasidism*, 127–33; R. Elimelekh of Leżajsk, *No'am Elimelekh*, 97–9; "Be-Ha'alotekha," 381–2; "Va-Etkhanan," 485–6.

57. On old-style hasidism, see Gershom Scholem, "Shtei eyduyot al havurot ha-Hasidim ve-ha-Besht," *Tarbiz* 20 (1949), Etkes, *Ba'al ha-Shem*, 169–78; Rosman, *Founder of Hasidism*; and Elhanan Reiner, "Hon, Ma'amad Hevrati, ve-Talmud Torah: ha-Kloyz be-Hevrah ha-Yehudit be-Mizrah Eiropah be- Me'ot 17–19," *Zion* 58 (1993), 287–328.

58. Jeremiah 15:19.

59. Israel Ba'al Shem Tov and Dov Ber of Międzyrzecz, *Zava'at ha-Ribash ve-hanhagot yesharot*, reprinted in *Sefarim kedoshim mi-kol talmidei Ha-Besht Ha-Kadosh*, vol. 91 (Brooklyn: Bet Hilel, 1993), 20.

60. See, for example, Elimelekh of Leżajsk, *No'am Elimelekh*, 261.

61. Gershon Hundert's assertion that "Hasidism was but one more of a multitude of movements of spiritual awakening, often of a mystical character" seems only applicable to the period before zaddikim became communal and supracommunal leaders (i.e., during the late eighteenth century). Hundert, "The Contexts of Hasidism," in Waldemar Kowalski and Jadwiga Muszyńska, ed., *Żydzi wśród chrześcijan w dobie szlacheckiej rzeczypospolitej* (Kielce: Kieleckie Towarzystwo, Naukowe, 1996), 183.

62. For theoretical approaches to the spread of Hasidism, see Rapoport-Albert, "Hasidism after 1772," in Rapoport-Albert, *Hasidism Reappraised*, 76–140; Immanuel Etkes, "Hasidism as a Movement—The First Stage," in Bezalel Safran, ed., *Hasidism: Continuity or Innovation?* (Cambridge, Mass.: Harvard University Press, 1988), and *Ba'al Ha-Shem*; Aaron Ze'ev Aescoly, *Hasidut be-Polin*, ed. David Assaf (Jerusalem: Magnes Press, 1998); Omeljan Pritsak, "Ukraine as the Setting for the Emergence of Hasidism," in *Israel among the Nations: Essays Presented in Honor of Shmuel Ettinger* (Jerusalem: Merkaz Zalman Shazar, 1987), 67–85; Chone Shmeruk, "Hasidism and the Kehilla," in Antony Polonsky, Jakub Basista, and Andrzej Link-Lenczowski, eds.,

The Jews in Old Poland, 1000–1795 (London: Tauris, 1993); Haviva Pedaya, "Le-hitpathuto shel had-degem ha-hevrati-da'ati-kalkali be-Hasidut: Ha-pidyon, ha-havurah, ve-ha-aliyah le-regel," in Menahem Ben-Sasson, ed., *Dat ve-kalkalah* (Jerusalem: Merkaz Zalman Shazar, 1995), 311–76; David Assaf, "Heyvetim histori'im ve-hevrati'im be-heker ha-Hasidut," in *Zaddik ve-eyda: Hebetim historiyim ve-Hevratiyim be-Heker ha-Hasidut* (Jerusalem: Merkaz Zalman Shazar, 2001) (offprint); Mor Altshuler, "The First Tzaddik of Hasidism: The Zlotchover Maggid and His Circle," *Jewish Studies Quarterly* 11 (2004), 127–93.

63. On Hasidic doctrine and the religious lives of its proponents, the English reader is referred to Hundert, *Essential Papers on Hasidism*, pt. 2; Rapoport-Albert, ed., *Hasidism Reappraised*, pts. 3–4; Green, "Typologies of Leadership," and "Teachings of the Hasidic Masters," in Barry Holtz, ed., *Back to the Sources: Reading the Classic Jewish Texts* (New York: Touchstone, 1984); Weiss, *Studies in Eastern Jewish Mysticism*; Schatz-Uffenheimer, *Hasidism as Mysticism*; Idel, *Hasidism*. For critical translations of Hasidic homiletic works, see Arthur Green, tr. and ed., *Menahem of Chernobyl's Upright Practices: The Light of the Eyes* (New York: Paulist Press, 1982); *The Language of Truth: the Torah Commentary of the Sefat Emet, Rabbi Yehudah Leib Alter of Ger* (Philadelphia: Jewish Publication Society, 1998).

64. Etkes, "The Zaddik," 159–67.

65. Piekarz, "Hasidism as a Socio-Religious Movement on the Evidence of *Devekut*," 226, 229, 231, 235, 238, 248, and *Biyemei zmihat ha-Hasidut* (Jerusalem: Mosad Bialik, 1978).

66. On aspects of the social impact of the rise of Hasidism, see Israel Halpern, "Havurot le-Torah ve-l'Mizvah ve-ha-T'nuah ha-Hasidit be-Hithapshutah," and "Yahaso shel R. Aharon ha-Gadol mi-Karlin kelapei mishtar ha-kehilot," in *Yehudim ve-Yahadut be-Mizrah Eiropa* (Jerusalem: Magnes Press, 1968), 313–339; David Kandel, "Żydzi w dobie utworzenia Królestwa Kongresowego," *Kwartalnik poświęcony badania przeszłości Żydów w Polsce* 1 (1912), 97–113, and "Komitet starozakonnych," in *Kwartalnik poświęcony badania przeszłości Żydów w Polsce*, (1912), 85–103; Schiper, *Przyczynki do dziejow chasydyzmu w Polsce*, ed. Zbigniew Targielski (Warsaw: PWN, 1992); Raphael Mahler, *Hasidism and the Jewish Enlightenment*, tr. Eugene Orenstein, Aaron Klein, and Jenny Klein (Philadelpia: Jewish Publication Society, 1985); Gries, "Hasidic Conduct (*Hanhagot*) Literature from the Mid–Eighteenth Century to the 1830s," 198–236, and *Sefer, Sofer ve-Sipur be-Reshit ha-Hasidut* (Ha-Kibbutz ha-Meyuhad, 1992); Zvi Meir Rabinowicz, *Bein Pshyskha le-Lublin* (Jerusalem: Kesharim, 1997); Hundert, "The Contexts of Hasidism," 171–84, and "Apta ve-Reshit ha-Hasidut Ad 1800," in Rachel Elior, Yisrael Bartal, and Chone Shmeruk, eds., *Zaddikim ve- Anshei Ma'aseh: Mehkarim be-Hasidut Polin* (Jerusalem: Mosad Bialik, 1994), 59–64; Eleonora Bergman, "Gora-Kalwaria (Gur)-ha-Yishuv ha-Yehudi be-Hazar ha-Rabi mi-Gor mi-Reshit ha-Mea 19 ad 1939," in Elior, Bartal, and Shmeruk, *Zaddikim ve- Anshei Ma'aseh*; W. Z. Rabinowitch, *Lithuanian Hasidism* (New York: Schocken Books, 1971); Mordecai Nadav, *Toledot Kehilat Pinsk, 1506–1880* (Tel Aviv, 1973); Mordecai Zalkin, "Between Dvinsk and Vilna: The Spread of Hasidism in Nineteenth-Century Lithuania" (in Hebrew), in Immanuel Etkes, David Assaf, Israel Bartal and Elchanan Reiner, eds., *Be-Magalei Hasidim: Kovez Mehkarim le-Zekhro shel Profesor Mordekhai Wilensky* (Jerusalem: Mosad Bialik, 2000), 335–349; (*Within Hasidic Circles: Studies in Hasidism in Memory of Mordecai Wilensky*) (Jerusalem: Bialik, 1999); Hayyim Gertner, "The Rabbinate and the Hasidic Movement in Nineteenth-Century Galicia: The Case of Shlomo Kluger," in Etkes et al., *Within Hasidic Circles*; Nafthali Loewenthal, *Communicating the Infinite: The Emergence of the Habad School* (Chicago: University of Chi-

cago Press, 1990); Assaf, *Zaddik ve-Eyda*; Marcin Wodziński, *Oświecienie żydowskie w Królestwie Polskim wobec chasydyzmu* (Warsaw: Wydawnictwo Cyklady, 2003), and "How Many *Hasidim* Were There in Congress Poland? On the Demographics of the Hasidic Movement in Poland During the First Half of the Nineteenth Century," *Gal-Ed* 19 (2004), 13–50 (offprint); and Yohanan Petrovsky, "Hasidism, Havurot, and the Jewish Street," Jewish Social Studies 10.2 (2004), 20–54.

67. Dubnow, *Toldot ha-Hasidut* (Tel Aviv: Devir, 1975), 8–9 and 36, and *History of the Jews in Russia and Poland*, vol. 1, tr. I. Friedlaender (Philadelphia: Jewish Publication Society, 1916), 220–34. See also Rabinowitch, *Lithuanian Hasidism*, 1–6.

68. Raphael Mahler, *Hasidism and the Jewish Enlightenment*, 1–16, and *A History of Modern Jewry, 1780–1815* (London: Vallentine, Mitchell, 1971), 364. On Dubnow's interpretation, see Robert Seltzer, "The Secular Appropriation of Hasidism by the East European Jewish Intellectual: Dubnow, Renan, and the Besht," *Polin* 1 (1986), 151–62.

69. Benzion Dinur, "The Origins of Hasidism and its Social and Messianic Foundations," in Hundert, *Essential Papers on Hasidism*, esp. 136–7.

70. Jacob Katz, *Tradition and Crisis*, ed. Bernard Dov Cooperman (New York: Schocken Books, 1993).

71. Shmeruk, "Hasidism and the *Kehilla*," 186–198; "Ha-Hasidut be-Askei Ha-Hakirut," *Zion* 35 (1970), 182–92. See also David Assaf and Israel Bartal, "Shtadlanut ve-ortodoksiyah: Zaddikei Polin be-mifgash im ha-zmanim ha-hadashim" in Elior, Bartal, and Shmeruk, *Zaddikim ve-anshe ma'aseh*, 67–8.

72. Weinryb, *The Jews of Poland to 1800*, 195–9.

73. Eisenbach, *Emancipation of the Jews in Poland*.

74. Eisenbach, *Emancipation of the Jews in Poland*. "Tolerated Jews" could send their children to Christian primary and secondary schools, and employ Christian servants. All Jews were freed from the poll tax and permitted to carry on any type of trade. But they were also required to stop using Hebrew and Yiddish in their records. Subsequent decrees abolished rabbinical autonomy, made Jews liable for military service, made them adopt German-sounding names, imposed taxes on kosher meat and candles, and upheld residence restrictions.

75. Mahler, *A History of Modern Jewry, 1780–1815*, 346.

76. Hundert, "The Contexts of Hasidism," 176. See also Hundert, "The Role of Jews in Commerce in Early Modern Poland-Lithuania," *Journal of European Economic History* 16 (1987), 246.

77. Mahler, *A History of Modern Jewry*, 346.

78. Robert Johnston, *Travels through Part of the Russian Empire and the Country of Poland* (New York, 1816), 382. Actually, the largest commercial enterprises in the eighteenth century were mainly in the hands of Germans, not Jews. See Hundert, "The Contexts of Hasidism," 176.

79. Tinsmiths.

80. Ostlers cared for guests' horses at inns.

81. J. T. James, *Journal of a Tour: 1813–1814* (London, 1827), 358.

82. James, *Journal of a Tour*, 420–421.

83. Stanisław Staszic, "Żydzi," and "O przyczynach szkodliwości żydów i srodkach usposobienia ich, aby się społeczeństwu użytecznymi stali," in Józef Kruszynski, ed., *Stanisław Staszic a kwestja Żydowska* (Lublin, 1926); "Żydzi," in *Przestroi dla Polska*, in Bogdan Suchodolski, ed., *Pisma filozoficzne i społeczne* (Warsaw: PWN, 1954), 298–303; Stanislaw Staszic (1755–1826), "Jews" (1790), in Harold Siegel, ed., *Stranger in Our Midst: Images of the Jew in Polish Literature* (Ithaca: Cornell University Press, 1996), 38–42.

84. Antoni Ostrowski, "Uwagi nad obyczaimi uspobieniem i charakterem żydów Polskich," in *Pomysły o potzrebie reformy towarzyskiey w ogólności i umianowiciey co do Israelitów w Polszcze* (Paris, 1834), 87–8. Johann Erich Biester wrote in 1791 that Poland has the Jews to thank for what little trade, industry, and finance there is. Johann Pilippe de Carosi claimed in 1778–80 that the Jews of Opatów had both large- and small-scale trade in their hands. See Nathan Michael Gelber, "Oyslenishe Rayunde Vegen Poylishe Yidn Inem Yahrhundert," in A. *Historishe Schriften* vol. 1 (Warsaw, 1929), 237–40. The claim about Opatów, however, is qualified by Hundert, who finds that specific trades were non-Jewish domains. *The Jews in a Polish Private Town: The Case of Opatów in the Eighteenth Century* (Baltimore: Johns Hopkins University Press, 1992), 46.

85. Mahler, *A History of Modern Jewry*, 349.

86. Artur Eisenbach, "Mobilność terytorialna ludności żydowskiej," in Witold Kula, ed., *Społeczeństwo Królestwa Polskiego* (Warsaw: PWN, 1966), vol. 2, 179–218; Eleonora Bergman, "The *Rewir* or Jewish District and the *Eyruv*," *Studia Judaica* 5:1 (2002), 86.

87. Mahler, *A History of Modern Jewry*, 344–362. Mahler argues that zaddikim appealed most of all to the poorer masses (364).

88. N. William Wraxall, *Memoirs of the Courts of Berlin, Dresden, Warsaw and Vienna, in the Years 1777, 1778, and 1779* (London, 1806), vol. 2, 9.

89. Ignacy Schiper, *Przyczynki do dziejów chasydyzmu w Polsce*, 68.

90. Shmuel Ettinger, "The Hasidic Movement: Reality and Ideals," in Hundert, *Essential Papers on Hasidism*, p. 229.

91. Yeshayahu Shahar, *Bikoret ha-hevrah ve-hanhagat ha-zibor be-sifrut ha-mussar ve-ha-derush be-Polin be-meah ha-18.*

92. Moshe Rosman, "Miedzyboz and Rabbi Israel Baal Shem Tov," in Hundert, *Essential Papers on Hasidism*, 209–25; "Social Conflicts in Międzyboż in the Generation of the Besht," in Rapoport-Albert, *Hasidism Reappraised* 51–62, and *Founder of Hasidism.*

93. Rapoport-Albert, "Hasidism after 1772," 85.

94. Steven Zipperstein, *The Jews of Odessa: A Cultural History, 1794–1881* (Stanford, Calif.: Stanford University Press, 1986), 4.

95. Arnold Eisen, *Rethinking Modern Judaism: Ritual, Commandment, Community* (Chicago: University of Chicago Press, 1998), 3.

96. Micha Berdychevski, "Le-korot ha-Hasidut," *Ozar ha-Sifrut* 3 (1899), 55.

97. See Eli Lederhendler, "The Decline of the Polish-Lithuanian *kahal*," *Polin* 2 (1987), 153.

98. Meetings over economic and residence concerns became increasingly frequent. Artur Eisenbach, "Ha-Nezigut ha-Merkazit shel ha-Yehudim be-Nesihut Varsheh, 1807–1815," in Israel Bartal and Israel Gutman, eds., *Kiyum ve-shever: Yehudei Polin le-doroteihem* (Jerusalem: Merkaz Zalman Shazar, 1997), 287–336.

99. Eisenbach, "Ha-Nezigut ha-Merkazit shel ha-Yehudim be-Nesihut Varsheh, 1807–1815," 287–336.

100. Shmeruk, "Ha-Hasidut be-Askei Ha-Hakirut."

101. Gershon Hundert, "On the Problem of Agency in Eighteenth-Century Jewish Society," in *Scripta Hierosolymitana 38: Studies in the History of the Jews in Old Poland in Honor of Jacob Goldberg* (Jerusalem: Magnes, 1998), 83.

102. Hundert, "On the Problem of Agency in Eighteenth–Century Jewish Society," 83–4. See also Hundert, *Jews in Poland-Lithuania in the Eighteenth Century* (Berkeley: University of California Press, 2004), 108–10; Adam Teller, "Radziwiłł, Ra-

binowicz, and the Rabbi of Świerz: The Magnates' Attitude to Jewish Regional Autonomy in the Eighteenth Century," in *Scripta Hierosolymitana* 38, 246–76.

103. On the decline of the rabbinate see Moshe Rosman, *The Lord's Jews: Magnate-Jewish Relations in the Polish-Lithuanian Commonwealth during the Eighteenth Century* (Cambridge, Mass.: Harvard University Press, 1990), 198–204; Adam Teller, "The Legal Status of the Jews on the Magnate Estates of Poland-Lithuania in the Eighteenth Century, *Gal Ed* 15 (1997), 56–60.

104. Hundert, "On the Problem of Agency in Eighteenth-Century Jewish Society," 89.

105. Hundert, "On the Problem of Agency in Eighteenth–Century Jewish Society," 89. Other attempts were made to replace the ailing institutions of Jewish autonomy, as well. Religious and charitable associations expanded their local activities, while yeshivas with a supracommunal scope were established in historic Lithuania. Assaf and Bartal, "Shtadlanut ve-ortodoksiyah, 67–8.

106. David of Maków, *Shever posh'im: Zot torat ha-kena'ot*, in Wilensky, *Hasidim u-Mitnaggdim* (Jerusalem: Mosad Bialik, 1990), 2:107.

107. Torsten Ysander, *Studien zum Bestschen Hasidismus in Seiner Religions geschichtlichen Sonderart* (Uppsala, 1933), 372–92); Yaffe Eliach, "Jewish Hasidim, Russian Sectarians: Non-Conformists in the Ukraine, 1700–1760" (Ph.D. diss., City University of New York, 1973).

108. Hundert, "The Contexts of Hasidism," 172–3; and more recently, *Jews in Poland-Lithuania*, 176–9.

109. Ze'ev Gries has offered pioneering studies of Hasidic printing efforts, but downplays their importance at the same time (see chapter 6 here). See "The Hasidic Conduct (*Hanhagot*) Literature," 198–236, and *Sefer, Sofer ve-Sipur*.

110. See, for example, Moshe Rosman, "Miedzyboz and Rabbi Israel Baal Shem Tov," in Hundert, *Essential Papers on Hasidism*, 209–25. Ignacy Schiper's manuscript from 1942 questions the older historiography. See Ignacy Schiper, *Przyczynki do dziejów chasydyzmu w Polsce*, 68.

111. Gershon Hundert's *Jews in Poland-Lithuania*, 186–95; 207–8.

112. The reader in search of a social history of Hasidism "proper"—with zaddikim and mass followings—must leap ahead to a period commencing almost a century after the death of the Besht: David Assaf, *The Regal Way*, originally in Hebrew, entitled *Derekh ha-Malhut: R. Yisrael mi-Ruzhin u-mekomo be-toldot ha-Hasidut* (Jerusalem: Merkaz Zalman Shazar, 1997).

113. Perhaps this had to do with a general disdain for historical writing among many traditional Jews. See Yosef Hayim Yerushalmi, *Zakhor* (Seattle: University of Washington Press, 1982).

114. Ira Robinson, "The Zaddik as Hero in Hasidic Historiography," in Menahem Mor, ed., *Crisis and Reaction: The Hero in Jewish History* (Omaha: Creighton University Press, 1995), 93–103.

115. See Rosman, *Founder of Hasidism*, 153–5, and Etkes's attempt to dismiss those concerns in *The Besht: Magician, Mystic, and Leader*, tr. Saadya Sternberg (Brandeis University Press, 2005), 235–43. See also Ada Rapoport-Albert, "Hagiography with Footnotes: Edifying Tales and the Writing of History in Hasidism," *History and Theory 27: Essays in Jewish Historiography* (1988), 119–59.

116. See *Founder of Hasidism*, 153–5, and Etkes's attempt to dismiss those concerns in *The Besht*, 235–43.

117. Isaac of Neskhiż, *Zikharon Tov* (Piotroków Trybunalski, Poland, 1892), 12, no. 6.

118. Neskhiż, *Zikharon Tov*, 18, no. 26.

119. Joseph Dan, *Ha-Sippur ha-Hasidi* (Jerusalem: Keter, 1975), 68–74.

120. Gedalyah Nigal, *Ha-Sipporet Ha-Hasidit: Toldoteha ve-Noseha* (Jerusalem: Hotsa'at Y. Markus, 1981), and "New Light on the Hasidic Tale and Its Sources," in Rapoport-Albert, *Hasidism Reappraised*; Chone Shmeruk, "Ha-Sipurim al R. Adam Ba'al Shem ve-Gilguleihem be-Nusahot Sefer 'Shivhei ha-Besht,' " in *Sifrut Yiddish be-Polin* (Jerusalem: Magnes Press, 1981), 119–46.

121. Shlomo Feinerman, "Ha-aiydot ha-Hasidiyot u-Mekoram," *Ha-Shiloah* 21 (1909), 437–41; Eli Yassif, *The Hebrew Folktale: History, Genre, Meaning*, tr. Jacqueline Teitelbaum (Bloomington: Indiana University Press, 1999), 385–98; Ben-Amos and Mintz, *In Praise of the Baal Shem Tov*, notes.

122. A Polish ethnographer writing at the turn of the twentieth century recorded a series of tales related by Christians about the Besht, who "lives on in the hearts and mouths of our people in Trościaniec." Helena Gruchowska, "Srul Rabi Bal-Szem," *Lud* 9 (1904), 50–8.

123. In one case, the protagonist of a peasant tale—an ice-cutter's daughter—is replaced by the Besht's daughter Adel in its Jewish recension. Ch. Chajes, "Baal-Szem-Tow u Chreścijan," *Miesięcznik Żydowski* 4 (1934), 450. A Polish analogue to R. Nahman of Bratslav's famous tale "The Seven Beggars" has been found; although R. Nahman's tales did not pretend to any historical veracity. Elisheva Sheinfeld, "Ma'asit Shivat ha-Kavzanim shel R. Nahman mi-Bratslav," *Yeda Am* 11 (1966), 65–77.

124. Yoav Elstein, "The Gregorius Legend: Its Christian Versions and Its Metamorphosis in the Hassidic Tale," *Fabula* 27:3–4 (1986), 195–215.

125. Alina Cała, "Polski i Żydowski Folklor: Wędrówka Wątków" (Jewish Historical Institute, forthcoming).

126. Immanuel Etkes argues that the Besht may have intentionally modeled his deeds on those described in *Shivhei Ha-Ari*. See *The Besht*, 246.

127. Assaf, *The Regal Way*.

128. Yassif, *The Hebrew Folktale*, 374–7; Etkes, *The Besht*, 235–43. According to Yassif, "reliability rests solely on the trustworthiness of the message-bearers. The closer they were to the event . . . and, importantly, the more pious—as such most unlikely to lie, especially in regard to as sacred a topic as the deeds of the zaddikim—the more one could rely upon what they said."

129. Yassif, *The Hebrew Folktale*, 374–7.

130. One hagiographer assures the audience that when Temerel hired the destitute R. Simha Bunem of Przysucha she made him a full partner in her enterprise. Another hagiographer, recalling that Temerel brought R. Simha Bunem and his disciples money, which enabled them to continue their stay at the Carlsbad baths, feels compelled to add that she also did their laundry. A third hagiographer acknowledges her instrumental role in the reversal of a ban against pilgrimages to Zaddikim, but cites R. Simha Bunem's pronouncement that the ban should have been left in place because it would have enabled him to serve God without distractions. See chapter three, below.

131. "Mare Kohen," p. 7, in Alexander Ziskind Ha-Kohen, *Torat Kohen* (Warsaw, 1939), app.

132. AGAD, CWW 1869, p. 11. The document refers to a non-Hasidic "main" prayer house/synagogue (the Hasidic petition invokes the terms interchangeably).

133. R. Alexander Zusya Kahana's distinguished lineage derived mainly from his mother's side. His mother, Zertel, was a daughter of R. Simha, an esteemed communal judge (*dayan*) in Warsaw. See "Mare Kohen," 1.

134. In formulating this argument, I have benefited immensely from discussions with scholars like Moshe Rosman, Israel Bartal, David Assaf, and Nehemia Polen.

135. Gwyn Prins, "Oral History," in Peter Burke, ed., *New Perspectives on Historical Writing* (University Park: Pennsylvania State University Press, 1992), 131–3.

136. On women's invisibility and source material, see Joan Wallach Scott, "The Problem of Invisibility," in S. Jay Kleinberg, ed., *Retrieving Women's History: Changing Perceptions of the Role of Women in Politics and Society* (Oxford: Berg, 1988), 5, 11.

137. Polish maskilim, it should be stated at the outset, present something of a semantic dilemma: few wrote in Hebrew—the chief language of Haskalah—or cultivated transregional relationships with other maskilim. I invoke the term "maskilim" as shorthand for "Polish Jewish advocates of integration, acculturation, and socioreligious reform."

138. Dubnow, *Toledot ha-Hasidut*, 34–6, and *History of the Jews in Russia and Poland*, 1:220–34. See also W. Z. Rabinowitch, *Lithuanian Hasidism* (New York: Schocken Books, 1971), 1–6. An embryonic form of the view appears in Heinrich Graetz, *History of the Jews*, vol. 5 (Philadelphia: Jewish Publication Society, 1895), 383, 392. Martin Buber imagines a "religious elite itself arising out of the mass of the people," forming a movement with a "democratic strain" that set aside the "existing 'aristocracy' of spiritual possession." See *The Origin and Meaning of Hasidism*, ed. and tr. Maurice Friedman (New York: Horizon Press, 1960), 58, 61. Benzion Dinur and Joseph Weiss characterize early zaddikim as members of a disenchanted secondary intelligentsia. See Dinur, "The Origins of Hasidism and Its Social and Messianic Foundations," 86–208; Joseph Weiss, "Some Notes on the Social Background of Early Hasidism," in *Studies in Eastern European Jewish Mysticism*, 12–7. Mahler stresses the "plebeian" origin of zaddikim, in *Hasidism and the Jewish Enlightenment*, 7–10.

139. R. Isaac Judah Jehiel Safrin, *Megillat Seterim*, ed. Nafthali Ben-Menahem (Jerusalem: Mosad Ha-Ravkuk, 1944), 11.

140. Assaf, *The Regal Way*, esp. 267–324.

CHAPTER I

1. Hence the nickname "Karliners" for Hasidim in anti-Hasidic bans.

2. Nahman Huberman, "Khasidim un Khasides in Bessarabia," *YIVO Bleter* 39 (1955), 278–83. R. Isaac Eizik Kalev (1751–1821) established that country's first fixed Hasidic presence, in the town of Nagykallo. See Michael Silber, "The Limits of Rapprochment: The Anatomy of an Anti-Hasidic Controversy in Hungary," *Studia Judaica* 3 (1994), 125–7; and, with caution, entries in Tzvi M. Rabinowicz, ed., *The Encyclopedia of Hasidism* (Northvale, N.J.: Aronson, 1996).

3. See the testimony of Israel Loebel and Mendel Lefin, below. On the alleged lateness of Polish Hasidism, see Dubnow, *Toledot ha-Hasidut*, 215; David Assaf, "Hasidut be-Hitpashtuta—Diyokano Shel R. Nehemia Jehiel Mi-Bihova ben 'Ha-Yehudi Ha-Kadosh," in Bartal, Mendelsohn, and Turnianski, *Ke-minhag Ashkenaz ve-Polin*, 275–6.

4. According to Mordecai Wilensky and various hagiographical accounts, the brothers became Hasidic in their youth. *Hasidim u-Mitnaggdim*, 1:84.

5. David Assaf, "Hasidut be-Polin be-Meah ha-19—Mazav ha-Mehkar ve-Skirah Bibliografit," in Rachel Elior, Yisrael Bartal, and Chone Shmeruk, eds., *Zaddikim ve-Anshe Ma'aseh: Mehkarim be-Hasidut Polin* (Jerusalem: Mosad Bialik, 1994), 357.

6. Assaf, "Hasidut be-Polin be-Meah ha-19, 357.

7. Assaf, "Hasidut be-Polin be-Meah ha-19, 357–79.

8. Zvi Rabinowicz, *Bein Pshyskha le-Lublin* (Jerusalem: Kesharim, 1997); Avraham Rubinstein, "He'arot le-Te'udah al Gviyot-Edut Neged ha-Hasidut," *Tarbiz* 32 (1963), 92–4, and "Hasidut ve Hasidim be-Varshe," *Sinai* 65 (1974) 61–84; and Rabinowicz, "Mekorot ve-Te'udot le-Toldot ha-Hasidut be-Polin," *Sinai* 82 (1978) 80–84; *Reshitah Shel Ha-Hasidut be-Polin Merkazit* (Ph.D. dissertation, Jerusalem: Hebrew University, 1960).

9. Aaron Aescoli, *Ha-Hasidut be-Polin*, ed. David Assaf (Jerusalem: Magnes Press, 1999).

10. Raphael Mahler, *Hasidism and the Jewish Enlightenment*, tr. Eugene Orenstein, Aaron Klein, and Jenny Klein (Philadelphia: Jewish Publication Society, 1985).

11. Bracha Sack, "Iyun ba-Torah Shel Ha-Hozeh Mi-Lublin," in Elior, Bartal, and Shmeruk, *Zaddikim ve- Anshei Ma'aseh*, 219–40; Rachel Elior, "Between *Yesh* and *Ayin*: The Doctrine of the Zaddik in the Works of Jacob Isaac, the Seer of Lublin"; Yehuda Gellman, "Hasidic Existentialism?" in Yaakov Elman and Jeffrey S. Gurock, eds., *Hazon Nahum: Studies in Jewish Law, Thought, and History Presented to Dr. Norman Lamm on the Occasion of His Seventieth Birthday* (New York: Yeshiva University Press, 1997), 393–417. On R. Israel of Kozienice, see Ze'ev Gries, "R. Yisrael ben Shabbetai mi-Kozienice ve-Peirushav le-Masekhet Avot," in Elior, Bartal, and Shmeruk, *Zaddikim ve-Anshe Ma'aseh*, 127–66. On R. Simha Bunem of Przysucha, see Alan Brill, "Grandeur and Humility in the Writings of R. Simhah Bunim of Przysucha," in Elman and Gurock, *Hazon Nahum*, 419–48. On Izbica, see Shaul Magid, *Hasidism on the Margin: Reconciliation, Antionmianism, and Messianism in Izbica/Radzin Hasidism* (Madison: University of Wisconsin Press, 2003).

12. "Ha-hasidut be-Hitpashtuta—Diyokano Shel R. Nehemia Jehiel Mi-Bihova ben 'Ha-Yehudi Ha-Kadosh," in Bartal, Mendelsohn, and Turnianski, *Ke-Minhag Ashkenaz ve-Polin*; David Assaf and Israel Bartal, " 'Hasidut Polin' o 'Ha-Hasidut be-Polin': Li-ve'ayat Ha-Geografya Ha-Hasidit be-Ikvot Ha-Kovets: Zaddikim be-Anshei Ma'aseh—Mehkarim Be-Hasidut Polin," *Gal-Ed* 14 (1995), 197–206; and " 'Ve-ha-Mitnaggdim Hitlozezu She-Nishtakher ve-Nafal': Nefilat Shel Ha-Hozeh Mi-Lublin Be-R'i Ha-Zikharon Ha-Hasidi ve-Ha-Satirah Ha-Maskilit", Immanuel Etkes, David Assaf, Israel Bartal and Elchanan Reiner, ed., *Be-Ma'aglei Hasidim*, 161–208; David Assaf and Israel Bartal, "Shtadlanut ve-Ortodoksyah: Zaddikei Polin be-Mifgash Im ha-Zemanim he-Hadashim," in Elior, Bartal, and Shmeruk, *Zaddikim ve-Anshe Maaseh*; Bergman, "Gora-Kalwaria (Gur)-ha-Yishuv ha-Yehudi be-Hazar ha-Rabi mi-Gor mi-Reshit ha-Mea 19 ad 1939"; Gries, "R. Israel ben Shabbethai Mi-Kozienice u-Perushav Le'Masekhet Avot."

13. Marcin Wodziński, " 'Sprawa chasydymów.' Z materiałów do dziejów chasydyzmu w Królestwie Polskim," in Krystyn Matwijowski, ed., *Z historii ludność Żydowskiej w Polsce i na Śląsku* (Wrocław, Poland: Uniwersytet Wrocławski, 1994); "Dybuk. Z Dokumentów Archiwum Głównego Akt Dawnych w Warszawie," *Literatura Ludowa* 36:6 (1992) 19–29, *Oświecenie żydowskie w Królestwie Polskim wobec chasydyzmu*; *Haskalah and Hasidism in the Kingdom of Poland: A History of Conflict*, tr. Sarah Cozens (Portland, Oregon: Littman Library of Jewish Civilization, 2005), "Ilu było chasydów w Królestwie Polskim około 1830 roku?" in Konrad Zieliński and Monika Adamczyk-Garbowski, *Ortodoksja, Emancypacja, Asymilacja: Studia Z Dziejów Ludności Żydowskiej na Ziemiach Polskich w Okresie Rozbiorów* (Lublin: Maria Curie-Skłodowski University, 2003), 25–48; "Hasidism, *Shtadlanut*, and Jewish Politics in Nineteenth–Century Poland: The Case of Isaac of Warka," *Jewish Quarterly Review*, 95:2 (2005).

14. Schiper, *Przyczynki do dziejow chasydyzmu w Polsce*.

15. Majer Bałaban, *Żydowskie miasto w Lublinie*, ed. Jan Doktor (Lublin: FIS Ma-

rek Gacka, 1991), 94; Zvi Meir Rabinowicz, *Bein Pshyskha ve Lublin: Ishim ve- Shitot be-Hasidiut Polin* (Jerusalem: Kesherim, 1997), 103. The place of birth is stated as Luków by Moses Menahem Walden, in *Nifla'ot ha-Rabi*, in *Sefarim Kedoshim mi-Talmide ha-Baal Shem Tov* 2 (Brooklyn, 1985), 71:184, upon which Rachel Elior relies, "Between *Yesh* and *Ayin*," 395.

16. David Assaf, " 'Ve-ha-Mitnaggdim Hitlozezu She-Nishtakher ve-Nafal': Nefilat Shel Ha-Hozeh Mi-Lublin Be-R'i Ha-Zikharon Ha-Hasidi ve-Ha-Satirah Ha-Maskilit," in Etkes et al., *Within Hasidic Circles*, 161–208.

17. David Assaf, "Hasidut be-Hitpashtuta—Diyokano Shel R. Nehemia Jehiel Mi-Bihova ben 'Ha-Yehudi Ha-Kadosh," in Bartal, Mendelsohn, and Turnianski, ed., *Ke-minhag Ashkenaz ve-Polin*, 269–98.

18. Aaron Aescoli, *Ha-Hasidut be-Polin*, ed. David Assaf (Jerusalem: Magnes Press, 1999), 89.

19. Marcin Wodziński, "Hasidism, *Shtadlanut*, and Jewish Politics"; Assaf and Bartal, "Shtadlanut ve-Ortodoksiyah: Zaddikei Polin be-Mifgash Im ha-Zmanim ha-Hadashim."

20. Assaf, "Hasidut be-Hitpashtuta," 273–4; " 'Hasidut Polin' o 'Ha-Hasidut be-Polin," 197–206.

21. Elior, "Between *Yesh* and *Ayin*"; Mahler, *Hasidism and the Jewish Enlightenment*, chap. 9; Rabinowicz, *Bein Pshyskha*, 257–92.

22. Jacob Isaac Horowitz of Lublin, *Zikharon Zot*. Munkac ed. (reprint, Jerusalem 1973), 75, "Vayikra," in *Torat Ha-Hozeh Mi-Lublin* (Jerusalem, 1979), 229, emphasis added. For more such texts, see Elior, "Between *Yesh* and *Ayin*," 438–9.

23. On the zaddik as high priest, see Arthur Green, "Typologies of Leadership and the Hasidic Zaddiq."

24. See Alan Brill, "Grandeur and Humility," 435 and 443–48.

25. Simha Bunem of Przysucha, *Kol Simha* (Breslau, 1859; reprint, Jerusalem, 1997), 9. For a similar teaching, see Simha Bunem of Przysucha, *Torat Simha*, 118; Shmuel of Sieniawa, *Ramataim Zofim*, vol. 1 (Warsaw, 1885), 2; and Brill, "Grandeur and Humility," 429–30.

26. See Martin Buber, *I and Thou*, tr. Walter Kaufman (New York: Scribner's, 1970), 73–5.

27. This point was argued by Alan Nadler at a University of Wrocław conference in Wrocław, Poland, August 23, 2004.

28. Yehuda Leib of Zaklików, *Likkutei Maharil* (Lublin, 1900; reprint, Jerusalem, 1971), parshat Yitro, 47.

29. As the holiday of Shavuot commemorates the reception of the Torah by the Israelites, it might be presumptuous to speak words of Torah right before that day.

30. Samuel of Sieniawa, *Ramataim Zofim*, 166.

31. Avraham Rubinstein, ed., *Shivhei Ha-Besht* (Jerusalem: Reuven Mas, 1991), 85–90; Rosman, *Founder of Hasidism*, 110.

32. Avraham Rubinstein, ed., *Shivhei Ha-Besht* (Jerusalem: Reuven Mas, 1991), pp. 85–90; Rosman, *Founder of Hasidism*, 110; *Shivhei Ha-Besht*, quoted in Etkes, *The Besht: Magician, Mystic, and Leader*, 126.

33. Abraham Gottlober, *Zikhronot u-Masa'ot* (Jerusalem: Mosad Bialik, 1976), vol. 1:222.

34. For a recent study of this problem, see Moshe Rosman, "The Indebtedness of the Lublin Kahal in the Eighteenth Century," *Scripta Hierosolymitana* 38, 166–83.

35. On the merit of designating certain Jewish modernizers in Central Poland "Maskilim," see Marcin Wodziński, "Good Maskilim and Bad Assimilationists, or To-

ward a New Historiography of the Haskalah in Poland," *Jewish Social Studies* 10:3 (2004), 87–122.

36. In an otherwise illuminating article, Ada Rapoport-Albert attempts to deny the relevance of the partitions for Hasidism, and even mis-cites the date of the second partition. See "Hasidism after 1772," 04.

37. Arthur Green, "Typologies of Leadership." in Green, *Jewish Spirituality*, 2:144. Green must mean the Polish-Lithuanian Commonwealth when he refers to the "Polish Kingdom."

38. Abraham Gottlober, *Zikhronot u-Masa'ot*, 1:165–7.

39. Rosman, *Founder of Hasidism*, 201. See also Rachel Elior, "Ha-mahlohet al Moreshet Habad," *Tarbiz* 49 (1980), 166–86. It should also be noted, however, that fourth son, Moses, of R. Jehiel Michael of Złoczów (d. 1781) established a Hasidic court and eventually a dynasty. See Altshuler, "The First Tzaddik of Hasidism," 134.

40. R. Israel resided in a palace in Ruzhin and a second one in Sadagora. Assaf, *The Regal Way*, 267–84.

41. Assaf, *The Regal Way*, 53.

42. R. Jehiel Michael of Złoczów (d. 1781), R. David Ha-levi of Stepan (d. 1810), R. Abraham Abba-Joseph of Soroca, R. Mordecai of Neskhiż (d. 1800), R. Samuel Ginzberg of David-Gorodok, R. Meir of Przemyślany (d. 1773), R. Shabbetai of Raszków (d. 1745), R. Phineas Shapiro of Korzec (d. 1791), R. Zvi Hirsch of Kamenka (d. 1781), R. Dov Ber of Międzyrzecz (d. 1772), R. Menahem Nahum of Chernobyl (d. 1798), R. Aaron Perlov "the Great" of Karlin (d. 1772), R. Solomon of Karlin (d. 1792), R. Mordecai of Lachowicze (d. 1810), R. Schneur Zalman of Liady (d. 1813), R. Menahem Mendel of Kosów (d. 1825), R. Isaac Eizik Eichenstein of Safrin (d. 1800). See chart in appendix to *Encyclopedia Judaica*, 1:160–69.

43. According to a decree on March 17, 1808, Jews were excluded from citizenship for ten years. Artur Eisenbach, *Emancypacja Żydów na żiemiach polskich, 1785–1870, na tle europejskim* (Warsaw: PIW, 1988), 141.

44. Wodziński, "Good Maskilim and Bad Assimilationists," 90–1; 106.

45. Wodziński, "Good Maskilim and Bad Assimilationists," 168. The Congress Kingdom was attached in personal union to imperial Russia. It had its own diet (*sejm*), national administration, judiciary, national army, and school system. But the character of the regime and economic and social relations remained much as before.

46. Wodziński, "Good Maskilim and Bad Assimilationists," chap. 5; Bolesław Limanowski, *Historya demokracyi Polskiej w epoce porozbiorowej* (Zurich, 1901), 112.

47. Jerzy Jedlicki, *A Suburb of Europe: Nineteenth–Century Approaches to Western Civilization* (Budapest: Central European University Press, 1999), 13–4. See also Barbara Szacka, *Teoria i utopia Stanisława Staszica* (Warsaw: PWN, 1965).

48. Jedlicki, *A Suburb of Europe*, 27.

49. Jedlicki, *A Suburb of Europe*, 82–6.

50. Jedlicki, *A Suburb of Europe*, 64.

51. John Stanley, "The Politics of the Jewish Question in the Duchy of Warsaw, 1807–1813," *Jewish Social Studies* 44 (1982), 49. However, Surowiecki proposed restrictions on Jewish settlement and occupations in the countryside.

52. Stanley, "The Politics of the Jewish Question in the Duchy of Warsaw, 1807–1813," 15.

53. Mahler, *Hasidism and the Jewish Enlightenment*, 272–8.

54. Mahler, *Hasidism and the Jewish Enlightenment*, 276.

55. Mahler, *Hasidism and the Jewish Enlightenment*, 276; and see chapter 3 here.

56. Traditional sources claim that he received his pharmaceutical license in Lemberg; however, Jews could not obtain pharmaceutical licenses in Galicia until 1832, five years after R. Simha Bunem's death. Aaron Marcus claims he earned it in Danzig. See Aaron Marcus, *Ha-Hasidut*, tr. M. Sheinfeld (Tel Aviv, 1954), 124; Eisenbach, *Emancipation of the Jews in Poland*, 204; Rabinowicz, *Bein Pshyskha*, 302, no. 15.

57. Menahem Boyim, *Ha-Rabi Rabi Bunem* (Bnei Brak, Israel: Torat Simcha Institute, 1997), 2:705–8 (app.). This fascinating document contains a provision in the event of a "change in regime" as a result of the impending Napoleonic War. The Sejm adopted a resolution on March 24, 1809, that introduced a tax on the ritual slaughter of cattle and poultry. This kosher meat tax was initially a tax on consumption, but was soon transformed into a direct tax and collected by lessors. See Eisenbach, *Emancipation of the Jews in Poland*, 142–3.

58. Zvi Meir Rabinowicz, "Mekorot ve-Teudot le-Toldot ha-Hasidut be Polin," *Sinai* 82 (1978), 85.

59. Mahler, *Hasidism*, 272; Abraham Issachar Benjamin of Powienic, *Meir Eynei ha-Golah* (Tel Aviv: Alter-Bergman, 1954), 1:39:137; 2:83:3]. And see chapter 3 here.

60. According to one tradition, R. Simha Bunem claimed, "I am amongst the merchants during their business, and everything that I say turns out to be so. And this is not the case with the other merchants, even in their own business affairs, for I have a business-sense." Israel b. Isaac Simha, "Or Simha," in *Simhat Yisraēl* (Petersburg, 1910; reprint, Jerusalem, 1986), 17:34. An example of R. Simha Bunem's advice appears in Samuel of Sieniawa, *Ramataim Zofim*, 215, when the zaddik counsels a serious Leipzig merchant to be more friendly and cheerful.

61. Yoez Kim Kadish, *Si'ah Sarfei Kodesh* (Piotroków Trybunalski, 1923) 1:33.

62. On the significance of Breslau, Leipzig, Frankfurt-on-the-Oder, and Danzig as points of contact between Polish and German-Jewish merchants, see Gershon Hundert, "An Advantage to Peculiarity? The Case of the Polish Commonwealth," *AJS Review* 6 (1981), 28–30.

63. Rabinowicz, *Bein Pshyskha*, 184–5.

64. Rabinowicz, *Bein Pshyskha*, 171, 195.

65. Wilensky, *Hasidim u-Mitnaggdim*, 1:59, no. 15.

66. Shalom Gutman, *Tiferet Bet Levi* (Jassy, 1909), 15.

67. Wodziński, "Good Maskilim and Bad Assimilationists," esp. 104–11.

68. See Israel Halpern, "Rabbi Levi Isaac of Berdyczów and the Royal Edicts of His Times" (in Hebrew), in *Yehudim ve-Yahadut be-Mizrah Eiropa*, 342. Although R. Levi Isaac no longer lived in Central Poland by this time, his contacts within the Warsaw mercantile elite may explain his involvement.

69. However, his advanced age and physical weakness prevented his making the journey. See chapter 3 here; and Artur Eisenbach, "Di Tsentrale Reprezentants-Argenen Fun Di Yiden in Warshaver Pirshtentum (1807–1815)," Yiddish version only, *Bleter Far Geschikhte* 2 (1938), 64–5; Rabinowicz, *Bein Pshyskha*, 206.

70. Avraham Hayyim Simha Bunem, ed., *Ohel Naphtali* (Lemberg, 1912), quoted in Paul Mendes-Flohr and Jehuda Reinharz, eds., *The Jew in the Modern World: A Documentary History* (New York: Oxford University Press, 1995), 137–8.

71. Kandel, "Komitet starozakonnych," 89–103.

72. Marcin Wodziński, "Hasidism, *Shtadlanut*, and Jewish Politics in Nineteenth-Century Poland"; Assaf and Bartal, "Shtadlanut ve-Ortodoksiyah"; David Assaf, "Hasidut be-Hitpashtuta," 273–4.

73. Elior, "Between *Yesh* and *Ayin*," 397.

74. Martin Buber, *For the Sake of Heaven (Gog u-Magog)* (Philadelphia: Jewish Publication Society, 1953). See also Shmuel Werses, "Ha-Hasidut be-Aspaklariyah Be-leteristit," in Elior, Bartal, and Shmeruk, *Zaddikim ve-Anshe Ma'aseh*, 317–56.

75. Morris Faierstein, *All Is in the Hands of Heaven: The Teachings of Rabbi Mordecai Joseph Leiner of Izbica* (Northvale, N.J.: Ktav, 1990).

76. That those acts were perceived by the masters as revolts seems to contradict Rapoport-Albert's theory of an inherently decentralized Hasidic leadership. In Galicia and Central Poland, establishing a court during the master's lifetime was indeed tantamount to rebellion. See Rapoport-Albert, "Hasidism after 1772," 95.

77. *Meir Eynei ha-Golah*, 23; 25–9. This was achieved on the order of the zaddik Jacob Isaac of Lublin. But the most prominent disciples, such as R. Isaac Meir Alter, future zaddik of Gór Kalwari (Gur), did not remain.

78. The Holy Jew's son Yerahmiel did succeed him, but was not able to attract a following on the scale of R. Simha Bunem's following. On another son of the Holy Jew, R. Nehemia Jehiel, whose following was also modest, see Assaf, "Ha-Hasidut be-Hitpashtuta."

79. The notion of a "founder" of a dynasty is somewhat paradoxical, as it is technically only applicable to a living zaddik who explicitly selected a son, son-in-law, or grandson as his successor.

80. See the letter of R. Abraham Moshe to R. Menahem Mendel printed in Samuel of Sieniawa, *Ramataim Zofim*, 201.

81. Letter from 1828, sent from Tomaszów, printed in *Nahalat Zvi* 11 (1995), 108.

82. AGAD, CWW 1871, 306–7.

83. Arthur Green upholds the traditional explanation that R. Isaac Meir sought a more religiously "safe" environment for his Hasidim by moving his court away from the secular snares of Warsaw. He rejects Elinora Bergman's explanation that R. Isaac Meir merely wished to wait until the death of his master, R. Menahem Mendel of Kotsk, before setting up a court in Gór. See Green's introduction to Judah Aryeh Leib Alter, *The Language of Truth: The Torah Commentary of the Sefat Emet, R. Yehudah Leib Alter of Ger* (Philadelphia: Jewish Publication Society, 1998), 24–5; and "Gora-Kalwaria (Gur)-ha-Yishuv ha-Yehudi be-Hazar ha-Rabi mi-Gor mi-Reshit ha-Mea 19 ad 1939."

84. Mahler, *Hasidism and the Jewish Enlightenment*, 311.

85. Assaf, *The Regal Way*, 57.

86. Andrzej Walicki, *The Enlightenment and the Birth of Modern Nationhood: Polish Political Thought from Noble Republicanism to Tadeusz Kosciuszko*, tr. Emma Harris (Notre Dame, Ind.: Notre Dame University Press, 1989), chaps. 3–5. Both thinkers did embrace the idea of a hereditary monarch; however, Kołłątaj 's monarch was to be weak in comparison to the Sejm, while Staszic professed a preference for a constitutional monarch.

87. Dubnow, *Toledot ha-Hasidut*, 3. He also indicated that in eastern Galicia and the Ukraine, Hasidim 'had conquered almost all of the communities" and in Romania and Hungary "a substantial portion of them." Only in greater Lithuania, including present-day Belarus, did he find mitnaggdim holding a decisive numerical edge.

88. The most suspect of them is the alleged weakness of Hasidism in Belarus, home to Lubavitch and Karlin Hasidism. See Mordecai Zalkin, "Mekomot shelo mats'ah adayin ha-hasidut ken la kelal? Bein Hasidim lemitnagdim belita bame'ah ha-19," in Immanuel Etkes et al., eds., *Be-Ma'agalei Hasidim: Kovets Lezikhro Shel Profesor Mordekhai Wilensky* (Jerusalem: Mosad Bialik, 1999), 161–208.

89. Warsaw: Wydawnictwo Cyklady, 2003. Translated with additions, as *Haska-*

lah and Hasidism in the Kingdom of Poland: A History of Conflict, tr. Sarah Cozens (Portland, OR: Littman Library of Jewish Civilization, 2005).

90. Wodziński, *Oświecenie żydowskie w Królestwie Polskim wobec chasydyzm*, 95–120, 175. On Buchner's anti-Hasidism see Mahler, *Hasidism and the Jewish Enlightenment*, 215.

91. Including moderate Galician Maskil Jacob Samuel Bik and the Ukrainian Maskil Eliezer Zvi Hakohen Zweifel.

92. Marcin Wodziński, "How Many *Hasidim* were there in Congress Poland? On the Demographics of the Hasidic Movement in Poland during the First Half of the Nineteenth Century," *Gal-Ed* 19 (2004), 46. See also Wodziński, *Oświecenie żydowskie*, 95–120, and "Ilu było chasydów w Królestwie Polskim około 1830 roku?" in Zieliński and Adamczyk-Garbowski, eds., *Ortodoksja, Emancypacja, Asymilacja*, 25–48.

93. Mahler, *Hasidism and the Jewish Enlightenment*, chap. 8.

94. Quoted in Wodziński, *Oświecenie żydowskie*, 154; and *Haskalah and Hasidism in the Kingdom of Poland*: 96.

95. Ibid.

96. The most obvious example of an ideologically enmeshed group of patrons is the Bergson family (see chapter three). Examples of more open attacks elsewhere include the imprisonment of R. Schneur Zalman Zalman of Liady (1798–1800), the expulsion of the Zaddik of Żydaczów from Zabaraż (1824), and the "Ushitsa Affair" (1838).

97. Wodziński's analysis of the activities of Maskilim is generally more sound than his analysis of Hasidism. See *Haskalah and Hasidism in the Kingdom of Poland*, chapter two, esp. 43–44.

98. See Moses Wassercug, "Korot Moshe Wassercug uNedivat Lev Aviv ha-Manoah R. Isserel Zal," ed. Henrich Loewe, *Jahrbuch der Jüdisch-Literarischen Gesellschaft* 8 (1910), 107; *Die Memoiren des Moses Wasserzug*, tr. Stefi Jersch-Wenzel and ed. Jakub Goldberg (Leipzig: 1999), 59.

99. See the case of Wodzisław, described in chapter 2 here.

100. To be sure, as Wodziński suggests, a small number of wealthy Hasidim in a given town may have swayed kahal elections disproportionately to their number, to but it is equally likely that those same influential Hasidim would advance the movement among the town's less affluent Jews. Wodziński. "How Many *Hasidim*?" 34–5.

101. See chapter 6.

102. Mahler, *Ha-Hasidut ve-ha-Haskalah* (Israel: Merhavya, 1961), 507.

103. See data in Schiper, *Żydzi Królestwa Polskiego w dobie powstania Listopadowego* (Warsaw: Instytut Nauk Judaistycznych, 1932), 6.

104. When R. Levi Isaac left Ryczywół in 1765, the Jewish population was 1,116. In 1790, it had dropped to 706. The Jewish population in Żelechów was 1,464 in 1765 and had dropped to 1,165 by 1790 (R. Levi Isaac departed in 1775). The Seer of Lublin left Wieniawa around 1790, and the Jewish population dropped from 403 in 1765 to 118 in 1790. Jadwiga Muszyńska, *Żydzi w miastach województwa sandomierskiego i lubelskiego w 18 wieku: Studium osadnicze* (Kielce, Poland, 1998), 151, 200–201.

105. Muszysńska, *Żydzi w miastach województwa sandomierskiego i lubelskiego w 18 wieku*, 150, 179, tables 5, 30. A higher count of 635 Jews in 1787 appears in the diocese records. See also Jan Jagielski's appendix to Schiper, *Przyczynki do dziejow chasydyzmu w Polsce*, 131–2. R. Meir resigned from his rabbinical post in Stopnica in 1817 but was succeeded by his son and continued to wield influence in the town. See chapter 2 here.

106. Abraham Zusman, *Barukh mi-Banim* (Vilna, 1869), 97–8.

107. Shimon Huberband, *Kiddush Hashem: Jewish Religious and Cultural Life in Poland During the Holocaust*, tr. David E. Fishman and ed. Jeffrey S. Gurock and Robert S. Hirt (New York: Yeshiva University Press, 1987), 307–8.

108. Leon Dembowski, *Moje wspomnienia* (St. Petersburg, 1898), 53–4.

109. Yizhak Szmulewicz's unpublished memoirs, quoted in Rabinowicz, *Bein Pshyskha*, 457–8.

110. The satire was probably augmented and edited by Joseph Perl. See David Assaf, " 'Ve-ha-Mitnaggdim Hitlozezu She-Nishtakher ve-Nafal'.

111. February 20, 1825. AGAD, KRSW 6635, pp. 16–7; Mahler, *Ha-Hasidut ve-ha-Haskalah*, app. 15e, pp. 495–7. Error in Mahler's rendition, first query (p. 496) should read *swoj* (not *skutek*) on line 14; *przyieżdzaiących* (not *przyeżdzaiących*) on line 18. The town's Jewish population was 1,377 in 1827.

112. For examples, see Gershon Hundert's *Jews in Poland-Lithuania*, 22.

113. On "sporadic Hasidim" see Assaf, *The Regal Way*, 279–80.

114. See Gershon Hundert, "Jewish Children and Childhood in Early Modern East Central Europe," in David Kraemer, ed., *The Jewish Family: Metaphor and Memory* (New York: Oxford University Press, 1989), 84.

115. See chapter 5.

116. Scott, "The Problem of Invisibility," 5.

117. See *Zemir Arizim* 14b, in Wilensky, *Hasidim u-Mitnagdim*, 2:211. Additional examples are in chapter 5.

118. AGAD, KRSW 6634, pp. 239–43; Mahler, app. to *Ha-Hasidut ve-ha-Haskalah*, 477–481; Wodziński, *Oświecenie żydowskie*, 268–71. See also Mahler, *Hasidism and the Jewish Enlightenment*, 318–21.

119. Schiper, *Żydzi Królestwa Polskiego*, 28–9.

120. August 4, 1824, AGAD, CWW 1871, p. 179. See also Marcin Wodziński, " 'Sprawa chasydymów,' " 239.

121. See the anti-Hasidic investigations described in chapters 2–3.

122. Ada Rapoport-Albert, "On Women in Hasidism: S. A. Horodecky and the Maid of Ludomir," in Rapoport-Albert and Zipperstein, *Jewish History*, 495–525. However, note the role of Temerel Sonenberg-Bergson, described in chapter 3.

123. AGAD, CWW 1871, 9–37. Compare with Wodziński, " 'Sprawa chasydymów,' " 230. He is more precise in "How Many *Hasidim*," 35–6.

124. Wodziński, "How Many *Hasidim*," 26.

125. Wodziński's claim of corroboration is for this reason misleading. See "How Many *Hasidim*," 37.

126. Wodziński, "How Many *Hasidim*," 36.

127. Cited in Hundert, "Jewish Children and Childhood," 85.

128. Wodziński only sees fit to quadruple the Podlasie figures, to obtain what he terms a "maximal estimate." Wodziński, "How Many *Hasidim*," 38–9.

129. Israel Loebel, "Kontres beGermanit shel R. Israel Loebel," in Wilensky, *Hasidim u-Mitnagdim*, 2:314, 338.

130. *Zemir Arizim* 2b–3a, in Wilensky, *Hasidim u-Mitnagdim*, 2:195.

131. Kandel, "Żydzi w dobie utworzenia Królestwa Kongresowego," 111. Quoted from a letter from Shakhna Neuding to Jan Glücksberg, no longer extant.

132. APK, RGR I 4399, pp. 16–21.

133. See Halpern, *Yehudim veYahadut beMizrah Eiropa*, 342.

134. A Jewish delegation to the Great Sejm, held in 1788–92, sought an amelio-

ration of Jewish legal status. See Eisenbach, *Emancipation of the Jews in Poland* (London, 1991), 21–112.

135. Mendel Lefin Satanower, *Essai d'un plan de reforme ayant pour objet d'eclairer la Nation Juive en Pologne et de redresser par la ses moeurs* (Warsaw, 1791), 30. Israel Halpern spots another reference in Lefin's essay: "Among the Jewish representatives [to the Great Sejm] was one of the rabbis of the *hasidim* who had recently left his community because of dissension and had traveled [to Warsaw] from deep in the Ukraine." Halpern identifies the rabbi as R. Levi Isaac. See Halpern, *Yehudim ve-Yahadut beMizrah Eiropa*, 342. See Emmanuel Ringelblum, "Khsides un Haskole in Varshe in 18-ten y.h.," *YIVO Bleter* 13:1–2 (1938), 125, for a dissenting view; also Samuel Dresner, *The World of a Hasidic Master: Levi Yitzhak of Berditchev* (Northvale, N.J.: Aronson, 1994), 68, 213.

136. Jacques Calmanson, *Uwagi nad niniejszym stanem Żydów Polskich y ich wydoskonaleniem* (Warsaw, 1797), 18–9.

137. Wodziński, "How Many *Hasidim*," 19–20.

138. Abraham Gottlober, *Zikhronot u-Masa'ot*, 1:63. He refers to a period before 1809, the year R. Levi Isaac of Berdyczów died.

139. Israel Zinberg, *A History of Jewish Literature: Hasidism and Enlightenment (1780–1820)* (Cincinnati: Ktav, 1976), 231.

140. AGAD, KRSW 6634, pp. 239–43; Mahler, *Ha-Hasidut ve-ha-Haskalah*, 477–81; Wodziński, *Oświecenie żydowskie*, 268–71. See also Mahler's paraphrase, *Hasidism and the Jewish Enlightenment*, 318–21.

141. *Otsar haSifrut* 3 (1888), 26. On the dispute resulting from Bik's perceived traitorous defense of Hasidism, see Natan Michael Gelber, *Arim ve-Imahot be-Yisra'el*, vol. 6, *Brody* (Jerusalem: Mosad ha-Rav Kook, 1957), 191–3; Shmuel Werses, "Bein Shnei Olamot: Yaakov Shmuel Bik bein Haskalah leHasidiut—Iyun Mehudash," *Gal-Ed* 9 (1986).

142. Article 1, no. 10. Text in Władysław Smoleński, *Ostatni rok Sejmu Wielkiego* (Kraków, 1897), 432.

143. APK, RGR I 4399, p. 12.

144. AGAD, CWW 1869, p. 7.

145. Jan Radomiński, *Co wstrzymuie reforme Żydów w kraiu naszym, i co ią przyspieszyć powinno?* (Warsaw, 1820), 63.

146. Wodziński, "How Many *Hasidim*," 22.

147. *The Jewish Expositor and Friend of Israel* 3 (1823) 8, 327.

148. See Wodziński, "How Many *Hasidim*," 23.

149. Quoted in Mahler, *Ha-Hasidut ve-ha-Haskalah*, 506. This document, probably no longer extant, mentions the reigning zaddikim as R. Menahem Mendel of Kock (Kotsk) and R. Yerahmiel of Przysucha (d. 1834). The letter was written between R. Menahem Mendel's succession, in 1827, and 1834.

150. Wodziński, " 'Sprawa chasydymów,' " 232. On R. Kahana's personal qualities, see Michaelson, "Mare Kohen," 4:17–9 and 9:31.

151. The nearest estimate is 377,754 for three years later, but was likely higher considering the incidence of census evasion. On Jewish population figures, see Bohdan Wasiutyński, *Ludność Żydowska w Polsce w wiekach XIX XX* (Warsaw, 1930), 8.

152. Wodziński, "How Many *Hasidim*," 28.

153. Wodziński, "How Many *Hasidim*," 17–8.

154. Dubnow, *Toldot ha-Hasidut*, 216. According to Ignacy Schiper, Dubnow "allowed himself to be hypnotized by the personality of the zaddik Levi Isaac, known

popularly as the Berdyczewer," crediting Żelechów, where R. Levi Isaac had served as rabbi, as Polish Hasidism's point of origin. See Schiper, *Przyczynki do dziejow chasydyzmu w Polsce*, 19.

155. Samuel Shmelke was also in Sieniawa, in Galicia, which Schiper erroneously places in Central Poland. See *Przyczynki do dziejow chasydyzmu w Polsce*.

156. The minute book of the Holy Society of Przysucha contains the signature of the future zaddik Simha Bunem, from 1793. Kadish, *Si'ah Sarfei Kodesh*, 1:58. The twenty-five–year-old R. Israel of Kozienice wrote a letter of adulation to his teacher in Przysucha, R. Abraham, in 1761. Letter printed in David Judah ben Raziel and Israel ben Feiga Sarah, *Kedushat Yisrael, Pe'er Yisrael* (Jerusalem, 1956), 8.

157. Schiper, *Przyczynki do dziejow chasydyzmu w Polsce*, 19–27. Czechów and Wieniawa are virtually the same town, according to Rabbinowicz, *Bein Pshyskha*, 104–5.

158. *Ir Hadash* is Yiddish for Nowe Miasto Korczyn, domain of the zaddik Uziel Meisels (1744–86). See Rabinowicz, *Bein Pshyskha*, 84.

159. *Meir Eynei ha-Golah*, 5, 15, 16.

160. Joseph Shaibowicz, "Towards a History of the Brzezin Kehilah (Jewish Community)," tr. Renee Miller (pp. 78–83 of the Brzeziny Record Book [Pinkas]); available: www.jewishgen.org/yizkor/brzeziny/brz078.html; Krzysztof Skwirowski, "Z 'Księgi Pamięnci Włodawy i okolic'. Włodawscy chasydzi," in *Zeszyty Muzealne. Muzeum Pojezime Łęczynsko-Włodawskiego*, vol. 7 (1997), 5; Eleonora Bergman and Jan Jagielski, *Zachowane synagogi i domy modlitwy w Polsce: Katalog* (Warsaw: Jewish Historical Institute, 1996), 51, 76, 112.

161. Ben-Amos and Mintz, trs. and eds., *In Praise of the Baal Shem Tov*, tale nos. 57, 117, and 120. On Chmielnik itself, see Jerzy Baranowski, "Synagoga w Chmielniku," *Biuletyn ŻIH* 36 (1960), 95–106.

162. The latter had taught R. Israel Kabbalah and introduced him to famous Hasidim (see no. 139). Letter printed in ben Raziel and ben Feiga Sarah, *Kedushat Yisrael, Pe'er Yisrael*, 8. R. Israel's father's name, Shabbetai, is followed by the phrase "Let my life be an expiatory sacrifice for him," a phrase appended to one's name during the first year after one's death, enabling David Judah and Israel to date it 1761.

163. Printed in *Maggid Meisharim al Massekhet Shabat* (Biłgoraj, 1937), 4.

164. Wilensky, *Hasidim u-Mitnaggdim*, 2:356.

165. Approbation to Zvi Hirsch Plinsker, *Zemah le-Avraham*, printed in Shlomo Zemah, "Ha-Hasidut ve-Plonsk," in *Iruvim* (Tel Aviv: Devir, 1984), 78–9.

166. Wilensky, *Hasidim u-Mitnaggdim*, 2:54, 102, 178, 235, and 356. R. Eleazar of Leżajsk (d. 1806) mentions R. Reuven of Grodzisk, who must send his daughter to the Maggid of Kozienice to expel a demon (*dybbuk*) from her. In Moshe Ha-Levi, ed., *Ayala Shluha, Kitvei Kodesh* (Bnei Brak, 1972), 11.

167. Yizhak Zinger, *Savah Razon* (Padgorze, Poland, 1901), 16, quoted in Yizhak Alfasi, "Haknasat Kala ve-Hatunot be-Hasidut," *Orayta* 15 (1986), 300.

168. "And after which Leib was received as rabbi of the holy community of Gąbin, because there was no peace between him and the Hasidim of Sierpc." Wassercug, "Korot Moshe Wassercug u-Nedivat Lev Aviv ha-Manoah R. Isserel Zal," 107.

169. Warka minute book, quoted in Huberband, *Kiddush Hashem*, 307–8.

170. The precise town in Polish is unknown. This is a guess based on the Hebrew spelling. Letter published by Zvi Rabinowicz, in *Sinai* 82 (1978), 84.

171. AGAD, CWW 1869, p. 11. The petition itself is from 1818.

172. APK, RGR I 4402, p. 5.

173. APK, RGR I 4402, pp. 1–7.

174. Wodziński, *Oświecienie żydowskie*, 110. Wodziński's archival analyses also add Chęcin, Łask, Suwałki, Chmielnik, Radzyn, Raczki, and Złoczew (see maps).

175. AGAD, CWW 1429, p. 165; and APK, RGR I 4402, pp. 8–14 and 30–2.

176. AGAD, CWW 1429; APR, RGR I 4399.

177. AGAD, CWW 1871, pp. 12–3. Probably R. Simon Deutch.

178. *Jewish Expositor* 8 (London, 1823), 414–5, 449–51.

179. Additional centers of Hasidism in Central Poland in 1820 are supplied by M. Kruszon in his unpublished master's thesis in the archives of the Jewish Historical Institute in Warsaw, "Chasydyzm na ziemiach Polskich", 1989: Krosno, Annopol, Leżajsk, Lublin, Kozienice, Mogielnica, Wolbórz, Opatów, Rymanów, (Nowy) Sącz, Ropczyc, Lelów, Sieniawa, Łęczna, Radoszyce, Przysucha, Kock, Warka, Góra Kalwaria, Alexandrów and Parysów. Several of these alleged courts could not be verified for that period.

180. On R. Levi Isaac's disputed itinerary, see Shalom Gutman, *Tiferet Bet Levi* (Jassy, Romania, 1909); Dubnow, *Toldot ha-Hasidut*, 151–2 and 216; Mordecai Wilensky, "Hearot le-Pulmusim Bein ha-Hasidim ve-ha-Mitnaggdim," *Tarbiz* 30 (1961), 396–404; Mordecai Nadav, "Kehilot Pinsk-Karlin Bein Hasidut le-Hitnaggdut," *Zion* 34 (1969), 98–108; Hayyim Liberman, "Hearot Bibliografyot le-Toldot R. Levi Yizhak mi-Berdytshev," in David Frankel, ed., *Sefer Ha-Yovel li-Khevod Alexander Marx: Li-melot lo shiv'im shanah* (New York: Jewish Theological Seminary, 1953), 15; Rabinowicz, *Bein Pshyskha*, 97–100. Beware the latter's error on p. 97 re: Ryczwół (date should be 1761, not 1831).

181. Gottlober, *Zikhronot u-Masa'ot*, 1:138. On the extremely vocal mode of Hasidic prayer, see later discussion.

182. Nahman of Bratslav, *Sihot ha-Ran* (Lemberg, 1901), p. 36, no. 63.

183. Around 1758, R. Jacob Emden charges that "now upstarts have arisen, a new sect of Hasidim in Volhynia and Podolia, and some of them have even come to this country [Germany]." Jacob Emden, *Mitpakhat Sefarim* (Altona, 1768), 31. Quoted in Shimon Dubnow, "The Maggid of Miedzyrzecz, His Associates, and the Centre in Vohlynia (1760–1772)," tr. Eli Lederhendler, in Gershon Hundert, ed., *Essential Papers on Hasidism*, 59 and 80, no. 2. See also Yehuda Friedlander, "The Struggle of the Mitnagedim and Maskilim against Hasidism: Rabbi Jacob Emden and Judah Leib Meises," in Shmuel Feiner and David Sorkin, eds., *New Perspectives on the Haskalah* (London: Littman Library of Jewish Civilization, 2001), 105–9.

184. Bedřich Nosek, "Shemuel Shmelke Ben Tsvi Hirsh Ha-Levi Horovits: Legend and Reality," *Judaica Bohemia* 21:2 (1985), 86. Another instructive case is that of R. Nathan Adler and his circle of pietists in Frankfurt. While not identical to Hasidism, the priests were similar in their dissemination of privileged Kabbalistic rite and their institution of separate prayer groups. R. Nathan and his circle were excommunicated by the Frankfurt community in 1779, and again in 1789. It has been suggested that the aversion to R. Nathan's circle had to do with fear of the messianic Frankist movement, whose leader Jacob Frank had recently settled in a fortress in nearby Offenbach. Rachel Elior, "R. Nathan Adler and the Frankfurt "Pietists: Pietist Groups in Eastern and Central Europe during the Eighteenth Century," in Karl E. Grözinger, ed. Jüdische Kultur in Frankfurt am Main (Harrassowitz Verlag: Wiesbaden, 1997) [offprint].

185. Hundert, "The Contexts of Hasidism," 182. However, the preeminent Polish Enlightenment reformer Stanislaw Staszic was not a nobleman, but an ex-priest.

186. Compare these phenomena with that of previous centuries, when the yeshivas of the Polish Commonwealth drew the youth of the West. Chone Shmeruk, "Ba-

hurim Mi-Ashkenaz Be-Yeshivot Polin," in Shmuel Ettinger et al., *Sefer-Yovel li-Yizhak Ber* (Jerusalem: Ha-Hevrah ha-Historit ha-Yisraelit, 1960), 304–17.

187. Hundert, "The Contexts of Hasidism," 177 and 182; Jews in Poland-Lithuania, 21–31.

1. Czernichów (Ukraine) is the town being discussed in the epigraph; however, those words might apply to towns throughout eastern and east central Europe. Hasidic liturgy is a combination of Ashkenazic and Sephardic liturgy. It is more accurately the rite initiated by R. Isaac Luria (1534–72) of Safed. As many Safed mystics were descendents of the refugees from Spain, the term *Nusah Sefarad* is inaccurately applied to Hasidic rite. See Louis Jacobs, *Hasidic Prayer* (New York: Schocken Books, 1975), 38–9; "Liturgy," in Tzvi M. Rabinowicz, *The Encyclopedia of Hasidism* (Northvale, N.J.: Aronson, 1996), 292–4.

2. Samuel of Sieniawa, *Ramataim Zofim*, 195; Rabinowicz, *Bein Pshyskha*, 516.

3. Shmuel Ettinger, "Hasidism and the Kahal," in Rapoport-Albert, *Hasidism Reappraised*, 63–75.

4. Yohanan Petrovsky-Shtern, "Hasidism, Havurot, and the Jewish Street," *Jewish Social Studies* 10:2 (2004), 20–54; Israel Halpern, "Havurot le-Torah ve-l'Mizvah ve-ha-Tenuah ha Hasidit be-Hithapshutah."

5. On the emergence of the Hasidic court as an institution, see David Assaf, *The Regal Way*, 267–324.

6. What Victor Turner terms "communitas." See *Dramas, Fields and Ritual Metaphors* (Ithaca: Cornell University Press, 1964), 45.

7. Gottlober, *Zikhronot u-Masa'ot*, 1:127. Enumeration added.

8. David of Maków, *Zemir Arizim*, in Wilensky, *Hasidim u-Mitnaggdim*, 1:47–8 and 68. The 1772 Brody and Lesznów decrees each mention an acceptable *shtibl*, where old-style hasidim have exclusive right to pray in Lurianic ritual. See also Nahum Gelber, *Arim ve-Imahot be-Yisrael*, vol. 6, *Brody*; Rosman, *Founder of Hasidism*; and Elhanan Reiner, "Hon, Ma'amad Hevrati," 287–328.

9. Elhanan Reiner, "Hon, Ma'amad Hevrati"; Rosman, *Founder of Hasidism*, 29.

10. Wilensky, *Hasidim u-Mitnaggdim*, 1:338, writes: "the term 'shtibl' as a house of worship of Beshtian Hasidim, as far as I can tell, does not appear in anti-Hasidic literature at the end of the eighteenth and beginning of the nineteenth centuries." In 1827, Peter Beer describes the Hasidic prayer house as a *kloyz*. See *Allgemeine Encyclopadie Wissenschaften und Kunste* (Leipzig, 1827), 196. Gottlober also refers to the *kloyz* as a place of worship. *Shtibl* and *bet midrash* are lumped together in Ephraim Dinard, *Zikhronot Bat Ami*, pt. 2 (New Orleans, 1920), 27.

11. AGAD, CWW 1723, pp. 3–5. Letter signed by Israel Rosen, I. Landshutter, R. Guttmann, S. L. Kronenberg, and I. Kohen. The Progressives first opened the prayer house in 1802, and established a synagogue in 1843. See Alexander Guterman, "The Origins of the Great Synagogue in Warsaw on Tłomackike Street," in Władysław Bartoszewski and Antony Polonsky, eds., *The Jews in Warsaw: A History* (Oxford: Blackwell, 1991), 181–211; Maria and Kazimierz Piechotka, "Polish Synagogues in the Nineteenth Century," *Polin* 2 (1987), 189.

12. APK, RGR I 4405. On later attempts to regulate prayer houses, see Jakób Kirszrot, *Prawa Żydów w Królestwie Polskiem* (Warsaw, 1917), 12–3.

13. AGAD, CWW 1441, contains a chart with names and address, including that of the Hasidic patroness Temerel Bergson. See also Maria and Kazimierz Piechotka,

"Polish Synagogues in the Nineteenth Century," 179–98; and complaints about prayer houses in *Jutrzenka* 6 (1861), 45, and *Jutrzenka* 13 (1861), 103.

14. AGAD, CWW 1597, pp. 266–8. Emphasis in original. On Abraham Stern, see Jacob Shatsky, "Avraham Ya'akov Shtern (1768–1842)," Joshua Starr Memorial Volume (New York: Conference on Jewish Relations, 1953), 203–11; and Mahler, *Hasidism and the Jewish Enlightenment*, 211 and 230.

15. See the dedication to the synagogue in "Akt darowizny bóżnicy przez Berka," in *Kwartalnik poświęcony badania przeszłości Żydów w Polsce* (1912), 180–2. The first such synagogue was not, however, constructed in 1830 by Berek (who at any rate died on November 19, 1822), an error repeated twice by the Piechotkas in "Polish Synagogues in the Nineteenth Century," 187 and 190; originating in Majer Bałaban, *Zabytki Historyczne Żydów w Polsce: Orz sprawozdanie Instytutu nauk judaistycznych w Warszawie za lata akademickie 1927/28–1928/29* (Warsaw: Nakładem Towarzystwa Krzewienia nauk judaistycznych w Polsce, 1929), 54.

16. Yehuda Moshe Tieberg mi-Aleksander, *Kedushat Yizhak: Yamei Hayyei Raboteinu ha-Kedoshim ha-Admorim mi-Alexander* (Jerusalem: Bi-defus Hershkoviz, 1952), 20, no. 13; Zenon Guldon, "Gminy wyznania mojżeszowego w powiecie radomskim w 16–18 wieku," in *Radom i region radomski w dobie szlacheckiej Rzeczpospolitej* (Radom, 1996), 2:158.

17. Warka minute book, in Huberband, *Kiddush Hashem*, 307–8.

18. Abraham Rubinstein's bibliography in *Hasidut: Reshima Bibliografit le-Shanah 1965* (Jerusalem: Mosad ha-Rav Kook, 1972), 353–4.

19. Synagogues were officially sanctioned and physically larger than prayer houses; however, prayer houses in Warsaw were officially sanctioned as well (AGAD, CWW 1441).

20. Gottlober, *Zikhronot u-Masa'ot*, 1:59. See also *Solomon Maimon: An Autobiography*, ed. Moses Hadas (New York: Schocken Books, 1967), 51–2: "The heads of the sect sent regular emissaries everywhere, whose duty it was to preach the new doctrine and win converts." The emissary Maimon met was the future zaddik Aaron of Karlin, according to Shmuel Ettinger, "Hasidism and the Kahal in Eastern Europe," in Rapoport-Albert, *Hasidism Reappraised*, 67.

21. *Shever Posh'im* 64a, in Wilensky, *Hasidim u-Mitnaggdim*, 2:159.

22. *Zemir Arizim* 3a, in Wilensky, *Hasidim u-Mitnaggdim*, 2:195. The reference is to the Seer of Lublin.

23. AGAD, KRSW 6634, pp. 239–43; Mahler, *Ha-Hasidut ve-ha-Haskalah*, app., 477–481; Wodziński, *Oświecenie żydowskie*, 268–71. See also Mahler's paraphrase, in *Hasidism and the Jewish Enlightenment*, 318–21.

24. *Kedushat Yizhak*, 19, no. 12. On R. Levi Isaac's clamorous prayer, see Gutman, *Tiferet Bet Levi*, 5.

25. The description originally applies to the Mishnaic sage R. Akiva.

26. Menakhem Bodek, *Seder ha-Dorot he-Hadash, Megilat Yuhasin* (Lemberg, 187–?). See also Gutman, *Tiferet Bet Levi* (Jassy, 1909), 5.

27. Bell, *Ritual Theory, Ritual Practice*, 116, 127, 204–23.

28. Shmeruk, "Hasidism and the *Kehilla*," 186–95; Isaiah Kuperstein, "Inquiry at Polaniec: A Case Study of a Hassidic Controversy in eighteenth Century Galicia," in *Bar Ilan Annual* 24–5, ed. Gershon Bacon and Moshe Rosman (Ramat Gan, Israel: Bar Ilan University, 1989), 25–40. Shaul Stampfer discusses the legalistic facet of Hasidic slaughtering, in "The Dispute over Polished Knives and Hasidic *Shehita*" (in Hebrew), in Immanuel Etkes, David Assaf, and Joseph Dan, *Mehkarei Hasidut* (Jerusalem: Magnes Press, 1999), 197–210.

29. Rubinstein, *Shivhei Ha-Besht*, 60, 73, and 215–6.

30. Gottlober, *Zikhronot u-Masa'ot*, 1:62. The cantorial function is described as a proving ground for aspiring zaddikim (1:61).

31. Walden, *Nifla'ot ha-Rabi*, 2:80, no. 229.

32. Witnessed by the zaddik Solomon Hakohen of Radomsko at the age of six. Yizhak Mordecai Rabinowicz, *Ohel Shlomo* (Piotroków, Poland, 1924), 5b, cited in Alfasi, "Haknasat Kala ve-Hatunot be-Hasidut," *Orayta* 15 (1986), 300–301.

33. See Assaf, *the Regal Way*, 82. The testimony is by Bonaventura Mayer, a convert to Christianity. It is from 1826.

34. The Belarusan zaddik Shneur Zalman of Liady, as provincial rabbi of the Polotsk province in 1786, was the highest provincial authority. He imposed fees and collections upon the region's inhabitants, enforced by threat of excommunication. See Fishman, *Russia's First Modern Jews*, 16–7.

35. See Elchanan Reiner, "Hon, Ma'amad Hevrati," 287–328; and R. Abraham Katzenellenbogen's letter from 1784, Wilensky, *Hasidim u-Mitnaggdim*, 1:128.

36. See Katz, *Tradition and Crisis*; Hundert, *The Jews of a Polish Private Town*. Although other groups, such as guilds and *havurot* (societies), organized separate *minyanim* as well, such groups were socially differentiated enough to avoid doing violence to the social hierarchy.

37. Piekarz, "Hasidism as a Socio-Religious Movement on the Evidence of *Devekut*," 232, and *Bi-yemei Zemihat Ha-Hasidut* (Jerusalem: Bialik, 1978), 390–2.

38. Archives pertaining to Hasidism were exploited by David Kandel, and Ignacy Schiper before the war, and by Raphael Mahler during a rare postwar visit. Kandel, "Żydzi w dobie utworzenia Królestwa Kongresowego," and "Komitet starozakonnych"; Schiper, *Przyczynki do dziejów chasydyzmu w Polsce*; Mahler, *Hasidism and the Jewish Enlightenment*, 317.

39. Warsaw, the tenth case, will be the focus of the next chapter.

40. Wassercug, "Korot Moshe Vaserzug ve-Nedivat Lev Aviv ha-Manoah R. Iserel"; Jakub Goldberg, "Eighteenth–Century Memoirs of Polish Jews. Memoirs of Mojżesz Wasercug from Great Poland," *Acta Poloniae Historica* 76 (1997), 28–9.

41. Eliyahu Eisenberg, ed., *Plozk: Toldot Kehillah Atikei Yamin be-Polin* (Tel Aviv: Menorah, 1967), 91–3; Ignacy Schiper, *Siedemset lat gminy żydowskiej w Płocku* (Lwów, 1938), 28–30. Schiper refers specifically to *Or Olam* (Frankfort on the Oder, 1777) and *Pri Tvu'ah* (Nowy Dwór, 1796). See also Shmuel Feiner, *The Jewish Enlightenment*, tr. Chaya Naor (Philadelphia: University of Pennsylvania Press, 2004), 37–8; 58–61; 349–51.

42. In *Bet Midot* (Szklów, 1785–86), Margaliot complains: "There are those disreputable *ba'alei shem* who wish to be thought of as men of God. They perform marvels before women and the light-headed through devious falsifications and lies. And as they falsify, they invoke the Royal seal (i.e., the name of God)." This is not, however, an attack against zaddikim. Compare Fishman, *Russia's First Modern Jews*, 120. See also Feiner, *The Jewish Enlightenment*, 284.

43. Mahler claimed that the Polish government's interest in Hasidism was not aroused until 1823. See *Hasidism and the Jewish Enlightenment*, 325.

44. *Polski Słownik Biograficzny* (Wrocław, Poland: Zakład Narodowy im. Ossolińskich, 1967), vol. 8:2, z. 57, pp. 157–8.

45. AGAD, CWW 1869, pp. 1–3.

46. AGAD, CWW 1869, p. 3.

47. Janusz Szczepański, *Dzieje społeczności żydowskiej powiatów Pułtusk i Maków Mazowecki* (Warsaw: Pułtuskie Towarzystwo Społeczno-Kulturalne, 1993), 27; Alek-

sander Kociszewski, *Mazowsze w epoce Napoleonskiej* (Czechanów, Poland: MOBN, 1985), 316; Stanley, "The Politics of the Jewish Question in the Duchy of Warsaw, 1807–1813." According to the latter, the date of the law was November 9, 1811.

48. AGAD, CWW 1869, p. 4.

49. Perhaps Senator Nowosilców.

50. AGAD, CWW 1869, p. 5. The initial might also read *K*; but it would not stand for Kobyliński.

51. AGAD, CWW 1869, p. 7.

52. AGAD, CWW 1869, p. 8.

53. AGAD, CWW 1869, p. 9.

54. AGAD, CWW 1869, p. 11.

55. AGAD, CWW 1869, p. 11. The Hasidic representatives are: Samuel Szaja, Szaie Michel, Nathan Cohn, Mendel Salomon, Meir David, Fiszel Moses, Moses Samuel, Ber Abraham, Aron Tabzidiwicz, and Izaak Abraham, "in the name of everyone." Wodziński speculates that the number of Hasidim in the town "could not have been much more than the ten signatories," a conclusion based, not very convincingly, on a similar document from Częstochowa. See *Oświecenie żydowskie w Królestwie Polskim wobec chasydyzmu*, III, no. 83.

56. Compare Kandel, "Komitet starozakonnych," 93.

57. AGAD, CWW 1869, p. 13. Mahler is mistaken in dating the attempt to ban Hasidic *minyanim* in Płock "in the spring of 1824." *Hasidism and the Jewish Enlightenment*, 395, no. 15. They occurred in the summer of 1818.

58. AGAD, CWW 1869, p. 14.

59. AGAD, CWW 1869, p. 16. Emphasis added.

60. No longer extant. The arguments of the Maskil are summarized for Zajączyk. AGAD, CWW 1869, p. 19.

61. AGAD, CWW 1869, p. 18.

62. Schiper, *Przyczynki do dziejow chasydyzmu w Polsce*, 115; Mahler, *Hasidism and the Jewish Enlightenment*, 198–200.

63. AGAD, PN 6, p. 484, protocol 274. Second version in AGAD, CWW 1869, p. 20. Both versions roughly identical.

64. AGAD, CWW 1869, p. 21.

65. AGAD, CWW 1723, pp. 3–5.

66. On the financial ties between the Hasidic patron Berek Sonnenberg-Bergson and Zajączek, see chapter 3. However, Wodziński accepts the constitutional rationalization at face value. See Marcin Wodziński, "Rząd Królestwa Polskiego Wobec Chasydyzmu: Początki 'Polityki Chasydzkiej' w Królestwie Polskim (1817–1818)," in *Żydzi I Judaizm we współczesnych badaniach Polskich*, vol. 3 (2004), 65–77.

67. AGAD, CWW 1869, pp. 22–4.

68. AGAD, CWW 1869, p. 25. David Kandel argues that Secretary General Sokołowski sought to "uproot superstition" in Płock, sending reports about miracle workers and their agents in the city. His efforts ended in 1823, when Hasidim were permitted to establish private prayer houses. This account does not seem to quite fit the documentary schema, however. See Kandel, "Komitet starozakonnych," 93–5.

69. AGAD, CWW 1444, pp. 11–8.

70. Russian Jewish communities were forced to accept "state rabbis" alongside their own "spiritual rabbis." See Chaeran Freeze, *Jewish Marriage and Divorce in Imperial Russia* (Hanover, N.H.: Brandeis University Press, 2002).

71. AGAD, CWW 1444, pp. 22–3.

72. AGAD, CWW 1444, p. 23.

73. Mahler argues that the government feared "the spread of liberal ideas . . . preferred Hasidism to Haskalah and correctly saw the Hasidic movement as a counterbalance to the activities of the Maskilim." *Hasidism and the Jewish Enlightenment,* 316.

74. In 1816, R. Israel Markus is listed as having been rabbi of Płock for twenty-five years (AGAD, CWW 1429). R. Kahana was succeeded, in 1832, by R. Aryeh Leib Zinz of Warsaw, a compromise appointee who was both a rationalistic Mitnagged and former teacher of the zaddik R. Isaac Meir Alter of Gur. Schiper, *Siedemset lat,* 34–5; Abraham Issachar Benjamin of Powienic, *Meir Eynei ha-Golah* (Tel Aviv: Alter-Bergman, 1954), 14.

75. Solomon Posner was one of several lessees of the oppressive kosher meat tax in 1818. He fought to preserve the authority to place tax evaders under ban of excommunication. In 1825, he was a member of the advisory chamber of the Jewish Committee. In 1840–50, he established two agricultural villages near Płock, where he settled 170 Jewish families. Mahler, *Hasidism and the Jewish Enlightenment,* 189–94; Schiper, *Przyczynki do dziejow chasydyzmu w Polsce,* 117; Bergman and Jagielski, *Zachowane synagogi i domy modlitwy w Polsce,* 105.

76. Deuteronomy 13:14, referring to those who tempt the Israelites to serve other gods.

77. Printed in *Meir Eynei ha-Golah,* 15.

78. See Eliyahu Eisenberg, *Plotsk: Toldot Kehillah Atikat Yamin be-Polin* (Tel Aviv: Menorah, 1967), 95.

79. Marcin Wodziński, "How Many *Hasidim,*" 32.

80. Michaelson, "Mare Kohen," 4.

81. Victor Turner observes four phases of social conflict, which he terms "social drama": (1) an initial breach, (2) an escalation of crisis, (3) redressive action, and (4) reintegration. See *Dramas, Fields, and Metaphors,* 37–42.

82. Wilensky, *Hasidim u-Mitnaggdim,* 1:230–1 and 1:239. Wilensky, however, incorrectly identifies Wodzisław as the Silesian town by the same name (1:239, no. 7). R. Avigdor was rabbi of Wodzisław (Yiddish: Lesli) before he replaced R. Levi Isaac in Pinsk, in 1786.

83. See Rabinowicz, *Bein Pshyskha,* 294–5.

84. APK, RGR I 4402, p. 5.

85. APK, RGR I 4402, p. 1.

86. APK, RGR I 4402, p. 2.

87. APK, RGR I 4402, p. 3.

88. APK, RGR I 4402, p. 3.

89. APK, RGR I 4402, pp. 4 and 7.

90. Ya'akov Hasdai, "The Origins of the Conflict between Hasidim and Mitnagdim," in Bezalel Safran, ed., *Hasidism: Continuity or Innovation?* (Cambridge, Mass.: Harvard University Press, 1988), 41. On separate prayer services by occupational guilds, see Rosman, *Founder of Hasidism,* 90–4. On old-style hasidic gatherings in Brody, see Reiner, "Hon, Ma'amad Hevrati," 287–328.

91. Urszula Dembińska did a great deal to encourage trade and industry, especially metal works. See Zenon Guldon, *Dzieje Przysuchy w XVIII wieku* (Przysucha, Poland: Muzeum im. Oskara Kolberga w Przysusze, 1995), 13.

92. Guldon, *Dzieje Przysuchy w XVIII wieku,* 7. The Jews played a significant role in the domestic and foreign trade.

93. Guldon, *Dzieje Przysuchy w XVIII wieku,* 12. The proportion of homeowners is high, considering that the total Jewish population was only 480 by 1790. See Mu-

szyńska, *Żydzi w miastach województwa sandomierskiego i lubelskiego w XVIII wieku*, 151 (table 5). On the Holy Jew, see Rabinowicz, *Bein Pshyskha*, 279–85; Elior, "Between Yesh and Ayin," 396–7.

94. See the letter printed in ben Raziel and ben Feiga Sarah, *Kedushat Yisrael, Pe'er Yisrael*, 8. On the dating of the letter, see chapter 1 here, number 161. The Maggid, who is referred to as "the youth" in the letter, would have been about twenty-five years old. According to the Potocka memoir cited later, the Maggid may have actually been a zaddik by that date; however, the account is somewhat garbled.

95. Printed in Kadish, *Si'ah Sarfei Kodesh*, 1:58. On the penetration of societies, or *havurot*, by early Ukrainian Hasidim, see Petrovsky, "Hasidism and the Traditional Jewish Societies in Nineteenth-Century Ukraine"; and Israel Halprin, "Havurot le-Torah ve-l'Mizvah ve-ha-T'nuah ha Hasidit be-Hithapshutah," in *Yehudim ve-Yahadut be-Mizrah Eiropa*.

96. AGAD, CWW 1871, p. 4. Published in full by Wodziński, " 'Sprawa chasydymów,' " 229. Only the response to the letter is published in Mahler, *Ha-Hasidut ve-ha-Haskalah*, app. 13a.

97. On R. Jacob Simon Deutch, see Abraham Issachar Benjamin of Powienic, *Meir Eynei ha-Golah*, 41.

98. AGAD, CWW 1871, p. 12–3.

99. According to Mahler, "Parczew did not occupy a prominent place in the history of Hasidism in Poland except in the period of the decline of the movement at the end of the nineteenth century, when the post of rabbi was held by grandchildren of *ha-Yehudi* of Przysucha." See *Hasidism and the Jewish Enlightenment*, 317. Mahler probably means the Holy Jew's great-grandson, R. Nathan David of Parczew (1868–1930).

100. James C. Scott, *Domination and the Arts of Resistance: Hidden Transcripts* (New Haven: Yale University Press, 1990), 122.

101. Report signed by Stanisław Grabowski, in AGAD, KRSW 6634; Mahler, *Ha-Hasidut ve-ha-Haskalah*, app. 13c, 476. See also decree from March 26, 1824, mentioned earlier.

102. AGAD, CWW 1871, 53. Decree from March 15, 1824. It was soon overturned, as described in the next chapter.

103. *Jewish Expositor and Friend of Israel* 10 (London, 1825), 28.

104. *Jewish Expositor and Friend of Israel* 10 (London, 1825), 29.

105. *Jewish Expositor and Friend of Israel* 10 (London, 1825), 29.

106. *Jewish Expositor and Friend of Israel* 10 (London, 1825), 29.

107. *Jewish Expositor and Friend of Israel* 10 (London, 1825), 30.

108. Kandel, "Komitet starozakonnych," 89–103.

109. Abraham Issachar Benjamin of Powienic, *Meir Eynei ha-Golah*, 39.

110. See appendix to Meir of Stopnicy, *Or Le-Shamayim* (Lublin, 1909).

111. APL, AML 2415, 1809–74, middle of folio. See also Robert Kuwałek, "Urzędowi rabini lubelkiego Okręgu Boznicznego 1821–1939," in Tadeusz Radzika, ed., *Żydzi w Lublinie* (Lublin: Uniwersytetu Marii Curie-Skłodowskiej, 1994), vol. 1 32. According to a decree from September 3, 1824, its members were exempt from fees.

112. The Seer of Lublin actually owned three-eighths of the house on 28 Szeroka street to which he attached his prayer house. Sąd Rejonowy w Lublinie, Wydział X Hipoteczny, Księga Hipoteczna Lublin, no. 264, available: http://kft.umcs.lublin.pl/stona.zydzi_lubelscy.html. Thanks to Robert Kuwałek for directing me to this source.

113. Kuwałek, "Społeczność Żydowska na Wieniawie," in Tadeusz Radzik, ed., *Żydzi w Lublinie* (Lublin: Wydawnictwo Uniwersytetu Marii Curie-Skłodowskiej, 1998), 2:175.

114. *Nifla'ot ha-Rabi*, 13:2. According to the tale, one of the Seer's followers was visited by an angelic maggid (messenger), who instructed him to inform the Seer that he must move to Wieniawa.

115. Alexander Tsederbaum, *Keter Kehunah* (Odessa, Russia, 1866), 124. See also Bałaban, *Żydowskie miasto w Lublinie*, 98. Bałaban's claim that the Seer arrived in Lublin accompanied one thousand followers seems quite exaggerated.

116. Rabinowicz, *Bein Pshyskha*, 110; Sholmo Barukh Nissenbaum, *Lekorot ha-Yehudim be-Lublin* (Lublin, 1900), 95.

117. Walden, *Nifla'ot ha-Rabi*, 86:283.

118. The decree was read in the Great Synagogue of Lublin, and recorded in the Great Synagogue's *pinkas* (as well as the *pinkas* of R. Zvi Hirsch b. Moses Doktor's synagogue). It is cited in Nissenbaum, *Lekorot ha-Yehudim be-Lublin*, 91–4.

119. R. Meir Margaliot, a disciple of the Besht.

120. *Nifla'ot ha-Rabi*, 42–3:77.

121. It is signed: Meir son of Mordecai, Zalman son of M. Zvi Hirsch, ___, Yizhak Isaac Hacohen, Tsvi Hirsch, Yekutiel Zalman son of Moses, Eliezer, Isaac Isaiah son of A. Zalman of Lublin. Note the absence of rabbinic honorifics.

122. 19 Av, 1803. *Besurot Tovot* (Lublin, 1927), letters nos. 2 and 9.

123. Rosman, "The Indebtedness of the Lublin Kahal in the Eighteenth Century," 166–83.

124. D. Miller, *Besurot Tovot* (Lublin, 1927) letter no. 10. The letter, signed by his widow and three sons, specifies the distribution of the Seer's estate, which included forty Torah scrolls. On the controversy surrounding the death of the Seer, see David Assaf, "One Event, Two Interpretations: The Fall of the Seer of Lublin in Hasidic Memory and Maskilic Satire" (in Hebrew), in Etkes et al., *Within Hasidic Circles*, 161–208.

125. In 1819, R. Joshua Hirschel Tarnopoler served as rabbi, followed by R. Meshullam Zalman Ashkenazy in 1829, neither of whom was Hasidic. Kuwałek, *Urzędowi rabini*, 32–3.

126. APL, AML 2419, p. 34.

127. Mahler, *Hasidism and the Jewish Enlightenment*, 325; APL, AML 2419, p. 56.

128. APL, AML 2419, p. 57.

129. APL, AML 2419, pp. 58–9. A copy of the report is scrawled on page 60, a copy of Viceroy Zajączek's general decree from August 30 following the statewide investigation of Hasidism. AGAD, CWW 1871, p. 231.

130. Casimir Stryienski, ed., *Memoirs of the Countess Potocka*, tr. Lionel Strachey (New York: Doubleday, 1900), 21–2. The astrologer tells the fortunes of Poniatowski's children, saluting an infant—Stanisław August—as the future king of Poland. This is not, however, possible—the Maggid of Kozienice (b. 1733 or 1737) was not even born or was a toddler when the future king of Poland (b. 1732) was an infant! Moreover, Poniatowski only become castellan of Cracow in 1752, when the future king was already twenty years old. Perhaps the narrator meant a different Poniatowski or Castellan?

131. The dates of birth ascribed to the Maggid are 1733 and 1737. This account seems to render the former more likely.

132. Muszyńska, *Żydzi w miastach*, 35.

133. *Dziennik Handlowy*, 1791, 1:162, 165–9, in Jacob Goldberg, *Jewish Privileges in the Polish Commonwealth*, vol. 2 (Jerusalem: Israel Academy of Sciences and Humanities), 95.

134. According to a Jewish petition from August 21, 1767, in APR, WAP, Zarząd

Dóbr Państwowich w Radomiu, 7, s. 144, the fire destroyed only fifteen Jewish homes, but also thirty-nine Jewish shops.

135. Muszyńska, *Żydzi w miastach*, 161 (table 12). Other population figures are 1,042 out of a total of 2,220 inhabitants by 1790, Muszyńska, *Żydzi w miastach*, 40; Guldon, "Gminy wyznania mojżeszowego w powiecie radomskim w 16–18 wieku," 158.

136. Ben Raziel and ben Feiga Sarah, *Kedushat Yisrael, Pe'er Yisrael*, 22. The year of the fire is given as 1778, an error repeated in Rabinowicz, *Bein Pshyskha*, 169. The fire of 1782 left one-third of the town's population homeless. See Muszyńska, *Żydzi w miastach*, 38.

137. Dariusz Wojciechowski, "Inwentarz Kozienic z 1784 roku," *Kieleckie Studia Historyczne* 13 (1995), 227. Registered as Izrael Sabsowicz (i.e., Israel, son of Shabbetai). The house is *niewjezdne*, meaning one of twenty-two houses that did not serve as guesthouses.

138. According to a letter written from R. Isaac, the *av bet din* of Cracow, to his son, *av bet din* of Tykocin. Rubinstein surmises that the letter was sent while R. Isaac was still in Chełma, for he did not become *av bet din* of Cracow until 1776. See "He'arot le-Te'udah al Gviyot-Edut Neged ha-Hasidut," *Tarbiz* 32 (1963), 96–7.

139. On the specific denunciation against inserting the *Keter* prayer, see R. Abraham Katzenellenbogen's letter to R. Levi Isaac from 1784, in Wilensky, *Hasidim u-Mitnaggdim*, 1:128, and commentary. During the *mussaf* service, the Hasidim replace the phrase "We worship and consecrate you" (*na'arizekha ve-nakdishekha*) with "A crown shall they give to you" (*keter yitenu lekha*), perhaps following the Sephardic liturgy. See also Rubinstein, "He'arot," 85; and Dubnow, *Toldot ha-Hasidut*, 131 and 156.

140. *Shever Posh'im*, 51a, in Wilensky, *Hasidim u-Mitnaggdim*, 2:138. According to tradition, the Żelechów fire occurred after R. Levi Isaac was expelled from the town, in 1775 (see *Tiferet Bet Levi*, 6; and Rubinstein, "He'arot," 94, for dating). This troubles Wilensky, *Hasidim u-Mitnaggdim*, 1:79, who seems to place too much stock in the tradition. Yiddish portions of the testimony are rendered in collaboration with Stephen Simons.

141. Rubinstein calculates that the Ashkenazic alternative to *keter* would have been *na'arizekha*. See "He'arot," 86.

142. A commentary to the legal codification *Shulhan Arukh*, "Yoreh Deah."

143. For a similar incident involving the Besht, see Rubinstein, *Shivhei Ha-Besht*, 215–6.

144. *Shever Posh'im*, 51a, in Wilensky, *Hasidim u-Mitnaggdim*, 2:139; and Rubinstein, "He'arot," 86–7. As Rubinstein points out, the decision protected the kosher slaughterer, whose livelihood would have been hurt by a nonkosher ruling. On slaughtering a non-Jew's animal, see Joseph Karo, *Shulhan Arukh*, "Yoreh Deah," 1, chap. 17, *Siftei Kohen*, no. 8. (Vilna, 1911).

145. The Maggid is also accused of using esoteric means to determine the ritual purity of his wife. *Shever Posh'im*, 53b, Wilensky, *Hasidim u-Mitnaggdim*, 2:141; and Rubinstein, "He'arot," 86–7.

146. See Shmeruk, "Hasidism and the *Kehilla*," 186–95.

147. Wilensky, *Hasidim u-Mitnaggdim*, 2:139.

148. Wilensky, *Hasidim u-Mitnaggdim*, 2:139.

149. On the Hasidic policy of restraint following the first bans, see Immanuel Etkes, *The Gaon of Vilna: the Man and His Image*, tr. Jeffrey M. Green (Berkeley: University of California Press), chap. 4; "The Gaon of Vilna and the Mitnagdim in the Eyes of the Hasidim," in Lempertas, ed., *The Gaon of Vilnius and the Annals of Jewish*

Culture, 81–7. The first bans occurred in 1772, in response to the establishment of a Hasidic prayer house in Vilna.

150. Hundert, *Jews in Poland-Lithuania in the Eighteenth Century*, 99–118. For a case during the rise of Hasidism, see Rosman, *Founder of Hasidism*, 93.

151. Muszyńska, *Żydzi w miastach*, 46–8; Guldon, "Gminy wyznania mojżesowego," 157.

152. Muszynska, *Żydzi w miàstach*, 46–8.

153. Muszynska, *Żydzi w miàstach*, 46–8.

154. AGAD, CWW 1429, p. 339. R. Solomon is also noted there as having been rabbi of Kozienice for forty-six years, i.e., since 1770. But we know that the post was to be left to him upon his father's death, after 1792. Moreover, in that agreement R. Solomon is described as Rabbi of Tarłów.

155. It was completed in 1794. See Guldon, "Gminy wyznania mojżeszowego," 158.

156. David of Maków, *Zemir Arizim*, 15a, in Wilensky, *Hasidim u-Mitnagdim*, 2: 213.

157. According to a version among the Polish peasantry, a citizen was robbed of money on the way to Warsaw. The Maggid ordered him to wait for three days, consulted his holy books, and found that the thief was among his guests. He asked the citizen to forgive 40 ducats, and the money was returned to him. According to another peasant tale, the Maggid consulted his holy books and discovered the whereabouts of stolen horses, an act of revenge against a thief who had cursed the Jews. See Józef Gluziński, *Włoscianie Polscy*, in *Archiwum domowe do dziejów i literatury-z rękopismów i dzieł najrzadszych* (Warsaw, 1856), 537.

158. Dembowski, *Moje wspomnienia*, 53–4.

159. Dembowski, *Moje wspomnienia*, 55. In 1778–80, a traveler named Johann Phillippe de Carosi recalls being assaulted by crowds of Jewish children in Kozienice. He dispersed them by pretending to be crazy and potentially dangerous. Nahum Gelber, "Oyslenishe Rayunde Vegen Poylishe Yidn Inem 18-Yahrhundert," 241.

160. Gelber, "Oyslenishe Rayunde Vegen Poylishe Yidn Inem 18-Yahrhundert," 241.

161. Gelber, "Oyslenishe Rayunde Vegen Poylishe Yidn Inem 18-Yahrhundert," 241.

162. Paweł Hertz calculates that Czartoryski's visit to Kozienice occurred from 1786 to 1787; however, Dembowski was not even born at that time. It is more likely that the visit occurred after the war of 1812 because Dembowski, loyal to Napoleon, only agreed to reenter Czartoryski's service after Bonaparte's demise. This would place the event slightly before R. Israel's death in 1814, when Dembowski was twenty-five years old. See "Rabbi Izrael z Kozienic i książę Adam Czartoryski," *W Drodze* 9: 133 (1984), 3–7. According to Hasidic tradition, the prince visited the Maggid to obtain a blessing in order that his wife might conceive, which occurred soon after. Prince Czartoryski's skeptical brother, however, mentioned his healthy son before the Maggid in jest, telling him that he was actually ill. The Maggid instructed him to run home, because his son was on the brink of death. Indeed, the skeptic found his son dead upon his return. David Ben Raziel and Israel ben Feiga Sarah, *Kedushat Yisrael, Pe'er Yisrael*, 21.

163. Abraham Issachar Benjamin of Powienic, *Meir Eynei ha-Golah*, 23. But the most prominent disciples, such as R. Isaac Meir Alter, future zaddik of Gur, soon transferred their allegiance to the zaddik Simha Bunem of Pryzsucha. See 25–9.

164. Mahler, *Ha-Hasidut ve-ha-Haskalah*, app. 13g, p. 486.

165. W. F. Becker, in *Jewish Expositor and Friend of Israel* 11 (1826), 229.

166. The case is summarized by Salezy Majmon "Luńe Kartki," *Izraelita* 40 (Warsaw, 1894), 329, but is marred by errors, omissions, and embellishments. I cite directly from APK, RGR I 4399.

167. On the Olkusz pact of 1680 (confirmed by King Sobieski in 1682), allowing Jews to export lead, see Hundert, "On the Jewish Community in Poland During the Seventeenth Century: Some Comparative Perspectives," *Revue des Etudes Juives* 142 (1983), 360.

168. Majer Bałaban, *Studja Historyczne* (Warsaw, 1927), 151–61.

169. A girl found lying in the forest that year claimed to have been attacked by a Jew with a knife. Although the surgeon could find nothing wrong with the girl, a Jewish tailor named Mortko was accused of attempted murder and was initially sentenced to death.

170. Bałaban, *Studja Historyczne*, 162–5, and "Die Poln. Juden in den Memoiren des Poln. Adels," in *Menorah Wien* 6:1 (1928), 32–38; Zenon Guldon and Jacek Wijaczka, "The Accusation of Ritual Murder in Poland, 1500–1800," *Polin* 10 (1997), 138–9.

171. Stanisław Wodzicki, *Wspomnienia z przeszłośći od r.1768 do r.1840* (Cracow, 1873), 204. Marcin Wodziński speculates that as Wodzicki's memoir was composed in 1840, he was likely confusing the event with the Damascus Affair of that year. See Wodziński, *Oświecienie żydowskie w Królestwie Polskim wobec chasydyzmu*, 150–1.

172. APK, RGR I 4399, p. 1.

173. APK, RGR I 4399, p. 2.

174. APK, RGR I 4399, p. 3–4.

175. APK, RGR I 4399, p. 12.

176. APK, RGR I 4399, pp. 14–5.

177. APK, RGR I 4399, pp. 16–21. The original forms of "Hasidim"—"Hussyty" or "Hassyty," and "Hussytów" or "Hassytów"—reflect spelling variants and Polish noun declensions.

178. *Sfarad* liturgy, a combination of the *Sephardic* and *Ashkenazic* (see n. 1).

179. *Ashkenazic* liturgy.

180. AGAD, CWW 1429, p. 167. The name appears as "Izyia Lande," either a relative of Joshua or Joshua himself. The rendering of Jewish names by the local officials was often not very precise.

181. This is confirmed in the official register of town rabbis from 1816, which lists the Olkusz rabbi as "Samuel Unger, born in Pilica, 54 years old, rabbi since three years ago, elected by the kahal Elders and community. But four months ago he left his office and returned to Pilica. The kahal has the responsibility to hold elections, without which there can be no succession." AGAD, CWW 1429.

182. There is an illegible portion of the document referring to an alleged decree by the Habsburg emperor. According to Mahler (*Hasidism and the Jewish Enlightenment*, 70–1), the Austrian government merely designated the Hasidim as "Freemasons" in 1814. In 1816, the new president of the court police commission accused the Hasidim of "strange, imaginary offenses" and deemed them "enemies of 'education.' " He asked the Galician governor's office to keep a close watch on the sect and "if possible to suppress it altogether"; but no further measures appear to have been taken.

183. APK, RGR I 4399, pp. 16–21.

184. AGAD, CWW 1429, p. 165; APK, RGR I 4402, pp. 8–14 and 30–2. But see later.

185. APK, RGR I 4399, p. 23.

186. Salezy, "Luźne Kartki," claims the authorities resolved that the Hasidim were "harmless." This does not, however, appear in the archival file, and is probably the author's conjecture.

187. Muszyńska, *Żydzi w miastach*, 150 (table 5). Tradition holds that he was born in Stopnica (see Rabinowicz, *Bein Pshyskha*, 370). However, the rabbinical register in AGAD, CWW 1429, lists R. Meir as "a native of Pacanów," slightly southeast of Stopnica.

188. Abraham Issachar Benjamin of Powienic, *Meir Eynei ha-Golah*, 25–7.

189. Abraham Issachar Benjamin of Powienic, *Meir Eynei ha-Golah*, 27.

190. Zvi Halevi Ish Horowitz, *Le-toldot ha-Kehillot be-Polin* (Jerusalem: Mosad Harav, 1978), 89. R. Abraham Joshua Heschel eventually settled in Międzybóż.

191. AGAD, CWW 1429, p. 165.

192. APK, RGR I 4402, p. 9.

193. APK, RGR I 4402, p. 10.

194. APK, RGR I 4402, pp. 12–4.

195. APK, RGR I 4402, pp. 8, 11, 30–2.

196. On the Landaus' domination of Opatów, see Hundert, *The Jews of a Polish Private Town*, esp. 118–9. On their renown as Mitnaggdim, see Abraham Issachar Benjamin of Powienic, *Meir Eynei ha-Golah*, 28–9: "And several days before the wedding, the aforementioned Rabbi Jacob Landau came to the city of Warsaw, and with him came several famous scholars from his family and friends, and all of them were great Mitnaggdim to the way of Hasidism." The zaddik Abraham Rafael Landau of Ciechanów actually adopted Landau—his wife's surname—as his own.

197. Hundert, "Apta ve-Reshit ha-Hasidut," 62; Abraham Yaairi, "Ner Tamid Societies in Poland and Lithuania," *Jewish Social Studies* 21:2 (1959), 118–31. An earlier work that mentions Hasidic leaders from Opatów is H. Horowitz, "Die judische gemeinde Opatow," in *Monatsschrift fur Geschichte und Wissenschaft des Judentums 38,* (1930), 110–23.

198. Jacob Emden, *Sefer Hitav'kut* (Altona, 1762; Lemberg, 1877), 80b, cited in Dubnow, "The Maggid of Miedzyrzecz," 76. See also Hundert, *The Jews of a Polish Private Town*, 127; and a discussion of Emden's position in Friedlander, "The Struggle of the Mitnagedim and Maskilim against Hasidism," 105–9. Friedlander doubts that Emden's position was directed toward the new Hasidism, analyzing passages in Emden's *Mitpakhat Sefarim* (1768). But Emden's explicit mention of R. Nahman would seem to indicate that he was referring to the new Hasidism.

199. Horowitz, *Le-toldot ha-Kehillot be-Polin*, 81. The death of the founder of the *bet midrash* led to a protracted legal discussion over whether the building could be used for secular purposes.

200. Hundert, "Apta ve-Reshit ha-Hasidut Ad 1800," in Elior, Bartal, and Shmeruk, *Zaddikim ve-Anshe Ma'aseh*, 62; Rabinowicz, *Bein Pshyskha*, 272.

201. The rabbinical agreement (*konsens*) is located in AGAD, Archiwum Gospodarcze Wilanowe, Administracja Dóbr Opatówskich, I/77, p. 19: "Now we find this Rabbi to be a renowned scholar in all training which is fitting for him to be Rabbi in Opatów, of the name Leybusz, descended from a great Family." See also Hundert, "Apta ve-Reshit ha-Hasidut Ad 1800," 62.

202. The rabbinical contract is printed in full in *Kovez Siftei Zaddikim* 4 (1992), 54–8. On Aaron of Opatów, see Hundert, "Apta ve-Reshit ha-Hasidut Ad 1800," 62.

203. AGAD, CWW 1871 (previously 1881), pp. 114–7; Wodziński, " 'Sprawa chasydymów,' " 233–4.

204. AGAD, CWW 1871, pp. 114–7; Wodziński, " 'Sprawa chasydymów,' " 233–4.

205. AGAD, CWW 1871, pp. 119–21; Wodziński, " 'Sprawa chasydymów,' " 234–5.

206. October 23, 1824. AGAD, CWW 1871, pp. 216–7; Wodziński, " 'Sprawa chasydymów,' " 242. Emphasis added. Mahler's claim that there was a "dramatic reversal in attitude toward the Hasidic movement" is not, however, borne out. See *Hasidism and the Jewish Enlightenment*, 329.

207. November 30, 1824, December 23, 1824, January 20, 1825. Mahler, *Ha-Hasidut ve-ha-Haskalah*, app. 15a–15d, 492–5. Errors in Mahler's transcription: 15b, line 2 of the body should read *Szkoły* (not *Sekty*); 15b, line 9 of the body should read *a* (not *że*); 15d, line 6 of the body should read *w zgromadzania się* (not *w zgrowadzaniu się*). Compare AGAD, KRSW 6635, pp. 10 and 15.

208. AGAD, KRSW 6635, pp. 18–22; Mahler, *Ha-Hasidut ve-ha-Haskalah*, app. 15f, 498–501. While the records only note "Pan Bergson," it was Jacob Bergson who acted as R. Meir's translator during the 1824 interrogation. See Wodziński, " 'Sprawa chasydymów,' " 237–8.

209. February 20, 1825. AGAD, KRSW 6635, pp. 16–7; Mahler, *Ha-Hasidut ve-ha-Haskalah*, app. 15e, pp. 495–7. Error in Mahler's rendition: first query (p. 496) should read *swoj* (not *skutek*) on line 14; *przyieżdzaiących* (not *przyeżdzaiących*) on line 18.

210. AGAD, KRSW 6635, p. 17; Mahler, *Ha-Hasidut ve-ha-Haskalah*, app. 15e, p. 497.

211. Mahler, *Hasidism and the Jewish Enlightenment*, 329.

212. AGAD, KRSW 6635, p. 23; Mahler, *Ha-Hasidut ve-ha-Haskalah*, app. 15g, p. 501.

213. This edition contained only portions of the work that has come down to us today as *Kedushat Levi Ha-Shalem*.

214. Wolf Jasni, ed., *Yizkor Bukh fun der Zelekhover Yiddische Kehille* (Chicago, 1953), 22; Dresner, *The World of a Hasidic Master*, 26–7.

215. In a letter to the Maggid of Kozienice, which has been dated between 1802 and 1807, the zaddik Asher of Stolin recalls: "when I was in the community of Żelechów, I had several mishaps, and with God's help I steered a middle course." The quarrel probably occurred when R. Asher took the side of R. Barukh of Międzyboż during the latter's conflict with R. Levi Isaac and R. Scheur Zalman of Liady. See R. Asher of Stolin's letter to the Maggid of Kozienice, printed in David Zvi Heilman, ed., *Iggerot Ba'al ha-Tanya* (Jerusalem, 1953), 184; W. Z. Rabinowitch, *Lithuanian Hasidism* (New York: Schocken Books, 1971), 49, 68, 71.

216. Alexander Sender of Komarno, *Zot Ha-Berakha* (Jerusalem, 1999), 23.

217. Alexander Sender of Komarno, *Zot Ha-Berakha*, 23–4. Perhaps this refers to R. Levi Isaac's famous rebuke of Poland's heavenly representative on Yom Kippur, according to the tradition mentioned in chapter 1.

218. Alexander Sender of Komarno, *Zot Ha-Berakha*, 24.

219. *Shever Posh'im*, 52b, in Wilensky, *Hasidim u-Mitnaggdim*, 2:140.

220. See *Hasidim u-Mitnaggdim*, 2:81; Rubenstein, "He'arot," 95. Rubinstein dates the testimony as 1773.

221. The Jewish population in Żelechów amounted to 1,464 in 1765, when R. Levi Isaac began his tenure. By 1790, that number had dropped to 1,165. See Muszyńska, *Żydzi w miastach*, 151 (table 5).

222. *Shever Posh'im*, 51a, in Wilensky, *Hasidim u-Mitnaggdim*, 2:138.

223. Wilensky, *Hasidim u-Mitnaggdim*, 1:79, 2:138. *Tiferet Bet Levi*, 6; and Rubinstein, "He'arot," 94.

224. Eleazer ben Elimeleh of Leżajsk, *Iggeret ha-Kodesh*, in appendix to *No'am*

Elimelekh. Based on translation by Louis Jacobs in *The Jewish Mystics* (New York: Schocken Books, 1990), 197–200.

225. Perhaps he is the Bigdor (Avigdor) Szlamowicz registered as a homeowner in Żelechów in 1789. See Muszyńska, *Żydzi w miastach*, 162 (table 13).

226. Abraham Zusman, *Barukh mi-Banim* (Vilna, 1869), 97–8.

227. Abraham Issachar Benjamin of Powienic, *Meir Eynei ha-Golah*, 41–7; Walden, *Nifla'ot ha-Rabi*, 37:66.

228. Zusman, *Barukh mi-Banim*, 97–8.

229. On that faulty designation, see Hundert, "The Contexts of Hasidism," 177 and 182.

230. Muszyńska, *Żydzi w miastach*, 168 (table 17).

231. Zusman, *Barukh mi-Banim*, 98.

232. AGAD, CWW 1871, pp. 12–3.

233. "Jabłonowski Maciej," quoted in Władysław Rostocki, "Rodowód i pozycja społeczna urzędników administracji państwowej i miejskiej w Warszawie (1807–1830)," in Ryszard Kołodziejczyk, Jan Kosim, and Janina Leskiewiczowa, eds., *Warszawa XIX wieku*, vol. 3 (Warsaw, 1974), 123.

234. Rodowód i pozycja Spoteczma, 124.

235. Rodowód i pozycja Spoteczma, 126.

236. AGAD, CWW 186, pp. 5–7.

237. On the conflicting policies of the Russian government and church with respect to demon possession (*klikushestvo*), see Christine Worobec, *Possessed: Women, Witches, and Demons in Imperial Russia* (DeKalb: Northern Illinois University, 2001), 20–63.

238. AGAD, CWW 186, p. 28.

239. AGAD, CWW 186, pp. 29–30.

240. AGAD, CWW 186, pp. 31–2.

241. AGAD, CWW 186, pp. 33–4.

242. Decree from November 10, 1910. AGAD, CWW 186, pp. 37–8.

CHAPTER 3

1. Dubnow, *Toldot ha-Hasidut*, 8–9 and 36, and *History of the Jews in Russia and Poland*, 220–34. See also Rabinowitch, *Lithuanian Hasidism*, 1–6. An embryonic form of the view appears in Graetz, *History of the Jews*, 5:383 and 392. On the allegedly humble origins of zaddikim, see Isaac Levitats, *The Jewish Community in Russia: 1772–1844* (New York: Columbia University Press, 1970), 162; Mahler, *Hasidism and the Jewish Enlightenment*, 7–10 and 272; Dinur, "The Origins of Hasidism and Its Social and Messianic Foundations," 86–208; Buber, *The Origin and Meaning of Hasidism*, 58 and 61; Harry Rabinowicz, *The World of Hasidism* (London: Vallentine, Mitchell, 1970), 183; Weiss, "Some Notes on the Social Background of Early Hasidism," 12–4.

2. Eisenbach, *Emancipation of the Jews in Poland*, esp. 207–72. See also N. M. Gelber, "Korot ha-Yehudim be-Polin mi-Reshit Halukatah ve-ad milhemet ha-Olam ha-Shniyah," in Israel Halperin, ed., *Bet Yisrael be-Polin* (Jerusalem, 1928), 1:112; Bina Garntsarska-Kadry, "Ha-yehudim ve-ha-Goramim le-Hitpathuta u-Mekoma shel ha-Ta'assiyah be-Varsha," *Gal-Ed* 2 (1975) 125–58, and "Ha-yehudim be-Hitpathuta ha-Kalkalit shel Polin," in Bartal and Gutman, *Kiyum ve-Shever*, vol. 1, esp. 335–6; Guterman, "The Origins of the Great Synagogue in Warsaw on Tłomackike Street," 181–211; Todd Endelman, "Jewish Converts in Nineteenth-Century Warsaw: A Quanti-

tative Analysis," *Jewish Social Studies* 4:1 (1997); and Mahler, *Hasidism and the Jewish Enlightenment*, 205–9.

3. Certain historians acknowledge wealthy Jewish entrepreneurs in the Hasidic movement, but fail to grasp the implication. See Aescoly, *Ha-Hasidut be-Polin*; Mahler, *Hasidism and the Jewish Enlightenment*; and Rabinowicz, *Bein Pshyskha*.

4. Schiper, *Przyczynki do dziejów chasydyzmu w Polsce*. See also Elior, Bartal, and Shmeruk, *Zaddikim ve-Anshe Ma'aseh*, 23–58; or Shmeruk's summary in "Yizhak Schiper's Study of Hasidism in Poland," in Rapoport-Albert, *Hasidism Reappraised*, 404–14.

5. Roman officials who protected the plebeian citizen from arbitrary action by the patrician magistrates.

6. Schiper, *Przyczynki do dziejów chasydyzmu w Polsce*, 68. Schiper was indebted to several articles in the journal *Kwartalnik poświęcony badaniom przeszłości Żydów* (1912), particularly those by David Kandel (cited later). See also Schiper, *Żydzi Królestwa Polskiego*, 21–45.

7. Dubnow shared this view of Hasidism with S. A. Horodetzky. See Deutsch, *The Maiden of Ludmir*, 23–33.

8. Rosman, *Founder of Hasidism*, 159–70.

9. Studies that accord with the Schiper conception include Rosman, *Founder of Hasidism*; Rubinstein, "Hasidut ve-Hasidim be-Varshe," *Sinai* 65 (1974), 61–84; Rabinowicz, *Bein Pshyskha*; Aescoly, *Ha-Hasidut be-Polin*, 75; Gershon Hundert, "Apta ve-Reshit he-Hasidut ad 1800," in Elior, Bartal, and Shmeruk, *Zaddikim ve-Anshe Ma'aseh*, 59–64; Shmuel Ettinger, "The Hasidic Movement—Reality and Ideals," in Hundert, *Essential Papers on Hasidism*, 226–43; Hasdai, "The Origins of the conflict between Hasidim and Mitnagdim," 27–46; and Rapoport-Albert, "Hasidism after 1772," 76–140.

10. The general Jewish opposition to integration, and Jewish requests for residence rights during the four-year Sejm, are noted by Hundert in *Jews in Poland-Lithuania*, 210 and 222. For a focus on the vanguard of integrationists, see Eisenbach, *Emancipation of the Jews in Poland*.

11. On Berlin's patrons of Haskalah, see Steven M. Lowenstein, *The Berlin Jewish Community: Enlightenment, Family, and Crisis, 1770–1830* (New York: Oxford University Press, 1994), 39. Occasionally, Western-oriented patricians were persuaded to support Hasidic initiatives. According to Hasidic tradition, Jacob Epstein helped avert an "evil decree" against an unspecified religious custom. See Moses Menahem Walden, *Ohel Yizhak* ([Jerusalem?], 1968), 53–4, no. 128.

12. Ireneusz Ihnatowicz, "Przemysł, Handel, Finanse," in Stefan Kieniewicz, ed., *Polska XIX Wieku: Państwo, Społeczeństwo, Kultura* (Warsaw: Wiedza Powszechna, 1977), 56–92; Jan Kosim, *Losy pewnej fortuny: Z dziejów burżuazji Warszawskiej w latach 1807–1830* (Wrocław: Zakład Narodowy im. Ossolińskich, 1972), 16 and 54.

13. Maria Bogucka, "Social Structures and Custom in Early Modern Poland," *Acta Poloniae Historica* 68 (1993), 100–101.

14. Jerzy Jedlicki, "Social Ideas and Economic Attitudes of Polish Eighteenth Century Nobility: Their Approach to Industrial Policy," *Fifth International Congress of Economic History* (Leningrad, 1970) 1:89–103; Witold Kula, *An Economic Theory of the Feudal System: Towards a Model of the Polish Economy, 1500–1800*, tr. Lawrence Garner (London: NLB, 1976), esp. 129–30 and chap. 7; Maria Bogucka, *The Lost World of the "Sarmatians"* (Warsaw: Polish Academy of Sciences, 1996). On nobles' attitudes toward industrialization, see Jedlicki, *A Suburb of Europe*.

15. Bogucka, "Social Structures and Custom," 112–3; *The Lost World*, 32.

16. Jedlicki, "Social Ideas and Economic Attitudes of Polish Eighteenth Century Nobility"; Bogucka, "Social Structures and Custom," 102; Jerzy Łukowski, *Liberty's Folly: the Polish Lithuanian Commonwealth in the Eighteenth Century* (London: Routledge, 1991), 67.

17. This may have been true of Jews in most modernizing societies. See David Hollinger, "Rich, Powerful and Smart: Jewish Overrepresentation Should Be Explained Rather Than Avoided or Mystified," *Jewish Quarterly Review* 94:4 (2004), 598.

18. Moshe Rosman, "Polish Jews in the Gdańsk Trade in the Late Seventeenth and Early Eighteenth Centuries," in Isadore Twersky, ed., *Danzig, between East and West* (Cambridge, Mass.: Harvard University Press, 1985), 111–20; Janina Bieniarzówna, "The Role of Jews in Polish Foreign Trade, 1648–1764), in Andzej Paluch, ed., *The Jews in Poland* (Cracow: Jagiellonian University Press, 1992), 1:101–9.

19. Ignacy Schiper, *Dzieje handlu Żydowskiego na ziemiach Polskich* (Warsaw, 1937; reprint, Cracow: Krajowa Agencja Wydawnicza, 1990), 291.

20. It has been calculated that well over one-third of the Jews who were engaged in trade were army purveyors by the early nineteenth century. Artur Eisenbach, "Jews in Warsaw at the End of the Eighteenth Century," in Bartoszewski and Polonsky, *Jews in Warsaw*, 95–126. See also Emanuel Ringelblum, *Żydzi w powstaniu Kościuszkowskiem* (Warsaw, 1938), 83–7.

21. For an overview of the phenomenon, see Garntsarska-Kadry, "Ha-yehudim ve-ha-Goramim."

22. See Gershon Hundert, "Jews, Money and Society in the Seventeenth-Century Polish Commonwealth: The Case of Kraków," *Jewish Social Studies* 43 (1981), 261–74.

23. On the nature of Jewish international trade a century earlier, see Rosman, "Polish Jews in the Gdańsk Trade," 111–20.

24. On the collapse of the grain market in the 1820s and the temporary ruin of Polish noblemen, see R. F. Leslie, *Polish Politics and the Revolution of November 1830* (London: University of London, 1956), 85.

25. Stanislaw Staszic (1755–1826): "Jews" (1790), in Siegel, *Stranger in Our Midst*, 38–42; Ostrowski, "Uwagi nad obyczaimi uspobieniem i charakterem żydów Polskich," 87–8.

26. Silesia, another area of substantial industrial development, was associated with the Germanies in this period.

27. Harro Harring, *Poland under the Dominion of Russia* (Boston, 1834), 113.

28. Harring, *Poland under the Dominion of Russia*, 113.

29. Nahman of Bratslav, "Hakham ve-Tam," in *Sippurei u-Ma'asiyot* (Ostróg, 1815; reprint, Jerusalem, 1991), 132, and "Sihot ha-Ran," in *Shivhei ha-Ran* (Lemberg, 1901), no. 28, p. 27.

30. Johnston, *Travels through Part of the Russian Empire and the Country of Poland*, 381–2. Franciscan Street reminded Harro Harring of the busy Jewish districts in Frankfort, Prague, Rome, Amsterdam, and Leghorn. Its Jews were "characterized by the same peculiarities, viz. uncleanliness, and the love of finery, avarice, and dishonesty; while the persecutions and insults to which they are exposed render them real objects of pity." Harring, *Poland under the Dominion of Russia*, 125.

31. A. N. Frenk, "Le-toldot ha-Yehudim be-Nesikhut Varshe," *Ha-Tekufah* 4 (1927), 471–80. Frenk's account includes a letter from Berek Sonenberg-Bergson requesting exemption from the ticket payments for his agent.

32. An allegation about Jewish "arrogance" and "conquest of all trade, crafts, and

distilleries" in Warsaw appears in Władysław Smoleński, *Mieszczaństwo warszawskie w końcu wieku 18* (Warsaw, 1976), 295–6.

33. Eisenbach, "Jews in Warsaw," 113.

34. The Warsaw *jurydyki* amounted to 28 when they were abolished in 1791. See Peter Martyn, "The Undefined Town within a Town," *Polin* 3 (1988), 26.

35. Eisenbach, "Jews in Warsaw"; Alexander Kraushar, *Kupiectwo Warszawskie* (Warsaw, 1929), 24. According to Harring in 1830, "[t]here are said to be ten thousand Jews in Warsaw; but their number may really be estimated much higher; for though some of them, by way of speculation, pretend to be converted to Chrisitianity, they secretly adhere to the Hebrew faith." The last may be a reference to either Frankists or assimilated Jews. See *Poland under the Dominion of Russia*, 124. On Jewish urbanization, see N. William Wraxall, *Memoirs of the Courts of Berlin, Dresden, Warsaw and Vienna, in the Years 1777, 1778, and 1779* (London, 1806), 2:9.

36. Eisenbach, "Mobilność terytorialna ludności żydowskiej," 179–218.

37. Mendel Lefin, *Essai d'un plan de Reforme ayant pour objet d'eclairer la nation juive en Pologne et de redresser par la ses moeurs* (Warsaw, 1791), 22–4, no. 5 and no. 6. Compare Nancy Sinkow, "Tradition and Transition: Mendel Lefin of Satanow and the Beginnings of the Jewish Enlightenment in Eastern Europe" (Ph.D. diss., Columbia University, 1996), 78; and Israel Bartal, "L'an Halakh Zror ha-Kesef? Ha-bikoret ha-Maskilit al-Hebeteha ha-Kalkalyim shel ha-Hasidut," in Menahem Ben-Sasson, ed., *Dat ve-Kalkalah*, 375–87.

38. AGAD, KRSW 6634, p. 240; Mahler, *Ha-Hasidut ve-ha-Haskalah*, app., 478.

39. Ephraim Fischel Fischelson, "Teyator fun Khsidem," in E. Tscherikower, ed., *Historische Schriften* vol. 1 (1929), 685; Mahler, *Hasidism and the Jewish Enlightenment*, 26.

40. Officials in charge of quartering soldiers in private homes.

41. Advice of a zaddik to his son. Isaac Ber Levinsohn, "Emek Refa'im," in *Yalkut Ribal* (Warsaw, 1878), 127.

42. Schiper, *Żydzi Królestwa Polskiego*, 28–9.

43. Chaim Wolf Reines, "Public Support of Rabbis, Scholars and Students in the Jewish Past," *Yivo Annual of Jewish Social Science* 7 (1952), 84–109; Adam Teller, "The Gaon of Vilna and the Communal Rabbinate in Eighteenth–Century Poland-Lithuania," in Lempertas, *The Gaon of Vilnius and the Annals of Jewish Culture*, 142–153.

44. Mahler, *Hasidism and the Jewish Enlightenment*, 205 and 223; and in greater detail, Shmuel Werses, "Portrait of a Maskil as a Young Man," in Feiner and Sorkin, *New Perspectives on the Haskalah*, 133–7. On Lefin's patronage by Adam Kazimierz Czartoryski, see Nancy Sinkoff, "Strategy and Ruse in the Haskalah of Mendel Lefin of Satanow," in Feiner and Sorkin, *New Perspectives on the Haskalah*, 98.

45. *Jewish Expositor and Friend of Israel* 9 (1824), 158 and 196.

46. Max Weber, "Theory of Social and Economic Organization," tr. A. R. Henderson and Talcott Parsons, in S. N. Eisenstadt, ed., *Max Weber on Charisma and Institution Building* (Chicago: University of Chicago Press, 1968), 52.

47. Rosman, *Founder of Hasidism*, 219, no. 48; Pinhas Katzenellenbogen, *Yesh Manhillim*, ed. I. D. Feld (Jerusalem, 1986), 88–9, 95–9, 107–8; Ben Amos and Mintz, *In Praise of the Ba'al Shem Tov*, 211, no. 211; Israel Halpern, "Bunty Woszczyłowskie," *Builetyn ŻIH* 26 (1958), 28–41, and "Gezerat Voshtzilo," in *Yehudim ve-Yahadut be-Mizrah Eiropa* (Jerusalem: Magnes Press, 1968), 277–88; Adam Teller, "The Sluck Tradition Concerning the Early Days of the Besht" (in Hebrew), in David

Assaf, Joseph Dan and Imanuel Etkes, ed., *Studies in Hasidism* (Jerusalem, Magnes 1999), 5–38.

48. Weiss, "Some Notes on the Social Background of Early Hasidism," 18. On occasional tours by zaddikim, see Assaf, *The Regal Way*, 296–8.

49. Haviva Pedaya, "Le-hitpathuto shel had-Degem ha-Hevrati-da'ati-kalkali be-Hasidut: Ha-Pidyon, ha-Havurah, ve-ha-Alyah le-Regel," in Menahem Ben-Sasson, ed., *Dat ve-Kalkalah* (Jerusalem: Shazar, 1995), 311–76; Israel Bartal, "L'an Halakh Zeror ha-Kesef? Ha-bikoret ha-Maskilit al-Hebeteha ha-Kalkaliyim shel ha-Hasidut," in Ben-Sasson, *Dat ve-Kalkalah*; David Assaf, " 'Money for Household Expenses': Economic Aspects of the Hasidic Courts," *Scripta Hierosolymitana* 38, 14–50. According to the last will and testament of David Halpern of Ostróg, executed in 1765, R. Aryeh Leib, the "Preacher of Połonne," R. Dov Ber, the "Great Maggid" of Międzyrzecz, R. Jehiel Michael of Złoczów, and R. Pinhas Shapiro of Korzec were each to receive 150 złoties. In the Land of Israel, R. Menahem Mendel of Przemyślany was to receive 200 złoties; and R. Nahman of Horodenka 150 złoties. Finally, the Besht's son, R. Zvi Hirsch, was bequeathed 100 złoties. In return, they were all to pray for Halpern's departed soul. See David Halpern of Ostróg, *Darkhei Ziyon* (Bartfeld, 1909), 2; and Hundert, *Jews in Poland-Lithuania in the Eighteenth Century*. According to Assaf, this will was printed to "encourage rich individuals to remember hasidic groups in their wills." See " 'Money for Household Expenses,' " 16, no. 9.

50. R. Isaac Meir Alter of Gur cofounded a factory that produced prayer shawls with the financially ruined Moses Halfan. See Abraham Issachar, *Meir Eyne ha-Golah* (Tel Aviv: Alter-Bergman, 1954), 1:10:33a, 1:39:137; 2:83:3.

51. See Issachar, *Meir Eyne ha-Golah*, 19:68, 10:33, 16:60, 18:63, and 19:67; and evidence brought later.

52. Abraham Issachar Benjamin, *Meir Eyne ha-Golah*, 19:68, 10:33, 16:60, 18:63, and 19:67, and see Israel Halpern, "Rabbi Levi Isaac of Berdyczów and the Royal Edicts of His Times" (in Hebrew), in *Yehudim ve-Yahadut be-Mizrah Eiropa*, 342. Halpern bases his dating (1791) on another document by Lefin. Ringelblum, "Khsides un Haskole in Varshe in 18-ten y.h.," 125, provides a dissenting view. See also Dresner, *The World of a Hasidic Master*, 68 and 213.

53. Ringelblum, "Khsides un Haskole in Varshe in 18-ten y.h.," 124–6; Mendel Lefin Satanower, *Essai D'un plan de reforme ayant pour objet d'eclairer la Nation Juive en Pologne et de redresser par la ses moeurs* (Warsaw, 1791), g and h, pp. 30–1.

54. R. Israel Loebel, *Sefer Vikuah*, 19b and 20b, in Wilensky, *Hasidim u-Mitnaggdim*, 316 and 318; Rubinstein, "Hasidut ve-Hasidim be-Varshe," 67–8.

55. Schiper, *Przyczynki do dziejów chasydyzmu w Polsce*, 26.

56. Rubinstein, "Hasidut ve Hasidim be-Varshe," 61–84. *Yizkor* (Memorial) accounts of Hasidism in Warsaw include Avraham Bik, "Etapen fun Hasidism in Varshe," in *Pinkes Varshe* (Buenes Aires: n.p., 1955), 1:179–86; Meir Shvartzmann, "Vi Hasides Hat Bazigt des Lomdishe Varshe," in *Das Amalike Yidishe Varshe* (Montreal: n.p., 1966), 750–5, on a later period; and Gabriel Waisman, ed., *Sefer Praga: A Memorial to the Jewish Community of Praga* (Hebrew/Yiddish) (Tel Aviv: Orli, 1974), 21–41 and 62–6. Jacob Shatzky cites questionable evidence in the reform pamphlets of the Maskil David Friedlander (1819), and the Polish writers Jan Radomiński (1820) and Jan Niepomucen Janowski (1830). Jacob Shatzky, *Geschikhte fun Yidn in Varshe*, 3:351–2. Friedlander and Radomiński do not mention Warsaw specifically. See Friedlander, *Uber die Verbesserung der Israeliten im Konigreich Pohlen* (Berlin, 1819), 38–42; and Radomiński, *Co wstrzymuie reforme żydów w kraiu naszym, i co ią przyspieszyć powinno?* 63.

57. AGAD, CWW 1869, p. 9.

58. *Jewish Expositor and Friend of Israel* 8 (1823), 327; 9 (1825), 218.

59. On March 21, 1827, R. Isaac Meir wrote a petition regarding his "prayer house for Jews at 1027 Grzybowska Street" and a request to authorize a new one at 959 Targowa Street. In 1828, he requested authorization for a prayer house on 1057 Grzybowska Street. Printed in Schiper, *Żydzi Królestwa Polskiego w dobie powstania Listopadowego*, 28.

60. Tieberg, *Kedushat Yizhak*, 12:1. That Danziger's allegiance to Hasidism was not absolute is suggested in his attending a lesson of the Mitnagged R. Akiva Eiger (Tieberg, *Kedushat Yizhak*, 13: 8). However, he married his son Feivel of Grojec to the daughter of the zaddik Simha Bunem of Pryzsucha; and his daughter to R. Levi Isaac of Berdyczów.

61. Tieberg, *Kedushat Yizhak*, 12:3, 13:5, 19:11, 19:12, 24:21. Feivel eventually began attending the synagogue of the Hasidim of the Seer of Lublin, in Warsaw. Tieberg, *Kedushat Yizhak*, 20, no. 13.

62. R. Levi Isaac debated at least twice in Warsaw. See Zvi Meir Rabinowicz, "Mekorot ve-Te'udot le-Toldot ha-Hasidut be-Polin," *Sinai* 82 (1978), 82–86. However, Ringleblum argues that the disputation provided an opportunity to expose the emptiness of Hasidism. "Khsides un Haskole in Varsheh in 18-ten y.h.,"

63. Page 7 of the record book of the society records that "on the intermediate days of Passover, 1744, the young boy Israel, son of R. Shabbatai, was admitted as a member. His father paid for him three *loit* of silver as admission fee." On page 12 is an inventory of holy vessels belonging to the society, including "a Torah plaque of R. Shabbatai, weighing five *loit* of silver." See Abraham Yaairi, "*Ner Tamid* Societies in Poland and Lithuania," *Jewish Social Studies* 21:2 (1959), 118–31.

64. Hundert, "Apta ve-Reshit he-Hasidut ad 1800," 62. On the Landau family, see Hundert, *The Jews of a Polish Private Town*, 124–31; H. Horowitz, "Die judische gemeinde Opatow und ihre Rabbiner," *Monatsschrift fur Geschikhte und Wissenschaft des Judentums* (1930), 110–23.

65. Rabinowicz, *Bein Pshyskha*, 206–7: "Mandelsberg employed about 500 families in his factory, received two medals from King Stanislaw Augustus, and had such intimate contacts with the authorities that he was able to warn the Maggid about the latest developments on the "Jewish question." Compare Meshulam Ze'ev Ashkenazi, *Bet Meshulam: Kavod Ha-Bayit* (Piotrków Trybunalski, 1905), 68–72.

66. The Maggid's appeal on behalf of a follower named Ze'ev Wolf, upon whom "the wheel of poverty has turned," appears in a letter in Rabinowicz's "Mekorot ve-Te'udot le-Toldot ha-Hasidut be-Polin," 82.

67. David of Maków, *Zemir Arizim* 17a (Warsaw, 1798), in Wilensky, *Hasidim u-Mitnaggdim*, 2:214.

68. The delegation, led by Berek Sonnenberg-Bergson (discussed later), lobbied Napoleon against various measures seen as threatening to traditional Jewish culture. See Artur Eisenbach, "Di Tsentrale Reprezentants-Argenen Fun Di Yiden in Warshaver Pirshtentum (1807–1815)" (Yiddish version only), *Bleter Far Geschikhte* 2 (1938), 64–5; Rabinowicz, *Bein Pshyskha*, 206.

69. Tieberg, *Kedushat Yizhak*, 12:2.

70. Tieberg, *Kedushat Yizhak*, 12:3.

71. Abraham Issachar Benjamin, *Meir Eyne ha-Golah*, 19:68; Rubinstein, "Hasidut ve-Hasidim be-Varshe," 22.

72. Abraham Issachar Benjamin, *Meir Eyne ha-Golah*, 10:33.

73. Abraham Issachar Benjamin, *Meir Eyne ha-Golah*, 16:60.

74. Abraham Issachar Benjamin, *Meir Eyne ha-Golah*, 18:63.

75. After marrying his daughter to their son Michael Joseph Bergson, the Hasidic scholar R. Aryeh Leibush of Stanisław (the Gral, 1809–79) was reproached by his aunt for making a match "for the sake of money." The Gral agreed to marry his other daughter to the son of the Hasidic patron Joseph Mandelsberg of Kuzmir, who possessed both wealth and *yihus* (distinguished lineage)—the ideal combination for a son-in-law. See Abraham Hayyim Michelzohn, *Ohel Naftali* (Lemberg, 1911), 147–8:410.

76. Nahum Sokolow, "Henri Bergson's Old-Warsaw Lineage," in Lucy Dawidowicz, ed., *The Golden Tradition: Jewish Life and Thought in Eastern Europe* (New York: Holt, Rinehart and Winston, 1967), 358.

77. Garntsarska-Kadry, "Ha-yehudim ve-ha-Gormim le-Hitpathuta ve-Mekoma shel ha-Ta'asyah be-Varshe," 39.

78. Sokolow, "Henri Bergson's Old-Warsaw Lineage," 352.

79. Schiper, *Dzieje handlu Żydowskiego*, 404.

80. Anna Michałowska, "Szmul Jakubowicz Zbytkower," *Biuletyn ŻIH* 2–3 (1992), 80. Emmanuel Ringelblum's estimate is less precise. See "Shmuel Zbytkower," *Zion* 3 (1938), 247.

81. Ignacy Schiper, "Z dziejów patrycjatu żydowskiego w Warszawie," *Nowe Słowo* 23:5 (1931); Jan Kosim, *Losy pewnej fortuny*, 17.

82. Schiper, *Dzieje handlu Żydowskiego*, 329. There is also evidence that Szmul supplied the Russian army in 1771 and 1772. See report by S. Potocki Prezes from October 6, 1810, in Tadeusz Mencel and Marian Kallas, eds., *Protokoły Rady Stanu Księstwa Warszawskiego* (Warsaw: Sejmowe, 1996), 3:2:98.

83. Michałowska, "Szmul Jakubowicz Zbytkower," 86.

84. Kosim, *Losy pewnej fortuny*, 17.

85. Teodor Ostrowski, ed., *Poufne wieści z oświeconej Warszawy: Gazetki pisane z roku 1782* (Wrocław: Zakład Narodowy im. Ossolińskich, 1972), 42–3.

86. Wilhelm Pohorille, "Dostawy wojkowe Szmula Jakubowicza Zbytkowera w latach 1792–4," in Majer Bałaban, ed., *Księga ku Czci Berka Joseliwicza* (Warsaw, 1934), 125–35.

87. Frenk, *Meshumadim in Poylin* (Warsaw, 1923), 22; Ringelblum, "Shmuel Zbytkower," 248.

88. Quoted in Ostrowski, *Poufne wieści*, 222.

89. Ringelblum, "Shmuel Zbytkower," 345–7.

90. See Gershon Hundert, "Was There an East European Analogue to Court Jews?" in Andzej Paluch, ed., *The Jews in Poland* (Cracow: Jagiellonian University Press, 1992) 1:67–76. Hundert gives a negative reply.

91. Ringelblum, *Żydzi w powstaniu Kościuszkowskiem* (Warsaw, 1938), 92–3 and 151; Aleksander Bocheński, "Protoplasta Finansjery Warszawskiej," *Wiedza i Życia* 9 (1983), 29. Tadeusz Korzon argues, however, that as Jews felt no connection to Poland, there is no reason to expect patriotism from Szmul. *Wewnętrzne dzieje Polski za Stanisława Augusta (1764–1794)*, 1:227–8 (Warsaw, 1897), 227–8.

92. The bank was established in his house on Przejazd Street, no. 643. Bocheński, "Protoplasta Finansjery Warszawskiej," 30; Frenk, *Meshumadim*, 21–3; Ringelblum, *Żydzi w powstaniu*, 150–1. On Szmul's kosher slaughterhouse, see also Ringelblum, "Yidn in varshe in 18-ton y.h. un zeyr rehleh-geschaftlehe lageh," 253. On his brickyard, see Schiper, *Dzieje Handlu Żydowskiego*, 328. On his minting enterprise, see Eisenbach, "Jews in Warsaw," 114. On his brewery and tannery, see Bocheński, "Protoplasta Finansjery Warszawskiej," 26–8. On the bank, see Stanisław Kempner,

Dzieje Gopodarcze Polski (n.p., 1920), 1:70; and Michałowska, "Szmul Jakubowicz Zbytkower," 84.

93. A pupil of Sokolow's grandfather's pupils recalled that "community leaders used to serve at his parties," a rather doubtful claim. Sokolow, "Henri Bergson's Old-Warsaw Lineage," 352.

94. Szmul's tombstone inscription, cited in Abraham Levinson, *Toldot Yehude Varshe* (Tel Aviv: Am Oved, 1953), 58; Ringelblum, "Shmuel Zbytkower," 250; and Shmuel Yevanin, *Nahalat Olamim* (Warsaw, 1882), 7; Rabinowicz, *Bein Pshyskha*, 299.

95. Tadeusz Korzon, *Wewnetrzne Dzieje*, 1:290; Ringelblum, "Shmuel Zbytkower," 255–7. Ringelblum speculates that the tradition about Szmul redeeming Jewish lives and corpses from Cossaks with jugs of money grew out of his use of connections with the Russian army—which he supplied—to save several Jews.

96. Levinson, *Toldot Yehude Varshe*, 58; Jacob Shatzky, *Geschikhte Fon Yidin in Varshe* (New York: Yidisher Visnshaftlekher Institut, Historishe Sektsye, 1947) 1:134.

97. Ringelblum, "Shmuel Zbytkower," 251–2; Levinson, *Toldot Yehude Varshe*, 58–9.

98. Frenk, *Meshumadim*, 27; Ringelblum, "Shmuel Zbytkower," 253–4; Schiper, *Cmentarze Żydowskie w Warszawie* (Warsaw: Maor, 1938), 4. See decree in Mathias Bersohn, *Diplomataryusz dotczacy Żydow w Dawnej Polsce* (Warsaw, 1910), 196–7, nos. 339–40; and Maurycy Horn, *Regesty dokumentów i ekscerpty z metryki koronnej do historii żydów w Polsce: 1697–1795* (Wrocław: Jewish Historical Institute, 1988), 2:2:15–16; 2:2:15–16; and Anonymous, "Z pinkasu Bractwa pogrzebowego praskiego," *Kwartalnik poświęcony* 1 (1912), 138–9.

99. Schiper, *Cmentarze Żydowskie w Warszawie*, 45–53; Frenk, *Meshumadim*, 28; Ringelblum, "Shmuel Zbytkower," 253–4; and Tadeusz Korzon, *Wewnętrzne dzieje*, 1:224–5. Szmul charged wealthy Jews 2,000 złoties for burial. His position as head of the cemetery and burial society also gave him an enormous amount of power, enabling him to threaten his enemies with the refusal to bury them or their family members.

100. Shatzky, *Geschikhte*, 1:135; Sokolow, "Henri Bergson's Old-Warsaw Lineage," 358.

101. Frenk, *Meshumadim*, 24 and 34.

102. Rubinstein, "Hasidut ve-Hasidim be-Varshe," 79; Schiper, *Żydzi Królestwa Polskiego w dobie powstania Listopadowego*, 38. H. Kirszenbaum argues that Szmul tolerated the rival burial society because it was Hasidic. See "Bractwo pogrzebowe na Pradze," *Kwartalnik poświęcony* 3 (1912), 133–46. Schiper discredits that speculation in *Cmentarze Żydowskie w Warszawie*, 32–3.

103. Frenk, *Meshumadim*, 21–37. Frenk demonizes Judyta as an opponent of "yiddishkeit," blaming her in great part for her children's apostasy. While accounts are confused and varied, it appears that Szmul had three wives—Sheindel, Leahen, and Judyta. Sheindel bore Abba, Berek, Isaac. All were Hasidic. All but one of Szmul's daughters from his second and third wives converted to Christianity after his death. Leihen's daughter Adele/Italia married the great banker Antoni Fraenkel (both converted in 1806). Of Judyta's three daughters, Anna and Barbara converted to Christianity (in 1813 and 1833, respectively); while Ludwiga married the acculturated "German" Jew Isaac Flatau and remained Jewish. For the most accurate accounts, see Ringelblum, "Shmuel Zbytkower," 248; and Schiper, "Z dziejów patrycjatu."

104. *Meir Eyne ha-Golah*, 17:61. The Maggid had to compose a melody to assist the one angel, created by Szmul's rescue of Jews during the Praga massacre, against

the demons created by his many sins, including possibly adultery. According to Rubinstein, Szmul's soul was only repaired because he was Berek's father. See also Rubinstein, "Hasidut ve-Hasidim be-Varshe," 74–6.

105. The surname Berek adopted in accordance with Prussian name legislation enacted during the Warsaw occupation.

106. Sokolow denies even Berek's allegiance to Hasidism, although he admits of Berek's contributions to the zaddik R. Isaac of Warka. See "Henri Bergson's Old-Warsaw Lineage," 358. On Berek's support of Hasidism, see also Schiper, *Przyczynki do dziejow chasydyzmu w Polsce*, 87; and *Żydzi Królestwa Polskiego w dobie powstania Listopadowego*, 23; and Rabinowicz, *Bein Pshyskha*, 200, 208, 301.

107. Ireneusz Ihnatowicz, *Obyczaj wielkiej burżuazji warszawskiej w XIX wieku* (Warsaw: PIW, 1971), 104. Berek and his wife Temerel may have composed literary works, according to Ihnatowicz.

108. Rabinowicz, "Mekorot ve-Te'udot le-Toldot ha-Hasidut be-Polin," 86.

109. Mahler finds that "in 1824 the legacy of Berek Samuel Sonnenberg included, besides cash, mortgages in the amount of 350,000 zlotys, six stone houses in Warsaw, and an estate in the district of Czersk" (194). See *Hasidism and the Jewish Enlightenment*, 189. On January 3, 1812, Berek's monopoly on the kosher meat tax (2,650,000 złoties per year), was confirmed. According to A. N. Frenk, he turned over the income from the kosher meat tax to the Warsaw kahal treasury in 1807. See Frenk, "Le-toldot ha-Yehudim be-Nesikhut Varshe," 455; Eisenbach, "Ha-Nezigut ha-Merkazit shel ha-Yehudim be-Nesikhut Varshe," in Bartal and Gutman, *Kiyum ve-Shever*, 304; Nahum Gelber, "The Jewish Question in Poland in the Years 1815–1830," (in Hebrew), *Zion* 13–4 (1948–49), 128; Ryszard Kołodziejczyk, *Piotr Steinkeller: 1799–1854* (Warsaw: PWN, 1963), 25; Eisenbach, *Emancipation of the Jews in Poland*, 211.

110. Barbara Grochulska, *Księstwo Warszawskie* (Warsaw: WP, 1966), 177–9.

111. Kosim, *Losy pewnej fortuny*, 22–5.

112. Kosim, *Losy pewnej fortuny*, 56–7.

113. Schiper, *Dzieje handlu Żydowskiego*, 368; "Z dziejów patrycjatu," part 3.

114. Emphasis added, as the term "citizen" was rarely applied to Jews. *Gazeta Warszawska* 101 (December 17, 1808).

115. AGAD, RMKW, serja 2-go—*Akta Spraw*, 115, p. 80; Kosim, *Losy pewnej fortuny*, 57. I would like to thank Francois Guennet for recommending the former source.

116. AGAD, RMKW, serja 2-go—*Akta Spraw*, 115, p. 77.

117. AGAD, RMKW, serja 2-go—*Akta Spraw*, 115, p. 79.

118. Grochulska, *Księstwo Warszawskie*, 180. One should accord Napoleon a hefty share of blame for the Duchy's desperate financial straits, including the imperative to maintain an army of fortythousand men (in 1808) and make exhorbitant interest payments to the French treasury (the Bayonne Sums). See Christopher A. Blackburn, *Napoleon and the Szlachta* (New York: Coloumbia University East European Monographs, 1998), 78.

119. Kosim, *Losy pewnej fortuny*, 56.

120. Five years later, Piotr Steinkeller and several Cracow merchants wrested it away from him. Kołodziejczyk, *Piotr Steinkeller*, 39–40.

121. Lubecki to Sobolewski, September 15, 1821. In Stanisław Smolka, ed., *Korespondencya Lubeckiego z ministrami sekretarzami stanu Ignacym Sobolewskim i Stefanem Grabowskim* (Cracow, 1909), 1.

122. Mieczysław Ajzen, *Polityka gospodarcza Lubeckiego* (Warsaw, 1932), 38–40.

123. Ostrowski, "Uwagi nad obyczaimi, uspobieniem i charakterem Żydów Polskich," 87; Schiper, "Z dziejów patrycjatu" (mis-citation there).

124. Kosim, Losy pewnej fortuny, 216–9.

125. Szymon Askenazy, Dwa Stulecie (Warsaw, 1910), 2:421–41 and 552–6.

126. For a summary of the debate, see John Klier, Russia Gathers Her Jews: The Origins of the "Jewish Question" in Russia (DeKalb: Northern Illinois University Press, 1986), 177–8. On Nowosilcow's liberal plan for improving Jewish legal status see Eisenbach, Emancipation of the Jews in Poland, 168–74; David Kandel, "Nowosilcow a Żydzi," Biblioteka Warszawska vol. 3, (1911), 144–50.

127. Jews were permitted by a subsequent decree of January 29, 1812, to pay 700,000 złoties annually in lieu of army service. See Szymon Askenazy, "Z dziejów Żydów polskich w dobie Księstwa Warszawskiego," Kwartalnik poświęcony 1:1 (1912), 1–14; and Schiper, Przyczynki do dziejów chasydyzmu w Polsce, 80. However, even the minister of war, Józef Poniatowski, felt that the exclusion of Jews from political life for ten years justified military exemption of a similar duration. See Stanley, "The Politics of the Jewish Question in the Duchy of Warsaw, 1807–1813," 56. The recruitment tax increased during the War of 1812 to 1,400,000 and remained in place after the war's conclusion, notwithstanding the efforts of Berek and his fellow representatives. See Eisenbach, "Ha-Nezigut ha-Merkazit," 311. Hasidic sources credit the eventual convert Stanisław Ezekiel Hoga (discussed later) with the reversal of the Napoleonic draft decrees. See B. Z. Lask Abrahams, "Stanislaus Hoga—Apostate and Penitent," in The Jewish Historical Society of England: Transactions 15 (London, 1946), 135.

128. Schiper, Przyczynki do dziejów chasydyzmu w Polsce; and see Kandel, "Nowosilcow a Żydzi," 142. After two years of deliberations and interventions, only Jews residing in cities possessing non tolerandis Judaeis were forbidden to trade in liquor, a contradiction that should not be missed! For memos, see Eisenbach, "Ha-Nezigut ha-Merkazit," 310.

129. Schiper, Żydzi Królestwa Polskiego w dobie powstania Listopadowego, 65; Przyczynk do dziejow chasydyzmu w Polsce, 106–7. The tsar granted audience to an unnamed Jew in connection with the denunciation of the ritual murder charge. Schiper guesses that this Jew was Berek.

130. Schiper, Przyczynki do dziejow chasydyzmu w Polsce, 119.

131. Walden, Ohel Yizhak, p. 10, no. 14.

132. Walden, Nifla'ot ha-Rabi, 75:202. No other sources mention Berek as having a prior wife who was Margaliot's daughter.

133. Walden, Or ha-Nifla'ot, 29:75. On "material zaddikism," see Elior, "Between Yesh and Ayin," 393–456.

134. Walden, Nifla'ot ha Rabi, 89:296.

135. Kadish, Si'ah Sarfe Kodesh, 2:15:24. See also Mahler, Hasidism and the Jewish Enlightenment, 272 (but Mahler mistakenly cites Temerel as Berek's mother); Meir Eidelboym, "Ha-Hasidut be-Einei Mitnagdeha," Tagim 3–4 (1962), 79; and a tale about how R. Bunem yielded to the sin of pride while in Danzig, in Walden, Ohel ha-Rabi, Or ha-Nifla'ot, 5:7.

136. The text of dedication on the synagogue's plaque is cited in Polish and Hebrew, in Anonymous, "Act darowizny boznicy przez Berka," Kwartalnik poświęcony 3 (1912), 180–2.

137. Schiper, "Z dziejów patrycjatu," part 3.

138. Warsaw's Jewish self-governing counsel was not officially a kahal. See Rafael Kempner, "Agonia kahal," Kwartalnik poświęcony 1 (1912), 71. In 1811, Berek was

one of several members of the Warsaw delegation, which acted as a supracommunal institution of self-government. In 1814, Berek was one of the Jewish representatives called to the Treasury office. See Artur Eisenbach, "Di Tsentralne Representanz-Organan fun di Yidn in Varshaver Firshtantom (1807–1815)," *Bleter far Geschikhte* 2 (Warsaw, 1938). In 1816, Berek was listed as an "Elder" in Warsaw. AGAD, CWW 1429, p. 13.

139. Dawid Kandel, "Żydzi w dobie Królestwa Kongresowego," 110–3. Summarized in Schiper, *Przyczyniki do dziejow chasydyzmu w Polsce*, 85–9; and Rubinstein, "Hasidut ve-Hasidim be-Varshe," 84.

140. On such alliances in tsarist Russia in 1843, see Michael Stanislawski, *Tsar Nicholas I and the Jews* (Philadelphia: Jewish Publication Society, 1983), 152. Other alliances also existed in this period: the Maskilim and Mitnaggdim managed to depose Berek and his brother Isaac from their position as elders in 1818. The Hasidim mobilized to defend the brothers, bringing a complaint before the mayor of Warsaw. The battle continued until the replacement of the kahal in 1821 by a "Synagogue Council." See Schiper, "Z dziejów patrycjatu," part 3, and *Przyczynki do dziejow chasydyzmu w Polsce*, 109–13. On alliances in general, see Fishman, *Russia's First Modern Jews*, chap. 6.

141. The residence restrictions were established in Warsaw by a decree from March 16, 1809, and later in other cities. The decree made exception for Jews who possessed over 60,000 złoties, owned a bank or mercantile firm, were literate in Polish, French, or German, sent their children to public schools, and did not possess distinguishing external Jewish marks (side–locks, etc.). Exemptions were also to be made for painters, doctors, and factory owners. See Adam Wein, "Żydzi poza rewirem Żydowskim w Warszawie (1809–1862), *Biuletyn ŻIH* 41 (1962), 46; Bergman, "The *Rewir* or Jewish District and the *Eyruv*," 85–97. Jews in Warsaw were concentrated onto even fewer streets by the tsar in 1821, and the restriction was extended to additional cities. Expulsions from certain streets were published in the bilingual Jewish newspaper *Dostrzegacz Nadwiślański* 3 and 37, on January 21 and September 15, 1824. Garntsarska-Kadary argues in a somewhat circular fasion that the imposition of the "ghetto" did not isolate Jews from the economy, but effected the transformation of the Jewish quarter into the heart of Warsaw industry. See "Ha-yehudim ve-ha-Goramim le-Hitpathuta ve-Mekoma shel ha-Ta'asyah be-Varshe," 31.

142. According to Adam Wein, eighteen Jewish families possessed that right during the period of the Duchy of Warsaw. See "Żydzi poza rewirem," 48. See also Wein, "Nabywanie i budowa nieruchomości przez Żydów w Warzawie (1821–1862)," *Biuletyn ŻIH* 64 (1967); and "Ograniczenie napływu Żydów do Warszawy," *Biuletyn ŻIH* 49 (1964); Eisenbach, *Emancipation of the Jews in Poland*, 226–7; Mahler, *Hasidism and the Jewish Enlightenment*, 179–181.

143. A. N. Frenk, *Yehude Polin be-Yame Milhemot Napoliyon* (Warsaw, 1912), 44; Sokolow, "Henri Bergson's Old-Warsaw Lineage," 353. See also Shatzky, *Geschikhte*, 1: 185. Napoleon frequently relied upon the capital of individual Jewish bankers. See Askenazy, "W dobie Ksiéstwa Warszawskiego," 7.

144. AGAD, KRSW 6628, p. 212.

145. Other wealthy traditionalists made similar requests, such as the traditionalist Maskil Michał Ettinger-Rawski. Eisenbach, *Emancipation of the Jews in Poland*, 222.

146. On Muskat's identity, see Eisenbach, *Emancipation of the Jews in Poland*, 226.

147. According to a list found by Wein, the street was either Królewski, Marszałkowski, Senatorski, Świentojerski, or Daniłewiczowski. "Żydzi poza rewirem," 48.

148. AGAD, KRSW 6628, p. 27. The petition is signed by Salamon Muskat.

149. See Eisenbach, *Emancipation of the Jews in Poland*, 220–1.

150. AGAD, KRSW 6628, p. 211. In this document, Lubecki acknowledges that the Saxon king, as duke of Warsaw, allowed Berek to acquire property "within the Warsaw city limits."

151. The petition reads: "My father Szmul Jakubowicz (Zbytkower), for his merits as a true Citizen, not only gained the grace of Kings like Stanisław Augustus, King of Poland, and the most gracious Catherine II, Empress of Mighty Russia, but additionally the present King of Prussia, who after political changes in this country, with his Privilege from the date February 27, 1798, deigned to award the family of this Szmul great freedom to trade, residence wherever they desired, and complete Civic Freedom. . . . I, the undersigned Son of this Szmul Jakubowicz, an image of my father, risking with the readiness of a mother every service to the Homeland and Government, to such a degree that today more than 600,000 złoties became the property of the Treasury, wait with great patience until the Government under the beloved scepter of Your Majesty will be able to repay me." AGAD, KRSW 6628, p. 212. Compare Eisenbach, *Emancipation of the Jews in Poland*, 222.

152. AGAD, KRSW 6628, pp. 212–3.

153. Eisenbach, *Emancipation of the Jews in Poland*, 224.

154. AGAD, KRSW 6628, p. 211. Unless Sokolow was in possession of a document that reversed that decision, we must doubt his assertion that "Alexander I restricted the privilege specifically only to Berek, and, after him, only to his eldest son." See "Henri Bergson's Old-Warsaw Lineage," 353.

155. Berek leased the Latowice *starostwo* (district subdivision) from Prince Adam Czartoryski for six years in the Duchy of Warsaw. In 1821, he bought the Suchowola and Lychowo farms (Czersk district) freehold. See Eisenbach, *Emancipation of the Jews in Poland*, 227; AGAD, KRSW 6628, p. 211.

156. AGAD, PRAKP, 9, s. 176, May 29, 1821.

157. Władysław Tatarzanka, "Przyczynki do historji żydów w Królestwie Kongresowem. 1815–1830 (I)," *Przegląd Judaistyczny* 1:4–6 (1922), 281.

158. AGAD, CWW 1012, p. 12; *Dostrzegacz Nadwiślański* 8 (1824), 59. Different calculations from those in Ihnatowicz, *Obyczaj*, 155. And see Marcin Wodziński, "Legat Berka Sonnenberga czyli o zaskakującej karierze mimowolnego dobroczyńcy," *Studia Judaica* 7:1 (2004), 183–206 [offprint].

159. AGAD, CWW 1012, p. 16.

160. AGAD, CWW 1012, p. 16–7.

161. Epitaph printed in Shmuel Yavnin, *Nahalat Olamim* (Warsaw, 1882), 12. It remains in the Warsaw Jewish cemetery.

162. On Berek's charitable enterprises, see Samuel Orgelbrand, ed., *Encyklopedyja Powszechna*, vol. 26 (Warsaw, 1861), Elżbieta Mazur, *Dobroczynność w Warszawie XIX wieku* (Warsaw: Instytut Archeologii i Etnologii Polskiej Akademii Nauk, 1999), 36–7.

163. *Kurjer Warszawski* 277, from November 19, 1822. Schiper is mistaken in claiming that Berek died in December 1823. See "Z dziejów patrycjatu," part 5.

164. Rubinstein, "Hasidut ve-Hasidim be-Varshe," 80. On her father, Abraham of Opoczna, whose name is inscribed on Temerel's tombstone, see Schiper, "Z dziejów patrycjatu."

165. Sokolow, "Henri Bergson's Old-Warsaw Lineage," 353.

166. Issachar, *Meir Eyne ha-Golah*, 17:62.

167. Hayyim Bezalel Panet, "Toldot Rabeinu Yehezkel," in *Derekh Yivhar*, (Mun-

kacz, 1894), first page. Temerel is also claimed to have studied Talmud. See Żor-Żor, "Żydzi na Pradze," *Echo Pragi* 13–4 (1916).

168. Schiper, "Z dziejów patrycju," part 5.

169. Marek Riverdil, the king's librarian, accompanied the king, who was curious about Jewish weddings, and described it in his memoir. See Aleksander Kraushar, *Dwa szkice historyczne* (Warsaw, 1905), 42.

170. AGAD, CWW 1012, p. 18. Parts of the Testament are published by Jan Papłońsky, "Życiorysy dobroczyńców Instytutu: Berek Szmulowicz Sonenberg," *Pamiętnik Warszawskiego Instytutu Głuchoniemych i Ociemniałych* 4 (1872–73), 106–12. A curious panegyric follows, having Berek exclaim, "I am a Jew! I know my nation, its faults and its misery, and yet I love it with all my spirit, and from a most pious heart I will not turn back, and before the most numerous hands I will not close mine!" (110).

171. AGAD, CWW 1012, p. 18.

172. Kosim, *Losy pewnej fortuny*, 219.

173. Schiper, *Dzieje handlu Żydowskiego na ziemiach Polskich* (Warsaw, 1937, reprint, Cracow: Krajowa Agencja Wydawnicza, 1990), 402. The salt company of which Temerel assumed control is mentioned in the Warsaw court records in 1823 when a barge carrying the salt was shipwrecked on the Wisła river, and most of the salt was stolen. A corrupt assistant to the chief of police, Birnbaum, found the thieves but kept a most of the fines for himself by registering the crime twice. When summoned before the court, he claimed ignorance about the matter. Bazyl Mochnacki, *Sprawa Birnbauma* (Warsaw, 1830), no. 72, p. 76.

174. AGAD, KRSWiD 5751, p. 86. Decree from August 11, 1810, granted to Temerel Sonenberg, "Money Lender." Whether her husband Berek was legally permitted to reside with her there remains unclear.

175. AGAD, PRAKP 15, s. 393.

176. AGAD, PRAKP 15, s. 679.

177. The acquisition was confirmed on January 31, 1828. AGAD, PRAKP 15, protokol 797.

178. Lynn Lubamersky, "Women and Political Patronage in the Politics of the Polish-Lithuanian Commonwealth," *Polish Review* 44:3 (1999), 259–75.

179. Schiper, "Dziejów patrycjatu" V.

180. AGAD, CWW 1441, p. 36. The service was led by her son, Michael Joseph; the sexton was Zalman Lewkiewicz of Ryczywół; and the cantor was Szulim Firkiel. Schiper, referring to a document in the destroyed Archive of the Warsaw Jewish Community, mentions that twenty-six of their relatives worshiped there.

181. Tieberg, *Kedushat Yizhak*, 17:23.

182. Jehiel Michael of Zakrotshtein, *Ez Avot, Megilat Yuhasin, Tahat ha-Ez* (Warsaw, 1898), 3a.

183. Boyim, *Ha-Rabi Rabi Bunem*, 2:589–90.

184. Issachar, *Meir Eyne ha-Golah*, 38. This may have represented an attempt to recruit R. Meir Alter for Przysucha Hasidism.

185. Buber, *Tales of the Hasidim*, vol. 2 272: "Temerel, a lady who lived in Warsaw and was known for her charitable works, visited Rabbi Bunem in Przysucha and gave him a sum of money to be distributed among worthy poor young men in his House of Study. The zaddik entrusted one of his pupils with this task. When he had just finished allotting the money, Rabbi Mendel arrived in a torn coat with the cotton showing through the ragged lining. 'What a pity!' cried the youth who had distributed the funds. 'I forgot about you and now I have no more money!' 'Money!' said Rabbi

Mendel and spat. For weeks afterward, the youth could not see a coin without feeling his gorge rise within him."

186. See Joseph Perl, *Megalle Temirin (Revealer of Secrets)* (Vienna, 1819), tr. Dov Taylor (Boulder, Colo.: Westview, 1997), letter no. 104; and Rubinstein's claims based on unpublished portions of the manuscript of *Revealer of Secrets*, in "Hasidut ve-Hasidim be-Varsheh, 91.

187. Yizhak Ewen, *Fun der gut Yidisher velt* (New York, 1917), 194.

188. Alexander Tsederbaum, *Keter Kehunah* (Odessa, 1866), 127–8; Rabinowicz, *Bein Pshyskha*, 301; Yonatan Halevi Eybeschutz, *Hedvat Simha* (Warsaw, 1930), approbation of Zvi Yehezkel Michaelson, iii; Simha, "Or Simha," 17:34.

189. *Nifla'ot ha-Rabi*, 90:304.

190. Rabinowicz, *Bein Pshyskha*, 293–369.

191. Walden, *Ohel Yizhak*, 24:96. R. Isaac of Warka suffered from recurring indebtedness. See also number 93.

192. Walden, *Ohel Yizhak*, 54:130; Mahler, *Hasidism and the Jewish Enlightenment*, 272. Harro Harring recalls: "The tobacco monopoly of Poland is purchased for some millions, how many I cannot precisely say; for numbers slip out of my memory as ducats out of my purse." *Poland under the Dominion of Russia*, 106.

193. Walden, *Ohel Yitshak*, 24:56. See also 10:17; Mahler, *Hasidism and the Jewish Enlightenment*, 272; Rabinowicz, *Bein Pshyskha*, 515.

194. Yehuda Leib Hakohen Levine, "Rav Pe'er," in *Y'khahen Pe'er* (Jerusalem, 1964), 30–1.

195. The zaddik Menahem Mendel of Kotsk dealt in hides, albeit unsuccessfully. In 1826, according to Schiper, he was "married to a daughter of a certain Warsaw moneylender and trading in textiles (or rather, his wife was trading in textiles)." R. Menahem Mendel owned a store on Wolowej Street, and a house and prayer house on 1027 Grzybowie Street. Schiper, *Żydzi Królestwa Polskiego*, 28; *Si'ah Sarfei Kodesh*, 1: 59:279. The zaddik Isaac Meir of Gur was a proprietor of a textile shop managed by his wife, a manufacturer of prayer shawls, and owner of a vinegar factory. R. Isaac Meir opened a store on Wolowej Street, which was destroyed during the 1830 uprising. The Russian government offered him a saloon as compensation; but R. Isaac Meir allegedly declined and, with his brother's backing, entered the more respectable book trade and became partner in a publishing house. Abraham Issachar Benjamin of Powienic, *Meir Eynei ha-Golah*, 1:38–9 and 2:83–4.

196. Shatzky, *Geschikhte fun yidn in Varshe* 2:124; Frenk, "Di Milhama Gegen der 'Hefkerut' in Amaligen Varshe," in *Almanah Zum 10-yahrigen Yubilum "Moment"* (Warsaw, 1921), 112; Rubinstein, "Hasidut ve-Hasidim be-Varshe," 82. The order is also attributed to R. Isaac of Warka.

197. Schiper, "Z dziejów patrycjatu," part 3.

198. On the wedding of Temerel's daughter and the grandson of R. Shmuel Shmelke, see Moses Menahem Walden, *Y'kaved Av* (Bnei Brak, 1968), 84–85. On Jacob's wedding, see Rabinowicz, *Bein Pshyskha*, 199–200.

199. Huberband, *Kiddush Hashem*, 307–8.

200. Huberband, *Kiddush Hashem*,

201. Isaac Ewen, *Fun der gut Yidisher velt* (New York, 1917), 194.

202. Schiper, "Z dziejów patrycjatu," part 3.

203. Shatzky, *Geschikhte fun Yidn*, 2:148.

204. Tombstone still extant in the Warsaw cemetery at Okopowa Street. Published by Schiper, "Z dziejów patrycju."

205. Marcin Wodziński, "Rząd Królestwa Polskiego Wobec Chasydyzmu: Poc-

zątki 'Polityki Chasydzkiej' w Królestwie Polskim (1817–1818)," *Żydzi I Judaizm we współczesnych badaniach Polskich* 3 (2004), 65–77.

206. AGAD, CWW 1012, p. 12; *Dostrzegacz Nadwiślański* 8 (1824), 59. I would like to thank Marcin Wodzinki for alerting me to the compulsion on the part of the government.

207. Meir of Opatów and Stopnica, *Or le-Shamayim* (Lublin, 1909).

208. Mose Elyakim Bryah of Kozienice, *Be'er Moshe* (Lemberg, 1918). Not *Kol Be'er Moshe* as indicated.

209. Simha Bunem of Przysucha, *Kol Simha* (Breslau, 1919).

210. Wilensky, *Hasidim u-Mitnaggdim*, 2:354.

211. Jacob Shatzky writes: "the legalization of Hasidic *shtiblah* (synagogues) in Warsaw is ascribed to this daughter-in-law of Szmul Zbytkower, a typical Woman of Valor who was connected with various statesmen or government officials." *Geschikhte*, 3:352–3. Leon Hollaenderski refers to "the rich Jewess named Bergson of Prague [*sic*]" who "obtained a permit of tolerance by the government during their quarrel with the Jewish rabbinists." *Les Israelites de Pologne* (Paris, 1846), 295. On Hollaenderski (1808/ 12–78), a Polish Maskil, see Abraham Duker, "Leon Hollaenderski's Statement of Resignation," *Jewish Social Studies* 15 (1953), 293–302.

212. This is only partly true. The Synagogue Council claimed that the "Hussites" were actually Hasidim, who had been in the country for a long time. Moreover, the Synagogue Council actually consisted of two Mitnaggdim and one Hasidic supporter, Temerel's son Jacob Bergson. See Schiper, *Żydzi Królestwa Polskiego w dobie powstania Listopadowego*, 24–5.

213. Mojżesz Feinkind, "Dysputa Żydowska za czasów Stanisława Staszyca," *Nasz Przegląd* (February 9, 1926). Although the date of a disputation is a fabrication, Feinkind must have seen at least one archival document because he correctly summarizes the contents of a report from February 24, 1824, in AGAD, KRSW 6634, p. 244, in which officials express the desire to ban Hasidism.

214. Feinkind, "Dysputa Żydowska"; Rabinowicz, *Bein Pshyskha*, 378; Frenk, *Meshumadim*, 72–9; Nahum Gelber, "She'elat ha-Yehudim be-Polin be-Shanot 1815– 1830," *Zion* 13 (1949), 132; Jehiel Michael of Zakrotsztein, *Ez Avot-Megillat Yuhasin* (Warsaw, 1898), 2b (and paraphrased in Boyim, *ha-Rabi Rabi Bunem*, 2:590–1).

215. R. Simha Bunem responded that Temerel thought she had rendered a great service for the world and no one can deny that her intentions were pure, but it would have been better if the ban had not been reversed and the zaddikim were locked up in a fortress guarded by Cossaks with guns and whips. That way, no one would be able to visit them and "confuse their thoughts." Frenk, *Meshumadim*, 78–79; Jehiel Michael of Zakrotsztein, *Ez Avot-Megillat Yuhasin*, 2b.

216. On the claim and the Hasidic counterclaim, see Alexander Tsederbaum, *Keter Kehunah* (Odessa, 1866), 123–4. The story is refuted, without mentioning Hoga by name, in Walden, *Nifla'ot ha-Rabi*, 44:79.

217. Boundaries around a neighborhood or city to make it permissible to carry objects on the Sabbath. See Hoge's explanation, in Bergman, "The *Rewir* or Jewish District and the *Eyruv*," 85–97.

218. Małgorzata Kośka, "Obyczaje żydowskie w świetle prawa obowiązującego w XIX wieku w Królestwie Polskim," in Jerzy Woronczak, ed., *Żydowskie gminy wyznaniowe* (Wrocław, 1995), 41.

219. Schiper, *Żydzi królestwa Polskiego w dobie powstania Listopadowego*, 49.

220. AGAD, CWW 1444, p. 33. See also Władysław Tatarzanka, "Przyczynki do historji żydów w Królestwie Kongresowem. 1815–1830 (I)," 284.

221. AGAD, *Rada Adminystracyjna Królestwo Polskiego* 12, s. 88. Other memos are cited in Kośka, "Obyczaje żydowskie w świetle prawa," 36.

222. Mahler, *Hasidism and the Jewish Enlightenment*, 219.

223. Jacob Tugenhold claimed that Hoga's date of conversion was 1824 ("seven years ago") but it was apparently 1825. Jacob Tugenhold, *Obrona Izraelitów przez Rabbi Menasse Ben Israel* (Warsaw, 1831), 65–6; Kandel, "Komitet starozakonnych," 97; Teodor Jeske-Choiński, *Neofici Polscy: Materyały historyczne* (Warsaw, 1904), 136. This is important, because Hoga was *not a convert* at the time of the alleged disputation. According to Choiński, Hoga was thirty-four years old. His wife Anna (twenty-three years old), and daughters Julia (age seven) and Antonina (age five) converted that same year.

224. *Proceedings of the London Society* 10 (1825), 276.

225. Tugenhold, *Obrona Izraelitów*, 65–66; Mahler, *Hasidism and the Jewish Enlightenment*, 219.

226. Stanisław Ezekiel Hoga, *Tu chazy, czyli rozmowa o Żydach* (Warsaw, 1830); Schiper, *Przyczynki do dziejów chasydyzmu w Polsce*, 103–8; B. Z. Lask Abrahams, "Stanislaus Hoga-Apostate and Penitent," *Jewish Historical Society of England: Transactions* 15 (London, 1946).

227. Abrahams, "Stanislaus Hoga-Apostate and Penitent," 137.

228. Hoga died in London on January 1, 1860, and was buried in the non-Jewish, nondenominational Highgate Cemetery where Karl Marx was buried. Many thanks to Sid (Shnayer) Leiman for the latter information. Hoga visited D. W. Marks of the West London Synagogue in 1844 and said, "I can bear my hypocrisy no longer, and henceforth I shall live as I was born, a Jew." See Abrahams, "Stanislaus Hoga-Apostate and Penitent," 137; and see N. Ben Menahem, "Shvilim be-Sadeh ha-Sefer," *Sinai* 60 (1967) 182–183. Rumor of the return to Judaism is mentioned in Tsederbaum, *Keter Kehunah*, 124. For recent work on Hoga, see Shnayer Leiman, "The Baal Teshuvah and the Emden-Eibeschutz Controversy," *Judaic Studies* (New York: Kew Gardens, 1985), 3–26.

229. Wodziński, " 'Sprawa chasydymów," 231–2. Stern, on the other hand, called Hasidic leaders swindlers.

230. Mahler's suggestion that Jacob's membership on the advisory chamber of the Jewish Committee influenced the investigation is misleading: the Committee was established a year after the investigation. See *Hasidism and the Jewish Enlightenment*, 316.

231. Schiper, *Przyczynki do dziejow chasydyzmu w Polsce*, 112. The other members of the Board were: Szaja Markus Posner (Hasidic) and Henryk Samelsohn (Maskil). The latter was replaced by Joseph Hayyim Halberstamm (Mitnagged).

232. Translated in Mahler, *Hasidism and the Jewish Enlightenment*, as Committee for Religions.

233. AGAD, KRSW 6634, p. 230. This letter, which Mahler neglected to cite, is the earliest mention of Dulfus's complaint. It is dated September 23, 1823. Mahler believes that the term "Hussytów" reflects the Ashkenazic Hebrew pronunciation.

234. Schiper, *Żydzi Królestwa Polskiego w dobie powstania Listopadowego*, 24–5; Mahler, *Hasidism and the Jewish Enlightenment*, 322. Mahler provides an incorrect date (December 20).

235. AGAD, KRSW 6634, p. 238; Mahler, *Ha-Hasidut ve-ha-Haskalah*, app., 475–6.

236. AGAD, KRSW 6634, pp. 249a–249b; Mahler, *Ha-Hasidut ve-ha-Haskalah*, app., 484–5. AGAD, CWW 1871, p. 53.

237. Bazyl Mochnacki, *Sprawa Birnbauma* (Warsaw, 1830), no. 31, p. 64; I. Warszawski, "Yidn in Kongress—Poylin," *Historische Shriften* 2 (Vilna, 1937–39), 346.

238. AGAD, CWW 1871, p. 65; Wodziński, " 'Sprawa chasydymów,' " 232.

239. Without the letter, Mahler could not explain why "before two months elapsed, the policy of the authorities toward Hasidism changed, and the decrees against it were nullified." See *Hasidism and the Jewish Enlightenment*, 325.

240. AGAD, KRSW 6634, p. 262; Mahler, *Hasidut*, app., 486.

241. Wodziński, " 'Sprawa chasydymów,' " 233.

242. AGAD, CWW 1871, pp. 169–73; Wodziński, " 'Sprawa chasydymów,' " 235–237.

243. AGAD, CWW 1871, pp. 173–8; Wodziński, " 'Sprawa chasydymów,' " 237–9. Lacking these materials, Mahler nevertheless correctly surmised that "there are grounds to assume that Hasidic leaders did appear before this committee." *Hasidism and the Jewish Enlightenment*, 326.

244. Mahler, *Hasidism and the Jewish Enlightenment*, 326. This idea reached fruition with the creation of the Warsaw Rabbinical School in 1826.

245. AGAD, KRSW 6635, p. 6; Mahler, *Ha-Hasidut ve-ha-Haskalah*, app., 491. Copy published in Wodziński, " 'Sprawa chasydymów,' " 241.

246. Jacob Isaac of Lublin, *Zot Zikharon* (Jerusalem, 1992), parshat Balak, 89–90.

247. Eric Wolf, "Kinship, Friendship, and Patron-Client Relations," in Michael Banton, ed., *The Social Anthropology of Complex Societies* (London: Tavistock, 1966), 16–7.

248. Assaf, " 'Money for Household Expenses,' " 27.

249. Klemens Junosza, *Nasi Żydzi w miasteczkach i na wsiach* (Warsaw, 1889), 67. Junosza refers to large gatherings at the zaddik's court on Rosh Hashanna and Yom Kippur.

250. Junosza, *Nasi Żydzi w miasteczkach i na wsiach*, 67; 68.

251. *Sefer Viku'ah* 21, Wilensky, *Hasidim u-Mitnaggdim*, II: 320.

252. Abraham Joshua Heschel, *Ohev Yisrael* (Jerusalem: n.p., 1962), Parshat Pinhas, 194.

253. David of Maków, *Shever Posh'im* 76, in Wilensky, *Hasidim u-Mitnaggdim*, II: 176–7.

254. Israel Loebel, *Kontres be-Germanit*, in Wilensky, *Hasidim u-Mitnaggdim*, II: 333–4.

255. Israel b. Isaac Simha, "Or Simha", in *Simhat Yisrael* (Petersburg, 1910: rpr. Jerusalem, 1986), 17: 34. An example of R. Simha Bunem's advice appears in Samuel of Sieniawa, *Ramata'im Zofim* (Warsaw, 1885), 215, when the Zaddik counsels a serious Leipzig merchant to be more friendly and cheerful.

256. Aescoly, *Ha-Hasidut be-Polin*, 75. Aescoly also suggests that Temerel "supported Hasidim and their zaddikim as a kind of sport and hobby of the rich."

257. Schiper, *Cmentarze Żydowskie w Warszawie*, 30–3.

258. Schiper, *Przyczynki do dziejów chasydyzmu w Polsce*, 84–6.

259. Feivel was the son of R. Simon, a respected judge (*dayyan*) in Brześć. See Abraham Issachar Benjamin of Powienic, *Meir Eynei ha-Golah*, 18; and his epitaph in *Nahalat Olamim*, 17. On Moses, see Abraham Issachar Benjamin of Powienic, *Meir Eynei ha-Golah*, 10.

260. Jacob Isaac of Lublin, *Zikharon Zot*, 55. R. Dov Ber, the Great Maggid of Międzyrzecz, was tolerant of merchants: "For sometimes a man studies because it is his nature that he has the desire to study; and also a man engages in mercantile busi-

ness, for he has a desire for this. And what is the difference between them? Each one fulfills his passion." See *Maggid Devarav L'ya'akov*, ed. Rivka Schatz-Uffenheimer (Jerusalem: Magnes Press, 1990), 169:97.

261. Israel Hopstein of Kozienice, *Avodat Yisrael Ha-Mefuar[al pi yad defus rishon]* (Bnei Brak, 1996), 156.

262. See Rapoport-Albert, "God and the Zaddik as Two Focal Points of Hasidic Worship," 318.

263. Brill, "Grandeur and Humility in the Writings of R. Simhah Bunim of Przysucha," 444–8.

264. Max Weber distinguishes between classes, which are determined solely by economic considerations, and status groups, which are "determined by a specific positive or negative social estimation of *honor*." See Eisenstadt, *Max Weber on Charisma and Institution Building*, 169–82.

265. A recent study on this subject is Endelman, "Jewish Converts in Nineteenth-Century Warsaw."

266. Assaf and Bartal, "Shtadlanut ve-Ortodoksiyah," 67–8.

267. Mahler, *Hasidism and the Jewish Enlightenment*, 210.

268. Szmul Zbytkower.

269. Feivel Kamienitzer Wohlberg.

270. Joseph Mandelsberg of Kuzmir.

CHAPTER 4

1. Weber, "Theory of Social and Economic Organization," 329; S. N. Eisenstadt, *Max Weber on Charisma and Institution Building*, xiii–xix and 48. On Hasidism, see Stephen Sharot, *Messianism, Mysticism, and Magic* (Chapel Hill: University of North Carolina Press, 1981); Rapoport-Albert, "Hasidism after 1772," 93; Assaf, *The Regal Way*, 47–65.

2. Assaf, *Regal Way*, 47–65.

3. See *Encyclopedia Judaica*, app., 1:160–9.

4. Rapoport-Albert, "Hasidism after 1772"; Sharot, *Messianism, Mysticism, and Magic.*

5. For different reasons, the Bratslaver Hasidim also achieved routinization through R. Nahman's "staff." Of course, patrons are only members of a leader's staff in a loose sense: ordinary displays of service and absolute submission are not required of patrons; nor are they directly responsible for the internal operations of an institution. But patrons do form part of the infrastructure of personnel that assists the charismatic leader in various ways.

6. E.g., the sons of R. Solomon Rabinowicz of Radomsko [d. 1866], R. Jehiel of Aleksander [d. 1894], R. Abraham Landau of Czechanów [d. 1875], R. Jacob Aryeh Guterman of Radzymin [d. 1874], and the grandson of R. Isaac Meir Alter of Gur [d. 1866]). Sons of the same deceased zaddik even began establishing lines simultaneously (e.g., the sons of R. Abraham Landau of Czechanów and R. Ezekiel Taub of Kazimierz). The Polish Zaddik R. Ezekiel Taub of Kazimierz [d. 1856] was succeeded by his son before 1862–63; however, the transition's success may be attributable to the new conditions, as well. *Encyclopedia Judaica*, app., 1:160–9.

7. Katz, *Tradition and Crisis*, 204; Scholem, *Major Trends in Jewish Mysticism*, 337; Mendel Piekarz, *Bi-yemei Zemihat Ha-Hasidut* (Jerusalem: Mosad Bialik, 1978); Rapoport-Albert, "Hasidism after 1772," 93.

8. Chaim Zytlowski, "A Note on Chassidism," in S. Ansky, *The Dybbuk: A Play*

in *Four Acts,* tr. Henry G. Alsberg and Winifred Katzin (New York: Liverlight, 1926), 19. See also 16.

9. Weiss also detects a "smell of Sabbatian heresy." Quoted in Ettinger, "The Hasidic Movement—Reality and Ideals," 229.

10. See Robert Seltzer, "The Secular Appropriation of Hasidism by the East European Jewish Intellectual: Dubnow, Renan, and the Besht," *Polin* 1 (1986), 151–2; Dubnow, *Toldot ha-Hasidut,* 34–6, and *History of the Jews in Russia and Poland,* 220–34. See also W. Z. Rabinowitch, *Lithuanian Hasidism,* 1–6. An embryonic form of the view appears in Graetz, *History of the Jews,* 5:383 and 392.

11. Dinur, "The Origins of Hasidism and Its Social and Messianic Foundations," 86–208; Weiss, "Some Notes on the Social Background of Early Hasidism," 12–4; Buber, *The Origin and Meaning of Hasidism,* 58 and 61; Rabinowicz, *The World of Hasidism,*183; Levitats, *The Jewish Community in Russia,* 162; Mahler, *Hasidism and the Jewish Enlightenment,* 7–10 and 272. Mahler attributed the Hasidic-Mitnaggedic rapprochement in Central Poland to Przysucha zaddikim, who were by this period "members of the well-to-do and middle classes." On Samuel Abba Horodezky's similar approach to that of these authors, see Deutsch, *The Maiden of Ludmir,* 23–33.

12. Gershon Hundert, in a tenuous way, posits a decline in the importance of lineage during the rise of Hasidism; David Assaf implies that ancestral lineage was not a factor during the formative stages of the movement, that is, up until early nineteenth-century Ukrainian Hasidism; and Arthur Green assumes that "[t]hose with the finest pedigrees of learning—and family—from Elijah Gaon in Vilna to Rabbi Ezekiel Landau in Prague, were known to be unsympathetic to the new movement (i.e., Hasidism) and its leaders." See Hundert, *The Jews in a Polish Private Town,* 155; Assaf, *The Regal Way,* 47–8; Green, "Typologies of Leadership," 130.

13. *Shivhei Ha-Besht,* tale no. 8, p. 21; "*im ploni almoni she lo nodah mekomo u mishpahato.*"

14. It was not inconceivable to match a *ba'al shem* of humble origins with R. Gershon's sister, who was a divorcee. According to a later tradition, the wife of R. Meir Margaliot refused to allow the Besht to procure a match between one of his children and a member of Margaliot family because of the Besht's lack of *yihus.* Meir Wunder, *Elef Margaliot* (Jerusalem: Ha-Makhon le-Hantsahat Yahadut Galitsyah, 1993), 24. See also Etkes, *The Besht,* 168.

15. A blatant fabrication of the Besht's lineage occurs in Nathan Zvi Friedman, *Ozar HaRabbanim* (Bnei Brak, n.d.), a work Wunder describes as containing "many mistakes in both content and arrangement." See "The Reliability of Genealogical Research in Modern Rabbinic Literature," (*Avotaynu* 11:4 [1995], 31–36). Friedman attempts to identify the Besht's father as Eliezer Isserles, a descendant of Moses Isserles (52). See also Aaron David Twersky, *Sefer Ha-Yahas Mi-Chernobyl ve-Ruzhin* (Lublin, 1938; reprint, Jerusalem, n.d.), 101. Samuel Horodezky describes the Besht as "a son of unknown parents, and not the 'son of famous ancestors.' " See *Leaders of Hassidism,* tr. Maria Horodezky-Magasanik (London: Hasefer, 1928), 5.

16. Rosman, *Founder of Hasidism,* 156–8. "The honorifics applied to the Besht by R. Meir, the scion of a very important rabbinic family, indicate that the Besht was a person of some fame and worthy of the respect of scholars." Moshe Rosman, "Social Conflicts in Miedzyboz," in Rapoport-Albert, *Hasidism Reappraised,* 51–62.

17. Reiner, "Hon, Ma'amad Hevrati," 39–41. Members of the Brody *kloyz* were exempted from a ban of excommunication threatened against those who engaged in kabbalistic practices.

18. Jacob Immanuel Schochet, *The Great Maggid* (Brooklyn: Kehot Publication

Society, 1974), 170–2. Schochet provides a fascimile of documents composed by Dov Ber. Based on these signatures, he deems R. Abraham "a scholar steeped in rabbinic learning" (21).

19. W. Z. Rabinowitch, *Lithuanian Hasidism*, 13–4.

20. For example, Schochet, *The Great Maggid*, 21.

21. Assaf, *The Regal Way*, 47–8. According to Assaf's schema, the first generation of zaddikim, "exemplified" by the Ba'al Shem Tov, arose by suddenly revealing their magical, prophetic, or charismatic abilities; the next generation—the generation of the Maggid of Międzyrzecz and his students—ascended by means of their intellectual abilities; while the third generation inherited leadership from their fathers, i.e., became zaddikim because of their *yihus*.

22. Etkes, *Ba'al ha-Shem*, chap. 1.

23. Levitats, *The Jewish Communitiy in Russia*, 113, 133, and 139. Levitats is, however, misleading in his characterization of early Hasidic leaders as "lowly folk," citing the Besht, Great Maggid, and Grandfather of Szpola as if they were typical (162).

24. Bedřich Nosek, "Shemuel Shmelke Ben Tsvi Hirsh Ha-Levi Horovits: Legend and Reality," *Judaica Bohemiae* 21:2 (1985), 75 and 89.

25. Ettinger, "The Hasidic Movement—Reality and Ideals," 240; Sharot, *Messianism, Mysticism, and Magic*, 169. Ettinger fails to note prominent exceptions like R. Jehiel Michael of Złoczów, R. Schneur Zalman of Liady, and certain descendants of the Besht.

26. Rapoport-Albert, "Hasidism after 1772," 77 and 93.

27. Nehemia Polen, "Rebbetzins, Wonder-Children and the Emergence of the Dynastic Principle in Hasidism," unpublished paper delivered at the Shtetl Conference at Boston University, Center for Judaic Studies, November 1, 2002 (Updated March 1, 2004, courtesy of the author).

28. Rosman, *Founder of Hasidism*, 201. See also Elior, "Ha-mahlohet al Moreshet Habad," 166-86. However, as mentioned earlier, the first hereditary transition occurred between R. Jehiel Michael of Złoczów and his son Moses in 1781. See Altshuler, "The First Tzaddik of Hasidism," 134.

29. *Altshuler, "The First Tzaddik of Hasidism,"* 204. Nafthali Loewenthal explains the adoption of hereditary succession in Lubavitcher Hasidism as owing to tendencies already present within the rabbinate, in addition to the monarchic and priestly models upon which the zaddik was based. See *Communicating the Infinite: The Emergence of the Habad School* (Chicago: University of Chicago Press, 1990), 104–8.

30. Anne Berger-Sofer, "An Exploration into the Lubavitcher Hasidic Leadership Kinship Alliance Network," *Working Papers in Yiddish and East European Jewish Studies* 27 (New York: YIVO Institute for Jewish Research 1977), 2.

31. Berger-Sofer, "An Exploration into the Lubavitcher Hasidic Leadership Kinship Alliance Network," 10.

32. Yoseph Salmon, "R. Naphtali Zevi of Ropczyce ('The Ropshitser') as a Hasidic Leader," in Rapoport-Albert, *Hasidism Reappraised*, 332–3.

33. R. Israel was the son of R. Shalom Shakhna of Pohrebyszcze, grandson of Abraham "the Angel," and great grandson of Dov Ber, "the Great Maggid" of Międzyrzecz.

34. Assaf, *The Regal Way*, 47–8.

35. David Assaf, "Manhigut ve-Yerushat Manhigut be-Hasidut be-Me'ah ha-19," in Hana Anit, ed., *On Leadership and Leaders* (in Hebrew) (Jerusalem: Ministry of Defence, 2000), 59–72.

36. Avraham Grossman, "From Father to Son: The Inheritance of Spiritual Lead-

ership in Jewish Communities in the Middle Ages," in David Kraemer, ed., *The Jewish Family: Metaphor and Memory* (New York: Oxford University Press, 1989), 115–32.

37. See Jacob Katz, "Nisuim Ve-Hayei Ishut Be-Mozei Yemei Ha-Benayyim," *Zion* 10 (1944–45), 33–48. Saul Bastomsky attempts to compare *yihus* to the Roman notion *dignatus* but the comparison, according to his own conclusion, is unfruitful. See Saul Bastomsky, "*Yihus* in the Shtetl and *Dignitas* in the Late Roman Republic," *Judaism* 39:1 (1990), 93–96. Isaac Levy writes apologetically: "The term has never borne the connotation of vain pride, but rather has acted as the guarantee that a union shall be established on firm foundations . . . which shall accord with the long cherished traditions associated with the Jewish home. It is because the influence of family background plays so large a part in domestic Jewish life." See "Marriage Preliminaries," in Peter Elman, ed., *Jewish Marriage* (London: Soncino Press, 1967), 43.

38. Mark Zborowski and Elizabeth Herzog, *Life Is with People* (New York: Schocken Books, 1952), 76.

39. This analysis does not consider *yihus azmo*—honorary *yihus* attained by virtue of one's own accomplishments.

40. According to Hundert, "[p]articularly during the first two-thirds of the eighteenth century, a kind of Polish-Lithuanian Jewish aristocracy existed. Members of a relatively small number of families held an astonishing number of rabbinical and communal offices. Among these families were the Ginzburgs, Heilperins, Horowitzs, Rapoports, and Katzenellenbogens." See *Jews in a Polish Private Town*, 117.

41. On father-son succession in the rabbinate, see Shaul Stampfer, "Inheritance of the Rabbinate in Eastern Europe in the Modern Period—Causes, Factors and Development over Time," *Jewish History* 13:1 (1999), 36–56; Sidney B. Hoenig, "Filial Succession in the Rabbinate," *Gratz College Annual of Jewish Studies* 1 (1972), 14–22; and Jefferey I. Roth, "Inheriting the Crown in Jewish Law: The Question of Rabbinic Succession," *Jewish Law Association Studies 9: The London Conference Volume* (1997), 237–59.

42. Polish village self-governing counsels were headed by the *wojt* or *soltys*, and assessors (so-called jurors), offices that frequently passed from father to son and were restricted to the most prosperous and well-connected with the noble town owner or administrator. They arbitrated legal disputes, collect taxes, and shaped the moral pattern that was binding on the village. See Bogucka, *The Lost World*, 33–4.

43. Marc Bloch, *Feudal Society* (Chicago: University of Chicago Press, 1961), 2: 283, 320–9. In 1790, however, barely 30,000 of the 120,000 noble families in the Polish-Lithuanian Commonwealth owned their land outright. Although all Polish nobles were theoretically equal, landless nobles were barred from election to public office, among other things. Nobility itself was not determined by property, which only served to stratify the nobility. See Jerzy Łukowski, *Liberty's Folly: the Polish Lithuanian Commonwealth in the Eighteenth Century* (London: Routledge, 1991), 9–37.

44. The fourth Mishnah of BT Kiddushin, for example, lists ten genealogical classes in order of prominence, and describes forbidden marriages. A Mishnah in BT Ta'anit 16b describes an ancient matchmaking ritual in which the women exclaimed to the men: "Do not set your eyes on beauty, but set your eyes on [good] family." But a Mishnah in BT Horayot 13a asserts: "the learned bastard takes precedence over the ignorant high priest." See also BT Eduyot 7b, Mishnah 7. One is discouraged against marrying above one's station in BT Kiddushin, 49a, and BT Kiddushin 70a: "he who takes a wife who is not fitting for him, the Torah reckons him as having ploughed the whole world and sown it with salt." One who marries below his station "disqualifies

his seed and blemishes his family." An uneven family status was understood as the cause of a bride's death (BT Ketubot 62b). The Talmud condones R. Ze'iri's decision not to marry his daughter into R. Johanan's family on the basis of the latter's inferior lineage. (BT Kiddushin 71b). One dictum states that when God causes his "divine Presence to alight," it is only upon families with *yihus* (BT Kiddushin, 70b); and another (BT Baba Batra 109b) states: "One should always cleave [i.e. through marriage] to good people [*tovim*]; for behold, from Moses who married the daughter of Jethro (an idolater) there descended Jonathan, while from Aaron, who married the daughter of Aminadab, there descended Phineas." In *Genesis Rabbah*, it is recorded in the name of R. Simon, "It is difficult for the Holy One, blessed be He, to upset a chain of *yihus*." The biblical Reuben lost his money, but not his noble descent. Others dissent (*Genesis Rabbah, Vayishlah* 82:11). *Bemidbar Rabbah, Naso* 8:9, teaches "even an idolater who converts and studies the Torah, behold, is like a High Priest."

45. The gemara explains the Bible's mention of the *yihus* of the officers of King David's army (1 Chronicles 7:40) as teaching that "their own merit and the merit of their fathers might aid them." BT Kiddushin 76b.

46. Grossman, "From Father to Son," 116. Many of these ideas are found in Grossman's other works, including *Hakhamei Ashkenaz Ha-Rishonim* (Jerusalem: Magnes Press, 1981), 400–440.

47. Israel Ta-Shma, "On the History of Polish Jewry in the Twelfth and Thirteenth Centuries," *Polin* 10 (1997); Hayyim Soloveitchik, "Three Themes in the *Sefer Hasidim*," *AJS Review* 1 (1976), 319–20.

48. Ephraim Kanarfogel, *Jewish Education and Society in the High Middle Ages* (Detroit: Wayne State University Press, 1992), 68. The German-born Judah Asheri (1250–1327/8) left a will with an extensive family history exhorting his children: "And the good name which your fathers bequeathed, uphold it and leave it to your children as a heritage." The children must toil in Torah or they will forsake their family tradition. See Israel Abrahams, *Hebrew Ethical Wills* (Philadelphia: Jewish Publication Society, 1926), 171–3.

49. In his responsa *Nodah Be-Yehuda* (Prague, 1776 and 1811), Ezekiel Landau (1713–93) claims: "Because I am from the stock of Rashi, I will interpret his sayings correctly." See section Yoreh Deah, no. 201. Cited in Judah Leib Hakohen Fishman, *Sarei Ha-Meah* (Jerusalem, 1944), 1:188. R. Jacob ben Asher (c. 1270–1340) argues that "to appoint despised families to lead the public" is to "despise the mizvah, as if the families with *yihus* in Israel are no more worthy than anyone else." That proclamation is hedged in by: "if he is a possessor of *yihus* and evil, what benefit is there before God in his *yihus*? And if he is from a lowly family and is a *zaddik*, it is good to bring a distant seed closer." See *Shulhan Arukh*, "Orah Hayyim," 53. R. Solomon Luria (c. 1510–74) argues that "in any case, if both of them are equal, of course the one with *yihus* comes before the one without *yihus*, and it is proper to be strict about this, for nothing is comparable to the prayer of a zaddik who is the son of a zaddik, etc." Maharshal, *Commentary on the Tur*, in *Bayit Hadash*, gloss on Orah Hayyim, 53.

50. Katz, "Nisuim Ve-Hayyei Ishut."

51. Salo Baron, *The Jewish Community* (Philadelphia: Jewish Publication Society, 1948), 3:132; Simha Assaf, "Le-Korot ha- Rabanut," in *Be-Ohalei Ya'akov* (Jerusalem: Mosad Ha-Rav, 1943), 40; Shalom Albeck, "Rabenu Tam's Attitude to the Problems of His Time" (in Hebrew), *Zion* 19 (61954), 128–30; and Gerald Bildstein, "Individual and Community in the Middle Ages: Halakhic Theory," in Daniel Elazar, ed., *Kinship and Consent* (Washington, D.C.: University Press of America, 1983), 217–58.

52. Shlomo Goittein has termed it a "religious democracy," meaning that

aristocratic-authoritative elements in Jewish communal government functioned thanks to communal sanction, but leadership was no less aristocratic or authoritative. Shlomo Dov Goitein, "Political Conflict and the Use of Power in the World of the Geniza," in Elazar, *Kinship and Consent*, 169–81. As Gershon Hundert puts it, "even the according of deference involves a measure of choice." See *Jews in a Polish Private Town*, 117.

53. Katz, "Nisuim Ve-Hayyei Ishut," 33–48. See also Chae Ran Freeze, *Jewish Marriage and Divorce in Imperial Russia* (Hanover, N.H.: Brandeis University Press, 2002), 36–41.

54. Katz, "Nisuim Ve-Hayyei Ishut," 33–48.

55. Stampfer, "*Heder* Study, Knowledge of Torah, and the Maintenance of Social Stratification in Traditional East European Jewish Society," 271–89.

56. Hayyim Hillel Ben Sasson, "Musagim ve-Meziyut be-Historiya ha-Yehudit be-Shilhei Yamei ha-Benayim," *Tarbiz* 29 (1959–60), 301.

57. *The Jews of A Polish Private Town*, 124–31.

58. Rosman, *The Lords' Jews* (Cambridge, Mass.: Harvard University Press, 1991), esp. 17 and 170.

59. Phineas Katzenellenbogen, *Sefer Yesh Manhillin*, ed. I. D. Feld (Jerusalem, 1986), 61–2.

60. Katzenellenbogen, *Sefer Yesh Manhillin*, 262. One chain stretches from a girl's father's father's father-in-law.

61. Katzenellenbogen, *Sefer Yesh Manhillin*, 156.

62. Katzenellenbogen, *Sefer Yesh Manhillin*, 181, 187, 207, 217, 243. One proposed match between R. Phineas and a rabbi's daughter was "a great thing, to draw me close [to him] and give me the sister of his wife, who was the daughter of great ones" (207). Later, R. Phineas merited the honor of clinging through marriage to the seed of a different rabbi (254–5).

63. Katzenellenbogen, *Sefer Yesh Manhillin*, 231.

64. *The Memoirs of Ber of Bolechów*, tr. Mark Vischnitzer (London: Humphrey Milford, 1922), 80.

65. *The Memoirs of Ber of Bolechów*, 69.

66. *The Memoirs of Ber of Bolechów*, 118.

67. *The Memoirs of Ber of Bolechów*, 126. "The grandfather of the bride was greatly pleased when he saw 'the house of my precious things,' and found that I was a man of substance. He thanked the Almighty that his grandchild was given to reliable people."

68. *Solomon Maimon: An Autobiography*, ed. Moses Hadas (New York: Shocken Books, 1967), 24–7.

69. Hayyim Hillel Ben Sasson, *Hagut ve-Hanhagah* (Jerusalem: Mosad Bialik, 1959), 96–7.

70. Ben Sasson, *Hagut ve-Hanhagah*, 97. Ephraim demarcates three types of "arrogant *yihus* possessors in Poland": those who are independently wealthy, those from a wealthy family, and those from a learned family.

71. BT Pesahim 49. "A man should always sell everything he has and marry his daughter to a scholar."

72. Samuel Shmelke Horowitz, *Shemen ha-Tov* (Piotroków Trybunalski, 1905), no. 153, p. 118.

73. Joseph Weiss, "Torah Study in Early Hasidism," in *Studies in East European Jewish Mysticism and Hasidism*, 56–68.

74. Elijah, the Vilna Gaon, *Commentary to Proverbs*, 11:20. Cited in *Ha-Hasidut Be-Mishnat ha-Rishonim*, "Shar ha-zaddik," (n.p., 1989), 28.

75. Hayyim of Volozhin, *Nefesh ha-Hayyim* (Bnei Brak, 1989), section *Ez Hayyim*, 448, no. 134.

76. Hayyim of Volozhin, *Nefesh ha-Hayyim*, section *Ez Hayyim*, 448, no. 137.

77. I.e., the covenant. Psalm 105:9.

78. The tradition begins: "I heard from S(imha) B(unem) . . .*av bet din* of Wislowiec, grandson of the great, holy Naftali Zvi Horowitz, *av bet din* of Ropczyce, that (R. Naftali Zvi) added the name Horowitz, after the surname of his mother's father . . . Isaac Halevi Horowitz, *av bet din* of Altona, Hamburg and Nadsavk." Hanokh Henokh Zilberschaz, ed., *Shemen Ha-Tov* (Pietrokóv, 1905), 106 no. 106 (misprinted as no. 100), a collection of sayings attributed to Samuel Shmelke Horowitz of Nikolsburg. Compare Isaac ben Asher, ed., *Sefer Nifla'ot Ha Yehudi: Bet zaddikim* (Jerusalem, 1907), 88, which acknowledges *Shemen Ha-Tov* as its source.

79. Naftali Horowitz, *Ohel Naftali* (Lwow: Zeidman and Oisshnit, 1910), 73 and 138; and *Responsa Imrei David*, introduction, no. 14, cited in A. J. Heschel, *The Circle of the Baal Shem Tov* (Chicago: University of Chicago Press, 1985), 163.

80. Ya'akov Margaliot, *Gedolim Ma'aseh Zadikim: Sipurim Hasidiyim*, ed. Gedalya Nigal (Jerusalem: Ha-Makhon le-Heker Ha-Sifrut Ha-Hasidut, 1991), no. 1. Rosman argues for the tale's authenticity because it does not presume a pedigree for the Besht. *Founder of Hasidism*, 156. Tale no. 10 has the Besht proclaim his special affection for the brothers.

81. When the Besht learned of a deceased Hasid's "young talented son who was being pushed into a marriage of low degree," he commanded the mother not to make the match. The Besht refused to be godfather at a circumcision ceremony because he perceived that the boy was an illegitimate offspring (*mamzer*). Once during a sermon, he exclaimed, "God O God, it is known and revealed to you that I do not preach this sermon for my honor (but for the honor of my father's and my mother's families)." See Ben-Amos and Mintz, *In Praise of the Baal Shem Tov*, tale no. 41, p. 54; no. 184, p. 195; no. 83, p. 107.

82. Ben Amos and Mintz, *In Praise of the Baal Shem Tov*, 258, no. 249. Yet according to a more edifying tale, the Besht vouchsafed "the mystical intent of a name composed of *alef-bet-gimel*, for I myself am this Name" to Zvi Hirsch later on in a dream. Phineas of Korzec, *Midrash Pinhas*, sec. 39, p. 30, cited in Gedalya Nigal, *Magic, Mysticism, and Hasidism*, tr. E. Levin (Northvale, N.J.: Aronson, 1994), 31.

83. Aharon of Apt, *Keter Shem Tov* (1794; reprint, Brooklyn, 1987), 59–60, no. 238. There is a controversy over the extent to which it contains authentic Besht teachings. See Rosman, *Founder of Hasidism*, p. 260, no. 69.

84. On R. Meshullam Feibush Heller's versions of the same parable, see Miles Krassen, *Uniter of Heaven and Earth: Rabbi Meshullam Feibush Heller of Zabarazh and the Rise of Hasidism in Eastern Galicia* (Albany: State University of New York Press, 1998), 96 and ns. 7–9.

85. Jacob Joseph Hakohen of Połonne, *Toldot Ya'akov Yosef* (Jerusalem, 1962), 393, parshat *Emor*.

86. Jacob Joseph Hakohen of Połonne, *Toldot Ya'akov Yosef*, 144, parshat *Va'ereh*.

87. The Great Maggid interprets the question "Why is there a zaddik who fares well, and a zaddik who fares ill?" (in BT Berakhot 7a, the question relates to the suffering of the righteous): "This means: why is there a zaddik who requires a great effort to break his bad qualities, and a zaddik who does not require a great effort for

this? And the teaching: 'zaddik son of a zaddik' seeks to convey that the son always has his father's nature; and, despite freedom of choice, even so, most have a nature similar to their fathers. And thus the teaching: 'A zaddik who is the son of a zaddik fares well,' for he already has his father's nature; while in the case of the 'zaddik son of an evildoer,' *his nature is reversed.*" See *Likkutim Hadashim,* 202a, cited in Moses Solomon Kasher, ed., *Mesillot Be-Mahshevat Ha-Hasidut* (Jerusalem, 1977), 22.

88. Ada Rapoport-Albert observes that R. Elimelekh has been incorrectly designated a proponent of hereditary succession.
See "The Problem of Succession in the Hasidic Leadership, with Special Reference to the Circle of Nahman of Bratslav" (Ph.D. diss., University of London, 1970), 128–30. Compare Samuel Horodezky, ed., *Shivhei Ha Besht* (Tel Aviv, 1947), notes, p. 190, n. 8.

89. Elimelekh of Leżajsk *No'am Elimelekh,* parshat *Emor,* tr. Shmuel Ettinger, "The Hasidic Movement," in Hundert, *Essential Papers on Hasidism,* 240. For a recent discussion on these teachings, see Assaf, *The Regal Way,* 51–3.

90. Elimelekh of Leżajsk, *No'am Elimelekh,* 104, parshat *Bemidbar.*

91. Elimelekh of Leżajsk, *No'am Elimelekh,* 104, parshat *Lekh Lekha.*

92. Elimelekh of Leżajsk, *No'am Elimelekh,* 350, parshat *Behar.* Cited in Rapoport-Albert, "Hasidism after 1772," 126–7.

93. Elimelekh of Leżajsk, *No'am Elimelekh,* 194, parshat *Bo.* R. Elimelekh furthermore hopes that the children of Israel will "watch over themselves carefully, and not watch over their ancestral merit, in order that there not come over them, God forbid, any boasting because of their *yihus.*" They should "look upon themselves as if they no ancestral merit at all." Otherwise, "they can defile the spirit." 340–1, parshat *Amor.*

94. Elimelekh of Leazzajsk, *No'am Elimelekh,* 197, parshat *Bo.* On the verse "a staff from each ancestral house"(Numbers 17:17), R. Elimelekh explains "that they will humble themselves and not pride themselves on the *yihus* of their fathers." 421, parshat *Korah.*

95. Elimelekh of Leżajsk, *No'am Elimelekh,* 417, parshat *Korah.*

96. According to Arthur Green, he "was not a great original thinker or spiritual teacher, but saw himself rather as custodian of the path that had been laid out by his grandfather, the Ba'al Shem Tov, and as heir to his authority." *Tormented Master,* 95. Gottlober, in *Zikhronot u-Masa'ot,* 1: 164–5, describes his argument with Shneur Zalman. Barukh allegedly proclaimed, "I am the grandson of the Besht and I should be shown respect." Shneur Zalman answered, "I, *too,* am the grandson of the Besht, his spiritual grandson, for the great Maggid was an outstanding disciple of the Besht and I am a disciple of the Maggid." Barukh of Międzybóż, "Mekor Barukh," in *Buzina Di-nehara Ha Shalem,* ed. Reuben Margaliot (Bilgoraj, n.d.), s. 9, 24, cited in Rapoport-Albert, "Hasidism after 1772," 111–2. Rapoport considers this "a piece of fictional writing by Rodkinson, inspired by the dynastic outlook which had become characteristic of Habad by the second half of the nineteenth century."

97. *Buzina Di-nehara,* toward the end; *Buzina Di-nehara Ha-Shalem,* 5, quoted in Ettinger, "The Hasidic Movement," 239. However, it is doubtful that R. Jacob Joseph intended his advice literally, for succession was undeveloped at the time.

98. "Abraham trusted in God that his son also would be illuminated in all the upper worlds, like him. And how did he trust in God that his son would also be like this? For to do this requires great effort and striving toward Godly ways. 'And he reckoned it to His charity (Genesis 15:6),' meaning: because Abraham did not think that by himself and his own deeds he came to be illuminated in all the upper worlds; and

that this was only thanks to the charity of God. And Abraham trusted that his son, too, could illuminate all the worlds." *Buzina Di-nehara* (Jerusalem, 1970), I.

99. Gottlober, *Zikhronot u-Masa'ot*, 1: 176. The recollection of the event is based on recent memory, however, as Gottlober was not born when the meeting occurred.

100. Letter from R. Asher of Stolin to R. Israel "the Maggid" of Kozienice, in David Zvi Heilman, ed., *Iggerot Ba'al ha-Tanya ve-Bnei Doro* (Jerusalem, 1953), 184. Rabinowitsh dates the letter between 1802 and 1807. See *Lithuanian Hasidism*, 68–70.

101. Nahman of Bratslav, *Shivhei ha Ran: Sihot ha Ran* (Lemberg, 1901), p. 60b no. 166; Rapoport-Albert, "Hasidism after 1772," 114–8.

102. Nahman of Bratslav, *Hayei Moharan: Nesiyato le-Erez Yisrael* (Jerusalem, 1962), p. 61, no. 1. Rapoport-Albert omits the crucial latter part of the tale: Nahman's mother asks him a second time when he will visit the Besht's grave, and he answers, "now I will not be at his grave, [but] during my return, with God's help, I will be at his grave." *Avaneihah Barzel* (Jerusalem, 1961), p. 17, no. 15. Cited in Rapoport-Albert, "Hasidism after 1772," 116.

103. Nahman of Bratslav, *Shivhei Ha-Ran* (Lemberg, 1901), 7, no. 25.

104. See Nahman of Bratslav, *Shivhei HaRan*, 7b: Once, R. Nahman denied having traveled to Kamienic-Podolsk to find letters of the Besht, for, he claimed, "I do not need them at all." In *Shivhei HaRan, Sihot HaRan*, 68b, "a certain old man from Slopkovitz [Solobkovtsy] who knew his grandfather, the holy R. Nahman Horodenker, of blessed memory, stood before our rabbi of blessed memory. He answered and said, 'They say that my teaching is from my grandfather, of blessed memory. If my grandfather R. Nahman himself heard my teaching, it would also be an innovation [*hidush*] for him."

105. Nahman of Bratslav, *Shivhei Ha-Ran*, p. 10, no. 11; p. 13, no. 19; p. 27, no. 22; p. 17, no. 24.

106. Nahman of Bratslav, *Haye Moharan*, 3:11; Green, *Tormented Master*, 166.

107. Nahman of Bratslav, *Likkutei Moharan*, 2, 97: " 'zaddik, ruling in the fear of God' (2 Samuel, 23:3). Everyone in Israel can reach this level of 'ruling' in his prayer; however, there are two hindrances. One is before prayer, i.e., he makes ready to pray in self-importance—because he has great *yihus* or because he toiled and labored in the service of the Creator—and because of this it is impossible to have governance in his prayer. One must rather forget all this, and it will seem to him as if he were only created today, and he is alone in the world. . . . 'For God has made me forget . . . all my father's house' (Genesis 41:51), this is *yihus*."

108. Nahman of Bratslav, *Likkutei Moharan*, 2, Torah 7, p. 13.

109. Nahman of Bratslav, *Sefer ha-Midot* (New York, 1967), 142.

110. Zvi Elimelekh of Dinów, *Responsa Bnei Yissakar* (Jerusalem, 1978), Month of Nissan 4:10, p. 94.

111. Rabinowitz, *Encyclopedia of Hasidism*, 451.

112. Salmon, "R. Naphtali Zevi of Ropczyce ('the Ropshitser') as a Hasidic Leader," 330.

113. Yehuda Leib of Zaklików, *Likkutei Maharil*, parshat Veyare (Lemberg, 1862), 11.

114. Assaf, *The Regal Way*, 61–2.

115. See Assaf, *The Regal Way*, 47–65.

116. Assaf, *The Regal Way*, 33, 51.

117. Perl, *Megalle Temirin*, 210, letter 127.

118. Advice of a zaddik to his son. Levinsohn, "Emek Refa'im," 127.

119. Cited in Assaf, " 'Money for Household Expenses,' " 14.

120. See Rabinowitsch, *Lithuanian Hasidism*, 101–102.

121. Stampfer, "Inheritance of the Rabbinate in Eastern Europe in the Modern Period."

122. On the verse "either his uncle or his uncle's son may redeem him" (Leviticus 25:49), R. Samuel Shmelke explained: "this is the zaddik, who is like a son to the Holy One Blessed Be He, or from his blood relations—his physical relatives—owing to there being a zaddik in his family." See Jacob Isaac Horowitz of Lublin, *Zikharon Zot*, parshat *Bahar*, 104.

123. Levi Isaac of Berdyczów, *Kedushat Levi ha-Shalem*, 200, parshat *Emor*.

124. Levi Isaac of Berdyczów, *Kedushat Levi ha-Shalem*, 154, parshat *Balak*.

125. Nahman of Bratslav, *Hayei Moharan*, 2, 3:93; Green, *Tormented Master*, 112.

126. As noted, Hundert tentatively interprets this episode as revealing the diminished significance of lineage in determining social status during the rise of Hasidism. Hundert, *The Jews in a Polish Private Town*, 155.

127. Israel Hopstein of Kozienice, *Tiferet Adam*, cited in M. Seinfeld, *Emet Mi-Kozk Tizmah* (Bnei Brak, 1961), 233. This tradition is conveyed by R. Menahem Mendel of Kotsk, who descended from R. Israel Halperin, *av bet din* of Ostróg and disciple of the Besht. However, see Shalom Gutman, *Tiferet Bet Levi*, 15. Levi Isaac similarly explains that "we are great *yihus* possessors, children of Abraham, Isaac and Jacob, while you [non-Jews] have nobody for a father." Thus, such expressions should not necessarily be taken at face value.

128. Israel Hopsten of Kozienice, *Tiferet Adam*, in Seinfeld, *Emet*, 155, parshat *Pinhas*.

129. Letter printed in Zvi Yehezkel Michaelson, *Siftei Kodesh* (Warsaw, 1929), 13.

130. Jacob Isaac Horowitz of Lublin, *Divrei Emet* (New York, 1946), parshat *Hay-ye Sarah*, beginning.

131. Horowitz, *Shemen Ha-Tov*, "Stories," no. 26, p. 66. This tradition is a further indication that a certain tension did result from Barukh's overemphasis of his Beshtian *yihus*.

132. Jacob Isaac Horowitz of Lublin, *Zikharon Zot*, 104, in *Torat ha-Hoze mi-Lublin*, 268.

133. Jacob Isaac Horowitz of Lublin, *Zot Zikharon*, 336.

134. Jacob Isaac Horowitz of Lublin, *Zikharon Zot*, 119, parshat *Korah*.

135. Jacob Isaac Horowitz of Lublin, *Zot Zikharon*, 15.

136. Barukh Yashar (Shlikhter), *Bet Komarna* (Jerusalem, 1965), 37. The betrothal contract is printed on pp. 37–9. See also the betrothal contract of the zaddik Abraham Joshua Heschel of Opatów, and another such contract signed by R. Nahman of Horodenka, in Heschel, "Umbakante Dokumenten Zu der Geschichte fon Khasides," 118–9. The contracts commence with detailed genealogical descriptions of the prospective bride and groom.

137. I have used the chart provided in the *Encyclopedia Judaica*, 1:160–9 as a guideline. Genealogical information is based on Levi Halevi Grossman, *Shem u-She'erit* (Tel Aviv, 1942); Wunder, *Elef Margaliot*, and *Ma'orei Galiziya—Enzyklopediya Le-Hakhmei Galicia*, 4 vols. (Jerusalem: Institute for the Commemoration of Galician Jewry, vol. 1, 1978; vol. 2, 1982; vol. 3, 1986; vol. 4, 1990), and "The Reliability of Genealogical Research in Modern Rabbinic Literature," *Avoteynu* 11:4 (winter 1995), 31–6; Aaron Walden, *Sefer Shem Ha- Gedolim He-Hadash* (Warsaw, 1879); Twersky, *Sefer Ha-Yahas Mi-Chernobyl ve-Ruzhin*; Yizhak Alfasi, *Ha-Hasidut* (Tel Aviv: Sifrit Maariv, 1974, 1979); Menahem Mendel Biber, *Mazkeret L'Gedole Ostraha* (Berdyczów, 1907);

Menahem Bodek, *Seder Ha-Dorot Mi-Talmidei ha-Besht* (Jerusalem, 1964–5); Abraham Yizhak Bromberg, *Mi-gedolei Ha-Hasidut* (Jerusalem: Haza'ot Hamahon L'Hasidut), vol. 18, *Bet Kozienice* (1961), vol. 19: *Ha-Hozeh Mi-Lublin* (1962); Solomon Buber, *Anshei Shem* (Cracow, 1895); Nathan Zvi Friedman, *Ozar Ha-Rabanim* (Bnei Brak, n.d.); Gutman, *Tiferet Bet Levi*; Hayyim Haikel of Indura, *Hayyim ve-Hesed* (Warsaw, 1790; reprint, Jerusalem, 1970); Hayyim Meir Heilman, *Bet Rabbi* (Tel Aviv, 1902); Heschel, *The Circle of the Baal Shem Tov: Studies in Hasidim*; Samuel Abba Horodezky, *Ha-Hasidut Ve-Toratah* (Tel Aviv: Dvir, 1951), and *Leaders of Hassidism*, M. H. Kleinman, *Shem Ha-Gedolim He-Hadash* (1977); Nathan Zvi Koenig, *Nevei zaddikim* (Bnei Brak, 1969); Shalom Hayyim Porush, *Encyclopedia of Hasidism, Ishim: Letters aleph to tet)*, ed. Yizhak Raphael (Jerusalem: Mosad HaRav Kook, 1980); Rabinowiz, *Encyclopedia of Hasidism*; Jacob Leib Shapiro, *Mishpahot Atikot be Yisrael* (1981); M. S. Slonim, *Toldot Mishpahat Ha-Rav mi-Liady* (Tel Aviv, 1946).

138. Ben-zion Dinur, *Be-Mifne Ha-Dorot* (Jerusalem: Mosad Bialik, 1954), 108; Gershon Hundert and Gershon Bacon, *The Jews of Poland and Russia: Bibliographical Essays* (Bloomington: Indiana University Press, 1984), 66.

139. Alexander Beider, *A Dictionary of Jewish Surnames from the Kingdom of Poland* (Teaneck, N.J.: Avotaynu, 1996), 33–4. Beider provides what he considers to be an exhaustive list, and claims that all but two (Gordon and Zak) originated in central and western Europe. He errs, however, in stating that "in other regions the role of bearers of rabbinical surnames was less important, since these areas were largely Hasidic, and most Hasidic dynasties were not related to the rabbinical families discussed above."

140. Only R. Eliezer Lipa and R. Dov Ber of Lubavitch seem to have married daughters of humble elementary school teachers; while R. Aryeh Leib of Szpola married the daughter of a Kosher slaughterer.

141. Closest approximation to Hebrew spelling.

142. He was a son of R. Abraham Eliezer Halevi, *av bet din* of Jozefów and Stolbtsy (Shverzna). His mother, Hinda Meitel, was daughter of Jacob Koppel of Lúków, who was purportedly offered the position of *av din* of Amsterdam, but turned it down. Shapiro, *Mishpahot Atikot be Yisrael*, 182; Walden, *Nifla'ot ha-Rabi*, 5. A tradition in the name of R. Elyahu Lehrman, heard from his grandfather via R. Abba Meiri, states, "it was inquired in heaven why they always fulfill the will of R. Jacob Isaac of Lublin ('*Izikel Lancuter*'). And they answered at length that he is the grandson of R. Jacob Kopel, may his memory be for a blessing, from the village of Lúków." Walden, *Nifla'ot ha-Rabi*, Walden, *Or ha-Nifla'ot*, 33:88.

143. R. Abraham and Meitel bore: (1) R. Jacob Isaac, the Seer of Lublin, (2) Asher Zelig of Belżyc, (3) R. Joseph, *av bet din* of Tarnogród, (4) the "Wise Man" of Izbice, (5) the wife of R. Reuven, *av bet din* of Żarnowiec and author of *Dodai be-Sadeh*, and (6) Ziviah, grandmother of several prominent rabbis (Walden, *Nifla'ot ha-Rabi*, 71:184; Grossman, *Shem u-She'erit*, 48). The Seer first married the daughter of R. Meir Halevi, *av bet din* of Most. His second wife, Tehila Shprinza, was daughter of R. Zvi Hirsch of Łańcut. The Seer married his son Israel of Lublin to Hanali, daughter of David, brother of the zaddik Moses of Przeworsk. He married his daughter Czirly to R. Samuel of Rzeszów; his son Joseph of Torczyn (Volhynia) to the daughter of R. Mordecai, *av bet din* of Dubienka, and then Korzec; his son Abraham to the daughter of Jacob Moses of Lublin; and his son Zvi Hirsch to the daughter of a certain Aryeh Leibush of Białystok.

144. R. Fishele Ephraim Shapiro's father, Joseph Leib, was a disciple of R. Jacob Joseph of Połonne and Rabbi of Biała Czerkiew. R. Fishele, a disciple of the Great

Maggid of Międzyrzec, married his second wife in Brzeziny, near the city of Łódz, where he spent the years of his *kest* before becoming Rabbi of nearby Stryków. He had two sons, R. Yekele and R. Izig of Żarnów, and a daughter. He married his son Yekele to the daughter of the doctor and eventual zaddik David Hayyim Bernard of Piotroków Trybunalski. He married his daughter to R. Reuven Kosher, rabbi in Ujazd. See Joseph Shaibowicz, "Towards a History of the Brzezin Kehilah (Jewish Community)," tr. Renee Miller (pp. 78–83 of the Brzezin Communal Record Book [Pinkas]), available: www.jewishgen.org/yizkor/brzeziny/brz078.html; Alfasi, *Ha-Hasidut*, 145.

145. His mother was Moteil, and his father was R. Asher Rabinowicz, *av bet din* of Przedbórz, whose genealogy extended back to R. Isaac Halevi Rabinowicz, brother of the author of *Turei Zahav* (R. David Halevi Rabinowicz). Rabinowicz only notes R. Asher as the Maggid of Przedborz. He served first as rabbi in Grodzisk. See Rabinowicz, *Bein Pshyskha*, 257.

146. The Holy Jew married Sheinedel, daughter of a wealthy innkeeper in Opatów. They married their son Yerahmiel of Przysucha to Golda, daughter of R. Dov, *av bet din* of Biała Czerkiew (Sadeh Lavan), and Sarah, sister of R. Barukh Frankel of Lipnik. He married his son Joshua Asher of Parysów to Lizi, daughter of R. Naftali Zvi Halberstadter. He married his son Nehemia Jehiel of Bychawa to the daughter of Hayyim of Biała Czerkiew. The Holy Jew married his daughter Rebecca Rachel to the zaddik Moses Biderman of Lelów, son of the zaddik David of Lelów. His daughter Sarah Leah married Samuel Raphael's of Lublin. R. Yerahmiel Rabinowicz of Przysucha married his son Nathan David of Szydlowiec to R. Samuel Shlitzky; and his son Jacob Isaac Elhanan of Przysucha to R. Dov Vertzi of Tłust/Korzec. R. Yerahmiel's brother R. Joshua Asher of Parysów married his son Jacob Zvi to the daughter of R. Solomon Halperin of Pinczów, son of the zaddik Menahem Mendel of Przemyślany. His son Aryeh Mordecai of Parysów/Jerusalem married the daughter of R. Samson of Zwolin, disciple of the Holy Jew; and then the daughter of the "wealthy" R. Naphtali Dov Penigstein of Warsaw. His son R. Meir Shalom of Kaluszyn married his brother Jacob Zvi's daughter. His son R. Abraham David Naphtali Yerahmiel of Parysów married the daughter of the "wealthy" Solomon of Reises. R. Nehemia Jehiel of Bychawa married his son Jacob Isaac of Bychawa to the granddaughter of R. Abraham "The Angel," son of R. Dov Ber, the "Great Maggid" of Międzyrzec. He married his son Hayyim Gedaliah of Bychawa to to the daughter of Nathan Leiv, son of R. Menahem Mendel of Rymanów.

147. R. Moses Leib was son of R. Jacob, and an eighth–generation descendant of R. Meir b. Abraham, *av bet din* of Lwów. See Horowitz, *Le-Toldot ha-Kehillot be-Polin*, 81. R. Moses married his daughter Pessi Leah to David of Zabludów, son of the zaddik Menahem Mendel of Kosów. The match of his other daughter, Temerel, is unknown. He married his son and successor as *av bet din* and zaddik in Sasów, R. Yekutiel Shmelke, to the daughter of a wealthy *yihus* possessor named Reuben Jaffee Essek, grandson of R. Mordecai Jaffee, author of the *Levushim* and son-in-law of R. David, *av bet din* of Satanów (son of Israel "Harif," a disciple of the Besht). R. Yekutiel married his daughter to R. Shraga Yair of Białobrzegi, author of *Aran Edat*. His sons Menahem Mendel and Alter Mordecai did not become zaddikim.

148. Letter from Zvi Cohen of Rymanów to Moses Leib, printed in Nahman Shapiro, ed., *Hidushe Ha-Ramal* (Israel, 1967), 42.

149. See *Tiferet Bet Levi*, 28.

150. R. Levi Isaac married his son Meir to Feige, daughter of R. Eliezer, *rosh yeshiva* of Karlin or Pinsk, and sister of R. Moses, *av bet din* and *rosh yeshiva* of Botosani, father-in-law of the zaddik Israel of Ruzhin. R. Levi Isaac married his son and

successor, R. Israel of Pików, to the daughter of R. Akiva of Mykolajów, son of R. Joseph, son of the Besht's disciple R. David of Mykolajów. Sources do not record the wife of R. Levi Isaac's third son, Dov Berish (who married his daughter to R. Eliezer Lipa, son of R. Meir, the "famous genius"). R. Levi Isaac married one of his daughters to Joseph Bunem Walish (who married his son Yekutiel Zalman to Beila, the daughter of R. Dov Ber of Lubavitch). R. Levi Isaac married his other daughter to R. Nathan of Kozienice.

151. R. Abraham Joshua Heschel's ancestors included the Maharam of Padua and R. Saul Wahl. His father, R. Samuel, was *av bet din* of Zamigród, and then Nowe Miasto Korczyn.

152. He had two sons and three daughters. He married Isaac Meir of Żynków to Mirel, daughter of Hayyim Jacob Strom, *av bet din* of Dukla. He married Joseph Moses of Międzyboż to the daughter of a member of the Przeworsk dynasty. His daughter Yokaved first married R. Kalman, son of R. Hayyim of Czernowice. They were divorced due to his apparent mistreatment of Yokaved, who then married Dan Jungerleib of Radzwił, son of R. Isaac of Radzywił. He married his daughter Dinah to Israel of Loczyniec, and married his third daughter Rachel to Mordecai Orenstein.

153. This name was used in official documents, but does not seem to denote his rabbinical descent.

154. Meir had four sons and three daughters. The wives of his sons Samuel of Drilice, R. Israel of Staszów, and Leibush Pesah of Lipsk/Jozefów are not known. R. Meir's son Phineas of Stopnicy married the daughter of R. Hayyim Jacob Strom, *av bet din* of Dukla. His three daughters married R. Menahem Mendel Rabin (or Reuben), *av bet din* of Głogów; R. Leibush Kizes (or Aryeh Leib Neuhaus), *av bet din* of Tomaszów; and R. Kopel, a nephew of the Seer of Lublin.

155. It is not known to whom they married their two daughters, or how long they lived. Levi Ha-Levi Grossman's *Shem u-She'erit* seems to say that their daughter married "Elimelekh, father of Itchela, father of R. Zvi, *av bet din* of Lipsk." Their son R. Abraham Moses of Przysucha married Breindel, daughter of R. Samuel Raphael of Lublin/Jozefów and Sara Leah, daughter of the Holy Jew of Przysucha. R. Abraham married his son Zvi Mordecai to the daughter of the zaddik Isaac of Warka. He married his son Jacob to the daughter of R. Fischel of Lubicz. And he married his daughter to Fischel, son of R. Isaac of Maków, son of R. Nathan Nata of Maków, who was the son-in-law of the zaddik Hayyim Heike of Indura.

156. Assaf, The *Regal Way*, 55.

157. Their eldest son Jacob David (1814–78) married Sarah Leah, daughter of R. Samuel of Parczew, and then Hayyah, daughter of R. Jacob of Jarnowice, and founded the Mszczonów (Amshinov) dynasty. After R. Isaac's death, however, most Warka Hasidim transferred their allegiance to his colleague/disciple Feivel Danziger of Grójec (d. 1849), founder of the Aleksandrów dynasty. Upon Feivel's death, Isaac's younger son Menakhem Mendel (the "Silent Zaddik," 1819–68), son-in-law of R. Zvi Aryeh of Warka," became the Warka zaddik. R. Isaac's daughters were: Zipporah, wife of Zvi Mordecai, son of Abraham Moses of Przysucha; Devorah, wife of R. Aaron Zakheim of Nadrożyn, son of the famous R. Moses Cohen of Warsaw; Sarah Hayyah, wife of R. Israel Zvi, *av bet din* of Białobrzeg; and Bluma, wife of R. Abraham Muskat, son of Isaiah Muskat of Praga, and in her second marriage, R. Geibush Librukh *av bet din* of Turchin.

158. Hayyah bore R. Menahem Mendel two daughters—Sarah Zina and Berakha— and two sons: Benjamin and Moses Yarokham. His son R. David of Kotsk was married to Hayyah Tova, daughter of R. Zvi Grunwald of Opoczno, known famously as

"Hirschele Diskes." Sarah Zina was married to the famous R. Abraham Bornstein, *av bet din* of Sochaczew. Berakha was married to R. Dov Ze'ev Hakohen, *av bet din* of Kotsk, grandson of "the Shakh." R. Benjamin was married to the daughter of R. Abraham Mordecai Alter of Gur Moses Yarokham married the daughter of the wealthy Isaac Blass of Goraj.

159. Gottlober, *Zikhronot u-Ma'asot*, 1: 56, 84 and 109.

160. Ezekiel Kotik, *Ma She-Raiti: Zikhronotav Shel Yehezkel Kotik*, ed. and tr. David Assaf (Tel Aviv: Tel Aviv University, 1999), 299–301.

161. Abraham Gottlober depicts the matchmaker as an aggressive salesman who frequently exaggerates the virtues of prospective matches. "Day after day," he recalls, the matchmaker would intimate to the father that "the time had already arrived to make a match for his son, and the daughter of such and such generous person suits him, and there is none as beautiful as she in all the land, and she speaks the Polish language fluently," the latter being an advantage in the marketplace. But all claims were of doubtful veracity: "the matchmaker who was an expert in his work increasingly uttered things of which the majority is lies." The Talmudic examination of the prospective match was frequently a farce, as "usually the groom departs in peace, for money answers everything." When the parents finally met the prospective match, they usually realized that "all the words of the matchmaker were lies and falsehood." Gottlober, *Zikhronot u-Ma'asot*, 1: 86–8 (composed in 1859). On matchmaking in eastern Europe, see Freeze, *Jewish Marriage and Divorce*, 19–25.

162. Alan Mintz, *"Banished from Their Fathers' Table": Loss of Faith and Hebrew Autobiography* (Bloomington: Indiana University Press, 1989), 27.

163. Mintz, *"Banished from Their Fathers' Table,"* 27. On the Yiddish author Y. L. Peretz's view toward arranged marriages, still occurring in his day, see Michael Taub, "Social Issues in Peretz's Short Dramas," *Yiddish* 10:1 (1995), 19.

164. Immanuel Etkes, "Marriage and Torah Study among the *Lomdim*," in Kraemer, *The Jewish Family*, 155.

165. Mordecai Levine, "Ha-Mishpaha Be-Hevra Mafkhanit Yehudit," *Me'asef* 13 (1982–83), 109–26; *Me'asef* 14 (1984) 157–71.

166. Levine, "Ha-Mishpaha," part 2, 160.

167. According to a Yiddish folksong, *yihus* was becoming incidental: "Perhaps you would like to know my yihus, / My grandfather was a Rabbi; / Let us get married / And put an end to this." Anonymous, cited in Yehoash Dworkin, "East European Yiddish Folk Love-Songs," in Raphael Patai, Francis Lee Utley, and Dov Noy, eds., *Studies in Biblical and Jewish Folklore* (Bloomington: Indiana University Press, 1960), 219. For more on the evolution of *yihus* in the late nineteenth century, see Freeze, *Jewish Marriage and Divorce*, 21–30.

168. Miriam Shomer Zunser, *Yesterday: A Memoir of a Russian Jewish Family* (New York: Harper and Row, 1978), 49.

169. On *yihus* in the twentieth century, see Zborowski and Herzog, *Life Is with People*, 77–9 and 272–3; Celia Stopnicka Rosenthal, "Social Stratification of the Jewish Community in a Small Polish Town," *American Journal of Sociology* 34 (1953), 1–10; Natalie F. Joffe, "The Dynamics of Benefice among East European Jews," *Social Forces* 27 (1948–49), 238–47; Nathan Hurvitz, "Marriage among Eastern European Jews Prior to World War I as Depicted in a *Briefenshteller*," *Journal of Marriage and the Family* 37 (1974), 422–30.

CHAPTER 5

1. The most famous example of a *ba'al shem* employed by the community is the Besht himself. See Rosman, *Founder of Hasidism*. Although kahals sometimes employed *maggidim* in a steady capacity, Joseph Weiss describes the humiliation suffered by *maggidim* who had to beg for the synagogue warden's permission to preach in every town they visited. See "Some Notes on the Social Background of Early Hasidism," 16–7.

2. Katz, *Tradition in Crisis*, 211.

3. See Assaf, " 'Money for Household Expenses,' " 46.

4. Assaf, " 'Money for Household Expenses,' " 46–7.

5. Peter Burke, *Popular Culture in Early Modern Europe* (New York: New York University Press, 1978), 272.

6. From Burke, *Popular Culture*, 281; Itzik Nakhmen Gottesman, *Defining the Yiddish Nation: The Jewish Folklorists of Poland* (Detroit: Wayne State University Press, 2003).

7. Note Gershom Scholem's refusal to distinguish between "the 'pure' Hasidism of the Ba'al Shem (Tov) and the 'depraved' zaddikism of his followers and their followers," allegedly sullied through magic and miracle working. See *Major Trends in Jewish Mysticism*, 342.

8. Compare Etkes, *Ba'al ha-Shem*, 275–91; and "Magic and Miracle Workers in the Literature of the Haskalah," in Feiner and Sorkin, *New Perspectives on the Haskalah*, 113–27. See also Rosman, *Founder of Hasidism*, 18; Ben-Amos and Mintz, *In Praise of the Ba'al Shem Tov*, 173–4, no. 152.

9. AGAD, CWW 186.

10. E. Henderson, *Biblical Researches and Travels in Russia; Including a Tour in the Crimea and The Passage of the Caucasus* (London, 1826), 227.

11. Gottlober, *Zikhronot u-Masa'ot*, 119.

12. On the practice of *kefizat ha-derekh* by *ba'alei shem*, see Nigal, *Magic, Mysticism, and Hasidism*, 33–50.

13. Gottlober, *Zikhronot u-Masa'ot*, 119–21.

14. Apparently a fictional town.

15. Samogitia district, near Kovno.

16. Norman Marsden, tr. and ed., *A Jewish Life under the Tsars: The Autobiography of Chaim Aronson, 1825–1888* (Totowa, N.J.: Allenheld, 1983), 83.

17. See Etkes's survey of known *ba'alei shem*, in *The Besht*, chap. 1; and Yohanan Petrovsky-Shtern, "The Master of an Evil Name: Hillel Ba'al Shem and His *Sefer Ha-Heshek*," *AJS Review* 28:2 (2004), 217–248.

18. The author was born in 1814. See Ludwig Kalisch, *Bilder meiner Knabenzeit* (Leipzig, 1872), 14.

19. Henryk Lew, "O lecznictwie i przesądach," *Izraelita* 31 (1896), 305.

20. Lew, "O lecznictwie i przesądach," 296.

21. Oscar Kolberg, *Dzieło wszystkie: Radomskie* Part 2 vol. 21 (Wrocław, 1964), 169. Reported in *Gazeta Kielecka*, August 2, 1884. See also Michał Zieleniewski, *O przesądach lekarskich ludu naszego* (Cracow, 1845), 66.

22. Etkes, *The Besht*, 41.

23. Etkes, *The Besht*, 47 and 53.

24. The term is an abbreviation of *dibbuk me-ru'ah ra'ah* (a cleavage of an evil spirit) or *dibbuk min ha-hizonim* (dybbuk from the outside). See Gershom Scholem, "Dibbuk," in *Encyclopedia Judaica*, 19–20; and Scholem's " 'Golem' ve 'Dibbuk' ba-

Milon ha-Ivri," *Leshoneinu* 6 (1934), 40–1. Other types of demons occupied houses and synagogues. Ben Amos and Mintz, *In Praise of the Ba'al Shem Tov*, tale no. 23 (p. 37), no. 84 (p. 107), no. 162 (pp. 180–1), no. 211 (pp. 211–2).

25. Moshe Idel, "Jewish Magic from the Renaissance Period to Early Hasidism," in Jacob Neusner, Ernest S. Frerichs, and Paul Virgil McCraken Flesher, ed., *Religion, Science and Magic in Concert and Conflict* (New York: Oxford University Pres, 1989), 107. Idel explains dybbuk possession as the inverse of possession by a Maggid, or angelic mentor.

26. Henryk Biegeleisen, *Lecznictwo ludu Polskiego* (Cracow, 1929), 197; Lew, "O lecznictwie," 352 and 364; Ignacja Piątkowska, "Ludoznawstwo żydowskie," *Wisła* 4 (1890), 806; Regina Lilientalowa, "Przesądy Żydowskie," *Wisła* 14 (1900), 320; B. W. Segel, "O chasydach i chasydyzmie," *Wisła* 8 (1894), 681; Gedalyah Nigal, *Sippurei "Dibbuk" be-Sifrut-Yisrael* (Jerusalem: Reuven Mas, 1994), 26–7.

27. Nigal, *Sippurei "Dibbuk,"* 35. Although young women figure prominently, Yoram Bilu's assertions that "possession trance provides socially deprived individuals, mostly women, with a golden opportunity to assume the spirit's identity and temporarily escape . . . the confines of their social roles" seems overstated. See Bilu, "Dybbuk and Maggid: Two Cultural Patterned [sic] of Altered Consciousness in Judaism," *AJS Review* 21/2 (1996), 346 and 348. In nineteenth–century Russian Christian society, however, it does seem that possession had become an "overwhelmingly female phenomenon." See Worobec, *Possessed*, 64; 66; 99.

28. Nigal, *Sippurei "Dibbuk,"* introduction, 12–25.

29. Toviyyah Hakohen, *Ma'aseh Toviyah* (Venice, 1707; reprint, Cracow, 1908), cited in Dubnow, *Toldot Ha-Hasidut*, 31.

30. Kolberg, *Dzieło wszystkie: Radomskie 2*, vol. 21, 143–66; Kolberg, *Dzieło wszystkie: Chełmskie 2*, vol. 34, 128–42; S. Matusink, *Lud* 14 (1908), 298–9.

31. Oscar Kolberg, *Dzieło wszystkie: Lubelskie 2*, vol. 17 (Wrocław, 1962), 103; S. Matusink, *Lud* 14 (1908), 298–9.

32. Kolberg, *Dzieło wszystkie: Radomskie* Part 2, vol. 21, 161. See also Biegeleisen, *Lecznictwo*, 207.

33. *Lud* 2 (1896), 315; Julian Tuwim, *Czary i Czarty Polskie* (Czytelnik, n.p., 1960), 300; Biegeleisen, *Lecznictwo*, 196; Benedeykt Chmielowski, *Nowe Ateny* (Cracow, n.d.), 100.

34. Biegeleisen, *Lecznictwo*, 108; Chmielowski, *Nowe Ateny*, 99–100; Tuwim, *Czary*, 303.

35. Tuwim, *Czary*, 21.

36. Biegeleisen, *Lecznictwo*, 211. Occasionally, Jewish demons were injurious, as well. The "Tale of the Evil Spirit in Korets," written in Prague, 1665, relates: "Then [the demon] broke her leg—oh my! / He twisted her brain and turned her face about." See Joachim Neugroschel, tr., *The Dybbuk and the Yiddish Imagination: A Haunted Reader* (New York: Syracuse University Press, 2000), 65.

37. Biegeleisen, *Lecznictwo*, 232–41.

38. Biegeleisen, *Lecznictwo*, 197, 206, 210. Aleksander Bruckner, *Dzieje kultury Polskiej* vol. 2 (Cracow, 1931), 112.

39. Chmielowski, *Nowe Ateny*, 147–8; Władysław Smolenski, *Przewrót umysłowy w Polsce wieku 18* (Warsaw, 1923), 20. Several handbooks contain verbatim exorcist prescriptions. See Tuwim, *Czary*, 311–2; Bruckner, *Dzieje kultury*, 112–3.

40. Biegeleisen, *Lecznictwo*, 197 and 213.

41. Nigal, *Sippurei "Dybbuk,"* 236.

42. S.U., "Wypędzanie czarta z opętanego," *Lud* 10 (1904), 215–6; Biegeleisen, *Lecznictwo*, 213.

43. Nigal, *Sippurei "Dybbuk,"* 234 and 239.

44. After the first blow, the girl freed her hands and dealt the zaddik two boxes on the ears. The zaddik then beat her face mercilessly with the *lulav*. See T. K. Oesterreich, *Possession: Demoniacal and Other* (New York: R. R. Smith, 1930), 209.

45. Oesterreich, *Possession*, 48–58. A classic exorcism, which may have formed the basis of S. Ansky's famous play *The Dybbuk*, is contained in Moses Gaster, *Ma'aseh Book* (Philadelphia: Jewish Publication Society, 1934), 301–3.

46. There is no evidence to back up Bilu's assertion that "the exorcist was always a revered rabbi." See "Dybbuk and Maggid," 348.

47. Ben Amos and Mintz, *Shivhei ha-Besht*, 34–5; Nigal, "New Light on the Hasidic Tale and Its Sources," in Rapoport-Albert, *Hasidism Reappraised*, 351; Rapoport-Albert, Gershon Bacon, and Moshe Rosman, "Al Ruhot Dibuk be-Sifrut Hasidim," in *Bar Ilan Sefer ha-Shanah*, 24–5 (Jerusalem, Bar Ilan University 1989), 53. It has been suggested that the Besht's *devekut* entailed a mild form of madness that allowed him to mediate more easily with dybbuks. Zvi Mark, "Dibuk ve-Devekut be-Shivhei ha-Besht: He'arot le-Fonomologiyah shel ha-Shygayon be-Reshit he-Hasidut," in Immanuel Etkes et al., eds., *Be-Ma'aglei Hasidim: Kovets Mehkarim Mukdash le-Zikhro Shel Mordekhai Vilensky* (Jerusalem: Mosad Bialik, 2000), 281.

48. Nigal, *Sippurei "Dybbuk,"* 46. In addition to the Besht, those zaddikim included the Maggid of Kozienice, Pinhas Elijah of Pilce, Shalom of Bełz, the Grandfather of Radoszyc, Hayyim "the Saraf" of Mogielnice, David of Tolna, Hanokh Henekh of Aleksander, Samuel Abba of Żychlin, Solomon of Bobówa, Israel of Ruzhyn, Barukh of Międzybóż, and Aaron of Kajdanów.

49. Letter from Eleazar of Leżajsk to Menahem Mendel of Rymanów, in Anonymous, *Imrei Shefer*, "Kitvei Kodesh" (Lemberg, 1884), 11–2. Nigal misattributes the letter to *Eliezer* of Leżajsk. See Nigal, *Sippurei "Dybbuk,"* 231.

50. Nigal, *Magic, Mysticism and Hasidism*, 96. Such was allegedly the fate of those who scorned the Hasidim of Kuty, R. Hayyim "the *Saraf*" of Mogielnice, R. Levi Isaac of Berdyczów, and the Holy Jew of Przysucha. Note, however, that the latter two are not included on Nigal's list of zaddikim who possessed knowledge of Names! On skepticism toward Hasidic exorcisms among Maskilim, see Etkes, *Ba'al ha-Shem*, 275–91; and "Magic and Miracle Workers in the Literature of the Haskalah," 113–27.

51. On the elite ties of these *ba'alei shem*, see Etkes, *The Besht*, 25–6, and 42.

52. AGAD, CWW 1424, pp. 2–5. Portions of these reports have been published by Marcin Wodziński in "Dybuk. Z Dokumentów Archiwum Głównego Akt Dawnych w Warszawie," *Literatura Ludowa* 36:6 (1992).

53. See Pesah Ruderman, *Ha-dibbuk* (Warsaw, 1878); Jakob Fromer, *Vom Ghetto zur modernen Kultur* (Charlottenburg, 1906), 57–72. Fromer was born in Łódz in 1865. See also Oesterreich, *Possession*, 207–10; Nigal, *Sippurei "Dybbuk,"* 248–50); and Ezekiel Kotik, *Ma she' Ra'iti*, 210–2. First published in Warsaw, 1912.

54. AGAD, CWW 1424, p. 5. On similar beliefs in Russian culture, see Worobec, *Possessed*, 50.

55. Several rabbinic authorities, including R. Meir b. Gedalyah, the Mahram of Lublin, went so far as to explore the legal ramifications of such unions, fearing that they might constitute adultery. Trachtenberg, *Jewish Magic*, 51–4; Nigal, *Magic, Mysticism and Hasidism*, 138–56.

56. AGAD, CWW 1424, p. 6.

57. AGAD, CWW 1424, pp. 7–8. The authorities were also annoyed that the *ba'al shem* had obtained his passport on the pretense of "private business matters" in Warsaw.

58. AGAD, CWW 1424, p. 8.

59. Worobec, *Possessed*, esp. 35. On the slightly later application of Russian psychiatry to the possessed, see 148–67.

60. AGAD, CWW 1424, p. 10.

61. Emphasis added. AGAD, CWW 1424, p. 10.

62. The village of Wola lay on Warsaw's western border, while Praga lay to the east, across the Vistula River.

63. AGAD, CWW 1424, pp. 11–2.

64. AGAD, CWW 1424, p. 13.

65. See Etkes, *The Besht*, esp. 7.

66. Mordecai Wilensky, "Hasidic-Mitnaggedic Polemics in the Jewish Communities of Eastern Europe: The Hostile Phase," in Hundert, *Essential Papers on Hasidism*, 244–71.

67. David of Maków, *Testament*, in Wilensky, *Hasidim u-Mitnaggdim*, 2:245–6 (emphasis added). Mitnaggdim also balked at the audacity of the zaddikim in claiming themselves capable of deriving materiality (*yesh*) from the supernal essence (*ayin*). See David of Maków, *Zemir Arizim*, 14b, in Wilensky, *Hasidim u-Mitnaggdim*, 2:211; and Elior, "Between *Yesh* and *Ayin*."

68. See Etkes, *The Besht*, 144–7.

69. Etkes, *The Besht*, 247.

70. Wilensky, *Hasidim u-Mitnaggdim*, 2:54–188. Dubnow only published fragments. According to Wilensky, R. David completed *Shever Posh'im* before 1800. See "The Polemic of Rabbi David of Makow against Hasidism," *Proceedings of the American Academy of Jewish Research*, vol. 25 (1956), 139.

71. On the use of *meliza* by Maskilim, see Moshe Pelli, "On the Role of *Melitzah* in the Literature of Hebrew Enlightenment," in Lewis Glinert, ed., *Hebrew in Ashkenaz: A Language in Exile* (New York: Oxford University Press, 1993).

72. "Zava'ato shel R. David mi-Makov," in Wilensky, *Hasidim u-Mitnaggdim*, 2:246. R. David was rabbi and maggid in Maków, and a disciple of R. Elijah, the Gaon of Vilna. See Wilensky, "The Polemic of Rabbi David of Makow."

73. Wilensky, "The Polemic of Rabbi David of Makow," 144, no. 36.

74. Israel Loebel, *Sefer Viku'ah*, in Wilensky, *Hasidim u-Mitnaggdim*, 2:313.

75. "*Behorah*," perhaps meaning that R. Levi Isaac was the first and worst of the zaddikim.

76. Usually denotes the honorary officer of a synagogue; but in the new context the *gabbai* was a zaddik's main attendant and organizer.

77. The language is reminiscent of the preparations for the Temple sacrifice.

78. Alternate translation of *ha-aliyah* is "that which is upon it." This is a description of Saul's feast.

79. Originally *mizbe'ah*, or "altar"!

80. David of Maków, *Zemir Arizim*, 3a–4a, in Wilensky, *Hasidim u-Mitnaggdim*, 2:196–7.

81. David of Maków, *Zemir Arizim*, 3a–4a, in Wilensky, *Hasidim u-Mitnaggdim*, 2:196–7.

82. Egypt is likened to a vegetable garden in the original verse.

83. "Until the time of your exodus from Egypt," i.e., midnight.

84. David of Maków, *Zemir Arizim*, 3a–4a, in Wilensky, *Hasidim u-Mitnaggdim*, 2:196–7.

85. David of Maków, *Zemir Arizim*, 3a–4a, in Wilensky, *Hasidim u-Mitnaggdim*, 2: 196–7.

86. David of Maków, *Zemir Arizim*, 17a (Warsaw, 1798), in Wilensky, *Hasidim u-Mitnaggdim*, 2:214.

87. " 'I have heard the groans of the children of Israel' (Exodus 6:16), that they complain that I have repeatedly endeavored 'to speak out against the staff of a Talmudic scholar' (Berakhot 19a), the holy Rabbi, the Maggid of Kozienice, 'dwelling . . . on the corner of a bed, and on a Turkish couch' (Amos 3:12) for his respite, 'because he is a Talmudic scholar, owing to his Torah and faith' (Sotah 21a), and 'spends nights like days' (Mo'ed Katan, 25b). And our Rabbis, may their memory be for a blessing, said, 'If you saw a Talmudic scholar who sinned,' etc. (Berakhot 19a), and they likewise said, elsewhere, 'conceal it as night' (Mo'ed Katan, 17a), and many similar teachings. To this, I return to their hearts, 'eternal penitence' (Sanhedrin 105a) 'and end your murmurings against me' (Numbers 17:25), 'and there was none that moved the wing, or opened the mouth' (Isaiah10:16), and do not 'respect any man's person, nor give flattering titles to anyone' (Job 32:21). 'Where there is a trace of blasphemy, one is not to bestow respect upon a rabbi' (Berakhot 19b)." David of Maków, *Zemir Arizim*, 10b–11a, in Wilensky, *Hasidim u-Mitnaggdim*, 2:207.

88. David of Maków, *Zemir Arizim*, 10b–11a, in Wilensky, *Hasidim u-Mitnaggdim*, 2:207.

89. R. David then compares the Maggid to the pseudoscholar Ahitofel from the Bible, who initially instructed King David but met with an early death. See BT Sanhedrin, 106b. David of Maków, *Zemir Arizim*, 11a, in Wilensky, *Hasidim u-Mitnaggdim*, 207.

90. David of Maków, *Zemir Arizim*, 14b, in Wilensky, *Hasidim u-Mitnaggdim*, 211.

91. David of Maków, *Zemir Arizim*, 12b, in Wilensky, *Hasidim u-Mitnaggdim*, 209.

92. David of Maków, *Zemir Arizim*, 11a, in Wilensky, *Hasidim u-Mitnaggdim*, 208.

93. The days between Rosh HaShannah and Yom Kippur.

94. David of Maków, *Zemir Arizim*, 2b–3a, in Wilensky, *Hasidim u-Mitnaggdim*, 195.

95. Rabbinowicz, *Bein Pshyskha*, 262. And see later discussion.

96. Rabbinowicz, *Bein Pshyskha*, 262.

97. Rabbinowicz, *Bein Pshyskha*, 262.

98. Shmeruk, "Hasidism and the *Kehilla*," 186–95; Stampfer, "The Dispute over Polished Knives and Hasidic *Shehita*," 197–210.

99. Teller, "The Gaon of Vilna and the Communal Rabbinate in Eighteenth-Century Poland-Lithuania," 142–53.

100. Prominent Mitnaggdim who served as rabbis of major towns include R. Avigdor of Pińsk, the renowned Mitnagged who was rabbi of Wodzisław before he replaced the zaddik Levi Isaac of Berdyczów as rabbi of Pińsk in 1786; and R. Abraham Katzenellenbogen, rabbi of Slutsk and Brisk, who debated R. Levi Isaac in Warsaw.

101. Hasdai, "The Origins of the Conflict between Hasidim and Mitnagdim," 41.

102. Their position was comparable to that of the Besht, who was also hired as a *ba'al shem* by the kahal and similarly refrained from social upheavals or criticism. Wilensky identifies David as a *maggid mesharim* and *moreh zeddek*, and notes claims that he also served as *av bet din*. See "The Polemic of Rabbi David of Makow," 144, no. 34.

103. Wilensky, *Hasidim u-Mitnaggdim*, 2:50–2 and 253.

104. On the merit of designating certain Jewish modernizers in Central Poland as "Maskilim," see Marcin Wodziński, "Good Maskilim and Bad Assimilationists," 87–122.

105. See Israel Bartal, "The Imprint of Haskalah Literature on the Historiography of Hasidism," in Rapoport-Albert, *Hasidism Reappraised*, 367–75. However, while Bartal notes a Haskalah tendency to depict Hasidism as a popular, folk movement (Bartal, "The Imprint of Haskalah Literature on the Historiography of Hasidism," 371), several Maskilim both acknowledged and resented Hasidism's links with the elite (see examples later).

106. Mendel Lefin Satanower, *Essai d'un plan de Réforme ayant pour objet d'éclairer la Nation Juive en Pologne et de redresser par là ses moeurs*, secs. 16–20, pp. 6–7. Published anonymously.

107. *Lefin Satanower, Essai d'un plan de Réforme ayant pour objet d'éclairer la Nation Juive en Pologne et de redresser par là ses moeurs*, sec. 22, p. 7.

108. *Lefin Satanower, Essai d'un plan de Réforme ayant pour objet d'éclairer la Nation Juive en Pologne et de redresser par là ses moeurs*, secs. 16–20, pp. 6–7.

109. *Lefin Satanower, Essai d'un plan de Réforme ayant pour objet d'éclairer la Nation Juive en Pologne et de redresser par là ses moeurs*, sec. 23, p. 7, and n. e, pp. 29–30.

110. *Lefin Satanower, Essai d'un plan de Réforme ayant pour objet d'éclairer la Nation Juive en Pologne et de redresser par là ses moeurs*, sec. 23, p. 7, and n. e, pp. 29–30.

111. Joseph Perl Archive, Jewish National and University Library Archives (JNULA), folder 72, pp. 2a–3b, translated and cited in Nancy Sinkoff, "Tradition and Transition: Mendel Lefin of Satanów and the Beginnings of the Jewish Enlightenment in Eastern Europe, 1749–1826" (Ph.D. diss., Columbia University, 1996), 142. The manuscript was written after the Great Sejm, which occurred from 1788 to 1792.

112. Joseph Perl Archive, JNULA, folder 72, p. 3b, cited in Sinkoff, *Tradition and Transition*, 143.

113. Joseph Perl Archive, JNULA, folder 72, p. 3b, cited in Sinkoff, *Tradition and Transition*, 143. See also Assaf, " 'Money for Household Expenses,' " 14–50.

114. Joseph Perl Archive, JNULA, folder 72, p. 3b, in Sinkoff, Tradition and Transition, 143.

115. Joseph Perl Archive, JNULA, folder 55, translated and quoted in Sinkoff, *Tradition and Transition*, 152.

116. Joseph Perl Archive, JNULA, folder 55, translated and quoted in Sinkoff, *Tradition and Transition*, 152.

117. Jacques Calmanson, *Uwagi nad niniejszym stanem Żydów Polskich y ich wydoskonaleniem* (Warsaw, 1797), 18–9.

118. The satire was probably augmented and edited by Joseph Perl. See David Assaf, " 'Ve-ha-Mitnaggdim Hitlozezu She-Nishtakher ve-Nafal': Nefilat Shel Ha-Hozeh Mi-Lublin Be-R'i Ha-Zikharon Ha-Hasidi ve-Ha-Satirah Ha-Maskilit," in Etkes et al., *Within Hasidic Circles*, 161–208.

119. Assaf, " 'Ve-ha-Mitnaggdim Hitlozezu She-Nishtakher ve-Nafal,' " 200.

120. Assaf, " 'Ve-ha-Mitnaggdim Hitlozezu She-Nishtakher ve-Nafal,' " 200–201.

121. His penis.

122. Assaf, " 'Ve-ha-Mitnaggdim Hitlozezu She-Nishtakher ve-Nafal,' " 202–3.

123. Assaf, " 'Ve-ha-Mitnaggdim Hitlozezu She-Nishtakher ve-Nafal,' " 181–3.

124. Wodziński has located an alternate version of this report in AGAD, CWW 1871. It is signed by Abraham Stern. See *Oświecenie żydowskie*, 268–71. Mahler incorrectly identifies the author as Abraham Buchner.

125. *Hersztów*—ringleaders. See Mahler, *Hasidism and the Jewish Enlightenment*, 321.

126. Mahler is unable to read the word, which is probably *pobierać*, meaning "to take or receive." AGAD, KRSW 6634, p. 243.

127. Mahler, *Hasidism and the Jewish Enlightenment*, 321.

128. Mahler, *Hasidism and the Jewish Enlightenment*, 321.

129. Levi Isaac of Berdyczów, *Kedushat Levi Ha-Shalem* (Jerusalem, 1993), parshat Hukat, 225. This is in contrast to ordinary people, whose souls alone yearn to perform commandments and thus leave behind a profane shell.

130. Shmuel Werses, "Bein Shnei Olamot."

131. Shmuel Yosef Fuenn, "Dor ve-Dorshav," in Shmuel Feiner, ed., *Me-Haskalah Lohemet le-Haskalah Meshameret: Nivhar Nikhteve R. Sh. Y. Fin* (Jerusalem: Merkaz Dinur, 1993), 80–4; Werses, "Portrait of a Maskil," 131.

132. Eliezer Zvi Hakohen Zweifel, *Shalom al Yisrael*, ed. Avraham Rubenstein (Jerusalem: Mosad Bialik, 1972).

133. Marcin Wodziński, "Jakub Tugenhold and the First Maskilic Defense of Hasidism," *Gal-Ed* 28 (2002), 35 (offprint).

134. Jacob Tugenhold, *Obrona Iszraelitów* (Warsaw, 1831), xxiii–xxiv.

135. N. M. Geleber, "Le-Toldot Ha-Rofeim be-Polin be-Meah ha-18," in *Shai Le-Yeshiyahu—Sefer Yovel Le-Y. Volfberg* (Tel Aviv: Ha-Merkaz le-Tarbut Shel Ha-Poel ha-mizrah; 1957), 355.

136. Rabinowitz, *Encyclopedia of Hasidism*, 42; Aviezer Borshtein, *Ha-Admor ha-Rofeh* (Tel Aviv: Alef, 1970). Schiper lists Bernhard among several assimilationists in the 1830s! See *Żydzi Królestwa Polskiego w dobie powstania Listopadowego* 175.

137. Wincenty Krasiński, *Apercu Sur les Juifs de Pologne l'an 1818* (Cracow, 1898), 28. On Krasiński, see Wodziński, "Jakub Tugenhold," 27–8.

138. Julian Ursyn Niemcewicz, *Levi and Sarah* (1821), in Segal, *Stranger in Our Midst*, 56.

139. Niemcewicz, *Levi and Sarah*, 59.

140. Niemcewicz, *Levi and Sarah*, 56–7.

141. Mahler, *Hasidism and the Jewish Enlightenment*, 396, no. 23. It does not appear to have survived in the original.

142. Archiwum Oświęcenia Publicznego, Akta Komitetu Starozak., vol. 65, cited in Mahler, *Ha-Hasidut ve-ha-Haskalah*, app., 488.

143. Mahler's rendering, *manów*, must be a misreading of *marów*, meaning "ghosts."

144. Approximately Hebrew for "amulets."

145. Archiwum Oświęcenia Publicznego, Akta Komitetu Starozak., vol. 65, cited in Mahler, *Ha-Hasidut ve-ha-Haskalah*, app., 488.

146. Mahler's rendering, *któl*, must be a misreading of *król*, meaning "king."

147. Archiwum Oświęcenia Publicznego, Akta Komitetu Starozak., vol. 65, cited in Mahler, *Ha-Hasidut ve-ha-Haskalah*, app., 488.

148. See, for example, Israel ben Shabbethai of Kozienice, *Avodat Yisrael Ha-Mefuar [al pi yad defus rishon]* (Bnei Brak, 1996).

149. Sabbath.

150. Archiwum Oświęcenia Publicznego, Akta Komitetu Starozak, vol. 65, cited in Mahler, Ha-Hasidut ve-ha-Haskalah, app., 488.

151. R. Simha Bunem of Przysucha and R. Isaac Meir of Gur acquired a degree of secular education. See Feivel Wettstein, *Halifat Mikhtavim* (Cracow, 1900), 81; and Abraham Issachar Benjamin of Powienic, *Meir Eynei ha-Golah*, 38.

152. Archiwum Oświęcenia Publicznego, Akta Komitetu Starozak., vol. 65, cited in Mahler, Ha-Hasidut ve-ha-Haskalah, app., 488.

153. Eisenbach, *Emancipation of the Jews in Poland*, 164–8, and "Attempts to Settle the Legal Status of the Jews during the Constitutional Period of the Congress Kingdom,' in *Jewish Social Studies* 50 (1988–92), 4–9. See also Raphael Mahler, "Ha-Mediniyut Klapei ha-Misiyonarim be-Polin ha-Kongresit be-Tekufat 'Ha-Brit Ha-Kedoshah,' " in Mikhal Handel, ed., *Sefer Shiloh: Kovez Ma'amarim L'zekhero* (Tel Aviv: Hug yedidim, 1961), 169–81.

154. Mahler, "Ha-Mediniyut Klapei ha-Misiyonarim be-Polin ha-Kongresit be-Tekufat 'Ha-Brit Ha-Kedoshah,' " 170 and 11.

155. Yitshak Fein, "Di Londoner Misyonerin-Gezelshaft far Yidn," *YIVO Bleter* 24 (1944), 41–2; and Endelman, "Jewish Converts in Nineteenth-Century Warsaw," 36–7. Endelman's significantly higher figures seem to derive from more rigorous investigation.

156. *Jewish Expositor and Friend of Israel*, vol. 8 (1823), 240. Their first allusion to Hasidism derives from Żytomir (the Ukraine) in 1818. Solomon observed that as a result of having been convinced of the insufficiency of their own religion to comfort their souls here and to save them hereafter, the Jews had begun to form various sects, different modes of worship, and "abstinent and tormenting lives" [probably old-style hasidim] and had "chosen themselves rabbies [sic], whom they almost worship as deities" [i.e., new Hasidim]. *Jewish Expositor and Friend of Israel* 3 (1818), 484.

157. *Jewish Expositor and Friend of Israel* 10 (1825), 140–1.

158. R. Simha Bunem of Przysucha began to go blind by the end of his life.

159. *Jewish Expositor and Friend of Israel* 10, 141.

160. *Jewish Expositor and Friend of Israel* 10, 141.

161. *Jewish Expositor and Friend of Israel* 10, 145.

162. *Jewish Expositor and Friend of Israel* 10, 145.

163. *Jewish Expositor and Friend of Israel* 10, 390. Wodziński accepts their initial statement as proof that "the Congress Kingdom was free of the hasidic dominance that characterized Russia" and even that "hasidim lacked any influence at all in Congress Poland." See *Haskalah and Hasidism in the Kingdom of Poland*, 99.

164. *Jewish Expositor and Friend of Israel* 11 (1826), 63.

165. *Jewish Expositor and Friend of Israel* 11, 64.

166. *Jewish Expositor and Friend of Israel* 8 (1823), 327.

167. *Jewish Expositor and Friend of Israel* 8, 327.

168. *Jewish Expositor and Friend of Israel* 11 (1826), 265–6.

169. For M. Gregoire's most extensive treatment of Hasidism, see *Histoire des Sectes Religieuses* (Paris, 1828), 3:321–35.

170. Henderson, *Biblical Researches and Travels in Russia*, 235.

171. Henderson, *Biblical Researches and Travels in Russia*, 235–6.

172. In missionary accounts, according to Wodzinski, "Russian Poland" usually meant the Pale of Settlement during this period. See Wodzinski, *Oświecenie żydowskie*, 106.

173. Podolia.

174. Wodzinski, *Oświecenie żydowskie* 236.

175. Clifford Geertz, *The Interpretation of Cultures* (New York: Basic Books, 1973), 112.

176. Solomon Maimon, "On a Secret Society, and Therefore a Long Chapter," in Hundert, *Essential Papers on Hasidism*, 20.

177. Attributed to the Great Maggid of Miedzyrzecz by Dubnow, "The Maggid of

Miedzyrzecz," 65; and *Toldot Ha-Hasidut*, 86; and by Rivka Shatz-Uffenheimer, *Hasidism as Mysticism: Quietistic Elements in Eighteenth-Century Hasidic Thought*, tr. Jonathan Chipman (Jerusalem: Magnes, 1993), 203. For a different identification of the "Maggid" in question, see Altshuler, "The First Tzaddik of Hasidism," 155.

178. Ze'ev Wolf of Żytomir, *Or ha-Meir*, "Rimzei Zav," (Brooklyn, 1975); quoted out of order in Dubnow, "The Maggid of Miedzyrzecz," 65; *Toldot Ha-Hasidut*, 86.

179. On this technique, see Rivka Schatz-Uffenheimer, "Divine Immanence and the Question of Prophecy," tr. Jonathan Chipman, in *Hasidism as Mysticism*, esp. 199–200. See also Benzion Dinur, "The Messianic-Prophetic Role of the Baal Shem Tov," 377–8 (esp. 385).

180. Samuel of Sieniawa, *Ramata'im Zofim* (Warsaw, 1885), 1: 193.

181. From the first blessing of the new month.

182. *Yohel* is the diminutive of *yoah*, which is a broth usually made from chicken or fish.

183. Psalm 130:7.

184. Yizhak of Neskhiż, *Zikharon Tov* (Piotroków Trybunalski, 1892), p. 12, no. 1. The event was recalled in 1867.

185. Yet one recollection serves as a reminder of the unreliability of memory-based accounts: R. Isaac allegedly once asked R. Levi Isaac if he knew the Maggid of Kozienice, and he answered, "I would like very much to meet him." But after agreeing to meet the Maggid, news arrived that he had died. This could not, however, have occurred, for the Maggid of Kozienice actually outlived R. Levi Isaac by five years. Moreover, testimony discussed in chapter 2 suggests that R. Levi Isaac and the Maggid were close colleagues. See Yizhak of Neskhiż, *Zikharon Tov*, p. 16, no. 13.

186. When R. Isaac Eizik's father entreated the Seer to intervene on his behalf so that he might have a son, the Seer warned him, "certainly if I decree a son for you, it shall be so. But you will not live long, for you both cannot coexist in the world." R. Isaac Eizik's father accepted this upon himself, and the Seer transmitted an "awesome Name that would draw my soul down, and said to him, 'You will have a son who will be a great light.' " Yizhak Isaac Yehudah Jehiel Safrin, *Megilat Seterim*, ed. Naftali Ben-Menahem (Jerusalem, 1944), 8. See also, with some caution, Morris Faierstein's translation, in *Jewish Mystical Autobiographies* (New York: Paulist Press, 1999).

187. Yizhak of Nezkhiż, *Zikharon Tov*, pp. 17–8, no. 23.

188. Possibly Dorohusk or Dorhucza.

189. Yizhak of Nezkhiż, *Zikharon Tov*, pp. 17–8, no. 23.

190. Yizhak Zinger, *Savah Razon* (Padgorze, 1901), 16, quoted in Alfasi, "Haknasat Kala ve-Hatunot be-Hasidut," 300. See also Buber's rewriting of this account in *Tales of the Hasidim*, 1: 306–7. Buber renders it in the first person with both additions and omissions, ostensibly for dramatic effect. For example, he decides to claim that "among the guests were more than two hundred zaddikim, as for the hasidim—you could not even have counted them."

191. "The Letter of the Rabbi Samuel Shmelke Horowitz, Rabbi of Nikolsburg, to the Brody kahal," in Wilensky, *Hasidim u-Mitnaggdim*, 1:85.

192. *ZemirArizim ve-Herevot Zurim* (1772), in Wilensky, *Hasidim u-Mitnaggdim*, 1: 47.

193. *ZemirArizim ve-Herevot Zurim* (1772), in Wilensky, *Hasidim u-Mitnaggdim*, 1: 88.

194. *ZemirArizim ve-Herevot Zurim* (1772), in Wilensky, *Hasidim u-Mitnaggdim*, 1: 88.

195. Literally, "as if we believe her," i.e., believing a woman found to not be a virgin at marriage, who claims that she was violated after the betrothal. R. Joshua (of the Mishna in Ketubot 12b) says "We do not live by her mouth" (we do not believe her). See the Vilna ban of 1772 in Wilensky, *Hasidim u-Mitnaggdim*, 1:37–44.

196. Vilna ban of 1772 in Wilensky, *Hasidim u-Mitnaggdim*, 1:86–7.

197. Vilna ban of 1772 in Wilensky, *Hasidim u-Mitnaggdim*, 1:86–7.

198. On the practice of metoposcopy by kabbalists in seventeenth–Century Safed, see Lawrence Fine, "The Art of Metoposcopy: A Study in Isaac Luria's Charismatic Knowledge," in Lawrence Fine, ed., *Essential Papers on Kabbalah* (New York: New York University Press, 1995).

199. Fine, "The Art of Metoposcopy," 9.

200. Yizhak Isaac Yehudah Jehiel Safrin, *Megilat Seterim*, 11. According to Morris Faierstein, the 3 *yuds* are a pun on 3 *yads* or "hands," which the Seer extended. See Faierstein, *Jewish Mystical Autobiographies*, 333, no. 21. However, the shape of the shank bone represented the letter *yud*.

201. The account is relayed by his grandson, R. Isaac Mordecai Rabinowitz.

202. Hebrew spelling unclear. May be Wlochy, Wloclawek (Leslau), or Wlodawa.

203. Yizhak Mordekhai Rabinowicz, *Ohel Shlomo* (Piotrków, 1924), 5b, cited in Alfasi, "Haknasat Kala ve-Hatunot be-Hasidut," 300–301.

204. Ibid., 294.

205. Turner, *Dramas, Fields and Metaphors*, 182–3.

206. Turner, *Dramas, Fields and Metaphors*, 45.

207. Turner, *Dramas, Fields and Metaphors*, 207.

208. Yizhak Isaac Yehudah Jehiel Safrin, *Megilat Seterim*, 13–4. The year was probably 1823.

209. The motivation of spiritual malaise is reflected in a tale by R. Nahman of Bratslav: "The son would sit in the attic and study, as is the way with the wealthy, and he would constantly study and pray; yet he felt deep down that he lacked something and did not know what, and he did not feel motivated in his study and prayer. And he told this to two youths, and they advised him to travel to the zaddik. . . . And the same son went and told his father how he was not feeling motivated in his worship, as stated, and that he lacked something and did not know what. Thus, he wished to travel to the zaddik. And his father answered him: 'Why should you want to travel to him? Are you not a greater scholar than he, and of greater yihus? It is not fitting for you to travel to him. Turn away from this path!' Until he prevented him from going. And he returned to his studies, and again felt the lack." Nahman of Bratslav, *Sippurei u-Ma'asiyot*, tale no. 8, "A Rabbi and His Only Son" (Ostróg, 1815/16), Bratslav ed. (Jerusalem, 1991), 122.

210. Author of *Pelei Yoez* (Łódz [sic?], 1856).

211. Yizhak Szmulewicz, unpublished memoirs, quoted in Rabinowicz, *Bein Pshyskha*, 457–8.

212. Liquor from the Near (and Far) East, similar to vodka, distilled from rice, molasses, or the sap of the cocoa palm.

213. Eleazar Hakohen of Pułtusk, "Ez Avot," in *Hidushei Maharakh* (Warsaw, 1898), 2.

214. BT Megillah 6b.

215. Eleazar Hakohen of Pułtusk, "Ez Avot," 3–4.

216. For an important discussion of this problem, see Rapoport-Albert, "On Women in Hasidism," 495–525.

217. Stefania Kowalska-Glikman, "Ludność żydowska Warszawy w połowie 19 w., w świetle akt stanu cywilnego," *Biuletyn ŻIH* 2:118 (1981), esp. 44–45.

218. Kowalska-Glikman, "Ludność żydowska Warszawy w połowie 19 w., w świetle akt stanu cywilnego," esp. 44–5. Wives of zaddikim were also saddled with the obligation to both financially support and raise their children. The wife of the zaddik Solomon of Radomsko for example, managed a store in town. See Yizhak Mordekhai Hakohen Rabinowitz, *Atarat Shlomo* (Piotrków Trybunalski, 1926), 40:27.

219. Yekutiel Kamelhar, "Bet Menahem," in *Em le-Binah* (Lemberg, 1909), 32. Kamelhar heard this from "the mouths of the elders of the city Rymanów."

220. Kamelhar, "Bet Menahem," 33.

221. See Elimelekh of Leżajsk, *No'am Elimelekh*, 108, 134–5, 279–81, and 285.

222. Joseph Perl, *Uiber das Wesen der Sekte Chassidim*, ed. Avraham Rubinstein (Jerusalem: Israel Academy of Sciences and Humanities, 1977), 106. According to Hasidic tradition, Perele prayed in a *tallit* and *girtel*, and fasted every Tuesday and Thursday. See Menasseh Unger, "Di Rebizen Perele Davent in Talit," in *Sefer Zikharon le-Kehillat Kozienice* (Tel Aviv, 1969), 112.

223. An *agunah* is a woman whose husband has disappeared without granting her a divorce, which is necessary for her to remarry. See Rubinstein, "He'arot," 96; or in greater detail, M. S. Geshuri, "Ha-Maggid Mi-Kozienice ve 'Tshuvat ha-Agunah' mi-Staszów," in *Sefer Staszów* (1962), 38–40. R. David of Maków denigrates the decision in *Shever Posh'im* 19a, in Wilensky, *Hasidim u-Mitnaggdim*, 2:84.

224. *Nifla'ot ha-Rabi*, 20:15; *Eser Orot*, 85:7.

225. Tsederbaum refers to Beila as "a pretty virgin from Lemberg." See *Keter Kahuna*, 125. The Maggid of Kozienice allegedly defended their controversial union on the grounds that it yielded another son.

226. *Ohel ha-Rabi*, "Or ha-Nifla'ot," 9:15.

227. The Seer was concerned that all her material needs be well taken care of upon his death. See his testament, composed posthumously by his offspring but seemingly in accordance with his wishes, in *Besurot Tovot*, no. 10.

228. August 4, 1824, in AGAD, CWW 1871, p. 179. See also Wodziński, " 'Sprawa chasydymów,' " 239.

229. Schiper, *Żydzi Królestwa Polskiego w dobie powstania Listopadowego*, 28–29.

230. *Si'ah Sarfei Kodesh*, vol. 1, pt. 2, 12:10.

231. Eleazar Hakohen of Pułtusk, "Ez Avot," in *Hidushei Maharakh* (Warsaw, 1898), 1.

232. Eleazar Hakohen of Pułtusk, "Ez Avot," 1.

233. Quoted in Wodziński, *Oświecenie żydowskie w Królestwie Polskim wobec chasydyzmu*, 154.

234. Introduction to *Torat ha-Yehudi*, cited in Rabinowicz, *Bein Pshyskha*, 270.

235. Mahler, *Hasidism and the Jewish Enlightenment*, 267; Rabinowicz, *Bein Pshyskha*, 260–5.

236. Piekarz, "Hasidism as a Socio-Religious Movement," 247.

237. Rabbinowicz, *Bein Pshyskha*, 262.

238. Wettstein, "Halifat Mihtavim Sh-Bein Weizenfeld ve-Reav," 80. "Romanit" probably refers to Latin. See also Samuel of Sieniawa, *Ramata'im Zofim* (Warsaw, 1885), 226.

239. On R. Samuel, see Menahem Boym, *Ha-rabbi Rabbi Bunem mi-Pshyskha*, 357.

240. The cited passages that follow are from Samuel of Sieniawa, *Ramata'im Zofim*, 163–84, reordered roughly chronologically.

241. The major exception R. Nahman of Bratslav's biographies, written by his disciple R. Nathan Shternharz, *Hayei Moharan* and *Sihot ha-Ran*, which form the basis of Green, *Tormented Master*.

242. Samuel of Sieniawa, *Ramata'im Zofim*, 2:28. This would be about 1813.

243. Samuel of Sieniawa, *Ramata'im Zofim*, 2:28.

244. BT Kiddushin 31a.

245. Samuel of Sieniawa, *Ramata'im Zofim*, 1:194.

246. BT Baba Kama 24a–24b.

247. R. Mordecai Benet (d. 1829), *av bet din* of Nikolsburg and grandson of the *Hahkam Zvi*. See Walden, *Sefer Shem ha-Gedolim He-Hadash*, 95–6.

248. Samuel of Sieniawa, *Ramata'im Zofim*, 1: 167.

249. R. Jeremiah of Maettersdorff, a native of Poland and author of *Moda'ah Rabba* (Lemberg, 1798), was invited to head the yeshiva of Maettersdorff in 1770, and presided over it for twenty-eight years. See Rabinowicz, *Bein Pshyskha*, 296.

250. I.e., Prussia.

251. R. Samuel describes R. Menahem Mendel: "And when the two holy brothers R. Elimelekh (of Leżajsk) and R. Zusya (of Annipol) had come to the aforementioned R. Menahem Mendel and did not reveal their identities, and approached him for charity, he gave it to them and told them their names and deeds, for he recognized them by their faces. And he had been a student of the holy R. Jehiel Michael of Złoczów in the latter's old age." See also Walden, *Sefer Shem ha-Gedolim He-Hadash*, 93.

252. R. Samuel of Sieniawa, *Ramata'im Zofim*, 1: 168.

253. Rubinstein, *Shivhei ha-Besht*, 216.

254. In Polish villages where few Jews lived, one was unlikely to find kosher food.

255. R. Samuel of Sieniawa, *Ramata'im Zofim*, 1: 170.

256. D. 1805.

257. R. Elimelekh's third son, R. Jacob, who became *av bet din* of Mogielnice.

258. R. Samuel of Sieniawa, *Ramata'im Zofim*, 1: 169–70.

259. On Jewish and non-Jewish cultural differences with respect to heroic types, see Daniel Boyarin, *Unheroic Conduct* (Berkeley: University of California Press, 1997), esp. 33–80.

260. That R. Simha Bunem was a bookkeeper for the Konsumpcja in the town of Siedlce is corroborated by a contract for the Konsumpcja that he drew up in 1812 (see chapter 3). The Sejm adopted a resolution on March 24, 1809, calling for a tax on the ritual slaughter of cattle and poultry. Initially a tax on consumption, this kosher meat tax was soon transformed into a direct tax and collected by lessors. See Eisenbach, *Emancipation of the Jews in Poland*, 142–3.

261. Kadish, *Si'ah Sarfei Kodesh*, 4:15:6.

262. On Jewish notions of the heroic as applied to *Shivhei Ha-Besht*, see Boyarin, *Unheroic Conduct*, esp. 33–80.

263. Rubinstein, *Shivhei Ha-Besht*, 50 and 57.

264. R. Moses Hayyim Ephraim of Sudziłków (1748–1800). R. Simha Bunem would have been under thirty-five years old.

265. A. Marcus, *Ha-Hasidut*, tr. M. Sheinfeld (Tel Aviv, 1954), 124; Rabinowicz, *Bein Pshyskha*, 302, no. 15; Eisenbach, *Emancipation of the Jews in Poland*, 204.

266. On account of his "German"-style clothing.

267. See Rashi on the verse. Everyone called him Esau, which has the same root as "made, completed," because Esau looked like a full-grown adult when he was born.

268. Esau represents a lie; thus, everyone was drawn (called) toward him.

269. R. Samuel of Sieniawa, *Ramata'im Zofim*, 1: 171–7.

270. Rubinstein, *Shivhei Ha-Besht*, 64–5. In this case, it is a dybbuk who recognizes the Besht's true self.

271. Ada Rapoport-Albert has argued that "the Besht himself may have wished to conform to the existing typology of mystical saintly lives and might have modeled himself on his illustrious predecessor, reenacting certain scenes from the life of [R. Isaac Luria] as recorded in the *In Praise of the Ari*." Ada Rapoport-Albert, "Hagiography with Footnotes: Edifying Tales and the Writing of History in Hasidism," *History and Theory* 27:4 (1988), 123. For another example of this trope, see Joseph Weiss, "Sense and Nonsense in Defining Judaism—The Strange Case of Nahman of Brazlav," in *Studies in Eastern European Jewish Mysticism*, 255–7.

272. For an application of this concept to the Besht, see Rapoport-Albert, "Hagiography with Footnotes," 136.

273. Probably Prussian Poland, referring to Napoleon's campaign of 1806–7, which resulted in Prussia's loss of lands it had gained during the second (1793) and third (1795) partitions of Poland. The treaties signed at Tilsit/Sovetsk on July 7–9, 1807, created the semiautonomous Duchy of Warsaw out of Prussia's territorial losses. The French also encamped in East Prussia in preparation for the campaign against Russia in May 1812. Thus, the alleged event would have occurred between 1806 and 1812.

274. R. Samuel of Sieniawa, *Ramata'im Zofim*, 1: 231–2.

275. R. Phineas of Magnuszew, a disciple of R. Elimelekh of Leżajsk and colleague of the Maggid of Kozienice. See Walden, *Sefer Shem ha-Gedolim He-Hadash*, 116.

276. Kabbalistic term for the world of emanation (the ten *sefirot*).

277. R. Samuel of Sieniawa, *Ramata'im Zofim*, 1: 178–83.

278. BT Shabbat 117b and 131b; Rosh Hashana 29b.

279. Moses balked at becoming a leader of Israel on account of his difficulties speaking in public.

280. R. Samuel of Sieniawa, *Ramata'im Zofim*, 1: 183–4.

281. Blessings preceding a wedding.

282. Phrase inserted in the blessing after the meal during a wedding.

283. 1815. This is not possible, however.

284. BT Eruvin 64a. R. Samuel of Sieniawa, *Ramata'im Zofim*, 1:162.

285. R. Samuel of Sieniawa, *Ramata'im Zofim*, 1:247.

286. R. Samuel of Sieniawa, *Ramata'im Zofim*, 1:52 and 68.

287. R. Samuel of Sieniawa, *Ramata'im Zofim*, 1:247. Cited in the name of the Rabbi of Łęczna.

CHAPTER 6

1. Scholem, *Major Trends in Jewish Mysticism*, 341–2. Moshe Idel concurs: "According to the Hasidic sources I am familiar with, Kabbalah is preeminently a paradigm of the human psyche and man's activities rather than a theosophical system." See Idel, *Kabbalah*, 152.

2. Jacob Isaac Horowitz of Lublin, *Zot Zikharon*, parshat *Mikez*, 189. See also parshat "*Shalah*," 275, where R. Jacob Isaac brings a similar teaching in the name of the Besht.

3. Levi Isaac of Berdyczów, *Kedushat Levi Ha-Shalem*, "*Drushim le-Hannukah*," 70; and "*Shalah*," 220–1.

4. Abraham Joshua Heschel, "Hasidism," *Jewish Heritage* 14:3 (1972), 14-6, quoted in Samuel Dresner, introduction to Heschel, *Circle of the Baal Shem Tov*, xiii.

5. Ze'ev Gries, "The Hasidic Managing Editor," in Rapoport-Albert, *Hasidism Reappraised*, 154. See also Gries, *Sefer, Sofer ve-Sipur*, chaps. 1 and 2.

6. Majer Bałaban, "Di Pruv zu Grinden di Erste Hebrayishe Drukerey in Varshe," in *Yidn in Poyln* (Vilna, 1932), 218. See also Szaja Friszman, "Drukarnie hebrajskie na Mazowszu od ich założenia do roku 1831," (master's thesis under the direction of Majer Bałaban, Warsaw University, archives of Jewish Historical Institute [ŻIH], no. 117/42), 10 and 51–2.

7. Gries does not consider the following works "Hasidic," even though their authors were Hasidic, presumably because they do not expound upon specifically Hasidic ideas (with the exception of Dov Ber of Lubavitch, *Lehavin Inyan ha-Hishtathut al Kevre zaddikim*): Schneur Zalman of Liady's legalistic work *Hilkhot Talmud Torah* (Szklów, 1794; Żółkiew, 1795; Lwów, 1798; Sławuta, 1798; Lwów, 1799); Hayyim ben Solomon Tyrer, *Sidduro Shel Shabbat* (Mohilów, 1813), Meir Margaliot, *Me'ir Netivim* (Połonne, 1791), Shabbetai of Raszków, *Sefer Klalot Tikkun ve-Aliyot ha-Olamot* (Lwów, 1778), and *Seder Tefillah mi-Kol ha-Shana* (Korzec, 1794), Schneur Zalman of Liady, *Shulhan Aruh- Hoshen Mishpat* (Kopys, 1814), and *She'alot ve-Teshuvot* (Kopys, 1815). I include them in appendix 3 in order to demonstrate the range of Hasidic literary creativity.

8. Gries, *Sefer, Sofer ve-Sipur*, 11–40.

9. Gries, "The Hasidic Managing Editor," 147–8; *Sefer, Sofer ve-Sipur*, 53.

10. Gries, *Sefer, Sofer ve-Sipur*, 11–40; 49; "The Hasidic Managing Editor," 142.

11. Dinard, *Zikhronot Bat Ami*, 14.

12. Dinard, *Zikhronot Bat Ami*, 14.

13. On the transitional phases toward a mass movement, see Etkes, "The Zaddik," 159–67.

14. Meir Wunder, "Ha-Ishor ha-Rishon le-Hadpasat Sifrei Hasidut," *Tagim* 1 (1969), 30.

15. Ben Amos and Mintz, *In Praise of the Ba'al Shem Tov*, 179.

16. Moshe Rosman, "A Prolegomenon to the Study of Jewish Cultural History," *Jewish Studies, an Internet Journal* 1 (2002), 121; Yohanan Petrovsky-Shtern, "The Master of an Evil Name: Hillel Ba'al Shem and His *Sefer Ha-Heshek*," *AJS Review* 28:2 (2004), 235.

17. Wunder, "Ha-Ishor ha-Rishon, 31–2.

18. Wunder, "Ha-Ishor ha-Rishon, 41.

19. Wunder, "Ha-Ishor ha-Rishon, 42. This is a play on *olamim*, which can mean both "forever" and "worlds," i.e., this world and the world to come. See Schatz-Uffenheimer, *Maggid Devarav le-Ya'akov le-Maggid Dov Ber mi-Mezhritch*, 3–4. In the continuation of the passage, R. Solomon admits to having been inspired by the publication of *Toldot Ya'akov Yosef* to finally print R. Dov Ber's teachings.

20. Schatz-Uffenheimer, *Maggid Devarav le-Ya'akov le-Maggid Dov Ber mi-Mezhritch*, 45.

21. Examples include R. Schneur Zalman of Liady and R. Jacob Isaac "the Seer" of Lublin. On this subject, see also Moshe Carmilly-Weinberger, *Censorship and Freedom of Expression in Jewish History* (New York: Yeshiva University Press, 1977), chap. 7.

22. The several attempts at Hasidic bibliography have been either defective or abortive. Hayyim Dov Friederberg's list at the end of *Bet Eked Sefarim* (Tel Aviv, Ha-Minkarha-Rashi M.A. Bar-Yuda, 1950) is, according to Ze'ev Gries, a "partial, deficient attempt." Pt. 1 of *Ha-Enziklopedyah le-Hasidut, aleph-tet* (Jerusalem, 1980), as

well as Gries's own project, remains incomplete. See Gries, "Hasidism: The Present State of Research and Some Desirable Priorities," *Numen* 34:1 (1987), 105.

23. According to Gries, *Alfa Beta*, where the study of *musar* (ethical) literature is preferred over traditional study, provoked condemnation. See Gries, "Hasidic Conduct (*Hanhagot*) Literature," 212–9.

24. Schatz-Uffenheimer, in *Hasidism as Mysticism*, devotes substantial space to Menahem Mendel of Vitebsk's *Pri ha-Arez*. The work supports her claims about quietism in early Hasidism, but how many Hasidim paid it heed?

25. Lieberman shows that no truly Hasidic printing presses existed in the Ukraine, Belarus, and Lithuania during the period up to 1837, with the exception of the Bratslav press, and that even those presses owned by Hasidim tended to print non-Hasidic, classical rabbinic books. In Korzec, the source of so many Hasidic books, he finds that printers were usually Mitnaggdim, Maskilim, or Christian. Hayyim Lieberman, "Badiya ve-Emet b'Divrei Batei ha-Defus ha-Hasidim," in *Ohel Rahel* (New York: n.p., 1984), vol. 2, 14–100. Johann Anton Krieger, a Christian printer from Warsaw, ran the Korzec press from 1781 to 1787. Table 6.1 reveals that three out of the twenty books printed during Krieger's tenure were Hasidic. See also Aryeh Tauber, "Defusei Korets," *Kiryat Sefer* 1 and 2 (1924/5, 1925/6).

26. Tauber, "Defusei Korets," 58. Lieberman repeats this error in "Le-She'elat Ya-has ha-Hasidut le-Lashon Yiddish," *Ohel Rahel*, 3:3: "In Galicia, accordingly, the printing of Hasidic books was completely absent" between 1815 and 1840.

27. Emanuel Ringelblum, "Restrictions on the Importation of Jewish Books Into Poland during the Eighteenth Century," *YIVO Annual of Jewish Social Science* 5 (1950), 34–5.

28. R. Jacob Orenstein of Lemberg endorsed *No'am Meggedim* and *Kedushat Levi*; R. Ephraim Zalman Margaliot of Brody endorsed *No'am Meggedim*, *Or Pnei Moshe*, and *Likkutei Moharan*; and R. Bezalel Margaliot of Ostróg endorsed *No'am Elimelekh* and *Or Pnei Moshe*. R. Issachar Dov Ber mi geza Zvi's *Bat Eyni* and *Mivasser Zedek* contain encomia by five Dubno judges (*dayanim*). The Ostróg *dayanim* lent their support to printings of *Shivhei ha-Besht*; while the Dubno *dayanim* endorsed *Bat Eyni* and *Mivasser Zeddek*. Surprisingly, old-style hasidim, members of the Ostróg *kloyz*, endorsed *Rav Yevi* (1792), *Me'ir Netivim* (1791), and *Sod Yakhin u-Voaz* (1794).

29. See Judah ben Samuel, *Sefer Hasidim*, ed. Reuben Margaliot (Jerusalem: Mossed Ha-Rav Kook, 1969–70), no. 586. In seventeenth-century Poland, *haskamot* with copyright warnings became customary when Moses Isserles imposed a ban on the purchasing of a rival edition of Moses Maimonides' *Mishneh Torah* to that printed by Meir Katzenellenbogen (Responsa Rema 10). See Menahem Elon, *The Principles of Jewish Law* (Jerusalem: Encyclopedia Judaica, 1975), 345. Elon errs on the date of Isserles's decree, putting it a century too early (fifteenth century). See also Nahum Rakover, *The "Haskamot" to Books as a Basis for the Rights of the Publishers* (in Hebrew) (Jerusalem: Misrad Ha-Mishpatim, 1970); and Israel Halpern, "Va'ad Arba Arzot be-Polin ve-ha-Sefer ha-Ivri," in *Yehudim ve-Yahadut be-Mizrah-Eiropa*, 78–87. In response to a papal bull against the Talmud in 1554, Jewish representatives met in Ferarra on June 21, 1554, and decided that no Hebrew book was to be published without the consent of three ordained rabbis. This was "the first provision made for the *haskamah*" (but not the first *haskamah*). William Popper, *The Censorship of Hebrew Books* (New York: Ktav, 1968); *Encyclopedia Judaica*, "Haskamah," 1452.

30. Wunder, "Ha-Ishor ha-Rishon," 35.

31. According to Ettinger, "in defiance of convention, it was published without the approbation of any rabbinic authority. This omission alone might have turned an

otherwise inoffensive publication into a provocative challenge to traditional authority, implicitly claiming the autonomous power to introduce new modes of worship and novel pietistic norms—a claim which soon became a major issue in the controversy." Shmuel Ettinger, "Hasidism and the *Kahal* in Eastern Europe," in Rapoport-Albert, *Hasidism Reappraised*, 70.

32. I have been unable to substantiate this rumored decree. Dov Ber of Międzyrzecz, *Maggid Devarov le-Ya'akov*, ed. Solomon of Lusk (Korzec, 1781), "Apology."

33. Shmuel Feiner, *The Jewish Enlightenment*, tr. Chaya Naor (Philadelphia: University of Pennsylvania Press, 2004), 73.

34. Barukh Abraham of Kosów's *Yesod Emunah*, composed in this period but not printed until 1854, contains fourteen *haskamot* from 1761–1765: Menahem Mendel of Przemyślany, Naftali Hirsch of Brody, Ephraim Zvi Ashkenazi of Brody, Menahem Mendel of Satanów, Aryeh Leibush of Białystok, Moses ben Yekutiel Zalman of Drogshtein/Sambor, Solomon Dov of Lawicz, Nahan of Aramil, Isaac Levi Ish Horowitz of Hamburg, Menahem Mendel Ish Horowitz of Lwów, Moses of Sambor, Nathan Nata of Rozdol, Joseph Moses ben Eliezer of Międzyrzecz, Shamri ben Isaac of Tiberia.

35. R. Moses of Sambor was son of the zaddik Isaac Aizik of Safrin (d.1800).

36. Eliezer Horowitz of Tarnogród, *No'am Meggedim* (Lwów, 1807), 4. R. Abraham Hayyim of Złoczów praises R. Moses of Sambor before the author, as does R. Simon Oder Berg.

37. R. Eliezer was a scion of the Horowitz family and a disciple of R. Jehiel Michael of Złoczów and R. Elimelekh of Leżajsk. See Gedaliya Nigal, "R. Eliezer mi-Tarnigrad ve-Sefarav," in *Mehkarim ba-Hasidut: Osef Ma'amarim* (Jerusalem: Ha-Makhon le-Heker ha-Sifrut Ha-Hasidut, 1999), 234–42.

38. Moses of Przeworsk, *Or Pnei Moshe* (Międzyrzecz, 1809), front matter, ii.

39. d. c. 1593.

40. Moses of Preeworsk, *or Pnei Moshe*, front matter.

41. On the subject of maggidim, or positive spirits, see Idel, "Jewish Magic from the Renaissance Period to Early Hasidism," 107; and Bilu, "Dybbuk and Maggid."

42. E.g., "the great, famous genius," "the famous Kabbalist, holy man of God," "the light, the great, famous, true holy genius," "son of holy ones," "of a chain of *yihus*."

43. See, for example, R. Levy Isaac of Berdyczów's endorsement of *Me'ir Netivim*: "From our teacher, the great and holy, famous, acute, genius, *hasid* and expert, our teacher R. Levi Isaac, may his light shine, *av bet din* and *rosh medina* of the holy community of Pinsk and the surrounding district, and at the present time *av bet din* in the holy community of Berdyczów, may He protect his going and coming. Residing in the home of the grandson of the great-uncle of the true genius, the author [R. Meir Margaliot], may his memory be for a blessing." Meir Margaliot, *Me'ir Netivim* (Połonne, 1791), i.

44. The approbation to Dov Ber of Międzyrzecz's *Or Torah* (Korzec, 1804) refers to *Likkutei Amarim: Maggid Devarov le-Yaakov* (Korzec, 1781).

45. For example, Menahem Mendel of Przemyślany, *Darkhei Yesharim* (Żółkiew, 1794); Aryeh Judah Leib of Połonne, *Kol Aryeh* (Korzec, 1798). Meir of Brody writes that R. Nahman "walks in the footsteps of his holy (great-grand)father," the Besht. See *Likkutei Moharan* (Ostróg, 1808).

46. Regarding R. Aaron of Apt, an endorser wrote: "And you shall take the breast of the ram of Aaron's consecration, and wave it for a wave offering before the Lord, and it shall be your part" (Exodus 29:26). Israel Baal Shem Tov (attributed), *Keter Shem Tov*, ed. Aaron Hirsch of Apt (Żółkiew, 1794), i.

47. " 'And I raised my eyes and looked, and behold there were two men standing before me' (Genesis 18:2), and in their hands was a thick scroll, written inside." Ze'ev Wolf of Leżajsk, to Elimelekh of Leżajsk, *No'am Elimelekh* (Lwów, 1788), i.

48. Eliezer Horowitz of Tarnogród, *No'am Meggedim*, 4.

49. For example, Jacob Tsvi of Oszwice, to *Amtahat Binyamin*.

50. Meir of Brody's endorsement of Uriel Feivel of Krasnopol, *Or Ha-Hokhma* (Laszczów, 1815).

51. Menahem Nahum of Chernobyl, *Me'or Eynayim*, 35. See also Reuven Aaron of Slapkowice in Benjamin of Złoczów, *Amtahat Binyamin* (Minkowice, 1796), 2.

52. Benjamin of Złoczów, *Hilkhat Binyamin* (Lwów, 1794).

53. Moses Hayyim Ephraim, *Degel Mahane Ephraim* (Berdyczów, 1808). The printing in Berdyczów suggests that Levi Isaac had a hand in the work's publication.

54. Abraham Hayyim of Złoczów to *No'am Meggedim*.

55. Jacob Isaac of Lublin, to Eliezer Horowitz of Tarnogród, *No'am Meggedim* (Lwów, 1807).

56. *Amtahat Binyamin*. The imitation of *haskamot* is also worth mentioning. Similar language of *haskamot* within the same work shows that endorsers read approbations that the publisher had already collected.

57. Mordecai b. Phineas of Korzec, to Ze'ev Wolf of Żytomir, *Or ha-Me'ir* (Korzec, 1798). Citation is from Job.

58. Yiddish version. See Jeremy Dauber, *Antonio's Devils: Writers of the Jewish Enlightenment and the Birth of Modern Hebrew and Yiddish Literature* (Stanford: Stanford University Press, 2004), 252, no. 1.

59. Ostróg *dayanim*, to *Shivhei ha-Besht*.

60. Meshullam Zusya of Annipol, encomium to Shneur Zalman of Liady, *Tanya* (Sławuta, 1796).

61. R. Nahman of Bratslav, *Sippurei Ma'asiyot* (Ostróg, 1816), 2.

62. Mishna *Avot*, 5:18.

63. Meir Halevi of Zelwa, to *Shivhei ha-Besht* (Berdyczów, 1815).

64. Israel of Kozienice, encomium to *Or Pnei Moshe*.

65. Ostróg *dayanim* to *Shivhei ha-Besht* (Berdyczów, 1815).

66. This phrase is based upon a saying by Moses Alsheikh, in his *Humshe Torah* (Lemberg, 1864), Deuteronomy "Va-Ethanan," on the verse "teach them diligently your children," 6:7.

67. Menahem Nahum of Chernobyl, *Me'or Eynayim* (Sławuta, 1798).

68. According to Mor Altshuler, the printers of R. Jacob Joseph's 1781 *Ben Porat Yosef* appended the Besht's second epistle, in which the Messiah promises he will come when the Besht's "springs are dispersed abroad," to hint at their messianic aim. Mor Altshuler, "Messianic Strains in Rabbi Israel Ba'al Shem Tov's 'Holy Epistle,' " *Jewish Studies Quarterly* 6 (1999), 69–70.

69. Based upon Song of Songs 7:10.

70. Jacob Orenstein, to *No'am Meggedim*.

71. Eliezer Horowitz of Tarnogród, to *No'am Elimelekh*.

72. Issachar Dov Ber mi Geza Tsvi, *Mivasser Zedek* (Dubno, 1798).

73. Issachar Dov Ber mi Geza Tsvi, *Mivasser Zedek*.

74. Asher Tsvi of Ostróg, to *Kol Aryeh* (Korzec, 1798).

75. Every reader, the *haskamot* promise, will find repose for his spirit, and healing for his body (Moses of Przeworsk, to *No'am Elimelekh*). Readers will receive "double blessings from heaven" (Levi Isaac, to *Hilkhat Binyamin*; Meir of Brody, to *Likkutei Moharan*). Some even ask "our brothers, children of Israel, to take their hands and

purchase the book" (Ostróg *Kloyz*, to *Me'ir Netivim*); and request readers to "strive to buy the books in generosity of heart" (Jacob Israel of Konstantin, to *Me'ir Netivim*). The Seer of Lublin proclaimed that he, himself, was giving the publisher money to buy the book (Jacob Isaac of Lublin, encomium to *No'am Meggedim*). R. Moses of Konstantin attested that the book is being sold at a bargain price (Moses Berin Shalom of Konstantin, encomium to ibid).

76. Only the *haskamot* to *Degel Mahane Ephraim* do not conclude with copyrights. Nearly every *haskamah* ends with the prohibition against "raising one's hand" to print this book without the permission of the publisher, and threatens curses and excommunication. A popular phrase was "I have come like Judah and others to declare a decree . . . ," referring to Judah b. Samuel the Hasid's decree in *Sefer Hasidim* regarding "trespassing your neighbor's boundary." Judah ben Samuel, *Sefer Hasidim*, 586. Despite a ten-year copyright, *No'am Elimelekh* was printed in Sławuta four years before the expiration. The endorsers admitted to having seen the original printing, but gave no indication that they had received the publisher's permission to reprint the book. See *Haskamot* to *No'am Elimelekh* (Sławuta, 1794). The Ostróg *dayanim* reasoned that, although *Shivhe ha-Besht* had already been printed in Żólkiew (*sic?*) a year earlier, it was not an attractive printing; therefore, the publishers committed no theft by re-printing it before the copyright expiration. See Ostróg *dayanim*, to *Shivhe ha-Besht* (Berdyczów, 1815).

77. The dates following copyrights sometimes preceded the date of printing by several years, reinforcing our sense of the lengthy process involved in bringing a work to print. Jacob Isaac of Lublin, Abraham Joshuah Heschel, and Menahem Mendel of Łuck each composed a *haskamah* to *Degel Mahane Ephraim* (Berdyczów, 1808) five years before the printing, in 1803.

78. Gries, "Between History and Literature—The Case of Jewish Preaching," *Journal of Jewish Thought and Philosophy* 4:1 (1994), 116.

79. Gries, "The Hasidic Managing Editor";

80. "Hebrew and the Habad Communication Ethos," in Glinert, ed., *Hebrew in Ashkenaz*; Dan Miron, "Sh. Y. Abramovitsh and His 'Mendele,' " in *The Image of the Shtetl* (New York: Syracuse University Press, 2000), 85–6.

81. Some Hasidic works were technically written by zaddikim, including R. Schneur Zalman of Liady's *Tanya*, and the works of the Maggid of Kozienice and the Seer of Lublin. But even those are likely based on oral sermons.

82. Shaul Stampfer, "What Did 'Knowing Hebrew' Mean in Eastern Europe?" in Glinert, *Hebrew in Ashkenaz*, 129–40.

83. See Naimo Seidman, *A Marriage Made in Heaven: The Sexual Politics of Hebrew and Yiddish* (Berkeley: University of California, 1997).

84. *Jewish Expositor* 6 (Warsaw, 1821), 477–8.

85. *Jewish Expositor* 10 (Warsaw, 1825), 465.

86. *Jewish Expositor* 10, 465.

87. *Jewish Expositor* 10, 465.

88. Hoff equated exceptional learnedness and Hebrew literacy: "We reckon that there were at least 200 Jews with us this day, many of them learned, as they asked for the tracts in Hebrew." *Jewish Expositor* 11 (1826), 220.

89. Naftali Loewenthal, "Hebrew and the Habad Communication Ethos," 168. Hebrew letters, according to R. Schneur Zalman, sustain all existence and instruct prophets. All speech in every language, according to R. Dov Ber of Lubavitch, is based on the Hebrew letters; and profane languages can be elevated by virtue of the fact that their root is Hebrew.

90. "Once he spoke with us on the subject of book printing in the present day, for printers have proliferated and they constantly print many books of the ancient and recent sages . . . and everyone buys books so that he can own them. . . . But they do not realize that if they do not *study* the teachings, the books are of no benefit at all; for owing to our many sins the study of Torah has declined greatly, and study is extremely limited now." Nahman of Bratslav, *Sihot ha-Ran*, no. 18, p. 25.

91. Gries, "R. Yisrael ben Shabbetai mi-Kozienice ve-Peirushav le-Masekhet Avot," 160–1.

92. Zvi Rabinowicz, *Bein Pshyskha*, 185; Gries, "R. Yisrael ben Shabbetai mi-Kozienice ve-Peirushav le-Masekhet Avot," 131. According to Tzvi M. Rabinowicz, Abraham Joshua Heschel "gave over sixty *haskamot* to printed books, covering a wide range of topics, but he did not endorse any work dealing with Kabbalah"(!) See *Encyclopedia of Hasidism*, 8. According to Samuel Dresner, "more books contain encomia by R. Levi Yitshak than from any other leader but R. Abraham Joshua Heschel of Apt." Dresner also notes that all of the twenty-eight books printed by the Berdyczów press contain the *haskamah* of either Levi Isaac or one of his sons. See *The World of a Hasidic Master*, 212–3.

93. AGAD, CWW 1871, pp. 37–8; Wodziński, " 'Sprawa chasydymów,' " 230.

94. The Maggid of Kozienice, the Seer of Lublin, Levi Isaac of Berdyczów, and R. Abraham Joshua Heschel of Opatów.

95. Stanislawski, *Tsar Nicholas I and the Jews*, 41–2; Carmilly-Weinberger, *Censorship and Feedom of Expression in Jewish History*, 117; Saul Ginsburg, *Drama of Slavuta* (Lanham, Md.: University Press of America, 1991), 30–6.

96. Mahler, *Hasidism and the Jewish Enlightenment*, 110. The manuscript was Perl's *Uber das Wesen der Sekte Chassidim.*

97. Mahler, *Hasidism and the Jewish Enlightenment*, 117.

98. Emanuel Ringelblum, *Projekty i próby przewarstwowienia Żydów w epoce stanisławowskiej* (Warsaw, 1934), 47.

99. Ringelblum, "Restrictions on the Importation of Jewish Books into Poland during the Eighteenth Century."

100. There is disagreement over the date of Krieger's relinquishing of the Nowy Dwór press. Ringelblum ends Krieger's activities as early as 1797. See his "Johann Anton Krieger, Printer of Jewish Books in Nowy Dwór," *Polin* 12 (2000), 198–211. Szaja Friszman finds that Krieger relinquished the press to Zvi Hirsch Nossanowicz in 1811–12. See "Drukarnie hebrajskie na Mazowszu," 14. Hayyim Dov Friedberg places the sale to Nossanowicz "in his old age." See *Toldot ha-Defus ha-Ivri be-Polanya*, 82. However, according to Vinograd's list in *Thesaurus of the Hebrew Book* (Jerusalem: ha-Makhan le-Biblyografy ah Memushavet, 1993), Krieger's seal appears on books printed in Nowy Dwór until the end of its functioning, in 1816.

101. Earlier, in 1776, Lazer had failed to gain enough *Jewish* support to open a press in Praga.

102. Ringelblum, "Johann Anton Krieger."

103. Natalalia Gąsiorowska, "Cenzura żydowska w Królestwie Kongresowem," in *Kwartalnik poświęcony badaniom przeszłości Żydów* vol. 1: 2 (Warsaw, 1912), 55. On presses in the Ukraine etc., see Lieberman, "Badiya ve-Emet be-Divrei Batei ha-Defus ha-Hasidim," 18.

104. The Nowy Dwór press was established by the Christian printer Johann Anton Krieger in 1780. See Ringelblum, "Johann Anton Krieger."

105. Established by Menahem Finkelstein in 1815. See Friedberg, *Toldot ha-Defus ha-Ivri be-Polaniyah*, 150.

106. Hebrew books were first printed in Warsaw by the Christian printer Piotr Zawadzki in 1796. See Lieberman, "Le-Toldot ha-Defus be-Varshe," 20. Although the precise year is not clear (see earlier discussion), Hirsch Nossonowicz seems to have purchased the Nowy Dwór press from Krieger and established presses at 1247 Bagno Street and 719 Leszno Street in Warsaw at least by 1818. Another short-lived enterprise published *Yesod Emuna ve-De'ah Anavah* in 1821. See Friszman, "Drukarnie hebrajskie na Mazowszu," 13 and 16.

107. The Lublin press only resumed briefly again in 1860. See Vinograd, *Thesaurus of the Hebrew Book*, "Lublin."

108. See Vinograd, *Thesaurus of the Hebrew Book*, 159. On Wax's legislative lobbying achievements, see Gąsiorowska, "Cenzura żydowska," 59–61.

109. Quoted in Friszman, "Drukarnie hebrajskie na Mazowszu," 46.

110. Friszman, "Drukarnie hebrajskie na Mazowszu," 46.

111. Mahler, *Ha-Hasidut ve-ha-Haskalah*, app., 507. The report mentions R. Menahem Mendel of Kotsk (d. 1859) and R. Yerahmiel of Przysucha (d. 1834) as "the most popular rabbis of the Hasidim," so it was issued between 1827 and 1834.

112. Mahler, *Ha-Hasidut*, app., 507.

113. Michał Bobrzyński, *Dzieje Polski* (Warsaw, 1931) III, 79–94. The decree is printed in Sefan Kieniewicz, *Przemiany społeczne i gospodarcze w Królestwie Polskim* (1815–1820), (Warsaw: Książka i Wiedza, 1951), 437–438.

114. Harring, *Poland under the Dominion of Russia*, 200–201.

115. Harring mistakenly refers to it as article 6.

116. Harring, *Poland under the Dominion of Russia*, 239–240.

117. APK, RGR I 4411, p. 1.

118. APK, RGR I 4411, p. 2.

119. According to Vinograd's list in *Thesaurus*, Hebrew book publishing virtually ceased in Cracow in 1670. Hebrew books only appeared in 1802, 1803, 1805, and 1810. Substantial publication only resumed in 1820, for several years.

120. APK, RGR I 4411, pp. 8–9.

121. Every printing press in the land, including Jewish ones, was in addition obligated to assemble three copies of any published work for the National Library. Finally, every press had to systematically print the registration in its books. APK, RGR I 4411, pp. 13–5. This copy of the decree was sent to the Cracow Commisssioner.

122. On Chiarni, see Schiper, *Przyczynki do dziejow chasydyzmu w Polsce*, 117–8.

123. Gąsiorowska, "Cenzura żydowska w Królestwie Kongresowem." For additional information on Jewish printing in nineteenth–century Poland, see Bernard Weinryb, "Zur Geschichte des Buchdruckes und der Zensur bei den Juden in Polen," *Monatsschrift fur Geschichte und Wissenschaft des Judentums* vol. 77 (1933) 273–300; and Bałaban, "Zu der Geschichte fun di Yudishe Drukerien in Poylin," *Almanakh zum 10 Yarung fur Moment* (1921), 189–208.

124. Friszman, "Drukarnie hebrajskie na Mazowszu," 35.

125. The Committee for Censorship of Hebrew Writings and Books.

126. Friszman, "Drukarnie hebrajskie na Mazowszu," 35–41.

127. Friszman, "Drukarnie hebrajskie na Mazowszu," 42–3.

128. See also Mahler, *Hasidism and the Jewish Enlightenment*, 211; Marcin Wodziński, "Jakub Tugenhold."

129. Mahler, *Hasidism and the Jewish Enlightenment*, 211.

130. Friszman, "Drukarnie hebrajskie na Mazowszu," 41.

131. Jacob Shatzky, "Avraham Ya'akov Shtern (1768–1842)," in *The Joshua Starr Memorial Volume* (New York: Conference on Jewish Relations, 1953), 208.

132. Shatzky, *Yidishe Bildungs-politik in Poylin* (New York: YIVO, 1943), 200. See also A. N. Frenk, "Di Milhama Gegen Der 'Hefkeros' in Amaligen Varshe," *Almanakh zum 10 Yarung fur Moment* (1921), 113.

133. From Psalms 116:14.

134. Script similar to Rashi, in which many Yiddish books were printed.

135. Gottlober, *Zikhronot u-Masa'ot*, 160–1.

136. See Chone Shmeruk, *Sifrut Yiddish be-Polin* (Jerusalem: Magnes Press, 1981), 119; and Moshe Rosman, "In Praise of the Ba'al Shem Tov: A User's Guide to the Editions of *Shivhei ha-Besht*," *Polin* 10 (1997).

137. Joseph Dan, *Ha-Sippur ha-Hasidi* (Jerusalem: Keter, 1975), 189–95.

138. Gries, *Sefer, Sofer ve-Sippur*, 37.

139. Dauber, *Antonio's Devils*, chaps. 6 and 7; Rosman, "The Editions of *Shvhei ha-Besht*," and "The History of a Historical Source: On the Editing of *Shivhei ha-Besht*," *Zion* 58 (1993), 210–2.

140. Letter from Jacob Samuel Bik, 1819, in Philip Friedman, "Di Erstere Kamfen Zweishen Haskole un Khsidism," *Fun Noentn Ovar* 4 (1938), 261–2.

141. Ira Robinson, "The Zaddik as Hero in Hasidic Historiography," in Mor, *Crisis and Reaction*, 93–103. Dan also cites the growing market for Hasidic nostalgia among increasing numbers of disaffected Jews from Hasidic backgrounds. See Joseph Dan, "A Bow to Frumkian Hasidism," *Modern Judaism* 11 (1991), 185.

142. They are more aptly categorized with the parable-tales that appeared in the works of R. Jacob Joseph of Połonne or the *Salma mul Eder*. See *Toldot Ya'akov Yosef*, parshat *Shoftim*, quoted in Dan, *Ha-Sippur ha-Hasidi*, 40–56; and *Ben Porat Yosef*, quoted in Gries, *Sefer, Sofer ve-Sippur*, 40–2. The tale in *Toldot Ya'akov Yoseph* is based upon a tale in Boccaccio's *Decameron*; while the tale in *Ben Porat Yosef* is based upon a tale in Proverbs 7 and *Zohar* 2, 163a. Werses compares the tales in *Salma mul Eder* (no. 165, earlier) to the *Tales of R. Nahman*. See "Towards A History of the Hebrew Novella in the Early Nineteenth Century: Studies in Zahlen's Salma Mul 'Eder' " in *Scripta Hierosolymitana* 27 (1978), 116.

143. Ben Amos and Mintz, *In Praise of the Ba'al Shem Tov*, 1–2.

144. *In Praise of the Ari* (Basel, 1629), a collection of tales about R. Isaac Luria (1534–72).

145. *In Praise of the Ari*.

146. Nathan Sternharz of Nemirów, *Sippurei Ma'asiyot*, editor's introduction (Jerusalem: n.p., 1993), 2.

147. On another tale collection of a piously didactic orientation, see Samuel Aryeh Zahlen, *Salmah mul Eder* (Warsaw, 1814; Prague, 1818). See Werses, "Towards the History of the Hebrew Novella".

148. Moses Hayyim Ephraim, *Degel Mahane Ephraim*, parshat *Veyashev* (Jerusalem: n.p. 1995), 50.

149. Nathan Shternharz, introduction to Nahman of Bratslav, *Sippurei Ma'asiyot* (Jerusalem, n.p., 1991), 4.

150. Nahman of Bratslav, *Sihot ha-Ran*, no. 138, p. 93.

151. Martin Buber, *Tales of the Hasidim*, vol. 1, pp. 68–70, 151, 191, 229, 263.

152. Rapoport-Albert, "Hasidism After 1772," 85. For a more subtle rendering of this idea, in which Moses and Aaron are said to possess an exclusive right to perform miracles (in contrast to the rest of the Israelites), see Abraham Joshua Heschel of Opatów, *Ohev Yisrael* (Jerusalem, 1962), 183–4.

153. Kalonymous Kalman Epstein, *Ma'or ve-Shemesh*, Parshat *Devarim* (Israel, 1964), 193. Quoted in Yizhak Buxbaum, *Storytelling and Spirituality in Judaism*

(Northvale: Jason Aronson Press, 1994), 117. But Buxbaum edits out the phrase "secular talk".

154. Nahman of Bratslav, *Likkutei Moharan*, 60:6. See also Green, *Tormented Master*, 345–6.

155. S. A. Horodezky, "Ha-Rikud ha-Hasidi," in Meir Shimon Geshuri, *La-Hasidim Mizmor: Me'asef sifruti ve-romanuti li-neginah . . . shel ha-Hasidim* (Jerusalem, 1936), 71–2; Michael Fishbane, "Mahol le-zaddikim: Torat ha-Rikud Ezel Rabi Nahman mi-Bratslav," in Etkes et al., *Be-Magalei Hasidim*, 335–49.

156. A. N. Birnboyim, "Ha-Shirah ve-ha-Zemirah Be-Hazarot Ha-zaddikim be-Polin," *Ha-Olam* 1 (1907), no. 1–17.

157. Geshuri, "Le-Toldot Nigunei ha-Hasidi be-Polin," in *Negina ve-Hasidut be-Vet Kuzmir u-Vanoteha* (Jerusalem: Ha-Heurah le-Hafatsat ha-Hasidut u-Neginatah, 1952), 9–14. Geshuri, "Ha-Niginah Ezel 'Ha-Hozei mi-Lublin,' " in *Negina ve-Hasidut be-Vet Kuzmir u-Vanoteha*, 15–29.

158. Meir of Opatów/Stopnica, *Or le-Shamayim* (Lublin, 1909), 111; Rabinowicz, *Bein Pshyskha*, 373–4; Birnboyim, "Ha-Shirah ve-ha-Zemirah Be-Hazarot Ha-zaddikim be-Polin," no. 1, p. 22.

159. Birnboyim, "Ha-Shirah ve-ha-Zemirah Be-Hazarot Ha-zaddikim be-Polin," 22. R. Abraham Moses also was said to have discovered the original music to the Davidic Psalms in a "foreign library." See Birnboyim, "Ha-Shirah ve-ha-Zemirah," 22.

160. Geshuri, *Ha-Nigun ve-Harikud be-Hasidut* (Tel Aviv: Hotsa'at Netsah, 1954), 88.

161. Birnboyim, "Ha-Shirah ve-ha-Zemirah" no. 4, p. 44.

162. Birnboyim, "Ha-Shirah ve-ha-Zemirah."

163. Abraham Issachar Benjamin of Powienic, *Meir Eynei ha-Golah*, 17.

164. Emphasis added. Nikos Papastergiadis, *The Turbulence of Migration: Globalization, Deterritorialization and Hybridity* (Malden, Mass.: Polity Press, 2000), 186. See Yuri Lotman, *The Universe of the Mind*, tr. A. Shukman (London: Tauris, 2001), 147.

165. Ch. Chajes, "Baal-Szem-Tow u Chreścijan," *Miesięcznik Żydowski* 4 (1934), 450. Chajes cites the Jewish version from *Kahal Hasidim* (Lwów, 1903), 84.

166. *Keter Shem Tov*, no. 8 (Brooklyn, 1972), 3.

167. Moses Hayyim Ephraim of Sudzyłków, *Degel Mahane Ephraim*, parshat *Lekh Lekha* (Jerusalem, 1995), 17. Emphasis added.

168. Nathan Shternharz, introduction to Nahman of Bratslav, *Sippurei Ma'asiyot* (Jerusalem: n.p., 1991), 4.

169. The pioneering ethnomusicologist Moshe Beregovski has demonstrated how Jewish folk music in general borrowed freely from Ukrainian folk music (and vice versa). Moshe Beregovski, "The Interaction of Jewish and Ukrainian Folk Music," (1930), tr. Mark Slobin, in *Jewish Instrumental Folk Music: The Collections and Writings of Moshe Beregovski* (Syracuse, N.Y.: Syracuse University Press, 2001), 513–29.

170. Moses Hayyim Ephraim of Sudzyłków, *Degel Mahane Ephraim*, parshat *Ve-Yarei*, 17–18.

171. R. Isaac Eizik is mentioned in the memoirs of the eighteenth century wine merchant Ber of Bolechów: "R. Eizik was a pretty little boy, who played and sang with a pleasant voice. When he grew up his singing made him famous among the Hasidim, as it is said: 'Sing unto the Lord a new song and His praise in the congregation of the saints (*Hasidim*). . . . ' R. Eizik became famous throughout the country on account of his piety. He was diligent in the study of rabbinical authors, and became a Rabbi and teacher in Israel; to this day he is Chief of the *Bet Din* in Nagy Kallo." See

The Memoirs of Ber of Bolechow, tr. Mark Vishnitzer (London: Humphrey Milford, 1922), 130.

172. In Chajes's version, the zaddik is R. Menahem Mendel of Rymanów, but most versions credit R. Isaac Eizik of Kallo. "God, God" is "Boże, Boże," which is close to "Róża, Róża." Chajes, "Baal-Szem Tow u Chreścijan," 453. Compare A. Z. Idelsohn, *Jewish Music in Its Historical Devlopment* (New York: Holt, 1929), 417–8. The last line of each version appears in Mordecai Stainman, *Niggun: Stories behind the Chasidic Songs That Inspire Jews* (Northvale, N.J.: Aronson, 1994), 24. Stainman replaces "God" with "*Shekhinah*."

173. R. Isaac Eizik only felt compelled to replace the very last line of the popular Hungarian folk song *Szol a kakas mar* ("The cock is already crowing"): "The cock is already crowing / It will soon be dawn / In the green forest / In the open field / A bird is walking / But what a bird / With yellow legs and wings of blue / It is waiting for me there / Wait, my rose, wait, always wait / If God willed me for you, I shall be yours / But when will this come to pass? / Yibonei ha-mikdash ir Zion Timalei" ("May the Temple be rebuilt and Zion be populated"). See Stainman, *Niggun*, 25–6; and 51–3. See also Albert Neuman, "The Rebbe's Song," and József Patai, "The Singing Saint," in Andrew Handler, ed. and tr., *Rabbi Eizik: Hasidic Stories about the Zaddik of Kallo* (Rutherford, N.J.: Fairleigh Dickinson University Press, 1977), 23–33.

174. Chajes, "Baal-Szem Tow u Chreścijan," 453.

175. Israel Loebel, *Sefer Vikuah*, in Wilensky, *Hasidim u-Mitnaggdim*, 2:305.

176. Gottlober, *Zikhronot u-Masa'ot*, 1:107.

177. Gottlober, *Zikhronot u-Masa'ot*, 1:107.

178. Dinard, *Zikhronot Bat Ami*, 14.

179. One new hybrid religion, called "Alleluiah," was not necessarily evidence that the indigenous group had succumbed to the dominant society, but arguably entailed a banner of cultural distinction and resistance. Susan Staats, "Fighting in a Different Way: Indigenous Resistance through the Alleluia Religion of Guyana," in Jonathan Hill, ed., *History, Power, and Identity: Ethnogenesis in the Americas, 1492–1992* (Iowa City: University of Iowa Press, 1996).

180. On cultural hybridity, see Pnina Werbner and Tariq Modood, *Debating Cultural Hybridity: Multi-Cultural Identities and the Politics of Anti-Racism* (London: Zed, 1997).

181. David Assaf concedes that local or regional varieties may be found in Hasidism on an ethnographic level. See " 'Hasidut Polin' o 'Ha-Hasidut be-Polin': Li-ve'ayat Ha-Geografya Ha-Hasidit be-Ikvot Ha-Kovets: Zaddikim be-Anshei Ma'aseh—Mehkarim Be-Hasidut Polin," *Gal-Ed* 14 (1995), 197–206.

CONCLUSION

1. A version of the allegory was also attributed to R. Uziel Meisels, in *Tiferet Uziel*. See Mor Altshuler, "The First Tzaddik of Hasidism," 159.

APPENDIX I

Sources for the information in this appendix include: Levi Halevi Grossman, *Shem u-She'erit* (Tel Aviv, 1942); Wunder, *Elef Margaliot* (Jerusalem: Ha Makhon Le-hantsahat Yahadut Galitsya, 1993), *Me'orei Galicia—Enzyklopediya Le-Hahmei Galitziya*, 4 vols. (Jerusalem: Institute for the Commemoration of Galician Jewry, vol. 1, 1978; vol. 2,

1982; vol. 3, 1986; vol. 4, 1990), and "The Reliability of Genealogical Research in Modern Rabbinic Literature," *Avoteynu* 11:4 (winter 1995), 31–6; Aaron Walden, *Sefer Shem Ha-Gedolim He-Hadash* (Warsaw, 1879); Aaron David Twersky, *Sefer Ha-Yahas Mi-Chernobyl ve-Ruzhin* (Lublin, 1938; reprint, Jerusalem, n.d.); Yizhak Alfasi, *Ha-Hasidut* (Tel Aviv: Sifrit Ma'ariv, 1974, 1979); Menahem Mendel Biber, *Mazkeret L'Gedole Ostraha* (Berdichev, 1907); Menahem Bodek, *Seder Ha-Dorot Mi-Talmudei ha-Besht* (Jerusalem: n.p., 1964–5); Abraham Yizhak Bromberg, *Mi-gedolei Ha-Hasidut* (Jerusalem: Hazaot Hamahon L'Hasidut), vol. 18, *Bet Kozienice* (1961), vol. 19, *Ha-Hozeh Mi-Lublin* (1962); Solomon Buber, *Aneshei Shem* (Cracow, 1895); Nathan Zvi Friedman, *Ozar Ha-Rabanim* (Bnei Brak, n.d.); Shalom Guttman, *Tiferet Bet Levi* (Jassy, 1909); Hayyim Haikel of Indura, *Hayyim ve-Hessed* (Warsaw, 1790; reprint, Jerusalem: n.p., 1970); Hayyim Meir Heilman, *Bet Rabbi* (Tel Aviv, 1902); Abraham Joshua Heschel, *The Circle of the Baal Shem Tov: Studies in Hasidim*, ed. S. H. Dresner (Chicago: University of Chicago Press, 1985), Samuel Abba Horodezky, *Ha-Hasidut Ve-Toratah* (Tel Aviv: Dvir, 1951), and *Leaders of Hassidism*, tr. Maria Horodezky-Magasanik (London: Hasefer, 1928); M. H. Kleinman, *Shem Ha-Gedolim Ha-Hadash* (Israel, 1977); Nathan Zvi Koenig, *Nevei zaddikim* (Bnei Brak, 1969); Shalom Hayyim Porush, *Encyclopedia of Hasidism, Ishim: Letters aleph to te)*, ed. Yizhak Raphael (Jerusalem: Mosad Ha-Rav Kook, 1980); Zvi Rabinowiz, *The Encyclopedia of Hasidism* (Northvale, N.J.: Jason Aronson Press 1996); Jacob Leib Shapiro, *Mishpahot Atikot be Yisrael* (Tel Aviv: Hatsa'at Hulyot, 1981); M. S. Slonim, *Toldot Mishpahat Ha-Rav mi-Liady* (Tel Aviv: n.p., 1946).

1. As mentioned in chapter 4, the most blatant fabrication of the Besht's lineage occurs in Nathan Zvi Friedman, *Ozar HaRabbanim* (Bnei Brak, n.d).

2. See tale no. 8 in Ben Amos and Mintz, *In Praise of the Ba'al Shem Tov*.

3. See Gelber, *Arim ve Imahot be-Yisrael*, vol. 6, *Brody*, 71. Samuel Hasid is also mentioned as the father of Zelig of Brody, who was killed in Safed. See letter from R. Yakir, son of R. Abrahm Gershon of Kuty to his in-law R. Moses Osterer, in Ya'akov Barnai, ed., *Iggerot Hasidim Mi-Arez Yisrael* (Jerusalem: Yad Yitshak Ben-Zvi, 1980), 51.

4. He is occasionally referred to as the son of Sima of Ulanów, as well. See *Shem u-She-erit*, 98.

5. Possibly Tytuvenai, in Lithuania. The main source for deciphering these towns has been Gary Mokotoff and Sallyann Amdur Sack, *Where Once We Walked: A Guide to the Jewish Communities Destroyed in the Holocaust* (N.J.: Avotaynu, 1991; reprint, 2002).

6. R. Barukh is known to have married a daughter of R. Aaron of Titów; Simha Husha is the only known daughter.

7. Of their other son, Abraham, we know nothing.

8. However, one son seems to have married a daughter or granddaughter of R. Nahman of Horodenka. R. Moses and R. Nahman were somehow related through marriage.

9. Arthur Green writes: "A marriage with the granddaughter of the Besht's only son seems like a move calculated to strengthen his authority, and perhaps to assure that male heirs from that line not serve as competitors to his own descendants. In fact Barukh had no male issue, and after his time the family lost its prominence in the Hasidic world." *Tormented Master*, 125. If Green is correct, then this reflects the superiority of patrilineal descent. However, at least through Isaac of Kałusz, husband of Barukh's daughter Hannah, the line endured for many generations. It included such zaddikim as Barukh of Jassy, Eliezer Hayyim of Skole, Barukh Phineas, and Isaac Eizik. See chart in *Encyclopedia Judaica*, 1:160–9.

10. Nahman of Horodenka was son of Hayyim of Horodenka, son of Saul, son of Hayyim, son-in-law of Isaac of Żółkiew, son of Samuel, son-in-law of Nafatali Katz (*av bet din* of Prostejov [Czech lands] and Lublin), son of Isaac, son of Samson Hakohen (*av bet din* of Prague), son-in-law of Judah Loewe, the Maharal of Prague. See Nathan Zvi Koenig, *Neve zaddikim* (Bnei Brak, 1969), 9.

11. Green, *Tormented Master*, 189. Nahman's purported descent from the House of David on both sides of his family bolstered his belief that this union would produce the messiah.

12. In the "Holy Epistle," a letter by the Besht, he writes the following to Gershon of Kuty: "And also my grandson, the important young man, the honorable Ephraim, a great prodigy at the highest level of learning; certainly, if the time is propitious, it would be fitting for you to come here yourself and see and be seen with him face to face and to rejoice in our joy as you promised me." *The Holy Epistle* of the Besht, cited in and translated by Rosman, *Founder of Hasidism*, 108.

13. Horodezky, *Leaders of Hassidism*, chapter on Dov Ber.

14. Horodezky, *Leaders of Hassidism*, chapter on Dov Ber.

15. Ben Amos and Mintz, *In Praise of the Ba'al Shem Tov*, 95, tale no. 75. There are several books entitled *Mishnat Hakhamim*. The likely authors here include Ze'ev Wolf Hokgelernter and Meshullam Feibush Horowitz.

16. Rapoport-Albert, "Hasidism after 1772," 91–3. R. Abraham appeared too holy for such a mundane task as leadership, embodying an old-style hasid. See Ben Amos and Mintz, *In Praise of the Ba'al Shem Tov*, 95, no. 75.

17. Probably Pogrebishche, in the Ukraine.

18. Legend ascribes this to Sarah having married an elderly scholar in order to escape the advances of the local squire's son, an act that earned her an illustrious son bearing her name. See Harry Rabinowicz, *The World of Hasidism* (London: Vallentine, Mitchell, 1970), 204.

19. Dubnow, *Toldot ha-Hasidut*, 159.

20. Dubnow, *Toldot ha-Hasidut*, 159, no. 2.

21. Dubnow, *Toldot ha-Hasidut*, 24.

22. According to legend, Aaron was named "the Silent" because he never spoke a profane word. See Alfasi, *Ha-Hasidut*, 115.

23. In a letter to Asher of Karlin, Israel of Kozienice praises either the daughter or widow of Aaron the Silent. See *Lithuanian Hasidism*, 77. Aaron was also a disciple of Uziel Meisels, author of *Tiferet Uziel* (Warsaw, 1862). See Hayyim Haikel's *Hayyim ve Hesed* (Warsaw, 1790; reprint, Jerusalem: n.p., 1970), 5.

24. Beider, *A Dictionary of Jewish Surnames from the Kingdom of Poland* (Teaneck, N.J.: Avotaynu, 1996).

25. Isaac Alfasi, *Entsyklopediya Le Hasidut: Ishim* (Jerusalem: Mosad Ha-Rav Kook, 1986), 169.

26. Alfasi, *Entsyklopediya Le Hasidut*, 169.

27. A beadle "carried out the orders of the warden, tended to the stove during the winter, went about collecting for the charities on weekdays, and kept order during services at all times. If educated, he also led the congregation in certain ceremonies during services, and where there was no *baal kore* on hand, he read from the scroll and inspected it on the eve of Sabbath." Levitats, *The Jewish Community in Russia, 1844–1917*, 171.

28. David Zvi Heilman, ed., *Iggerot Ba'al ha-Tanya ve-Bnei Doro* (Jerusalem, 1953), 186; Rabinowitch, *Lithuanian Hasidism*, 77. Among the writings found in Stolin is "a letter (dated the day after Sukot, 1801) from R. Yisrael of Kozhenits to

R. Asher after the death of the latter's wife, in which the writer expresses a high regard for the widow of R. Aharon 'the Silent' of Zhelihov (or for his daughter?)."

29. Gottlober, *Zikhronot u-Masa'ot*, 176. The recollection of the event is based on
recent memory, however, as Gottlober was not yet born.

30. Levi Halevi Grosman, *Shem U-She'erit* (Tel Aviv: n.p., 1943), 101.

31. Probably Medwjedowka, in the Ukraine.

32. Alfasi, *Entsiklopediyah*, 332.

33. Horodezky, *Leaders of Hassidism*, p. 68.

34. Yet there is reason to doubt Aryeh's inclusion in the category of *yihus azmo*.
His father's surname, Gerundi, may signify membership in an old Spanish family.
The Gerundi family is described in the work *Tiferet Bet David* as "of the descendants
of the Exile from Jerusalem, who live in Spain." From the Gerundi family came ancestors of both the Horowitz and Epstein families. M. Y. Weinstock, *Tiferet Bet David:
Divre Yemehem Shel ha-Admorim le-Vet Lelov be-Erets Yisrael* (Jerusalem: n.p., 1968),
cited in Neil Rosenstein, "Ashkenazic Rabbinic Families," *Avotaynu* 3:3 (summer
1987), 7.

35. Hayyim Meir Heilman, *Bet Rebbe* (Tel Aviv, 1902), 133.

36. A detailed exposition of this family, which describes the links to Rashi, is
found in Jacob Leib Shapiro's *Mishpahot Atikot*, 19–47.

37. Technically, Phineas should not be referred to as a zaddik, for he and other
intimates of the Besht's circle were not zaddikim as the term came to be known. As
explained, I have used the term "zaddik" as a shorthand for all early Hasidic leaders.

38. Also known as Rydzyna, south of Poznan.

39. Shapiro, *Mishpahot Atikot*, 147. R. Jonah Weill's grandfather was Moses Meir
Weill, known as the "Maharam of Shtinglen." R. Jonah was the uncle of the author of
Korban Natanel (Karlsruhe, 1756).

40. Shapiro, *Mishpahot Atikot*, 137.

41. I have been unable to determine if this is the daughter of the same Jacob
Joseph of Połonne, author of *Toldot Ya'akov Yosef*. But it seems that such a fact would
have been publicized.

42. Closest approximation is the town of Waniowice, 75 kilometers southwest of
Lwów.

43. Closest approximation is the town of Kolin, Czech lands.

44. Sixty-two kilometers NEE of Uman. Two more sons, Eliyahu and Mordecai,
are listed by Friedman in *Ozar HaRabbanim*; but these cannot be corroborated. I have
not seen other mention of these sons.

45. Also known as Nesuhoyezhe, located near Rovno.

46. Their daughter married R. Samuel Jehiel, grandson of R. Isaac of Radziwiłów and R. Abraham Joshua Heschel of Opatów. This was the "Great Wedding in
Ustilla." See Aescoly, *Ha-Hasidut be-Polin*, 82–8.

47. Possibly Botosani, in Romania.

48. "Margoliouth," *Encyclopedia Judaica*, 963.

49. Also known as Pomortsy.

50. Again, we are relying upon Friedman alone.

51. Location unknown.

52. Location unknown. Closest approximation is Remel.

53. Prominent Hasidim from two other aristocratic families—Halpern and Landau—will not be included, because it cannot be established that they were Hasidic
leaders. (1) Joel Halpern, *av bet din* of Leszniow, son of Israel Harif Halpern, *av bet
din* of Zaslaw and Ostrog, was a disciple/colleague of the Besht. He married his

daughter to the zaddik Phineas Horowitz. (2) David Halpern, another early disciple/colleague of the Besht, inherited his position of rabbi of Ostróg from his father, Israel (probably the same Israel in no. 1, making him Joel's brother). David was a forbear of the zaddik Menahem Mendel of Kock (d. 1859). (3) Zvi Aryeh Landau of Alik, son of Abraham Landau of Alik, was a disciple of Jehiel Michael of Złoczów. He married his son to the daughter of the zaddik Mordecai of Krzemieniec, his teacher's son.

54. Wunder, *Enziklopedia Le Hakhame Galizya*, letters "tet" through "ayin,":531. I have been unable to locate *Min Shamayyim* in any list or database.

55. I have not been able to confirm this, however. Some biographers describe Samuel as Mordecai's in-law.

56. Wunder, *Enziklopedia Le Hakhame Galizya*, letters "tet" through "ayin,": 46–60.

57. Also known as Ozhiran, in the Ukraine.

58. Menahem Mendel Bodek, *Seder Ha-Dorot*, 58. Rapoport-Albert views the story as an example of Elimelekh attempting to groom his son for future leadership. See "The Problem of Succession in the Hasidic Leadership, with Special Reference to the Circle of Nahman of Bratslav," 85.

59. But see Ettinger, who claims that Elimelekh "himself acted on the principle of transferring authority to a disciple: there is a tradition that 'the rabbi Rabbi Melekh in his old age ordered all who were sick or embittered to come to his disciple R. Izikel of Lancut (the "seer" of Lublin). Until he accustomed everyone to come to Lancut. And they ceased to come to him. And he waxed very wroth' (*Ohel Elimelekh* [Jerusalem, 1967], 165)"; cited in Hundert, *Essential Papers on Hasidism*, 240. Both Ettinger and Rapoport-Albert rely on dubious sources. But judging by the additional fact that Elimelekh's son Eleazar succeeded him in Leżajsk, Rapoport-Albert's view is the more likely one.

60. R. Reuben successfully performed an exorcism. See *Imrei Shefer* (Lemberg, 1884), 11 (app.); reprinted in Nigal, *Sipurei "Dybbuk,"* 231–3.

61. Probably her brother Eleazar's father-in-law from his first marriage.

62. Perhaps Vienzindziai.

63. Wunder, *Entsiklopedia Le Hakhame Galizya*, letters "aleph" through "dalet," 33. The Urbachs were a prominent Jewish family—the Besht claimed that R. Aryeh Leib Urbach (d. 1750), uncle of Meir Margaliot, had the soul of the talmudic sage R. Abayye.

64. See, for example, Heschel, *Circle of the Baal Shem Tov*, chap. 4.

65. R. Jehiel Michael might have been a member of the Rabinowitz family, because that name is attached to one of his descendants, Barukh Rabinowitz of Jassy.

66. Location unknown.

67. Shapiro, *Mishpahot Atikot be Yisrael*, 38. Ephraim Fischel was son of Samuel, *av bet din* of Indura, Minsk and the Galil, author of *Responsa Shmuel*. Samuel's father was Joseph, *av bet din* of Fiorda; and his grandfather, Samuel, was one of the greatest rabbinic legislators of the seventeenth century, author of *Bet Shmuel*.

68. Green, *Menahem of Chernobyl's Upright Practices*, 21.

69. Menahem Nahum's connection to the Katznellenbogen family is only noted by Friedman in *Ozar Rabbanim*. The Katzenellenbogen claim is absent in Twersky, *Sefer Ha Yahas Mi Chernobyl ve-Ruzhin.*

70. Rapoport-Albert, "Hasidism after 1772," 129. R. Jehiel Michael of Złoczów died in 1786, and several of his sons became zaddikim.

71. Twersky, *Sefer Ha Yahas Mi Chernobyl ve-Ruzhin*, 18.

72. Horodezky writes that R. Nahum "lived in dire poverty. The records of the

hevra kadisha, the Burial Society in Chernobyl, contain a very characteristic note in this regard. Rabbi Nahum was admitted as a member, but being unable to pay the contribution of 3 Rubles in cash, he was obliged to give as security the book *Sefer Hassidim.*" See *Leaders of Hassidism,* 128.

73. Heilman, *Bet Rebbe,* 17. Barukh was son of Moses of Posen, son of Yudel (author of *Kol Yehudah*), son of Moses, son of Zvi Hirsch, son of Joseph Yoske (*av bet din* of Lublin), son-in-law of Judah Loebe, the Maharal of Prague.

74. Heilman, *Bet Rebbe,* 108.

75. Precise name and location unknown.

76. Location unknown.

77. Location unknown.

78. Heilman, *Bet Rebbe,* 111.

79. Sixty-two kilometers west of Witebsk.

80. Gottlober, *Zikhronot u-Ma'asot,* 151; David Assaf, "Momer o-Kadosh? Ma'aseh be-Ikvot Moshe Beno shel R. Schneur Zalman mi-Liady," *Zion* 64:4 (2000).

APPENDIX 2

Source: AGAD, CWW 1424, pp. 2–5.

1. Such a time would be market day.

2. Wodziński's reading is "Pac, Pacjak, Tatarjack" (p. 19). See "Dybuk Z Dokumentów Archiwum Głównego Akt Dawnych w Warszawie," Literatura Ludowa 36:6 (1992), 19. On the use of the names of angels for magical purposes, see Trachtenberg, *Jewish Magic,* 97–100; and Anonymous, *Sefer ha-Razim: The Book of Mysteries,* tr. Michael Morgan (Chico, Calif.: Scholars Press, 1983).

3. A *shofar.*

4. On the use of amulets in such cases, see Nigal, *Magic, Mysticism and Hasidism,* 123–4.

5. Member of the upper Polish nobility, suggesting that magnates continued to be feared in spite of the tsarist hegemony.

6. An acculturated Jew. Thanks to Marcin Wodziński for this interpretation.

7. Such delays may have been intended to increase opportunities to collect money from the bystanders.

8. In an exorcism in Korzec, a *dybbuk* recalls that he fled into the body of a ritually clean animal: "I thought to myself that now I shall gain atonement, believing as I did that the animal would be killed by a Jew, and thus I would be redeemed by the blessing to be uttered by the *shohet* over the ritual slaughter. But, as my bad fortune would have it, the animal was killed by one uncircumcised." Quoted in Nigal, *Magic, Mysticism, and Hasidism,* 90–1.

9. The following note is appended here: "These are threads that a Jew binds to his Clothes, wearing them in the form of a shawl."

APPENDIX 3

This list is primarily based upon Yeshayahu Vinograd, *Thesaurus of the Hebrew Book* and *Ha-sefer Ha-Ivri* (CD-ROM) (Jerusalem: EPI and Institute for Hebrew Bibliography, 1994). Other sources include Hayyim Dov Friedberg, *Bet Eked Sepharim* (Tel Aviv, 1951); Abraham Yairi, "Ha-Defus ha-Ivri be-Berdyczów," *Kiryat Sefer* 21 (1944–45) 100–24; and Aryeh Tauber, "Defusei Korets," *Kiryat Sefer* 1 and 2 (1924/5, 1925/6) 302–306; Hayyim Lieberman, "Nusafot le-'Hadefus ha-Ivri be-Szklów,' " *Kiryat Sefer*

25 (1949), 315–320. I have also picked up stray references in Gries, "The Hasidic Conduct (*Hanhagot*) Literature." The date 1815 is chosen as a cutoff because by this time most of the disciples of Dov Ber of Międzyrzecz had passed away.

1. Every effort has been made to examine actual books, which has been possible in the case of about 85 percent of the editions. In other cases, I rely upon prior lists, which may impugn the complete accuracy of the list.

As the books listed do not supply precise printing information, dates of publication are approximates based on the assumption that printings followed shortly after the dates cited in the publishers' introductions or *haskamot*. In addition, as the Hebrew calendar does not correlate exactly with ours, books printed in the months of Tishri, Heshvan, Kislev, and Tevet might have actually been printed one year earlier (according to our calendar) than is cited.

2. This is "apparently a commentary on the *Tanya*." See Hundert, *The Jews in a Polish Private Town*, 84.

3. Cited twice by Vinograd, *Thesaurás of the Hebrew Book*.

4. In Yiddish. Friszman, "Drukarnie hebrajskie na Mazowszu," 25, and Hayyim Dov Friedberg, *Bet Eked Sefarim*. Hayyim Lieberman considers this an error, because "It is known that R. (Dov) Ber did not print any of books during the lifetime of his father, the Elder *Admor* (R. Schneur Zalman of Liady)." However, according to our list, this assumption must be questioned. Naftali Loewenthal notes the first edition as "around" 1817; while Vinograd lists the first edition as Szklów (Shklov), 1832. See Lieberman, "Le-She'elat Yahas ha-Hasidut le-Lashon Yiddish," 2; and Loewenthal, "Hebrew and the Habad Communication Ethos," 183 and 188, no. 6. Elsewhere, Loewenthal records the date as 1816. See "Early Habad Publications in their Setting," in Hebrew *Studies, British Library Occasional Papers* 13, ed. Diana Rowland Smith and Peter Salinger (London: British Library, 1991), 101.

5. According to Hayyim Lieberman, the first edition of Elimelekh of Leżajsk, *No'am Elimelekh*, appeared in Szklów without date or place of publication. See *YIVO Bleter* 34 (1950), 187.

6. Printed with *Likkutei Shoshana*. See Lieberman, "Dafus Bilti Yaduah," *Kiryat Sefer* 36 (1961), 543–4.

7. Meshullam Feibush's text appeared between pages 19d and 31a of the Lemberg edition; however, this was not indicated until the Żółkiew edition. His first principal work, *Yosher Divrei Emet*, consisted of two letters (written in 1777 and 1782) that were included in the Lemberg edition of *Likkutim Yekarim*. The first letter was censored; and significant material was added to the Żółkiew version. For a full discussion, see Krassen, *Uniter of Heaven and Earth*, 38–9.

8. Based on Hundert, who explains that the first complete editions (parts 1 and 2) were published in Korzec, 1797, without approbations. Hundert holds that parts 1 and 2 were published in Żółkiew in 1794 and 1795, respectively. However, I have adhered to Vinograd's dates. See *Jews in a Polish Private Town*, 84.

9. Judah b. Zvi Hirsch, Aryeh Leib b. Hayyim Segal, Aaron b. Yerahmiel, Abraham b. Isaac.

10. Mordecai b. Moses, Moses b. Eliezer Lipman Halpern, Moses Ze'ev Dov Ber, Judah Leib ben liezer, Mordecai ben Phineas.

11. Hayyim Lieberman, "Nusafot le-'Hadefus ha-Ivri be-Shklov,' " *Kiryat Sefer* 25 (1949), 320.

12. Contains *Rav Yevi* glosses.

13. Nathan b. Shmalke, Mordecai b. Abraham Lemil (son-in-law of author), Mordecai b. Simon ha-Levi Horowitz, Judah b. Zvi Hirsch, Joel b. Ze'ev Wolf.

14. *Kedushat Levi* was first printed in Sławuta, and comprised only sermons on Hannukah and Purim. According to Wilensky, it was reprinted in 1806, along with sermons on *Eser Kedushot*. The 1810/11 printing by R. Levi Isaac's sons in Berdyczów contains his commentary on the Pentateuch. See Wilensky, "The Polemic of Rabbi David of Maków against Hasidism," *PAAJR* (1956), 140.

15. This is a commentary upon various "remembrances" to be recited during prayer (keeping the Sabbath, the giving of the Torah, etc.). R. Levi Isaac's commentary is printed alongside that of R. Raphael b. Zechariah Mendel, author of *Marpeh le-Nefesh*. A first edition, probably with R. Raphael's commentary alone, appeared in Żółkiew 1764. The Mezyrów 1794 edition is mentioned as the *first* edition in its introduction, where the publisher describes his excitement over having found the commentary of R. Levi Isaac, presently *av bet din* of Berdyczów.

16. Published with *Iggeret ha-Kodesh*.

17. Asher Zvi b. David, Nathan Natan b. Samuel Shmelke, Mordecai b. Simon Halevi Horowitz, Mordecai Safra, Judah b. Zvi Hirsch.

18. Nathan Nata b. Samuel Shmelke, Joel b. Nahman Hacohen, Judah Leib b. Abraham Aveli of Krzemienice, Mordecai b. Abraham of Lemil, Israel Jacob b. Moses Judah.

19. Nowe Miasto Korczyn.

20. The Laszczów edition of *Darkhei Yesharim* claims to be the second edition, but no date is given. Mordecai Ziskind of Laszczów wrote the approbation.

21. Location and precise spelling unknown.

22. Location and precise spelling unknown.

23. Signatures supplied by: Israel Hayyim of Ludmir, Zvi Hirsch Eichenstein of Żydaczów, Leib of Minkowicz, Isaac of Hassyn, Samuel of Tulczyn, Reuven of Żytomir, Isaac b. Jehiel Michael of Nadworna, Benjamin Ze'ev Wolf of Zabarazh, Moses b. Jehiel Michael of Międzyrzecz, Moses Bezalel of Ludmir, Abraham Judah Leib of Brzerzyn, Jehiel Michael and his brother Joseph Halpern of Brzerzyn, Aryeh Leib Halpern, Issachar Dov Ber b. Abraham Solomon Halpern, Isaac of Międzyrzecz, Aaron of Międzyrzecz, Mendel of Międzyrzecz, Israel Issermetchin.

24. Pt. 1 only.

25. Pt. 2.

26. The alleged printing in Sławuta, 1809, actually occurred in Lemberg or Żółkiew, 1830–1890. The falseness of the alleged date was revealed because the printers noted R. Nahman (d. 1810) as deceased. See David Assaf, *Bratslav: Bibliografyah Mo'eret* (Jerusalem: Merkaz Zalman Shazar, 2000), 4.

27. Bilingual (Hebrew and Yiddish). Alternate places of printing are Berdyczów and Mohilów.

28. Attached to *Sefer ha-Midot*. Actually composed by Nathan Shternharz. See Assaf, *Bratslav*, 7.

29. Assaf, *Bratslav*, 3–4.

30. An anthology of Lurianic Kabbalah.

31. Approbations state date of publication as 1795.

32. According to Gershom Scholem.

33. Not included in Yehoshua Mondshein, *Torat Habad*, vol. 2, *Sifrei ha-Halakha shel Admor ha-Zaken* (Brooklyn: Ozar ha-Hasidim, 1984).

34. Not included in Mondshein, *Torat Habad*, vol. 2, *Sifrei ha-Halakha shel Admor ha-Zaken*.

35. Not included in Mondshein, *Torat Habad*, vol. 2, *Sifrei ha-Halakha shel Admor ha-Zaken*.

36. Not included in Mondshein, *Torat Habad,* vol. 2, *Sifrei ha-Halakha shel Admor ha-Zaken.* However, a Sudzyłków edition is noted as "approximately" 1820 (p. 8).

37. Questioned by Mondshein, in *Torat Habad: Bibliyografiyot* (Brooklyn: Kohot, 1981), 58.

38. According to Naftali Loewenthal, there are no remaining copies of this edition. See "Hebrew and the Habad Communication Ethos," 94.

39. According to Mondshein, *Torat Habad,* vol. 2, *Sifrei ha-Halakha,* 206.

40. According to Mondshein, *Torat Habad,* vol. 2, *Sifrei ha-Halakha,* 20. According to Vinograd, the printing was in Kopys.

41. Republished by his son R. Dov Ber of Lubavitch as *Seder Tefilot mi-Kol ha-Shanah* in Kopys, 1816. This included a revised version of *Luhot Birkhot ha-Nehenin,* entitled *Seder Birkhot ha-Nehenin.* See Mondshein, *Torat Habad,* vol. 2, *Sifrei ha-Halakha shel Admor ha-Zaken,* 66; Loewenthal, "Hebrew and the Habad Communication Ethos," 100.

42. Hanokh Henokh signed anti-Hasidic ordinances. See Fishman, *Russia's First Modern Jews,* 20.

43. Location and precise spelling unknown.

Bibliography

BIBLIOGRAPHIES AND BIBLIOGRAPHICAL ESSAYS

Anonymous. *Ha-sefer Ha-Ivri*. CD-ROM. Jerusalem: EPI and Institute for Hebrew Bibliography, 1994).

Assaf, David. *Bratslav: Bibliografyah Mo'eret* (Jerusalam: Merkaz Zalman Shazar, 2000).

———. "Hasidut be-Polin be-Meah ha-19—Mazav ha-Mehkar ve-Skirah Bibliografit." In Rachel Elior, Yisrael Bartal, and Chone Shmeruk, eds., *Zaddikim ve-Anshe Ma'aseh: Mehkarim be-Hasidut Polin* (Jerusalem: Mosad Bialik, 1994), 357–79.

———. "Heivetim Histori'im ve-Hevrati'im be-heker ha-Hasidut. In David Assaf, ed., *Zaddik ve-Eyda* (Jerusalem: Merkaz Zalman Shazar, 2002 [offprint]).

Bałaban, Mayer. *Bibliography on the History of the Jews in Poland and in Neighboring Lands: Works Published during the years 19001–930* (Warsaw, 1930; reprint, Jerusalem, 1978).

———. "Przegląd literatury doyczącej Żydowskich gmin wyznaniowych w Polsce." *Miesięcznik Żydowski* 10 (1931) 374–85.

———. "Przegląd literatury historyi Żydów w Polsce, 1891–1907." *Kwartalnik Historyczny* vol. 12:2–3 (1908), 494–524.

———. "Przegląd literatury historyi Żydów w Polsce: 1. 1907–1909. 2. 1909–1911." *Pregląd Historyczny*, vol. 15 and vol. 16 (1912–13), 231–48 and 369–85.

Ben Amos, Dan. "Jewish Folklore Studies." *Modern Judaism* 11 (1991), 176–5.

Corrsin, Stephen. "Works on Polish Jewry, 1990–1994: A Bibliography." *Gal-Ed* 14 (1995), 131–233.

Friederberg, Hayyim Dov. *Bet Eked Sefarim* (Tel Aviv, Ha Mimkarkha-Rashi M. A. Bar-Yuda 1950).

———. *Toldot ha-Defus ha-Ivri be-Polaniyah* (Tel Aviv, Ha Mimkar ha-Rashi M. A. Bar-Yuda 1950).

Friedman, Philip. "Polish Jewish Historiography between the Two Wars (1918–1939)." *Jewish Social Studies* 11:4 (1949).

Goldberg-Mulkiewicz, Olga. *Ethnographic Topics Relating to Jews in Polish Studies*, Studies on Polish Jewry series (Jerusualem: Magnes Press, 1989).

Hundert, Gershon, and Gershon Bacon. *The Jews in Poland and Russia: Bibliographical Essays* (Bloomington: Indiana University Press, 1984).

Lerski, George and Halina. *Jewish-Polish Co-Existence, 1772–1939: A Topical Bibliography* (New York: Greenwood, 1986).

Lieberman, Hayyim. "Badiya ve-Emet b'Divrei Batei had-Defus ha-Hasidim." In *Ohel Rahel* (New York, 1984).

———. "Nusafot le-'Hadefus ha-Ivir be-Szklów.' " *Kiryat Sefer* 25 (1949) pp. 315–320.

Loewenthal, Nafthali. "Early Habad Publications in Their Setting." In *Hebrew Studies*. British Library Occasional Papers 13, Diana Rowland Smith and Peter Salinger, eds. (London: British Library, 1991).

Mondshein, Yehoshua. *Torat Habad: Bibliyografiyot* (Brooklyn: Kohot, 1981).

———. Torat Habad vol. 2: *Sifrei ha-Halakha shel Admor ha-Zaken* (Brooklyn: Ozar ha-Hasidim, 1984).

Muszyńska, Katarzyna, ed. *Bibliographies of Polish Judaica: International Symposium, Cracow 5–7 July 1988 (Proceedings)*. Studia Polono-Judaica: Series Bibliographica, 1 (Cracow: Jagiellonian University Press, 1993).

Pilarczyk, Krzysztof. *Przewodnik po Bibliografiach Polsckich Judaików: Guide to Bibliographies of Polish Judaica*. Studia Polono-Judaica: Series Bibliographica, 1 (Cracow: Jagiellonian University Press, 1992).

Rabinowicz, Tzvi M., ed. *The Encyclopedia of Hasidism* (Northvale, N.J.: Aronson), 567–83.

Rapoport-Albert, Ada, ed. *Hasidism Reappraised*: (Portland, Oregon: Littman Library of Jewish Civilization, 1997), 465–91.

Rubinstein, Abraham. *Hasidut—Reshima Bibliografit le-Shanah 1965* (Jerusalem: Mosad ha-Rav Kook, 1972), 353–4.

Ruta, Magdalena. *Judaika Wydane w Polsce*. Studia Polono-Judaica: Series Bibliographica, 6 (Cracow: Jagiellonian University Press, 1993).

Tauber, Aryeh. "Defusei Korets." *Kiryat Sefer* 1 and 2 (1924/5, 1925/6), pp. 302–306.

Vinograd, Yeshayahu. *Thesaurus of the Hebrew Book* (Jerusalem: ha-Makhon le-Bibliyografyah Memuhshevet, 1993).

Walden, Aaron. *Shem Ha-Gedolim he-Hadash* (Jerusalem: n.p., 1965), vol. 2: Ma'arekhet Sefarim.

Weinreich, Uriel, and Beatrice Weinreich. "Yiddish Language and Folklore: A Selective Bibliography for Research." In Cornelis Van Schooneveld, ed., *Janua Linguarum* 10 (1959), 42–60.

Wierzbieniec, Wacław. *Judaika Polskie z XIX wieku: Materiały do bibliografii I: druki w językach nie-Żydowskich*. Studia Polono-Judaica: Series Bibliographica, 5/1 (Cracow: Jagiellonian University Press, 1999).

Wodziński, Marcin. *Groby cadyków w Polsce* (Wrocław: Towarzystwo Przyjaciól Polonistyki Wrocławskiej, 1998), 240–1.

Wunder, Meir. "The Reliability of Genealogical Research in Modern Rabbinic Literature." *Avoteynu* 11:4 (winter 1995), 31–6.

Yaairi, Abraham. "Ha-Defus ha-Ivri be-Berdychev." *Kiryat Sefer* 21 (1944–5).

PRIMARY SOURCES

Archival

Unpublished

Archiwum Główne Akt Dawnych (AGAD), Centralne Władze Wyznaniowe (CWW), 1869.
AGAD, CWW 1429.
AGAD, CWW 1871.
AGAD, CWW 1723.
AGAD, CWW 1869.
AGAD, CWW 1424.
AGAD, CWW 1441.
AGAD, CWW 1597.
AGAD, CWW 1444.
AGAD, CWW 186.
AGAD, CWW 1012.
AGAD, Komisya Rządowa Spraw Wewnętrznych (KRSW) 6628.
AGAD, KRSW 6634.
AGAD, KRSW 6635.
AGAD, KRSW 5751.
AGAD, Archiwum Gospodarcze Wilanowe, Administracja Dóbr Opatówskich, I/77.
AGAD, Protkoły Rady Aministracyjnej (PN) 6.
AGAD, Rada Ministrów Księstwa Warszawskiego (RMKW), serja 2-go—Akta Spraw, 115.
AGAD, Protokołów Rada Administracyjna Królestwo Polskiego (PRAKP) 9.
AGAD, PRAKP 15.
AGAD, PRAKP 12.
Archiwum Państwowe w Kielcach (APK), Radomski Rząd Gubernialny I (RGR I) 4399.
APK, RGR I 4402.
APK, RGR I 4405.
APK, RGR I 4399.
APK, RGR I 4411.
Archiwum Państwowe w Lublinie (APL), Akta Miasta Lublina (AML) 2419.
APL, AML 2415.
Archiwum Państowe w Radomiu (APR), WAP, Zarząd Dóbr Państwowich w Radomiu 7.
Sąd Rejonowy w Lublinie, Wydział X Hipoteczny, Księga Hipoteczna Lublin, no. 264. Available: http://kft.umcs.lublin.pl/stona.zydzi_lubelscy.html.

Published

Borzymińska, Zofia, ed. *Dzieje Żydów w Polsce, 19 wiek:wybór tekstów żródłych* (Warsaw: Jewish Historical Institute, 1994).
Friedman, Philip. "Di Erstere Kamfen Zweishen Haskole un Khsidism." *Fun Noentn Owar* 4 (1938), 259–275.
Gluzinski, Józef. *Włoscianie Polscy*, in *Archiwum domowe do dziejów i literatury- z ręko-pismów i dzieł najrzadszych* (Warsaw, 1856).

Heschel, Abraham Joshua. "Umbakante Dokumenten Zu der Geschichte fon Kha-sides: Vegen dem Khasides-Arkhiv fun Yivo." *Yivo Bleter* 36 (1952), 113–133.

Horn, Maurycy. *Regesty dokumentów i ekscerpty z metryki koronnej do historii żydów w Polsce: 16971–795*, vol. 2:2 (Wrocław: Zakład Narodowy im. Ossolińskich, 1988).

Jeske-Choiński, Teodor. *Neofici Polscy: Materyały historyczne* (Warsaw, 1904).

Kirszrot, Jakób. *Prawa Żydów w Królestwie Polskiem* (Warsaw, 1917).

Majmon, Salezy. "Luźne Kartki." *Izraelita* 40 (Warsaw, 1894), p. 329.

Mencel, Tadeusz, and Marian Kallas, eds. *Protokoły Rady Stanu Księstwa Warszaws-kiego*, vol. 3:2 (Warsaw: Sejmowe, 1996).

Ostrowski, Teodor, ed. *Poufne wieści z oświeconej Warszawy: gazetki pisane z roku 1782* (Wrocław: Zakład Narodowy im. Ossolińskich, 1972).

Rabinowicz, Tzvi Meir. "Mekorot ve-Te'udot le-Toldot ha-Hasidut be-Polin." *Sinai* 82 (1978), 82–86.

Wojciechowski, Dariusz. "Inwentarz Kozienic z 1784 roku." *Kieleckie Studia History-czne* 13 (1995), 219–230.

Nineteenth–Century Newspapers and Periodicals

Allgemeine Zeitung des Jundenthums
Dostrzegacz Nadwiślański
Gazeta Kielecka
Gazeta Warszawska
Izraelita
Jewish Expositor and Friend of Israel
Jutrzenka
Kurjer Warszawski
Lud
Ozar ha-Sifrut
Pamiętnik Warszawskiego Instytutu Głuchoniemych i Ociemniałych.
Wisła

Dissertations and Articles

Eliach, Yaffe. "Jewish Hasidim, Russian Sectarians: Non-comformists in the Ukraine, 17001–760" (Ph.D. diss., City College of New York, 1973).

Friszman, Szaja. "Drukarnie hebrajskie na Mazowszu od ich założenia do roku 183" (Master's thesis written under the direction of Majer Bałaban, Archives of the Jewish Historical Institute, no. 117/42, Warsaw University).

Kruszon, M. "Chasydyzm na ziemiach Polskich." Master's thesis in the Archives of the Jewish Historical Institute in Warsaw (Poznań, 1989).

Polen, Nehemia. "Rebbetzins, Wonder-Children and the Emergence of the Dynastic Principle in Hasidism," unpublished paper delivered at the Shtetl Conference at Boston University, Center for Judaic Studies, November 1, 2002. Updated March 1, 2004, courtesy of the author.

Rapoport-Albert, Ada. "The Problem of Succession in the Hasidic Leadership, with Special Reference to the Circle of Nahman of Bratslav" (Ph.D. diss., University of London, 1970).

Sinkoff, Nancy. "Tradition and Transition: Mendel Lefin of Satanow and the Begin-nings of the Jewish Enlightenment in Eastern Europe" (Ph.D. diss., Columbia University, 1996).

Medieval and Early Modern Sources

Abraham Ibn Ezra, *The Commentary of Ibn Ezra on the Pentateuch,* tr. Jay Shachter (Hoboken, N.J.: KTAV, 1986).
Alsheikh, Moses. *Humshe Torah* (Lemberg, 1864).
Bahya. Sefer Rabeina Bahya al Ha-Torah (Jerusalem, 1992).
Emden, Jacob. *Mitpahat Sefarim* (Altona, 1768).
———. *Sefer Histavkut* (Altona, 1762; Lwów, Poland, 1877).
Eybeschutz, Jonathan Halevi. *Hedvat Simha* (Warsaw, 1930).
Gellis, Yaakov. Tosafot Shalem (Jerusalem: Hotsa'at Mifal Tosafot ha-Shalem, 1982).
Joseph Bechor Shor. Perush L'Humishei Torah (Jerusalem: Makor, 1978).
Judah ben Shmuel. *Sefer Hasidim,* ed. Ruben Margaliot (Jerusalem: Mossad Ha-Rav Kook, 1969–70).
Karo, Joseph. *Maggid Mesharim al Massekhet Shabat* (Biłgoraj, 1937).
———. *Shulhan Arukh,* section "Yoreh Deah" vol. 1, chap. 17, commentary *Siftei Kohen* (Vilna, 1911).
Katz, Shabbetai. Commentary *Siftei Kohen Shulhan Arukh,* "Yoreh Deah" vol. 1, chap. 17 (Vilna, 1911).
Landau, Ezekiel. *Nodeh Be-Yehuda Mahadorah Tanina* (Prague, 1776 and 1811).
Nahmanides. Perushe Ha-Torah (Jerusalem: Mosad Ha-Rav Kuk, 1969).
Rosin, David, ed. Perush Ha-Torah Asher Katav Rashbam (Jerusalem, 1970).
Silbermann, A. M., ed. Chumash with Targum Onkelos, Haphtorot and Rashis' Commentary (Jerusalem, (1978).
Singer, Sholem Alchanan. *Medieval Jewish Mysticism: The Book of the Pious* (Northbrook, Ill.: Whitehall, 1971).

Hasidic Texts: Homiletics, Hagiography, Correspondence

Abraham Joshua Heschel of Apt, Ohev Yisrael (Jerusalem, 1962).
Aharon of Apt. *Keter Shem Tov* (1794, reprint, Brooklyn, 1987).
Alexander Sender of Komarno. *Zot Ha-Berakha* (Jerusalem: Mekhon Hekhal ha-berakhah, 1999).
Anonymous. *He-Hasidut ve-Mishnat ha-Rishonim.* "Shar ha-zaddik" (n.p., 1989).
———. *Imrei Shefer,* "Kitvei Kodesh" (Lemberg, 1884).
Ashkenazi, Meshulam Ze'ev. *Bet Meshulam: Kavod Ha-Bayit* (Piotrokòw Trybunalski, Poland, 1905).
Barnai, Ya'akov, ed. *Iggerot Hasidim Mi-Erez Yisrael* (Jerusalem: Yad Yitshak Ben-Zvi, 1980).
Barukh Yashar (Shlichter). *Bet Komarna* (Jerusalem: [s.n.], 1965).
Barukh of Międzybóż. *Buzina Di-nehara* (Jerusalem, [s.n.], 1970).
———. *Buzina Di-nehara Ha-Shalem.* Ed. Reuben Margaliot (Bilgoraj, n.d.).
Ben-Amos, Dan, and Jerome Mintz, tr. and ed. *In Praise of the Ba'al Shem Tov (Shivhei ha-Besht)* (Bloomington: Indiana University Press, 1970).
Benjamin of Złoczów. *Amtahat Benyamin* (Minkowice, 1796).
———. *Hilkhat Binyamin* (Lwów, Poland, 1794).
Bodek, Menahem Mendel. *Seder ha-Dorot he-Hadash, Megilat Yuhasin* (Jerusalem, [s.n.] 1965).
Buber, Martin. *For the Sake of Heaven (Gog u-Magog)* (Philadelphia: Jewish Publication Society, 1953).

————. *Tales of the Hasidim. Vol. 1, The Early Masters,* Tr. Olga Marx (New York: Schocken Books, 1948).

————. *Tales of the Hasidim. Vol. 2, The Later Masters.* Tr. Olga Marx (New York: Schocken Books, 1948).

David ben Raziel, and Israel ben Feiga Sarah. *Kedushat Yisrael, "Pe'er Yisrael"* (Jerusalem, 1956).

Dov Ber of Międzyrzecz. *Maggid Devarav le-Ya'akov la-Maggid Dov Ber mi-Mezhritch.* Ed. Rivka Schatz-Uffenheimer. (Jerusalem: Magnes Press, 1990).

Eleazer ben Elimelekh of Leżajsk. *Iggeret ha-Kodesh.* Appendix to *No'am Elimelekh,* ed. Gedalyah Nigal (Jerusalem: Mosad Ha-Rav Kook, 1978).

Eleazar Hakohen of Pułtusk. "Ez Avot." In *Hidushei Maharakh* (Warsaw, 1898).

Eliezer Horowitz of Tarnogród. *No'am Meggedim* (Lwów, 1807).

Elimelekh of Leżajsk. *No'am Elimelekh.* Ed. Gedalyah Nigal (Jerusalem: Mosad Ha-Rav Kook, 1978).

Epstein, Kalonymous Kalman. *Ma'or ve-Shemesh,* parshat Devarim (Tel Aviv, 1964).

Green, Arthur, tr. and ed. *The Language of Truth: The Torah Commentary of the Sefat Emet, R. Yehudah Leib Alter of Ger* (Philadelphia: Jewish Publication Society, 1998).

————. *Menahem of Chernobyl's Upright Practices, the Light of the Eyes* (New York: Paulist Press, 1982).

Gutman, Shalom. *Tiferet Bet Levi* (Jassy, Romania, 1909).

Halevi, Moshe, ed. *Ayala Shluha, Kitvei Kodesh* (Bnei Brak, Israel, 1972).

David, Halperin, of Ostróg. *Darkhei Ziyon* (Bartfeld, 1909).

Hayyim Haikel of Indura. *Hayyim ve-Hesed* (Warsaw, 1790; reprint, Jerusalem: Makor, 1970).

Heilman, David Zvi, ed. *Iggerot Ba'al ha-Tanya ve-Bnei Doro* (Jerusalem, [s.n.] 1953).

Heller, Meshullam Feibush. *Likkutim Hadashim* (Lemberg, 1792).

Hibner, Jehiel Mikhal. *Nahalah le-Yisrael* (Lemberg, 1876).

Horodezky, Samuel, ed. *Shivhei Ha-Besht* (Tel Aviv: Devir, 1947).

Horowitz, Shmuel Shmelke. "The Letter of the Rabbi Samuel Shmelke Horowitz, Rabbi of Nikolsberg, to the Brody Kahal." In Mordechai Wilensky, ed., *Hasidim u-Mitnaggdim,* vol.1 (Jerusalem: Mosad Bialik, 1990).

————. *Shemen Ha-Tov* (Piotroków Trybunalski, 1905).

Isaac ben Asher, ed. *Sefer Nifla'ot Ha-Yehudi: Bet zaddikim* (Jerusalem, 1907).

Isaac of Neskhiź. *Zikharon Tov* (Piotroków Trybunalski, 1892).

Israel Ba'al Shem Tov and Dov Ber of Międzyrzecz. *Za'avat ha-Ribash ve-Hanagot Yesharot.* Reprinted in *Sefarim Kedoshim mi-Talmidei Ba'al Shem Tov.* Vol. 91 (Brooklyn: Bet Hilel 1993).

Israel b. Isaac Simha. "Or Simha." In *Simhat Yisrael* (Piotroków, 1910; reprint, Jerusalem, 1986).

Israel Hapstein of Kozienice. *Avodat Yisrael Ha-Mefuar[al pi yad defus rishon]* (Bnei Brak: Makhon Mofet Tsufim, 1996).

Issachar Dov Ber mi-Geza Tsvi. *Mivasser Tsedek* (Dubno, Lithuania, 1798).

Jacob Isaac Horowitz of Lublin. *Divrei Emet* (New York, 1946).

————. *Toraf ha-Hoze mi-Lublin* (Jerusalem: Hotsa'at Hekhon Torani, 1979).

————. *Zikharon Zot* Munkac ed. (reprint, Tel Aviv, 1973).

————. *Zot Zikharon* (Tel Aviv, 1987).

Jacob Joseph Hakohen of Połonne. *Toldot Ya'akov Yosef* (Jerusalem, 1962).

Jaffee, Israel. *Shivhei ha-Besht* (Berdyczów, 1815).

Kadish, Yoets Kim. *Si'ah Sarfe Kodesh* (Piotroków Trybunalski, 1923).

Kamelhar, Yekutiel. "Bet Menahem." In *Em la-Binah* (Lemberg, 1909).

Levi Isaac of Berdyczów. *Kedushat Levi ha-Shalem* (Jerusalem: Makhon Kedushat Levi, 1993).

Lieber, Akiva Hakohan. *Imrei Shefer* (Lemberg, 1884).

Margaliot, Meir. *Kol Aryeh* (Korzec, Russia, 1798).

———. *Meir Netivim* (Połonne, Russia, 1791).

———. *Sod Yakhin u-Voaz* (Berdichev, Russia, 1902).

Margaliot, Ya'akov. *Gedolim Ma'aseh Zaddikim: Sipurim Hasidiyim*. Ed. Gedalya Nigal (Jerusalem: Ha-Makhon le-Heker Ha-Sifrut Ha-Hasidut, 1991).

Meir of Opatów/Stopnica. *Or le-Shamayim* (Lublin, 1909).

Menahem Mendel of Kotsk. *Ohel Torah* (Jerusalem: Nofet Tsufim, 1997).

Michaelson, Zvi Yehezkel. "Mare Kohen." Appendix in Alexander Ziskind Ha-Kohen, *Torat Kohen* (Warsaw, 1939).

———. *Siftei Kodesh* (Warsaw, 1929).

Michelzohn, Abraham Hayyim. *Ohel Naftali* (Lemberg, 1911).

Miller, D. *Besurot Tovot* (Lublin, 1927).

Miscellaneous. *Kovets Nahalat Zvi* 2 (1995) and 11 (1995): correspondence.

———. *Kovets Siftei Zaddikim* 4 (1992): correspondence.

Mose Elyakim Bryah of Kozienice. *Be'er Moshe* (Lemberg, 1918).

Moses Hayyim Ephraim of Sudzyłków. *Degel Mahaneh Ephraim* (Jerusalem: Hotsa'at Mir, 1995).

Moses of Przeworsk. *Or Pnei Moshe* (Międzrzecz, Russia, 1809).

Nahman of Bratslav. *Avaneihah Barzel* (Jerusalem, 1961).

———. *Hayei Moharan: Nesiyato le-Erez Yisrael* (Jerusalem: Hamol, 1962).

———. *Sefer ha-Midot* (New York: Hamol, 1967).

———. *Sihot ha-Ran* (Lemberg, 1901).

———. *Sippurei Ma'asiyot* (Ostróg, 1816; reprint, Jerusalem: Mekhon Torat ha-Netsah 1991).

———. *Shivhei ha Ran: Sihot ha-Ran* (Lemberg, 1901).

Panet, Hayyim Bezalel. "Toldot Rabeinu Yehezkel," in *Derekh Yiuhar* (Munkacz, Poland, 1894).

Phineas of Korzec. *Imrei Pinhas Ha-Shalem*. Ed. Ezekiel Shraga Frankel (Ramat Gan, Israel: Yehezkel Shraga Frenkl, 1988).

———. *Midrash Pinhas* (Ashdod: Yehezkel Shraga Frenkl 1989).

Rabinowitz, Yizhak Mordekhai Hakohen. *Atarat Shlomo* (Piotroków Trybunalski, 1926).

———. *Ohel Shlomo* (Piotroków Trybunalski, Poland, 1924).

Rubinstein, Avraham, ed. Dov Ber ben Samuel of Linits, *Shivhei Ha-Besht* (Jerusalem: Reuven Mas, 1991).

Seinfeld, M. *Emet Mi-Kotsk Tizmah* (Bnei Brak, Israel: Netsah, 1961).

Shapiro, Nahman, ed. *Hidushe Ha-Ramal* (Jerusalem [s.n.] 1967).

Shmuel of Sieniawa. *Ramata'im Zufim* (Warsaw, 1885).

Shneur Zalman of Liady. *Tanya* (Sławuta, Russia, 1796).

Simha Bunem of Przysucha. *Kol Simha* (Jerusalem, 1997).

Steinman, Eliezer. *Sefer Be'er Ha-Hasidut* (Tel Aviv: Keneset, 1950).

Tieberg, Yehuda Moshe mi-Aleksander. *Kedushat Yizhak: Yamei Hayyei Raboteinu ha-Kedoshim ha-Admorim mi-Alexander* (Jerusalem: Bi-defus Hershkovits, 1952).

Walden, Moses Menahem. *Nifla'ot ha-Rabi* (Warsaw, 1911), reprinted in *Sefarim Kedoshim mi-Talmide ha-Ba'al Shem Tov* (Brooklyn: Bet Hilel, 1985).

———. *Or ha-Nifla'ot* (Warsaw, 1911). Reprinted in *Sefarim Kedoshim mi-Talmide ha-Ba'al Shem Tov* vol. 2 (Brooklyn: Bet Hilel, 1985).

———. *Y'kaved Av* (Bnei Brak, Israel, 1968).

———. *Ohel Yizhak* ([Jerusalem?], 1968).

Jehiel Michael of Zakrotsztein. *Ez Avot, Megilat Yuhasin, Tahat ha-Ez* (Warsaw, 1898).

Yehuda Leib Hakohen Levine. "Rav Pe'er." In *Y'khahen Pe'er* (Jerusalem, 1964).

Yehuda Leib of Zaklików. *Likkutei Maharil* (Lemberg, 1862).

Yizhak Isaac Yehudah Jehiel Safrin. *Megilat Seterim.* Ed. Nafthali Ben-Menahem (Jerusalem: Mosad ha-Rav Kuk, 1944).

———. *Jewish Mystical Autobiographies: Book of Visions and Book of Secrets.* Tr. Morris Faierstein (New York: Paulist Press, 1999).

Yizhak of Nezkhiż. *Zikharon Tov* (Piotroków Trybunalski, Poland, 1892).

Ze'ev Wolf of Żytomir. *Or ha-Meir,* "Rimzei Zav" (Korzec, Russia, 1798; reprint, Brooklyn, 1975).

Zevin, Shlomo Yoseph. *Sippurei Hasidim* (Tel Aviv: A. Tsiyoni, 1957).

Zinger, Yizhak. *Sava Razon* (Padgorze, Poland, 1901).

Zusman, Abraham. *Barukh mi-Banim* (Vilna, 1869).

Zvi Elimelekh of Dinów. *Responsa Bnei Yissakar* (Jerusalem: Mifale Sefarim li-yetsa, 1978).

Mitnaggdic Texts

Anonymous. *Zemir Arizim ve-Harevot Zurim* (1772). In Mordechai Wilensky, ed., *Hasidim u-Mitnaggdim,* vol. 1 (Jerusalem: Mosad Bialik, 1990).

David of Maków. *Shever Posh'im: Zot Torat ha-Knaot.* In Mordechai Wilensky, ed., *Hasidim u-Mitnaggdim,* vol. 2 (Jerusalem: Mosad Bialik, 1990).

———. *Zemir Arizim* (Warsaw, 1798). In Mordechai Wilensky, ed., *Hasidim u-Mitnaggdim* vol. 2 (Jerusalem: Mosad Bialik, 1990).

———. "Zivato shel R. David mi-Makov." In Mordechai Wilensky, ed., *Hasidim u-Mitnaggdim,* (Jerusalem: Mosad Bialik, 1990).

Hayim of Volozhin. *Nefesh ha-hayim* (Bnei Brak, 1989).

Leibel, Israel. *Kontres be-Germanit shel R. Israel Leibel.* In Mordechai Wilensky, ed., *Hasidim u-Mitnaggdim,* vol. 2 (Jerusalem: Mosad Bialik, 1990).

———. *Sefer Vikuah,* vol. 2 In Mordechai Wilensky, ed., *Hasidim u-Mitnaggdim* (Jerusalem: Mosad Bialik, 1990).

Haskalah Texts and Proposals for Jewish Reform

Anonymous. *Di Genarte Velt* (1815).

Bik, Jacob Samuel. "Mikhtavim." *Ozar ha-Sifrut, Sefer Shanati,* vol. 3 (Kraków, 1888).

Calmanson, Jacques. *Uwagi nad niniejszym stanem Żydów Polskich y ich wydoskonaleniem* (Warsaw, 1797).

David Friedlander. *Uber die Verbesserung der Israeliten im Konigreich Pohlen* (Berlin, 1819).

Fischelson, Ephraim Fischel. "Teyator fun Khsidim." *Historische Schriften* 1, E. Tscherikower, ed. (1929) 645–94.

Fuenn, Shmuel Yosef. "Dor ve-Dorshav." In Shmuel Feiner, ed., *Me-Haskalah Lohemet le-Haskalah Meshameret: Nivhar Nikhteve R. Sh. Y. Fin* (Jerusalem: Merkaz Dinur, 1993).

Hoge, Stanisław Ezekiel. *Tu chazy, czyli rozmowa o Żydach* (Warsaw, 1830).

Lefin Satanower, Mendel. *Essai D'un plan de reforme ayant pour objet d'eclairer la Nation Juive en Pologne et de redresser par la ses moeurs* (Warsaw, 1791).

Levinsohn, Isaac Ber. "Emek Refa'im." In *Yalkut Ribal* (Warsaw, 1878).

Ostrowski, Antoni. "Uwagi nad obyczaimi uspobieniem i charakterem żydów Polskich." In *Pomysły o potzrebie reformy towarzyskiey w ogólnośći i umianowiciey co do Israelitów w Polszcze* (Paris, 1834).

Perl, Joseph. *Megalle Temirin (Revealer of Secrets)*, (Vienna, 1819). Tr. Dov Taylor (Boulder, Colo.: Westview, 1997).

———. *Uiber das Wesen der Sekte Chassidim*. Ed. Avraham Rubinstein (Jerusalem: Israel Academy of Sciences and Humanities, 1977).

Radominski, Jan. *Co wstrzymuie reforme Żydów w kraiu naszym, i co ią przyspieszyć powinno?* (Warsaw, 1820).

Staszic, Stanisław. "Żydzi,"and "O przyczynach szkodliwości żydów i srodkach usposobienia ich, aby się społeczeństwu użytecznymi stali." In Józef Kruszynski, ed., *Stanisław Staszic a kwestja żydowska* (Lublin, 1926).

Tsederbaum, Alexander. *Keter Kehunah* (Odessa, 1866).

Tugenhold, Jacob. Introduction to *Obrona Izraelitów przez Rabbi Menasse Ben Israel* (Warsaw, 1831).

———. *Rys myśli poważnych* (Warsaw, 1848).

Memoirs, Yizkor Books, and Travel Diaries

Bik, Avraham. "Etapen fun Hasidism in Varshe." In *Pinkes Varshe* (Buenos Aires, 1955), 1:179–86.

Birkenthal, Dov Ber. *The Memoirs of Ber of Bolechów*. Tr. Mark Vischnitzer (London: Humphrey Milford, 1922).

Dembowski, Leon. *Moje wspomnienia* (St. Petersburg, 1898).

Dinard, Ephraim. *Zikhronot Bat Ami*, pt. 2 (New Orleans, 1920).

Eisenberg, Eliyahu. *Plotsk: Toldot Kehillah Atikat Yamin be-Polin* (Tel Aviv: Menorah, 1967).

Ewen, Yizhak. *Fun der gut Yidisher velt* (New York, 1917).

Fromer, Jakob. *Vom Ghetto zur modernen Kultur* (Charlottenburg, 1906).

Fuen, Samuel Joseph. *Dor ve-Dorsav Me-Haskalah Lohemet le-Haskalah Meshameret: Nivhar Nikhteve R. Sh. Y. Fin*. Ed. Shmuel Feiner (Jerusalem: Merkaz Dinur, 1993).

Gelber, Nahum. "Oyslenishe Rayunde Vegen Poylishe Yidn Inem 18th Yahrhundert." In A. Tserikover, ed., *Historishe Schriften* vol.1 (Warsaw, 1929).

Gluckl of Hameln. *Memoirs of Gluckl of Hameln*. Tr. Marvin Lowenthal (New York: Schocken Books, 1977).

Goldberg, Jacob, ed. and tr. *Die Memoiren des Moses Wasserzug* (Leipzig: Leipziger Universitatsverlag, 1999).

Gottlober, Avraham. *Zikhronot u-Ma'asot* (Jerusalem: Mosad Bialik, 1976).

Harring, Harro. *Poland under the Dominion of Russia* (Boston, 1834).

Henderson, E. *Biblical Researches and Travels in Russia; Including a Tour in the Crimea and the Passage of the Caucasus* (London, 1826).

Huberband, Shimon. *Kiddush Hashem: Jewish Religious and Cultural Life in Poland during the Holocaust*. Tr. David E. Fishman. Ed. Jeffrey S. Gurock and Robert S. Hirt. (New York: Yeshiva University Press, 1987).

James, J. T. *Journal of a Tour in Germany, Sweden, Russia and Poland, 1831–34* (London, 1827).

Jasni, Wolf, ed. *Yizkor Book fun der Zelechover Yiddische Kehille* (Chicago: Aroysgegebn fun der Tsentraler Zshelekhover landsmanshaft in Shikago, 1953).

Johnston, Robert. *Travels through part of the Russian Empire and the Country of Poland* (New York, 1816).

Kalisch, Ludwig. *Bilder meiner Knabenzeit* (Leipzig, 1872).

Katzenellenbogen, Pinhas. *Yesh Manhillim*. Ed. I. D. Feld. (Jerusalem, 1986).

Kotik, Yehezkel. *Ma She-Raiti . . . Zikhronotav Shel Yehezkel Kotik*. Ed. and tr. David Assaf (Tel Aviv: Tel Aviv University Press, 1999).

Maimon, Solomon. *Solomon Maimon: An Autobiography*. Ed. Moses Hadas (New York: Shocken Books, 1967).

Marsden, Norman. *A Jewish Life under the Tsars: The Autobiography of Chaim Aronson, 18251–888* (Totowa N.J.: Allanheld, 1983).

Shaibowicz, Joseph. "Towards a History of the Brzezin Kehilah (Jewish Community)." Tr. Renee Miller. Pap. 78–83 of the Brzezin Communal record book (Pinkas). Available: www.jewishgen.org/yizkor/brzeziny/brzo78.html., ed. Fay Bussgang.

Shvartzmann, Meir. "Vi Khasides Hat Bazigt das Lomdishe Varshe." In *Das Amalike Yidishe Varshe* (Montreal: Farband of Jews in Montreal, 1966).

Stryienski, Casimir, ed. *Memoirs of the Countess Potocka*. Tr. Lionel Strachey (New York: Doubleday, 1900).

Waisman, Gabrie, ed. *Sefer Praga: A Memorial to the Jewish Community of Praga* (Tel Aviv: Orli, 1974).

Wassercug, Moshe. "Korot Moshe Wassercug u-Nedivat Lev Aviv ha-Manoah R. Isserel Zal." In Henrich Loewe, ed., *Jahrbuch der Judisch-Literarischen Gesellschaft* 8 (1910), 441–446.

Wodzicki, Stanisław. *Wspomnienia z przeszłości od r. 1768 do r. 1840* (Kraków, 1873).

Wraxall, William N., *Memoirs of the Courts of Berlin, Dresden, Warsaw and Vienna, in the Years 1777, 1778, and 1779*, vol. 2 (London, 1806).

Yavnin, Shmuel. *Nahalat Olamim* (Warsaw, 1882).

Zunser, Miriam Shomer. *Yesterday: A Memoir of a Russian Jewish Family* (New York: Harper and Row, 1978).

SECONDARY SOURCES

Encyclopedias, Gazetteers, Biographical Dictionaries, and Genealogies

Alfasi, Yizhak. *Ha-Hasidut* (Tel Aviv: Sifriyat Ma'ariv, 1974, 1979).

———. *Entsyklopediya Le-Hasidut: Ishim*, letters "alef"—"tet" (Jerusalem: Mosad Ha-Rav Kuk, 1986).

Beer, Peter. *Allgemeine Encyclopadie Wissenschaften und Kunste* (Leipzig, 1827).

Beider, Alexander. *A Dictionary of Jewish Surnames from the Kingdom of Poland* (Teaneck, N.J.: Avotaynu, 1996).

Bergman, Eleanor, and Jan Jagielski. *Zachowane synagogi i domy modlitwy w Polsce: Katalog* (Warsaw: Jewish Historical Insitute, 1996).

Biber, Menahem Mendel. *Mazkeret Li Gedole Ostraha* (Berdichev, 1907).

Bodek, Menahem Mendel. *Seder Ha-Dorot Mi-Talmide ha Besht* (reprint, Jerusalem [s.n.], 1964–5).

Bromberg, Abraham Yizhak. *Mi-gedolei He-Hasidut*. Vol. 18. *Bet Kozienice* (Jerusalem: Haza'ot Hamahon L'Hasidut, 1961). Vol. 19, *Ha-Hozeh Mi-Lublin* (Jerusalem: Haza'ot Hamahon L'Hasidut, 1962).

Buber, Solomon. *Aneshei Shem* (Cracow, 1895).

Encyclopedia Judaica (New York: Macmillan, 1971).

Friedman, Nathan Zvi. *Ozar Ha-Rabanim* (Bnei Brak, n.d.).

Grossman, Levi Halevi. *Shem u-She'erit* (Tel Aviv, 1943).

Guttman, Shalom. *Tiferet Bet Levi* (Jassy, 1909).

Heilman, Hayyim Meir. *Bet Rabi* (Berdyczów, 1902).

Horodezky, Samuel. *Ha-Hasidut Ve-Toratah* (Tel Aviv: Dvir, 1951).

Koenig, Nathan Zvi. *Nevei zaddikim* (Bnei Brak: Kolel Bratslav, 1969).

Mokotoff, Gary, and Sallyann Amdur Sack. *Where Once We Walked: A Guide to the Jewish Communities Destroyed in the Holocaust* (Teaneck, N.J.: Avotaynu, 1991; reprint, 2002).

Orgelbrand, Samuel, ed. *Encyklopedyja Powszechna* (Warsaw, 1861).

Polski Słownik Biograficzny. Polska Akademia Umiejętności. (Cracow: Polska Akademia Umejętności; Wrocław: Zakład Narodowy im. Ossolińskich, 1967; Skład główny w księg, Gebethnera I Wolffa, 1967).

Porush, Shalom Hayyim. *Encyclopedia of Hasidism, Ishim: Letters aleph to tet.* Ed. Yizhak Raphael (Jerusalem: Mosad Ha-Rav Kook, 1980).

Shapiro, Jacob Leib. *Mishpahot Atikot be-Yisrael* (Tel Aviv: Hotsaot Hulyot, 1981).

Slonim, M. S. *Toldot Mishpahat Ha-Rav mi-Liady* (Tel Aviv, 1946).

Sulmierski, Filip, ed. *Słownik Geograficzny Królestwo Polskiego* Vol. 3 (Warsaw, 1882).

Twersky, Aaron David. *Sefer Ha-Yahas Mi-Chernobyl ve-Ruzhin* (Lublin, 1938; reprint, Jerusalem, n.d.).

Walden, Aaron. *Sefer Shem Ha-Gedolim He-Hadash* (Warsaw, 1879).

Wunder, Meir. *Elef Margaliot* (Jerusalem: Ha Makhon Le-hantsahat Yahadut Galitsya, 1993).

———. *Me'orei Galicia—Enzyklopediya Le-Hahmei Galitziya.* 4 vols. (Jerusalem: Institute for the Commemoration of Galician Jewry, vol. 1, 1978; vol. 2, 1982; vol. 3, 1986; vol. 4, 1990).

Books and Journal Articles

Abrahams, B. Z. Lask. "Stanislaus Hoga-Apostate and Penitent." In *The Jewish Historical Society of England: Transactions* 15 (London, 1946), 121–148.

Abrahams, Israel. *Hebrew Ethical Wills* (Philadelphia: Jewish Publication Society, 1926).

Abraham Issachar Benjamin of Powienic. *Meir Eynei ha-Golah* (Tel Aviv: Alter-Bergman, 1954).

Aescoly, Aaron Ze'ev. *Ha-hasidut be-Polin.* Ed. David Assaf (Jerusalem: Magnes Press, 1999).

Ajzen, Mieczysław. *Polityka gospodarcza Lubeckiego* (Warsaw: Warszawa Nakładem Towarzystwa Naukowego Warzawskiego, 1932).

Albeck, Shalom. "Rabenu Tam's Attitude To the Problems of His Time" (in Hebrew). *Zion* 19 (1954), 104–141.

Alfasi, Yizhak. *Gur: Toldot Hasidut Gur* (Tel Aviv: Sinai, 1978).

———. "Haknasat Kala ve-Hatunot be-Hasidut." *Orayta* 15 (1986), 289–310.

Alon, Gedaliah. *The Jews in Their Land.* Tr. Gershon Levi. (Cambridge, Mass.: Harvard University Press, 1990).

Altshuler, Mor. "Messianic Strains in Rabbi Israel Ba'al Shem Tov's 'Holy Epistle.' " *Jewish Studies Quarterly* 6 (1999), 55–70.

Anonymous. "Akt darowizny bóżnicy przez Berka." *Kwartalnik poświęcony badania przeszłości Żydów w Polsce* 1 (1912), 180–2.

———. "Bractwo pogrzebowe na Pradze." *Kwartalnik poświęcony badania przeszłości Żydów w Polsce* 3 (1912), 133–46.

Anonymous. Ha-Hasidut be-Mishnat ha-Rishonim: Mekorot le-Hanhagot Ha-Hasidut me-Hazal Rishonim ve-Aharonim (Jerusalem: [s.n.], 1989).

———. *Sefer ha-Razim: The Book of Mysteries.* Tr. Michael Morgan. (Chico, CA: Scholars Press, 1983).

———. "Z pinkasu Bractwa pogrzebowego praskiego." *Kwartalnik poświęcony badania przeszłości Żydów w Polsce* 1 (1912), 138–9.

Aschheim, Steven. *Brothers and Strangers: The East European Jew in German and German Jewish Consciousness, 1800–1923* (Madison: University of Wisconsin Press, 1982).

Askenazy, Szymon. *Dwa Stulecie,* vol. 2, (Warsaw: Nakładem Gebethnera I Wolffa, 1910).

———. "Z dziejów Żydów polskich w dobie Księstwa Warszawskiego." *Kwartalnik poświęcony badania przeszłości Żydów w Polsce* 1:1 (1912), 1–14.

Assaf, David. *Derekh ha-Malkhut: R. Yisrael mi-Ruzhin.* (Merkaz Zalman Shazar: Jerusalem, 1997).

———. "Hasidut be-Hitpashtota—Diyokano Shel R. Nehemia Jehiel Mi-Bihova ben 'Ha-Yehudi Ha-Kadosh." In Israel Bartal, Ezra Mendelsohn, and Chava Turnianski, eds., *Ke-minhag Ashkenaz ve-Polin: Sefer Yovel le- Chone Shmeruk: Kovets Mehkarim be-Tarbut Yehudit* (Jerusalem: Merkaz Zalman Shazar, 1993), 269–98.

———. " 'Money for Household Expenses': Economic Aspects of the Hasidic Courts." *Scripta hierosolymitana* 38 (1998), 14–50.

———. "Momer u-Kadosh? Ma'aseh be-Ikvot Moshe Beno shel R. Schneur Zalman mi-Liady." *Zion* 64:4 (2000), 453–515.

———. *The Regal Way: The Life and Times of Rabbi Israel of Ruzhin* (Stanford, Calif.: Stanford University Press, 2002).

———. " 'Ve-ha-Mitnaggdim Hitlozezu She-Nishtakher ve-Nafal': Nefilat Shel Ha-Hozeh Mi-Lublin Be-R'i Ha-Zikharon Ha-Hasidi ve-Ha-Satirah Ha-Maskilit." In Immanuel Etkes, David Assaf, Israel Bartal, and Elchanan Reiner, eds., *Be-Ma'aglei Hasidim: Kovets Mehkarim Mukdash le-Zikhro Shel Mordekhai Vilensky* (Jerusalem: Mosad Bialik, 1999), 161–208.

Assaf, David, and Israel Bartal. " 'Hasidut Polin' o' 'Ha-Hasidut be-Polin': L'bayat Ha-Giyografiah Ha-Hasidit be-Ikvot Ha-Kovets: Zaddikim be-Anshei Ma'aseh—Mehkarim Be-Hasidut Polin." *Gal-Ed* 14 (1995), 197–206.

———. "Manhigut ve-Yerushat Manhigut be-Hasidut be-Me'ah ha-19." In Hana Anit, ed., *On Leadership and Leaders* (in Hebrew) (Jerusalem: Ministry of Defence, 2000), 59–72.

———. "Shtadlanut ve-Ortodoksiyah: Zaddikei Polin be-Mifgash Im ha-Zmanim ha-Hadashim." In Rachel Elior, Yisrael Bartal, and Chone Shmeruk, eds., *Zaddikim ve-Anshe Ma'aseh: Mehkarim be-Hasidut Polin* (Jerusalem: Mosad Bialik, 1994).

Assaf, Simha. "Le-Korot ha-Rabanut." In *Be-Ohalei Yaakov* (Jerusalem: Mosad Ha-Raw Kuk, 1943).

Bacon, Gershon. "Prolonged Erosion, Organization and Reinforcement: Reflections on Orthodox Jewry in Congress Poland." In Yisrael Gutman, ed., *Major Changes within the Jewish People in the Wake of the Holocaust* (Jerusalem: Yad Vashem, 1996).

Bałaban, Majer. "Die Poln. Juden in den Memoiren des Poln. Adels." In *Menorah Wien* 6:1 (1928) 382–383.

———. *Żydowskie miasto w Lublinie.* Ed. Jan Doktor (Lublin: FIS Marek Gacka, 1991).

———. *Studja Historyczne* (Warsaw: M. J. Freid, 1927).

———. *Yidn in Polin: Shtudyes un shilderungen fun fargangene tkufes: mit 45 bilder oyf 32 bleter* (Vilna: B. Klezkin, 1932).

————. *Zabytki Historyczne Żydów w Polsce: orz sprawozdanie Instytutu nauk judaisty-cznych w Warszawie za lata akademickie 1927/28–1928/29* (Warsaw: Nakładem Towarzystwa Krzewienia nauk judaistycznych w Polsce, 1929).

————. "Zu der Geschichte fun di Yudishe Drukerien in Poylin." *Almanach zum 10 Yarung fur Moment* (1921), 189–208.

Baranowski, Jerzy. "Synagoga w Chmielniku." *Biuletyn ŻIH* 36 (1960), 95–106.

Baron, Salo. *The Jewish Community, Its History and Structure to the American Revolution.* Vol. 3 (Philadelphia: Jewish Publication Society, 1948).

Bartal, Israel. "The Imprint of Haskalah Literature on the Historiography of Hasidism." In Ada Rapoport-Albert, ed., *Hasidism Reappraised* (London: Littman Library of Jewish Civilization, 1997).

————. "L'an Halakh Zeror ha-Kesef? Ha-bikoret ha-Maskilit al-Hebeteha ha-Kalkaliyim shel ha-Hasidut." In Menahem Ben-Sasson, ed., *Da'at ve-Kalkalah* (Jerusalem: Merkaz Zalman Shazar, 1995).

Bastomsky, Saul. "*Yihus* in the Shtetl and *Dignitas* in the Late Roman Republic." *Judaism* 39:1 (1990), 93–96.

Bell, Catherine. *Ritual Theory, Ritual Practice* (New York: Oxford University Press, 1992).

Ben Menahem, N. "Shvilim be-Sadeh ha-Sefer." *Sinai* 60 (1967), 182–183.

Ben Sasson, Hayyim Hillel. *Hagut ve-Hanhagah* (Jerusalem: Mosad Bialik, 1959).

————. "Musagim ve-Mitsyot be-Historya ha-Yehudit be-Slah Yamei ha Benayim." *Tarbiz* 29 (1959), 296–312.

Berdychevski, Micah Yosef. "Le-Korot ha-Hasidut." *Ozar ha-Sifrut* 3 (1899), 51–62.

Beregovski, Moshe. "The Interaction of Jewish and Ukrainian Folk Music" (1930). Tr. Mark Slobin. In *Jewish Instrumental Folk Music: The Collections and Writings of Moshe Beregovski* (Syracuse, N.Y.: Syracuse University Press, 2001), 513–29.

Berger, Israel. Zekhut Yisrael ha-nikra Eser Orot (New York: [s.n.], 1976).

Berger-Sofer, Anne. "An Exploration into the Lubavitcher Hasidic Leadership Kinship Alliance Network." *Working Papers in Yiddish and East European Jewish Studies* 27 (New York: YIVO Institute for Jewish Resaerch, 1977).

Bergman, Eleonora, and Jan Jagielski. "Dokumentacja synagog i cmentarzy Żydowskich w Polsce." In Krzysztof Pilarczyk, ed., *Żydzi i Judaizm we współczesnych badaniach Polskich Materiały z Konferencji* (Kraków: Księgiarnia Akademicza, 1995).

————. "Gora-Kalvarya (Gur): Ha-Yishuv ha-Yehudi ve-Hazer ha-Rabi mi-Gur mi-Reshit ha-Meah 19 ad 1939." In Rachel Elior, Yisrael Bartal, and Chone Shmeruk, eds., *Zaddikim ve-Anshe Ma'aseh: Mehkarim be-Hasidut Polin* (Jerusalem: Mosad Bialik, 1994).

————. "The *Rewir* or Jewish District and the *Eyruv*." *Studia Judaica* 5 (2002), 85–97.

————. *Zachowane synagogi i domy modlitwy w Polsce: Katalog* (Warsaw: Jewish Historical Institute, 1996).

Biegeleisen, Henryk. *Lecznictwo ludu Polskiego* (Cracow: Polska akademja umiejętności, 1929).

Bieniarzówna, Janina. "The Role of Jews in Polish Foreign Trade, 1648–1764). Ed. Andzej Paluch. *The Jews in Poland.* Vol. 1 (Cracow: Jagiellonian University Press, 1992).

Bildstein, Gerald. "Individual and Community in the Middle Ages: Halakhic Theory." In Daniel Elazar, ed., *Kinship and Consent* (Washington, D.C.: University Press of America, 1983).

Bilu, Yoram. "Dybbuk and Maggid: Two Cultural Patterned [*sic*] of Altered Consciousness in Judaism." *AJS Review* 21:2 (1996), 341–366.

Blackburn, Christopher A. *Napoleon and the Szlachta* (New York: Columbia University East European Monographs, 1998).

Bloch, Marc. *Feudal Society*. Vol. II (Chicago: University of Chicago Press, 1961).

Bobrzyński, Michał. *Dzieje Polski* 3 (Warsaw, 1931).

Bocheński, Aleksander. "Protoplasta Finansjery Warszawskiej." *Wiedza i Życia* 9 (1983), 25–31.

Bogucka, Maria. *The Lost World of the "Sarmatians"* (Warsaw: Polish Academy of Sciences, 1996).

———. "Social Structures and Custom in Early Modern Poland." *Acta Poloniae Historica* 68 (1993), 100–101.

Borshtein, Aviezer. *Ha-Admor ha-Rofeh* (Tel Aviv: Alef, 1970).

Boyim, Menahem. *Ha-Rabi Rabi Bunem* (Bnei Brak: Torat Simcha Institute, 1997).

Brill, Alan. "Grandeur and Humility in the Writings of R. Simhah Bunim of Przysucha." In Yaakov Elman and Jeffrey S. Gurock, eds., *Hazon Nahum: Studies in Jewish Law, Thought, and History Presented to Dr. Norman Lamm on the Occasion of His Seventieth Birthday* (New York: Yeshiva University Press, 1997).

Bruckner, Aleksander. *Dzieje kultury Polskiej* 2 (Cracow, 1931).

Buber, Martin. *The Origin and Meaning of Hasidism*. Ed. and tr. Maurice Friedman (New York: Horizon Press, 1960).

Burke, Peter. *Popular Culture in Early Modern Europe* (New York: Harper and Row, 1978).

Buxbaum, Yizhak. *Storytelling and Spirituality in Judaism* (Northvale, N.J.: Aronson, 1994).

Cała, Alina. "Polski i Żydowski Folklor: Wędrówka Wątków" (Warsaw: Jewish Historical Institute, forthcoming).

Calmanson, Jacques. *Uwagi nad niniejszym stanem Żydów Polskich y ich wydoskonaleniem* (Warsaw, 1797).

Carmilly-Weinberger, Moshe. *Censorship and Freedom of Expression in Jewish History* (New York: Yeshiva University Press, 1977).

Chajes, Ch. "Ba'al-Szem-Tow u Chreścijan." *Miesięcznik Żydowski* 4 (1934), 440–459.

Chmielowski, Benedeykt. *Nowe Ateny* (Cracow, n.d.).

Dan, Joseph. *Ha-Sippur ha-Hasidi* (Jerusalem: Keter, 1975), 189–95.

———. *Mehkarei Hasidut* (Jerusalem: Magnes Press, 1999), 197–210.

Dinur, Benzion. *Be-Mifne Ha-Dorot: Mehkarim ve-Iyunim be-Reshitam shel ha-Zemanim ha-Hadashim* (Jerusalem: Mosad Bialik, 1954).

———. "The Messianic-Prophetic Role of the Baal Shem Tov." In Marc Saperstein, ed., *Essential Papers on Messianic Movements and Personalities in Jewish History* (New York: New York University Press, 1992), 377–88.

———. "The Origins of Hasidism and its Social and Messianic Foundations." In Gershon D. Hundert, *Essential Papers on Hasidism* (New York: New York University Press, 1991), 86–208.

Doktór, Jan. "Jakub Frank, a Jewish Heresiarch and His Messianic Doctrine." *Acta Polonaie Historica* 76 (1997), 53–74.

Dresner, Samuel. *The World of a Hasidic Master: Levi Yitzhak of Berditchev* (Northvale, N.J.: Aronson, 1994).

———. *The Zaddik: The Doctrine According to the Writings of Rabbi Yaakov Yosef of Polonoy* (London: Abelard-Schuman, 1964).

Dubnow, Simon. *History of the Jews in Russia and Poland*. Vol. 1. Tr. I. Friedlaender (Philadelphia: Jewish Publication Society, 1916).

————. "The Maggid of Miedzyrzecz." Tr. Eli Lederhendler. In Gershon Hundert, ed., *Essential Papers on Hasidism* (New York: New York University Press, 1991).

————. *Toldot ha-Hasidut* (Tel Aviv: Devir, 1975).

Duker, Abraham. "Leon Hollaenderski's Statement of Resignation." *Jewish Social Studies* 15 (1953), 293–302.

Dworkin, Yehoash. "East European Yiddish Folk Love-Songs." In Raphael Patai, Francis Lee Utley, and Dov Noy, eds., *Studies in Biblical and Jewish Folklore* (Bloomington: Indiana University Press, 1960).

Eidelboym, Meir. "Ha-Hasidut be-Einei Mitnagdeha." *Tagim* 34 (1962), 47–81.

Eisen, Arnold. *Rethinking Modern Judaism: Ritual, Commandment, Community* (Chicago: University of Chicago Press, 1998).

Eisenbach, Artur. "Attempts to Settle the Legal Status of the Jews during the Constitutional Period of the Congress Kingdom." *Jewish Social Studies* 50 (1988–92).

————. *Emancipation of the Jews of Poland.* Ed. Antony Polonsky. Tr. Janina Dorosz. (Oxford: Blackwell, 1991).

————. *Emancypacja Żydów na żiemiach polskich, 1785–1870, na tle europejskim* (Warsaw: PIW, 1988).

————. "Ha-Nezigut ha-Merkazit shel ha-Yehudim be-Nesihut Varsheh, 1807–1815." In Israel Bartal and Israel Gutman, eds., *Kiyum ve-Shever: Yehudei Polin le-Doroteihem* (Jerusalem: Merkaz Zalman Shazar, 1997).

————. "Jews in Warsaw at the End of the Eighteenth Century." In Władysław Bartoszewski and Antony Polonsky, eds., *Jews in Warsaw: A History* (Oxford: Blackwell, 1991).

————. "Mobilność terytorialna ludności żydowskiej." In Witold Kula, ed., *Społeczeństwo Królestwa Polskiego* (Warsaw: PWN, 1966).

————. "Di Tsentrale Reprezentants-Argenen Fun Di Yiden in Warshaver Pirshtentum (1807–1815)." *Bleter Far Geschikhte* 2 (1938), 33–88.

Eisenstadt, S. N., ed. *Max Weber On Charisma and Institution Building* (Chicago: University of Chicago Press, 1968).

Elior, Rachel. "Bein 'hitpashtut ha-gashmiyut' le-bein 'hitpashtut ha-ahavah gam be-gashmiyut.' " In Israel Bartal, Hannah Turniansky, and Ezra Mendelssohn, eds., *K'minhag Ashkenaz ve-Polin: Sefer yovel le-Chone Shmeruk* (Jerusalem: Merkaz Zalman Shazar, 1993).

————. "Between *Yesh* and *Ayin*: The Doctrine of the zaddik in the Works of Jacob Isaac, the Seer of Lublin." In Ada Rapoport-Albert and Steven Zipperstein, eds., *Jewish History: Essays in Honor of Chimen Abramsky* (London: Halban, 1988).

————. "Changes in Religious Thinking in Polish Hasidut: A Comparison between 'Fear' and 'Love' and 'Depth' and 'Surface' " (in Hebrew). *Tarbiz* 62–3 (1993), 381–431.

————. "Ha-mahlohet al Moreshet Habad." *Tarbiz* 49 (1980), 166–186.

————. "Hasidism—Historical Continuity and Spiritual Change." In Peter Schafer and Joseph Dan, eds., *Gershom Scholem's "Major Trends in Jewish Mysticism" Fifty Years After: Proceedings of the Sixth International Conference on the History of Jewish Mysticism* (Tubingen: Mohr, 1993).

————. *The Paradoxical Ascent to God—The Kabbalistic Theosophy of Habad* (Albany: State University of New York Press, 1992).

————. "R. Nathan Adler and the Frankfurt "Pietists: Pietist Groups in Eastern and Central Europe during the Eighteenth Century." In Karl E. Grözinger, ed., *Jüdische Kultur in Frankfurt am Main* (Wiesbaden: Harrassowitz Verlag, 1997) (offprint).

Elior, Rachel, Yisrael Bartal, and Chone Shmeruk, eds. *Zaddikim ve-Anshe Ma'aseh: Mehkarim be-Hasidut Polin* (Jerusalem: Mosad Bialik, 1994).

Elon, Menahem. *The Principles of Jewish Law* (Jerusalem: Encyclopedia Judaica Press, 1975).

Endelman, Todd. "Jewish Converts in Nineteenth-Century Warsaw: A Quantitative Analysis." *Jewish Social Studies* 4:1 (1997), 367.

Etkes, Immanuel. *Ba'al Ha-Shem: Ha-Besht—Magyah, Mystikah, Hanhagah* (Jerusalem: Merkaz Zalman Shazar, 2000).

———. "The Historical Besht: Reconstruction or Deconstruction?" *Polin* 12 (1999), 297–306.

———. "Magic and Miracle Workers in the Literature of the Haskalah." In Shmuel Feiner and David Sorkin, eds., *New Perspectives on the Haskalah* (London: Littman Library of Jewish Civilization, 2001).

———. "Marriage and Torah Study Among the *Lomdim*." In David Kraemer, ed., *The Jewish Family: Metaphor and Memory* (New York: Oxford University Press, 1989).

———. "The Role of Magic and *Ba'alei Shem* in Ashkenazic Society in the Late Seventeenth and Early Eighteenth Centuries." *Zion* 60 (1995), 69–104.

Ettinger, Shmuel. "The Hasidic Movement—Reality and Ideals." In Gershon Hundert, ed., *Essential Papers on Hasidism: Origins to the Present* (New York: New York University Press, 1991), 226–43.

———. "Hasidism and the Kahal in Eastern Europe." In Ada Rapoport-Albert, ed., *Hasidism Reappraised* (London: Littman Library of Jewish Civilization, 1997).

Faierstein, Morris. *All Is in the Hands of Heaven—The Teachings of Rabbi Mordechai Joseph Leiner of Izbica* (Hoboken, N.J.: Ktav, 1990).

Fein, Yitshak. "Di Londoner Misyonerin-Gezelshaft far Yidn." *YIVO Bleter* 24 (1944), 27–46.

Feiner, Shmuel, and David Sorkin, eds. *The Jewish Enlightenment*. Tr. Chaya Naor (Philadelphia: University of Pennsylvania Press, 2004).

———. *New Perspectives on the Haskalah* (London: Littman Library of Jewish Civilization, 2001).

Feinerman, Shlomo. "Ha-aiydot ha-Hasidiyot u-Mekoram." *Ha-Shiloah* 21 (1909), 437–441.

Feinkind, Mojżesz. "Dysputa Żydowska za czasów Stanisława Staszyca." *Nasz Przegląd* (February 9, 1926), 7.

Fine, Lawrence. "The Art of Metoposcopy: A Study in Isaac Luria's Charismatic Knowledge." In *Essential Papers on Kabbalah* (New York: New York University Press, 1995).

Fishbane, Michael. "Mahol le-zaddikim: Torat ha-Rikud Ezel Rabi Nahman mi-Bratslav." In Imanuel Etkes, David Assaf, Israel Bartal and Elchanan Reiner, eds., *Be-Magalei Hasidim: Kovets Mehkarim le-Zekhro shel Profesor Mordekhai Wilensky* (Jerusalem: Mosad Bialik, 2000).

Fishman, David. *Russia's First Modern Jews: The Jews of Shklov* (New York: New York University Press, 1995).

Fishman, Judah Leib Hakohen, *Sha'are Ha-Meah*. Vol. 1 (Jerusalem: Mosad Ha-Rav Kuk, 1944).

Freeze, ChaeRan. *Jewish Marriage and Divorce in Imperial Russia* (Hanover, N.H.: Brandeis University Press, 2002).

Frenk, Azriel Nathan. "Di Milhama Gegen der 'Hefkerut' in Amaligen Varshe." In *Almanakh Zum 10-yahrigen Yubilum "Moment"* (Warsaw, 1921).

———. "Ha-yehudim be-Hitpathuta ha-Kalkalit shel Polin." In Israel Bartal and Israel Gutman, eds., *Kiyum ve-Shever* Vol. 1 (Jerusalem: Merkaz Zalman Shazar, 1997).

———. "Le-toldot ha-Yehudim be-Nesikhut Varshe." *Ha-Tekufah* 4 (1927), 451–88.

Friedlander, Yehuda. " 'The Words of the Talebearer are as Wounds': On Megillat Yuhasin Attributed to Rabbi Mendel Landsberg of Kremnitz" (in Hebrew). *Hebrew Union College Annual* 37 (1986), 21–37.

———. *Meshumadim in Poylin* (Warsaw, 1923).

———. "The Struggle of the Mitnagedim and Maskilim against Hasidism: Rabbi Jacob Emden and Judah Leiv Mieses." In Shmuel Feiner and David Sorkin, eds., *New Perspectives on the Haskalah* (London: Littman Library of Jewish Civilization, 2001).

———. *Yehude Polin be-Yame Milhemot Napoliyon* (Warsaw, 1912).

Garntsarska-Kadry, Bina. "Ha-yehudim ve-ha-Goramim le-Hitpathuta ve-Mekoma shel ha-Ta'asiyah be-Varshe." *Gal-Ed* 2 (1975), 25–58.

Gąsiorowska, Natalalia. "Cenzura żydowska w Królestwie Kongresowem." In *Kwartalnik poświęcony badaniu przeszłości Żydów* 1:2 (1912), 55–65.

Gaster, Moses, ed. *Ma'aseh Book* (Philadelphia: Jewish Publication Society, 1934).

Geertz, Clifford. *The Interpretation of Cultures* (New York: Basic Books, 1973).

Gelber, Natan Michael. *Arim ve-Imahot be-Yisrael.* Vol. 6, *Brody* (Jerusalem: Mosad ha-Rav Kook, 1957).

———. "Oyslenishe Rayunde Vegen Poylishe Yidn Inem 18-Yahrhundert." In A. Tserikower, *Historishe Schriften* vol. 1 (Warsaw, 1929), 233–251.

———. "She'elat ha-Yehudim be-Polin be-Shanot 1815–1830." *Zion* 13–4 (1948–49), 106–142.

———. "Korot ha-Yehudim be Polin mi-Reshit Halukatah ve-ad milhemet ha-Olam ha-Shniyah." In Israel Halperin, ed., *Bet Yisrael be-Polin*, vol. 1 (Jerusalem: Ha-Mahlakah le-inyene ha-no'ar Shelha-Histadrut, 1948–53).

Geshuri, Meir Shimon. "Be-Shvilei ha-Nigun ve-ha-Zemer le-Vet Kozience." In *Sefer Zikharon le-Kehillat Kozience* (Tel Aviv, 1969).

———. "Erekhei Negina be-Hasidut." In *La-Hasidim Mizmor* (Jerusalem, 1936), 92–9.

———. "Ha-Maggid Mi-Kozience ve 'Tshuvat ha-Agunah' mi-Staszów." In *Sefer Staszów* (Tel Aviv, 1962).

———. "Ha-Niginah Ezel 'Ha-Hozei mi-Lublin.' " In *Negina ve-Hasidut be-Vet Kuzmir u-Vanoteha* (Jerusalem: Ha-Hevrah le-Hafatsat ha-Hasidut u-Neginatah, 1952).

———. *Ha-Nigun ve-Harikud be-Hasidut* (Tel Aviv: Hotsa'at Netsah, 1954).

———. *La-Hasidim Mizmor: Me'asef sifruti ve-romanuti li-neginah . . . shel ha-Hasidim* (Jerusalem, 1936).

———. "Le-Toldot Nigunei ha-Hasidi be-Polin." In *Negina be-Hasidut be-Vet Kuzmir u-Vanoteha* (Jerusalem: Ha-Hevrah le-Hafat sat ha-Hasidut u Neginatah, 1952).

Gellman, Yehuda (Jerome). "Hasidic Existentialism?" In Yaakov Elman and Jeffrey S. Gurock, eds., *Hazon Nahum: Studies in Jewish Law, Thought, and History Presented to Dr. Norman Lamm on the Occasion of His Seventieth Birthday* (New York: Yeshiva University Press, 1997).

Ginsburg, Saul. *Drama of Slavuta* (Lanham, Md.: University Press of America, 1991).

Gluziński, Józef. *Włoscianie Polscy,* in *Archiwum domowe do dziejów i literatury- z rękopismów i dzieł najrzadszych* (Warsaw, 1856).

Goitein, Shelomo Dov. "Political Conflict and the Use of Power in the World of the Geniza." In Daniel Elazar, ed., *Kinship and Consent* (Washington, D.C., University Press of America, 1983).

Goldberg, Jacob. "Gminy Żydowskie (Kahały) w systemie władztwa dominalnego w szlacheckiej Rzeczypospolitej." In M. Drozdowski, ed., *Między historią a teorią* (Warsaw: PWN, 1988).

Gottesman, Itzik Nakhmen. *Defining the Yiddish Nation: the Jewish Folklorists of Poland* (Detroit: Wayne State University Press, 2003).

Graetz, Heinrich. *History of the Jews* (Philadelphia: Jewish Publication Society, 1895).

Green, Arthur. *Tormented Master* (Tuscaloosa: University of Alabama Press, 1979. Reprinted in Woodstock, Vt.: Jewish Lights, 1992).

———. "The Zaddik as Axis Mundi in Later Judaism." In Lawrence Fine, ed., *Essential Papers on Kabbalah* (New York: New York University Press, 1995).

———. Typologies of Leadership and the Hasidic Zaddiq. In Arthur Green, ed., *Jewish Spirituality*, vol. 2 (New York: Crossroad, 1986–87).

Gries, Ze'ev. "Between History and Literature—The Case of Jewish Preaching." *Journal of Jewish Thought and Philosophy* 4:1 (1994), 113–122.

———. "The Hasidic Conduct (Hanhagot) Literature from the Mid-Eighteenth Century to the 1830s" (in Hebrew). *Zion* 46 (1981), 198–236.

———. "The Hasidic Managing Editor." In Ada Rapoport Albert, ed., *Hasidism Reappraised* (London: Littman Library of Jewish Civilization, 1997).

———. "Hasidism: The Present State of Research and Some Desirable Priorities." *Numen* 34:1 (1987), 96–108, *Numen* 34:2 (1987), 180–213.

———. "R. Yisrael ben Shabbetai mi-Kozienice ve-Peirushav le-Masehet Avot." In Rachel Elior, Yisrael Bartal, and Chone Shmeruk, eds., *Zaddikim ve-Anshe Ma'aseh: Mehkarim be-Hasidut Polin* (Jerusalem: Mosad Bialik, 1994).

———. *Sefer, Sofer ve-Sipur be-Reshit ha-Hasidut* (HaKibbuz ha-Meyuhad, 1992).

Grochulska, Barbara. *Księstwo Warszawskie* (Warsaw :Wiedza Powszechna, 1966).

Grossman, Avraham. "From Father to Son" (in Hebrew). *Zion* 50 (1985) 9–23.

———. "From Father to Son: The Inheritance of Spiritual Leadership in Jewish Communities in the Middle Ages." In David Kraemer, ed., *The Jewish Family: Metaphor and Memory* (New York: Oxford University Press, 1989).

———. *Hakhamei Ashkenaz Ha-Rishonim* (Jerusalem: Magnes Press, 1981).

Gruchowska, Helena. "Srul Rabi Bal-Szim." *Lud* 9 (1904), 50–58.

Guldon, Zenon. *Dzieje Przysuchy w 18 wieku* (Przysucha: Muzeum im. Oskara Kolberga, 1995).

———. "Gminy wyznania mojżeszowego w powiecie radomskim w 16–18 wieku." In *Radom i region radomski w dobie szlacheckiej Rzeczpospolitej*, vol. 2 (Radom: Radomskie Towarzystwo Naukowe Muzeum wsi Radomskie, 1996).

Guldon, Zenon, and Jacek Wijaczka. "The Accusation of Ritual Murder in Poland, 1500I–800." *Polin* 10 (1997), 99–140.

Guterman, Alexander. "The Origins of the Great Synagogue in Warsaw on Tłomackike Street." In Władysław Bartoszewski and Antony Polonsky, eds., *The Jews in Warsaw: A History* (Oxford: Blackwell, 1991).

Halpern, Israel. "Bunty Woszczyłowskie." *Builetyn ŻIH* 26 (1958), 28–41.

———. "Gezerat Voshtzilo." In *Yehudim ve-Yahadut be-Mizrah Eiropa* (Jerusalem: Magnes Press, 1968).

———. "Havurot le-Torah ve-l'Mizvah ve-ha-T'nuah ha-Hasidit be-Hithapshutah." In *Yehudim ve-Yahadut be-Mizrah Eiropa* (Jerusalem: Magnes Press, 1968).

———. "Rabbi Levi Isaac of Berdyczów and the Royal Edicts of His Times" (in Hebrew). In *Yehudim ve-Yahadut be-Mizrah Eiropa* (Jerusalem: Magnes Press, 1968).

———. "Va'ad Arba Arzot be-Polin ve-ha-Sefer ha-Ivri." *Yehudim ve-Yahadut be-Mizrah-Eiropa* (Jerusalem: Magnes Press, 1967), 78–87.

———. "Yahaso shel R. Aharon ha-Gadol mi-Karlin Kelapei mishtar ha-kehilot." In *Yehudim ve-yahadut be Mizrahłiropa*.

Hakohen, Toviyah. *Ma'aseh Tovayyah* (Kraków, 1908).

Hasdai, Ya'akov. "The Origins of the Conflict between Hasidim and Mitnagdim." In Bezalel Safran, ed., *Hasidism: Continuity or Innovation?* (Cambridge, Mass.: Harvard Uiversity Press, 1988).

Hertz, Paweł. "Rabbi Izrael z Kozienic i książę Adam Czartoryski." *W Drodze* 9:133 (1984), 3–7.

Heschel, A. J. *The Circle of the Ba'al Shem Tov: Studies in Hasidism*. Ed. Samuel Dresner. (Chicago: University of Chicago Press, 1985).

———. *Kotsk: In Gerangl far Emesdikeyt* (Tel Aviv: Ha-Menorah).

Hoenig, Sidney B. "Filial Succession in the Rabbinate." *Gratz College Annual of Jewish Studies* 1 (1972), 14–22.

Hollaenderski, Leon. *Les Israelites de Pologne* (Paris, 1846).

Horodezky, Samuel. *Leaders of Hassidism*. Tr. Maria Horodezky-Magasanik (London: Hasefer, 1928).

Horowitz, H. "Die judische gemeinde Opatow und ihre Rabbiner." In *Monatsschrift fur Geschichte und Wissenschaft des Judentums* vol. 38 (1930), 102–3.

Huberman, Nahman. "Hasidim un Hasidut in Bessarabia." *YIVO Bleter* 39 (1955) 278–283.

Hundert, Gershon David. "Apta ve-Reshit ha-Hasidut Ad 1800." In Rachel Elior, Yisrael Bartal, and Chone Shmeruk, eds., *Zaddikim ve-Anshe Ma'aseh: Mehkarim be-Hasidut Polin* (Jerusalem: Mosad Bialik, 1994).

———. "The Contexts of Hasidism." In Waldemar Kowalski and Jadwiga Muszyńska, eds., *Żydzi wśród chrześcijan w dobie szlacheckiej Rzeczypospolitej* (Kielce: Kieleckie Tow. Naukowe, 1996).

———. *Jews in Poland-Lithuania in the Eighteenth Century: A Genealogy of Modernity* (Berkeley: University of California Press, 2004).

———. "Jews, Money and Society in the Seventeenth-Century Polish Commonwealth: The Case of Kraków." *Jewish Social Studies* 43 (1981), 261–274.

———. *The Jews of a Polish Private Town: The Case of Opatów in the Eighteenth Century* (Baltimore: Johns Hopkins University Press, 1992).

———. "On the Problem of Agency in Eighteenth-Century Jewish Society." *Scripta Hierosolymitana 38: Studies in the History of the Jews in Old Poland in Honor of Jacob Goldberg* (Jerusalem: Magnes Press, 1998).

———. "Was There an East European Analogue to Court Jews?" In Andzej Paluch, ed., *The Jews in Poland*, vol. 1 (Cracow: Jagiellonian University Press, 1992).

Hurvitz, Nathan. "Marriage Among Eastern European Jews Prior to World War I as Depicted in a *Briefenshteller*." *Journal of Marriage and the Family* 37 (1974), 422–30.

Idel, Moshe. "Jewish Magic from the Renaissance Period to Early Hasidism." In Jacob Neusner, Ernest S. Frerichs, and Paul Virgil McCraken Flesher, eds., *Religion, Science and Magic in Concert and Conflict* (New York: Oxford University Press, 1989).

———. *Hasidism: Between Ecstasy and Magic* (Albany: State University of New York Press, 1995).

———. *Kabbalah: New Perspectives* (New Haven: Yale University Press, 1988).

———. "Music and Prophetic Kabbalah." In Israel Adler and Bathja Bayer, eds., *Yuval Studies of the Jewish Music Research Centre* vol. 4. (Jerusalem: Jewish Music Research Center, 1982).

Idelsohn, A. Z. *Jewish Music in Its Historical Devlopment* (New York: Holt, 1929).

Ihnatowicz, Ireneusz. *Obyczaj wielkiej burżuazji warszawskiej w 19 wieku* (Warsaw: PIW, 1971).

———. "Przemysł, Handel, Finanse." in Stefan Kieniewizc, ed., *Polska 19 Wieku: Państwo, Społeczeństwo, Kultura* (Warsaw: Wiedza Powszechna, 1977).

Ish Horowitz, Zvi Halevi. *Le-toldot ha-Kehillot be-Polin* (Jerusalem: Mosad Ha-Rav Kook, 1978).

Jacobs, Louis. "Hasidism and the Dogma of the Decline of the Generations." In Ada Rapoport-Albert, ed., *Hasidism Reappraised* (London: Littman Library of Jewish Civilization).

Jasni, Wolf, ed. Yizkor Bukh fun der Zelekhover Yiddische Kehille (Chicago: Aroysgegebn fun der Tsentraler Zshelekhover landsman Shaft, 1953).

Jedlicki, Jerzy. "Social Ideas and Economic Attitudes of Polish Eighteenth Century Nobility: Their Approach to Industrial Policy." In *Fifth International Congress of Economic History*. Vol. 1 (Leningrad, 1970).

———. *A Suburb of Europe: Nineteenth–Century Approaches to Western Civilization* (Budapest: Central European University Press, 1999).

Joffe, Natalie F. "The Dynamics of Benefice among East European Jews." *Social Forces* 27 (1948–9), 238–47.

Jost, J. M. *Geschichte der Israeliten seit der Zeit der Maccabaer bis auf unsre Tage* (Berlin, 1828).

———. *Neuere Geschichte der Israeliten* (1847).

Junosze, Klemens. *Nasi Żydzi w miasteczkach i na wsiach* (Warsaw, 1889).

Kanarfogel, Ephraim. *Jewish Education and Society in the High Middle Ages* (Detroit: Wayne State University Press, 1992).

Kandel, David. "Żydzi w dobie utworzenia Królestwa Kongresowego." *Kwartalnik poświęcony badaniu przeszłości Żydów w Polsce* 1 (1912), 95–113.

———. "Komitet starozakonnych." *Kwartalnik poświęcony badaniu przeszłości Żydów w Polsce* r.1, z.2 (1912), 85–103.

———. "Nowosilcow a Żydzi." *Biblioteka Warszawska* (1911), vol. 3, 144–50.

Kaplan, Marion. "For Love or Money: The Marriage Strategies of Jews in Imperial Germany." *Leo Baek Institute Yearbook* 28 (1983), 263–300.

Kasher, Moses Solomon, ed. *Mesillot Be-Mahshevat Ha-Hasidut* (Jerusalem: Bet Torah Shlemah, 1977).

Kassow, Samuel D. "Community and Identity in the Interwar *Shtetl*." In Yisrael Gutman, and Ezra Mendelsohn, eds., *The Jews of Poland Between Two World Wars* (Hanover, N.H.: Brandeis University Press, 1989), 200–204.

Katz, Jacob. "Nisuim Ve-Hayei Ishut Be-Motsei Yamei Ha-Benayyim." *Zion* 10 (1944–45), 33–48.

———. *Tradition and Crisis*. Ed. Bernard Dov Cooperman (New York: Schocken Books, 1993).

Kempner, Rafael. "Agonia Kahal." *Kwartalnik poświęcony badania przeszłości Żydów w Polsce* 1 (1912), 67–73.

Kempner, Stanisław. *Dzieje Gopodarcze Polski porozbiorowey w zarysie* (Warsaw: K. Kowalewski, 1920).

Kieniewicz, Stefan. *Przemiany społeczne i gospodarcze w Królestwie Polskim: 1815–1820* (Warsaw: Książka i Wiedza, 1951).

Klier, John. *Russia Gathers Her Jews: The Origins of the "Jewish Question" in Russia* (Dekalb: Northern Illinois University Press, 1986).

Kociszewski, Aleksander. *Mazowsze w epoce Napoleonskiej* (Czechanów: RSW PKR, 1985).

Kolberg, Oscar. *Dziełe wszystkie: Radomskie* Part 2. Vol. 21 (Wrocław, 1964); *Chełmskie* Part 2. Vol. 34 (Wrocław, 1964); *Lubelskie* Part 2. Vol. 17 (Wrocław, 1962).

Kołodzijczyk, Ryszard. *Piotr Steinkeller: 1799–1854* (Warsaw: PWN, 1963).

———. "Przemiany społeczno-kulturowe w środowisku luności Żydowskiej w Królestwie Polskim w XIX wieku." In Marta Meducka, ed., *Kultura Żydów Polskich XIX wieku* (Kielce, 1992).

Korzon, Tadeusz. *Wewnętrzne dzieje Polski za Stanisława Augusta (1764–1794)* (Warsaw, 1897).

Kosim, Jan. *Losy pewnej fortuny: Z dziejów burżuazji warszawskiej w latach 1807–1830* (Wrocław: Zakład Narodowy im. Ossolińskich, 1972).

Kośka, Małgorzata. "Obyczaje żydowskie w świetle prawa obowiązującego w XIX wieku w Królestwie Polskim." In Jerzy Woronczak, ed., *Żydowskie gminy wyznaniowe* (Wrocław: Przyjaciół Polonistyki Wrocławskie, 1995).

Kowalska-Glikman, Stefania. "Ludność żydowska Warszawy w połowie XIX w., w świetle akt stanu cywilnego." *Biuletyn ŻIH* 2:118 (1981), 37–49.

Krasinski, Wincenty. *Apercu Sur les Juifs de Pologne l'an 1818* (Cracow, 1898).

Krassen, Miles. *Uniter of Heaven and Earth: Rabbi Meshullam Feibush Heller of Zabarazh and the Rise of Hasidism in Eastern Galicia* (Albany: State University of New York Press, 1998).

Kraushar, Alexander. *Kupiectwo Warszawskie* (Warsaw: F. Hoesick, 1929).

Kula, Witold. *An Economic Theory of the Feudal System: Towards a Model of the Polish Economy, 1500–1800.* Tr. Lawrence Garner (London: NLB, 1976).

Kuperstein, Isaiah. "Inquiry at Polaniec: A Case Study of a Hassidic Controversy in Eighteenth–Century Galicia." *Bar Ilan Annual* 24–25, Gershon Bacon and Moshe Rosman, eds. (Ramat Gan, Bur Ilan University, 1989), 25–40.

Kuwałek, Robert. "Spoleczność Żydowska na Wieniawie." In Tadeusz Radzik, ed., *Żydzi w Lublinie* vol. 2 (Lublin: Wydawnictwo Uniwersytetu Marii Curie-Skłodowskiej, 1998).

———. "Urzedowi rabini lubelkiego Okregu Boznicznego 1821–1939." In Tadeusz Radzika, ed., *Żydzi w Lublinie* (Lublin: Wydawnictwo Uniwersytetu Marii Curie-Skłodowskiej, 1994).

Lachower, Abraham. "Jewish Burial Associations in Moldavia." *YIVO Annual* 10 (1955), 300–18.

Lamm, Norman. *The Religious Thought of Hasidism: Texts and Commentary* (New York: Yeshiva University Press, 1999).

Lederhendler, Eli. "The Decline of the Polish-Lithuanian *Kahal.*" *Polin* 2 (1987), 150–155.

Leiman, Shnayer Z. "The Ba'al Teshuvah and the Emden-Eibeschutz Controversy." In *Judaic Studies* (New York: Kew Gardens, 1985).

Leslie, R. F. *Polish Politics and the Revolution of November 1830* (London: University of London Press, 1956).

Leszczyński, Anatol. "The Terminology of the Bodies of Jewish Self-Government." In Antony Polonsky, Jakub Basista, and Andrzej Link-Lenczowski, eds., *The Jews in Old Poland, 1000–1795* (London: Tauris, 1993).

Levi-Strauss, Claude. *The Elemenatary Structures of Kinship* (London: Eyre and Spottiswoode, 1969).

Levine, Mordekhai. "Ha Mishpaha Be-Hevra Mafkhanit Yehudit." *Ma'asef* 13 (1982–3) 109–26; and *Ma'asef* 14 (1984), 157–71.

Levinson, Abraham. *Toldot Yehude Varshe* (Tel Aviv: Am Oved, 1953).

Levitats, Isaac. *The Jewish Community in Russia: 1772–1844* (New York: Columbia University Press, 1970).

Levy, Isaac. "Marriage Preliminaries." In Peter Elman, ed., *Jewish Marriage* (London: Soncino Press, 1967).

Lew, Henryk. "O lecznictwie i przesądach." *Izraelita* 31 (1896), 296–97; 305–306; 315–316; 352–353, 364–65; 373–74, 381–82; 391–92; vol. 32 (1897), 362–63; 381–82, 394–95, 406–407; 446–47, 475–76 vol. 34 (1899), 443–44.

Lieberman, Chaim. "He'arot Bibliografyot le-Toldot R. Levi Yitshak mi-Berdytshev," and "Le-Toldot ha-Defus be-Varshe." In David Frankel, ed., *Sefer Ha-Yovel li-Khevod Alexander Marx: Li-melot lo shiv'im shanah* (New York: Jewish Theological Seminary, 1953).

———. "Le-She'elat Yahas ha-Hasidut le-Lashon Yiddish." In *Ohel Rahel* vol. 3 (New York [s.n], 1984).

———. "Truth and Fabrication in the Words of Hasidic Printing Houses" (in Hebrew). *YIVO Bleter* 34 (1950) 15–103.

Lilientalowa, Regina. "Przesądy Żydowskie." *Wisła* 14 (1900), 639–44.

Limanowski, Bolesław. *Historya demokracyi Polskiej w epoce porozbiorowej* (Zurich, 1901).

Loewenthal, Nafthali. *Communicating the Infinite: The Emergence of the Habad School* (Chicago: University of Chicago Press, 1990).

———. "Hebrew and the Habad Communication Ethos." In Lewis Glinert, ed., *Hebrew in Ashkenaz: A Language in Exile* (New York: Oxford University Press, 1993).

———. "Spirituality, Melody and Modernity in *Habad* Hassidism." In Steven Stanton, ed., *Proceedings of the First International Conference on Jewish Music* (London: City University, 1997).

Lubamersky, Lynn. "Women and Political Patronage in the Politics of the Polish-Lithuanian Commonwealth." *Polish Review* 44:3 (1999), 259–75.

Lukowski, Jerzy. *Liberty's Folly: The Polish Lithuanian Commonwealth in the Eighteenth Century* (London: Routledge, 1991).

Magid Shaul. *Hasidism on the Margin: Reconciliation, Antinomianism, and Messianism in Izbica/Radzin Hasidism* (Madison: University of Wisconsin Press, 2003).

Mahler, Raphael. *Ha-Hasidut ve-ha-Haskalah* (Merhavya: Sifriyat Po'alim, 1961).

———. "Ha-Mėdiniyut Klapei ha-Misiyonarim be-Polin ha-Kongresit be-Tekufat 'Ha-Brit Ha-Kedoshah.' " In Mikhal Handel, ed., *Sefer Shiloh: Kovetz Ma'amarim L'zekhero* (Tel Aviv: Hug Yedidim be-shiftufim ha-makhlakah le-hinukh, 1961).

———. *Hasidism and the Jewish Enlightenment*. Tr. Eugene Orenstein, Aaron Klein, and Jenny Klein (Philadelphia: Jewish Publication Society, 1985).

———. *A History of Modern Jewry, 1780–1815* (London: Vallentine, Mitchell, 1971).

Mark, Zvi. "Dibuk ve-Devekut be-Shivhei ha-Besht: He'arot le-Fonomologiyah shel ha-Shygayon be-Reshit he-Hasidut." In Immanuel Etkes, David Assaf, Israel Bartal, and Elchanan Reiner, eds., *Be-Ma'aglei Hasidim: Kovets Mehkarim Mukdash le-Zekhero Shel Mordechai Vilensky* (Jerusalem: Mosad Bialik, 2000).

Martyn, Peter. "The Undefined Town within a Town." *Polin* 3 (1988), 25–45.

Mazor, Ya'akov, and Moshe Taube. "A Hassidic Ritual Dance: The Mitsve Tants." In Israel Adler, Frank Alvarez-Pereyre, Edwin Seroussi, and Lea Shalem, eds., *Yuval: Studies of the Jewish Music Research Centre* 6 (Jerusalem: Jewish Music Research Center, 1994).

Mazur, Elżbieta. *Dobroczynność w Warszawie XIX wieku* (Warsaw: Instytut Archeologii i Etnologii Polskiej Akademii Nauk, 1999).

Michałowska, Anna. "Szmul Jakubowicz Zbytkower." *Biuletyn ŻIH* 23 (1992) 79–90.

Mintz, Alan. "Guenzburg, Lilienblum, and Haskalah Autobiography." *AJS Review* 4 (1979), 71–110.

———. *"Banished from Their Fathers' Table": Loss of Faith and Hebrew Autobiography* (Bloomington: Indiana University Press, 1989).

Miron, Dan. "Sh. Y. Abramovitsh and His 'Mendele.' " In *The Image of the Shtetl* (New York: Syracuse University Press, 2000).

Mochnacki, Bazyl. *Sprawa Birnbauma* (Warsaw, 1830).

Morley, David, and Kuan-Hsing Chen, eds. *Stuart Hall: Critical Dialogues in Cultural Studies,* (London: Routledge, 1996).

Muszyńska, Jadwiga. *Żydzi w miastach województwa sandomierskiego i lubelskiego w 18 wieku* (Kielce: Wyższa Szkoła Pedagogiczna, 1998).

Nadav, Mordechai. "Kehilot Pinsk-Karlin Bein Hasidut le-Hitnaggdut." *Zion* 34 (1969), 99–108.

Neugroschel, Joachim, ed. and tr. *The Dybbuk and the Yiddish Imagination: A Haunted Reader* (New York: Syracuse University Press, 2000).

Neuman, Albert. "The Rebbe's Song." In Andrew Handler, ed. and tr., *Rabbi Eizik: Hasidic Stories about the Zaddik of Kallo* (Rutherford, N.J.: Fairleigh Dickinson University Press, 1977).

Niemcewicz, Julian Ursyn. *Levi and Sarah* (1821). In Harold B. Segal, tr. and ed., *Stranger in Our Midst: Images of the Jew in Polish Literature* (Ithaca: Cornell University Press, 1996).

Nigal, Gedaliya. "Al Ruhot Dibuk be-Sifrut Hasidiim." In Gershon Bacon and Moshe Rosman, eds., *Bar Ilan Sefer ha-Shanah* 24–5 (Jerusalem: Bar Ilan University (1989), 51–60.

———. *Ha-Siporet ha-Hasidit: Toldoteha ve-Noseha* (Jerusalem: Ha-Makhan he-Heker ha-Sifrut ha-Hasidit, Hotsa'at Y. Markus, 1981).

———. *Magic, Mysticism, and Hasidism.* Tr. E. Levin (Northvale, N.J.: Aronson, 1994).

———. New Light on the Hasidic Tale and Its Sources." In Ada Rapoport-Albert, ed., *Hasidism Reappraised* (London: Littman Library of Jewish Civilization, 1997).

———. "R. Eliezer mi-Tarnogród ve-Sefarav." In *Mehkarim be-Hasidut: Osef Ma'amarim* (Jerusalem: Ha-Makhon le-Heker ha-Sifrut Ha-Hasidut, 1999).

———. *Sippurei "Dybbuk" be-Sifrut-Yisrael* (Jerusalem: Reuven Mas, 1994).

Nissenbaum, Sholmo Barukh. *Lekorot ha-Yehudim be-Lublin* (Lublin, 1900).

Nosek, Bedřich. "Shemuel Shmelke Ben Tsvi Hirsh Ha-Levi Horovits: Legend and Reality." *Judaica Bohemia* 21:2 (1985), 75–94.

Nussbaum, Hillary. *Historyja Żydów od Mojżesza do epoki obecnej. Vol. 5, Żydzi w Polsce* (Warsaw, 1890), 306.

———. *Skice historyczne z Życia żydów w Warszawie* (Warsaw, 1881).

Oesterreich, T. K. *Possession: Demoniacal and Other* (New York: R. R. Smith, 1930).

Papastergiadis, Nikos. *The Turbulence of Migration: Globalization, Deterritorialization and Hybridity* (Malden, Mass.: Polity Press, 2000).

Papłońsky, Jan. "Życiorysy dobroczyńców Instytutu: Berek Szmulowicz Sonenberg." *Pamiętnik Warszawskiego Instytutu Głuchoniemych i Ociemniałych* 4 (1872–3), 106–12.

Passamaneck, Stephen M. "Some Medieval Problems in *Mamzeruth.*" *Hebrew Union College Annual* 37 (1966) 121–45.

Patai, Józef. "The Singing Saint." In Andrew Handler, ed. and tr., *Rabbi Eizik: Hasidic Stories about the Zaddik of Kallo* (Rutherford, N.J.: Fairleigh Dickinson University Press, 1977).

Pedaya, Haviva. "Le-hitpathuto shel had-Degem ha-Hevrati-da'ati-kalkali be-Hasidut: Ha-Pidyon, ha-Havurah, ve-ha-Alyah le-Regel." In Menahem Ben-Sasson, ed., *Da'at ve-Kalkalah: Yahasei Gomlin: Kovets Ma'amarim* (Jerusalem: Merkaz Zalman Shazar, 1995).

Pelli, Moshe. "On the Role of *Melitzah* in the Literature of Hebrew Enlightenment." In Lewis Glinert, ed., *Hebrew in Ashkenaz: A Language in Exile* (New York: Oxford University Press, 1993), 99–110.

Petrovsky-Shtern, Yohanan. "Hasidism, Havurot, and the Jewish Street." *Jewish Social Studies* 10:2 (2004), 205–4.

Piechotka, Maria and Kazimierz. "Polish Synagogues in the Nineteenth Century." *Polin* 2 (1987), 179–98.

Piątkowska, Ignacja. "Ludoznawstwo żydowskie," *Wisła* 4 (1890), 803–810.

Piekarz, Mendel. *Biyemei Zmihat ha-Hasidut* (Jerusalem: Mosad Bialik, 1978).

———. "Hasidism as a Socio-Religious Movement on the Evidence of *Devekut*." In Ada Rapoport-Albert, ed., *Hasidism Reappraised* (London: Littman Library of Jewish Civilization, 1997).

Pohorille, Wilhelm. "Dostawy wojkowe Szmula Jakubowicza Zbytkowera w latach 1792." In Majer Bałaban, ed., *Księga ku Czci Berka Joseliwicza* (Warsaw, 1934).

Popper, William. *The Censorship of Hebrew Books* (New York: Ktav, 1968).

Poppers, H. L. "The Declasse in the Babylonian Jewish Communities." *Jewish Social Studies* 20 (1958), 153–79.

Pritsak, Omeljan. "Ukraine as the Setting for the Emergence of Hasidism." In Yitzhak Baer, ed., *Israel Among the Nations: Essays Presented in Honor of Shmuel Ettinger* (Jerusalem: Merkaz Merkaz Zalman Shazar, 1987), 67–85.

Rabbinowitz, Harry. *The World of Hasidism* (London: Vallentine, Mitchell, 1970).

Rabinowicz, Zvi Meir. *Bein Pshyskha ve Lublin: Ishim ve- Shitot be-Hasidiut Polin* (Kesherim: Jerusalem, 1997).

———. "Mekorot ve-Te'udot le-Toldot ha-Hasidut be-Polin." *Sinai* 82 (1978), 182–86.

Rabinowitch, W. Z. *Lithuanian Hasidism: From Its Beginnings to the Present Day*. Tr. M. B. Dagut (London: Vallentine, Mitchell, 1970).

Rakover, Nahum. *The "Haskamot" to Books as a basis for the Rights of the Publishers"* (in Hebrew) (Jerusalem: Misrad Ha-Mishpatim, 1970).

Rapoport-Albert, Ada. "Hagiography with Footnotes: Edifying Tales and the Writing of History in Hasidism." *History and Theory 27: Essays in Jewish Historiography* (1988), 119–59.

———. "Hasidism after 1772: Structural Continuity and Change." In Ada Rapoport-Albert, ed., *Hasidism Reappraised* (London: Littman Library of Jewish Civilization, 1997), 76–140.

———. "On Women in Hasidism: S. A. Horodecky and the Maid of Ludomir." In Ada Rapoport-Albert and Steven Zipperstein, eds., *Jewish History: Studies in Honor of Chimen Abramsky* (London: Halban, 1988), 495–525.

———. "The Zaddik as a Focal Point of Divine Worship." In Gershon Hundert, ed., *Essential Papers on Hasidism* (New York: New York University Press, 1991), 299–329.

Reiner, Elhanan. "Hon, Ma'amad Hevrati, ve-Talmud Torah: Ha-Kloyz be-Hevrah Ha-Yehudit Be- Mizrah Eiropah be-Meot 171–9." *Zion* 58 (1993), 287–328.

Reines, Chaim Wolf. "Public Support of Rabbis, Scholars and Students in the Jewish Past." *Yivo Annual of Jewish Social Science* 7 (1952), 84–109.

Reinharz, Jehuda and Shulamit. "Leadership and Charisma: The Case of Theodor Herzl." In Jehuda Reinharz and Daniel Swetschinski, eds., *Mystics, Philosophers, and Politicians: Essays in Jewish Intellectual History in Honor of Alexander Altmann* (Durham, N.C.: Duke University Press, 1982).

Ringelblum, Emmanuel. "Johann Anton Krieger, Printer of Jewish Books in Nowy Dwór." *Polin* 12 (2000), 199–211.

———. "Khsides un Haskole in Varshe in 18-ten y.h." *YIVO Bleter* 13:12 (1938), 124–32.

———. *Projekty i próby przewarstwowienia Żydów w epoce stanisławowskiej* (Warsaw: Instytut Badań Spraw Narodowościowych, 1934).

———. "Restrictions on the Importation of Jewish Books Into Poland During the Eighteenth Century." *YIVO Annual of Jewish Social Science* 5 (1950), 31–40.

———. "Shmuel Zbytkower." *Zion* 3 (1938), 247–66; *Zion* 4 (1939), 337–55.

———. "Yidn in Varshe in 18-ten y.h. un zeyr rehleh-geschaftlehe lagen." In E. Tschernikower, ed., *Historishe Schriften* vol. 2 (Vilna, 1937).

———. *Żydzi w powstaniu Kościuszkowskiem* (Warsaw: Księgarnia Popularna, 1938).

Rivkind, Isaac. "Mishpatei-Kubiustusim." *Horev* 2:1 (1935), 60–5.

Rosenstein, Neil. "Ashkenazic Rabbinic Families." *Avotaynu* 3:3 (summer 1987), 7–13.

Rosenthal, Celia Stopnicka. "Social Stratification of the Jewish Community in a Small Polish Town." *American Journal of Sociology* 34 (1953), 1–10.

Rosman, Moshe. *Founder of Hasidism* (Berkeley: University of California Press, 1996).

———. "The History of a Historical Source: On the Editing of *Shivhei ha-Besht*" (Hebrew). *Zion* 58 (1993), 175–214.

———. "In Praise of the Ba'al Shem Tov: A User's Guide to the Editions of *Shivhei ha-Besht*." *Polin* 10 (1997), 183–99.

———. *The Lords' Jews* (Cambridge, Mass.: Harvard University Press, 1991).

———. "Miedzyboz and R. Israel Ba'al Shem Tov (Besht)" (in Hebrew). *Zion* 52:2 (1987), 177–89.

———. "Miedzyboz and Rabbi Israel Ba'al Shem Tov." In Gershon Hundert, ed., *Essential Papers on Hasidism* (New York: New York University Press, 1991), 209–25.

———. "Polish Jews in the Gdańsk Trade in the Late Seventeeth and Early Eighteenth Centuries." In Isadore Twersky, ed., *Danzig, between East and West* (Cambridge, Mass.: Harvard University Press, 1985), 111–20.

———. "Social Conflicts in Międzyboż in the Generation of the Besht." In Ada Rapoport-Albert, ed., *Hasidism Reappraised* (London: Littman Library of Jewish Civilization).

Rostocki, Władysław. "Rodowód i pozycja społeczna urzędników administracji państwowej i miejskiej w Warszawie (1807–1830)." In Ryszard Kołodziejczyk, Jan Kosim, and Janina Leskiewiczowa, eds., *Warszawa XIX wieku*, vol. z. 3 (Warsaw: PWN, 1974).

Roth, Jefferey I. "Inheriting the Crown in Jewish Law: The Question of Rabbinic Succession." *Jewish Law Association Studies 19: The London Conference Volume* (1997), 237–259.

Rubinstein, Avraham. "Hasidut ve Hasidim be-Varshe." *Sinai* 65 (1974), 61–84.

———. "He'arot le-Te'udah al Gviyot-Edut Neged ha-Hasidut." *Tarbiz* 32 (1963), 92–4.

———. *Reshitah Shel Ha-Hasidut be-Polin Merkazit* (Jerusalem: Hebrew University, 1960).

Ruderman, Pesah. *Ha-dibuk* (Warsaw, 1878).

Salmon, Yoseph. "R. Naphtali Ze'evi of Ropczyce ('The Ropshitser') as a Hasidic Leader." In Ada Rapoport-Albert, ed., *Hasidism Reappraised* (London: Littman Library of Jewish Civilization, 1997), 321–4.

Schatz-Uffenheimer, Rivka. *Hasidism as Mysticism.* Tr. Jonathan Chipman (Princeton, N.J.: Princeton University Press, 1993).

Schiper, Ignacy. *Cmentarze Żydowskie w Warszawie* (Warsaw: Maor, 1938).

———. *Dzieje handlu Żydowskiego na ziemiach Polskich* (Warsaw, 1937; reprint, Cracow: Krajowa Agencja Wydawnicza, 1990).

———. *Przyczynki do dziejow chasydyzmu w Polsce,* ed. Zbigniew Targielski (Warsaw: PWN, 1992).

———. "R. Yisrael Ba'al Shem Tov: Demuto ve-Sifrut ha-Hasidut ha-Keduma." Tr. Ma. Y. *Ha-Doar* 28 (1960), 525–53.

———. *Siedemset lat gminy żydowskiej w Płocku* (Lwów, 1938).

———. "Z dziejów patrycjatu żydowskiego w Warszawie." *Nowe Slowo* 23:5 (1931).

———. *Żydzi Królestwa Polskiego w dobie powstania Listopadowego* (Warsaw: Instytut Nauk Judaistycznych, 1932).

Schochet, Elijah Judah. *Bach—Rabbi Joel Sirkes: His Life, Works and Times* (Jerusalem: Feldheim, 1971).

Schochet, Jacob Immanuel. *The Great Maggid: The Life and Teachings of Rabbi Dov Ber of Mezhirech* (Brooklyn: Kehot Publication Society, 1974).

Scholem, Gershom. "Dibbuk." In *The Encyclopedia Judaica.*

———. " 'Golem' ve 'Dibbuk' be-Milon ha-Ivri." *Lashoneinu* 6 (1934), 40–1.

Scott, Joan Wallach. "The Problem of Invisibility." In S. Jay Kleinberg, ed., *Retrieving Women's History: Changing Perceptions of the Role of Women in Politics and Society* (Oxford: Berg, 1988).

———. *Major Trends in Jewish Mysticism* (New York: Schocken Books, 1974).

———. *The Mystical Shape of the Godhead* (New York: Schocken Books, 1991).

———. "Shtei Eyduyot al Havurot ha-Hasidim ve-ha-Besht." *Tarbiz* 20 (1949), 228–41.

Segel, B. W. "O chasydach i chasydyzmie." *Wisła* 8 (1897), 305–310.

Shakhar, Yishayahu. *Bikoret Ha-hevrah v'Hanhagat Ha-Zibor b'Sifrut Ha-Mussar ve-Ha-Drush Be'Polin be-Meah ha-Shmonah Asar* (Jerusalem: Merkaz Dinur, 1992).

Sharot, Stephen. *Messianism, Mysticism, and Magic* (Chapel Hill, N.C.: University of North Carolina Press, 1981).

Shatzky, Jacob. "Avraham Ya'akov Shtern (1768–1842), in *The Joshua Starr Memorial Volume: Studies in History and Philology* (New York: Conference on Jewish Relations, 1953).

———. *Geschikhte fun Yidn in Varshe,* vols. 1–3 (New York: Yidisher Visnshaftlekher Institut, Historishe Sektsye, 1947).

———. *Yidishe Bildungs-politik in Poylin* (New York: YIVO Insititute, 1943).

Sheinfeld, Elisheva. "Ma'asit Shivat ha-Kavzanim shel R. Nahman mi-Bratslav." *Yeda Am* 11 (1966), 657–7.

Shila, S. "Ha Shadkhan Be-Mishpat Ha-Ivri." *Mishpatim* 4 (1973), 361–73.

Shils, Eward. "Charisma, Order and Status." *American Sociological Review* 30 (1965), 199–212.

Sherwin, Byron L. *Mystical Theology and Social Dissent* (Rutherford, N.J.: Farleigh Dickinson University Press, 1982).

Shmeruk, Chone. "Bahurim Mi-Ashkenaz Be-Yeshivot Polin." In Shmuel Ettinger, Salo Baron, Ben Zion Dinur, and Y. Hailperin, eds., *Sefer Yovel le-Yitshak Ber: bi-Melot lo Shiv'im shanah* (Jerusalem: Ha-Hevrah ha-Historit ha-Yisraelit, 1960).

————. "Ha-Hasidut be-Askei Ha-Hakirut." *Zion* 35 (1970), 182–92.

————. "Hasidism and the *Kehilla*." In Antony Polonsky, Jakub Basista, and Andrzej Link-Lenczowski, eds., *The Jews in Old Poland, 1000–1795* (London: Tauris, 1993).

————. *Sifrut Yiddish be-Polin* (Jerusalem: Magnes Press, 1981).

————. "Yitshak Schiper's Study of Hasidism in Poland." In Ada Rapoport-Albert, ed., *Hasidism Reappraised* (London: Littman Library of Jewish Civilization, 1997).

Sif (Shvert), Eleazar. "Le-Toldot ha-Nigun ha-Hasidi." In Meir Geshuri, ed. *La-Hasidim Mizmor: Me'asef sifruti ve-romanuti li-neginah . . . shel ha-Hasidim* (Jerusalem, 1936), 47–51.

Sinkoff, Nancy. "Strategy and Ruse in the Haskalah of Mendel Lefin of Satanow." In Shmuel Feiner and David Sorkin, eds., *New Perspectives on the Haskalah* (London: Littman Library of Jewish Civilization, 2001), 86–102.

Skwirowski, Krzysztof. "Z 'Księgi Pamięnci Włodawy i okolic'. Włodawscy chasydzi." In *Zeszyty Muzealne. Muzeum Pojezime Łęczynsko-Włodawskiego*, Vol. 7 (1997).

Smoleński, Władysław. *Mieszczaństwo warszawskie w końscu wieku 18* (Warsaw: PIW, 1976).

————. *Ostatni rok Sejmu Wielkiego* (Cracow, 1897).

————. *Przewrót umysłowy w Polsce wieku 18* (Warsaw: WK, 1923).

Smolka, Stanisław, ed. *Korespondencya Lubeckiego z ministrami sekretarzami stanu Ignacym Sobolewskim i Stefanem Grabowskim* (Cracow: NAU, 1909).

Sokolów, Nahum. "Henri Bergson's Old-Warsaw Lineage." In Lucy Dawidowicz, ed., *The Golden Tradition: Jewish Life and Thought in Eastern Europe* (New York: Holt, Rinehart and Winston, 1967).

Soloveitchik, Hayyim. "Three Themes in the *Sefer Hasidim*." *AJS Review* 1 (1976), 311–357.

Staats, Susan. "Fighting in a Different Way: Indigenous Resistance through the Alleluia Religion of Guyana." In Jonathan Hill, ed., *History, Power, and Identity: Ethnogenesis in the Americas, 1492–1992* (Iowa City: University of Iowa, 1996).

Stampfer, Shaul. "The Dispute over Polished Knives and Hasidic *Shekhita*." In Imanuel Etkes, David Assaf, and Joseph Dan, *Mehkarei Hasidut* (Jerusalem: Hebrew University, 1999), 197–210.

————. "*Heder* Study, Knowledge of Torah, and the Maintenance of Social Stratification in Traditional East European Jewish Society." *Studies in Jewish Education* 3 (1988), 271–89.

————. "Inheritance of the Rabbinate in Eastern Europe in the Modern Period—Causes, Factors and Development over Time." *Jewish History* 13:1 (1999), 136–56.

————. "What Did 'Knowing Hebrew' Mean in Eastern Europe?" In Lewis Glinert, ed., *Hebrew in Ashkenaz: A Language in Exile* (New York: Oxford University Press, 1993), 129–40.

Stanley, John. "The Politics of the Jewish Question in the Duchy of Warsaw, 1807–1813." *Jewish Social Studies* 44 (1982), 47–62.

Stępkowski, Lech. "Kozienice w czasach Stanisława Augusta. Główne czynniki rozwoju osady w latach 1764–1794." *Ziema Kozienicka* 2 (1992), 3–11.

S. U. "Wypędzanie czarta z opętanego." *Lud* 10 (1904), 215–216.

Szacka, Barbara. *Teoria i utopia Stanisława Staszica* (Warsaw: PWN, 1965).

Szczepański, Janusz. *Dzieje społecznośći żydowskiej powiatów Pułtusk i Maków Mazowecki* (Warsaw: Pułtuskie Towarzystwo Społeczno-Kulturalne, 1993).

Ta-Shma, Israel. "On the History of Polish Jewry in the Twelfth and Thirteenth Centuries" (in Hebrew). *Zion* 53 (1988), 347–69.

————. "On the History of Polish Jewry in the Twelfth and Thirteenth Centuries." *Polin* 10 (1997), 287–317.

Tatarzanka, Władysław. "Przyczynki do historji żydów w Królestwie Kongresowem. 1815–1830." (1). *Przegląd Judaistyczny*, 1:46 (1922), 271–94.

Taub, Michael. "Social Issues in Peretz's Short Dramas." *Yiddish* 10:1 (1995), 18–23.

Teller, Adam. "Radziwiłł, Rabinowicz, and the Rabbi of Świerz: The Magnates' Attitude to Jewish Regional Autonomy in the Eighteenth Century." *Scripta Hierosolymitana* 38 (Jerusalem: Magnes, 1998).

————. "The Sluck Tradition Concerning the Early Days of the Besht" (in Hebrew). In David Assaf, Joseph Dan, and Imanuel Etkes, eds., *Studies in Hasidism* (Jerusalem: Hug le-Mahshevet Yisrael, 1999).

Trachtenberg, Joshua. *Jewish Magic and Superstition: A Study in Folk Religion* (New York: Atheneum, 1974).

Turner, Victor. *Dramas and Ritual Metaphors: Symbolic Action in Human Society* (Ithaca: Cornell University Press, 1967).

Tuwim, Julian. *Czary i Czarty Polskie* (Warsaw: Czytelnik, 1960).

Unger, Menasseh. "Di Rebizen Perele Davent in Talit." In *Sefer Zikharon le-Kehillat Kozienice* (Tel Aviv, 1969).

Walicki, Andrzej. *The Enlightenment and the Birth of Modern Nationhood: Polish Political Thought from Noble Republicanism to Tadeusz Kosciuszko*. Tr. Emma Harris (Notre Dame, Ind.: Notre Dame University Press, 1989).

Warszawski, I. "Yidn in Kongress—Poylin." *Historische Shriften* vol. 2 (Vilna, 1937–9).

Wein, Adam. "Żydzi poza rewirem Żydowskim w Warszawie (1809–1862). *Biuletyn ŻIH* 41 (1962), 45–70.

————. "Nabywanie i budowa nieruchomości przez Żydów w Warzawie (1821–1862). *Biuletyn ŻIH* 64 (1967), 33–53.

————. "Ograniczenie napływu Żydów do Warszawy." *Biuletyn ŻIH* 49 (1964), 3–34.

Weinryb, Bernard. *The Jews of Poland to 1800* (Philadelphia: Jewish Publication Society, 1982).

————. Zur Geschichte des Buchdruckes und der Zensur bei den Juden in Polen." *Monatsschrift fur Geschichte und Wissenschaft des Judentums* 77 (1933), 173–300.

Weiss, Joseph. "A Circle of Pneumatics in Pre-Hasidism." In *Studies in Eastern Jewish Mysticism*, ed. David Goldstein (Oxford: Oxford University Press, 1985).

————. "The Saddik—Altering the Divine Will." In *Studies in Eastern European Jewish Mysticism*, ed. David Goldstein (London: Littman Library of Jewish Civilization, 1985).

————. "Sense and Nonsense in Defining Judaism—The Strange Case of Nahman of Brazlav." In *Studies in Eastern European Jewish Mysticism*, ed. David Goldstein (London: Littman Library of Jewish Civilization, 1985).

————. "Some Notes on the Social Background of Early Hasidism." In *Studies in Eastern European Jewish Mysticism*, ed. David Goldstein (Oxford: Oxford University Press, 1985).

————. "Torah Study in Early Hasidism." in *Studies in Eastern European Jewish Mysticism*.

————. *Studies in Eastern Jewish Mysticism*. Ed. David Goldstein (Oxford: Oxford University Press, 1985).

Werbner, Pnina, and Tariq Modood. *Debating Cultural Hybridity: Multi-Cultural Identities and the Politics of Anti-Racism* (London: Zed, 1997).

Werses, Shmuel. "Bein Shnei Olamot: Yakov Shmuel Bik Bein Haskalah le-Hasidiut-Iyun Me-Hodesh." *Gal-Ed* 9 (1986), 27–76.

———. "Ha-Hasidut be-Aspaklariyah Beleteristit." In Rachel Elior, Yisrael Bartal, and Chone Shmeruk, eds., *Zaddikim ve-Anshe Ma'aseh: Mehkarim be-Hasidut Polin* (Jerusalem: Mosad Bialik, 1994).

———. "Portrait of a Maskil as a Young Man." In Shmuel Feiner and David Sorkin, eds., *New Perspectives on the Haskalah* (London: Littman Library of Jewish Civilization, 2001).

———. "Towards the History of the Hebrew Novella in the Early Nineteenth Century: Studies in Zahlen's *Salma Mul 'Eder.*" *Scripta Hierosolymitana* 27 (1978), 107–124.

Wettstein, Feivel. *Halifat Mikhtavim* (Cracow, 1900).

Wilensky, Mordechai. "Bikoret al Sefer Toldot Ya'akov Yosef." In *Alexander Marx: Jubilee Volume on the Occasion of His Seventieth Birthday* (New York, 1950).

———. "Hasidic-Mitnaggedic Polemics in the Jewish Communities of Eastern Europe: The Hostile Phase." In Gershon Hundert, ed., *Essential Papers on Hasidism* (New York: New York University Press, 1991).

———. "He'arot le-Pulmusim Bein ha-Hasidim ve-ha-Mitnaggdim." *Tarbiz* 30 (1961), 396–409.

———. *Hasidim u-Mitnaggdim* (Jerusalem: Mosad Bialik, 1990).

———. "The Polemic of Rabbi David of Makow against Hasidism." *Proceedings of the American Academy of Jewish Research* (1956), 137–56.

Willner, Ann Ruth and Dorothy. "The Rise and Role of Charismatic Leaders." *Annals of the American Academy of Political Science* 358 (March 1965), 77–88.

Wodziński, Marcin. "Dybuk. Z Dokumentów Archiwum Głównego Akt Dawnych w Warszawie." *Literatura Ludowa* 36:6 (1992), 19–29.

———. "Hasidism, Shtadlanut, and Jewish Politics in Nineteenth Century Poland: the Case of Isaac of Warka," *Jewish Quarterly Review*, 95/2 (2005).

———. *Haskalah and Hasidism in the Kingdom of Poland: A History of Conflict*, tr. Sarah Cozens (Portland, Ore.: Littman Library of Jewish Civilization, 2005).

———. "How Many *Hasidim* were there in Congress Poland? On the Demographics of the Hasidic Movement in Poland During the First Half of the Nineteenth Century." *Gal-Ed* 19 (2004) (offprint).

———. "Ilu było chasydów w Królestwie Polskim około 1830 roku?" In Konrad Zieliński and Monika Adamczyk-Garbowski, *Ortodoksja, Emancypacja, Asymilacja: Studia Z Dziejów Ludności Żydowskiej na Ziemiach Polskich w Okresie Rozbiorów* (Lublin: Maria Curie-Skłodowski University Press, 2003).

———. "Jakub Tugenhold and the First Maskilic Defense of Hasidism." *Gal-Ed* 18 (2002) (offprint).

———. *Oświecenie żydowskie w Królestwie Polskim wobec chasydyzmu* (Warsaw: Wydawnictwo Cyklady, 2003).

———. "Rząd Królestwa Polskiego Wobec Chosydyzmu: Początki 'Polityki Chasydzkie,' " w Krókstwie Polskim (1817–1818). In Krzysztof Pilarczyk, ed., *Żydzi i Judaizm w Współczesnych badaniach Polskich*, vol. 3 (Cracow: Księgarnia Akademicka, 2004).

———. " 'Sprawa chasydymów.' Z materiałów do dziejów chasydyzmu w Królestwie Polskim." In Krystyn Matwijowski, ed., *Z historii ludność Żydowskiej w Polsce i na Śląsku* (Wrocław: Uniwersytet Wrocławski, 1994).

Wolf, Eric. "Kinship, Friendship, and Patron-Client Relations." In Michael Banton, ed., *The Social Anthropology of Complex Societies* (London: Tavistock, 1966).

Worobec, Christine. *Possessed: Women, Witches, and Demons in Imperial Russia* (DeKalb: Northern Illinois University Press, 2001).

Wunder, Meir. "Ha-Ishor ha-Rishon le-Hadpasat Sifrei Hasidut." *Tagim* 1 (1969), 30–35.

———. "The Reliability of Genealogical Research in Modern Rabbinic Literature." *Avotaynu* 11:4 (1995), 31–36.

Yaairi, Abraham. "*Ner Tamid* Societies in Poland and Lithuania." *Jewish Social Studies* 21:2 (1959), 118–31.

Yassif, Eli. *The Hebrew Folktale: History, Genre, Meaning,* Jacqueline Teitelbaum, tr. (Bloomington: Indiana University Press, 1999).

Ysander, Torsten. *Studien zum Bestschen Hasidismus in Seiner Religions geschichtlichen Sonderart* (Uppsala, 1933).

Yuval, Yisrael Yakov. *Hakhamim Be-Doram* (Jerusalem: Magnes Press, 1988).

Zborowski, Mark, and Elizabeth Herzog, *Life Is with People* (New York: Schocken Books, 1952).

Zemah, Shlomo. "Ha-Hasidut be-Plonsk." In *Iruvim* (Tel Aviv: Devir, 1984).

Zieleniewski, Michał. *O przesądach lekarskich ludu naszego,* (Cracow, 1845).

Zinberg, Israel. *A History of Jewish Literature: Hasidism and Enlightenment (1780–1820).* Tr. and ed. Bernard Martin (Cincinnati: Hebrew Union College, 1976).

Żor-Żor. "Żydzi na Pradze." *Echo Pragi* 13–4 (1916).

Index